THOMSON

COURSE TECHNOLOGY

Professional ■ Trade ■ Reference

# HACKING THE

## TiVo

**Warning:** Doing almost any of the procedures discussed in this book requires opening your TiVo, which instantly *voids* your TiVo warranty *forever*. Also, you can get a serious electrical shock if you're not careful while poking around inside your TiVo, just as you can with any electrical device. Never work on your TiVo while it's plugged in.

## SECOND EDITION

William von Hagen

*Important:* Thomson Course Technology PTR cannot provide software support. Please contact the appropriate software manufacturer's technical support line or Web site for assistance.

Thomson Course Technology PTR and the author have attempted throughout this book to distinguish proprietary trademarks from descriptive terms by following the capitalization style used by the manufacturer.

Information contained in this book has been obtained by Thomson Course Technology PTR from sources believed to be reliable. However, because of the possibility of human or mechanical error by our sources, Thomson Course Technology PTR, or others, the Publisher does not guarantee the accuracy, adequacy, or completeness of any information and is not responsible for any errors or omissions or the results obtained from use of such information. Readers should be particularly aware of the fact that the Internet is an ever-changing entity. Some facts may have changed since this book went to press.

Educational facilities, companies, and organizations interested in multiple copies or licensing of this book should contact the publisher for quantity discount information. Training manuals, CD-ROMs, and portions of this book are also available individually or can be tailored for specific needs.

ISBN: 1-59200-481-4

Library of Congress Catalog Card Number: 2004108010

Printed in the United States of America

04 05 06 07 08 BH 10 9 8 7 6 5 4 3 2 1

Thomson Course Technology PTR,
a division of Thomson Course Technology
25 Thomson Place
Boston, MA 02210
http://www.courseptr.com

**THOMSON**

COURSE TECHNOLOGY™

Professional ■ Trade ■ Reference

**SVP, Thomson Course Technology PTR:**
Andy Shafran

**Publisher:**
Stacy L. Hiquet

**Senior Marketing Manager:**
Sarah O'Donnell

**Marketing Manager:**
Heather Hurley

**Manager of Editorial Services:**
Heather Talbot

**Acquisitions Editor:**
Megan Belanger

**Associate Marketing Managers:**
Kristin Eisenzopf and Sarah Dubois

**Project and Copy Editor:**
Marta Justak

**Technical Reviewer:**
Eric McDonald (AKA musclenerd)

**Thomson Course Technology PTR Market Coordinator:**
Amanda Weaver

**Interior Layout:**
Danielle Foster

**Cover Designer:**
Mike Tanamachi

**CD-ROM Producer:**
William von Hagen

**Indexer:**
Sharon Hilgenberg

**Proofreader:**
Dan Foster

# Trademarks and Copyrights

*For my wife and best friend—I love you, Dorothy, and I always will.*

# Acknowledgments

I'd like to thank my wife for putting up with my TiVo obsession and for never carrying out any of her threats. Five TiVos in a two-person house seems just about right to me. And you thought that the Lisp Machines in the dining room were bad!

I'd like to thank musclenerd (AKA Eric McDonald) for his excellent technical editing and suggestions for the second edition of this book. I would also like to continue to thank embeem (AKA Mike Baker) for his technical edits and suggestions for the first edition of this book. Their participation made this book far better than it would have been without them—all of the errors are mine, but many improvements are theirs. I'd also like to thank the TiVo hacking community in general, which has freely and selflessly contributed ideas, hacks, and time towards making the TiVo a fun machine. Special thanks to AlphaWolf, Andrew Tridgell, dubbya, Dylan, ElectricLegs, embeem, geowar, Ingineer, JohnnyDeath, Josh Graessley, Kazymyr, lightn, mactivo, MuscleNerd, Otto, ronnythunder, Tyger, and countless others. Thanks to embeem and lightn (AKA Josha Foust) specifically for substantial contributions to the MFS information in Chapter 9. Like everyone, I'd like to thank Linus Torvalds and the Open Source community for Linux. I'd also like to thank the folks at TiVo, Inc. for making a great product and actively supporting the TiVo hacking community. (What's up with that hashing stuff, guys? C'mon!)

I would also like to thank the folks at Course Technology PTR for letting me write this book and for letting me update it in a second edition. Special thanks to my agent, Marta Justak, for helping me through another project and for fixing up my prose as the copy editor. Like the old song, I was born to wander…. Thanks, too, to Sharon Hilgenberg for impressive work making it possible to find things in this book and to Danielle Foster for making this book look great.

# About the Author

**William von Hagen** is a senior product manager at TimeSys Corporation. He has been a UNIX® devotee for over 20 years and a Linux fanatic since the early 1990s. He has worked as a system administrator, writer, developer, systems programmer, drummer, and content manager. He has written books on such topics as Linux® Filesystems, SGML, Mac OS X, and Red Hat® Linux, and has written for publications including *Linux Magazine, Mac Tech, Linux Format, Mac Format,* and *Mac Home.* An avid computer collector specializing in workstations, he owns more than 200 computer systems. You can reach Bill at vonhagen@vonhagen.org.

# Contents at a Glance

Introduction ...................................................... xix

1  Know Your TiVo ..................................................1

2  Just Do It! ........................................................25

3  TiVo Tips and Tricks...........................................43

4  Exploring Your TiVo Hardware...........................87

5  The Hacker's Tool Chest of TiVo Tools ...........139

6  Backing Up and Restoring TiVo Data ............. 177

7  Expanding Your TiVo's Storage Capacity .......221

8  Connecting the Universe to Your TiVo ...........245

9  Working with Your TiVo from Windows
   and Macintosh Systems....................................313

10  Linux and the TiVo .........................................361

11  Getting and Installing New Software
    for Your TiVo ................................................411

12  Extracting, Inserting, and Playing TiVo
    Recordings.......................................................433

**13 TiVo Repairs and Troubleshooting** .................. **479**

**14 Other TiVo Hacking Resources** ....................... **489**

**Index** ............................................................... **517**

**About the CD** .................................................. **543**

# Contents

**Introduction** ......................................................... xix

**Chapter 1**     **Know Your TiVo** ........................................................1

Why TiVo? ...............................................................2

What's This TiVo Service I Keep Hearing About? ...............3

     TiVo Service Fees....................................................4

     TiVo Service Levels ................................................5

     Identifying Your TiVo...............................................7

     TiVos and Your Viewing Habits ..................................8

A Short Course in TiVo History .....................................10

TiVo Business Partners and Integrators............................12

     Partnering with the Networks ....................................13

     Showcasing Upcoming Broadcasts...............................13

     TiVo Software Licensing ...........................................14

     TiVo's Software Partners .........................................15

TiVo Hardware Models and Features................................16

Identifying Your TiVo Software Version .............................19

TiVo and the Competition............................................21

     NDS, Sky+, and XTV ...............................................21

     ReplayTV ..............................................................22

     UltimateTV.............................................................23

     Software Competitors ..............................................23

Future Trends .........................................................24

**Chapter 2**     **Just Do It!** ..........................................................25

Opening a TiVo .......................................................26

Removing TiVo Disk Drives...........................................29

Putting a TiVo or Other Disk in Your PC .............................35

Adding a Larger Disk to Your TiVo ...................................38

Adding a Second Disk to Your TiVo ................................. 40

**Chapter 3    TiVo Tips and Tricks.........................................43**

Using the TiVo Remote Control.......................................... 44

TiVo Remote Control Shortcuts ...................................... 46

Resolving Remote Control Problems ............................... 46

Using a PDA as a Remote Control ..................................48

Secret TiVo Commands and Modes ....................................49

Activating Backdoor Mode................................................51

Using Clear-Clear-Enter-Enter Codes ...........................61

Using Clear-Enter-Clear Codes .....................................62

Using Enter-Enter Codes ................................................65

Using Select-Play-Select Codes........................................67

Using Thumb-Thumb-Thumb Codes..............................69

The Irritating AutoTest Mode .......................................72

Sorting the Now Playing List in V. 3.x TiVos ...................72

Automating Backdoor Mode and Other Codes .................74

Legendary TiVo Monitor and Diagnostic Commands ..........78

TiVo Scheduling Tips and Tricks .......................................81

Using TiVo WishLists .....................................................83

Activating and Using Advanced WishLists .......................83

**Chapter 4    Exploring Your TiVo Hardware .........................87**

Attaching a Terminal Emulator or Serial Console ................88

Opening the TiVo...............................................................91

Working with TiVo Disk Drives ..........................................92

How Large Can TiVo Disks Be? .....................................92

Removing TiVo Disk Drives.............................................93

Attaching TiVo Disk Drives to Your PC.........................97

Unlocking TiVo Hard Drives ........................................100

Adding Disk Drives to Your TiVo ....................................101

Power Considerations in TiVo Series 2 TiVos ................103

Heat Considerations in TiVo Series 2 TiVos .................104

Dealing with Modems ...........................................................105

Networking Your TiVo ..........................................................106

Networking 101 .................................................................107

Networking Series 1 TiVos ................................................111

Networking Series 2 and DVD TiVos ............................ 120

Using the Network to Make Daily Calls ..........................124

TiVo Hardware Supplies on the Net ....................................134

9thTee.com ......................................................................135

Hinsdale ..........................................................................135

PTVupgrade.com ...............................................................136

TiVo Store .......................................................................136

Weaknees.com ..................................................................137

TiVo Sites Outside the United States ..............................137

Other Sources for TiVo Hardware ...................................138

**Chapter 5**   **The Hacker's Tool Chest of TiVo Tools ..........139**

TiVo Tools Overview ...........................................................141

BlessTiVo ........................................................................141

Bootpage .........................................................................144

MFS Tools .......................................................................147

TiVoMad Utilities ............................................................160

TPIP ..............................................................................162

Useful Linux Tools Outside Most Tools Disks ................164

Boot Disks .........................................................................166

BATBD—Bill's Accumulated TiVo Boot Disk ...............169

Dylan's Boot Floppy ........................................................173

Johnny Death's Boot CD ..................................................173

Kazamyr's Boot CD ..........................................................173

Knoppix Linux ............................................................ 174

PTVUpgrade.com ........................................................ 174

Sleeper's ISO ............................................................... 175

TiVo Hacking for PPC ................................................ 175

**Chapter 6**   **Backing Up and Restoring TiVo Data ............. 177**

Overview ..................................................................... 179

When to Back Up? ...................................................... 181

Finding Room for Backups ......................................... 182

File Size Limitations Under Linux and Windows .......... 185

Creating Image Backups Using dd ............................. 186

Creating Backups Using MFS Tools ........................... 190

Creating a Simple Backup Using MFS Tools .............. 191

Creating a Compressed Backup Using MFS Tools ......... 193

Backing Up an Entire TiVo Disk Using MFS Tools ....... 194

Backing Up Multiple-Disk TiVo Systems ....................... 195

Advanced Backup Options ........................................... 196

Backing Up Selected Information from Your TiVo ............. 198

Finding Backups of the TiVo Software ........................... 200

General Information about Restoring TiVo Data ............... 202

Restoring Image Backups Using dd ............................. 203

Restoring Backups Created Using MFS Tools ................. 205

Restoring an MFS Tools Backup Without
Adding New Space ....................................................... 205

Restoring an MFS Tools Backup to a Larger Drive ........ 207

Restoring an MFS Tools Backup to a
Two-Drive TiVo .......................................................... 209

Advanced MFS Tool Restore Options ........................... 211

Verifying TiVo Disks Restored Using MFS Tools .......... 216

Connecting Backup and Restore Commands
Using a Pipe ............................................................... 217

Changing TiVo Operating System Versions
Using Backups ............................................................ 219

**Chapter 7**    **Expanding Your TiVo's Storage Capacity .......221**

Overview..................................................................................222

TiVo Disk Capacity by Model and Software Version ..........223

What You'll Need for Your TiVo Upgrade .........................225

Replacing an Existing TiVo Disk with a Larger One..........226

Upgrading a Disk Without Using Backup Files .................229

Expanding Drives Using Disk Images................................233

     Expanding a Drive from a Disk Image............................233

     Using Disk Images Without Intermediate
     Backup Files................................................................236

Adding a Second Drive to Your TiVo................................238

     Using the MFS Tools Utilities to Add a
     Second Drive................................................................239

     Using the BlessTiVo Utility to Add a Second Drive ........242

**Chapter 8**    **Connecting the Universe to Your TiVo ...........245**

Getting a Command Prompt on Your TiVo .......................246

     Getting a Command Prompt on a Series 1 TiVo ...........248

     Getting a Command Prompt on a Series 2 TiVo............252

     Two-Kernel Monte for the Series 2 TiVo .......................260

Starting FTP and Telnet on Your TiVo..............................274

Integrating Your TiVo with AOL Instant Messenger..........275

Caller ID and Your TiVo ...................................................280

News, Sports, Weather, and Your TiVo..............................281

Programming Your TiVo over a Network Using
   TiVoWebPlus.....................................................................283

     Installing TiVoWebPlus.................................................284

     Exploring the TiVoWebPlus Menus ..............................288

     Changing the Appearance of TiVoWebPlus ....................290

     Browsing and Recording Upcoming Shows Using
     TiVoWebPlus................................................................291

     Undeleting Recordings Using TiVoWebPlus ..................298

Getting Status Information about Your TiVo in
TiVoWebPlus ................................................................ 300

Enabling Internet Access to Your TiVo .........................301

Using TiVo's Home Media Features ....................................302

Playing Music or Displaying Photos Using
Your TiVo ....................................................................303

Scheduling Recordings on Your TiVo over the Internet
Using Home Media Features ........................................ 304

Multiroom Viewing on Your TiVo .................................309

**Chapter 9      Working with Your TiVo from Windows
and Macintosh Systems ...................................313**

Communicating with Your TiVo from Windows ................ 314

Serial Communications from Windows Systems .............315

Transferring Files over a Serial Connection
from Windows ................................................................318

Networked Communications from Windows ..................321

Creating TiVo Tools Disks under Windows .........................327

TiVo Disks and Windows Systems .....................................333

Exploring ext2 Disk Images under Windows ..................333

Accessing Windows Disks from Your TiVo.....................335

Integrating Windows Systems with TiVo's
Home Media Features .........................................................337

Installing and Using the Windows TiVo Desktop...........337

Playing Windows Audio Formats other than MP3 .........342

TiVos and Mac OS X .........................................................345

TiVo Disks and Mac OS X Systems .................................... 346

ext2 Filesystem Support for Mac OS X.......................... 346

Putting Series 1 and Series 2 Disks in Your
Mac OS X System...........................................................347

Mounting and Exploring ext2 Partitions under
Mac OS X.......................................................................349

Exploring ext2 Filesystem Images under Mac OS X.......351

Mounting and Exploring MFS Partitions under Mac OS X ...................................................................354

Blessing a Disk under Mac OS X ................................356

Creating TiVo Tools Disks under Mac OS X .......................357

Integrating Macintosh Systems with TiVo's Home Media Features .......................................................359

**Chapter 10   Linux and the TiVo .........................................361**

Introduction to Linux and Open Source Software ..............362

Overview of the Linux Boot Process ...............................363

Linux Filesystems and Initial RAM Disks.....................364

The Linux Boot Sequence for Initial RAM Disks ..........366

Obtaining the Source Code for TiVo's Linux ................367

Overview of the TiVo Application Environment.................367

The TiVo Startup Process...............................................368

TCL and iTCL...............................................................369

TiVo's TiVoSH Application ............................................370

TiVo Disk Information .....................................................371

TiVo Disk and Partition Map ........................................372

MFS—TiVo's Media File System .....................................374

Exploring MFS...............................................................375

Using Serial Communications under Linux.....................382

Using minicom for Serial Communications.....................383

Transferring Files Using minicom .................................385

Using a Linux Shell ...........................................................386

Job Control in the Bash Shell .......................................388

Running Commands in the Background ..........................388

Managing Commands in the Bash Shell .........................389

Popular Linux Software for the TiVo ...............................391

Busybox..........................................................................391

Emacs .............................................................................392

FTP .................................................................................393

GCC ........................................................................395

NFS ........................................................................395

Rsync .....................................................................397

Telnet .....................................................................398

Wget ...................................................................... 400

Burning CDs on Linux Systems ..................................... 400

Working with TiVo's Home Media Features
from Linux ...........................................................402

The Personal TiVo Home Media Option ....................... 403

The Java Home Media Option ..................................... 404

**Chapter 11** **Getting and Installing New Software
for Your TiVo** ...............................................**411**

Mounting the BATBD CD on Your System ......................412

Installing Software on Your TiVo ................................... 414

Identifying Binary File Formats .................................... 414

Uncompressing ZIP and GZ Files ................................415

Extracting Files from TAR and TGZ Archives .............. 417

Installing Software Packaged with TPM .......................420

Installing Hacks from the BATBD CD .........................421

Safe Locations for Storing Your TiVo Hacks ..................422

Installing Cross-Compilers for TiVo Development ............423

Selecting and Installing a Cross-Compiler for
the TiVo Series 1 .........................................................424

Selecting and Installing a Cross-Compiler for
the TiVo Series 2 .........................................................425

Cross-Compiling Software on a Linux System ..............427

Stand-alone TiVo Tools and Development Projects ...........428

An Alternate UI in the TiVo Web Project .....................428

The TiVo Enhancement Development Team ..................428

The Personal TiVo Home Media Option ........................429

The Java Home Media Option .....................................429

Closed Captioning Support Using TiVoVBI ...................430

TiVo Utilities Home Page................................................431

**Chapter 12**  **Extracting, Inserting, and Playing TiVo
Recordings ........................................................433**

Overview: Extraction, Insertion, and Conversion ...............434

Video File Formats .............................................................436

TiVo Video File Formats ................................................436

Identifying TiVo Video Files on Linux and
Mac OS X Systems .....................................................437

Target Video File Formats ..............................................439

Saving Recordings to Media—Built-In Methods .............. 440

Saving Recordings to Videotape ......................................441

Saving Recordings to DVD on DVD TiVos ................. 442

Using a TV Tuner Card and Video Capture
Software...................................................................... 442

Overview: Extracting Recordings from Your TiVo ............447

Overview of Extraction and Processing Software........... 448

Tips for Extracting Recordings over a Network ..............449

Extracting Recordings Directly from a TiVo Disk .........449

Disabling Video Encryption .............................................455

Using TyTool.................................................................... 460

Using TyStudio .................................................................467

Using mfs_ftp ...................................................................471

Playing TY Files with mplayer .........................................476

**Chapter 13**  **TiVo Repairs and Troubleshooting .................. 479**

Dealing with a Blown Modem ........................................... 480

Using External Modems with the TiVo..........................481

TiVo Troubleshooting........................................................485

No Picture or Welcome Screen .......................................485

Your TiVo Is Stuck at the Welcome Screen .....................485

Your TiVo Is Stuck at the Second Welcome Screen.........487

Your TiVo Displays a Green Screen.................................488

**Chapter 14 Other TiVo Hacking Resources.........................489**

A Byte of Fun—TiVo Advocacy Articles.............................491

Online Forums for TiVo Information and Discussion.........492

The alt.org Forums ......................................................494

AVS Forum...................................................................495

The DealDatabase Forums ...........................................497

MacTiVo Forums ......................................................... 500

PTVupgrade Forums ....................................................501

pvrhax0r Forums..........................................................502

SiliconDust Forums ......................................................502

TiVo Community Forums .............................................504

TiVo.net Forums ..........................................................507

TiVo Hardware Web Sites .................................................508

Various TiVo FAQs and Help Sites ...............................509

Hacking the TiVo FAQ.................................................510

Hinsdale FAQs ............................................................510

OzTiVo Site .................................................................511

Seth's TiVo FAQ .........................................................511

TiVo Network Hack How-to Guide...............................511

TiVoHelp.com .............................................................512

Weaknees Interactive TiVo Upgrade Instructions ..........512

DirecTiVo Sites and Information........................................512

TiVo Software Download Sites ..........................................512

Sites Specific to Video Extraction, Archiving, Processing, and Insertion................................................................514

**Index ...............................................................517**

**About the CD.................................................543**

# *Introduction*

What exactly is TiVo (pronounced tee-vo), and where did it come from? A TiVo system records cable and satellite television instantly on a hard drive rather than on a videotape, enabling you to store and record an endless number of television program in one place. But that's not all it does. TiVo also offers a host of other features that make it a truly useful, timesaving device rather than simply a replacement for your aging VCR. In fact, TiVo represents the most exciting revolution in personal entertainment technology since the VCR or the television itself.

Some of the many advantages of TiVo over a VCR include:

◆ More durable recording capabilities than videotape

◆ Far easier to use (and expand) than a VCR

◆ More storage than a stack of videotapes

◆ Automatically locates and records your favorite programs, regardless of when or where they were broadcast

◆ Able to leap tall buildings in a single bound

◆ Optionally selects programs to record, based on your previous viewing habits

TiVo, Inc. and its hardware partners have been shipping TiVo units since 1999 with many different TiVo models available. At the time of this book's writing, these models fell into two general classes, known as *TiVo Series 1* and *TiVo Series 2*. (More details about these in Chapter 1, "Know Your TiVo.") Both of these classes can be hacked, er, "upgraded." TiVo, Inc. is continually updating its operating system and its capabilities while it matures as a company. The former is a win for TiVo customers, while the latter can present impediments to aspiring TiVo hackers. For example, Series 2 models are faster and sexier than Series 1 models, but it is more difficult to get command-line access to Linux on the Series 2 models due to "features" like kernel signing and hashed application size information stored in the TiVo filesystem. Luckily, many of the features that "needed" to be added to the Series 1 class and that required command-line access now are provided automatically by Series 2 models. As I'll explain later, however, there are ways around almost everything.

This book does not attempt to replace your TiVo documentation. It doesn't explain how to set up or configure your new TiVo, nor does it explain all the features of the TiVo and how to use them. (The documentation that came with your TiVo does a good job of all of that.) Instead, I'll explain how you can hack your TiVo—that is, how you can extend its capacity and capabilities beyond those that are provided out of the box. You'll also learn how to use certain features after you've hacked them or extended their capabilities through various TiVo backdoors (think "cheat codes," which are available in different versions of the TiVo software). Think of this book as a companion volume to your TiVo documentation.

Although you can find much of this information on the Internet, this book is designed to make your life easier by culling the resources and presenting them in one place—and then tailoring the hacking instructions so almost anyone can do it.

I'm not conducting a TiVo cheerleading session. Where appropriate, I'll point out the caveats, downsides, and costs of owning and using TiVo. However, like most TiVo owners, I feel that the benefits of owning and using TiVo far outweigh the disadvantages. Your mileage may vary.

## How To Use This Book

This book is intended for anyone with some computer experience and curiosity about what's inside their TiVo. It starts with an illustrated, hands-on chapter for people who don't really like to read, but just want to hack their TiVos and then use this book to press flowers. I'm fine with that. Or, if you're nervous about playing with hardware, the next chapter explains how to activate secret commands and modes of operation that help you get more out of your TiVo without even opening the box. Subsequent chapters then explain how to inexpensively add disk space to your TiVo, increasing the amount and quality of recordings that you can store. You'll learn how to install and run many freely-available, open source applications on your TiVo, so that you can schedule recordings over the Web, get news, sports, and weather displayed on your TiVo screen, and even check your portfolio while not missing an instant of your favorite broadcast television.

The focus of the book is how Linux, Macintosh, and Windows users can all work on and get the most out of their TiVos. The software for each platform is organized into system-specific sections, and much of it is provided on the CD that came with the book. If you've never experimented much with hardware, it isn't "hard."

Later chapters explain how to install and run different versions of the TiVo operating system and software on your TiVo so that you can take advantage of specific new (or old) features. Your TiVo is a full-fledged computer system—why not make the most of it?

To get started using this book, follow the hand-on tutorials in Chapter 2 for a quick overview, take a tour of TiVo history in Chapter 1, or look at Chapter 3 to see how to get the most out of the TiVo's user interface. Next, read Chapters 6 and 7 to learn how to use the included CD to back up your TiVo and add a bigger disk yourself—for far less than what others might charge. Finally, look at some of the programs described in Chapters 5 and 8, to see what you might find useful to have running on your TiVo. Your TiVo is a home entertainment device, a home computer, and this book will help you fine-tune its capabilities. Have a good time!

## Let's Have Some Fun

Like any smart appliance (and even most video games), there are plenty of tips and tricks that can help you get more out of your TiVo, even if you decide that you don't ever want to open the box.

To make it easier to find hot tips or usability suggestions, this book identifies this kind of information as tips and tricks with special "TiVo Guide" icons to differentiate them from the standard text of the book. These sections look like the following examples:

 **TiVo Guide**

Did you know that your TiVo has many special commands built into its remote control, providing shortcuts to your favorite TiVo commands and even to some hidden menus? To activate these... read the book.

If this information is specific to a certain model or software version of TiVo, these tips identify where, when, and how you can expect to use them. TiVo, Inc. is constantly upgrading its software, so different versions of the TiVo hardware can do different things.

## Hacking Is a Good Thing

Many people are confused by the word "hacking" (most notably the media), viewing it as an activity done by eccentric geeks with no social skills. This could not be further from the truth. That hype sells newspapers, magazines, and gets viewers for the evening news, but it isn't the way that anyone with a frontal lobe uses the word.

"Hacking" can be defined as using your ingenuity to explore and improve the capabilities of application software, operating systems, or hardware. You can hack your car by adding a new carburetor, "souping" up the fuel injection ratio, or adding some high-performance accessory. You can hack your home cable setup by splitting the cable and running it to multiple points in your house. If you don't like your house, you can hack it by adding a new room or moving the doors around. That's what this book is about—expanding the capacity and capabilities of your TiVo and interacting with it in new ways.

This book is *not* about "cracking," which means stealing services or information and doing something illegal, unethical, or immoral with them. Those kinds of activities are the computer equivalent of shoplifting—and they are just plain wrong.

Installing a new or modified version of your operating system and application software or adding new storage devices to your TiVo are tasks that are as American as apple pie. Roll the "America the Beautiful" soundtrack please....

## This Book, Your TiVo Warranty, and a Few Warnings

You do not have to be a Linux hacker or own a single Ministry or KMFDM T-shirt in order to hack your TiVo. This book provides clear, easy-to-follow instructions for a variety of enhancements that almost anyone can perform. Where relevant, each procedure described in this book also lists potential problems that you may encounter and explains how to correct them.

>  **WARNING**
>
> The procedures discussed in this book require opening your TiVo, which instantly voids your TiVo warranty *forever*. You can get a serious electrical shock if you're not careful while poking around inside your TiVo, just as you can with any electrical device. Never work on your TiVo while it's plugged in. Think of this book as the equivalent to a book on home television or automotive repairs, both of which can be dangerous. You can be hurt if you're not careful!

Here are a few other rules to satisfy the lawyers:

**Caution:** Never work on your TiVo while drinking hot beverages or while driving. Hot beverages may be hot. Don't drink and drive. Look both ways before you cross the street or open your TiVo. A penny saved is a penny earned. Don't run with scissors.

**Caveat:** Neither the publisher nor I am responsible for any damage to you or your TiVo if you attempt to follow the procedures discussed in this book. Nor are we responsible if a meteor strikes you while reading this book. This book is made of paper, and thus is flammable. We are not responsible for any resulting damage or injuries if you accidentally set this book on fire or drop it on your foot.

# This Book and TiVo, Inc.

The folks at TiVo had nothing to do with this book except as an inspiration. They are smart people who deserve your support. This book does not explain how to get around the TiVo service or in any way avoid paying TiVo the money that they deserve for their excellent service. TiVo deserves your support for pioneering an awesome device and a new way of interacting with broadcast media (although it would have been nice if they had left the Series 2 TiVo models as accessible as the Series 1 models). TiVo also deserves cultural kudos for not suppressing the hundreds of bulletin boards and Web sites that have sprung up discussing TiVo hacking and tips and tricks. In many cases, the people at TiVo go out of their way to contribute to and host community Web sites where TiVo internals are discussed. I can't think of any other company that has been so cool about its products. If you attempt to cheat TiVo, you hurt everyone. Please don't do that.

This version of the book explains how to back up and edit recorded video from your TiVo's hard drive. Since the latest TiVos from Pioneer include a DVD burner and TiVos have always provided the capability to save recordings to videotape, it seems silly not to discuss how to back up your recordings using alternate, unofficial methods. To keep the losers in the Recording Industry Association of America (RIAA), the whiners at the Motion Picture Association of America (MPAA), and the boneheads who voted for the Digital Millennium Copyright Act (DMCA) happy, do not sell or give away any recordings that you made with your device. Always force people to watch commercials, watch them yourself, and buy every product advertised, as many times as possible. Most importantly, do not always take the author of this book seriously.

I do not own stock in TiVo, although I've certainly considered it. This book is an attempt to share various experiences with TiVo, Linux, the Mac OS, and even Microsoft Windows. The goal of this book is to help you enhance the capacity and, in most cases, the capabilities of your TiVo. You've paid for your TiVo, and you can do whatever you want to the physical device. If you break it... well, you've already bought it, and you get to keep both pieces. Buy another one. The folks at TiVo shouldn't be too upset about that.

# HACKING THE TiVo

## Chapter 1

SECOND EDITION

## Know Your TiVo

So you've got a TiVo or you're thinking about getting one—now what? If you already have a TiVo, congratulations! This chapter provides some interesting reading about the TiVo, its history, and the features of the TiVo models, including a discussion of the hackability of various TiVo models. If you're still thinking about getting a TiVo, this chapter is definitely for you because it explores the answers to such questions as the following: Which one should you choose? What do different models do? Why would you prefer one particular model to another?

# Why TiVo?

TiVo systems are the best example of the most exciting revolution in personal entertainment technology since the VCR or the television itself. Like a VCR, TiVos enable you to record cable and satellite television, but TiVos offer a host of other features that make them a true home recording appliance rather than simply a replacement for your aging VCR.

Like any new terminology, the name for the class of devices that the TiVo belongs to is still adapting. New devices require new terminology, and it usually takes a while for the "right" term to be adopted—think "horseless carriage" as opposed to a "car" or an "automobile." TiVo and TiVo-like devices are referred to as *PVRs* (Personal Video Recorders), *PTVs* (Personal Television Receivers), *PDRs* (Personal Digital Recorders), *HDRs* (Hard Disk Recorders), *DVRs* (Digital Video Recorders), or the somewhat arcane *IEDs* (Intelligent Entertainment Devices). Regardless of what you call them, TiVo devices are the front-runners in the next generation of home video recording. Throughout this book, I'll try to use the acronym DVR, since that seems to be the most popular term for this class of devices,  and it has the added benefit of being the term used on the majority of TiVo Web sites (which should count for something).

DVRs are to VCRs as a refrigerator is to a block of ice. Some of the many advantages of DVRs over a VCR include the following:

◆ Far easier to use than a VCR

◆ More storage capacity than a videotape

◆ Simultaneous access to a library of recordings

◆ High quality recordings that do not degrade over time

DVRs would be impressive even if they were simply a replacement for your VCR, but they are much more than that. While DVRs from different manufacturers provide different capabilities, they generally provide some features that no VCR can touch, such as automatically locating and recording your favorite programs and those programs it has selected for you based on your viewing habits, regardless of when they are broadcast or on what channel. DVRs can even locate and record programs that feature your favorite actors, directors, or genre.

DVRs are revolutionizing the way that people watch, record, and interact with broadcast and cable television. A TiVo (or similar device) enables you to watch your favorite programs whenever you want—sometimes referred to as *time-shifting* because you can watch what you want when you want, rather than when it was originally broadcast. VCRs can do this to some extent, but they are limited to what fits on a single videotape (unless you happen to have a videotape-changing robot in your living room).

One of the greatest things about the TiVo is that it represents a stellar example of *convergence*, which is basically the techno-speak term for the tendency of technologies to combine by absorbing and adding related capabilities from each other.

As electronic devices become cheaper and more powerful, each generation of electronic devices tends to be smaller and more capable than previous generations, which is an amazing combination. Think about it—the portable phones of 15 years ago look like field radios from World War II. Today's cell phones fit in your pocket and can be used from almost anywhere in the world; you can browse the Internet, capture and transmit video, and they are available in hundreds of designer colors. In the computer industry, this is humorously referred to as *creeping featurism* (adding more and more features to an existing product), but today's sophisticated electronics and heightened connectivity expectations mean that people expect devices to do more. Why should you need a separate remote control for every electronic device in your house? Why shouldn't your cell phone provide Internet access, tell you the time and date, and let you play games?

The TiVo is all about convergence. Inside each TiVo lurks a fully functional computer system that serves as the brains of your TiVo. The TiVo operating system coordinates the input signal coming from your cable or satellite system and the commands you issue from your remote control to the hard disk where your recordings are stored. Your TiVo can record video on its hard drive while displaying an existing recording. A TiVo system that is integrated with DirecTV systems can even record satellite broadcasts while you watch another live broadcast.

Luckily, the TiVo does not have the standard usability or system crash problems that plague many home computer systems. The TiVo is as reliable as a telephone and easier to use than a VCR. A TiVo runs an advanced, popular computer operating system called *Linux*, about which you need to know absolutely nothing in order to use your TiVo. For most people, the relationship between Linux and your TiVo is the same as the relationship between electricity and your telephone. You don't have to know how your telephone works to order a pizza over the phone—the Linux operating system for TiVo is similarly invisible.

If you've ever worked on your own car or opened up your home PC to fix or add something, the use of Linux will give you some similar opportunities for customizing and enhancing your TiVo experience. I've saved a lot of money and had a lot of fun expanding and experimenting with my TiVo, and you can too. If you have ever added a board, hard drive, or CD-ROM drive to your computer system, chances are that you can easily save yourself some money and feel quite virtuous by following the procedures discussed in this book. If you have any interest or expertise in programming, you can add even more capabilities to your TiVo. No other device provides as much potential for enhancement while improving your lifestyle by its very existence.

# What's This TiVo Service I Keep Hearing About?

Like any computer-based device, a TiVo has both hardware and software components. The hardware component is obvious—it's the black or silver box that you got when you purchased your TiVo. On the software side, TiVo, Inc. provides Linux, lots of behind-the-scenes system software, and an impressively useful and intuitive user interface that is what you see when you hook up your TiVo to your television and wield the TiVo remote control.

In addition to the software that runs on the TiVo itself, TiVo adds one more bit of software, which is a subscription to a service that provides television listings to your TiVo system. The TiVo service provides much more than just a set of television listings (the same listing you can get by reading your *TV Guide* or by looking up local television listings on some Web site). It provides detailed listings for every channel on your local cable or satellite network, including information about the genre of each show, the actors that appear in each show, information about the director (where applicable), and summary information about the subject of the show itself. Using this enhanced, specially formatted information enables your TiVo to automatically record exactly what you're interested in, as long as you've subscribed to an appropriate level of the TiVo service.

 **TIP**

When watching a program on your TiVo, you can always press the Enter or Display keys on your remote to get detailed information about the show you're watching.

The extra programming information provided by the TiVo service enables the TiVo to perform many of the smart recording features that most people have come to expect from TiVo, such as the following:

◆ TiVo Season Passes, which subscribe to a series of shows so that you'll never miss an episode, and also provide smart features, such as recording episodes only the first time that they are broadcast and automatically skipping repeated episodes

◆ TiVo Suggestions, which record shows that match some aspect of your viewing preferences, as compiled from the TiVo's history of the shows that you have previously watched and/or recorded

◆ TiVo WishLists, which tell the TiVo to record shows that match various keywords in the show's title or description, feature certain actors, are directed by specific directors, and so on.

# TiVo Service Fees

TiVo, Inc. charges for their listings service in two different ways: as a recurring monthly charge, or as a single charge for the life of a specific TiVo. How (and if) you have to pay for the TiVo service depends on what type of TiVo you have:

◆ If you have a DirecTiVo with a basic level of DirecTV programming, you have to pay $5.99 per month, per DirecTiVo, for the TiVo programming information. If you have a more advanced level of the DirecTV programming, usually known as their TOTAL CHOICE package, the TiVo programming information is free—there are no monthly charges.

◆ If you have a stand-alone TiVo, you have to pay $12.99 per month for TiVo programming information, which you can hardwire to a credit card to simplify payment. As of June, 2004, if you have multiple stand-alone TiVos, you can get the TiVo service for up to 5 additional TiVos at $6.95 per month. You can also pay a one-time subscription charge of $299 for a lifetime subscription (i.e., no monthly charges), where lifetime means the lifetime of a single registered TiVo machine—not, as we might prefer, our personal lifetimes.

 **TIP**

If you've just bought your first TiVo and it's a Series 2, I'd recommend that you pay for lifetime service and do it now. Series 1 TiVos feature older, slower hardware and have just been around for a while. The Series 2s are the future of TiVo— Series 1s, though, are easier to hack, have a shorter lifespan, and so on.

From early 2003 through June, 2004, TiVo also offered a Home Media Option (HMO) that added some useful features to a Series 2 TiVo. As of June, 2004, the features previously known as the Home Media Option are now built into the standard TiVo service as its Home Media Features. More about this in the next section.

# TiVo Service Levels

The requirement that you pay for the TiVo service is the most commonly cited irritant by TiVo detractors, and is also one of the reasons that so many TiVo-like systems and open source software projects have sprung up. TiVo-like systems have a variety of mechanisms for populating their devices with guide information, many of which involve a subscription service that may or may not have an associated charge. The open source TiVo alternatives usually obtain guide data by retrieving it from online sites that display programming information. This retrieval is often done by what is known as *scraping* such Web sites, which means that programs retrieve HTML pages from these sites, parse through the Web content, and convert it into a format that can be used by a particular project. Nothing wrong with that, except that any changes to the format of the data on the target Web site require a change to the program that retrieves and parses the information. Still, you can't beat the price!

However, TiVo didn't get to be incredibly popular and successful by ignoring its customers. Beginning in early 2004, TiVo added a new, entry-level service that provides basic programming information for some newer TiVos but does not provide all of the capabilities of the classic TiVo service. For TiVo systems that come with the TiVo Basic service, TiVo renamed its standard service level to be *TiVo Plus*.

The next sections explore the current levels of TiVo service at the time this book was updated and also discuss the cost and capabilities of add-on service levels such as TiVo's Home Media Option. Table 1.1 summarizes the primary differences between these three service levels.

# TiVo Basic

Recognizing that some people will settle for fewer TiVo features if there is an associated cost savings, the vendors of newer DVD-enabled TiVo systems, such as the Pioneer and Toshiba

TiVos, offer a free, entry-level TiVo service called *TiVo Basic*. There is no cost for the TiVo Basic service, which features enough functionality to enable you to retrieve basic programming information and record and watch television. As shown in Table 1.1, the TiVo Basic service level doesn't provide some of the capabilities that make the TiVo a truly impressive device, such as TiVo Season Passes, Suggestions, and WishLists (described previously), but you can't beat the price. When you install a DVD-enabled TiVo that comes with the TiVo Basic service level, you can try the TiVo Plus service level (what most of us think as the standard TiVo service) free for 45 days, at which point you will probably not want to go back to the TiVo Basic service level.

## TiVo Plus

Let's not forget that TiVo is an actual commercial entity that would like to survive, and thus needs a revenue stream of some sort. The newer TiVos for which TiVo Basic service is available have renamed the standard TiVo service level *TiVo Plus* and charge the same fees for TiVo Plus that users of previous TiVos were accustomed to for the "standard" TiVo service. The TiVo Plus service level provides all of the fun conveniences that most people have come to expect from TiVo, such as Season Passes, Suggestions, and WishLists described earlier.

On the newer TiVos for which TiVo Basic service is available, you must also be subscribed to the TiVo Plus service in order to upgrade to other features such as TiVo's Home Media Option.

For a comparison of the TiVo Basic and TiVo Plus service levels straight from the horse's mouth, see **http://customersupport.tivo.com/tivoknowbase/root/public/tv199.htm**.

## What Was TiVo's Home Media Option?

TiVo's Home Media Option (HMO), introduced in early April, 2003, extended the basic capabilities and network awareness of Series 2 machines. TiVo's Home Media Option required that your Series 2 was running Version 4.0 or better and that your TiVo was running a service level greater than the TiVo Basic service level. As of June, 2004, HMO capabilities (now known as Home Media Features) are now built into the standard TiVo service for Series 2 machines at no extra cost. These capabilities are the following:

◆ Share recordings between networked Series 2 TiVos, known in TiVo terms as *multiroom viewing*. You can record a show on one of your TiVos and easily watch it on another by transferring it over your home network. You can also browse the Now Playing lists of other networked Series 2 TiVos to more easily select shows from the lists.

◆ Schedule recordings over the Internet by connecting to tivo.com to schedule recordings up to 30 minutes before the actual broadcast—if your Series 2 TiVo is on a home network with an always-on, broadband connection to the Internet.

◆ Access online music and digital photographs from any Series 2 TiVo. This is especially attractive to TiVo owners whose TiVo is part of a high-quality, home theater setup (although it works for me, too).

◆ Export collections of MP3 files and playlists from Windows and Macintosh systems, using platform-specific software called the *TiVo Desktop*. You can play online audio files in MP3 format and can use playlists in the ASX, M3U, and PLS formats used by most online audio players.

◆ Export collections of digital photographs from Windows and Macintosh systems by using platform-specific software called the *TiVo Desktop*. You can view digital photographs saved in the BMP, DIB, GIF, JPG, and PNG file formats.

---

 **NOTE**

See Chapter 9, "Working with Your TiVo from Windows and Macintosh Systems," for information about integrating various types of computer systems with Series 2 TiVos running v4.0 or better of the TiVo software.

---

 **Don't Despair, Linux Lovers!**

Although TiVo itself doesn't offer Linux-side software that works with its Home Media Features, open source software comes to the rescue! See the discussion in Chapter 10 entitled "Working with TiVo's Home Media Features from Linux" for software that makes it easy to integrate your Linux-based audio files and digital photo collections with TiVo's Home Media Features.

---

 **NOTE**

If you have one or more stand-alone Series 2 TiVos and a DVD-enabled TiVo such as the Pioneer 57 or 810, you can use the TiVo's multiroom viewing capability to transfer shows between them. Unfortunately, at the time this book was updated, you cannot save shows to DVD that were originally recorded on your stand-alone Series 2s due to differences in the bit-rates at which shows are recorded on these types of machines and corresponding limitations in the TiVo software. At best, this is infuriating and hopefully something that TiVo will fix in updated versions of the software for the DVD-enabled TiVos.

---

# Identifying Your TiVo

The TiVo can be identified by an internal serial number, known as the *TiVo service number*, which is stored in a programmable, read-only memory chip in your TiVo as well as printed on a label on the back of your system. This service number is used by TiVo to track your subscription status, any customer support issues that you may have raised, and to identify any add-on services (such as the TiVo Home Media option) that you may have purchased for that particular TiVo. TiVo also uses this information whenever it needs to download a

**Table 1.1   Comparing TiVo Service Levels**

| Feature | TiVo Basic | TiVo Plus |
|---|---|---|
| Browse by Time and Channel | No | Yes |
| Digital Music and Photos | No | Yes |
| Multiroom Viewing | No | Yes |
| Program Information | Up to 3 days | Up to 14 days |
| Remote Scheduling | No | Yes |
| Search by Title | No | Yes |
| Season Passes | No | Yes |
| Sort Now Playing List | No | Yes |
| TiVo Suggestions | No | Yes |
| WishLists | No | Yes |

new version of the TiVo operating system. The first field of a TiVo service number identifies the model of your TiVo, so you don't accidentally get a version of the operating system that is incompatible with your TiVo hardware.

While a TiVo's serial number can be changed, each TiVo also contains a cryptographic chip that stores the public and private encryption keys specific to that unit. This allows TiVo, Inc. to transmit content, such as the Home Media option, that can only be loaded by a specific unit.

# TiVos and Your Viewing Habits

Your TiVo automatically downloads program listings and advanced paid programming from the TiVo service weekly, through a local phone call, over the Internet, or as part of a data stream such as DSS or the embedded stream that provides VCRPlus+ information. Direc-TiVo and TiVo Basic systems do not need access to a phone line to retrieve programming information, but all stand-alone TiVos and TiVos running the TiVo Plus service level or better need to regularly retrieve programming information over a phone line or the Internet. These TiVos schedule these downloads to occur during off-peak hours because, once downloaded, the information is reformatted and indexed to improve the speed at which you can search for or simply display television programming information. Whenever the TiVo scheduled download is supposed to occur, the TiVo first checks whether it is currently recording something, and reschedules the download for a later time if that's the case. Next, the TiVo displays a screen informing you that it wants to download information and giving you the option of deferring the download until a later time. The latter is useful if you are actively watching a show or planning to record something in the next hour or so.

When downloading programming information and updates, your TiVo also uploads two diagnostic files to TiVo central:

◆ A diagnostic log file for the TiVo hardware and software that describes the relative health of your TiVo system.

◆ A viewing information file that contains information about viewer-related events (channel changes, etc.) occurring on your TiVo during the lifetime of the log file. This file is anonymous and does not include information about your TiVo serial number (though, to be honest, that information could be resurrected from Web and FTP logs if anyone really cared).

## TiVo, Privacy Concerns, and Advertising

Many people today are concerned about who has information about them and what is being done with that information. When users discovered that TiVo was sending this information back to TiVo headquarters (regardless of how anonymous it was), the Internet exploded with crankiness. In response, TiVo clarified its privacy policy by making sure that users knew that they could opt out of the automatic collection of data from their systems. You can do this by calling the TiVo Customer Care telephone number (877-FOR-TIVO) and requesting that they not track or use this information from your TiVo.

TiVo systems can also display pop-up messages, known as *Pre-TiVo-Central Messages* (PTCMs). These messages display on your TiVo screen whenever you first press the TiVo button on your remote—in other words, before you get to the TiVo Central menus, as the name suggests. After you read them, these messages are stored in a special section of the TiVo Central menu system, and can be reviewed (and subsequently deleted) by going to the TiVo Messages & Setup menu and selecting TiVo Messages. This screen displays all undeleted marketing/advertising messages on your screen. You can view any message by highlighting the message title, clicking Select to view the message, and then using the arrow wheel to select Delete Message when you've finished reading it. If you want to save the message, simply select Done and click the Select button.

TiVo PTCMs can be service-related messages, such as those that can remind you that your TiVo needs to "phone home" to get updated programming listings, but they also can contain advertising. Many people resent paying for the TiVo service and then having advertising piped into their homes. Therefore, like the TiVo data collection, you can opt out of receiving advertising PTCMs by calling TiVo Customer Care (877-FOR-TIVO) and requesting that you no longer receive them. You will still occasionally receive quality-of-service PTCMs, but you won't be subjected to those that are essentially spam.

**WARNING**

The viewing information file provides information that TiVo may make available to ratings services, analysts, and so on. Some people may find this odious because TiVo can (in theory) profit from this information by reselling it without your permission, or because they are simply invading your privacy by snooping on your viewing habits. I personally could care less. My TiVo has revolutionized my television viewing habits by freeing me from the tyranny of a clock and a calendar. As far as I'm concerned, they're welcome to the few scraps of demographic data that may fall from my plate.

# A Short Course in TiVo History

The idea of personal desktop video on a computer system is not unique to TiVo, Inc., although TiVo has made it practical. Personal desktop video systems are the outgrowth of two separate trends of the early 1990s—personal desktop video creation and editing, and the interest of cable/media companies in delivering more than just cable TV to customers' desktops (and charging for it, of course).

In 1989, Avid Technology unveiled the Avid One Media Composer, an advanced video editing system running on Macintosh computers. In October of 1990, a company named NewTek amazed the US video production community by shipping a breakthrough product called the *Video Toaster* for the Commodore Amiga computer. These products enabled users to add text or graphics to an existing video without the need for a separate character generator. Users could modify and create video graphics, and multiplex, combine, and edit existing video sources. These solutions cost exponentially less than any similar video-editing solution, and worried companies like Chryon, which produced substantially more expensive video-editing hardware and software packages.

High-performance video workstations, such as Silicon Graphics machines, were capable of doing the same sorts of things as the Media Composer and Video Toaster (and more, of course), and already were doing it for expensive, high-budget projects such as the *Jurassic Park* movies. These groundbreaking products put video-editing capabilities in the hands of aspiring video producers (and low-budget cable channels) everywhere.

As companies like Avid and NewTek were pioneering an affordable desktop video-editing device, the companies that were already delivering video to their customers were trying to identify the next big way of making money from their customers. In December of 1993, Time-Warner executive Gerald Levin announced a consuming new initiative for Time-Warner called the *Full Service Network (FSN)*. Combining the power of cable television, cable telephony, on-demand video and film, and home shopping, the Full Service Network was piped into a few thousand test homes and businesses in the Orlando, Florida area.

The Full Service Network was not the first attempt at expanding the horizons of home video service, but it was certainly the most impressive in its scope and the most extensive investment to date from a major consumer firm. Companies like TCI had previously tested video on demand, where customers could request specific videos from their homes and have them piped directly to their televisions. The TCI experiment in this regard was especially humorous, consisting of an armada of employees on roller skates feeding videos into a wall of VCRs whenever a customer requested a specific video. GTE pioneered a short-lived interactive television home shopping service known as *Main Street*, whose name was meant to prophesy how home shopping would eclipse physical shopping malls, just as those malls had once eclipsed downtown streets lined with stores.

The most interesting development that eventually came out of the Full Service Network was the relationship that evolved between two executives from Silicon Graphics, the company that made the set-top boxes that the Full Service Network depended upon. With years of experience in high-bandwidth video delivery and display, Silicon Graphics was a natural choice to provide this technology. TiVo founders Mike Ramsay (former Senior Vice President of the Silicon Desktop Group at SGI and former president of SGI's Silicon Studio, Inc.) and Jim Barton (vice president of SGI's Systems Software Division and the lead system software architect of the Full Service Network) met in the context of the Full Service Network.

 **TIP**

For more information on the Full Service Network and the big media companies' involvement, including experiments and losses in interactive television and other pre-Internet technologies, John Motavelli's *Bamboozled at the Revolution* (Viking, 2002, ISBN 0-670-89980-1) is an excellent read.

Working against Time Warner's Full Service Network was the sheer fact of how revolutionary its goals were at the time. In late 1993, the Internet boom had barely begun, but the potential for the Internet to eclipse many of the FSN goals was already evident. Also working against FSN was the fact that no special box was required, only a high-speed connection. The number of big media firms and startups that made—and subsequently lost—money trying to broadcast video over the Internet is only superseded by the number of people who have made fortunes delivering porn over the Internet (probably the Internet's most profitable niche to date).

The "eureka moment" that occurred to Ramsay and Barton was that people didn't necessarily need special content piped into their homes—they just needed a better way of interacting with it—namely, by liberating viewers from the constraints of the broadcasting schedule. After all, by the mid 1990s, most viewers were getting a hundred or more channels of television delivered to their homes. The TiVo folks put it this way on their Web site:

> "...As the pioneer in digital video recording services, TiVo Inc. was founded on one driving vision: to create and continually enhance a new, easy—and much better—way to watch television. The idea that everyone, no matter how busy life gets, deserves to enjoy the television entertainment of their choice on their time, established the cornerstone of the TiVo philosophy: watch what you want, when you want...."

This basic TiVo concept is an idea that is elegant in its simplicity, giving viewers a way of more easily recording larger amounts of broadcast media and then watching it whenever they want. The keys to this concept are service, software, and affordability. If consumers were receiving cable broadcasts already, what benefits could an auxiliary service provide that would make people willing to pay for it? What benefits could a new piece of hardware for the home provide that would make it attractive to consumers?

In January, 1999, TiVo unveiled its Personal Television Service at the National Consumer Electronics Show in Las Vegas, Nevada. Since then, in partnership with hardware manufacturers such as Philips Consumer Electronics, Thomson, and Sony, and through broadcast alliances with vendors such as AOL, DirecTV, and a variety of broadcast channels, the TiVo has become the leading Personal Video Recorder available today. Originally known as *TeleWorld*, this term is now used to identify special TiVo broadcasts, and TiVo is the name known throughout the industry. Its combination of affordable hardware and elegant, easy-to-use way of interacting with TiVo viewers, as well as its partnerships with various cable and broadcast channels have earned TiVo a passionate group of devotees who would never return to the primitive simplicity of pure cable television and VCRs.

Today, TiVo is actively adding features that extend its capabilities, and it is pursuing software partners that increase the accessibility of TiVos from other systems and software packages. These innovations help preserve the TiVo's leading edge as a hub for digital entertainment in the home and might even make money for TiVo along the way. Some of these, such as remote scheduling and the upcoming ability to watch TiVo recordings on devices other than a TiVo, were probably at least partially inspired by the hacks described in this book, but the folks at TiVo, Inc. are also smart people who would probably like to stay in business and thus have their own R&D and business development plans. Though ReplayTV may largely have bitten the big one, as described later in this chapter, other competitors to TiVo are continually emerging and, like any high-tech company, TiVo must continue to innovate and provide a superior product in order to survive.

Liberté, egalité, and better TV! Vive la TiVolution!

# TiVo Business Partners and Integrators

As anyone who has ever tried to pioneer a new type of computer system or computer-based home appliance has discovered, software and hardware are expensive. Most startup hardware companies who don't want to (or can't) handle the sole expense of hardware production develop a "reference platform," which is basic proof-of-concept hardware required to support their software. If the focus of the company is on software or service (which the TiVo strategy was originally), they license this hardware design to various manufacturers who specialize in hardware production and partner with them to provide the associated software and services.

TiVo, Inc. writes the software that runs on TiVo machines. They are therefore responsible for software updates, supporting the TiVo service, and general system setup information. As a home appliance, TiVo is very interested in making your initial experience with the TiVo positive, and getting you to connect to the TiVo service as quickly as possible. TiVo makes the majority of its money from subscriptions to the TiVo service, and only recently has begun directly manufacturing TiVo hardware. Until later Series 2 TiVo systems, all of the hardware manufacturing for TiVo was outsourced to other companies. Philips, Sony, Thomson, and Hughes manufacture Series 1 TiVo hardware units, and they make their money selling the hardware. They are responsible for hardware problems and repairs, upgrades to the hard drive, and so forth. Series 2 TiVo models have been manufactured directly under the TiVo brand name as well as Sony. Hughes and TiVo codeveloped the Series 2 DirecTiVo. (The next section explains the differences between various models of TiVo hardware and how to identify the model you have.)

Interestingly enough, TiVo does not generate its own program schedule information. TiVo gets up-to-date programming information from a company called Tribune, although it may eventually use other sources of programming information. The core features of the TiVo service are the depth and detail provided by its scheduling information and how the TiVo stores and indexes that information to make it easy to identify programs that you want to record based on a variety of features.

## Partnering with the Networks

In addition to hardware and internal software partnerships, TiVo also is actively involved in partnering with existing broadcast networks so they can deliver custom or special interest content to TiVo customers. TiVo is working with networks such as NBC, Showtime, and Starz, to provide advanced scheduling and interaction mechanisms that simplify recording broadcasts from those networks. These active partnerships and positive relationships with existing broadcast systems are the primary reasons that the TiVo does not automatically provide features that enable you to automatically skip commercials, which is available on competing ReplayTV devices. Like any recording mechanism for broadcast media, the TiVo offers a fast-forward (in three impressive speeds) that enables you to fast-forward through advertising. Also, as you'll learn later in this book, various versions of the TiVo operating systems offer ways of easily skipping forward in 30-second increments, which is (ironically) the lowest common denominator of the time required for most modern TV commercials.

## Showcasing Upcoming Broadcasts

The best examples of TiVo's customized programming are its Showcases, which are available on your TiVo by selecting Showcases after pressing the TiVo Central button on your TiVo remote. These Showcases are divided into sections dedicated to items identified as features by TiVo headquarters, and a number of sections associated with specific broadcast media such as Showtime, NBC, Starz, the Discovery Channel, HBO, The Movie Channel (TMC), Encore, The Learning Channel (TLC), Cinemax, Flix, Westerns, and the Sundance channel. These broadcasters use the interactive TiVo platform as a new way to reach a select group of users, freeing themselves from traditional 30-second TV advertisements. The TiVo Showcases enable broadcast media partners to present highlights of their products and schedules in a new way, targeting people who are obviously interested enough in television viewing to have bought a TiVo. Some of the best known examples of TiVo Showcases have been promotions for new movies such as *Austin Powers in Goldmember*, *Mr. Deeds*, and music videos from popular artists such as Sheryl Crow and Counting Crows (no relation). In these cases, the associated TiVo Showcases included video and audio footage that were available nowhere else. But let's face it—the TiVo Showcases are essentially advertising, although it is advertising available only to a relatively select group of people who are obviously interested in television—TiVo owners like us. TiVo's Showcases include its own *TiVolution* Showcase, which discusses items of special interest to TiVo users.

One of the more irritating developments on the TiVo recently has been the continuing emergence of "gold star" TiVo advertising, which is a set of advertising messages that are downloaded to the TiVo. These appear as items prefaced by a gold star on the initial TiVo Central menu. Recent advertisers have included Porsche, which says something about the demographic expectations of TiVo owners (congratulations to all of us!). Unfortunately, this type of advertising is as exciting as the subscription and special offer cards that fall out of magazines you've purchased. This is particularly true in the case of a TiVo, especially if you've bought your TiVo to liberate yourself from putting up with advertising in real time.

## TiVo Software Licensing

With newer TiVos, such as the DVD-enabled Pioneer 57H, 810H, and the Toshiba SD-H400, TiVo has also begun licensing different levels of the TiVo service and its capabilities to hardware manufacturers. The specific capabilities of the first of these, the TiVo Basic service level, were described earlier in this chapter.

TiVo's support of other service levels can be a very good thing for TiVo, because each system bundled with the Basic service level is able to optionally upgrade to the full TiVo service, supporting WishLists, Season Passes, and smart searches based on actor, director, and so on. Manufacturers that bundle the Basic service with their hardware aren't expected to pass any monthly cost to buyers, which is a great way for TiVo to get its service into homes without the monthly cost requirement that is a stumbling block for many people when purchasing a stand-alone TiVo. I wondered about this before I bought my first TiVo. At this point, I personally find the TiVo service cost to be just another monthly utility bill (for the one machine on which I haven't paid for lifetime service).

Unfortunately, the availability of the new Basic service level is a business-to-business feature, and therefore doesn't benefit existing TiVo users. At the time of this book's writing, TiVo doesn't plan to offer a less expensive version of this service to owners of existing Series 1 and Series 2 models.

# TiVo's Software Partners

TiVo is increasing its efforts to extend the accessibility of its offerings with software packages from a variety of different vendors. The introduction of network-enabled Series 2 TiVos and TiVo's Home Media Features have made TiVos inherently accessible from other systems—now we all just have to wait to see how far TiVo and media-related software vendors are willing to go to fulfill the promise of true convergence.

TiVo maintains a list of current software partners on the TiVo site at **http://www.tivo.com/4.9.17.asp**. This page lists official partners from TiVo's perspective, but it does not include all of the companies who have taken advantage of the open specifications for TiVo's Home Media Features (available at **http://www.tivo.com/developer**) to enable their software to interoperate with it. Following is a list of software packages that interoperate with TiVo systems at the current time:

- **Adobe Photoshop Album 2.0 (http://www.adobe.com/tivo)** is an easy-to-use Windows software package for organizing digital photographs, and includes a "Publish To TiVo DVR" button so that you can view photos on your TV through a networked TiVo DVR.

- **MoodLogic (http://www.moodlogic.com/tivo.html)** is an interesting remixing Windows software package that makes it easy to browse your MP3 collection and remix songs that it contains by using your remote control. Although many people simply want to play their MP3s, if you want to play with them first, MoodLogic has some fun features.

- **Media Jukebox (http://www.musicex.com/mediajukebox/index.html)**, from MusicExchange.com software, uses J. River's Music Exchange technology (**http://www.musicex.com/labels.html**) to export audio files in a variety of different formats from Windows systems so that they can be played on your television or home entertainment center through TiVo's Home Media Features. Using this package is discussed in the section of Chapter 9 entitled "Playing Windows Audio Formats Other than MP3."

- **Picasa Digital Picture Organizer (http://www.picasa.net/ads/tivo3.php)** for TiVo is an extremely simple and easy-to-use Windows software package that helps you organize digital photographs, create slideshows, set those slideshows to music, and export them to a networked Series 2 TiVo.

As you can see from this list, the current focus of most TiVo-enabled software is enhanced integration with the audio and still photography capabilities of TiVo's Home Media Option. At the Consumer Electronics Show in spring 2004, TiVo announced even more exciting capabilities and related software partnerships, including TiVo programming over cell phones (yawn) and its TiVo ToGo software (wow!). Although not available at the time this book was written, TiVo ToGo is supposed to extend interoperability to recorded video by enabling network-enabled TiVos to share recordings from a TiVo to other computer systems. As announced, TiVo ToGo will consist of a TiVo security key and TiVo-enabled versions of software packages such as Sonic Solution's MyDVD and CinePlayer applications.

While a conceptually exciting development, how useful this is remains to be seen. (It would help if it were actually available when I was writing this, but what can I say?) In the first place, the security key is rumored to be a physical device (known as a *dongle*) that plugs into a USB port on the TiVo, and which the TiVo will use to obtain authentication information. Dongles have been used for years in the software industry (traditionally on classic serial or parallel ports), and are universally recognized as a hassle because they can be misplaced, lost, or chewed and eaten by less discerning pets. Let's hope that TiVo comes up with a less kludgy, long-term solution—maybe a (gasp!) software solution?

The announced software perspective is equally disappointing. Both the MyDVD and CinePlayer applications are Windows-only applications, which leaves users of the best-known platform for Audio/Video display and editing—the Macintosh—without an out-of-the-box solution. The folks at Apple are as smart as anyone and will presumably address this limitation in short order, but TiVo's announced Windows-centric focus is, as always, disturbing and disappointing. Check the Web page for this book (**http://www.vonhagen.org/tivo**) for a discussion of new developments as they emerge.

Windows-only software also leaves Linux lovers such as myself out in the dark, but we're used to that. I'm sure that the army of Linux TiVo hackers will start fixing this problem a few minutes after the software is released, and the video extraction packages discussed in Chapter 12 are already available. Still, an official, open TiVo solution for displaying recorded video on other types of systems would be what we in the software industry call "The Right Thing."

# TiVo Hardware Models and Features

Different TiVo models have different capabilities and can be hacked to different extents and in different ways. Take a look at the various models of TiVo that have been sold during its history.

Although TiVo has had a number of hardware partners over the past few years, all TiVo units fall into two general classes: TiVo Series 1, which use an IBM PowerPC 403GCX processor running at 50 MHz, and TiVo Series 2, which use a NEC MIPS processor running at 162 MHz. In addition to these fundamental differences, there are two other basic TiVo classes: those made for use with any cable service (often simply referred to as a *stand-alone TiVo*), and those made for use with DirecTV dish receivers (often referred to as the *DirecTiVo*).

The connectors on the back of the Series 1 and Series 2 TiVo systems are very similar, as shown in Table 1.2.

The Audio Right/Left and Video inputs and outputs both use RCA-style connectors. Both controller outputs use 305 mm minijack sockets. The S-Video inputs and outputs use the same mini DIN connectors. The telephone connectors are standard RJ-11 connectors. Stand-alone TiVo units have a standard Channel 3/Channel 4 selector switch next to the RF input.

DirecTiVo units also provide two internal inputs, two coaxial audio outputs, two coaxial video outputs, one standard analog TV input, and a Dolby Digital optical output (using a TosLink con-

**Table 1.2   TiVo Connectors**

| Input/Output | Series 1 | Series 2 |
|---|---|---|
| Audio Right/Left, Video Inputs | 2 | 2 |
| Audio Right/Left, Video Outputs | 2 | 2 |
| Infrared Control Output | 1 | 1 |
| Serial Control Output | 1 | 1 |
| S-Video Output | 1 | 1 |
| S-Video Input | 1 | 1 |
| RF Output | 1 | 1 |
| RF Input | 1 | 1 |
| USB Ports | 0 | 2 |
| Telephone Connector | 1 | 1 |

nector). DirecTiVo units contain two separate tuners, so that you can watch one show live while you record another, but can only record from DTV sources. On all TiVo units, you can watch a show that you have already recorded while recording something that is currently being broadcast, but only on the DirecTiVos can you watch one live broadcast while recording another.

Nowadays, all TiVo models sold as new through TiVo or consumer electronics shops, such as Best Buy or Circuit City, should be TiVo Series 2 machines; however, if you're buying a used TiVo somewhere, you will want to ask whether it is a TiVo Series 1 or Series 2 unit. The easiest way to tell the difference between them is the presence of the USB connectors on all TiVo Series 2 units. Series 1 models do not have these.

The amount of storage that comes with your TiVo (assuming that it has yet to be hacked) is based on the manufacturer and the model number. In most cases, you can identify your machine's manufacturer by looking at the front panel of your DVR, which typically displays the manufacturer's logo. If your front panel only displays a TiVo logo, then you have a Series 2 system made by TiVo. You can also extrapolate the manufacturer of your TiVo from the TiVo service number (which is unique to each unit and is present on the back of each TiVo, on a sticker on the outside of the original shipping materials for the TiVo). Alternatively, you can connect the TiVo to a television, turn on both, and look at the onscreen TiVo Central menu (press the TiVo button on the TiVo's remote control, select Messages & Setup, and then select System Information).

Table 1.3 shows the relationship between the first three digits of a TiVo serial number and the manufacturer and model of each TiVo. In general, the first number represents the hardware generation, the second is the brand of TiVo you're using, and the third digit is the type of TiVo. (For example, all DirecTiVo prefixes end with '1'.)

**Table 1.3   TiVo Model Numbers**

| Digits | Manufacturer | Model |
|--------|--------------|-------|
| 000 | Philips | HDR110 or HDR310 Series 1 stand-alone (14 or 30 hours recording capacity, respectively) |
| 001 | Philips | DSR6000 Series 1 DirecTV receiver with TiVo (35 hours recording capacity) |
| 002 | Philips | HDR112, HDR212, HDR312, HDR612 Series 1 stand-alone (14, 20, 30, or 60 hours recording capacity, respectively) |
| 010 | Sony | SVR-2000 Series 1 Digital Video Recorder stand-alone (30 hours recording capacity) |
| 011 | Sony | SAT-T60 Series 1 DirecTV receiver with TiVo  (35 hours recording capacity) |
| 023 | Thomson | PVR10UK Series 1 stand-alone, 40 hours, UK only |
| 031 | Hughes | GXCEBOT Series 1 DirecTV Digital Satellite Receiver |
| 101 | Phillips | DSR7000 (DIRECTV DVR with TiVo (35 hours) |
| 110 | Sony | SVR-3000 Series 2 stand-alone (80 hours) |
| 121 | RCA | DirecTV DVR with TiVo |
| 130 | TiVo | TCD130040 Series 2 stand-alone (40 hours) |
| 140 | TiVo | TCD140060 Series 2 stand-alone (60 hours) |
| 151 | Hughes | Series 2 DirecTV Digital Satellite Recorder (40 hours) |
| 230 | TiVo | TCD230040 Series 2 stand-alone (40 hours) |
| 240 | TiVo | TCD240040 Series 2 or TCD240080 Series 2 stand-alones (40 or 80 hours, respectively) |
| 250 | TiVo | TCD540140 Series 2 stand-alone (140 hours) |
| 264 | Toshiba | Digital Media Server with TiVo |
| 275 | Pioneer | Pioneer, all models |
| 301 | Philips | DSR704 (35 hours) or DSR708 (80 hours) |
| 321 | RCA | DirecTV DVR with TiVo |
| 351 | Hughes | DirecTV DVR with TiVo |
| 381 | Samsung | DirecTV DVR with TiVo |

The hardware expandability of each TiVo model differs somewhat. The recording capacity of all TiVos can be upgraded in different ways:

- By replacing the disk in a single-disk system with a higher-capacity drive
- By replacing both disks of a dual-disk system with higher-capacity drives
- By replacing the two disks of a dual-disk system with a single, higher-capacity drive
- By adding a second disk to an existing single-disk system

Most unhacked TiVo machines have a single disk drive, with the exception of the stand-alone Philips HDR312 and HDR612 TiVo models and some Philips DSR6000 and Sony SAT-T60 DirecTiVo units.

Adding a second drive to any single-disk TiVo Series 1 machine requires that you buy a special mounting bracket for the second drive. Sources for these brackets are listed in the section of Chapter 4 entitled "TiVo Hardware Supplies on the Net."

TiVo Series 2 machines are somewhat quirkier. The 60-hour TCD140060 Series 2 model, the 40-hour TCD130040 AT&T Series 2 model, and the Sony SVR-3000 have internal brackets with space to accommodate a second drive—all you need are a few screws to mount the drives. The TCD230040 and TCD240080 TiVo Series 2 systems and Hughes HDVR2 systems do not have space for a second drive on their existing configuration, but on the Net you can buy slightly "Frankensteinian" brackets that will hold two drives for these systems. Sources for these brackets are also given in the section of Chapter 4 entitled "TiVo Hardware Supplies on the Net."

 **NOTE**

New Series 2 TiVos are still appearing from other hardware partners, which is a good thing for TiVo and a vote of confidence in TiVo technology for us all. Humax's T800 and T2500 models (**http://www.humaxusa.com/Products_framset.html**) are Series 2-based TiVos that can save up to 80 and 250 hours of recordings respectively. Both Humax and Toshiba have announced TiVo-powered DVD recorders scheduled for 2004.

# Identifying Your TiVo Software Version

TiVo has been constantly improving and upgrading its software since the first TiVo crawled out of the ocean long ago. Different versions of the TiVo software are hackable to different degrees, and you may find that you'd prefer one version to another. Software is, after all, inherently "soft," and can thus be changed in the sense that you can usually install a specific, older version of the TiVo software on a compatible machine if you can locate one.

## TiVo Choosing the TiVo That's Right For You

With such a bewildering assortment of old and new TiVo models, it's difficult to determine which one you should actually buy. While this is a personal choice, here are a few tips that might help you decide.

Choosing between stand-alone and DirecTiVo models is somewhat easy:

- ◆ If you have DirecTV, you probably want a DirecTiVo system.

- ◆ If you have DirecTV and watch a lot of HDTV programming, you probably want one of the HDTV-enabled DirecTiVos.

- ◆ If you desperately want to record one live broadcast while watching another, you will need to buy a DirecTiVo, since this is the only type of TiVo with two separate tuners. You will also need to buy a dual-LNB dish with your DirecTV installation.

- ◆ If you only have cable and never plan to get DirecTV service, you will want to buy a stand-alone TiVo. DirecTiVo units will not work with standard cable service.

Choosing between TiVo Series 1 and Series 2 models is somewhat trickier. Here are a few guidelines:

- ◆ Both Series 1 and Series 2 machines can be expanded easily to increase their storage capacity.

- ◆ If you simply want to take advantage of the latest and greatest TiVo features (such as the Home Media Option), you must buy a Series 2 TiVo. Series 1 TiVo models do not support the Home Media Option.

If your goal is hacking a TiVo and having a bit of fun while taking advantage of the world's coolest DVR, I prefer the Series 1 models. TiVo Series 1 models are no longer being produced, their software is no longer being actively upgraded, and they feature slower, less-powerful hardware; however, they are a more open hardware and software platform. Hacking TiVos Series 2 machines is quite possible (as explained in detail later in this book), but it is harder to do—and you also are susceptible to new TiVo software upgrades that may override your carefully hacked system.

To identify the version of the software that is currently running on your TiVo system, go to TiVo Central by pressing the TiVo button on your TiVo remote control. Next, highlight Messages & Setup (shown as TiVo Messages and Setup in some versions of the TiVo software), and then press the Select button. Finally, highlight System Information and press Select again.

**NOTE**

The capabilities and hackability of different versions of the TiVo software are discussed in Chapter 4, "Exploring Your TiVo Hardware."

# TiVo and the Competition

DVRs are the wave of the future, and several similar products to TiVo are already available, with more on the way.

That said, this is a book on hacking TiVo machines, not hacking DVRs. I believe the TiVo to be far and away the best of all currently available DVRs, and expect that trend to continue. (It would be nice if TiVo would lighten up a bit regarding the hashing and signature checks in their latest software, but I guess they forgot to ask me.)

For TiVo fans, the core differentiators between TiVo and other DVR systems are the following:

◆ TiVos run Linux, a popular open source operating system. The growing popularity of Linux and its fundamental power as a Unix-like system gives TiVo users access to thousands of open source software projects, many of which you easily can recompile and install on hacked TiVo systems. The fact that TiVos use Linux for their operating system does not mean that the TiVo software is an open source project.

◆ The TiVo user interface is consistent, easily navigable, and attractive.

◆ TiVo's Season Passes, WishLists, and general features for locating shows in which users are (or might be) interested are more powerful and usable than those on any other DVR.

Your mileage may vary. A generally good source of comparative information about different DVRs is the PVR Compare site at **http://www.pvrcompare.com**. This is an excellent site with detailed comparisons among the different DVRs, and it tries to maintain its objectivity (unlike the author of this book).

# NDS, Sky+, and XTV

In early June, 2004, DirecTV sold all of its shares in TiVo, Inc., heightening speculation that DirecTV may seek an alternative to TiVo for future DVRs. The obvious contender for this is an implementation of NDS's XTV (**http://www.nds.com/personal_tv/personal_tv.html**) such as that used by Sky (http://www.sky.com) on its Sky+ systems. DirecTV was acquired by News Corp. late in 2003, which also owns the NDS Group. It therefore wouldn't be at all surprising if future DirecTV devices offer Sky+ or some other XDS-based service as an alternative to or replacement for the TiVo service.

# ReplayTV

ReplayTV systems are the best-known and closest TiVo competitor. Originally designed and manufactured by a company called SONICblue (**www.sonicblue.com**), the end of dot.com mania and the decline of many high-tech stocks hit SONICblue hard, and the ReplayTV business was sold to D&M Holdings in April, 2003. D&M Holdings is the parent company of Denon and Marantz, a well-known Japanese company specializing in consumer audio and video electronics, so ReplayTV systems may have found a good home.

ReplayTV systems feature good hardware and good support for many common hardware interfaces (USB, FireWire, and so on). In addition, they are easily expanded and provide good network connection support. ReplayTV systems run an operating system called *Sutter*, which is a custom real-time operating system that makes extensive internal use of XML for data representation and storage. As a custom operating system, Sutter is highly customized to make the most of the underlying ReplayTV hardware. The downside of a custom operating system is, of course, that you can hold a meeting of all of the world's Sutter experts, programmers, and its complete code base in a very small room.

The single ReplayTV feature that gets the most press is its automatic 30-second skip feature. This button makes it easy to skip over commercials without fast-forwarding. (A similar, undocumented feature can be activated on most TiVo models, as explained in Chapter 4.) While users love this feature, broadcast media companies hate it, since they get much of their revenue from selling advertising. SONICblue has been in court for a few years as the result of a lawsuit over this feature by companies whose names you might recognize, such as Paramount Pictures Corporation, Disney Enterprises, Inc., National Broadcasting Company, Inc., NBC Studios, Inc., Showtime Networks Inc., The United Paramount Network, ABC, Inc., Viacom International Inc., CBS Worldwide, Inc., CBS Broadcasting, Inc., and more. TiVo has gone out of its way to maintain good relationships and even partnerships with many of these companies.

ReplayTV systems offer similar capabilities to TiVo systems in terms of searching for shows by time, title, and even wildcards, although all of these work slightly differently than TiVo. ReplayTV's Zones are roughly equivalent to the TiVo's WishList feature.

ReplayTV systems offer some excellent features that the TiVo does not. For example, ReplayTV's buffer for live television is limited only by the amount of available disk space, rather than being limited to 30 minutes as TiVo is. ReplayTV systems also provide slightly better quality video recording in its highest quality-recording mode, which HDTV owners may find extremely attractive.

Some excellent Internet resources on ReplayTV systems are found at the following:

- ◆ ReplayTV FAQ at **http://replayfaq.leavensfamily.com** (also available simply as **http://www.replaytvfaq.com**)
- ◆ ReplayTV Advanced FAQ at **http://replayfaq.reidpix.com/faq.asp**
- ◆ ReplayTV Revealed at **http://www.widemovies.com/replaytv.html**
- ◆ ReplayTV versus TiVo comparison at **http://egotron.com/ptv**

- ReplayTV and TiVo FAQ at **http://www.sgsw.com/misc/faq.html**
- AVS Forum at **http://www.avsforum.com/avs-vb/forumdisplay.php?s= &forumid=27**

## UltimateTV

UltimateTV was a Microsoft-backed DVR that is now sold only by DirecTV as an alternative to the DirecTiVo systems (although software updates for older systems are still being released, or were as of April, 2003). For the most part, though, it appears that Microsoft largely has shut down UltimateTV. While it's hard to avoid celebrating the failure of any Microsoft-backed enterprise, this section attempts to do so.

UltimateTV systems were a competitor to the DirecTiVo systems, providing integration with WebTV or Dish Network satellite systems. Like DirecTiVo systems, UltimateTV systems can record one live broadcast while you are watching another live broadcast because they provided two physical tuners in each UltimateTV unit. UltimateTV systems did not provide rich programming guide information or a very usable or friendly mechanism for locating and identifying shows of interest. They also lacked features that many DVR owners consider critical—for example, buffering live TV broadcasts while you view a previously recorded program. (UltimateTV systems could do this, but only when the picture-in-picture display was being used.)

UltimateTV systems used a version of Windows CE in their set-top boxes, which provided users with a familiar user interface but was not easy for users to experiment with and expand. As a Microsoft product, there is much less community spirit and open sharing of information on the Internet regarding UltimateTV. Some useful links are listed below:

- UltimateTV Hacking Forum at **http://www.dealdatabase.com/forum**
- TiVo versus UltimateTV comparison at **http://www.pvrcompare.com/ tivoutvframe.html**
- TiVo, ReplayTV, and UltimateTV feature comparison at **http://www. pvrcompare.com/featurechart.html**

## Software Competitors

A number of software competitors to the TiVo are already available (see the section of Chapter 12 entitled "Using a TV Tuner Card and Video Capture Software"). These software packages run on various types of computer systems and work in conjunction with a video capture card or some similar device. At the moment, none of these offer the advanced capabilities of the TiVo features such as WishLists and Season Passes, but let's face it—it's only a matter of time and effort until they do.

# Future Trends

Because most families today subscribe to some sort of cable or satellite television service, the easiest way to convince people to purchase DVRs is to incorporate them into set-top cable or satellite boxes. Although DVR companies such as TiVo and UltimateTV pioneered this idea, this approach is being used by EchoStar Communications Corporation, the owners of Dish Network, one of the leading satellite broadcasting systems. EchoStar provides integrated single-tuner DVRs (which it calls *PVRs*) in its DishPVR 501, 508, and 721 set-top boxes. These systems provide the same sorts of capabilities as the TiVo and the other DVRs discussed previously, including pausing, rewinding, and recording broadcast television on internal hard drives. Developed by EchoStar, its DVRs owe no royalties to anyone, and they are conceptually easier to set up than stand-alone systems such as stand-alone TiVo and ReplayTV systems. Similarly, TimeWarner is selling recording capability through its digital-cable set-top boxes from Scientific Atlanta. Charter Communications has a startup division called *Digeo* that is offering a DVR. Comcast purchased access to Gemstar-TV Guide's interactive programming guide and offers a DVR. Things are heating up—everyone sees the value of the concepts that TiVo pioneered and wants their own slice of the pie.

Ubiquitous home computing presents a similar problem for stand-alone devices like the TiVo. As hardware and software prices continue to drop and storage and processing capabilities continue to increase, single-board DVR products from a number of companies are beginning to emerge. Many of my friends no longer own stereo systems, instead using their home computers as the basis of their home entertainment centers. Sophisticated video boards bundled with DVR software present the same sort of potential problem to dedicated entertainment devices like the TiVo.

The ball is in TiVo's court to maintain their edge by doing things like the following:

◆ Innovate features, staying ahead of the competition in terms of the capabilities of the software, accessibility from other types of computer systems, and so on. For example, why not enable the TiVo to access video files in other formats that are stored on networked computer systems? Right now, even proposed solutions like TiVo ToGo are out-bound, pushing TiVo recordings to other devices. As digital movie cameras become ubiquitous, more and more homes will have collections of MP2 or other video files on their computers that people would naturally love to easily integrate with their TiVos and home entertainment centers.

◆ Provide innovative ways of packaging the core TiVo service with new hardware as it is released. Many people will always prefer a complete out-of-the-box solution to one that requires work. The TiVo GUI is easy-to-use and installation is a breeze. Though I use packages like MythTV on my Linux systems, they are a bear to configure and use compared to any TiVo from day one.

◆ Leverage their expertise by identifying and opening new markets.

The future provides significant challenges for TiVo. By continuing to expand the capabilities, capacity, and interoperability of their systems and software, TiVo will survive as a stand-alone concern for quite a while. Whether TiVo will be able to maintain its edge is anyone's guess. But you can only take my TiVos when you can pry them from my cold, dead fingers.

# HACKING THE TiVo

## Chapter 2

## Just Do It!

**D**ifferent people use computer books like this one in various ways. Some prefer not to read the entire book and just home in on the particular nugget of information that they're looking for. Others read the whole thing from cover to cover before doing anything. A third group jumps around, looks for some relevant procedures to follow, follows them, reads a bit, experiments with the software on the CD that accompanies the book, and then keeps the book around for occasional reference or amusement.

If you're not a cover-to-cover reader, this chapter is for you. This chapter is designed to help you do the most common TiVo tasks, such as opening a TiVo, increasing the amount of space on your TiVo by adding a larger or second disk, and getting a command prompt on various TiVos. There is an entire book full of general information wrapped around this chapter if you're interested in why you're performing each of these steps—this chapter simply focuses on what to do and how to do it.

**NOTE**

This section focuses on working with standard TiVo kernels, V4.x and earlier, used on current Series 1 TiVos and DirecTiVos, stand-alone Series 2 TiVos, and Series 2 DirecTiVos.

**WARNING**

Please unplug your TiVo before working on it! Not doing so might give you a serious electric shock and a smoking Van der Graf Generator Afro, and can also cause damage to your TiVo. TiVo power supplies are not shielded; in other words, all their components are out in the open, with no enclosing case like those around most PC power supplies. While working on your TiVo, be careful not to touch any part of the TiVo supply because some of the components store a charge that can be painful or even fatal in rare cases.

**NOTE**

Following the procedures in this chapter voids your warranty. Please see the introduction of this book for other legal warnings and caveats.

# *Opening a TiVo*

When you need to read this section:

◆ If you are going to replace your existing TiVo drive(s) with one or two larger drives, you will need to open your TiVo case and remove the drive(s) that it contains.

◆ If you are simply adding a second drive to a single-drive TiVo, you will need to open the case, but you do not have to remove the existing drive.

To open the case, you will need the following tools:

◆ Number 10 Torx screwdriver (Series 1 and Series 2 TiVos)

◆ Number 15 Torx screwdriver (Series 1 and most Series 2 TiVos)

◆ Phillips screwdriver (DVD-enabled Series 2 TiVos)

Although the case styles and number of screws differ slightly between various TiVo models, opening the case is essentially the same on all TiVos:

1. Disconnect your TiVo from your television and put it on a flat surface with the back of the TiVo facing you. Figure 2.1 shows the rear of a Series 1 TiVo.

2. Removing the screws that attach the top of the TiVo case to its frame is easy, but differs on various TiVo models:

   ◆ On a Series 1 TiVo, use a Torx screwdriver to remove the three Torx screws that hold the top of the TiVo case to the rest of its frame. Looking at the back of the TiVo, there is one screw in the center of the top of the trim and one in the center of each side of the trim on the back. Don't remove any of the other screws, since they hold the internals of the TiVo together. If your Series 1 TiVo still features a sticker saying "Warranty void if this sticker is broken," remove the sticker. You are voiding your warranty. Figure 2.1 shows the rear of a Series 1 TiVo with the screws removed.

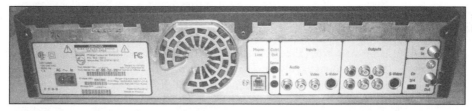

**FIGURE 2.1**   *The rear of a Series 1 TiVo*

   ◆ On a Series 2 TiVo, use a Torx screwdriver to remove the four Torx screws that hold the top of the TiVo case to the rest of its frame. Looking at the back of the TiVo, there are two screws along the top of the trim and one in the center of each side of the trim on the back. Don't remove any of the other screws, since they hold the internals of the TiVo together. Figure 2.2 shows the rear of a Series 2 TiVo with the screws removed.

**FIGURE 2.2**   *The rear of a Series 2 TiVo*

   ◆ On a DVD-enabled Series 2 TiVo, use a Phillips screwdriver to remove the eight Phillips screws that hold the top of the TiVo case to the rest of its frame. Looking at the back of the TiVo, there are two screws along the top of the trim and one in the center of each side of the trim on the back. There are also two screws on each side of the TiVo. Don't remove any of the other screws, since they hold the internals of the TiVo together. Figure 2.3 shows the rear of a Pioneer 810H with the screws removed.

**FIGURE 2.3**   *The rear of a Series 2 TiVo from Pioneer*

3.  Separate the top of the case from the rest of the TiVo. This step is not necessary on Series 2 TiVos from Pioneer. On Series 1 and other Series 2 TiVos, slip the end of a flat screwdriver or tack puller between the trim around the top of the TiVo case and the back of the TiVo and wiggle it gently until the top of the case begins to slide away from the back of the TiVo. You will want to do this at several points so that the top is evenly separated from the rest of the TiVo. Figure 2.4 shows the top of the TiVo case being separated on a Series 1 TiVo.

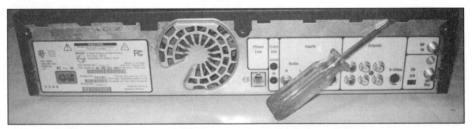

**FIGURE 2.4**   *Separating the top of a Series 1 TiVo from the case*

 **TIP**

The tops of Series 1 TiVos use slotted tabs to ensure a tight fit with the rest of the TiVo case. One of these is located near the bottom of the trim on each side of the back of the TiVo; the rest are along the top. You will therefore want to gently pry the top away from the rest of the case near the bottom of the trim on each side and at several points along the top.

4.  On Series 1 and non-Pioneer Series 2 TiVos, once the top of the TiVo is slightly separated from the back of the TiVo, pull the top of the TiVo case back a half inch or so to separate it from the front of the TiVo (see Figure 2.5). You can then lift

the rear of the top of the case up to expose the internals of your TiVo, as shown in Figure 2.6. This step is the same for most Series 2 TiVos. On Pioneer Series 2 TiVos, grab the bottom rear of the sides of the case, lift out slightly, and lift up the back of the top of the case (see Figure 2.7).

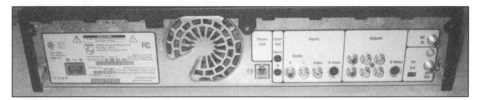

**FIGURE 2.5**  *Pulling back the top of a Series 1 TiVo*

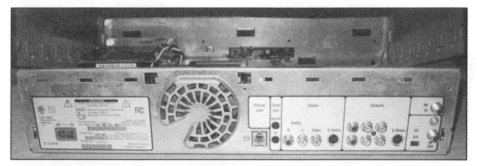

**FIGURE 2.6**  *Lifting off the top of a Series 1 TiVo*

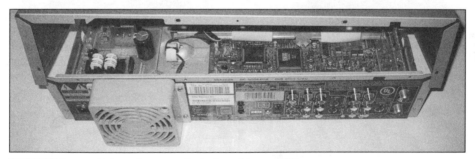

**FIGURE 2.7**  *Lifting off the top of a Series 2 Pioneer TiVo*

# Removing TiVo Disk Drives

When you need to read this section:

◆ If you are going to replace your existing TiVo drive(s) with one or two larger drives, you will need to remove the drive(s) that your TiVo contains.

To remove the drive(s) from your TiVo, you will need the same tools as in the previous section:

◆ Number 10 Torx screwdriver (Series 1 and Series 2 TiVos)

◆ Number 15 Torx screwdriver (Series 1 and most Series 2 TiVos)

◆ Phillips screwdriver (DVD-enabled Series 2 TiVos)

Although disk drives are mounted differently in various TiVo models, removing the disk drives is essentially the same on all TiVos:

1. After opening the case, remove the IDE and power connections that are attached to the TiVo drive. Figure 2.8 shows the IDE and power connections on a single-drive Series 1 TiVo. The IDE connection is the flat or multistrand ribbon cable at left in the figure, and it is connected to your TiVo's motherboard. The power connection is the four-strand cable at right. These look the same on any model of TiVo, but the location of your drive will differ based on the model of TiVo that you are working with. In some Series 2 TiVos, you won't be able to disconnect these until you have removed the drive bracket as described later in this section.

**FIGURE 2.8**  *IDE and power connections to a Series 1 TiVo hard drive*

2. On DirecTiVo and some older Series 2 machines, you will also have to disconnect the two-pin connector between a fan on the drive bracket and your TiVo's motherboard. Make sure that you reconnect this when reassembling your TiVo—not doing so will cause the TiVo to overheat and can cause glitches in operation.

**NOTE**

If your TiVo contains more than one drive, one is the master (boot) drive and the other is a slave drive that provides additional storage. Make sure that you keep track of which is which. If you are facing the rear or the TiVo, the drive at the left is typically the master drive—its jumpers should already be set to indicate that. The drive at the right is typically the slave drive—which its jumpers should also indicate. I suggest getting a marker of some sort and writing "Master" on the top of the master drive and "Slave" on the top of the slave drive. Though you are probably going to be replacing these with larger drives, you'll want to keep these drives as backups and will need to know which was which if you ever put them back in a TiVo.

3.  Remove the screws that hold the bracket(s) containing your TiVo's hard drive(s). TiVo hard drives are mounted in a bracket that is screwed to the frame of the TiVo. The number and type of screws that hold the bracket to the frame differ based on which type of TiVo you are working with:

    ◆ On Series 1 stand-alone TiVos, the drive bracket is attached to the frame by two Torx screws near the front of the case (see Figure 2.9).

**FIGURE 2.9**   *Screws attaching the drive bracket to a Series 1 TiVo case*

    ◆ On most Series 2 stand-alone TiVos, the drive bracket is attached to the frame by two Torx screws, as shown in Figure 2.10. Series 2 stand-alone TiVos from AT&T use a different type drive bracket, which is still is attached to the frame by two Torx Screws (see Figure 2.11).

**FIGURE 2.10** *Screws attaching the drive bracket to a Series 2 TiVo case*

**FIGURE 2.11** *Screws attaching the drive bracket to a Series 2 AT&T TiVo case*

◆ On Series 2 TiVos from Pioneer, the drive bracket is attached to the frame by four Phillips screws, two on either side of the drive. The two screws at the right of the drive are shown in Figure 2.12.

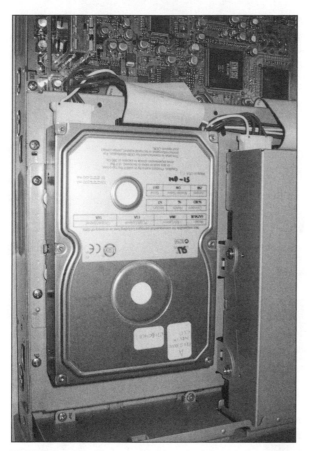

**FIGURE 2.12** *Screws attaching the drive bracket to a Series 2 Pioneer TiVo case*

4. Remove the drive bracket from the TiVo case. Series 1 and most Series 2 stand-alone TiVo drive brackets are also attached to the TiVo frame by two tabs that slip through the drive bracket. To remove the drive bracket on most TiVos, use a finger to lift the portion of the bracket from which you removed the screws, as shown in Figures 2.13 and 2.14. You should then be able to remove the bracket by lifting it up and out of the case.

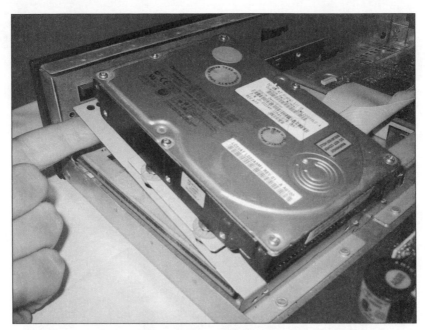

**FIGURE 2.13** *Lifting the drive bracket off the tabs in a Series 1 TiVo*

**FIGURE 2.14** *Lifting the drive bracket off the tabs in most Series 2 TiVos*

To remove a drive bracket that looks like the bracket in Figure 2.11, use a finger to lift the end of the bracket as shown in Figure 2.15. Pull the bracket out about an inch to separate it from the sockets at the other end of the bracket, detach the fan, IDE, and power connectors from the drive, and lift the bracket out of the case.

**FIGURE 2.15**   *Lifting the drive bracket in a Series 2 AT&T TiVo*

5.  Turn the bracket over and remove screws that hold the drive(s) to the bracket(s). Again, the type and number of screws differ depending on the model of TiVo that you are working with.

Congratulations! You've removed the drive(s) from your TiVo! You are now ready to put the drive in your PC and use the software included on the BATBD CD that accompanies this book to increase the storage capacity of your TiVo!

# Putting a TiVo or Other Disk in Your PC

When you need to read this section:

◆  If you are going to replace your existing TiVo drive(s) with a larger drive, you will need to put your TiVo disk(s) and the new drive in your PC so that you can copy your TiVo operating system and data from the old disk(s) to the new disk.

◆  If you are going to keep your original TiVo disk but want to add a second drive to your TiVo, you will need to put the new disk in your PC so that you can format the new disk correctly.

To put other disk drives in your PC, you will need the following tools:

- A Phillips screwdriver.
- Spare jumpers if your TiVo drive(s) or new drive do not have any. If you need these, you can purchase them at any computer or electronics store.
- A second IDE cable, if your computer system only has one. If you need this, you can purchase one at any computer store.

After you've removed a drive from your TiVo or have purchased a new drive that you can use for additional storage on your TiVo, the key to working with it is to attach it to another type of computer system. This section focuses on how to attach a TiVo disk to a desktop x86 personal computer so that you can boot from the BATBD and clone your TiVo disk to a larger one.

---

 **NOTE**

This tutorial section provides a fast and easy way of attaching TiVo and new drives to your PC, is intended for the novice computer hacker, and simplifies things by having you disconnect any hard drives that are currently attached to your PC. This is often unnecessary, but makes the instructions simpler and easier to explain. Please do not flame the author for unnecessary steps or in general. I am trying to be helpful.

For a more detailed discussion of attaching TiVo and new drives to your PC without disconnecting your existing hard drive(s), see Chapter 4. For example, you will want to have a PC hard drive attached to your system if you want to create files that contain a backup of your TiVo drive. The instructions in this chapter explain how to install a larger or second drive without creating backup files.

---

Although a variety of different cases are used with today's PCs, the procedure for putting other disks in the PC is essentially the same:

1. Check your PC's BIOS to make sure that it is configured to boot from your CDROM drive first. You will need to be able to boot from the BATBD CD that accompanies this book in order to follow the instructions in any subsequent section of this chapter. This setting is usually located on the advanced BIOS options screen of your PC's BIOS display screen. To access your PC's BIOS, reboot the PC and immediately press the appropriate key on your keyboard—usually either Delete or F1 on your keyboard. The appropriate key should be listed on the screen after you reboot your PC. Once you see the BIOS screen, use the arrow key to display the Advanced BIOS Options screen and check the Boot Sequence entry (or a similar entry) to make sure that the system boots from the CD first.

2. Shut down the PC and remove the side cover (tower systems) or top (for desktop systems) to give you access to the disk drives, motherboards, and cards.

3. Locate your computer's IDE cables. These are one or two flat (sometimes round in new PCs) 40-pin cables with the same sort of connectors at both ends and a second, similar connector near one of the ends. IDE cables are connected to your motherboard at one end (or, in rare cases, to an IDE or EIDE controller card) and to your PC's disk and CD-ROM drive(s) at the other end. Your IDE connectors are referred to as IDE-1 and IDE-2, and are usually labeled in this way on the motherboard or controller card. The cable from each IDE connector on a motherboard or controller card can be attached to a maximum of two hard or CD-ROM drives. Figure 2.16 shows two IDE cables connected to a generic PC motherboard.

**FIGURE 2.16**   *IDE cables connected to a PC motherboard*

4. Follow the cables to see how they connect to your PC's hard disk and CD-ROM drive. In order to add any drive to your PC, you'll have to connect it so that it does not conflict with the drives that are already installed. When two drives are attached to a single IDE cable, they must be configured differently by connecting pins known as *jumpers* that are located on the back or bottom of the hard drive or CD-ROM drive. *Master* is the term used for the first drive on an IDE interface; *slave* is the term used for the second drive on an IDE interface.

5. Disconnect any hard drives in your PC hard drive by unplugging the IDE and power cables from the back of the drive. Write down which IDE cable they were connected to so that you can use this information when you are finished hacking your TiVo and want to reassemble and use your PC again.

6. Check the jumpers on your CD-ROM drive to see how the drive is currently configured and write down that setting so that you can restore it when you are finished hacking your TiVo and want to reassemble and use your PC again. A guide to the meaning of the jumper settings on your hard and CD-ROM drives is usually

printed on the top or back of the hard or CD-ROM drive. If your CD-ROM drive is currently set to a jumper setting known as *Cable Select* (CSEL) or *Single Drive*, change that jumper so that it is the master on that IDE interface.

7. Connect the TiVo disk(s) (if you are replacing your TiVo disk(s) with a larger disk) and the new disk to your PC's IDE cables, making sure that they are jumpered according to the settings in Table 2.1. You will have two TiVo disks only if your TiVo currently contains two drives. If your TiVo only contains one disk, that's fine—use the settings in the Master TiVo Disk column and ignore the column and settings for the Slave TiVo Disk.

**Table 2.1 Jumper Settings for TiVo and New Hard Drives in a PC**

| CD-ROM | Master TiVo Disk | Slave TiVo Disk | New Drive |
|---|---|---|---|
| Master, IDE-1 | Slave, IDE-1 | Master, IDE-2 | Slave, IDE-2 |
| Master, IDE-2 | Master, IDE-1 | Slave, IDE-1 | Slave, IDE-2 |

8. Attach your master (or only) TiVo disk to the cable attached to IDE-1 in your PC and attach a power connector to the drive.

9. If your TiVo contained two hard drives, attach your slave TiVo disk to the IDE cable identified in Table 2.1 and attach a power connector to the drive.

10. Attach your new drive to the cable attached to IDE-2 in your PC and attach a power connector to the drive.

 **TIP**

When adding other drives to your PC during this tutorial chapter, you can temporarily slip the drive into an empty space in your PC if you have enough room, temporarily attach the drive to your PC case by using two Phillips screws if you want, or even simply set the drive on top of a sheet or cardboard or other insulating material in the bottom of your PC. Be very careful when handling disk drives!

Congratulations! You are now ready to add a larger disk to your TiVo or prepare a second disk for use with an existing TiVo disk, as explained in the following sections.

# *Adding a Larger Disk to Your TiVo*

This section explains how to copy the data from your existing TiVo drive(s) to a new, larger disk.

Adding a larger disk is an easy procedure if you followed the instructions in the previous sections correctly.

1. Turn on your PC and put the BATBD CD in your PC's CD-ROM drive. When the initial BATBD boot screen displays, press Return or Enter to boot from the default BATBD boot setting.

**TIP**

If you are working with a Pioneer 810, you will need a backup image of the Pioneer 57H software and should restore this to your new disk. Some people have been able to upgrade an 810 with the actual 810 software, but this is problematic. See the section of Chapter 6 entitled "Finding Backups of the TiVo Software" for more information about finding specific TiVo backups. See the sections of Chapter 7 on restoring from MFS Tools backups for more detail—sorry, but that's outside the scope of the quick tutorials in this chapter.

2.  Clone your TiVo disk(s) to the new drive by issuing the appropriate **mfstool backup** command. (The MFS Tool commands are explained in detail in Chapter 5.) The specific command you execute depends on the jumper settings you used for your TiVo drive(s) and the new drive, as shown in Table 2.1 and described in the previous section of this chapter:

    ◆  If you installed a single drive from your TiVo and jumpered it according to the settings in the first row in Table 2.1, issue the following command:

        ```
        mfstool backup-o - -a/dev/hdb¦mfstool restore-i - -C-x/dev/hdd
        ```

    ◆  If you installed two drives from your TiVo and jumpered them according to the settings in the first row in Table 2.1, issue the following command:

        ```
        mfstool backup-o - -a/dev/hdb/dev/hdc¦mfstool restore-i - -C-x/dev/hdd
        ```

    ◆  If you installed a single drive from your TiVo and jumpered it according to the settings in the second row in Table 2.1, issue the following command:

        ```
        mfstool backup-o - -a/dev/hda¦mfstool restore-i - -C-x/dev/hdd
        ```

    ◆  If you installed two drives from your TiVo and jumpered them according to the settings in the second row in Table 2.1, issue the following command:

        ```
        mfstool backup -o - -a/dev/hda/dev/hdb¦mfstool restore-i - -C-x/dev/hdd
        ```

 **WARNING**

Type these commands exactly as shown, being very careful about spacing. For example, the entry after the –o and –i options in each command is a single dash, preceded and followed by a space. There must be spaces between each of the items on the command line. Similarly, the vertical bar character (found on most keyboards over the backslash) is very important for Linux reasons. For more information about this type of command, see the section of Chapter 7 entitled "Upgrading a Disk without Using Backup Files."

3. Depending on the size of your TiVo drives, this command can take an hour or two. If this command only takes a few minutes, something has gone wrong. If you are upgrading the drives from a very old Series 1 TiVo, you may need to unlock the drives. See the section of Chapter 4 entitled "Unlocking TiVo Hard Drives" for more information. Nowadays, TiVo drives are rarely locked and explaining how to work around this problem is unfortunately outside the scope of this quick tutorial.

Once the backup operation completes, remove the BATBD CD and shut down your PC. Remove the new disk and test it by jumpering it for Cable Select and putting it in your TiVo. Connect its IDE and power cables and turn on the TiVo. If your TiVo boots successfully and looks exactly as it did when you used your original TiVo disks, congratulations, you've hacked your TiVo and have much more storage space available for your precious recordings. All of your existing recordings should still be playable, but now you have room for much, much more!

If this is all you want to do with your TiVo at the moment, shut it down, reattach the drive to the drive bracket, reattach the bracket to the TiVo frame, and put the top back on your TiVo. Next, rejumper and reattach the drives in your PC as they were originally (you did write that down as instructed, right?) and turn on your PC to test it before putting the case back together. Don't panic if your PC doesn't restart correctly—it is very easy to mix up jumper settings and which IDE cable a drive is connected to. If you have a problem restarting your PC, turn it off and double-check the jumper settings and which IDE cable each hard drive and CD-ROM drive is attached to. Make sure that the IDE cables are firmly seated in the sockets on your motherboard or on your controller card.

# Adding a Second Disk to Your TiVo

When you need to read this section:

◆ If you are going to keep your original TiVo disk but want to add a second drive to your TiVo.

◆ If you have followed the instructions in the previous section to clone your existing TiVo drive(s) to a new disk and then subsequently want to add a second drive to your TiVo.

To add a second disk drive to your TiVo, you will need the following:

◆ A bracket to hold the new drive, unless your TiVo is a Series 2 TiVo from AT&T. Sources for additional drive brackets are listed in the section of Chapter 4 entitled "Adding Disk Drives to Your TiVo."

This section explains how to prepare a second disk for use with an existing TiVo disk. When you add a second disk to a TiVo that already contains a single disk, information about the second drive is added to the first drive, and the two drives must always be used together in the future. The disks in a two-disk TiVo are referred to as being *married*. As always, divorce is painful.

**NOTE**

This tutorial section provides a fast and easy way of preparing a second drive for use with an existing TiVo drive and is intended for the novice computer hacker. This can be done at the same time that you prepare a larger TiVo disk but is explained separately in this tutorial to make the instructions simpler and easier to explain. Please do not flame the author for unnecessary steps or in general. I am trying to be helpful. For a more detailed discussion of different, more sophisticated ways of adding a second drive to your TiVo, see Chapter 7.

Preparing a second drive is an easy procedure if you followed the instructions in earlier sections of this chapter correctly and jumpered your drives as shown in Table 2.1.

1. Turn on your PC and put the BATBD CD in your PC's CD-ROM drive. When the initial BATBD boot screen displays, press Return or Enter to boot from the default BATBD boot setting.

2. Prepare the new disk for use with your TiVo by issuing the following command:

```
BlessTiVo /dev/hdd
```

 **NOTE**

When you execute the BlessTiVo command, the program first checks to see if the drive exists and can be opened. If you see error messages such as "No device specified," "Too many command line options," or "Unable to connect to /dev/hdx," these usually mean that you accidentally specified the wrong drive on the BlessTiVo command line or you specified the name of the drive.

3. If the drive you are blessing already contains DOS or Linux partitioning information, the BlessTiVo command warns you of this fact and asks if you want to proceed. Answer "Y" if you do, or thank your lucky stars and answer "N" if you do not. Although this extra paranoia may be irritating if you're sure that you know what you're doing, this extra verification step is quite handy if you picked up the wrong spare disk for use with your TiVo or didn't detach your PC hard drive(s) before beginning, as explained in "Putting a TiVo or Other Disk in Your PC." You will be very unhappy if you accidentally format a drive that contains data that you may want to use again in the future.

4. The BlessTiVo command asks you to verify that you want to proceed even if the specified disk contains no partitioning information. Answer "Y" to continue. The BlessTiVo command then formats and partitions the new drive. When this completes, the BlessTiVo command displays a final summary message listing the amount of storage available on the newly formatted drive.

**WARNING**

The summary message displayed at the end of the BlessTiVo process is very important—you should always check this value to make sure that it is within 3 GB of the total size of the disk that you are adding. If the size of the disk that you are blessing is not reported as being within 3 GB of the actual size of the disk, do not add this drive to your TiVo. If you do add it, the two drives will be married, and you will not be able to take advantage of the storage that is actually available on the second disk.

Once the BlessTiVo operation completes, remove the BATBD CD and shut down your PC. Remove the new disk and test it by jumpering it as a slave and putting it in your TiVo along with your original drive. Connect its IDE and power cables and turn on the TiVo. If your TiVo boots successfully and looks exactly as it did when you used your original TiVo disks, congratulations, you've hacked your TiVo and have much more storage space available for your precious recordings!

If this is all you want to do with your TiVo at the moment, shut it down, reattach the drive to the drive bracket, reattach the bracket to the TiVo frame, and put the top back on your TiVo. Next, rejumper and reattach the drives in your PC as they were originally (you did write that down as instructed, right?), and turn on your PC to test it before putting the case back together. Don't panic if your PC doesn't restart correctly—it is very easy to mix up jumper settings and which IDE cable a drive is connected to. If you have a problem restarting your PC, turn it off and double-check the jumper settings and which IDE cable each hard drive and CD-ROM drive is attached to. Make sure that the IDE cables are firmly seated in the sockets on your motherboard or on your controller card.

# HACKING THE TiVo

SECOND EDITION

# Chapter 3

## TiVo Tips and Tricks

**A**lthough most of this book is about the physical hacking of your TiVo or installing new commands and software, there are a number of cool things that you can do with your TiVo without opening it.

Some of the items discussed in this chapter are simply informational. The remote control shortcuts discussed in the first section of this chapter provide quick access to portions of TiVo Central that otherwise require a little menu walking, but aren't listed in the TiVo documentation. Similarly, later in this chapter I'll provide suggestions for optimal ways of scheduling programs to guarantee that your TiVo finds your desired programming. The TiVo makes it extremely easy to pick scheduled shows by name within the timeframe of the current programming/guide data that your TiVo currently contains. TiVos also provide some impressively powerful ways of creating WishLists that you can store on your TiVo, and which continue to work, regardless of the programming/guide data that your TiVo currently contains. These lists enable you to use special wildcard characters to match words or sequences of words in upcoming programming titles. For example, have you always wished that you could record every movie with the word "Hacker" in the title? TiVo WishLists are the ticket, but learning to use the special characters that WishLists provide for matching terms can be tricky.

Other TiVo tips and tricks, such as the secret TiVo commands and modes discussed in the next section, change the behavior of your TiVo, what it displays on the screen, or how it responds to various buttons on your remote control. Some of these are dangerous (a warning that will be repeated throughout this chapter). Make sure that you have a disk-copy backup before you attempt any of these tips and tricks. (See Chapter 6, "Backing Up and Restoring TiVo Data," for a discussion of the various ways in which you can back up your TiVo.) Similarly, the section titled "Legendary TiVo Monitor and Diagnostic Commands" in this chapter tells you how to access the TiVo boot monitor, which provides some interesting information about your TiVo and its configuration but also enables you to trash your TiVo's boot information, rendering it unusable. Be careful—be very, very careful when poking around in the boot monitor.

# Using the TiVo Remote Control

The TiVo remote control provides an impressively dense collection of specialized and general-purpose buttons. There are two basic models of TiVo remote controls, as shown in Figure 3.1. The remote control on the left is a TiVo Series 1 remote control (a DirecTiVo, in this case), while the one on the right is for a TiVo Series 2 system. Some of TiVo's hardware partners, such as Sony, have made custom remote controls for their TiVo-based hardware, as shown in the middle of Figure 3.1. The Sony remote is a much heavier, more solid remote than the ones from TiVo and also provides extra features such as a button that lets you jump directly to the "Now Playing" list of recorded programs. It is also a smarter remote, meaning that it can learn the codes required to control your television by scanning through a series of available codes and "watching" for a reaction from your television. The shape of all TiVo remotes makes them quite comfortable to hold in your hand during even the longest TiVo marathon.

Comparing the TiVo Series 1 and Series 2 remotes shows that relatively little has changed since day one. The Series 2 remotes are longer, so the buttons are spaced out a bit more on the remote. Some of the buttons that had double functions on the TiVo Series 1 remote now have separate buttons (Live TV and Guide, for example). The Series 2 remotes also have a

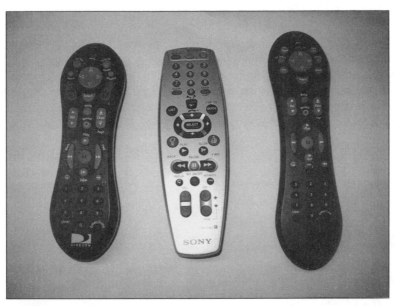

**FIGURE 3.1** *Various TiVo remote controls*

control switch that enables you to hardwire a specific remote to a specific TiVo. This feature is especially handy if you have two TiVos in the same room since they would otherwise both respond to any remote like some twisted high-tech synchronized swimming performance. The Series 2 remote control also features a PIP/Window button (presumably for "picture in picture"), which appears to be reserved for future expansion—it currently does nothing.

The remote controls provided with the latest TiVo-based systems, the Pioneer 57-H and 810-H, are very similar to the standard TiVo Series 2 remote, but they provide buttons related to viewing and controlling DVDs on their systems. The Sony remote is a different animal altogether, but many people prefer it to the standard TiVo remote. Some of the features that I specifically like are its List button, which takes you directly to the Now Showing List, and the fact that its base fits nicely in the palm of my hand. Your mileage may vary if you have smaller hands.

 **TIP**

If you lose your TiVo remote, your dog eats it, or you simply want to consolidate the functionality of several remotes into one, there are a number of universal remotes that work with the TiVo. Though many of these are available, a great one is the Harmony H688 Universal Remote, which is available from various vendors including WeaKnees.com (**http://www.weaknees.com/harmony_details.php**). Another great site for replacement remotes (and probably the most informative) is **http://www.hifi-remote.com/ofa**, which features TiVo-capable replacement remotes from One For All and Radio Shack. They even work with ReplayTV systems if you're using one of those instead of a BetaMax.

# TiVo Remote Control Shortcuts

In addition to the clearly labeled controls provided on the TiVo remote, TiVo remotes also offer some undocumented shortcut commands. Pressing the TiVo Central button at the top center of the remote followed by pressing any numeric key takes you to a specific portion of the TiVo menu hierarchy. Even though the menus are quite easy to navigate, it's also handy to be able to jump directly to different points that you may want to access quickly. The different number keys on the remote take you to the following locations:

- ◆ 0 - Shows the "TiVo Guy" introductory animation on all stand-alone TiVos and some pre-3.1 DirecTiVos.
- ◆ 1 - Season Pass Manager
- ◆ 2 - ToDo List
- ◆ 3 - Search Using WishLists
- ◆ 4 - Search By Title
- ◆ 5 - Browse By Channel
- ◆ 6 - Browse By Time
- ◆ 7 - Record Time/Channel
- ◆ 8 - TiVo's Suggestions
- ◆ 9 - Showcases

Being undocumented and hence unsupported, these shortcuts could conceivably stop working in some future release of the TiVo software, but the majority of them have remained the same since at least Version 2.5 of the TiVo software, so we'll just keep our fingers crossed.

# Resolving Remote Control Problems

Getting your first TiVo is typically a great experience, but it does have its irritating aspects. Stand-alone TiVos interact with home cable boxes by sending signals through the TiVo's Infrared Blaster, which is the L-shaped IR device that you position over your cable box's IR input. Your TiVo remote controls the TiVo, so when you tell the TiVo to change channels, it does so by sending the appropriate signal out over the IR Blaster, which feeds the appropriate codes into your cable box, and "the right thing happens." Usually, that is.

 **NOTE**

This section is relevant only to stand-alone TiVo owners. DirecTiVos are obviously integrated with the DirecTV receiver. If you are using a stand-alone TiVo with a generic DirecTV receiver, you've probably connected the two with a serial cable and therefore aren't using IR at all.

All cable boxes have different control codes, so your TiVo offers a number of possible controller codes for use when you initially configure your remote. The suggested code list generally uses choices that vary by the sequence of the control codes that they send and the speed at which they send the control codes through the IR Blaster. You may have to experiment a bit with the available choices until you find the optimal set for your cable box. Few things are more irritating than telling the TiVo to change channels and having it change to Channel 16 instead of 162, for example. Just ask my wife, who wanted to take a hatchet to our first TiVo until we found the control codes that best matched our cable box.

The following are some suggestions that should help you set up your TiVo, IR Blaster, and cable box so that they work together optimally. If you are having trouble changing channels on your cable or satellite box using the TiVo, try the following:

◆ If the TiVo seems to be trying to change the channels but nothing actually happens, make sure that the IR Blaster is plugged into the correct port on the back of your TiVo. It should be plugged into the lower of the two $1/8$" jacks under the Cntrl Out label on the back of the TiVo—the top one is for a serial connection, and it won't work with the IR Blaster. On some TiVos, the ports on the back are actually labeled IR and Serial.

◆ Make sure that one of the IR Blaster emitters is correctly positioned over the IR receiver on your cable or satellite box. If you aren't sure where the IR receiver is on your cable or satellite box, look for a small square red plastic shape on the front of the box. If you still can't locate it, shine a flashlight or other bright light source onto the front of the cable or satellite box, looking for a transparent section behind which you can see a small, round lens.

◆ Make sure that the IR Blaster emitter you're using is positioned far enough out from the front of your cable or satellite box so that it actually shines into the box's IR receiver. Typically, you attach the IR Blaster so that its lens can shine into the cable or satellite box's IR receiver by attaching it to the top or bottom of the cable or satellite box by using one of the pieces of double-sided adhesive provided in the IR Blaster pack in your TiVo cable kit.

◆ Consider buying a flat IR emitter and using that rather than the IR Blaster provided with your TiVo. These flat IR emitters come with a transparent adhesive strip that enables you to directly attach them over the IR receiver on your cable or satellite box. They are available from a number of vendors, but I recommend the 8160/ 8170/8170S emitters from SmartHome (**http://www.smarthome.com/8170.html**). These are single emitters instead of the double-headed IR Blaster that comes with the TiVo. Equivalent double-headed models (8171S/8172) are also available from SmartHome.

◆ If you are using the IR Blaster that came with your TiVo, tuck the second head behind the TiVo to ensure that it isn't causing distortion accidentally.

◆ Consider building a small hood (also known as a *tent* or *fort*) around the cable or satellite box IR receiver so that it can't receive signals from anything other than the IR Blaster or replacement emitter.

◆ Make sure that the front of the TiVo isn't in direct sunlight or in a position where it may receive signals from any other IR sources that you may be using, such as audio system remote controls, DVD system remotes, and so on.

◆ Try alternate settings for the remote control codes that your TiVo uses to communicate with your cable or satellite box. These alternate settings are available by navigating through the following TiVo menus: Messages & Setup, Recorder & Phone Setup, Cable/Satellite Box, Cable Box Setup menu. Try slower settings if your TiVo only seems to transmit a subset of the digits of your desired channel.

◆ Configure the TiVo to send three digits rather than just two (in the same TiVo menu as the previous bullet: Messages & Setup, Recorder & Phone Setup, Cable/Satellite Box, Cable Box Setup menu). This causes the TiVo to send leading zeroes in single- or double-digit channel requests.

◆ Configure your TiVo to require that you press Enter after selecting a new channel in order to change to your desired channel. This is useful if your TiVo sends channel change requests to the cable or satellite box prematurely. For example, use this configuration if you try to change to channel 162 and the TiVo always changes to channel 16 before you've pressed the final digit. If this is happening to you, you should try to locate a slower control code, as suggested earlier in this list.

## Using a PDA as a Remote Control

One of the most impressive and interesting things about the TiVo is the tremendous amount of user loyalty and pure creativity that it inspires. You only have to search the Web for "TiVo" or look at the tremendous number of posts on TiVo sites, such as the TiVoCommunity and DealsDatabase Forums (see Chapter 14, "Other TiVo Hacking Resources"), to see the huge number of people who are hacking their TiVos, porting open source software to them, and developing software that runs on operating systems such as Microsoft Windows and Apple's Mac OS. They all have one thing in common— they want to interact with their TiVos. As discussed in Chapter 4, companies like 9thTee.com, PTVupgrade.com, SiliconDust, and Weaknees.com are churning out TiVo upgrade kits and add-ons, continuing the hardware side of the convergence concept that was discussed in Chapter 1, "Know Your TiVo."

Though not actually TiVo hardware, a truly cool hardware-related TiVo add-on is a piece of software called OmniRemote Pro, an optional infrared (IR) amplifier that enables you to use your Palm to control your TiVo. The Web page for this package is at **http://www.pacificneotek.com/omniProfsw.htm**. If you're one of the many road warriors who has a Palm or compatible PDA in your holster at all times, this could be just the ticket for unifying all the remotes in your house. The software requires PalmOS 3.0 or better and works on Palms and compatible PDAs, such as the Palm III, IIIx, Palm V, Palm VII, Sony Clie, and Handspring Visor. I use it with an old Palm 3C, and it's great. One of its coolest aspects is that the OmniRemote software actually turns your PDA into a Universal Remote so that you can configure the software and add buttons to create a software remote that controls any and every IR device in your house—you're only limited by the screen real estate on your PDA. The OmniRemote software is also *skinnable*, which means that you can easily change its appearance by creating or importing your own backgrounds using a variety of Macintosh and PC software packages.

Figure 3.2 shows two sample skins for the OmniRemote Pro software, side by side, to give you an idea of just how flexible this software is on PDAs with color and higher screen resolutions. This is a fun piece of software that I highly recommend. It also prevents you from having to panic if your dog eats your remote (speaking from personal experience).

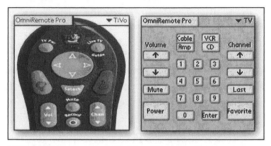

**FIGURE 3.2**   *Sample OmniRemote Pro screens*

# Secret TiVo Commands and Modes

Let's talk about some of the special remote control codes that activate or modify the behavior of your TiVo, the things that it displays onscreen, and so on. These are not officially supported by TiVo, so they could vanish or change in any new release of the TiVo software. However, they range from being interesting to being downright useful, and can help you enrich your TiVo experience.

The secret commands and modes are simple examples of what are commonly referred to as *Easter eggs*. In the software biz, Easter eggs are undocumented features available in a program or operating system that are activated on a date or at a preset time, after a specific or random interval, or in response to an arcane combination of key strokes that most users would never press. Software Easter eggs get their name from the Easter festivities held for children in the United States and other countries, where part of the Easter celebration involves kids getting up and trying to find the Easter candy that the Easter Bunny (or, occasionally, the children's parents) hides for them.

 **WARNING**

TiVo's secret commands and modes are not accidental—they're in there for a reason. Typically, these sorts of hidden features are there for diagnostic or developmental purposes. As diagnostic tools, they provide access to low-level capabilities that can cause data loss or, in extreme cases, put your TiVo into a state where it must be repaired by TiVo service in order to unscramble it. Be very careful when activating any of the secret commands, codes, or modes discussed in this chapter.

Some of the secret TiVo commands and modes are only available if other modes already have been activated, while others are available at any time. Some commands persist even after you have restarted your TiVo and must be disabled by using other codes, while still others must be re-enabled each time you reboot the TiVo. (The section later in this chapter, "Automating Backdoor Mode and Other Codes" explains how to automatically re-enable your favorite secret TiVo modes each time you restart your TiVo.)

The various codes available on different versions of the TiVo are typically grouped together, and, accordingly, are named based on the initial key sequence that you must enter using your remote control to activate them. As a quick summary, the next few sections discuss the following modes and codes:

- *AutoTest mode* These codes cause your TiVo to randomly generate key presses and are presumably used by TiVo QA and system test personnel. These codes are uninteresting and irritating because you often have to reboot your TiVo in order to stop AutoTest mode. They are listed last in this section because I don't see why anyone would knowingly activate AutoTest mode twice. This mode is also known as "Bullwinkle" mode.

- *Backdoor mode* This is a special mode on the TiVo that displays additional information about your TiVo, providing insights into the state and behavior of the system. Backdoor mode must be enabled before you can access some of the other TiVo modes and commands.

- *Clear-Clear-Enter-Enter (CCEE) codes* These codes primarily activate diagnostic features. Some of these codes require that backdoors be enabled, while others do not.

- *Clear-Enter-Clear (CEC) codes* These codes seem targeted for use by TiVo quality assurance and system test personnel, and require that backdoors be enabled to use them.

- *Enter-Enter (EE) codes* These codes enable you to set variables used by the TiVo, and they require that Backdoor mode be enabled in order to use them.

- *Select-Play-Select (SPS) codes* These codes affect the behavior of the TiVo and include what is probably the most famous and popular TiVo key sequence—the value used to turn the Skip Forward button into a 30-second skip button, which is eminently desirable in order to avoid viewing commercials when replaying a stored recording. Don't skip this section! These codes work regardless of whether Backdoor mode is enabled.

- *Thumb-Thumb-Thumb (TTT, or Triple Thumb) codes* These codes reveal hidden screens, expired recordings, and expired showcases on your TiVo. They can be both useful and interesting, and the folks at TiVo would probably be happy if you would re-watch some of the old promotions and commercials that are stored on your TiVo. Backdoors must be enabled in order to use these codes.

Some of these codes can be entered directly from the remote control, while others must be entered from what is known as the Ouija screen. This is the text-entry screen that is used by TiVo when specifying, selecting, or browsing entries from various Pick Programs To Record screens (TiVo Central, Pick Programs To Record). My favorite is the Ouija screen in the Search By Title section, because it contains a complete set of numbers, the entire alphabet, and a space.

As you'd expect from undocumented features, such as secret codes and Easter eggs, some of the secret control codes are specific to certain versions of the TiVo software. If that's the case, the explanatory text identifies the version of the operating system to which they are specific. This chapter focuses on codes that work on Versions 3.0 and later of the TiVo software. Codes that worked on previous versions of the TiVo software are also identified, but are listed primarily for historical completeness.

---

 **NOTE**

---

The codes listed in this section were found through the hard work and consistent experimentation of TiVo users all over the world. Special thanks go to Otto, a former senior member of the AVS TiVo Forum, for compiling a centralized list of the codes that was the initial inspiration for this section.

## Activating Backdoor Mode

Backdoor mode is one of the more interesting TiVo modes, and must be enabled before you can use some of the other codes discussed in this section. Backdoor mode is a special mode in which a variety of extra TiVo commands, settings, and capabilities are available. The key sequence required to activate Backdoor mode is specific to each version of the TiVo software and can be downright tricky to activate in the latest versions. It's tricky because different versions of the TiVo software use different hash values (also known as *hash keys*) to verify the backdoor code. (See the next section, "Hashing 101," if you want more detail about what hashing is and what it does.)

Enabling backdoors causes a good deal of new and more detailed information to display throughout the TiVo menu hierarchy. After backdoors are enabled, the System Information screen not only states that they are enabled but also displays new information, such as the amount of time that your TiVo has been running without rebooting, the value of many internal variables, pending and past system software updates, whether or not you've opted to disallow receiving PTCMs (Pre-TiVo Central Messages, discussed in Chapter 1), and so on. Other portions of the TiVo menu hierarchy also show additional information. More importantly, enabling backdoors facilitates the use of some of the other special commands and modes that can be activated only when Backdoor mode is enabled.

Most of the hash codes for releases of the TiVo software up to and including V3.0 are known quantities (see "Activating Backdoor Mode on V3.0 and Earlier TiVos"). To activate Backdoor mode on a TiVo model running a more recent version of the TiVo software (most are), you'll actually have to get your hands dirty in hackerland. For details, see the section later in this chapter on "Activating Backdoor Mode on V3.1 and Later TiVos."

**TIP**

After activating Backdoor mode as described in the next few sections, try pressing the Channel Down key a number of times to display an in-house joke about the game ZeroWing.

## Hashing 101

*Hashing* is a standard computer science term for using an algorithm to transform a sequence of characters into a fixed-length value. The idea behind hashing is that using a sufficiently complex but fast hashing operation will produce unique values, even from similar inputs. These values can then be used to quickly access or verify data. Most databases use a hashing algorithm to generate the index keys used to locate specific database records. For example, without using hashing or an equivalent operation, looking up "von Hagen, Bill" in a database containing entries for both "von Hagen, Bill" and "von Hagen, Connie" would require a laborious set of character comparisons until a unique character was encountered (in this example, "B"). It's much faster to use hashing to generate a unique value for each of these names and then use that hash value to find the appropriate record in the database.

The checksums used to verify the integrity of downloaded files are another example of the use of hash values. When a file is uploaded, a checksum is calculated based on the original contents of the file. When someone downloads the file, they can compare it against the checksum to verify that the file is the same as the original—in other words, that it was not modified on the download site and that it was not somehow damaged during the download process. The TiVo uses hashing for both encryption and data verification purposes, but the codes necessary to activate Backdoor mode are an example of hashing for encryption. (See the discussion of the TiVo startup procedure in Chapter 9 for a discussion of hashing used for data verification purposes.) All serious hashing algorithms used in encryption are one-way—meaning, you can't easily decipher the original input from a given hash value; you can only compare the output of the hash algorithm in multiple cases to see if they are the same. TiVos use a well-known hashing algorithm known as *SHA1*, the Secure Hash Algorithm, Version 1.0. For more information about this algorithm, see **http://www.w3.org/PICS/DSig/SHA1_1_0.html** for both encryption and verification.

TiVo hash values are impressive. As an example, the following example shows the TiVo resource that contains the hash value for enabling backdoors on systems running Series 3.2 software.

```
ResourceItem 999074/174 {
  Id = 131251
  String = 96F8B204FD99534759A6C11A181EEDDFEB2DF1D4
}
```

The "String" is the output of the SHA1 hashing algorithm from the 3.2 backdoor code. This is not the sequence of characters you have to type when enabling backdoors—this is the sequence of characters that must be generated by the SHA1 algorithm in response to the backdoor code. Therefore, to determine the code, all you have to do is find the random-length string of random characters that generates this output when processed by the SHA1 algorithm. Don't despair. As explained in the next section, the backdoor codes for many TiVo software releases are well known (and listed in this book).

 **NOTE**

If you're curious about the other aspects of the resource shown above, see the information in Chapter 10 on TiVo's MFS filesystem.

If your TiVo is running a TiVo software release for which the backdoor codes are not known, there are two possible approaches. Brute force attempts to identify the backdoor code are certainly possible, but my supercomputer is down at the moment. For a solution that involves a bit of hacking but is eminently doable, see "Activating Backdoor Mode on V3.1 and Later TiVo Models" (also known as "If You Can't Find the Key, Change the Lock") later in this chapter.

## Activating Backdoor Mode on V3.0 and Earlier TiVos

If your TiVo is running a version of the software up to and including V3.0, you're in luck—the hash codes for these versions of the operating system are well known. Known backdoor codes can be entered by using the remote, but the TiVo must currently be displaying one of the TiVo screens that enable you to enter text, such as the Search By Title or Browse By Name screens. To activate backdoors on a V3.0 or earlier TiVo system (using Search By Title as an input screen), do the following:

1. Click the TiVo button to display the TiVo Central menu.
2. Navigate down to the Pick Programs To Record menu entry and press Select.
3. Search By Title should be highlighted. Press Select.
4. All Programs should be highlighted. Press Select. The Ouija screen displays, as shown in Figure 3.3. (You could have also gotten here by using the TiVo-4 shortcut discussed earlier.)
5. On this screen, enter one of codes shown in the following table, based on the type of TiVo that you have and the version of the software that you are running. (You can identify your software version by following the instructions in Chapter 1, "Identifying Your TiVo Software Version".)

Enter the strings exactly as shown between the double quotation marks, including any spaces (don't enter the double quotation marks). (Note that all of the "0s" in the Backdoor codes are zeroes, not uppercase "Os.") If you have entered the correct code, the TiVo will bong a few times and display the message "Backdoors enabled!" as shown in Figure 3.4. The TiVo will then return to TiVo Central.

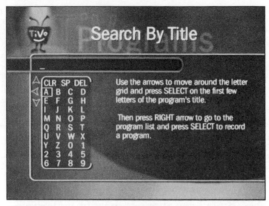

**FIGURE 3.3** *Ouija Screen in the Search By Title screen*

**FIGURE 3.4** *Enabling backdoors in the Search By Title screen*

**Table 3.1 Known TiVo Backdoor Codes**

| TiVo Software Release | Code |
| --- | --- |
| 1.3 (US) | Enter "0V1T" and press Thumbs Up. |
| 1.5.0 or 1.51 (UK) | Enter "0V1T" and press Thumbs Up. |
| 1.5.2 (UK) | Enter "10J0M" and press Thumbs Up. |
| 2.0 | Enter "2 0 TCD" and press Thumbs Up. |
| 2.5 (US) | Enter "B D 2 5" and press Thumbs Up. |
| 2.5.5 (UK) | Enter "B D 2 5" and press Thumbs Up. |
| 2.5.2 (DirecTiVo) | Enter "B M U S 1" and press Thumbs Up. |
| 3.0 | Enter "3 0 BC" and press Thumbs Up. |

If you're the paranoid sort, the easiest way to verify that the backdoor feature is indeed enabled is to navigate to the System Information screen. If it is enabled, the first entry in this screen will state that it is enabled (see Figure 3.5).

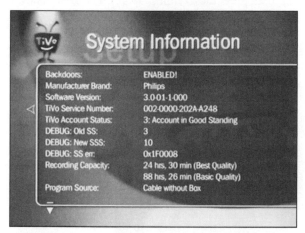

**FIGURE 3.5**   *System Information screen indicating that Backdoor mode is enabled*

## Activating Backdoor Mode on V3.1 and Later TiVo Models

As mentioned previously, the backdoor codes for versions of the TiVo software newer than V3.0 are unknown, which is probably a situation that will continue with future TiVo software releases. Fortunately, since we're all hackers here, a relatively simple solution is available for people (like me) who simply must enable backdoors on their TiVo systems.

 **NOTE**

At the time this book was updated, no one knew the hash strings for DVD-equipped TiVos such as the Sony SVR-2000, the Sony SVR-3000, the Pioneer 57-H, and the Pioneer 810-H. Therefore, backdoors *cannot* currently be enabled on those systems. These systems all run versions of the TiVo software later than 4.0.x, which is the last TiVo software release for which the hash strings are known. Check the TiVo forums discussed in Chapter 14, "Other TiVo Hacking Resources," for updates—chances are good that some enterprising TiVo hacker is looking for the answer to the same problem right now.

Prior to Version 4.0 of the TiVo software, backdoors were interesting and occasionally useful, but now Version 4.0 of the TiVo software provides an extremely useful screen that can only be seen when backdoors are enabled. This is a Disk Space Usage screen that you can access from the Pick Programs To Record screen off TiVo Central. Until now, "guesstimating" the amount of remaining free space on your TiVo was truly a black art—depending on the number of recordings you have, the quality level at which they were recorded, the size of your disk drive minus the space TiVo uses for system partitions, and the sacrifice of a chicken. No more! To display this screen (only available on V4.0 systems), enable backdoors as described in this section, navigate to the Pick Programs To Record screen, press Zero on your remote control, and then press the Thumbs Up key. The Disk Space Usage screen shown in Figure 3.6 displays!

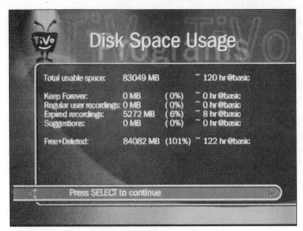

**FIGURE 3.6**  *The Disk Space Usage screen—a good place to get information*

 **NOTE**

TiVo machines run Linux, which, like all Unix-like systems, reserves some amount of extra space in each filesystem for use during emergencies. (The amount of extra space allocated can be changed—or eliminated—when you create a new Linux partition.) So, the calculations shown on the Disk Space Usage screen may not identify the exact amount of free space available down to the last byte, but the values shown are accurate as far as the system's perception of available space is concerned.

If you enable backdoors on a TiVo running 4.x+, another special code enables you to get various information about the Home Media Features. Going to the Now Playing screen and pressing 0-Thumbs Up (that's zero followed by the Thumbs Up key) displays information about the status of the Home Media Features on your system and also lists the other systems available on your network. If the Home Media Features aren't working on your system, this screen will simply say that permission to transfer to/from this system is not currently enabled, and it suggests that you contact TiVo.

The process of enabling backdoors on TiVo V3.1 and later systems involves some techniques explained later in this book, which you may not have encountered yet if you're a front-to-back or random-access reader. Where necessary, each of the following steps provides cross-references to the appropriate sections of the book.

**WARNING**

The instructions in this section for enabling backdoors require that you use a hexadecimal editor to actively modify data in raw Linux partitions. Making a mistake during this process can render your TiVo disk unusable, turning your TiVo into an expensive electric paperweight. I strongly suggest that you either clone your disk to an identical disk and work on the copy (by using the Linux **dd** utility to save an exact image of your disk to a spare drive with enough free space to hold it), or you use the **mfstool** utility to back up your TiVo disk before performing the following instructions. (See Chapter 6, "Backing Up and Restoring TiVo Data" for a discussion of backup alternatives before proceeding. Some backup methods will cause you to lose any recordings that you may have stored on your TiVo disk.) Do not proceed without backing up your drive unless you are extremely comfortable with working on disks at a very low level or just don't care. Don't make me say, "I told you so."

To make it possible to enable backdoors on TiVo systems running V4.x of the TiVo software, do the following:

1. After backing up your TiVo drive or throwing caution to the winds, remove your TiVo hard drive and put it in an x86 or IA/32 PC, as described in Chapter 4, "Working with TiVo Disk Drives." Make sure that you've jumpered the drive correctly so that it does not conflict with any other drive on your system! See Chapter 8, "Working with Your TiVo from Windows and Macintosh Systems," for information about trying to do this on a Macintosh. (I apologize in advance for the fact that this section is PC-centric. I love my G4 and iBooks as much as anyone, but PCs are ubiquitous and easier to use for hacking purposes.)

2. Obtain and burn one of the TiVo boot disks containing the tools that you need to edit the TiVo partitions. See the section of Chapter 5 entitled "Boot Disks" for a discussion of the various boot disks. If you are not using a boot disk that includes the hexedit utility (in other words, the BATBD disk), make sure that you have access to a Linux partition on the boot disk of your PC where you have downloaded or built a statically-linked copy of the hexedit utility. Chapter 4 also provides more detailed information on the hexedit utility.

3. Boot using the TiVo CD that you created in the previous step, selecting a byte-swapped boot configuration from the boot menu. If your TiVo is a Series 1 stand-alone or DirecTiVo, you must boot with the TiVo disk byte-swapped in order to access the partitions used by the TiVo. After booting your system using the TiVo boot CD, follow any other instructions (such as mounting the CD) that are associated with the specific boot CD that you are using.

4. Use the **pdisk** utility to display the partition map on the TiVo drive; then write down all of the partitions that are identified as MFS Application partitions. These are the partitions that you will search through for backdoor hash values. For example, consider the following pdisk output:

```
Partition map (with 512 byte blocks) on '/dev/hdd'

#:                 type  name                        length base        ( size )

1:   Apple_partition_map  Apple                           63 @ 1

2:                Image  Bootstrap 1                       1 @ 64

3:                Image  Kernel 1                       8192 @ 65        (  4.0M)

4:                 Ext2  Root 1                       262144 @ 8257      (128.0M)

5:                Image  Bootstrap 2                    4096 @ 270401    (  2.0M)

6:                Image  Kernel 2                       4096 @ 274497    (  2.0M)

7:                 Ext2  Root 2                       262144 @ 278593    (128.0M)

8:                 Swap  Linux swap                   131072 @ 540737    ( 64.0M)

9:                 Ext2  /var                         262144 @ 671809    (128.0M)

10:                 MFS  MFS application region       524288 @ 933953    (256.0M)

11:                 MFS  MFS media region           50770944 @ 1458241   ( 24.2G)

12:                 MFS  Second MFS application region 524288 @ 52229185 (256.0M)

13:                 MFS  Second MFS media region    64477184 @ 52753473  ( 30.7G)

14:                 MFS  New MFS Application             1024 @ 117230657

15:                 MFS  New MFS Media              42852352 @ 117231681  ( 20.4G)

16:          Apple_Free  Extra                          2495 @ 160084033 (  1.2M)
```

In this example, you would have to search and potentially update both the partitions /dev/hdd10 and /dev/hdd12.

---

 **TIP**

If the list of partitions on your disk is too long to fit on a single screen, you can scroll back to previous messages by holding down the Shift key and pressing the Page Up key on your keyboard.

5. If you're not using the BATBD, make sure that you have access to a statically-linked version of the **hexedit** utility (or one that is compiled against the same libraries and library versions as those used on your boot disk).

6. Use the **hexedit** application to edit each of the partitions identified in Step 4, specifying the name of the partition that you want to edit as a command-line argument. The following example command edits partition 12 on a hard drive attached as a slave drive on the PC's second IDE interface:

```
# hexedit /dev/hdd12
```

 **NOTE**

If you're not sure how to identify the partition you should be editing, see Chapter 4's discussion of Linux disk-drive naming conventions for more information.

7. After the **hexedit** application starts, your screen will look something like that shown in Figure 3.7. Use the following commands to locate and replace the appropriate strings from Table 3.2:

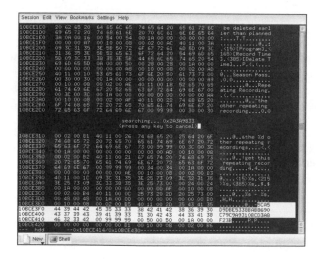

**FIGURE 3.7**   *Editing a partition using the Linux hexedit utility*

**Table 3.2   TiVo Software Releases and Hashes**

| TiVo Software Release | String To Search For |
| --- | --- |
| 3.1 | 96F8B204FD99534759A6C11A181EEDDFEB2DF1D4 |
| 3.2 | 96F8B204FD99534759A6C11A181EEDDFEB2DF1D4 |
| 4.0 | 61508C7FC1C2250E1794624D8619B9ED760FFABA |

◆ 7.1. After starting **hexedit**, press the Tab key to move the cursor from the hexadecimal section of the display to the ASCII section of the display.

◆ 7.2. Press Ctrl-s (hold down the Ctrl key and press the letter "s") to display the search prompt, press the Caps Lock key to ensure that what you type is completely in uppercase, and then enter one of the strings shown in Table 3.2. The string that you enter depends on the version of the TiVo software that your TiVo disk is running.

◆ 7.3. After the **hexedit** application locates the specified string, it will position the cursor at the beginning of the search string. Enter the following string as the new hash:

5CA5D9DBE5338BAB8690C79C9A9310BCD3A8F23B

Simply typing in the ASCII display will overwrite the existing values there.

◆ 7.4. After you have entered the new string, release the Caps Lock key and press Ctrl-s to search for the specified string again. The **hexedit** utility will prompt you as to whether you want to save your modifications—double-check that you have entered the string correctly, and answer "Y" to save the modified partition, if that's the case.

◆ 7.5. Repeat the previous three steps twice, once for each instance of the backdoor hash in the TiVo filesystem.

◆ 7.6. After you reach the end of the partition, press Ctrl-x (hold down the Ctrl key and press the letter "x") to save all of your modifications to the file and return to the Linux command prompt. If you do not want to save your changes and wish to exit at any time, press Ctrl-c (hold down the Ctrl key and press the letter "c").

8. After repeating Step 7 for every partition that you identified in Step 4, shut down the Linux system by executing the Shutdown Now command.

 **NOTE**

The next time you boot your PC, press the CD drive's Eject button to remove the CD to ensure that your PC doesn't accidentally reboot from the CD.

9. Remove the hard drive and restore any jumpers on the drive to the pins where they were located when you removed the drive from the TiVo.

10. Put the drive back in your TiVo and plug in the TiVo. It should go through its standard boot sequence.

11. After the TiVo boots, follow the procedure described earlier in "Activating Backdoor Mode on V3.0 and Earlier TiVo Models," using the backdoor code "3 0 BC." This should enable backdoors on your system!

Congratulations! You are now a bona fide TiVo hacker, and can access the "Free Disk Space" screen.

# Using Clear-Clear-Enter-Enter Codes

Like the majority of the other special TiVo codes discussed in this chapter, the name of this class of TiVo codes is based on the sequence of keys that you must press on your remote in order to activate them. These codes are all initiated by pressing the Clear key on your remote, the Clear key again, the Enter key, and the Enter key again. You then enter an additional key to activate a specific feature. Clear-Clear-Enter-Enter (CCEE) codes must be entered from the TiVo System Information screen (TiVo Central, Messages & Setup, System Information).

Most of the CCEE codes activate diagnostic features, although few of them actually seem to work in Versions 3.0 and later of the TiVo software on which this book focuses. Most of the CCEE codes also require that Backdoor mode be enabled, even though some work regardless. The following list explains each of the CCEE codes that has been discovered in the various TiVo software releases:

◆ *C-C-E-E 0*   In versions of the TiVo software prior to Version 3.0, this option enabled you to enter a specific Dial-in Configuration Code, presumably to send logs and other information back to TiVo support. This option no longer does anything in Versions 3.0 and later of the TiVo software. Pressing this key sequence with backdoors enabled still makes the triple-ding that indicates success, but nothing seems to happen.

◆ *C-C-E-E 2*   In versions of the TiVo software prior to Version 3.0, this key sequence toggled a Special mode: DEBUG option in the System Information screen. After activating this feature, you had to exit and then re-enter the System Information screen in order to see the message. When this option was enabled, debugging output was written to the file `/var/log/tvdebuglog` on the TiVo system. Once set, this option would survive across reboots but shouldn't be left on for long because it could fill up your TiVo `/var` partition. This option no longer seems to work in V3.0 and later TiVo software releases, regardless of whether you have enabled backdoors.

◆ *C-C-E-E 3*   In versions of the TiVo software prior to Version 3.0, this key sequence was supposed to initiate a special call to TiVo headquarters. This option required that backdoors be enabled, but it no longer seems to do anything obvious in Versions 3.0 and later of the TiVo software. Pressing this key sequence with backdoors enabled still makes the triple-ding that indicates success, but nothing seems to happen.

◆ *C-C-E-E 7*   Still supported in Versions 3.0 and later of the TiVo software, this option causes a timestamp message to be written to the `/var/log/tverr` log file. It is assumed that this option is used by TiVo customer support to generate timestamp messages in TiVo logs to help identify problems. Messages written to the `tverr` log file have the following format:

`SetupDebugContext:OnNumber[NNN]: USER PROBLEM LOGSTAMP`

◆ *C-C-E-E 8*   In versions of the TiVo software prior to Version 3.0, this key sequence displayed the Channels You Watch screen with no channels selected, providing a quick and easy way to clear your current list of selected channels. This key sequence doesn't do anything in Versions 3.0 and later of the TiVo software, regardless of whether you have enabled backdoors.

# Using Clear-Enter-Clear Codes

The name of this class of TiVo codes is based on the sequence of keys that you must press on your remote control in order to activate them. These codes are all initiated by pressing the Clear key on your remote, the Enter key, and the Clear key again. You then enter an additional key to activate a specific feature. Clear-Enter-Clear (CEC) codes must be entered from the TiVo System Information screen (TiVo Central, Messages & Setup, System Information).

Most of the CEC codes affect the behavior of the TiVo, and all of them require that you have enabled backdoors. All of the CEC codes work in Versions 3.0 and later of the TiVo software, although few of them do anything that would interest most people. Like many of the TiVo special modes, the CEC codes seem targeted for use by TiVo quality assurance and system test personnel. The following list explains each of the CEC codes that have been discovered:

◆ *C-E-C 0*  Turns off listing Schedule Suggestions in the ToDo List screen. Schedule Suggestions are items listed on the TiVo Suggestions screen (TiVo Central, Pick Programs To Record, Schedule Suggestions) that the TiVo plans to record. The resulting list only displays scheduled items from your WishLists or Season Passes.

◆ *C-E-C 1*  Performs the same tasks as C-E-C 0.

◆ *C-E-C 2*  Turns on displaying Schedule Suggestions in the ToDo List screen. Normally, this will only take effect the next time the TiVo updates the ToDo List. See the "ThumbsDown-ThumbsDown-ThumbsUp Instant Replay Code" later in this chapter for information on rebuilding the ToDo List.

◆ *C-E-C 3*  Performs the same tasks as C-E-C 2.

◆ *C-E-C 4*  Forces the TiVo Suggestions screen to rebuild.

◆ *C-E-C 5*  Toggles overshoot correction when fast-forwarding. Overshoot correction is an automatic feature of the TiVo that backs up the current recording a small amount if you press Play while fast-forwarding; it is intended to correct for the amount of time between the point at which you see that commercials are over and your show starts, and the time when you actually hit the Play button. Overshoot correction is very useful, unless you have the reflexes of a cobra or video game addict.

◆ *C-E-C 6*  Displays the Node Navigator, which is a hidden mechanism that provides direct access to the TiVo menu internals. The Node Navigator is shown in Figure 3.8. Using the Node Navigator can be extremely dangerous to the health of your TiVo—simply exploring the TiVo menu hierarchy can occasionally break things even if you don't think that you've changed anything. Don't use the Node Navigator without a complete backup of your TiVo disk(s). On the other hand, now that I've satisfied my conscience, you can do a few cool things in the Node Navigator, such as visiting Node 1 in V3.0 and later TiVo software releases to specify an exact value for the overshoot correction discussed in the entry for the C-E-C 5 key sequence in this section. For another cool feature doable via the Node Navigator, see the section later in this chapter entitled "Activating and Using Advanced WishLists."

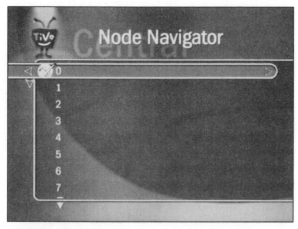

**FIGURE 3.8**    *The TiVo Node Navigator screen*

◆ *C-E-C FastForward*    Reboots the TiVo. This works quite well and can be equally useful if you have hacked your TiVo and want the new changes to take effect without actually pulling the plug and plugging it back in again. Rebooting the machine using this key sequence is easier on your hardware.

◆ *C-E-C SkipForward*    Causes the TiVo to behave as if it has run out of guide data and is often referred to as *Boat Anchor Mode*. This is probably intended for use by the TiVo QA and System Test folks—it's not something that you and I would want to do.

◆ *C-E-C Slow*    Creates a file called /tmp/mwstate on your TiVo, which provides a snapshot of the state of the **myworld** application and is used by the TiVoWeb application and some TiVo test code (/tvlib/tcl/tv/screenTestsFramework.tcl). The following is an example of an **mwstate** Insert file:

```
context {
    id {121}
    pTextM {(null)}
    mode {1}
    currentPos {0}
    duration {0}
    replayStart {0}
    replaySize {0}
    playStatus {0}
    fShowRecordingDotM {false}
    fTrickPlayEnabledM {true}
    beginTime {
        pTextM {0:00}
    }
```

```
        middleTime {
            pTextM {(null)}
        }
        endTime {
            pTextM {1:00}
        }
        title {Farscape}
        startTimeM {12152 14400}
        endTimeM {12152 18000}
        recordingDurationM {3600}
    }
    recorder {
        nAction {0}
        nCache {1}
        cache0 {
            idRecording {1510079/-1}
            idProxy {2}
        }
    }
}
```

◆ *C-E-C ThumbsUp*    Enables you to display and explore the TiVo log files on your
TV screen from anywhere in the TiVo menu hierarchy. Figure 3.9 shows an example
of a TiVo log file displayed using this key sequence. After a log file is displayed,
the up and down arrows enable you to scroll through the information in each log;
the right arrow takes you to the next log file, and the left arrow returns you to the
standard TiVo menus. The ThumbsUp and ThumbsDown keys take you to the top
and bottom of whatever log file is currently displayed. Viewing the log files can be
quite useful if your TiVo seems to be behaving strangely or responding slowly—examining the log files often can help you identify failing hardware or other problems
that may require a call to TiVo customer support.

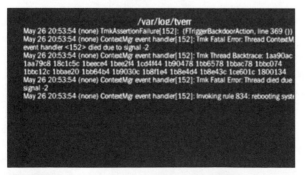

**FIGURE 3.9**    *Displaying log files on the TiVo screen*

◆ *C-E-C ThumbsDown*   Shuts down the **myworld** (**tivoapp**) program on your TiVo, which is the program responsible for almost all of the TiVo functions. If you have a bash shell running on your TiVo, you can re-execute the **myworld** (**tivoapp**) command to restart the TiVo—otherwise, your only alternative is to power-cycle the TiVo (that's geek-speak for turning it off and on again).

# Using Enter-Enter Codes

The name of this class of TiVo codes is based on the sequence of keys that you must press on your remote control to activate them. These codes are all initiated by pressing the Enter key twice on your remote, followed by an additional key to activate a specific feature. Enter-Enter (EE) codes must be entered from the Ouija screen in the TiVo Search by Title screen (TiVo Central, Pick Programs To Record, Search By Title, Category), and they require you to have backdoors enabled. The specified prompt displays in the text entry area at the top of the screen—after entering a value, you press the same EE code again for the code to be accepted. An example of this screen is shown in Figure 3.10. Since the Enter-Enter codes all take numeric values, you can enter them by using the numeric portion of the TiVo remote control keypad, rather than navigating through the Ouija screen.

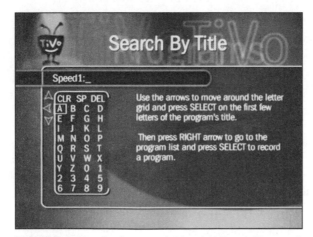

**FIGURE 3.10**   *Setting a variable using Enter–Enter codes*

All of the EE codes are used to set internal values used by the TiVo, and still work in Versions 3.0 and later of the TiVo software. Unlike many of the TiVo special modes, the EE settings can be quite useful in tailoring the TiVo's behavior exactly the way you want it. The following alphabetical list explains each of the EE codes that have been discovered:

◆ *E-E 1*   Displays the Speed1: prompt and turns on the Record LED on the front of your TiVo until you supply a value. The Speed1 setting enables you to specify a three-digit number that represents the percentage of the TiVo's normal playback speed that the first fast-forward speed consists of. (The TiVo fast-forward button has three speeds, which you step through each time you press the fast-forward button.) For example, specifying a value of "400" would set the first fast-forward speed to 4 times the normal playback speed. Specifying a "1" would set the first fast-forward speed to 1 percent of the TiVo normal speed (which could hardly be considered fast-forward). The default setting for the first fast-forward speed is 300% of normal speed. After entering the new value using the TiVo remote control's numerals (or the Ouija screen, if you insist), press Enter-Enter-1 for the TiVo to accept the new value and turn off the red LED on the front of the machine. These values are reset to their default values whenever your TiVo reboots.

◆ *E-E 2* Displays the Speed2: prompt, which enables you to set the second of the TiVo fast-forward speeds. This is the percentage of the TiVo's default playback speed that the second fast-forward speed consists of. The default setting for the second fast-forward speed is 2000% of normal speed. After entering the new value, press Enter-Enter-2 again for the TiVo to accept the new value.

◆ *E-E 3* Displays the Speed3: prompt, which enables you to set the third of the TiVo fast-forward speeds. This is the percentage of the TiVo's default playback speed that the third (highest) fast-forward speed consists of. The default setting for the third fast-forward speed is 6000% of normal speed. After entering a value, press Enter-Enter-3 again for the TiVo to accept the new value.

◆ *E-E 4* Displays a Rate1: prompt, whose function is unknown.

◆ *E-E 5* Displays a Rate2: prompt, whose function is unknown.

◆ *E-E 6* Displays a Rate3: prompt, whose function is unknown.

◆ *E-E 7* Displays an Inter: prompt, which enables you to specify the duration of TiVo interstitials. Examples of TiVo interstitials were animations featuring the TiVo mascot that displayed between each menu screen in early versions of the TiVo software, but they are no longer used. The only remaining Interstitial is the opening TiVo animation that displays whenever you restart your TiVo, or in response to pressing "0" when the TiVo Central menu displays. This setting is vestigial and not very useful. If you insist on entering a value, you must press Enter-Enter-7 again for the TiVo to accept the new value.

◆ *E-E 8* Displays an Open: prompt, whose function is unknown.

◆ *E-E 9* Displays an **int.disabled** or **int.enabled** prompt that toggles interstitials. Toggling the value of this variable doesn't seem to have an effect in Versions 3.0 and later of the TiVo software, although you must still press Enter-Enter-9 again for the TiVo to accept the new value.

◆ *E-E FastForward* Displays a Delay: prompt that enables you to tweak one of the values used to calculate overshoot correction. The default value for this variable is 957. When overshoot correction is enabled, the delay and offset (set using the E-E-Rewind key sequence, discussed next) values are used in overshoot correction calculations. (See the C-E-C-5 and C-E-C-6 codes discussed earlier in this chapter for other settings related to overshoot correction.) After setting the delay and offset values, you must display any recorded program, play it, pause it, and press

FastForward for the new values to take effect. The delay and offset values used in TiVo software Version 1.3 (750 and 1000, respectively) are remembered fondly by many long-time users and are worth experimenting with.

♦ *E-E Rewind*   Displays an Offset: prompt that enables you to tweak one of the values used to calculate overshoot correction. The default value for the offset is 2000. See the explanation of the E-E-FastForward code for additional information about how this value is used.

♦ *E-E TiVo*   Enables you to set the TiVo clock, using the same format as that used by the TiVo **settime** command, which is YYYYMMDDhhmm[ss]. Be careful when setting this value, as setting it incorrectly could cause your TiVo to believe that all of its guide data has expired. If you accidentally munge the time using this command, use the Make Test Call command (TiVo Central, Messages & Setup, Recorder & Phone Setup, Phone Connection, Make Test Call) to automatically set the clock correctly without reloading your guide data.

# Using Select-Play-Select Codes

The name of this class of TiVo codes is based on the sequence of keys that you must press on your remote control to activate them. All of these codes are initiated by pressing the Select key on your remote, pressing the Play key, and then pressing the Select key again. Then you enter an additional key to activate a specific feature and press the Select key again. All of these codes are best entered while playing back a recording, since the Select key is used to, er, select things in the TiVo menus, and the Play key is irrelevant when you already are playing back a recording.

All of the Select-Play-Select (SPS) codes activate cool features, and can be used regardless of whether you have enabled backdoors. The following list explains each of the SPS codes that has been discovered:

♦ *S-P-S 9 S*   Toggles between displaying a clock and elapsed time display in the bottom right corner when replaying recordings or watching live TV (see Figure 3.11). After you activate this, repeating the same key sequence will turn off the clock, but you have to pop back to another menu and then return to playing back the recording for the display to actually go away. When using this code on systems running TiVo V3.0 and 3.1 software releases, only a clock displays, while TiVo V3.2 and later software releases display both a clock and an elapsed time display. The latter is handy when resuming the playback of a recording that you've already started watching because it tells you where you are in the recording.

♦ *S-P-S 30 S*   Toggles 30-second Skip mode, and it is the TiVo's most famous Easter egg. ReplayTV owners tend to go on and on about this feature, and after activating this key sequence, we rave too. Entering this key sequence turns the SkipForward button into a 30-second skip button. This button is very handy in skipping through commercials when playing back a recorded program.

**FIGURE 3.11**   *A clock displayed in a Playback screen*

◆ *S-P-S InstantReplay S*   Toggles between displaying a cryptic status message in the bottom right corner while playing back a stored program or displaying that same message while watching live TV (see Figure 3.12). The status message provides information about the routine that the TiVo is currently executing and gives you the feeling that you're watching television inside a debugger. Like the S-P-S-9-S clock display, you can press this key sequence again to disable the status message, but you must pop back to another menu and then return to playing back the recording for the display to actually go away.

**FIGURE 3.12**   *The status messages displayed in a playback screen*

◆ *S-P-S Pause S*   Toggles between whether the Play bar vanishes quickly or lingers for a few seconds. The Play bar provides a graphical representation of where you are in the playback of a stored recording or where you are in the TiVo live TV buffer. You should only activate this feature if you have good peripheral vision or a photographic memory, because when active, this option causes the Play bar to display for something like only a quarter of a second.

# Using Thumb-Thumb-Thumb Codes

The name of this class of TiVo codes is based on the sequence of keys that you must press on your remote control to activate them. These codes are all initiated by pressing some combination of the ThumbsUp and ThumbsDown keys, followed by an additional key to activate a specific feature. These codes perform different tasks based on the location from where you activate them.

The Thumb-Thumb-Thumb (TTT) codes activate a variety of features, including new screens, expired recordings, expired Showcases, and a few general interface changes. The TTT codes require that backdoors be enabled before the codes can be used. The following list explains each of the TTT codes that have been discovered:

- ◆ *ThumbsDown ThumbsDown ThumbsUp InstantReplay*  If entered in the ToDo List (TiVo Central, Pick Programs To Record, ToDo List), this code activates the display of Scheduled Suggestions in the list. Scheduled Suggestions are items from the TiVo's Suggestions screen (TiVo Central, Pick Programs To Record, TiVo's Suggestions) that the TiVo is planning to record, and which are present in the ToDo List (TiVo Central, Pick Programs To Record, ToDo List). If this code is entered in the Now Playing list (TiVo Central, Now Playing), this code displays hidden recordings. These consist of advertisements, promotional messages from TiVo, and so on that are stored in reserved space on your TiVo disk. These hidden recordings are normally displayed as star messages on the main TiVo screen or within messages from TiVo for a fixed period of time. If you're interested in reviewing these, you can display any of the hidden recordings by navigating to the recording and pressing the right arrow key on your remote. Figure 3.13 shows a sample screen containing these entries as activated by this code sequence.

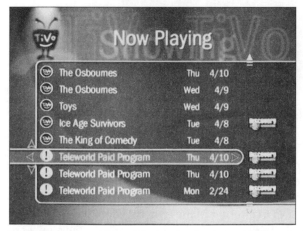

**FIGURE 3.13**  *A Now Playing list displaying hidden recordings*

**NOTE**

If you activate this code in the ToDo list, you'll see *Teleworld Paid Programming* and *Advanced Paid Programming* entries. *Teleworld Paid Programming* entries are the video clips that are recorded for Showcase items and gold star promotions.

If you activate this code in the Now Showing screen, the Teleworld recordings are added to the end of the Now Playing list. The most interesting aspect of this code is to view expired Teleworld items or, occasionally, to catch a glimpse of promotional items before they're enabled.

◆ *ThumbsDown ThumbsUp ThumbsDown Instant Replay*  Entering this code from the Now Playing screen (TiVo Central, Now Playing) causes the TiVo to display a new screen, Clips On Disk. This screen contains the same files as shown by the previous code but organizes them based on the names of the files that contain the clips. You can view any of these clips by navigating to the clip and pressing the right arrow key. Unfortunately, if your system has no hidden clip files, this code sequence reboots your TiVo. Figure 3.14 shows a sample Clips On Disk screen.

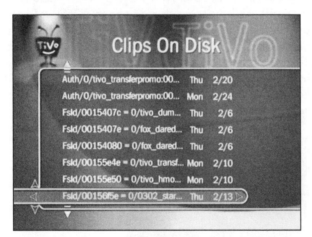

**FIGURE 3.14** *The hidden Clips On Disk screen*

◆ *ThumbsDown ThumbsUp ThumbsDown Record*  Entering this code from the Showcases screen (TiVo Central, Showcases) results in the TiVo displaying all Showcases on the machine, regardless of whether they have expired. You can hide these by re-entering the code. Entering this code sequence from the TiVo Central menu causes the TiVo to display a Menu Item backdoor screen, as shown in Figure 3.15. This screen displays the current date in two formats: the number of days since January 1, 1970 (the standard Unix beginning of time) and also in the normal style. If there is a star menu item at the bottom of the TiVo Central screen, this screen also displays information about that item, including its expiration date (the date beyond which it will no longer display on your TiVo screen). To close this screen, simply use the left arrow key.

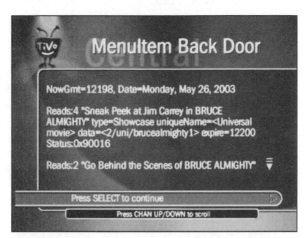

**FIGURE 3.15**    *The Menu Item backdoor screen*

◆ *ThumbsDown ThumbsUp ThumbsDown Clear*    Entering this code from the TiVo Central screen changes all of the screen display fonts to Helvetica Italic (see Figure 3.16). Entering this code again returns them to the standard Helvetica screen font.

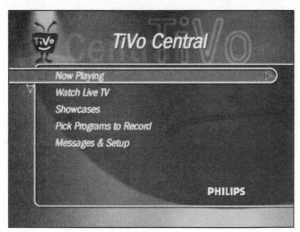

**FIGURE 3.16**    *TiVo screens using an italic font*

◆ *ThumbsDown ThumbsDown ThumbsDown Enter*    Writes debug messages to the TiVo log file, /var/log/tvlog. I didn't see any direct correlation between the messages in this file and the times I entered this key combination, but your mileage may vary. It's not very interesting, though.

# The Irritating AutoTest Mode

AutoTest mode must be entered while viewing a description from the Now Playing screen (TiVo Central, Now Playing). Once this mode is entered, the TiVo randomly generates key presses to simulate someone using the TiVo. Backdoors must be enabled to start AutoTest mode, which is presumably present for TiVo QA, System Test, or burn-in use.

To enter AutoTest mode, go to the Now Playing screen, view the description of any stored recording, and press the 1, 2, and 3 keys on your remote, followed by the ChannelDown button. A message is written to the log file, stating "***** Auto_test mode unlocked! *****". You can then press 4 to initiate the automatic key-press generation. After you are in AutoTest mode, you can press 5 to change the test, press 7 or 8 to change the delay between key presses, or press 4 again to terminate the test. When you are in AutoTest mode, it is difficult to completely exit it without rebooting your TiVo—for example, pressing 4 again may restart the automatic test.

# Sorting the Now Playing List in V3.x TiVos

By default, the items in the Now Playing list (TiVo Central, Now Playing) are sorted based on the date when they were recorded. This is less than useful, since you're more likely to be looking for a specific show by name than you are to search for something that you recorded on a specific date (unless your memory is lots better than mine). Version 4.0 of the TiVo software builds in the capability to sort the items in the Now Playing list based on recording date, expiration date, or name. Luckily, a special key sequence in all 3.x versions of the TiVo software enables you to do the same thing. This secret key sequence doesn't require backdoors to be enabled—it works anytime, as long as you're running some 3.x version of the TiVo software.

 **NOTE**

Version 4.0 of the TiVo software now enables you to group entries by name, which reduces the size of your Now Playing list; for example, if you have a Season Pass to a specific show and have multiple episodes of the same show on your TiVo. Versions 3.x described in this section don't provide the grouping feature.

To enable the sorting feature of the Now Playing list in a TiVo machine running version 3.x of the TiVo software, do the following:

1. Navigate to the Now Playing list from TiVo Central.
2. Enter the following key sequence: Slow 0 Record ThumbsUp. The second character is a Zero. Check out the initials - S0RT! The screen shown in Figure 3.17 displays.
3. Press the Display or Enter button to display the Now Playing Options screen (see Figure 3.18).

**FIGURE 3.17**  *The Now Playing list after activating sorting*

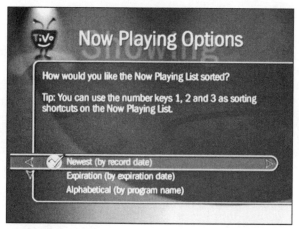

**FIGURE 3.18**  *Sorting options for the Now Playing Options list*

4. Select the way in which you'd like items in the Now Playing list to be sorted and press Select. The Now Playing list redisplays, sorted based on your selection. Figure 3.19 shows a version 3.x Now Playing list sorted alphabetically.

**FIGURE 3.19** *An alphabetically sorted Now Playing list*

After you've activated sorting on your version 3.x system, you can re-sort the entries in the list from the Now Playing screen without entering the Now Playing Option screen by selecting a number corresponding to the type of sorting in which you're interested. Press 1 on your TiVo remote to re-sort the list based on the time that you recorded the program. Press 2 on the TiVo remote to re-sort the list based on the recording's expiration date (useful if you want to see what the TiVo is most likely to delete if it runs low on space and "needs" to record something). Press 3 on the TiVo remote to re-sort the list alphabetically.

This special sorting mode is not permanent; it goes away if you reboot your TiVo (or if the TiVo reboots itself). You can manually re-enable it at any time; you can also disable it yourself by repeating the same key sequence that you used to activate it. See the next section for information about automatically re-enabling various features when your TiVo reboots.

## Automating Backdoor Mode and Other Codes

As interesting and useful as the commands are that you can access from the TiVo Backdoor mode, Backdoor mode itself is not permanent. If your TiVo reboots due to a scheduled software upgrade or because the power goes out, you must manually re-enable Backdoor mode. This isn't a huge hassle, but why do something manually if you can configure your TiVo to do it automatically?

One approach to automatically enabling Backdoor mode on a hacked TiVo is to install a modified version of the TiVo's **tivoapp** binary that has been patched to enable backdoors (this is available from posts on the DealDatabase forum discussed in Chapter 14). However, this isn't very flexible, because it only turns on backdoors and doesn't enable you to automatically enable any other settings.

My preferred approach is to install the TiVoWebPlus application on a hacked TiVo and then take advantage of its built-in Web server and Web-based remote control to automatically execute the key sequences necessary to turn on enable 30-Second Skip mode, enable backdoors, and so on. Unfortunately, this only works on versions of the TiVo software prior to V4.x, but if you're using a DirecTiVo, a stand-alone Series 1 TiVo, or a stand-alone Series 2 on which you're still running TiVo software prior to V4.0, this is a fun and flexible way to have your TiVo automatically enable features. (See Chapter 8 for more information about TiVoWebPlus and its predecessor, TiVoWeb.) The TiVo system provides an application called **http_get**, which is normally used to retrieve updates from TiVo headquarters. However, you can also use this command in your /etc/rc.d/rc.sysinit startup script to send the correct commands to the TiVoWeb Web server and its component applications by using the TiVo loopback Ethernet interface address, 127.0.0.1. All Unix and Unix-like systems provide a loopback address as a convenience for connecting to the local system over an internal interface that is always at the IP address 127.0.0.1. Using **http_get** to send these commands to the Web server's **sendkey** command via the loopback interface enables you to automatically (although somewhat slowly) enable various TiVo modes, as in the following example from my **rc.sysinit** script, which starts 30-Second Skip mode:

```
#
# Activate 30-Second skip mode using TiVoWeb and http_get
#
# Give TiVoWeb time to initialize
#
sleep 120
#
# Get to a well-known location in the menu hierarchy
#
http_get -T 0 -C 0 -D . -U http://127.0.0.1:80/sendkey/livetv
#
# Begin viewing a recorded show
#
http_get -T 0 -C 0 -D . -U http://127.0.0.1:80/sendkey/tivo/tivo/select/
select
#
# Give the show time to start
#
sleep 10
#
```

```
# Enable 30-second skip
#
http_get -T 0 -C 0 -D . -U http://127.0.0.1:80/sendkey/select/play/select
http_get -T 0 -C 0 -D . -U http://127.0.0.1:80/sendkey/num3/num0/select
#
# Go back to TiVo Central
#
http_get -T 0 -C 0 -D . -U http://127.0.0.1:80/sendkey/tivo
```

 **NOTE**

The commands in this example are broken up to make them more readable—you can actually send as many commands as you want to TiVoWeb's sendkey module.

The **http_get** command's -T and -C options are mandatory arguments that ordinarily identify the transaction code and the call id, which are irrelevant in this case, so we simply supply a value of 0. Similarly, the -D option identifies the directory relative to which the command should be executed. When retrieving files as part of a daily or weekly call, this directory is typically /var/packages, but it is irrelevant in this case, so I simply pass an argument of '.', which means "the current directory" in Unix/Linux-speak. The important argument is the URL that you want to contact, which is specified using the -U command-line argument. The URL for each **http_get** command in this example begins with the string "http://127.0.0.1:80/sendkey", which means "use the HTTP protocol to contact the host at the address 127.0.0.1, using port 80, and tell it to execute the **sendkey** command there." The values after the **sendkey** command on each line represent a sequence of TiVo remote commands that the **sendkey** command should execute.

The previous example automatically turns on 30-Second Skip mode whenever I restart my TiVo. You can enable backdoors by doing the same thing, as in the following example:

```
#
# Enable backdoors on 3.0 box - long
#
# Go to Pick Programs to Record, Search By Title
#
http_get -T 0 -C 0 -D . -U http://127.0.0.1:80/sendkey/down/down/down
http_get -T 0 -C 0 -D . -U http://127.0.0.1:80/sendkey/select/select
#
# Go to Talk Shows -> Don't Specify a Subcategory, or anything
# that never has a show that begins with a 3 in your area.
#
http_get -T 0 -C 0 -D . -U http://127.0.0.1:80/sendkey/down/down/down/down
```

```
http_get -T 0 -C 0 -D . -U http://127.0.0.1:80/sendkey/down/down/down/
down/down

http_get -T 0 -C 0 -D . -U http://127.0.0.1:80/sendkey/down/down/down/
down/down

http_get -T 0 -C 0 -D . -U http://127.0.0.1:80/sendkey/down/down/select/
select
#
# Backdoor code begins here. Hack and Laboriously crawl through the Ouija
screen...
#
#   Enter 3
#
http_get -T 0 -C 0 -D . -U http://127.0.0.1:80/sendkey/num3
#
#   Pick Space
#
http_get -T 0 -C 0 -D . -U http://127.0.0.1:80/sendkey/up/right/select
#
#   Enter 0
#
http_get -T 0 -C 0 -D . -U http://127.0.0.1:80/sendkey/num0
#
#   Pick Space (Still positioned there in Ouija)
#
http_get -T 0 -C 0 -D . -U http://127.0.0.1:80/sendkey/select
#
#   Enter B
#
http_get -T 0 -C 0 -D . -U http://127.0.0.1:80/sendkey/down/select
#
#   Enter C and Thumbs Up
#
http_get -T 0 -C 0 -D . -U http://127.0.0.1:80/sendkey/right/select/
thumbsup
```

 **NOTE**

This example assumes that your TiVo uses "3 0 BC" as the code to enable back-doors. If your TiVo uses a different code for backdoors, you'll have to change the letters and numbers sent in all of the lines after the one that says "Backdoor code begins here."

If you want to activate your own favorite backdoors by using this mechanism in your /etc/ rc.d/rc.sysinit file, but are unsure what commands to send, see the discussion of the TiVoWebPlus application in Chapter 8 for more information about starting TiVoWebPlus and displaying its Web-based remote control (currently available only on a Series 1 TiVo running TiVoWebPlus or running an older version of TiVoWeb). To see the command that you should send for any key on the Web-based remote, simply position your cursor over that key on the TiVoWeb or TiVoWebPlus Web page and observe the URL shown in the status bar at the bottom of the screen.

# Legendary TiVo Monitor and Diagnostic Commands

Aside from the secret commands and modes discussed earlier, stand-alone TiVo models also provide some other hidden commands of interest in the TiVo boot (ROM) monitor, which you can access by using the serial connection provided on the back of your TiVo.

**NOTE**

To be honest, the commands that you can access through the ROM monitor are fairly uninteresting with the exception of the **bootparams** command, but they are included here for completeness. The examples in this section are taken from a Series 1 TiVo—Series 2 TiVos provide more of a command-line interface to the boot PROM and are very different from those on a Series 1.

To access the TiVo ROM monitor:

1. Connect the serial Channel Change port on the back of your TiVo to a 9-pin serial port on your PC using the cable that came with your TiVo. You will need to get a null-modem adapter on your TiVo as well as a gender changer to mate the null-modem connector to your PC serial port.

2. Start a terminal emulator on your PC—minicom on Linux systems and Hyper-Terminal on Windows systems are usually present by default. After starting the terminal emulator, configure it for 9600 baud, 8-bit word length, no parity, and 1 stop bit. Most terminal emulators offer a setting for the latter three settings labeled something like 8N1. You should also disable hardware and software flow control, and verify that the terminal emulator is configured to use the serial port to which you've connected your TiVo. This is usually COM1 on Windows systems or /dev/ttyS0 on Linux systems.

3. Plug in the TiVo and immediately press the Return or Enter key on your keyboard.

4. The TiVo displays a Verify password: prompt on Series 1 TiVos, and a "what is password?" prompt on Series 2 TiVos. Enter a password of "factory" (without the quotation marks) and press Enter. (The default bootrom password for S2 combo

boxes is not known but can still be set via the crypto command discussed later.)
This should display a message like the following:

```
Console switched to DSS port
  ------- System Info --------

 Processor speed = 50 MHz

 Bus speed      = 25 MHz

 Amount of DRAM  = 16 MBytes
 Video configuration 3, Serial number 0
 Enet MAC address= 0:4:ac:e3:0:54
 Hostname       = debug-13
 Auto disk locking disabled
 ---------------------------
IDE err = 0x4
IDE drive 0 doesn't challenge security..  Assume insecure device
IDE drive 1 challenges with 0x10001
Respond with 0x6f576955
Check keys a few more times
Respond with 0x6f576955
Respond with 0x6f576955
Respond with 0x6f576955
Drive should be unlocked now.
 --- Device Configuration ---
 Power-On Test Devices:
   000  Enabled   System Memory [RAM]
 ---------------------------
 Boot Sources:
   002  Enabled   EIDE disk Controller [EIDE]
gateway: 192.168.1.227
 ---------------------------
  B - Boot from disk
  N - Network (tftp) boot
  X - print extended menu
->
```

If the "factory" password doesn't work, you can set the ROM monitor password from a bash shell prompt on a hacked TiVo by executing a command like the following:

```
crypto -u -srp password
```

where "password" is the password that you want to set for ROM monitor access.

Once the ROM monitor prompt displays, you can display a larger menu of available options by entering the "X" (for extended) command. The following menu displays:

```
B - Boot from disk
N - Network (tftp) boot
U - Update flash from tftp flash image
T - Teleworld menu
V - Print TiVo Prom Version
W - Word Write
R - Word Read
P - Change Boot Parameters
M - Configure Memory
C - Configure Video
E - Configure Ethernet
K - Set backdoor password
k - Verify backdoor password
z - Change Serial Number
Z - Run memory tests
1 - Enable/disable tests
2 - Enable/disable boot devices
3 - Change IP/MAC addresses
4 - Ping test
5 - Toggle auto disk locking
6 - Toggle automatic menu
7 - Display configuration
8 - Save changes to configuration
9 - Unlock TiVo Secure Disk
0 - Exit menu and continue
```

 **WARNING**

Be very careful when poking around in the ROM monitor. If you are not careful, you can accidentally set or change the TiVo boot parameters and configuration to the point that it will not boot.

Some of the more interesting of these commands are the following:

- ◆  *p*   Enables you to change the TiVo boot partition. Pressing "p" displays the following:

```
->p
Old: root=/dev/hda4
New( - to abort): -
```

This information tells us that my TiVo boots from /dev/hda4. To change this to the other boot partition (/dev/hda7), enter root=/dev/hda7 at the New: prompt. To exit from this menu item without changing the boot partition, you *must* enter a dash ("-"). Simply pressing Enter changes the value of the boot partition variable to null, which would be bad—your TiVo wouldn't boot. You can also change the boot partition from a hacked TiVo by using the **bootparam** command.

- ◆  *v*   Displays the TiVo PROM version.

- ◆  *8*   Saves any changes that you've made to the configuration.

# TiVo Scheduling Tips and Tricks

The capability of TiVo to record programs identified by a number of criteria makes it a powerful tool for customizing your television viewing experience. Its basic ability to time-shift shows, recording them so that you can watch them at your convenience rather than scheduling your life around the *TV Guide*, lets you watch what you want to watch when you want to watch it.

The TiVo's ability to compile a local database of the kinds of things that you like to watch and to automatically record shows that it "thinks" that you would like is a great feature. After you've had your TiVo for a while (and providing that you have some free space on its disk), you'll find that you are pleasantly surprised by what your TiVo has recorded for you.

The fact that the TiVo continually maintains a 30-minute buffer of broadcast television is a great convenience if you're watching live TV; this feature enables you to pause the television and return to it within 30 minutes without losing anything. You can combine this feature with the TiVo recording capabilities in a variety of interesting ways. For example, I generally like to watch the evening news but don't always get home in time to see the beginning. My solution to this is to program the TiVo to always record one minute of the evening news on my favorite channel, only keeping one copy of this one-minute recording around. This causes the TiVo to only waste a minute's worth of disk space, but, more importantly, it forces the TiVo to always tune to my favorite local news channel and begin loading the 30-minute buffer with the news from the right channel. Whenever I get home, I rewind the TiVo to the beginning of the buffer and fast-forward through the 30-minute buffer, only stopping for the news items that interest me. No commercials, no local "cat-up-a-tree," human interest *crapola*. I also set this to "Record at Most" one instance of these, so that my disk doesn't accidentally fill up with old news.

The TiVo makes it extremely easy to schedule the recording of shows that you can locate through the commands on its Pick Programs to Record menu. Locating and selecting shows to record is well documented in the *TiVo Viewer's Guide* that comes with your TiVo; however, it's important to understand the basic capabilities of different types of scheduled recordings. Below is a quick reference for the various methods for locating shows that you want your TiVo to record, while highlighting the differences among them.

With your TiVo, you have four basic ways of scheduling programs to record:

◆ Scheduling a recording of specific duration on a specific channel at a specific time. This is accomplished by using the Record By Time Or Channel menu (TiVo Central, Pick Programs To Record, Record By Time Or Channel). This menu provides three options:

　◆ *Browse By Time* enables you to browse through shows that will broadcast at a specific time on any of the channels that you receive.

　◆ *Browse By Channel* enables you to browse through shows that are to broadcast on a specific channel that you receive.

　◆ *Manually Record Time/Channel* enables you to record what is broadcast on a specific channel for a specific period of time.

◆ Explicitly identifying shows by name and scheduling them to be recorded. This recording option enables you to browse through available shows by genre or simply browse through all upcoming shows for shows of interest.

◆ Explicitly identifying shows by name and then getting a Season Pass to a number of broadcasts of that show on a specific channel at a specific time. Season Passes enables you to automatically schedule recording 1, 2, 3, 4, 5, or All episodes of a specific show on a specific channel at a specific time. (The TiVo Version 4.0 software also enables you to schedule recording up to 10 episodes of a selected show.) This is a powerful recording option that makes can automatically record every episode of your favorite prime-time drama or comedy.

◆ Defining a WishList is a powerful, flexible mechanism for recording all instances of a show regardless of when or on what channel they are broadcast. This option makes it easy for you to tell your TiVo to record every instance of any show based on specific criteria, including portions of its title, portions of its description, actors performing in the show, the director of a show, or even the type of show (movies, sports, comedy, and so on).

With the exception of the explicitly scheduled recording of a program at a specific time period, Season Passes, and WishLists, all of the TiVo's recording options depend on the guide data stored on the system. So, the recording options locate shows to record only within roughly a two-week period. TiVo's WishLists are its most flexible and powerful mechanism for finding shows in which you're explicitly interested.

# Using TiVo WishLists

TiVo's WishLists enable you to define sets of keywords, actors, and directors to identify shows that you'd like to record. The guide data provided on the TiVo is more extensive than that used by any other DVR, so you can quickly find shows you're interested in recording, regardless of when or on what channel they're being broadcast. TiVo WishLists are not tied to specific channels or times, but provide a general way of searching whatever guide data your TiVo contains at any time.

When creating WishLists , keep in mind the following handy tips:

◆ The "*" (generated by pressing Slow on your TiVo remote control) is a wildcard character that matches any sequence of characters. For example, if you want to create a single WishList that will record both episodes of *King of the Hill* and *King of Queens*, you could enter the title keyword "King." If you wanted to expand this to also catch the movie *Kings of Oblivion*, you could enter "King*" as your title keyword, which would match all three.

◆ You can use double quotation marks (generated by pressing the Pause key on your TiVo remote control) to restrict your WishList to multiple words appearing in a specific order. For example, if you only wanted to record episodes of *Perry Mason* but not the *Mason Perry Summer Special*, entering "Perry Mason" inside double quotes would record only the former.

◆ Special characters such as hyphens, slashes, and periods that may appear in show titles should be replaced by spaces in your WishList entries. Dollar signs in program names should be replaced with a capital "S." With the exception of double quotes and the asterisk, any other characters that are not present on the Ouija screens that you use to create WishLists are simply ignored.

Having the ability to loosely define shows you're interested in recording based on portions of the title, show description, or an actor or director involved in the show provides a flexible mechanism for telling your TiVo what you want to record. The capability of using wildcards and quotation marks to refine the shows that your WishLists will match provides additional power. However, as described below, WishLists have an even more powerful, hidden feature—they can create WishLists that combine any or all of these ways to describe what you want to record.

# Activating and Using Advanced WishLists

WishLists make it quite handy to locate shows that you want to record based on a keyword, or specific actor or director names, but TiVo gives you even more power in its WishLists—in an undocumented feature, of course. This feature, known as *TiVo Advanced WishLists*, enables you to combine all of these types of searches into complex WishLists. Only interested in recording science fiction movies starring Arnold Schwarzenegger? No problem. Only want to record *Star Trek the Next Generation* shows that feature Wil Wheaton as Wesley Crusher? No problem!

To access the TiVo Advanced WishLists, enable backdoors on your system. Next, begin creating a WishList by going to the TiVo Central, Programs to Record, Search Using WishLists page. Select Create New WishList. When the Create WishList screen displays, press "0" on your remote control, and the screen shown in Figure 3.20 is shown.

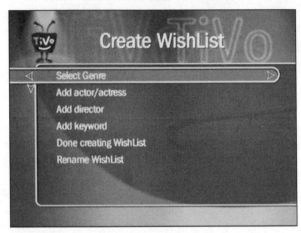

**FIGURE 3.20** *The advanced Create WishList screen*

From this screen, you can create an advanced WishList by using any combination of the items that you use to create standard WishLists. By default, the advanced WishList uses a logical or to match shows—in other words, selecting the genre science fiction and fantasy and the actor Wil Wheaton would match any shows that contained those items. This is probably not what you want to do. To make any item in the list mandatory, select the Edit List option (see Figure 3.21). Following the instructions at the top of the screen, select any items that you want to make mandatory and press ThumbsUp while they are highlighted.

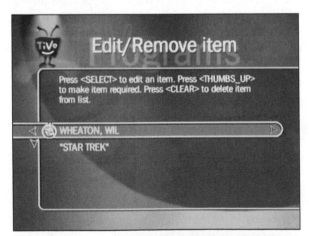

**FIGURE 3.21** *Making items mandatory in an advanced WishList*

Figure 3.22 shows the finished WishList used as an example in this section. With the power of advanced WishLists, you can create WishLists for very precise combinations of specific items so that you don't record more than you want but always record the exact broadcasts that you love best.

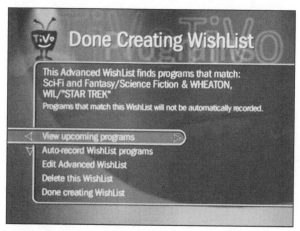

**FIGURE 3.22**    *A completed advanced WishList*

# HACKING
## THE
# TiVo

SECOND
EDITION

# Chapter 4

## *Exploring Your TiVo Hardware*

The previous chapters provided a general introduction to TiVo culture, your TiVo hardware and software options, and keys to opening up some of the hidden features of the TiVo software. Now, it's time to actually crack the nut (or the TiVo, in this case). This chapter explains how to physically open your TiVo, work with its existing hardware, and add networking hardware to various types of TiVos. It generally paves the way for the storage and software modifications discussed later in the book.

**NOTE**

In this chapter, I provide generic descriptions for working with your TiVo, which means that you should be able to use them on TiVo Series 1, Series 2, and DirecTiVo models. Discussions regarding TiVo software apply through release 5.2, which is the release of the TiVo software used on the latest Pioneer 57-H and 810-H systems at the time this book was written. Although things will surely change in future TiVo releases, this chapter focuses mainly on existing hardware (which can't change) and contains relatively few references to the TiVo software.

Before opening TiVo, please refer to this book's Introduction, especially the section entitled "This Book, Your TiVo Warranty, and a Few Warnings." In a nutshell, once you open your TiVo, your warranty is null and void—only a pleasant memory.

# Attaching a Terminal Emulator or Serial Console

As you follow the instructions in this book, you may want to set your TiVo to display a serial prompt over its primary serial port. Doing so enables you to access your TiVo from a terminal emulator such as minicom on Linux systems, HyperTerminal on Windows systems, and other similar applications. Of course, if you still have an ancient computer terminal sitting around, as I do, you can attach it to your TiVo.

As I mentioned in Chapter 3, "TiVo Tips and Tricks," attaching a terminal emulator to your TiVo is easy. After doing so, you will still have to follow one of the procedures described in Chapter 8 to display a command prompt on your TiVo—this section only discusses the hardware side of things.

Most TiVos come with a 10-foot cable that has a $^1/_8$-inch male jack at one end and a 9-pin male serial connector at the other. If you have such a cable, you'll need two additional components—a null-modem connector and a 9-inch gender changer, usually referred to as a *gender bender*. The null-modem connector is necessary because the TiVo serial port is wired to enable devices to control your TiVo, not to enable passive devices to communicate with it. Null-modem connectors simply swap two of the wires between the two systems, thereby enabling communications. The gender bender is necessary because most PC serial ports also have male connectors—the gender bender converts a male connector to a female connector or vice versa (hence the name) so that you can connect two devices with the same type of pins (in this case, the TiVo serial cable and the null-modem connector that you attached to your PC's serial port).

Connect the $^1/_8$-inch jack on one end of the serial cable to the serial Cntrl Out port on the back of your TiVo, which is the uppermost of the two connectors. Do not connect the jack to the IR port, which you probably will be using to control your TiVo. On the 9-pin end of the cable, connect the gender bender to the cable's 9-pin connector and then connect the null-modem adapter to the end of the gender bender. You can then connect the gender bender to the 9-pin serial port on your PC using the cable that came with your TiVo.

**NOTE**

If your gender bender or null modem connector has a screw connector that enables you to firmly connect multiple connectors, you may need to remove the screw connector in order to make a secure connection between the null modem adapter, the gender bender, and your PC's serial port.

After you've made the connection between your TiVo and your PC, you'll need to start a terminal emulation program on the PC in order to communicate with your TiVo. The most commonly used terminal emulation and serial communications software packages are minicom, which usually come by default with Linux systems, and HyperTerminal, which comes with Windows systems.

**NOTE**

Most Macintosh systems don' t have standard serial ports, so they are not covered here. If you're a Macintosh user and want to communicate with your TiVo, your best bet is to put your TiVo on your home network and communicate with it using a Macintosh program like FAT Telnet (on older Macs) or Telnet (on Mac OS X systems).

After starting the terminal emulator on your Windows or Linux system, configure it for 9600 baud, 8-bit word length, no parity, and 1-stop bit. Most terminal emulators offer a setting for the latter three settings, labeled something like 8N1. You should also disable hardware and software flow control and verify that the terminal emulator is configured to use the serial port you've connected to your TiVo, which is usually COM1 on Windows systems or **/dev/ttyS0** on Linux systems.

Unless you just want to examine the output of the TiVo's ROM monitor (as explained in "Legendary TiVo Monitor and Diagnostic Commands," in Chapter 3), you'll also need to have a program running on the TiVo with which you can communicate, such as the Linux command interpreter, as explained in Chapter 8, "Connecting the Universe to Your TiVo."

### TiVo Making Your Own Serial Cable

If your TiVo didn't come with a serial cable, you can buy one from one of the vendors discussed at the end of this chapter or simply make your own by buying the appropriate connectors at your local electronics store. You'll need a male DB9 connector, a @bf1/8-inch male jack, and a length of cable containing at least three wires. You'll probably have to buy cable with four or more wires and just ignore the extra strands.

To create a serial cable that is analogous to the one that should have come with your TiVo, wire it up as shown in Table 4.1

**Table 4.1   Standard TiVo Serial Cable Wiring**

| $1/8$-inch Jack | 9-Pin Connector |
| --- | --- |
| $1/8$-inch Tip | DB9 Pin 3 |
| $1/8$-inch Ring | DB9 Pin 2 |
| $1/8$-inch Sleeve | DB9 Pin 5 |

Of course, if you're making your own TiVo serial cable, you might as well make a custom one that eliminates the need to add a null-modem connector at the end. As explained earlier, the null-modem connector just swaps two of the wires between a serial cable and another connector (like your PC's serial port). To create a custom serial cable that connects your TiVo to your PC, wire it up as shown in Table 4.2.

**Table 4.2   Null Modem TiVo Serial Cable Wiring**

| $1/8$-inch Jack | 9-Pin Connector |
| --- | --- |
| $1/8$-inch Tip | DB9 Pin 2 |
| $1/8$-inch Ring | DB9 Pin 3 |
| $1/8$-inch Sleeve | DB9 Pin 5 |

For general reference, TiVos have three or four serial ports, depending on whether they are Series 1 or Series 2 systems, as shown in the following table. The type of TiVo you are hacking determines the serial port to which you should direct certain applications on the hacked TiVo, such as the TiVo/Linux program that displays a command prompt. Table 4.3. shows the names and uses of the serial ports on different models of the TiVo.

**Table 4.3   TiVo Serial Ports**

| Device | Description |
|--------|-------------|
| **/dev/ttyS0** | IR port on the front of your TiVo and the IR Cntrl (IR Blaster) port on the back of your TiVo |
| **/dev/ttyS1** | TiVo modem |
| **/dev/ttyS2** | Debug port on the TiVo Series 1. DSS Serial port on the back of TiVo Series 2 models |
| **/dev/ttyS3** | DSS serial port on the back of the TiVo Series 1 |

# Opening the TiVo

Drum roll, please! Now the fun really begins. Experimenting with hidden commands and control codes is certainly interesting, but the key to expanding your disk storage or adding new software to your TiVo is physically getting inside it.

 **NOTE**

Please refer to this book's Introduction, especially the section "This Book, Your TiVo Warranty, and a Few Warnings," before opening your TiVo. In a nutshell, once you open your TiVo, your warranty is null and void—only a pleasant memory. You will find plenty of places that can repair TiVos (and even do the upgrade for you, if you're truly paranoid) at the end of this chapter, but keep in mind that by opening your TiVo, you're eliminating the folks at TiVo as one of these places.

The only tools that you'll need to open your TiVo and remove the disk drive(s) are a number 10 Torx screwdriver and a number 15 Torx screwdriver, or just a Phillips screwdriver if you're working with one of the Pioneer DVD-enabled Series 2 TiVos. A Torx screwdriver has a six-point, star-shaped head and provides superior gripping power and protection from stripping than do standard slotted or Phillips-head screwdrivers. Sets of Torx screwdrivers are available at most computer stores, Sears, your local Home Depot, and almost any larger auto parts stores. The Torx screws on the TiVo case are number 10 Torx screws; the screws that hold the drive(s) in place and on the drive bracket are a combination of number 10 and number 15 screws.

Both Series 1 and Series 2 TiVo models come apart easily. To remove the cover, use the number 10 Torx screwdriver to detach the three (Series 1) or four (most Series 2) screws on the black edge on the back of the machine. On Pioneer TiVos, all of the case and drive bracket screws are Phillips screws—thanks, Pioneer!— but you will also have to remove four screws, two on each side of the machine.

After you remove these screws, pull the top straight back an inch or so and lift it up and off when you can see into the front of the machine. I sometimes use a regular screwdriver to pry between the case trim and the back of the machine. You can also use a screwdriver to carefully separate the top from the machine's plastic front panel, but be careful when doing so—the plastic front panel is lightly attached to the steel frame of the TiVo.

 **NOTE**

You will find a silver sticker labeled "Warranty void if this seal is broken" spanning the black and silver portions on the back of Series 1 TiVo machines. Given that you're opening the machine, you may as well peel this sticker off or break it. Series 2 models do not have such a sticker, but it's clear that the same idea applies when simply opening the machine.

# Working with TiVo Disk Drives

By now, I'm sure that you are eager to find out how to physically remove and replace the disks in your TiVo and how to add another disk to single disk systems. Though some early TiVos came with two disks, single-disk systems are much more common nowadays—and prime for upgrading by adding a second disk!

You will usually remove your TiVo drive to back it up or to replace it with another, larger disk. You should back up your TiVo as soon as possible after buying it (see Chapter 6, "Backing Up and Restoring TiVo Data," for the details). The longer you wait, the greater the amount of data you will have to back up—if you want to preserve shows that you've recorded.

## How Large Can TiVo Disks Be?

Before going into the details of removing disks from your TiVo and putting them in a PC for backup and expansion purposes, let's take a moment to explore the maximum disk capacity supported by various TiVo models. Disk drive prices are always coming down, and yesterday's large disks are today's swap space. Regardless of how cheap disks are, there's no point in buying a larger drive than your TiVo can use.

The core issue with TiVo disk capacity is that all of the TiVo kernels through TiVo software Version 4 (including 4.0.1 and 4.0.1b) do not provide support for 48-bit logical block addressing (generally referred to as LBA48). Logical block addressing is a technique that enables a computer to address large hard disks by referring to sectors on the disk by block number, starting with 0, instead of the classic CHS (Cylinder:Head:Sector) geometry of a disk. These logical block numbers are mapped to CHS values by the firmware on the hard disk. This capability is only present in Linux kernel Versions 2.4.19 and above, which is a later version of the Linux kernel than that used on all Series 1 and non-DVD Series 2 TiVos.

Here's a quick breakdown of maximum TiVo disk capacity:

◆ *Series 1 TiVo/DirecTiVo*   All Series 1 TiVos that run stock versions of the TiVo operating system are limited to 137 GB of storage per disk drive, giving you a maximum capacity of 274 GB of storage per TiVo. As I'll explain in Chapter 7, "Expanding your TiVo's Storage Capacity," newer kernels are available for these systems that remove this limitation, but they are not a part of the stock TiVo software. If you use these, you'll be able to use any large IDE drive with your TiVo, but if TiVo ever updates the software for these units again, you may be SOL. (In other words, unless TiVo releases a kernel for these units that supports LBA48, you may lose data on your larger disks. Be *very* careful about using nonstock TiVo kernels without preventing automatic software upgrades from occurring.) Chapter 7 explores these issues in detail and provides some ways of protecting yourself against unwitting updates.

◆ *Non-DVD Series 2 TiVos/DirecTiVos*   At the time this book was updated, all "classic" Series 2 TiVos are limited to 137 GB of storage per disk. Since these systems use hashing to verify kernel signatures, it isn't easy to replace these kernels with customized kernels that support larger hard drives unless you use Monte and have access to a custom-built Linux kernel for the TiVo. More about that in the section of Chapter 8 entitled, "Two-Kernel Monte for Series 2 TiVos."

◆ *Series 2 TiVos with Integrated DVD Drives*   The Pioneer 57-H and 810-H Series 2 TiVos use a later version of the Linux kernel that supports larger disks. I'm using a single 250 GB disk in my upgraded Pioneer 810-H with no problems.

For stock Series 1 and Series 2 TiVo upgrades, I tend to use 160 GB disks even though I can't use all of the storage that they provide. The next lower standard disk size is 120 GB, which is less than the maximum that TiVos support, and 120 GB disks aren't all that much cheaper. As of this writing, 160 GB disks are cheap—less than $100 per drive at most sources on the Web. They certainly won't get more expensive in the future.

# Removing TiVo Disk Drives

The interiors of TiVo systems are very different depending on the model. Figure 4.1 shows the inside of a single-drive TiVo Series 1 (shown from the top). To remove the disk drive, use the number 15 Torx screwdriver to remove the two screws near the front of the TiVo that attach the disk drive bracket to the TiVo frame.

 **NOTE**

For goodness sake, unplug your TiVo before working on it! Not doing so might give you a serious electric shock and a smoking Van der Graf Generator Afro, as well as causing damage to your TiVo. Similarly, TiVo power supplies are not shielded; in other words, all their components are out in the open, with no enclosing case like those around most PC power supplies. Be careful not to touch any part of the TiVo supply because some of the components store a charge that can be painful or even fatal in rare cases.

**FIGURE 4.1** *The inside of a single-drive TiVo Series 1 machine*

After removing these screws, remove the two cables on the back of the disk drive that attach the TiVo to the motherboard and the power supply. The four-wire connector is the power connector; the other cable is an IDE (Integrated Drive Electronics) cable that transfers data to and from the motherboard. Series 1 machines use a multistrand IDE cable (each wire is a separate strand), whereas most PCs and Series 2 machines use a flat cable known as a *ribbon cable*. Don't worry about remembering which way these cables attach to the drive; both of these connectors are shaped so that they can only attach to the drive in a specific way.

 **NOTE**

On DirecTiVo and some older Series 2 machines, you will also have to disconnect a fan on the drive bracket that is connected to the motherboard by a small connector. Make sure that you reconnect this when reassembling your TiVo—not doing so will cause the TiVo to overheat and cause glitches in operation.

After you've detached the cables, you can remove the disk drive and bracket by sliding it one-half inch toward the back of the machine and then lifting it straight up. Be careful when handling the disk drive—it contains your TiVo data!

 **NOTE**

All Series 1 machines are designed to have two disk drives, but they provide only a mounting bracket for each drive that is currently in the system. If your Series 1 TiVo has only a single drive and you want to add a second one, you'll need to buy another bracket to mount the second drive. Sources for drive brackets (and more) are listed in the section "TiVo Hardware Supplies on the Net" later in this chapter.

Series 2 TiVos are very different from Series 1 models, and there's lots of variety among the different Series 2 models. Figure 4.2 shows an AT&T Series 2 TiVo (model TCD140060) with the top off. Note that the drive in the system is mounted in a totally different way than those on the Series 1, being located on a removable bracket. This bracket comes predrilled with holes that enable you to mount a second drive without any special hardware except for a few screws and washers.

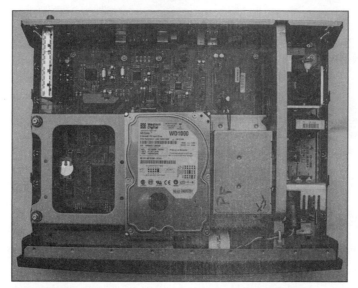

**FIGURE 4.2**   *A single-drive Series 2 60-MB AT&T TiVo*

To remove the drive from this type of Series 2 machine (after removing the lid, of course), use the number 15 Torx screwdriver to remove the two screws that attach the drive bracket to the machine and detach the wire that connects the fan to the motherboard. The remainder of the bracket is held in place by two pins at the end of the bracket farthest from these screws, which protrude through the vertical bracket between the TiVo motherboard and the power supply.

To remove the bracket and the drive from the TiVo, put the fingers of one hand under the end of the bracket nearest the power supply and lift the opposite end of the bracket (where you removed the screws). You can then wiggle the bracket from side to side, pulling toward the end where you removed the screws until the drive and bracket slip out of the machine.

Figure 4.3 shows a TiVo-branded Series 2 machine with the top off. Note that the drive in the system is mounted in a totally different way than those on the Series 1 or the AT&T Series 2 shown earlier. Also notice that this model of TiVo is designed to hold only one disk drive. Luckily, it can easily hold two when used with custom drive brackets that you can buy over the Internet, as I'll describe in the section "TiVo Hardware Supplies on the Net" later in this chapter.

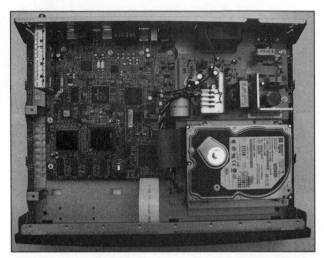

**FIGURE 4.3** *A single-drive Series 2 40-MB TiVo from TiVo*

To remove the drive from this type of TiVo Series 2 machine, use the number 10 Torx screwdriver to remove the two screws that attach the drive bracket to the base of the TiVo (near the front of the machine). After disconnecting the fan, IDE, and power cables, you can remove the bracket holding the drive by sliding it one-fourth inch toward the power supply and then lifting it straight up and out of the machine.

The latest TiVo systems from vendors such as Sanyo and Pioneer come with integrated DVD players (the former) and DVD burners (the latter). Removing the hard drives from these types of systems is slightly more complex because you have to remove the DVD drive in order to get access to the TiVo's hard drive. Figure 4.4 shows a Pioneer 810-H Series 2 machine with the top off.

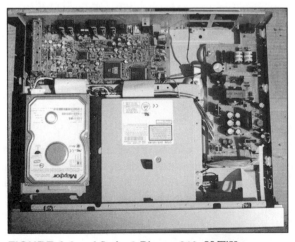

**FIGURE 4.4** *A Series 2 Pioneer 810-H TiVo*

To remove the drive from these types of TiVo Series 2 machines, remove the four Phillips screws that attach the drive frame to the TiVo case, disconnect the IDE and power connections to the drive, and lift the drive and bracket out of the machine.

After removing the drive from whatever model of TiVo you have, disconnect it from the bracket on which it is mounted (Torx screws on Series 1 and most Series 2 TiVos, Phillips screws on Pioneer Systems) so that you can put it in your PC for backup purposes. Attaching a TiVo drive to your PC is described in the next section. See Chapter 6 for various methods for backing up your TiVo.

# Attaching TiVo Disk Drives to Your PC

PCs are the preferred hardware platform for hacking your TiVo because they are ubiquitous, fast, and cheap. After removing a disk drive from your TiVo, attaching it to your PC is easy to do because TiVos and modern PCs use the same types of IDE drives.

To put a TiVo drive in your PC, shut down the PC and remove the top (for desktop systems) or the side cover that gives you access to the disk drives, motherboards, and cards. Next, locate the IDE cables that are attached to the IDE interfaces on your motherboard (or, in rare cases, to an IDE or EIDE controller card). IDE cables are flat, 40-pin ribbon cables with the same sort of connectors on the ends that you saw in your TiVo when you removed its drive.

In order to add your TiVo drive to your PC, you'll have to connect it so that it does not conflict with drives that are already installed in your PC. Most PCs have two IDE interfaces, known as *primary* (IDE-1) and *secondary* (IDE-2). The cable from each IDE interface can be attached to a maximum of two hard or CD-ROM drives. If two drives are attached to a single cable, they must be configured as master and slave drives by connecting pins known as *jumpers* that are located on the back or bottom of the hard drive or CD-ROM drive. *Master* is the term used for the first drive on an IDE interface; *slave* is the term used for the second drive on the IDE interface.

Although the hard drives used by different operating systems are physically the same, the way in which data is stored on them by each operating system is different. Modern Windows PCs store data using disk formats known as FAT-32 (32-bit File Allocation Table) and NTFS (NT File System). Linux systems store data in a variety of formats, most commonly the EXT2 or EXT3 filesystem formats. If you are attaching your TiVo hard drive to your PC to back it up, you will also need to access a hard drive in the PC once you boot from a TiVo tools disk—so that you will have a place to save the backup file. In order to do so, you must have at least one FAT-32, EXT2, or EXT3 partition in your PC at the same time that you attach the TiVo drive. The FAT-32, EXT2, or EXT3 drive in your system must have sufficient free space for the backups. The space required to save a backup of a TiVo drive ranges from 200MB to the total size of the disk drive you are backing up. Backups of most of my TiVos, once I've been using them, are between 800 and 900 MB in size. For more information on backing up your TiVo, see Chapter 6.

**NOTE**

Whether your PC normally runs Microsoft Windows or Linux, all of the bootable tools disks available for hacking the TiVo actually boot your PC into a miniature version of Linux. Don't believe anything you've heard about Linux being cryptic or hard to use (hey, telling you exactly what to do is the purpose of this book). Just follow the instructions carefully, and you'll be a white-belt TiVo hacker in no time.

To continue attaching your TiVo drive to your PC, you must set the jumper (or jumpers) on the TiVo drive so that it does not conflict with any existing drive in your PC. To do so, you must know how the current drives are connected. You can determine how the hard drive and the CD-ROM drive are connected in one of two ways: automatically or manually.

The PC automatically tells you how the drives are connected—just look at the information in your PC's BIOS (Basic Input Output System), which is the chip that controls the PC's configuration. To examine the drive configuration using the BIOS, reboot the PC (without attaching the TiVo hard drive yet—you'll do that in a minute or two) and immediately press the appropriate key on your keyboard to enter the PC's BIOS screen—usually either Delete or F1 on your keyboard; the appropriate key should be listed on the screen after you reboot your PC. After you see the BIOS screen, it should display entries for Primary Master, Primary Slave, Secondary Master, and Secondary Slave. The values beside these entries should explicitly identify the drives that are attached to these interfaces or display the word "Auto," which means that the drives attached to each interface will be detected automatically when you boot your PC. If Auto displays, you can use the arrow keys to navigate to each of these entries and press Enter (or Return) to force the system to probe that interface to see what's connected.

By tracing cables and examining jumpers, you can manually identify how the drives are connected. To do so, turn off the PC and follow each of the IDE cables from your PC back to the hard drive and the CD-ROM drive. The hard drive that your PC boots from is known as the *boot drive*, and it is usually connected as the master on the first IDE interface on your system. If connected to the same IDE cables as your hard drive, your CD-ROM drive is probably jumpered as the slave on the primary IDE interface (IDE-1). If your CD-ROM drive is connected to your other IDE cable (IDE-2), it is probably jumpered as the master on that interface.

Once you know how your current drives are connected, you can proceed to jumper your TiVo drive so that it does not conflict with existing drives in your PC. A guide to the jumpers on your hard drive that will cause the drive to be recognized as a master or slave drive is usually printed on the top of the hard drive.

 **WARNING**

Be careful when reading the jumper information; though they are usually written from left to right, just as the jumpers are physically located on the hard drive, some jumper settings are listed relative to a jumper key, which is a single pin on the left or right side of the hard drive jumpers.

TiVo drives should be jumpered as indicated in Table 4.4, depending on how your PC hard drive and CD-ROM drive are currently connected.

**Table 4.4   Jumper Settings for TiVo Hard Drives in a PC**

| Hard Drive | CD-ROM Drive | TiVo Drive Setting |
| --- | --- | --- |
| Master, IDE-1 | Slave, IDE-1 | Master, IDE-2 |
| Master, IDE-1 | Master, IDE-2 | Slave, IDE-1 |
| Master, IDE-1 | Slave, IDE-2 | Slave, IDE-1 |
| Single Drive, IDE-1 | Master, IDE-2 | Slave, IDE-1; Rejumper HD as Master, IDE-1 |
| Single Drive, IDE-1 | Slave, IDE-2 | Slave, IDE-1; Rejumper HD as Master, IDE-1 |
| Cable Select, IDE-1 | Master, IDE-2 | Slave, IDE-1; Rejumper HD as Master, IDE-1 |

After you jumper your TiVo drive and attach it to your PC, you can verify that it is jumpered and attached correctly by rebooting the PC, entering the BIOS, and examining the Primary and Secondary IDE interfaces as described earlier in this section.

 **WARNING**

If you are adding a TiVo drive to a Windows system, *do not* let the Windows system boot into Windows with the TiVo drive attached. Windows may decide to reformat or damage the TiVo drive, because it cannot identify the format of the TiVo drive. To ensure that this does not occur, put a bootable floppy in the PC's floppy drive or a bootable CD (such as one of the TiVo boot disks discussed in Chapter 5, "The Hacker's Toolchest of TiVo Tools") in the PC's CD-ROM drive before starting the PC.

After following the instructions in this section and verifying that your PC can correctly find all of its drives, follow the instructions in Chapter 6 to back up the drive. After you complete the backup, you can shut down the PC and return the drive to your TiVo—that is, if you are just doing a backup. If you want to restore the backup to a new, larger disk and make more space for storing recordings available to your TiVo, you can turn off the PC and insert the new, larger drive and follow the procedure described in Chapter 7, "Expanding Your TiVo Storage Capacity."

## 📺 Simplify Adding and Removing Drives with Mobile Racks

If you plan on doing much TiVo hacking, you'll be spending a fair amount of time inserting and removing TiVo drives from your PC. To simplify these procedures, I put drive racks in my PC. *Drive racks* are trays that enable you to insert and remove disk drives from the front of your machine, and they look like the hi-tech equivalent of desk drawers. Also known as *mobile racks,* they fit into the kinds of slots in which you insert CD drives in the front of your machine, and they are connected to your motherboard with a standard IDE cable. To add a drive, put it into a tray (provided with the rack) and connect it to the power and IDE cables inside the tray. Then slide the tray into the rack, push down on the handle to lock it in place, and use a circular key (much like an old-style PC key) to turn it on and make it available to your PC. Figure 4.5 shows a sample drive rack with the tray inserted.

**FIGURE 4.5**   *A removable hard drive rack with tray inserted*

Whenever I build a new PC, I attach a rack to each of the secondary IDE interfaces in the PC and configure the boot and CD-ROM drives as masters on each IDE interface. I then jumper whatever drive I want to use as a slave, put it in one of the racks, and access it as the slave on whichever IDE interface the rack is connected. No fuss, no muss.

Drive racks are available at most component-level computer stores, various online component dealers (check **http://www.pricewatch.com** and search for "Mobile Rack" to do comparison shopping), and online sites like eBay for between $10.00 and $20.00.

# Unlocking TiVo Hard Drives

The hard drives used in some TiVos go through a lock/unlock step as part of the TiVo firmware boot process. The unlock process makes all of the disk's capacity available to your TiVo. You can determine whether you have one of these drives by putting it in your PC and examining the size of the hard drive in the PC's BIOS. If your drive shows up as being 9 GB (9000 MB) or so in size, you have a locked TiVo drive.

The DOS directory on the BATBD CD that accompanies this book contains applications to unlock older TiVo disk drives. After booting from the BATBD CD, you must mount the CD in order to access this directory, as explained in the section of Chapter 11 entitled "Mounting the BATBD CD on Your System."

The classic utility for unlocking disks (specifically Quantum disks) is **QUNLOCK.EXE**, which is included on the CD. However, a more flexible program for unlocking multiple types of disk drives is **DISKUTIL.EXE**, which is also provided on the BATBD CD. For more information about using **DISKUTIL.EXE**, see the file diskutil.txt in the same directory on the BATBD CD or on the floppy disk as the file DISKUTIL.TXT.

Both of these are DOS utilities, which therefore require that you boot to DOS, run the utility, and then reboot from the BATBD CD in order to actually work with the unlocked hard drive. Since bootable DOS floppy disk images can be somewhat hard to come by nowadays (you can't even create them under Windows 2000 or XP), the DOS directory on the BATBD CD includes an image of a bootable FreeDOS floppy with these utilities already installed. FreeDOS is a complete, free, 100% MS-DOS compatible operating system. Thank God for the open source community!

To write the FreeDOS floppy image to a floppy disk from a Linux or other Unix-like system, mount the BATBD CD as explained in Chapter 11, change directory to its DOS directory, and use the following command:

```
dd if=FDODIN06.IMG of=/dev/fd0 obs=18k
```

You can then boot your PC from the floppy drive (make sure that your BIOS is set to try booting from the floppy drive—A:—first) and run the **DISKUTIL.EXE** program to unlock your drive. Then remove the floppy disk and reboot your system from the BATBD CD to proceed with the upgrade process.

 **NOTE**

More information about the FreeDOS project is available at **http://www.freedos.org**. Retro, but useful! The FreeDOS disk image provided on the BATBD CD is a slightly-enhanced version of Steve Nickolas's ODIN 0.6 one-disk FreeDOS distribution, which I obtained from **http://fd-odin.dosius.com/**. Thanks, Steve!

# Adding Disk Drives to Your TiVo

This section explains how to physically add a second disk to your TiVo. See Chapter 7 for information on preparing the disk so that the TiVo can use it to store recorded programs—simply adding a drive to your TiVo won't help unless it's prepared for use by the TiVo as described in that chapter. Before continuing, however, here is a list of what you may need to add a second drive:

- ◆ Number 10 Torx screwdriver
- ◆ Number 15 Torx screwdriver

◆ Phillips screwdriver (for Pioneer TiVos)

◆ Disk drive jumpers

◆ Drive mounting bracket and screws, depending on your TiVo model

◆ Screws for mounting new drives, depending on your TiVo model

◆ Plastic/rubber washers for suppressing drive noise (optional)

◆ Two-connector IDE cable

◆ Y-power cable

Physically adding a second drive to a TiVo is easy. As mentioned earlier, all Series 1 machines come with room for mounting two drives, but they use a special bracket to physically attach each drive to the frame of the TiVo. Series 2 models are somewhat more complex because different models have different requirements. The AT&T TiVos don't require a special bracket and come predrilled so that you can easily add a second drive without special hardware other than four screws. The Series 2 machines manufactured by TiVo are designed to hold only a single drive, but they can be expanded to hold two drives through the use of the special brackets shown in Figure 4.6. All special brackets that you need for the Series 1 and Series 2 machines are readily available from the sources mentioned in the section "TiVo Hardware Supplies on the Net" later in this chapter. The folks at Weaknees.com make the black plastic bracket shown in Figure 4.6, which is the best bracket for adding a second drive to the Series 2 machine from TiVo. The metal ones shown in Figure 4.6 will also do the job, but they're just too clunky for me.

**FIGURE 4.6** *Mounting brackets for Series 2 machines*

After you've prepared the second drive as described in Chapter 7, "Expanding Your TiVo's Storage Capacity," and attached it to the appropriate mounting bracket for your TiVo, make sure that you set the jumpers on the drive so that the new drive is identified as a slave drive. The jumper settings necessary to do so depend on the type of drive you are adding, and they are usually printed on the label at the top of the drive. If your drive didn't come with jumpers, you can purchase a pack of them at your local Radio Shack or other electronics store.

If you are adding a second drive to a Series 1 machine, you'll need to liberate the power cable from the TiVo frame. As shipped, the power connector for the second drive is tie-wrapped to the bottom of the TiVo case. Carefully clip the tie-wrap with a pair of diagonal cutters and free the power connector. You will need to remove the IDE cable from the plastic clip that holds it to the bottom of the TiVo case so that you can run it over the second drive in order to connect it. You will also need to flip the connector over so that you can attach it to the IDE connector on the new drive. Don't worry—you can easily connect it only one way: the plastic nub at the top of the connector fits into a similar notch on the IDE connector on the drive.

TiVo Series 2 models are somewhat more complex. The IDE cables shipped with any Series 2 machine have only a single connector and are capable of being connected only to a single drive. To attach a second drive, you must acquire a new IDE cable with two drive connectors. Luckily, suitable IDE cables are usually provided when you purchase a new disk drive and also with most of the Series 2 drive brackets. If necessary, you can also obtain a two-connector IDE cable at most electronics or computer stores. You can then disconnect the original IDE cable in your TiVo and insert the new one in your TiVo. (Be careful when seating the cable on the motherboard—pushing too hard might crack the motherboard and kill your TiVo.) You can then attach each of the IDE connectors on the new IDE cable to each of the drives. Again, don't worry; they are easily connected only one way because the plastic nub on the top of each connector fits into a similar notch on the IDE connector on each drive.

Similarly, most Series 2 machines don't have a spare power connector for the disk drive. You may need to buy a Y-power cable, often referred to as a *splitter*, in order to run DC power to your second disk drive. These are also readily available at most electronics or computer stores. In order to use a splitter, remove the power connector from your existing disk drive and plug it into the male end of the splitter. You can then run one of the ends of the Y to your original disk drive and the other end to the new drive.

Most Series 2 TiVos will require one of the special brackets shown in Figure 4.5 to mount the new drive and remount your existing one. I prefer the black bracket shown in Figure 4.6 (from Weaknees.com) for adding drives to Series 2 machines from TiVo. This bracket is superior to any other bracket for the Series 2, because it comes with new power and IDE cables and is (optionally) available with fans to increase the cooling inside your TiVo. It also comes with clear, detailed instructions for installing the bracket.

Series 2 60-MB AT&T TiVos don't require a special bracket because there is already room for a second drive on the existing bracket. If you have one of these TiVos, you will need to buy screws to attach the drive to the bracket. You may also want to purchase some plastic or rubber washers to use when attaching the drive, in order to reduce noise from the drive that might otherwise be transmitted through the mounting bracket.

# Power Considerations in TiVo Series 2 TiVos

The power supplies in stand-alone Series 2 machines are less powerful than those in Series 1 machines, which is understandable because all Series 1 models were designed with two drives in mind, whereas all Series 2 machines ship with only one drive, and (as explained in the previous section) some don't even provide space for a second drive without a special bracket. Some users who have put a second drive in stand-alone Series 2 machines have reported power supply failures. DirecTiVo Series 2 machines have more robust power supplies than the stand-alone Series 2 units and rarely need additional help after adding a second drive, but the techniques discussed in this chapter certainly can't hurt.

The point at which disk drives require the maximum amount of power is shortly after you turn them on. Much like starting a car requires an initial burst of power to get the engine started, disk drives require initial bursts of power to start the platters inside the drive rotating (known as *spinning up the drive*) and then launch the drive heads so that they can read and write data. If you are putting two disk drives in a Series 2 machine, you want to stagger the point at which the drives spin up so that they draw their initial bursts of power at slightly different times.

There are two easy ways to ensure that both your drives don't spin up and launch their heads at the same time. The first approach is to make sure you use two different disk drives, from different manufacturers, inside your TiVo. Because the drives are physically different, they will spin up and launch at slightly different times, so you shouldn't have a problem.

If you want to be almost totally safe, you can also buy (or make) a device that induces a delay between the times when the two drives spin up. Doing so will enable you to safely use two identical drives and will also protect you from the off chance that two drives from two different manufactures have exactly the same spin up and launch timing. The folks at Weaknees.com make such a device, which they call *PowerTrip*. The folks at PTVupgrade.com make a very similar device, known as a *SmartStart Power Supply Protector*. (They cost the same amount but differ in that the *PowerTrip* uses a mechanical relay while the *SmartStart* is a solid-state device.) Both of these devices are small units with power connectors at each end—one male and one female. To connect either of them, you simply insert it between the power connector and your primary disk drive by plugging the power connector into the appropriate connector from the *PowerTrip* or *SmartStart* and plugging the other connector into the disk drive. Doing so induces a slight initial delay between the time that the *PowerTrip* or *SmartStart* supplies power to the disk drive to which the device is connected. Voila! No worries.

 **NOTE**

I am not an employee of 9thTee.com, PTVupgrade.com, or Weaknees.com and am not being paid to promote their products. However, I do know a good thing when I see one (or two, in this case).

# Heat Considerations in TiVo Series 2 TiVos

Adding a second drive to any TiVo increases the amount of heat generated by the TiVo. This is an especially important issue if you are adding a second drive to one of the Series 2 TiVos distributed by TiVo, since many of these provide a minimal amount of cooling in the first place. Some of the AT&T Series 2 TiVos, shown in Figure 4.2, mount the drives on a separate bracket that includes an auxiliary fan and also provides space for air circulation under the drive(s). Series 2 systems from TiVo, shown in Figure 4.3, mount the drive without much space for air circulation, and don't provide much of a fan in the first place.

If you are adding a second drive to a Series 2 system from TiVo, you'll need a special bracket for mounting two drives in the system. Some of these are shown in Figure 4.6. I strongly suggest that you get one of the black plastic brackets from Weakness.com as shown in this figure. This bracket is easy to install and comes with an auxiliary cooling fan that will help keep your TiVo cool, calm, and operational for years to come.

# Dealing with Modems

When you initially install a TiVo, you walk through a series of steps known as *Guided Setup*. The TiVo walks you through this process if it notices that it has no guide or connectivity information. TiVo's Guided Setup helps you configure your remote control and television to work together, collects information about your cable or satellite service, and lets you specify your zip code so that the TiVo can locate local numbers that you can use to obtain regular programming guide information and updates. During Guided Setup, any TiVo with the full TiVo service connects to TiVo HQ using an 800 number (in the United States) and uses the zip code information that you provided to download a list of local numbers that the TiVo can call for these updates.

## TIVO Updating TiVo Configuration Information

If you buy a used TiVo, change cable or satellite providers, or move to a different area, you will need to reconfigure your TiVo. This enables you to identify your new location to TiVo HQ so that the TiVo knows your cable provider and can download guide information that reflects your cable or satellite provide. Doing so also causes the TiVo to attempt to find new (local) phone numbers to call for programming and guide updates. Getting weekly programming updates via a toll call can be quite expensive. You can redo the TiVo's Guided Setup process at any time by selecting this command from the TiVo's Restart or Reset System menu (select TiVo Central, Messages & Setup, Restart or Reset System, Guided Setup).

TiVos with the full TiVo service always require a phone line in order to run through the initial Guided Setup process. Newer TiVos with the TiVoBasic service level (discussed in the section of Chapter 1 entitled "TiVo Service Levels") do not require access to a phone line at all, receiving their programming information from your cable service over the same stream as the VCRPlus+ data. DirecTiVos only require access to a phone line when you first configure them using Guided Setup, and only subsequently in order to pay for Pay-Per-View (PPV) movies. In theory, they also require phone line access with programming packages like NFL Sunday Ticket, but that doesn't seem to be enforced.

By default, stand-alone TiVos with the full TiVo service require continuous access to a phone line in order to make daily and occasional weekly calls for programming and guide updates. If you put your TiVo on a home network with access to the Internet, you can eliminate the need for a phone line by following the instructions later in this chapter in the section entitled "Using the Network to Make Daily Calls."

### TIP

If you have a DirecTiVo and disconnect the phone line after going through Guided Setup, after 30 days you will begin to receive once-daily reminders that you really should connect the phone line to the DirecTiVo. You can eliminate this warning by installing and running a script that convinces the DirecTiVo that the call has succeeded. Sample scripts that do this, `fakecall31.tcl` and `fakecall40.tcl`, are provided in the TPM/`tpm_packages` directory on the BATBD CD that accompanies this book, in the TPM packages `fakecall31-1.0-5.tivo.tpm` and `fakecall40-1.0-5.tivo.tpm`. For more information about TPM and installing software packaged using TPM, see the section of Chapter 11 entitled "Installing Software Packaged with TPM."

Unless your house is more modern than mine, you have a limited number of telephone jacks available. If you're reasonably handy, you can easily run a new phone line from one of your existing phone jacks to somewhere near your TiVo. This may not always be feasible for aesthetic reasons and may not be physically possible if you're renting or own a condo that you don't feel like drilling holes through.

A great solution in these cases is a wireless phone jack. These jacks consist of two parts: a base unit that you plug into an electric outlet anywhere in your house and attach to an existing phone jack, and an extension unit that you plug into an electric outlet near your TiVo and connect to the TiVo using the extension unit's phone jack. Hooray! Instant phone connection at your TiVo without running any additional wires, tearing up or stapling phone cords to your baseboards, and drilling holes in your floor. Wireless phone jacks work by using your home's electric wiring to transmit and receive specially encoded phone signals, which they encrypt and decrypt between base and extension units.

Wireless phone jacks are available from many different manufacturers, including the General Electric Company, Phonex, and RCA. My favorites are the 920 and 930 units made by RCA, which offer built-in surge suppression. These and similar wireless phone jacks are available from your local electronics store or on eBay, where they typically go for about $25 to $30.

## Networking Your TiVo

You may want to put your TiVo on your home network for a variety of reasons, including the following:

◆ Because it's there.

◆ To more easily transfer files of one sort or another to and from your TiVo.

◆ To more easily connect to the TiVo from any system in your house (not just one with a serial connection to the TiVo).

◆ To use TiVoWeb or TiVoWebPlus to control your TiVo from a browser on any other machine on your home network.

◆ To use the network for obtaining programming and guide data instead of a much slower modem that requires a phone line.

Any and all of these reasons are great for connecting your TiVo to your home network, but the last one is probably the most pragmatic. Modems are reliable but slow and obviously require access to a phone line. If you have your TiVo on your home network and your home network has a constant connection to the Internet (as with cable or DSL broadband connections), you can bypass using the modem altogether by configuring your TiVo to make your daily and weekly calls over the network. See the section "Using the Network to Make Daily Calls" later in this chapter for specific information on the settings necessary to use a network rather than a modem for these calls.

As you might expect, because of fundamental hardware differences, different models of TiVos are networked in different ways. Series 1 TiVos are networked through a diagnostic port located on the Series 1 TiVo motherboard. Series 2 machines are networked by using wired or wireless USB adapters.

# Networking 101

Like most modern computer systems, TiVos can communicate with other systems and devices over a type of network called *Ethernet*, using the TCP/IP (Transmission Control Protocol/Internet Protocol) and UDP (Universal Data Packet) protocols. Ethernet was invented by Xerox Corporation at Xerox PARC (Palo Alto Research Center) in the early 1970s. Like most things they've invented—except for the photocopier—Xerox failed to make money from Ethernet, which was actually commercialized by many companies (like 3COM, which was founded by the inventor of Ethernet networking, Bob Metcalf, who knew a good thing when he invented it).

Until a few decades ago, the Internet was a fairly techie term, used only by people whose employers or academic experience offered connectivity to the Internet or its predecessor, the Arpanet. The creation and popular explosion of the World Wide Web and the advent of e-mail as a replacement for phone calls changed all that; suddenly, there was a reason for people to want (or perhaps even need) access to the Internet.

Early home Internet connectivity was primarily done through dial-up connections that emulated TCP/IP connections over dial-up lines using protocols such as SLIP (Serial Line Internet Protocol), CLSIP (Compressed SLIP), or PPP (Point-To-Point Protocol). Unless you were a serious computer geek, developer, or researcher, a home network was somewhat rare, but the advent of broadband access to the Internet through cable and telephone providers changed all that. A few years ago, my home network was connected to the Internet through a Linux system that I'd set up as an on-demand SLIP gateway that also regularly dialed out to my ISP, connected using command scripts, and retrieved my mail to a local mail server. Hardly nerdy at all. Today, like many people, I have always-on connectivity to the Internet through a $100 Linksys gateway that connects all the machines on my home network to the Internet via my cable modem.

The point of this trip down memory lane is that home networks are becoming more common, but most people have never needed to set one up before now. If you use a single PC, Mac, or workstation as your sole home machine, a straight connection to a cable or DSL modem works just fine. However, the instant you want to enable multiple machines to communicate over a home network, you may encounter unfamiliar terms like hubs, switches, 10-BaseT, RJ45, cross-over-cables, uplink ports, packets, gateways, routers, Cat5, and a variety of others that pass for popular nouns among nerdier users. This section provides a quick overview of these terms. It tells you how to set up a trivial home network and makes you comfortable with the network-related terms that are used throughout this book. For more detailed information, consult any of the hundreds of books available on home networking.

The basic element of a modern network connection is a standard Ethernet cable, which is just a length of multistrand cable with connectors on either end that enable you to connect a network card in your personal computer (or whatever type) to another network device. The most common connectors used today are plastic connectors known as RJ-45 connectors, which are transparent plastic jacks that look like a fatter version of a standard telephone cable connector. Ethernet cables that use these connectors are often known as 10-BaseT, 100-BaseT, or even 1000-BaseT, where the numeric portion of the name indicates the speed of your network—the cables are the same. 1000-BaseT is more commonly known as gigabit Ethernet, and if you actually use gigabit Ethernet in your house, I'm proud to know you. 10/100 (that is, 10 megabit or 100 megabit) Ethernet is the standard nowadays. If you run across the term Cat5 when buying or researching Ethernet cables, that term stands for Category 5 cabling, which has to do with shielding that insulates the cable from outside electromagnetic influence—and also with not giving off poisonous smoke if the plastic exterior of the cable burns off, which isn't a big concern for most home networks; if your house is on fire, you probably have bigger worries than inhaling the smoke from your smoldering Ethernet cables.

 **NOTE**

As another historical note, you may also encounter the term 10-Base2 when researching network cards. This is an older type of 10-megabit Ethernet cabling that uses shielded BNC (Bayonet Neill-Concelman, or Baby N Connector) cables. Unless you are using some really old Ethernet cards or need to connect older workstations to your home network, you should stay away from these cards unless they also have 10/100 BaseT connectors and, in most cases, even then since these cards typically offer only 10-megabit network communication speeds.

The best way to visualize the Internet or any Ethernet network is as an extremely long piece of cable to which some huge number of computers and network devices are attached. In the simplest case, you must use a device called a *hub*, *switch*, or *router* to attach multiple machines to an Ethernet. A *hub* is a device with multiple incoming connectors for attaching the Ethernet cables from different machines, with a single output connector that attaches it to another Ethernet device such as a cable modem, another hub, or a switch, router, or gateway. Network communications on any incoming port of the hub are broadcast to all other devices on the hub and are also forwarded through the outgoing connection. *Switches* are much like hubs on steroids because they keep track of how network connections between different machines are made and reserve dedicated internal circuitry for established connections. Switches are, therefore, both typically faster and more expensive than hubs because they do more.

*Gateways* and *routers* are similar to hubs and switches, but are designed to provide connectivity between different networks. If a machine that you are trying to connect to isn't immediately found on your local network, the request is forwarded through your gateway, which then sends it on. Network communication is done using discrete units of information that are known as *packets*. Packets contain the IP (Internet Protocol) address of the host that they are trying to contact. IP addresses are in the form of NNN.NNN.NNN.NNN, and are the network equivalent of a post office box, uniquely identifying a specific machine. Packets for an unknown local host are sent through your gateway. Routers are expensive, sophisticated pieces of hardware that direct network communication between multiple networks, translate packets between different network communication protocols, and limit network traffic to relevant networks so that your request to retrieve a file from a machine in your son's bedroom isn't broadcast to every machine on the Internet.

The most common way to connect machines on a home network is to use a hub or a home gateway that is connected to your cable or DSL modem. The difference between these is that a hub simply forwards packets through its outgoing connector (known as an *uplink port* because it links the network connections on that device with those on another and is, therefore, wired differently). A home gateway may convert internal network addresses to addresses that are compatible with the outside world before sending the information on through its outgoing or uplink connector. If you're using a hub to connect your home network to your cable or DSL modem, each machine on your home network would require an IP address that is unique on the Internet. This can be expensive, since most ISPs charge money for each unique host that can be connected to the Internet from your home at any given time. Home gateways provide a way around this because they enable your home network to use a special type of IP addresses known as nonroutable IP addresses to assign unique internal network addresses. The gateway then internally translates these to appropriate external addresses if you're trying to connect to a machine on the Internet. The most common nonroutable IP addresses are in the form of 192.168.*X*.*Y*, where *X* and *Y* are specific to how you've set up your network.

 **TIP**

If you're really interested, you can get more information about nonroutable IP addresses and address translation in the Internet RFCs (Request for Comment) that defined them, 1597 and 1918. Use your favorite Internet search engine to find relevant information, or check out links such as **http://www.safety.net/ sum1597.html** and **http://www.howstuffworks.com/nat2.htm**.

IP addresses are assigned to computer systems in two basic ways, either statically or dynamically. *Static addresses* are addresses unique to your home network that are always assigned to a particular machine. *Dynamic addresses* are addresses that are automatically assigned to a computer system or network device when you turn it on. Most ISPs use dynamic addresses because only a limited number of IP addresses are available on the Internet. Using dynamic IP addresses enables your ISP to recycle and reassign IP addresses as people turn their machines off and on. Most dynamic IP addresses nowadays are assigned using a protocol called *DHCP* (Dynamic Host Control Protocol), which fills out the network information for your system when it activates its network interface, including things like the IP address of a gateway system and the IP addresses of DNS (Distributed Name Service) servers that translate between hostnames and the IP addresses that they correspond to.

In order to use static addresses on your home network, you simply assign each machine a unique, nonroutable IP address from a given family of nonroutable IP addresses. For example, most of my home machines have static addresses in the form of 192.168.6.Y. Since I use a home gateway, I've configured it to do address translation (more specifically known as *NAT*, or Native Address Translation) to correctly translate between these addresses and the external IP address of my home gateway box.

If you want to use Dynamic IP addresses on a home network, one of the machines on your home network must be running a DHCP server. Most home gateways, such as those from DLink or Linksys, have built-in DHCP servers that you simply configure to hand out IP addresses from a specific range of addresses (192.168.6.240 through 192.168.6.250, in my case). Once you activate address translation on your home gateway, your gateway will route packets appropriately. Remember that your home gateway is probably getting its IP address by contacting your ISP's DHCP server, whereas hosts on your internal network will get their IP addresses from your DHCP server. Don't set up hosts on an internal network to contact your ISP's DHCP server unless you have only a single machine on your home network or want every one of your machines to be visible on the Internet. (An obvious security problem because anyone who knows the address can get to your machine. I'm totally ignoring network security here; that topic deserves its own book or three, which you can get from your local bookstore.)

To return to the subject of this particular book (TiVos, remember?), TiVos are usually configured to obtain IP addresses via DHCP. If you're using a Series 1 machine, you can assign it a static address when you install the network-related software(see next section). A bit more work is involved in convincing Series 2 models to use a static IP address, since Series 2 TiVos running Versions 3.X and later of the TiVo software provide USB network support out of the box. I tend to use DHCP for systems such as the TiVos because it's simply easier, although figuring out the IP address assigned to your TiVo can be tricky if you haven't hacked it to provide a command prompt. Figuring out your TiVo's dynamic IP address is discussed later in this chapter in the debugging portion of the section "Using the Network to Make Daily and Weekly Calls."

The overview information in this section should have familiarized you with basic home networking terms and concepts. If you have a Series 2 machine and have purchased TiVo's Home Media Option (discussed later in this book), TiVo provides a good overview of setting up a small home network on the TiVo HQ Web site at **http://www.tivo.com/4.9.8.asp**. As you might expect, the Internet is knee-deep in Web sites that provide more general information about home networking. For truly detailed information about setting up and configuring a home network on a specific type of machine and operating system, see any of the hundreds of books on those topics at your local bookstore.

# Networking Series 1 TiVos

If you've hacked into a TiVo and examined the `/etc/rc.d/rc.sysinit` startup script, you know that TiVos have been networked at TiVo headquarters from day one. No big surprise—they are Linux boxes, after all. However, this capability was denied the rest of us until a pioneering effort by Andrew Tridgell (Tridge) developed the original network adapter for the TiVos that enabled people to use certain types of older PC-style ISA networking cards to put their TiVos on the network. This effort was especially groundbreaking because TiVos don't have an ISA bus, so the device worked by adding a single ISA bus slot to the TiVo motherboard through the clever use of a diagnostic edge connector that the board provided. You could then put a standard NE2000 or compatible ISA network card in this slot, load a few drivers that Tridge provided, execute standard Linux IP configuration commands, and suddenly your TiVo was wired.

Today, all of the commonly-encountered Ethernet solutions for Series 1 models are from 9thTee.com, which has partnered with Tridge and a company called *SiliconDust.com* to bring you easy-to-install, easy-to-use cards that help you get your Series 1 machines up on your home network. Beyond just the hardware, all of these cards share a common install program called *nic_install*, which is available from the 9thTee.com site in ISO format and is also provided on the TiVo Series 1 sections of the TiVo boot disk that accompanies this book. More about that later. First, let's discuss the hardware.

 **NOTE**

Just to be perfectly clear, the networking cards discussed in this section can be used only with Series 1 stand-alone and DirecTiVos. They cannot be used with Series 2 machines, which I'll discuss in the next section.

Tridge's original adapter design was cleaned up and commercialized thanks to the TiVo fanatics at 9thTee.com, who named their version the TiVoNet board. TiVoNet boards are no longer being manufactured, though they still work fine—if you find one on eBay and also buy a compatible ISA network card. Since the original TiVoNet cards, two other network adapters have been developed and released (developed by the folks at SiliconDust.com and available from 9thTee) that are far easier to configure, install, and use. These are the TurboNet and AirNet cards.

Figure 4.7 shows a TurboNet network card for the Series 1. Like all Series 1 network adapters, this one also fits onto the diagnostic port of the Series 1 motherboard. TurboNet cards have a built-in RJ-45 Ethernet connector and don't require that you purchase a separate network adapter. TurboNet cards are easy to install and similarly easy to configure and use, but still require that you run a 10-BaseT Ethernet cable to your TiVo from a hub or switch on your home network.

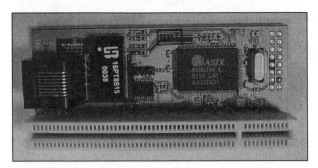

**FIGURE 4.7**   *A TurboNet network adapter for Series 1 TiVos*

As shown in Figure 4.8, an even more sophisticated RJ-45 Ethernet adapter is available in SiliconDust's CacheCard. The CacheCard is a wired Ethernet adapter that also includes a DIMM (Dual Inline Memory Module) slot in which you can insert up to 512 MB of high-performance SDRAM to expand your Series 1 TiVo's cache, which is used during operations such as displaying menus, sorting programs and Season Passes, and so on. If you are willing to use a wired connection to your home Ethernet (which is much faster than a wireless connection but obviously limits the mobility of your TiVo), the CacheCard is the ultimate wired Ethernet adaptor for Series 1 TiVos

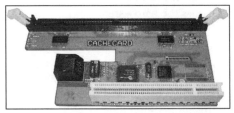

**FIGURE 4.8**   *A CacheCard network adapter for Series 1 TiVos*

 **NOTE**

When buying a CacheCard, make sure that it is at least revision 2.2. Earlier revisions of the CacheCard had some firmware and hardware growing pangs, are much more sensitive to the types of SDRAM that you can use with them, and are generally not as reliable as revision 2.2 and later of the card. Be especially careful if you are buying a used CacheCard from an auction site such as eBay—the revision level is printed on the circuit board, in the upper right-hand corner of the CacheCard.

Shown in Figure 4.9, AirNet cards are the height of TiVo Series 1 network evolution as far as I'm concerned. AirNet cards provide a PCMCIA adapter that enables you to use a standard laptop wireless Ethernet card to put your Series 1 machine on your home network as long as the wireless PCMCIA card uses the Intercil Prism2 or Prism2.5 chipset, which includes most of the 802.11b cards on the market. AirNet cards will not work with Cisco 802.11b cards because Cisco cards use their own MAC chipset. It will also not work with 802.11b cards from Dell, because these are actually made by Cisco.

 **NOTE**

AirNet cards for DirecTiVos are slightly different than AirNet cards for stand-alone Series 1 TiVos. Make sure that you buy the right one. Although Figure 4.9 shows a wireless PCMCIA Ethernet card in the AirNet card, you can also buy them without the PCMCIA card and add your own from the list in Table 4.7.

**FIGURE 4.9**   *An AirNet network adapter for Series 1 machines*

Table 4.7 shows some inexpensive and common PCMCIA 802.11b cards that use the Prism2 chipset, and should therefore work fine with an AirNet card.

Whenever possible, consider buying a PCMCIA card with an antenna, or at least with the capability of attaching one. Though an antenna costs extra, it can enable you to maximize the distance between your TiVo and your wireless access point.

Regardless of which Series 1 network card you buy, installing it in your TiVo is simple. Once you've installed it, you can install the necessary software on your TiVo drive by removing it from your TiVo and putting it in your PC, as described in the section "Working with TiVo Disk Drives" earlier in this chapter.

If you've decided to use the installer to simplify things, after you've burned a CD of the installation software and installed the TiVo drive in your PC, use the following procedure to install the software for your TiVoNet, TurboNet, CacheCard, or AirNet card:

1.  Run the network interface card (NIC) installation command by executing the **/nic_install/nic_install** command, followed by the name of the network card that you want to install, which is either TiVoNet, TurboNet, or AirNet. For example, to install the drivers and support software for an AirNet card, execute the following command:

    ```
    /nic_install/nic_install
    ```

**Table 4.7   Common Prism2 PCMCIA Cards Compatible with AirNet**

| Manufacturer | Model | Antenna |
| --- | --- | --- |
| Addtron | AWP-100 | No |
| Addtron | AWP-101 | No |
| Asanté | AL1011 | No |
| Belkin | F5D6020 | No |
| Compaq | WL100 | No |
| CellVision | WLC-100 | No |
| Demarc | Relia-Wave | No |
| D-Link | DW-655H | No |
| D-Link | DWL-650 | No |
| LinkSys | WPC11 | No |
| Proxim | RangeLAN-DS 8434-05 | Yes |
| Proxim | RangeLAN-DS 8433-05 | No |
| SMC | SMC2532W-B | No |
| SMC | SMC2632W | No |
| Teletronics | WL-11000 | Yes |
| Zcomax | XI-300 | Yes |
| Zcomax | XI-300B | No |
| Zcomax | ZFE-300 | No |
| Zcomax | XI-325 | Yes |
| Zcomax | XI-325H | Yes |
| Zcomax | XI-325H1 | Yes |
| ZoomAir | 4105 | Yes |

**TIP**

An easy-to-use installer for the software required for using a TurboNet Card or AirNet card in your TiVo can be downloaded as an ISO image from 9thTee.com or SiliconDust.com. URLs for this software are **http://www.silicondust.com/terms_of_use.html** and **http://www.9thtee.com/nic_cd_20030223.iso**. If you are installing a CacheCard using this procedure, you will also want to download the incremental CacheCard installer from the URL **http://www.silicondust.com/nic_install_pc_20040331.zip**. If you are installing a CacheCard, you will want to download and install the contents of this file, as it contains the driver used to enable caching on the CacheCard.

IMPORTANT NOTE: Series 1 TiVos running v3.+ of the TiVo software already contain the modules for using networking, so you do not need to use the installer—however, the installer discussed in this section also installs software such as telnet and FTP for you, automatically updates your rc.sysinit file, and so on. I'd suggest using it, since it's easy to use and doesn't hurt anything. If you are using the installer, you must burn a CD of it in order to boot your PC from it. Burning CDs from ISO images on different types of home computer systems is explained elsewhere in this book. If you are installing a CacheCard, you will also need to format a DOS floppy and extract the contents of the incremental CacheCard installer to the floppy disk using the **unzip** program.

2. The installation program then probes your system, locates your TiVo drive, and analyzes its structure, as shown in the following output:

```
TiVo TurboNet/AirNet Installation - 20020907
Copyright 2002 Silicondust Engineering Ltd. All rights reserved.
Detecting TiVo hard drive...
     Trying /dev/hdb...
             Not a tivo drive.
     Trying /dev/hdc...
             Unable to open.
     Trying /dev/hdd...
             kernel=/dev/hdaFigure 3.
             root=/dev/hda4 .
     Found TiVo hard drive - /dev/hdd (Secondary Slave).
Detecting TiVo partitions...
     Active kernel partition = /dev/hddFigure 3.
     Inactive kernel partition = /dev/hdd6.
     Active root partition = /dev/hdd4.
```

```
        Inactive root partition = /dev/hdd7.
        Var partition = /dev/hdd9.
Determining software version...
Partition table:
     0: /dev/hdd start=   933952 length=  1048576
     1: /dev/hdd start=  1982528 length= 56650752
     2: /dev/hdd start= 58895488 length=     8192
     3: /dev/hdd start= 58903680 length= 97397760
Zone table:
     0: inode    size=1
     1: stream   size=18
     2: file     size=66
     3: stream   size=34
          Philips SA running .0-01-1-000
```

3. After the script completes its probe of the system, it checks to see whether the system boots with an initial RAM disk and prompts you to disable it, which must be done in order to correctly install the drivers for your network card. (For more information about initial RAM disks [aka *initrds*], see Chapter 10, "The TiVo Startup Process.") The output of this section looks like the following:

```
Scanning for initrd...
     Initrd found to be active
Initrd must be disabled to install the airnet drivers
Ok to disable [y/n]?
```

4. Enter **y** and press Enter (Return) to continue the installation process. At this point, the installation script mounts the partitions that it needs to modify on your TiVo disk, installs the drivers, and prompts you to supply any customizations that you want to make to the card's network configuration. (This example is from an AirNet card installation; your options will differ if you are installing a TurboNet, CacheCard, or TiVoNet card.) Output from this section looks like the following:

```
Disabling initrd...
     Complete.
Mounting partitions...
     Root successfully mounted.
     Var successfully mounted.
Checking network script...
     Complete.
Current/New Configuration:
     timing setting = normal
```

```
    SSID            = wlan
    encryption      = none
    key             =
    ip address      = dhcp
    ip subnet mask  = dhcp
    ip gateway      = dhcp
    debug level     = off
    daily call      = network
Options
    1: Change timing setting
    2: Change SSID
    3: Change encryption
    4: Change IP address/gateway
    5: Change debug logging option
    6: Change daily call option
    7: Dump log file
    0: Apply and exit
[0..7]?
```

 **NOTE**

The options displayed in this list are dependent on the type of network card that you are installing. The examples in this section are taken from an AirNet installation. TiVoNet, TurboNet, and CacheCard installations are very similar—the only difference is the list of options available and the numbers that you have to type to select them.

5. To change the options from this list, enter the number of the option and press Enter (Return). The current setting for the specified variable is displayed, followed by a prompt that enables you to specify a new value, as in the following example:

```
[0..7]? 2
SSID is currently set to "wlan".
New SSID? wvh
```

 **NOTE**

The SSID value is specific to the AirNet card and identifies the name of the wireless network you want to join. This option applies only when you're using a wireless network and will not be listed if you are installing a TiVoNet or TurboNet card.

### TIP

The most common values that you may want to consider changing from this list are the card's IP address and associate gateway information. As shown in the following example, all TiVoNet, TurboNet, and AirNet cards are initially configured to obtain dynamic IP address information from a Dynamic Host Control Protocol (DHCP) server. Installing the TiVoNet/TurboNet/CacheCard/AirNet software to use DHCP will automatically start a DHCP client on your TiVo. You will want to change these options if you are not running a DHCP server on your home network or if you simply want to assign a single, well-known address to your TiVo.

6. If you want to manually assign an IP address to your network card, enter **4** and specify an IP address that is compatible with your network, a subnet mask used to mask bits in that address, and the address of your network's gateway to external IP addresses (required for calling out over the network), as in the following example:

```
[0..7]? 4
IP address is currently set to "dhcp".
Subnet mask is currently set to "dhcp".
Gateway address is currently set to "dhcp".
New IP address [x.x.x.x dhcp]? 192.168.1.30
New Subnet mask [x.x.x.x dhcp]? 255.255.255.0
New Gateway address [x.x.x.x dhcp]? 192.168.1.1
Current/New Configuration:
     timing setting = normal
     SSID           = wvh
     encryption     = none
     key            =
     ip address     = 192.168.1.30
     ip subnet mask = 255.255.255.0
     ip gateway     = 192.168.1.1
     debug level    = off
     daily call     = network
Options
     1: Change timing setting
     2: Change SSID
     3: Change encryption
     4: Change IP address/gateway
     5: Change debug logging option
     6: Change daily call option
```

```
    7: Dump log file
    0: Apply and exit
```

7. Consider changing the Daily call option. In most cases, you will want the TiVo's daily call to be made over the network unless you do not have an always-on connection to the Internet. This is the default value when installing a TiVoNet, TurboNet, CacheCard, or AirNet card. If you have a broadband connection to the Internet through a system that is not always on, change the Daily call option to dial-up, which will cause your TiVo to continue to use the modem for its daily calls.

8. When you finish changing all the options you want to change, enter **0** and press Return to cause the nic_install program to actually write its changes to your TiVo configuration and startup file, as in the following example:

```
[0..7]? 0
Copying files...
    Complete.
Verifying route executable...
      Complete.
Writing network script...
    Complete.
Updating startup script...
    Complete.
Clear the log file on the tivo [y/n]? n
Unmounting partitions...
    Root successfully unmounted.
    Var successfully unmounted.
Installation Complete.
```

 **TIP**

If you see a message similar to `"Error — Unable to find complete string"` after the `"Updating startup scripts"` entry, this means that your `/etc/rc.d/rc.sysinit` script probably doesn't contain the following string:

echo **"rc.sysinit is complete"**

The **nic_install** program looks for this line in order to determine where to insert the network startup commands. If this line is not present, usually you have already modified your `/etc/rc.d/rc.sysinit` script. To enable the **nic_install** program to complete successfully, you must reinsert this command as the last line of your `/etc/rc.d/rc.sysinit` file.

If you are installing a CacheCard, you still have a few steps left to go. As mentioned earlier, you must download the latest drivers from the SiliconDust forums, which you can find at **http://www.silicondust.com/forum**. Download the zip file containing the latest CacheCard drivers, format a floppy disk in DOS format, and do the following:

1. Insert the floppy disk and mount... type:

```
mkdir /mnt/fd0
mount -t vfat /dev/fd0 /mnt/fd0
cd /mnt/fd0
```

2. Run the version of the nic_install script on the floppy disk:

```
chmod +x nic_install
./nic_install cachecard
```

3. Follow the instructions in the previous section to answer the various questions you are prompted for. At the end of the script, press "0" to save your changes and exit.

Congratulations! You're a few seconds from having your TiVo on the network! If you have a DirecTiVo, you must run the **tivoflash** utility after running the nic_install script, as in the following example. (Do *not* run this utility on any stand-alone, non-DirecTiVo system.)

```
/tivoflash/install
```

Almost there—just a few minutes more! Shut down your PC, remove your TiVo hard drive, reset the jumpers (if necessary), and put the drive back in your TiVo. The next time you turn it on, your TiVo should be available on your network. The nic_install program installs both the TiVo FTP daemon and a lite version of the Telnet daemon so that you can, respectively, transfer files to and from the remote machine and log in on the remote machine over the network. Neither the TiVo FTP daemon nor Telnet require authentication, so be careful about who has access to your network and thus your TiVo. A malicious and knowledgeable person on your network could easily delete all or some of the TiVo filesystem, which would probably force you to reinstall the TiVo from backups.

# Networking Series 2 and DVD TiVos

Thanks to TiVo, its desire to modernize its products, and the march of time in general, Series 2 TiVos are much easier to network than Series 1 machines. Series 2 models provide USB ports that enable you to quickly and easily attach a variety of USB adapters to your TiVo system. Figure 4.10 shows a sample wired USB adapter (left) and wireless USB adapter (right).

Table 4.8 shows a list of USB Ethernet adapters that are compatible with the Series 2 machines. (A big thanks to the folks on the AVS Forum for compiling the genesis of this list.)

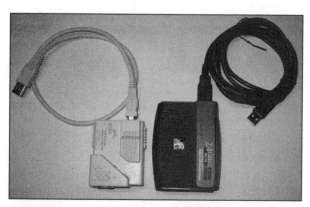

**FIGURE 4.10**   *Wired and wireless USB network adapters for Series 2 machines*

**Table 4.8   Wired USB Ethernet Adapters Compatible with Series 2 Machines**

| Manufacturer | Model |
|---|---|
| 3Com | 3C460B |
| ABOCOM | USB 10/100 Fast Ethernet |
| ABOCOM | USB HPNA/Ethernet |
| Accton | USB 10/100 Ethernet Adapter |
| Accton | SpeedStream USB 10/100 Ethernet |
| ADMtek | ADM8511 Pegasus II USB Ethernet |
| ADMtek | AN986 Pegasus USB Ethernet (eval. board) |
| Allied Telesyn | AT-USB100 |
| Belkin | F5D5050 |
| Billionton | USB-100 |
| Billionton | USBE-100 |
| Billionton | USBEL-100 |
| Billionton | USBLP-100 |
| Compaq | iPAQ Networking 10/100 USB |
| Corega | FEter USB-TX |
| D-Link | DSB-650 |
| D-Link | DSB-650TX |
| D-Link | DUB-E100 |

**Table 4.8    Wired USB Ethernet Adapters Compatible with Series 2 Machines (*continued*)**

| Manufacturer | Model |
| --- | --- |
| Elsa | Micolink USB2Ethernet |
| Hawking | UF100 10/100 Ethernet |
| Hawking | UF200 10/100 Ethernet |
| IO DATA | USB ET/TX |
| IO DATA | USB ET/TX-S |
| Kingston | KNU101TX Ethernet |
| LANEED | USB Ethernet LD-USB/T |
| LANEED | USB Ethernet LD-USB/TX |
| Linksys | USB100M |
| Linksys | USB200M |
| Linksys | USB100TX |
| Linksys | USB10TX |
| MELCO | BUFFALO LUA2-TX |
| MELCO | BUFFALO LUA-TX |
| Microsoft | MN-110 |
| NetGear | FA101 |
| NetGear | FA120 |
| Siemens | SS1001 |
| SmartBridges | SmartNIC 2 PnP Adapter |
| SMC | 202 USB Ethernet |
| SMC | SMC2208 |
| SOHOware | NUB100 Ethernet |

Of course, wireless USB adapters are also available, as shown at the right of Figure 4.9. Table 4.9 shows a list of wireless USB Ethernet adapters that are compatible with Series 2 TiVos. This table also lists the Series 2 TiVos on which each adapter is known to work. Wireless USB adapters are slightly more sensitive to differences in the USB hardware provided on various types of TiVos. If you want to put your TiVo on your network and are buying a wireless USB adapter explicitly for that purpose, I'd strongly suggest that you use a wireless USB adapter that is known to work. If you already have other wireless USB adapters available and want to try them out, do so by all means, and let me know if you discover others that work. I have been able to identify quite a few that do not work, largely the cheap, brand-X wireless adapters that I can't seem to resist trying.

**Table 4.9   Wireless USB Ethernet Adapters Compatible with the Series 2**

| Manufacturer | Model | Known to Work On |
| --- | --- | --- |
| Belkin | F5D6050 | All Series 2 models |
| D-Link | DWL-120 V.A | SVR-3000, TCD130040, TCD140060 |
| D-Link | DWL-120 V.D | TCD230040, TCD240040 |
| D-Link | DWL-120 V.E | All Series 2 models |
| Hawking | WU250 | TCD230040, TCD240040 |
| Linksys | WUSB11 V2.6 | All Series 2 models |
| Linksys | WUSB12 | TCD230040, TCD240040 |
| Microsoft | MN-510 | TCD230040, TCD240040 |
| NetGear | MA101 V.A | SVR-3000, TCD130040, TCD140060 |
| NetGear | MA101 V.B | All Series 2 models |
| SMC | 2662W V.2 | All Series 2 models |

The version of the TiVo software that your Series 2 is running is critical to whether your TiVo will automatically recognize and configure the network adapter.

Drivers for the USB network adapters listed in the previous two tables are included with TiVo software Versions 3.0 and greater for Series 2 models. If you are only interested in getting programming and guide updates over your home network, putting Series 2 machines running these software versions on your network is trivial. To do so, simply turn off the TiVo and attach your wired or wireless USB Ethernet adapter. If you're using a wired USB Ethernet adapter, make sure that it's correctly connected to your home network and that you're running a DHCP server, as explained earlier in this chapter in the section "Networking 101."

 **TIP**

Wireless USB adapters are officially supported only under TiVo software Version 4+, though I have not had problems using them with Series 2 TiVos running Version 3.x of the TiVo software. If you encounter problems using a wireless USB adapter under earlier versions of the TiVo OS, try using a wired USB adapter or upgrade the version of the TiVo OS that you are running.

Next, power up the TiVo again. The Series 2 should recognize your USB adapter, though it won't say anything about it unless you're running TiVo software Version 4+. If you're running TiVo software version 4+, go into the TCP/IP Settings or Wireless Settings menus (available through TiVo Central, Messages and Setup, Settings, Phone & Network Settings, Edit Phone or Network Settings) to verify that your network adapter was detected. You should then try to switch your TiVo to using the network for its daily and weekly calls, as described in the next section. This is the easiest way to test that both the TiVo and your network are configured correctly. If your goal is to be able to use the network to connect and transfer files to your Series 2 model, you'll need to read the first section of Chapter 8, "Connecting the Universe to Your TiVo," which discusses getting a command prompt on Series 2 systems so that you can install network-related software such as Telnet and FTP. Chapter 8 also discusses the specific TiVo software that provides network support in the TiVo's Linux operating system, in case you're working with a version of the TiVo software older than 3.0.

## Using the Network to Make Daily Calls

After you've put your Series 1 or Series 2 TiVo on your home network, you can easily configure it to use the network to make its daily and weekly calls. This enables your TiVo to receive programming and guide data updates without requiring access to a phone line. Unless you're using an AirNet card on a Series 1 or a wireless USB adapter on a Series 2, you'll still need access to an Ethernet cable connected to your home network, but, hey, progress is process. Even a wireless Ethernet connection is much faster than a phone line, and wired connections are tremendously faster.

 **NOTE**

Configuring your TiVo to be able to receive programming and guide updates over the network is not the same thing as putting your TiVo on the network so that you can log into it and transfer files back and forth. If you're using a TurboNet or AirNet card on a Series 1 machine and used the standard **nic_install** program to configure your system, the **nic_install** program also configured your system automatically to enable FTP and Telnet access—thanks, SiliconDust! However, getting FTP and Telnet access on Series 2 machines is a totally different kettle of fish, "thanks" to PROM and system software updates that have made it much harder to hack into the last few versions of the TiVo software on Series 2 systems (that is, software Versions 3.1 and later). Don't despair, however—it's certainly doable, and this book tells you how in Chapter 8. For now, enable programming and guide updates via the network and enjoy this performance improvement while you read Chapter 8 and begin to flex your hacking muscles.

Configuring your TiVo to use the network to make its daily calls for programming information is quite easy, but works slightly differently on Series 1 and Series 2 TiVos, due to differences in the versions of the TiVo software available for these systems. The next two sections explain how to do this on each type of system.

# Using the Network for Daily Calls on a Series 1 TiVo

To enable using the network to receive programming and guide updates on a Series 1 TiVo, all you have to do is go to the Dial Prefix screen and enter a dialing prefix of **,#401**, which is entered as Pause Enter 4 0 1, and click Select. For TiVo Version 3.x and earlier systems, the Dial Prefix is located in the Change Dial Options menu (TiVo Central, Messages and Setup, Recorder & Phone Setup, Phone Connection, Change Dial Options). Next, make a test call to test the new dial options—unlike many computer-related tasks, "it should just work." If the call fails, here are a few things to try, in order, before giving in to panic and changing every possible configuration setting:

1. Make sure that a DHCP Server is running on your home network (see "Networking 101" for more information about DHCP servers, the services that they provide, and where to run them).

2. Make sure that your network adapter is firmly connected to your Series 1 TiVo. It requires a bit of effort to firmly seat TiVoNet, TurboNet, CacheCard and AirNet adapters on the Series 1 motherboards. This is, of course, by design so that they don't come loose easily. I tend to slide mine on at one end and then rock it back and forth, with my fingers between the front of the TiVo and the back of the card. If you're using an AirNet card, make sure that your PCMCIA card is a Prism 2/2.5 card and that it's firmly seated in the AirNet adapter.

3. If you are using a wired Ethernet adaptor such as a TurboNet or CacheCard, verify that your TiVo is correctly connected to a hub or switch on your home network and that these are correctly connected to your home network. Not connecting your hub to your DSL or cable modem using the Uplink port is a common mistake. Integrating a hub or switch into your home network was explained in the section "Networking 101," earlier in this chapter.

4. Verify network connectivity from the network adaptor's point of view. To do this, check that the Link and Power lights are active on your network adapter, if available. TurboNet cards and CacheCard network adapters feature a green LED that lights up to indicate Ethernet connectivity. If you're using an AirNet card, the connectivity and power indicators are usually located on the PCMCIA Ethernet card that you plugged into the AirNet card.

5. Make sure that you entered the exact string `",#401"` for your dial prefix. It would be embarrassing to share how many times I left out the comma when I was first experimenting with this on my original Series 1, so I'll just claim that I've never made that mistake. Oops! If you find that you entered the wrong string, don't tell anybody—simply correct it and try making another test call.

6. If you've jumped ahead in this book and followed the instructions in Chapter 8 to get a command prompt on your TiVo, connect to your TiVo's serial port and make sure that its network configuration is correct using the `ifconfig` command, as in the following example:

```
bash-2.02# ifconfig -a
lo          Link encap:Local Loopback
```

```
              inet addr:127.0.0.1  Bcast:127.255.255.255  Mask:
255.0.0.0
              UP BROADCAST LOOPBACK RUNNING  MTU:3584  Metric:1
              RX packets:1078 errors:0 dropped:0 overruns:0 frame:0
              TX packets:1078 errors:0 dropped:0 overruns:0 carrier:0
coll:0


eth0     Link encap:Ethernet  HWaddr 00:40:36:01:B0:11
              inet addr:192.168.6.248  Bcast:192.168.6.255  Mask:
255.255.255.0
              UP BROADCAST RUNNING MULTICAST  MTU:1500  Metric:1
              RX packets:0 errors:0 dropped:0 overruns:0 frame:0
              TX packets:0 errors:0 dropped:0 overruns:0 carrier:0
coll:0
         Interrupt:29
```

This example shows that the Ethernet connection eth0 is working fine on my TiVo, and that the TiVo has the IP address 192.168.6.248. If you don't see an entry for "eth0", this means that your TiVo didn't initialize its Ethernet interface correctly. Use a text editor, such as vim or emacs, to check the file /var/log/kernel for a message containing the string "eth0" to see if there was a problem recognizing your Ethernet card or loading one of the network-related kernel modules. If this is the case on your Series 1, turn off the TiVo and try reseating everything.

7. If you still suspect a DHCP problem and are running a Linux system, use **ethereal**, **tcpdump,** or some similar Linux network packet-sniffing utility to check that your TiVo is actually sending and receiving packets over the network, as well as where they're going. For example, my DHCP server has the IP address 192.168.6.200 on my home network. When I boot a TiVo, I see a packet like the following on my home network (this output is cut from one of the windows displayed by the Linux ethereal utility):

```
192.168.2.200    255.255.255.255    \
       Syslog LOCAL1.INFO: 0C8E 400 DHCP SERVER Offered...
```

If you select that packet in ethereal, you'll see output indicating the IP address that the DHCP server offered to your TiVo—for example, something like this:

```
Message: 08CE 400 DHCP SERVER Offered \
       Offering: 192.168.6.248 To: FFFFFFFFFFFF \
                      By: 192.168.6.200
```

This traffic indicates that my DHCP server (which isn't running on my Linux system, but is running on an Apple Airport wireless access point) just handed out the IP address 192.168.6.248.

If you still can't successfully make a daily call, your best bet is to skip ahead to Chapter 8. In order to really diagnose what's happening on your TiVo, you'll need command-line access to it, which is easy to set up on Series 1 TiVos.

## Using the Network for Daily Calls on a Series 2 TiVo

As explained earlier, Series 2 TiVos are much easier to network than Series 1 machines. Series 2 models provide USB ports that enable you to quickly and easily attach a variety of USB adapters to your TiVo system. Because Series 2 TiVos are essentially network-aware, similar improvements have been made to the TiVo software to make it easy to take advantage of the network for obtaining daily programming and guide data.

If you are running any version of the TiVo software earlier than v4.0 on your Series 2 TiVo and don't want to upgrade (or if you're using a Series 2 DirecTiVo), the procedure for making daily calls over the network is the same as is on Series 1 TiVos, as discussed in the previous section. If you are running any v4.0 or better version of the Series 2 TiVo software, it's even easier!

 **TIP**

Unless you have a specific reason to assign a static IP address to your TiVo, I suggest that you always use DHCP to dynamically assign an IP address to your TiVo, even if you are installing network software such as FTP, Telnet, TiVoWebPlus, various servers for extraction purposes, and so on. DHCP is simply easier. The section later in this chapter entitled "Figuring Out Your TiVo's DHCP Address" provides a simple shell script that you can run from a Linux or Mac OS X system to locate active systems in the range of IP addresses that are allocated by your DHCP server.

From TiVo Central, select Messages & Setup, Settings, and Phone & Network Setup. The Connect via: setting at the top of the screen shows whether your TiVo is currently configured to connect to the TiVo service over the phone or the network, as shown in Figure 4.11, which shows a system that is configured to use the network.

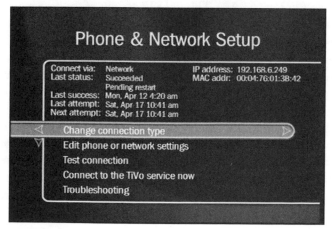

**FIGURE 4.11**   *The Phone & Network Setup screen for TiVo Software 4+*

If the value beside this label is Phone, do the following:

1. Select the Change connection type menu entry and select Network. The Phone & Network Settings screen redisplays. If this screen now shows a value in the MAC addr field (the hardware address of your Ethernet adapter), your network adaptor was detected. If this screen shows a numeric IP address in the IP address field, you're done, and can skip the rest of this section unless you want to assign a static IP address to your TiVo. If no IP address is displayed, proceed to the next step.

2. Select the Edit Phone or Network settings menu entry.

3. Select the TCP/IP Settings menu entry. If you are using a DHCP server to automatically assign a network address to your TiVo's network adapter, make sure that the Obtain IP address automatically menu entry is selected and skip to the next step. If you want to assign a static IP address to your TiVo, select the Specify static IP address entry. In this case, you will need to know:

   ◆ The IP Address that you want to assign to your TiVo. This must be an IP address that is valid on your home network, and which your home gateway knows how to provide address translation for. Make sure that you do not specify the same IP address that another system in your home is using, or any IP address that is in the range dispensed by any DHCP server that you are running on your home network.

   ◆ The Subnet Mask used on your home network. This is usually 255.255.255.0 if you are using a home gateway that does Native Address Translation (NAT) to enable your home systems to access the Internet.

   ◆ Your Gateway (Router) Address. This is the internal IP address of your home gateway, which is often 192.168.1.1 for out-of-the-box home gateways (unless you've changed something—for example, I use 192.168.6.x for my home network, so my home gateway is at 192.168.6.1).

   ◆ DNS (Name Server) Address. This is the IP address of the system on your home network that maps IP addresses to host names. If you do not have one, you can enter the IP address of one of your ISP's DNS Servers.

4. If you are using DHCP and your ISP requires a DHCP client ID, use the ouija screen and enter that here. If you are using a home gateway that provides a DHCP server, you generally do not have to specify a DHCP client ID. In the latter case, select I don't have a DHCP client ID.

5. If you're comfortable with the settings you've chosen, select Accept these settings to proceed with the TiVo network configuration. If you want to change something, select Restore the previous settings and reselect the TCP/IP Settings menu entry to rerun TCP/IP configuration.

6. If you are using a wired USB Ethernet device, press the left arrow to return to the Phone & Network Setup menu. Your TiVo should now display an IP address and MAC address.

7. If you are using a wireless USB Ethernet device, select the Wireless Settings menu option. An information screen displays, telling you the information that you will need to know in order to proceed. Press Select to continue. You'll need to know:

   ◆ The name and password (optional) for your internal wireless network, if any

   ◆ The level of encryption for your internal wireless network, if any

8. If your home wireless network is open (does not require a password or level of encryption), its name should display at the bottom of the list shown on the screen that displays. This is actually the Secure Set Identifier (SSID) for that network. If one is displayed, select its name, click Accept these settings, and press the left arrow to return to the Phone & Network Setup screen. If an IP address is displayed on this screen, skip to Step 12. If one is not, reselect the Phone & network settings menu entry, reselect Wireless Settings, and select Connect to a closed wireless network.

9. Use the ouija screen to enter the SSID (name) of your home wireless network. When finished, navigate to the Done entering text entry.

10. Use the ouija screen to enter the password for your home wireless network. When finished, navigate to the Done entering text entry.

11. Select the level of encryption for your home wireless network. This is the length of the key used to secure connections to your home network.

12. Click Accept these settings and press the left arrow to return to the Phone & Network Setup screen. If an IP address is displayed on this screen, congratulations! If one is not, verify the information about your home network and re-enter it on the Connect to a closed wireless network screen.

If your TiVo doesn't detect the presence of your USB network adaptor, here are a few things to try:

1. After powering down your Series 2 TiVo and attaching a USB adaptor, make sure that the USB connector is pushed in all the way on the back of your TiVo and power your TiVo back up.

2. Verify network connectivity. To do this, check that the Link and Power lights are active on your network adapter. Most USB network adapters feature a green LED that lights up to indicate Ethernet connectivity, and they also provide a yellow power LED that lights up when the adapter is receiving power through the USB port.

3. Verify that your TiVo is correctly connected to a hub or switch on your home network and that these are correctly connected to your home network. Not connecting your hub to your DSL or cable modem using the uplink port is a common mistake. Integrating a hub or switch into your home network was explained in the section "Networking 101," earlier in this chapter.

4. If you want to use DHCP to dynamically assign IP addresses, make sure that a DHCP Server is running on your home network (see "Networking 101" for more information about DHCP servers, the services that they provide, and where to run them). Most home gateways have a built-in DHCP server that you may need to explicitly activate.

5. If you've jumped ahead in this book and followed the instructions in Chapter 8 to get a command prompt on your TiVo, connect to your TiVo's serial port and make sure that its network configuration is correct using the ifconfig command, as in the following example:

```
bash-2.02# ifconfig -a
lo        Link encap:Local Loopback
          inet addr:127.0.0.1  Bcast:127.255.255.255  Mask:
255.0.0.0
          UP BROADCAST LOOPBACK RUNNING  MTU:3584  Metric:1
          RX packets:1078 errors:0 dropped:0 overruns:0 frame:0
          TX packets:1078 errors:0 dropped:0 overruns:0 carrier:0
coll:0


eth0      Link encap:Ethernet  HWaddr 00:40:36:01:B0:11
          inet addr:192.168.6.248  Bcast:192.168.6.255  Mask:
255.255.255.0
          UP BROADCAST RUNNING MULTICAST  MTU:1500  Metric:1
          RX packets:0 errors:0 dropped:0 overruns:0 frame:0
          TX packets:0 errors:0 dropped:0 overruns:0 carrier:0
coll:0
          Interrupt:29
```

This example shows that the Ethernet connection eth0 is working fine on my TiVo, and that the TiVo has the IP address 192.168.6.248. If you don't see an entry for "eth0," this means that your TiVo didn't initialize its Ethernet interface correctly. Use a text editor such as vim or emacs to check the file /var/log/kernel for a message containing the string "eth0" to see if there was a problem recognizing your Ethernet card or loading one of the network-related kernel modules. If this is the case on your Series 1, turn off the TiVo and try reseating everything. If this is the case on your Series 2, try another USB Ethernet adapter—yours may simply be bad.

6. If you still suspect a DHCP problem and are running a Linux system, use ethereal, tcpdump, or some similar network packet-sniffing utility to check that your TiVo is actually sending and receiving packets over the network, as well as where they're going. For example, my DHCP server has the IP address 192.168.6.200 on my home network. When I boot a TiVo, I see a packet like the following on my home network (this output is cut from one of the windows displayed by the Linux ethereal utility):

```
192.168.2.200   255.255.255.255   \
     Syslog LOCAL1.INFO: 0C8E 400 DHCP SERVER Offered...
```

If you select that packet in ethereal, you'll see output indicating the IP address that the DHCP server offered to your TiVo—for example, something like this:

```
Message: 08CE 400 DHCP SERVER Offered \
        Offering: 192.168.6.248 To: FFFFFFFFFFFF \
                        By: 192.168.6.200
```

This traffic indicates that my DHCP server (which isn't running on my Linux system, but is running on an Apple Airport wireless access point) just handed out the IP address 192.168.6.248.

# Figuring Out Your TiVo's IP Address

DHCP is very handy if you have a variety of machines on your home network and don't want to manage your IP addresses manually. However, if you're using DHCP and want to hack your TiVo to install software like FTP, Telnet, extraction servers, and TiVoWebPlus, figuring out the IP address that was dynamically assigned to your TiVo can be somewhat tedious. Some DHCP servers enable you to configure them so that they always assign specific IP addresses to specific MAC addresses, which is a great one-time solution to this problem as long as you remember the IP address you've assigned to your TiVo's MAC address. However, if your DHCP server can't be configured in this way and you want to take advantage of the flexibility provided by DHCP, it's still useful to have a tool that probes your DHCP addresses and tells you whether a system is currently using each.

The following is a shell script that I use on my Linux, Mac OS X, and Windows (Cygwin) systems to identify the active machines whose IP addresses are within the range of IP addresses assigned by my DHCP server:

```
#!/bin/sh

base_addr="192.168.6"
start_range="240"
end_range="250"

loop_val=$start_range
end_range=`expr $end_range + 1`
systype=`uname`

if [ x$systype = "xDarwin" ] ; then
    echo ""
    echo "NOTE: No command-line ping timeout on OS X."
    echo ""
```

```
    fi

    while [ $loop_val != $end_range ] ; do

      addr=$base_addr"."$loop_val

      if [ x$systype = "xDarwin" ] ; then
        ans=`ping -q -c 3 $addr ¦ grep loss ¦ sed -e 's;.*, \(.*% packet loss\).*;\1;'`
      else
        ans=`ping -q -c 3 -w 1 $addr ¦ grep loss ¦ sed -e 's;.*, \(.*% packet loss\).*;\1;'`
      fi

      if [ "x$ans" = "x100% packet loss" ] ; then
       output="  Nobody home at $addr"
      else
       output="$addr is alive!"
      fi
      echo "  $output"

      loop_val=`expr $loop_val + 1`

    done
```

A copy of this script is located in the scripts directory at the top level of the BATBD CD that accompanies this book. (You'll have to mount the CD to access this directory, as explained in the section of Chapter 11 entitled, "Mounting the BATBD CD.") This script would certainly be more succinct if written in Perl but is more generic as a standard Un*x shell script.

The settings at the beginning of this script reflect my home network, which is probably configured differently than yours. To modify this script to work with your home network and DHCP server settings, change the *base_addr* string's value to the nonroutable Class C network that you are using at home and modify the *start_range* and *end_range* variables to reflect the beginning and end, respectively, of the range of IP addresses on that network that are handed out by your DHCP server.

**TIP**

If you are using Windows, the Angry IP Scanner utility is a great (and free) utility that enables you to probe your home network in much the same way as my sample script does. It is available from **http://www.angryziber.com/ipscan**. Its developer's page is at **http://ipscan.sf.net/**. The binary for this utility is provided in the connectivity directory on the BATBD CD that accompanies this book. The name of the binary is **ipscan.exe**.

## Managing IP Addresses for Networked TiVos

If you don't want to run a DHCP server on your home network for some reason or if you simply decide that you'd prefer to assign your TiVo a specific IP address, you can force the TiVo to use a specific IP address in different ways. On Series 2 TiVos running v4.x+ of the TiVo software, you can set the TiVo's IP address manually on the TiVo Messages & Setup, Setup, Phone & Network Setup screen. On TiVos running an older version of the TiVo software, you will need to modify one of the TiVo startup files. If you used the **nic_install** script to install networking support on your TiVo, I suggest that you modify the file /etc/rc.d/rc.net. If you did not run the **nic_install** script, you should modify the file /etc/rc.d/rc.sysinit.

**NOTE**

To modify either of these files on your TiVo, you will have to remount the / partition so that it is writable by using the command **mount –o rw,remount /** when logged in on the TiVo. Once you have completed your modification, you should remount the root partition as read-only, using the command **mount –o ro,remount /**. (Don't type the period.)

To modify the file /etc/rc.d/rc.net, open it in a text editor. This script uses DHCP by default, and will look something like the following:

```
#
#!/bin/sh
#

if /sbin/insmod -f /lib/modules/airnet.o ssid=wvh timing=6 ; then
        export DYNAMIC_NET_DEV=eth0
        mkdir -p /var/state/dhcp
        /sbin/dhclient -q eth0 2>/dev/null &
fi
```

Change the script so that it looks like the following:

```
#
#!/bin/sh
#

if /sbin/insmod -f /lib/modules/airnet.o ssid=wvh timing=6 ; then
        export DYNAMIC_NET_DEV=eth0
        ifconfig eth0 fixed-IP-address netmask 255.255.255.0 up
     route add default gw your-gateway-address
fi
```

Replace *fixed-IP-address* with the IP address that you want to assign to your TiVo, which should be a non-routable IP address that is valid on your home network (and which is not used by any other device on the network). Replace *your-gateway-address* with the IP address of your home gateway, which is probably 192.168.1.1 (or 192.168.6.1 in my case, since I use the 192.168.6 network at home).

To modify the file /etc/rc.d/rc.sysinit, open it in a text editor and search for the section that looks like the following:

```
unset DYNAMIC_NET_DEV
if [ -f /etc/rc.d/rc.net ]
then
  echo "Configuring network..."
  source /etc/rc.d/rc.net
fi
```

Immediately after this section, add the following lines:

```
 ifconfig eth0 fixed-IP-address netmask 255.255.255.0 up
 route add default gw your-gateway-address
```

Replace *fixed-IP-address* with the IP address that you want to assign to your TiVo, which should be a non-routable IP address that is valid on your home network (and which is not used by any other device on the network). Replace *your-gateway-address* with the IP address of your home gateway, which is probably 192.168.1.1 (or 192.168.6.1 in my case, since I use the 192.168.6 network at home).

# TiVo Hardware Supplies on the Net

As discussed throughout this chapter, there are thousands of TiVo fanatics and TiVo-related Web sites on the Internet. Many of these discuss how to hack various aspects of the TiVo software, but some actually provide the hardware that you'll need to do things like add disk drives to various models of TiVos, and will also do this for you if you're really paranoid about opening up your TiVo or simply don't have the time. This section discusses the best sites that I've found on the Internet for buying TiVo parts, getting your TiVo repaired, and for general TiVo expertise. These are, therefore, my favorite sites—if you have a similar site and it isn't listed here, I apologize in advance, and please let me know. More knowledge is always better as far as I'm concerned.

The United States sites in this section are listed alphabetically to avoid any suggestion of prejudice. I've bought things from all of these sites and prefer certain items from each. If you're creating a new TiVo site, maybe you'll want to register AAATiVo.com for better placement in the next version of this book?

# 9thTee.com

9thTee is one of the premiere sites for TiVo information, software, repairs, upgrades, and parts, and it has been in business since 1992 selling networking components, cool stuff, and (apparently) whatever else interests them. As discussed earlier in this chapter, 9thTee was the original commercial vendor for the TiVoNet cards (dealing with Tridge directly), and is also the sole distributor for the TurboNet and AirNet cards from SiliconDust.com. If you want to put your Series 1 TiVo on the network, buy a card from these guys—recently, bootleg TurboNet (and probably AirNet) cards have appeared for sale, but buying these is essentially ripping off both 9thTee and Nick at SiliconDust (aka jafa on the TiVo AVS forums). This book is about hacking the TiVo for fun, not about stealing. The people who did the hard work to design the hardware and software and to manufacture and distribute cool TiVo add-ons like these cards deserve your support.

9thTee offers pretty much every TiVo part and add-on you can think of, including modem repair kits for the truly technically inclined who don't want to simply cable up an external modem as described earlier in this chapter. 9thTee has brackets, tools, cables, and whatever else you might need to hack your TiVo yourself, repairs TiVos if you have one that is out of warranty or just want yours repaired *fast*, and will even upgrade your TiVos or sell you an upgrade kit if you want to save some time.

Check out their site at **http://www.9thTee.com**.

# Hinsdale

Hinsdale provides upgrade services and kits for all models of TiVo, provides a speedy repair service for ailing TiVos, and is perhaps best known for its how-tos, which describe how to do the upgrade yourself. Not only is this a truly exemplary illustration of most of the good things about the Internet and people in general, it demonstrates their detailed knowledge and expertise. I've heard nothing but good things about Hinsdale in TiVoLand.

Hinsdale accepts all major credit cards and also accepts PayPal payments. If you're looking for something to do with the profits from an eBay auction, a Hinsdale upgrade might be just what you're looking for.

Check out **http://www.newreleasesvideo.com/hinsdale-how-to/upgradeservice.html** or just search for Hinsdale TiVo in your favorite Internet search engine.

## PTVupgrade.com

PTVupgrade.com is a great site for purchasing TiVo kits, getting your TiVo upgraded, and getting a variety of hardware and software-related TiVo information. They are more actively involved in kernel hacking than most of the other TiVo service sites, recently announcing a breakthrough that enables you to use more than 137 GB of a given hard drive with your TiVo. (See Chapter 7 for a discussion of hard drive limitations in stock TiVo software distributions). These guys clearly love TiVos and probably know them better at the operating system level than any other site.

PTVupgrade.com specializes in expanding and repairing TiVos and also sells complete upgraded units. The 9thTee site actually resells PTVupgrade.com's upgrade kits and services. Series 1 TiVo upgrade kits from PTVupgrade.com are identified as NetReady, which means that they come with popular TiVo networking software such as ftp and Telnet.

PTVupgrade.com also distributes a version of the TyTool extraction software that they call *DVRchive*—it's slightly older than the latest downloadable version, but it's nice to be able to get support for TyTool through the PTVupgrade.com forums (discussed in Chapter 14, "Other TiVo Resources on the Net"). More information about DVRchive is available at **http://www.ptvupgrade.com/products/DVRchive**.

 **TIP**

One especially cool service provided by PTVupgrade.com is that you can send them a disk of any supported size, and they will install a virgin copy of the latest TiVo OS for the system of your choice on that disk. This is known as a drive recertification—more information about this service is available at **http://www.ptvupgrade.com/db/upgrade/category/products/product_detail_html?product_id=68**. If you want to upgrade your TiVo and don't want to play around with the disks yourself, this is a fast and convenient alternative. Also, if you are interested in hacking a Pioneer 810-H and need a disk with the Pioneer 57-H software, this service is for you.

Check out their site at **http://www.PTVupgrade.com**—it's definitely worth a visit.

## TiVo Store

As you might suspect, TiVo repairs its own hardware and also offers items such as USB network adapters that are guaranteed to work with Series 2 systems, replacement remotes and cables, and cool accessories like TiVo shirts and toys. All of these items are available through the TiVo store at **http://store.tivo.com**.

If you have a problem with your TiVo hardware, the TiVo site is less than exciting. The primary TiVo customer support site is located at **http://customersupport.tivo.com/ userWelcome.asp** and features a troubleshooting guide for hardware and software problems. Unfortunately, if you're looking for instant help with a dead Series 1 box, you'll wander through a few menus until you finally find out how to contact support from the actual manufacturer of your TiVo. Though I'm somewhat cranky about this, it's not totally surprising—as I discuss in Chapter 1, TiVo makes the majority of its money from selling the TiVo service. Since it doesn't make most of its hardware, we can't really expect them to fix someone else's. They'll be happy to fix Series 2 systems that they manufactured, especially those that are still under warranty. If you have an older TiVo, contact 9thTee or Weaknees for repairs and to talk to certified TiVo fans.

## Weaknees.com

Weaknees.com is the other premiere TiVo hardware and software site on the Web. Weaknees is entirely TiVo-related and, thus, is much easier to navigate than any other TiVo supplier's site. It provides an excellent selection of TiVo hardware, software, and information, and it features TiVo repair and upgrade services. In my opinion, the Series 2 expansion brackets from Weaknees are better than anyone else's, and the Weaknees bracket features additional cooling fans to keep your TiVo cool even when recording the longest *Farscape* or *Rockford Files* marathon. Weakness is also the creator of the PowerTrip device that helps protect upgraded Series 2 systems from the vagaries and power demands of additional drives when you expand your TiVo's storage capacity.

Weaknees offers pretty much every TiVo part and add-on you can think of, including external modem kits people need to cable up an external modem, as described earlier in this chapter. Weaknees has brackets, tools, cables, and whatever else you might need to hack your TiVo yourself, repairs TiVos if you have one that is out of warranty or just want yours repaired *fast*, and will even upgrade your TiVos or sell you an upgrade kit if you want to save some time.

Check out their site at **http://www.weaknees.com**.

## TiVo Sites Outside the United States

As I mention in Chapter 1, TiVo partnered with Thompson Electronics to provide TiVo hardware in the United Kingdom. If you're a TiVo fan living in the United Kingdom or anywhere outside the United States that uses the same type of power as the UK, you may want to have your TiVo repaired or upgraded by someone in your own neighborhood. PACELink is an excellent firm in the United Kingdom that will be glad to do this for you. Its URL is **http://www.pacelink.co.uk**. It also offers a variety of services, software, and accessories that enable you to more easily interact with the hardware and services in the United Kingdom, such as the DigiBox.

# Other Sources for TiVo Hardware

There are plenty of other sites on the Internet for obtaining TiVo upgrades, service, and general information. The ones listed previously are sites that I've specifically heard good things about, or that I've personally dealt with. (I have never paid for an upgrade, so can't vouch for that aspect of any site I've discussed.) If you have some spare time, google (search) for TiVo Upgrade Kits and surf through the 10 or 20 pages of results. Happy hunting.

One good source of used TiVos and inexpensive, competitive upgrades is eBay.com. I've bought a few used TiVos there and have been happy with the results. As the largest flea market and auction site in the known universe, eBay is a great starting point for getting an upgrade or used TiVo. It's certainly the easiest place to get a Series 1 system for pure hacking pleasure at this point.

### TiVo | Used TiVos and Lifetime Service

One nice aspect of buying a used TiVo on the Internet is that you can often buy TiVos there with lifetime service already paid for—as mentioned earlier, lifetime TiVo service travels with a specific machine (in most cases), and you can avoid having to pay for the service yourself if you buy such a machine there. You might think that this would make TiVo cranky, but it actually shouldn't. I assume that everyone who's selling their old TiVos with lifetime service on eBay is doing so because they've bought a newer TiVo or DirecTiVo system, and, therefore, TiVo is still getting the appropriate amount of service revenue.

# HACKING THE TiVo

SECOND EDITION

# Chapter 5

## The Hacker's Tool Chest of TiVo Tools

Thanks to the efforts of hundreds of dedicated TiVo hackers and the miracle of the Internet for instant information and file sharing, TiVo hackers today have hundreds of pieces of software from which to choose. Regardless of the model and type of TiVo you're using, you can choose from a tremendous variety of recompiled Linux utilities, TiVo-only software, and personal computer software for operating systems, such as Microsoft Windows, Apple's Mac OS, and Linux that all interact with your TiVo in interesting and often useful ways.

The corollary of this idea is that the Internet is a tremendous collection of unsorted, essentially random information that isn't verified or kept up-to-date. I could post a page tomorrow explaining how to transmute lead into gold by sacrificing a chicken in a graveyard, and the truly gullible would have no way of knowing whether it was true and useful information unless they actually tried it. The same thing is true about TiVo-related information on the Internet—you have no way of knowing whether the information is up-to-date, complete, or even applies to your machine unless you actually try out the posted instructions and see what happens. This can take a fair amount of time, can be a total waste of that time, and (with instructions explaining how to modify your operating system) can be downright dangerous.

A good example of obsolete information is Frequently Asked Questions, better known as *FAQs*. In TiVo-Land, one of the best-known FAQs is the "Hacking the TiVo FAQ" (no relation to this book or this author). This FAQ was written a long time ago and hasn't been maintained for years, although it was recently updated to state explicitly that it was out-of-date. It also discusses hacking techniques and software that are largely specific to the Series 1 TiVos. However, because it was written when there was essentially only one type of TiVo and because its authors couldn't see into the future, it doesn't say that it *is* for the Series 1 TiVo. The techniques and environment variables described in that FAQ for getting a command-line prompt on your TiVo 1 won't work on a Series 2 TiVo.

Like most computer system software, software for the TiVo can be divided into two general classes: application software and system software. Application software typically consists of utilities that are run by users and don't require any special privileges in order to execute them. Testing application software is generally fairly safe on systems with reasonable security because normal users can't access or modify resources that they shouldn't.

System software is a whole different ballgame. Not only will software compiled for the Series 1 not run on Series 2 machines, but also you can potentially screw up your Series 2 machine if you overwrite Series 2 software with equivalent Series 1 software on a Series 2 machine. Also, the idea of user-level security is nonexistent on a TiVo because all of the TiVo hacks that give you command-line access to TiVos do so as the root user (aka the superuser). On a TiVo, like any other Linux or Unix system, the superuser has privileges to do anything to any file or device on the machine, including bad things.

This chapter is designed to introduce the most popular hacking software for the TiVo, explain what type of TiVo for which it is relevant, and explain any limitations involved in using the software on different types of TiVos.

This chapter also discusses the various bootable TiVo tools disks that you can find on the net, as well as the bootable BATBD disk that accompanies this book. All of the software discussed in this chapter is found on the BATBD disk, and some subsets of it can be found on various other tools disks. The discussion of each tools disk explains which type of TiVo it is intended for use with, what tools and versions of those tools that each disk includes, and provides an overview of using each tools disk. Not surprisingly, since the author assembled the BATBD disk for use with this book, it is the most complete and up-to-date of any of the tools disks, and gets the most extensive discussion.

# TiVo Tools Overview

This section discusses software that is designed to run on an x86-based Linux system, and which can be used to interact with TiVo disks that have been attached to those systems as described in Chapter 4, "Exploring Your TiVo Hardware." These are the tools required to actually do many of the procedures discussed in subsequent chapters, such as backing up and restoring disks, cloning existing disks to larger ones, and examining and otherwise modifying TiVo disk partitions and data.

## BlessTiVo

Written by Mike Hill, BlessTiVo is a utility that enables you to prepare quickly and easily a second disk for use with your TiVo. The BlessTiVo utility takes its name from the fact that attaching a second drive to a TiVo requires that the drive be prepartitioned, contain special boot information in the drive's boot sectors, and that the third partition on the drive contains a special TiVo ID string. Among TiVo hackers, the sum of all three of these actions is known as "blessing" the drive for use with your TiVo—hence the name. You typically run the BlessTiVo program from a PC that you have booted from a TiVo tools floppy or a TiVo tools CD, such as the BATBD CD that was included with this book. Versions of the BlessTiVo program are also available for Mac OS 9 and Mac OS X. You can download the Mac OS X version of the BlessTiVo program from the URL **http://www.weaknees.com/mactivo.php**. It is also in the Macintosh directory of the BATBD CD, for your convenience.

 **NOTE**

As mentioned previously, after booting your TiVo for the first time with a second drive attached, the two drives in that TiVo are permanently associated with each other (well, at least until you reformat them). The software side of this association is accomplished by the main TiVo drive recording the TiVo ID string of its partner.

The most common way to prepare a second drive for use in your TiVo is by using the MFS Tools, discussed later in this chapter. When restoring or expanding a backup to a new, larger drive using MFS Tools, you can automatically prepare and add a second drive at the same time by appending its name to the MFS Tools command line. This is a fine solution if you are using a PC to restore and expand the backups, and that system has two free IDE connectors so that you can mount both of the drives intended for the TiVo at the same time.

If your PC only has a single free IDE connector, you can do the same thing in two steps by using both the MFS Tools and the BlessTiVo program. First, you attach the new hard drive to a PC and restore and expand your backup image to that drive. Next, you shut down the PC, remove the newly prepared TiVo disk, and insert the second drive that you want to use with your TiVo. After rebooting, you use the BlessTiVo program to prepare the second drive by itself. At this point, you can shut down the PC again, remove the second TiVo drive, and insert both drives into your TiVo after setting their jumpers correctly.

Similarly, if you are not a Pentium-class PC user, you can use the **BlessTiVo** command to prepare a second drive to use with your TiVo with the BlessTiVo program. Unfortunately, the MFS Tools commands are not yet available for Macintosh systems, but the Macintosh version of BlessTiVo at least makes it possible to augment your existing TiVo storage from a Macintosh. (See Chapter 8, "Working with Your TiVo from Windows and Macintosh Systems," for more information about TiVo-related applications for the Macintosh and using your Macintosh to work with TiVo storage.)

Using the **BlessTiVo** command on a PC is quite straightforward—after attaching the drive you want to bless to your PC or Mac OS X system, reboot the system from a TiVo tools disk. When you see the command prompt ('#'), execute the **BlessTiVo** command, specifying the name of the drive that you want to prepare for use as a second disk in your TiVo on the command-line after the **BlessTiVo** command, as in the following example:

```
BlessTiVo /dev/hdX
```

In this example, *X* represents the identifier for the disk that you want to format. The device names used by the **BlessTiVo** command are /dev/hdb for a TiVo drive attached as a slave on your primary IDE interface, /dev/hdc for a TiVo drive attached as a master on your secondary IDE interface, and /dev/hdd for a TiVo drive attached as a slave on your secondary IDE interface. As a safety feature, the **BlessTiVo** command does not allow you to specify /dev/hda as the drive to be formatted, because this drive is typically the boot disk used by your PC or Mac OS system.

For example, if the drive that you want to prepare for use in your TiVo is attached as a slave on your secondary IDE interface, you would execute the following command:

```
BlessTiVo /dev/hdd
```

When you execute the **BlessTiVo** command, the program first checks to see if the drive exists and can be opened. If you see error messages such as "No device specified," "Too many command line options," or "Unable to connect to /dev/hdx," these usually mean that you accidentally specified the wrong drive on the **BlessTiVo** command line, you specified the name of the drive incorrectly (no spaces in device names!), you set the jumpers on the drive incorrectly when you put it in your PC or Mac, or you do not have sufficient privileges to write to the drive. Recheck the command-line arguments that you specified, verify that the drive jumpers are set correctly, and, if you are not running from the BATBD disk, make sure that you are executing the **BlessTiVo** command as a Linux or Mac OS X user with superuser or administrative privileges.

Once the BlessTiVo program verifies that it can find the specified drive, it then examines the drive to determine whether the drive already contains DOS or Linux partitioning information. If the drive already contains valid partitions, the **BlessTiVo** command warns you of this fact and asks if you want to proceed. Although this extra paranoia may be irritating if you're sure that you know what you're doing, this extra verification step is quite handy if you've accidentally specified the wrong disk name and are attempting to overwrite the wrong drive, for example, your primary Windows partition or other data that you may want to use again in the future.

The **BlessTiVo** command also asks you to verify that you want to proceed even if the specified disk contains no partitioning information. This can be handy if the disk you have specified contains data partitioned in a format that the **BlessTiVo** command does not understand, such as Mac OS X partitions.

If you reply "y" to whichever of these confirmation requests you see, the TiVo blesses the specified drive by performing the following operations:

◆ Erases the first few sectors of the drive to eliminate any existing partitioning information.

◆ Writes a valid boot page to the first sector of the drive.

◆ Creates three partitions on the drive.

◆ Writes the TiVo ID string to the third partition.

The **BlessTiVo** command displays a status message as it completes each of these steps and displays a final summary message as it exits. This summary message displays the amount of storage available on the newly formatted drive.

 **WARNING**

The summary message displayed at the end of the BlessTiVo process is very important. You should always check this value to make sure that it is within 3 gigabytes of the total size of the disk that you are adding. If the size of the disk that you are blessing is not reported as being within 3 GB of the actual size of the disk, do not add this drive to your TiVo. If you do so, the two drives will be married, and you will not be able to take advantage of the storage that is really available on the second disk without backing up the drives, reformatting them, and so on.

If the **BlessTiVo** command reports the drive size incorrectly, this is usually due to one of two problems:

◆ The drive is not jumpered to take advantage of Logical Block Addressing (LBA), which is commonly used on newer, larger hard drives. Check the manual that came with your drive or check the jumper settings. You may accidentally have set the wrong jumper when configuring the drive to add it to your PC or Mac OS X system.

◆ The Linux kernel that you are booting from is not capable of recognizing disks with the storage capacity of the hard drive that you are trying to format. This is not a problem if you have booted from a TiVo tools disk, such as the BATBD disk included with this book, but may be a problem if you are executing the **BlessTiVo** command from the command line of an older Linux system.

Assuming that the amount of storage reported as available on the new drive is within 3 GB of the physical size of the drive, you can now shut down the system by pressing the Ctrl-Alt-Delete keys on a PC or by executing the shutdown command on your Mac. After the system shuts down, you can remove the drive from your desktop system, verify or set the jumpers so that the drive is configured as a slave drive, and insert it into your TiVo. After you power up the TiVo, the startup process may take slightly more time than is normally required while the TiVo integrates the new storage and updates its internal drive and capacity information. After the TiVo boots, you should be able to go to the System Information screen (TiVo Central, Messages & Setup, System Information) and verify that the storage capacity of your TiVo has increased. If it has not, turn off your TiVo and verify that you set the jumpers correctly so that the drive is identified as a slave disk. This is a common oversight in the excitement of TiVo hacking and expanding your TiVo's storage capacity before the next *Star Trek* or *South Park* marathon begins.

For experienced TiVo hackers, the **BlessTiVo** command provides some additional command-line options that enable you to individually execute each of the stages of the BlessTiVo process. These options can be specified on the command line after the name of the drive that you want to bless, and they consist of the following:

◆ *erase* Erase the first few sectors of the drive to eliminate any existing partitioning information. This stage of the BlessTiVo process does the same thing as the Linux/Unix **dd** command that is often used to wipe the partition map on an existing drive.

◆ *bpage* Write a valid bootpage to the first sector of the drive. This stage of the BlessTiVo process is the equivalent of the **bootpage** command discussed later in this chapter.

◆ *part* Create three partitions on the drive. This stage of the BlessTiVo process is the equivalent of the actions of the **pdisk** program discussed later in this chapter.

◆ *id* Write the TiVo ID string to the third partition. This stage of the BlessTiVo process is the equivalent of the **GenAddDiskTiVoID** program that is found on some TiVos or a subset of the actions of the MFS Tools **mfstool add** command.

# Bootpage

The bootpage utility reads and writes TiVo boot information from the first sector of the master disk in your TiVo, which is the disk from which your TiVo boots. The information in the master drive's boot sector is as follows:

◆ The partition where the bootable kernel for your TiVo is located

◆ An alternate partition from which to load a kernel if booting from the primary bootable kernel fails

◆ The network hostname of your system

◆ The default IP address of your system

◆ The default MAC address of your system

The boot and alternate boot partition information in your master boot disk's boot sector is critical to the TiVo boot process. The boot partition is not the partition from which the Linux kernel (the actual operating system) is loaded but instead identifies the partition that the running kernel uses as the root filesystem for your TiVo. Like any Linux or Unix system, the TiVo's boot partition is where startup information and the basic commands necessary for the TiVo boot process are stored. The network-related information stored in your master disk's boot sector is rarely used. Items that can be configured using the TiVo's system software, such as your system's hostname and IP address, are typically overridden by explicit commands in your TiVo's startup files.

---

 **NOTE**

There are at least two different versions of the **bootpage** command. These share most of the options discussed in this section, but differ in one or two areas. The standard TiVo **bootpage** command comes as part of your TiVo's root filesystem, and is the file `/sbin/bootpage`. This version of the **bootpage** command doesn't display a usage message if you execute it without any options, and assumes that you are referring to a default TiVo hard drive (`/dev/hda`) if you don't specify one on the command line. The other version of the **bootpage** command was originally written by Andrew Tridgell ("Tridge" of Samba fame), and it is available in source form. Tridge's bootpage has some built-in help if you can't remember the available options (or don't have this book handy—simply execute it with no arguments), requires that you specify the name of the TiVo drive that you're querying or updating, and only updates the bootpage if you specify the items that you want to update on the command line, along with the –C switch. For example, the following stock TiVo **bootpage** command updates the TiVo's hostname to "wvhtivo:"

```
/sbin/bootpage -H wvhtivo
```

The equivalent command using the Series 2 version of Tridge's bootpage utility provided on the BATBD CD is the following:

```
bootpage.s2 -H wvhtivo -C /dev/hda
```

Similarly, the values passed to the –A and –B options differ between versions of the **bootpage** command. The number you give to TiVo's version of the **bootpage** command has to be 3 or 6. The number you give to Tridge's version of **bootpage** must be 4 or 7.

Tridge's version of the **bootpage** command is provided in the `bootpage` directory of the BATBD CD that accompanies this book, precompiled for Series 1 (**bootpage.s1**), Series 2 (**bootpage.s2**), and desktop x86 (**bootpage.x86**) systems. Which one you use is up to you—I prefer Tridge's version of the **bootpage** command because I have no short-term memory, and therefore it's handy to be able to get a listing of available options.

---

As you might expect, any changes made in the boot sector of a TiVo hard disk will only take effect the next time you boot your TiVo using that hard drive as the master/boot drive.

The general syntax of the **bootpage** command is the following:

```
bootpage [options] device
```

As specified on the **bootpage** command line, *device* is the base name of a disk, not the name of any specific partition. Valid device names are therefore of the form /dev/hda, /dev/hdb, and so on. When a partition is required, you need only specify the number corresponding to that partition on your TiVo drive—for example, you would specify "6" rather than "/dev/hda6."

The **bootpage** command's command-line options are listed below:

◆ *-A partition device* Sets the number of the alternate boot *partition* identified in the boot sector of the specified *device*. Check the value returned by the −a option before using this option, since TiVo's version of bootpage requires different values than the open source version.

◆ *-a device* Displays the number of the alternate boot partition identified in the boot sector of the specified *device*.

◆ *-B partition device* Updates the number of the boot partition identified in the boot sector of the specified *device* to *partition*. Check the value returned by the −b option before using this option, since TiVo's version of bootpage requires different values than the open source version.

◆ *-b partition device* Displays the number of the current boot *partition* identified in the boot sector of the specified *device*.

◆ *-C device* (Tridge's bootpage only) Writes the bootpage of the specified *device*. If you are using Tridge's version of the bootpage utility, you must always specify this option on the command line with the items that you want to update or the TiVo bootpage will not be updated.

◆ *-f device* Switches ("flips") the primary and alternate boot partitions of the specified *device*, making the former boot partition the alternate boot partition, and making the former alternate boot partition the primary boot partition.

◆ *-H hostname device* Sets the default hostname of the TiVo to *hostname* in the boot sector of the specified *device*. This option is really only useful if you have set up your home network to netboot your TiVo using **bootp** or some similar service.

◆ *-h device* Displays the default hostname of the TiVo, as identified in the boot sector of the specified *device*.

◆ *-I ipaddress device* Sets the default IP address of the TiVo to *ipaddress* in the boot sector of the specified *device*. This option is really only useful if you have set up your home network to netboot your TiVo using **bootp** or some similar service.

◆ *-i device* Displays the default IP address of the TiVo, as identified in the boot sector of the specified *device*.

◆ *-M macaddress device* Sets the default MAC address (hardware network address) of the TiVo to *macaddress* in the boot sector of the specified *device*. This option is really only useful if you have set up your home network to netboot your TiVo using **bootp** or some similar service.

- ◆ *-m device*   Displays the default MAC address of the TiVo, as identified in the boot sector of the specified *device*.

- ◆ *-P params device*   Sets current boot parameters to the list of parameters specified in *params*. As you'll see later in this book, clever manipulation of the TiVo's boot parameters is the key to successfully hacking into later versions of the TiVo's Linux operating system.

- ◆ *-p device*   Gets a list of the boot parameter information stored in the boot sector of the disk identified by *device*. These boot parameters are typically just a string of command-line arguments that can be passed to the Linux kernel at boot time.

- ◆ *-q device*   (Standard TiVo bootpage only) Displays a summary of the information in the boot sector of the specified *device*.

- ◆ *-W filename device*   Writes the bootpage information from the specified *device* to the file *filename*.

The TiVo's use of duplicate kernel and root filesystem partitions, discussed in more detail in Chapter 10, "Linux and the TiVo," is a clever way of ensuring the dependability and reliability of your TiVo in almost any circumstances except severe hardware failures. Because the TiVo is a consumer appliance designed for regular daily use, TiVo, Inc. can't afford to have the system get into a state where you would have to locate and invoke your local Linux wizard in order to correctly configure it. TiVos therefore use primary and alternate boot partitions, both to simplify upgrades and for protection from hardware problems. When TiVo, Inc. releases an upgraded version of the TiVo's Linux kernel, that kernel is loaded into your system's alternate boot partition as part of the upgrade process. If this kernel is downloaded and installed successfully, the TiVo uses the **bootpage** command to set the partition containing the updated kernel as your TiVo's new boot partition and sets the partition where the current kernel is located as the new alternate partition. Should a problem occur, the system always can fall back to the previous kernel by loading it from the alternate partition.

# MFS Tools

Ah, the near-legendary MFS Tools utilities! The MFS Tools are the Swiss Army Knife of TiVo utilities, and were written by Steven Lang, aka *Tiger*. The MFS Tools utilities are a tremendously powerful and eminently useful set of utilities for your TiVo that largely replace all other disk backup, disk restore, disk expansion, and disk addition utilities for the TiVo. They take their name from the Multimedia File System (MFS), which is the partition format and organization used by the TiVo to store and locate your recordings. (For more information about MFS, see Chapter 9.)

**NOTE**

The MFS Tools are organized around a single utility named **mfstool** that actually provides a suite of commands that perform various, related functions. A *command suite* is the term used to describe a command whose first argument specifies the function that the command is to perform, with subsequent command-line arguments being specific to the way in which the command suite is used. Confusing? Many other people think so, too, but this simplifies program maintenance in many ways.

Since the **mfstool** utility performs multiple functions and the notion of command suites may be alien to most users, many tools disks (including the one provided with this book) create multiple links to the **mfstool** executable with names that indicate the specific function that they are intended to perform. Supported links for the mfstool program are things like **backup**, **restore**, and **mfsadd**. To minimize or at least change the amount of confusion related to these commands, this chapter (and the rest of this book) specifies the full, generic command-line syntax for each example of the **mfstool** utility.

As of early 2004, the source code for the MFS Tools utilities was released to the open source community by Tiger, and is available at **http://sourceforge.net/projects/mfstools/**. The actual project site is at **http://mfstools.sourceforge.net/** has a few links to downloadable binaries, but the best way to get the source is through CVS (Concurrent Versioning System), the source code control system in which all of the source code for SourceForge projects is stored. You can retrieve a copy of the MFS Tools source using the following commands from a Linux or Mac OS X system (or a Windows system if you are running Cygwin):

```
cvs -d:pserver:anonymous@cvs.sourceforge.net:/cvsroot/mfstools login
(press return to enter blank password)
cvs -z3 -d:pserver:anonymous@cvs.sourceforge.net:/cvsroot/mfstools co
mfstools
```

These commands will create a directory called mfstools that contains the current MFS Tools sources as checked into SourceForge.

As you'd expect, various TiVo hackers are pounding on the source for MFS Tools, adding various bells, whistles, and significant enhancements. The primary thread on the Dealdatabase forum where fixing and enhancing MFS Tools is discussed is at **http://www.dealdatabase.com/forum/showthread.php?t=33080**. TiVo hacker ronnythunder has made especially significant contributions, adding built-in capabilities for streaming backups over the net, fixing bugs, and so on. The src directory on the BATBD CD contains an `mfstools` directory that contains three archives of the MFS Tools source:

◆ *mfstools_15jun04.tgz* A snapshot of the MFS Tools source code from SourceForge as of 15 June, 2004.

◆ *mfstools_orig.tgz*   a snapshot of the MFS tools source code as originally released by Tiger.

◆ *mfstools_rt.tgz*   A snapshot of ronnythunder's enhanced MFS Tools source code, which was used to build the version of the MFS Tools utilities found on the BATBD CD.

The version of the MFS Tools utilities provided on the BATBD CD was compiled from ronnythunder's source, adding compilation flags to support large files and to compile the binaries statically for ease of use and portability.

 **TIP**

Like any active piece of open source software, the MFS Tools utilities are being actively worked on. The version on the BATBD CD has worked for me with no problems. However, if you encounter problems, the BATBD CD also includes a binary version of the "original" MFS Tools utilities. If you boot from the BATBD CD and select the **bigs2** or **bigs1** boot options, you can execute the original 2.0 version of the MFS Tools utilities by executing the command **old_mfstool** instead of **mfstool** in any of the command examples given in this book. You won't be able to create backup files larger than 4 GB, but this at least gives you a safety net of sorts in case some of the latest MFS Tools enhancements are incompatible with your system for some reason. When using the old version of the **mfstool** command, you will not need to use the **–C** option specified in all **mfstool restore** command examples—this option is only available in the new version of the **mfstool** command.

The **mfstool** command suite performs the following basic functions, which are also the keywords that you must supply as the first argument on the **mfstool** command line in order to invoke those functions:

◆ *add*   Enables you to add partitions to a TiVo disk to take advantage of all space available. Also enables you to add a second TiVo disk to an existing TiVo disk.

◆ *backup*   Backs up TiVo disks in a special format that minimizes the space required to store the backups or the number and type of files that are actually backed up.

◆ *d*   Dumps raw data from a specified MFS volume (new MFS Tools only; not in 2.0).

◆ *info*   Provides information about the status of the MFS volumes on one or more TiVo disks.

◆ *mls*   provides information about the MFS disks and volumes specified in the MFS_DEVICE and MFS_DEVLIST environment variables (new MFS Tools only; not in 2.0).

◆ *restore*   Restores TiVo data from backup files in the format created by the mfstool **backup** command.

When specifying the names of TiVo disks on any mfstool command line, you must use the standard convention /dev/hda for a drive attached as a master on your primary IDE interface,

/dev/hdb for a drive attached as a slave on your primary IDE interface, /dev/hdc for a drive attached as a master on your secondary IDE interface, and /dev/hdd for a drive attached as a slave on your secondary IDE interface. The **mfstool** commands that accept partition names on the command line use the same naming conventions, except that the numeric identifier(s) for the specific partition(s) must be appended to the basic device name.

Other features common to all of the commands in the mfstool suite are default values for the disk(s) that you are working with and two environmental variables that can be used to override these default values. If no disk drives are specified on the command line of any command in the mfstool command suite, the default disk(s) /dev/hda and /dev/hdb are used. If you want to work with other disks but still don't want to specify them on the command line for some reason, you can override these default values by setting the values of the **MFS_HDA** and **MFS_HDB** environment variables to the name of the device(s) or file(s) that contain the data with which you are working. This occasionally can be useful when you are working with specific partitions or partitions with nonstandard device names. Setting environment variables in Linux is explained in Chapter 9.

There have been three major releases of the MFS Tools utilities: Versions 1.0 and 2.0 and subsequent utilities improvements. Version 2.0 was created when Series 2 machines first appeared and adds features such as being able to deal with byte-order differences between Series 1 and Series 2 systems. The third "release" covers the incremental improvements to the MFS Tools utilities that have been made since they were released as open source, such as the version provided by default on the BATBD CD. One of the especially cool features of the MFS Tools utilities is that they do not require the use of a special kernel, boot parameters, and so on. Given sufficient privileges on any Linux system, the MFS Tools can make all of the disk modifications that they require to correctly restore backup data (whether byte-swapped or not), create new partitions, and so forth.

The next few sections explain each of the primary mfstool commands in more detail, discussing the command-line options specific to each. The information in these sections is provided as reference information for these commands. For information about using these commands to back up and restore data from your TiVo, see Chapter 5. For information about using these commands to expand the storage on an existing TiVo, see Chapter 6.

## The mfstool add Command

The **mfstool** suite's **add** command enables you to expand the set of MFS volumes on one or two TiVo disks. The **mfstool add** command is typically used in one of two ways:

- ◆ To increase the number of MFS volumes available on a new, larger disk after an existing TiVo disk has been copied to it using the Linux **dd** command (as explained in the section of Chapter 6 entitled "Expanding an Existing TiVo Disk without Losing Anything").

- ◆ To add a second drive to an existing single-drive TiVo system. When used in this fashion, the **mfstool add** command is a complete replacement for the **BlessTiVo** command discussed earlier in this section.

Using the **mfstool add** command to perform these functions is explained in Chapter 6.

Command-line options for the **mfstool add** command are as follows:

◆   *-r scale*   This option enables you to trade off between the amount of RAM required to track disk usage on your TiVo drives and the efficiency of the storage used on those drives. The TiVo's MFS partitions can store data in 1, 2, 4, 8, or 16 MB allocation units. Choosing a smaller allocation unit size increases the efficiency of your TiVo's storage, because less space will be "wasted" when recordings do not completely fill an allocation unit. However, because more allocation units are required to store a recording if the allocation units themselves are smaller, the TiVo uses more memory when tracking smaller allocation units. For example, assume that the allocation unit was 16 MB and the TiVo was trying to store a recording that required 20 MB of disk space. This would require two allocation units and would completely fill the first one but waste 12 MB of disk space in the second. In order to keep track of the recording, the TiVo would have to keep information about both allocation units in memory. On the other hand, with an allocation unit of 4 MB, the recording would require five allocation units but no disk space would be wasted. However, the TiVo would have to keep information about five allocation units in memory to keep track of that recording.

Acceptable values for this option are 0 (corresponding to a 1 MB allocation unit), 1 (corresponding to a 2 MB allocation unit), 2 (corresponding to a 4 MB allocation unit), 3 (corresponding to an 8 MB allocation unit), and 4 (corresponding to a 16 MB allocation unit). In general, the larger the allocation unit value, the less RAM used (making the TiVo more responsive when displaying menus, changing and processing options, and so on), but the greater the amount of storage that may be wasted when storing recordings.

 **WARNING**

The partitions created by TiVo when preparing a system use the allocation unit size of 1 MB (scaling value 0). However, when adding partitions, the **mfstool add** command uses a value of 4 MB (scaling value 2) in order not to overload your TiVo's memory when tracking relatively huge amounts of disk storage. To be safe, you should not use allocation unit values lower than 4 MB in most cases (scaling value "2"), so that the system has enough memory to perform maintenance and self-repair procedures whenever the system restarts. This is especially true on Series 1 machines, which have much less memory (16 MB) than Series 2 systems (32 MB).

◆   *-x drive1 drive2*   This option expands the set of MFS volume to use all available space on all drives listed in the **mfstool add** command line. This option creates extra partitions on each drive in order to use all existing space, and it also adds the new partitions to the list of partitions available to the TiVo. If a second drive is specified on the command line and that drives does not contain existing MFS volumes, the disk's partition table will be erased and recreated with only MFS volumes present. Any existing data on any new drive that is added to the MFS volume set will be lost.

◆ *-X drive*   This option expands the set of MFS volumes to use all available space on a single drive. This option is much like the -x option, but only creates TiVo partitions on a single drive, adding them to the storage available to hold recordings on that drive. This option can be specified multiple times on the same command line (as in the sample command, **mfstool add -X /dev/hda -X /dev/hdb**), but that's somewhat silly.

◆ *NewApp NewMedia*   These two command-line options enable you to specify the device names of a pair of MFS partitions (one application region, NewApp, and one associated media region, NewMedia) that will then be immediately added to the existing set of MFS volumes. In order for this command to work correctly, both partitions must already exist, and the partitions must be of the type "MFS."

## The mfstool backup Command

The mfstool suite's backup command enables you to back up the contents of one or more TiVo disks. If a single disk is specified, it must be the first or only disk from your TiVo; if two disks are specified, they must be specified in the order that they would be encountered on your TiVo (i.e., master first, and slave second).

Backups created using the **mfstool backup** command can be saved as files on various types of storage device (disk, tape, DVD, etc.) and can also be written to standard output so that the output of the mfstool backup command can immediately be used as input by a parallel **mfstool restore** command. This can be useful if you simply want to clone one disk to another or collapse two disks to a single disk without requiring the intermediate storage space that would otherwise be required by a backup file.

Given that you have to physically remove the drive(s) from your TiVo to back them up, TiVo backups aren't something that you want to perform as regularly as we all back up the personal data on our personal computers. (We all do back up our personal computers, right?) How to use the **mfstool backup** command to back up TiVo disks and when you should consider doing so is explained in Chapter 6, "Backing Up and Restoring TiVo Data." Using the mfstool backup command to provide input to a **mfstool restore** command in order to clone a disk is explained in the section of Chapter 6 entitled "Connecting Backup and Restore Commands Using a Pipe".

Command-line options for the **mfstool backup** command are as follows:

◆ *-[1-9]*   Create a compressed backup, with lower numbers indicating lower compression. While compressing a backup reduces the amount of space required to store the backup, it also increases the time required to perform the backup. Acceptable values for this option are −1 through −9; the recommended compression value is -6, which seems to provide the best trade-off between space savings and decreased performance due to the overhead of compressing the data.

- *-a*   Back up all of the data on the original disk(s). This maximizes the space required for the backup but preserves any recordings that you may have on the original disk(s).

- *-fN*   When backing up data from the specified disk(s), include all video streams with a filesystem identifier (**fsid**, in MFS terms) below *N*. The default value for *N* is 2000, because most of the nonprogrammatic filesystem data required for generic TiVo operation (primarily background animations and graphics files) has identifiers whose IDs are less than this value. These are rarely included in filesystem updates received from TiVo due to their size—TiVo assumes that you already have them on the system you are updating. They must therefore be included in backups to guarantee standard operation.

 **TIP**

When using the MFS Tools utilities to back up HDTV and DVD-enabled TiVos, you should use a higher FSID value than the default of 2000. A value of 5700 is often suggested—I tend to use 6000, just to be on the safe side, since 5700 doesn't seem to get all of the wireless-related settings.

- *-lN*   When backing up data from the specified disk(s), include all video streams whose size is less than *N* megabytes. Common values are 32 or 64 (MB). Using this option overrides any value specified with the -f option.

- *-o file*   Specifies the name of the output *file* to which backup data should write. Most backup files require between 200 and 900 MB of disk space. As with most Linux applications, a dash ('-') can be specified instead of a filename, which indicates that the backup should be written to standard output. In this case, the output of the **mfstool backup** command can be piped to an **mfstool restore** command, enabling you to clone one TiVo disk to another without requiring any intermediate disk space for the backup image.

- *-s*   Reduces the size of the backup image by shrinking the number and size of the TiVo volumes that you are backing up. This operation condenses all of the volumes recorded in the backup file, usually enabling multidisk backups to subsequently be restored to single disks that are at least the size of the original TiVo A drive. Any MFS filesystems that are not used will not be included in the backup.

- *-T*   Used with the -l option to specify that the number used for video stream size calculation will be the total amount of space allocated to a given video stream, rather than the amount of space that is actually used by the data that it contains. This option also causes the entire amount of space allocated to each file to be included in the backup, rather than the amount of space that is actually used by the data in the file.

- *-t*   Used with the -l option to specify that the number used for video stream size calculation will be the total amount of space actually used by that video stream, rather than the amount of space that is allocated to a given file on the disk. This option is especially useful in versions of the TiVo software greater than Version 2.0, where video streams could span multiple files.

◆ *-v* Excludes the /var directory from the backup. This directory is normally included because it is used by many system functions, but all of the necessary files and directories that it can contain will be recreated by your TiVo if the directory is not found when you power on your TiVo. Depending on the size of your /var directory, excluding it from backups using this option can reduce the size of your backups by up to 128 MB. Since most TiVo hacks are stored in the /var directory, this option can also be used to guarantee that a TiVo backup is as generic as possible, without including the fruits of your hacking experiments.

## The mfstool info Command

The mfstool suite's **info** command displays information about the MFS volumes on one or more disks that you identify on the command line. This is the same sort of information displayed by the **pdisk** command's "p" command, but does not display information about the standard Linux or swap volumes present on the specified disk(s).

## The mfstool restore Command

The mfstool suite's **restore** command restores backup files created using the **mfstool backup** command, and also automatically allocates any free space remaining on the target disk(s) to the TiVo MFS filesystem. This command will automatically create any MFS volume pairs necessary to enable your TiVo to take advantage of any free space available on the target disk(s), minus any fragments that fall outside the allocation boundaries of the MFS filesystem. Such fragments are portions of the free space on your disk that are smaller than the size of the allocation unit used when creating the MFS filesystem(s). You can think of these as the remainder of dividing the amount of free space on your disk by the size of your allocation units.

As you might expect, the **mfstool restore** command is the most complex and powerful of the commands in the mfstool command suite. Creating backup files is one thing, but restoring them, correctly handling any byte-swapping present in the backup file, analyzing any free space remaining on the target disk(s) when the operation completes, and automatically creating new MFS partitions to fill that space is a complex set of operations. However, doing all of these tasks using Version 2.0 or better of the MFS Tools command suite is far easier and less nerve-wracking than performing each of these tasks manually and in the right order.

Command-line options for the **mfstool restore** command are as follows:

◆ *-B* Disables automatic detection of byte swapping, forcing the restore to be done with byte-swapping.

◆ *-b* Disables auto-detection of byte swapping, forcing the restore to occur without byte-swapping. This option is necessary when restoring backups made to the TiVo Series 2 with Version 1 of MFS Tools.

◆ *-C* Restricts the restore process to use LBA28 rather than LBA48, even if 48-bit logical block addressing is supported by the kernel. This option is only available in the latest versions of the MFS Tools utilities (such as the one on the CD that accompanies this book), and should be used when restoring backups to disks that will be used in TiVos running software Versions 4.x and earlier.

◆ *-i file*   Identifies the file from which backup data should be read. As with most Linux applications, a dash (-) can be specified instead of a filename, which indicates that the backup should be read from standard output. In this case, the **mfstool restore** command can read backup information piped to it from an **mfstool backup** command, enabling you to clone one TiVo disk to another without requiring any intermediate disk space for the backup image.

◆ *-l*   Does not fill up the partition table on the target drive, providing the opportunity to subsequently add another pair of MFS volumes to the target disk(s). Of course, this option cannot guarantee that there will actually be free space available on the target drive(s), so it can not guarantee that it will be possible to add additional MFS volumes. This option is implied when the **-x** option is used.

◆ *-p*   Causes the restore process to attempt to optimize the partition layout to provide optimal performance based on the disk/data access patterns used by TiVo machines. Using this option attempts to minimizes disk head movement by positioning frequently-accessed application data in the middle of the disk(s) and storing video data on the outside cylinders of the disk(s).

◆ *-q*   Suppresses the progress display that is typically displayed when executing a restore operation. Specifying this option twice suppresses all status information, displaying only error messages if any occur.

◆ *-r scale*   This option enables you to trade off between the amount of RAM required to track disk usage on your TiVo drives and the efficiency of the storage used on those drives. The TiVo's MFS partitions can store data in 1, 2, 4, 8, or 16 MB allocation units. Choosing a smaller allocation unit size increases the efficiency of your TiVo's storage, because less space will be "wasted" when recordings do not completely fill an allocation unit. However, because more allocation units are required to store a recording if the allocation units themselves are smaller, the TiVo uses more memory when tracking smaller allocation units. For example, assume that the allocation unit was 16 MB and the TiVo was trying to store a recording that required 20 MB of disk space. This would require two allocation units and would completely fill the first one but waste 12 MB of disk space in the second. In order to keep track of the recording, the TiVo would have to keep information about both allocation units in memory. On the other hand, with an allocation unit of 4 MB, the recording would require 5 allocation units but no disk space would be wasted. However, the TiVo would have to keep information about 5 allocation units in memory to keep track of that recording.

Acceptable values for this option are 0 (corresponding to a 1 MB allocation unit), 1 (corresponding to a 2 MB allocation unit), 2 (corresponding to a 4 MB allocation unit), 3 (corresponding to an 8 MB allocation unit), and 4 (corresponding to a 16 MB allocation unit). In general, the larger the allocation unit value, the less RAM will be used (making the TiVo more responsive when displaying menus, changing and processing options, and so on), but the greater the amount of storage that may be wasted when storing recordings.

◆ *-s size* Specifies the size in megabytes of the swap partition to create when restoring from backups. The default size of a TiVo swap partition is 64 MB, but can be increased up to 511 MB by using this option. A swap partition larger than 64 MB is required when your TiVo contains drives that provide more than 120 MB of storage for recordings. Larger swap partitions can also provide substantial performance improvements on TiVo machines with large drives or ones that run relatively large numbers of programs (e.g., TiVoWeb, FTPD, and Telnet come to mind). When upgrading TiVo drives, it is always a good idea to set the swap space to 128 MB (by specifying a numeric value of 127, like any good C program would expect).

 **WARNING**

Version 2 of the MFS Tools has a bug in which using any value larger than 127 does not correctly initialize the swap partition header. You can allocate larger swap partitions when using the **mfstool restore** command, but they will not work correctly until initialized on your TiVo using the **mkswap** command on your TiVo or by using the **tpip** utility discussed later in this chapter.

◆ *-v size* Specifies the size in megabytes of the /var partition that should be created when restoring from backups. The default size of the /var partition is 128 MB, which you may want to increase if you are planning to install significant amounts of extra software (such as your favorite hacks).

◆ *-X drive* Extends the MFS volume set to fill the specified *drive*. This is similar to the -x option but only fills a single drive rather than all available drives. Multiple instances of this command can be specified on the **mfstool restore** command line (for example, -X /dev/hda -X /dev/hdb), which is interesting but rarely useful.

◆ *-x* Extends the MFS volume set to fill all of the drives onto which backup data is restored. Using this option creates extra pairs of FS partitions on the target drive(s) and adds entries for them to the table of usable space available on the TiVo, even if they are not actually required to save the data that you are restoring.

◆ *-z* Zeroes out any partitions that were not backed up, such as the inactive bootstrap, kernel, and root partitions, as well as the **/var** partition if it is not in use. Swap space is automatically recreated, and is not zeroed out. Using this option may slightly increase the time required to restore your TiVo data but ensures that the TiVo cannot attempt to use these partitions.

## Pdisk

The **pdisk** (Partition Disk) utility was originally developed for users of early versions of Linux on Macintosh and other systems that used processors in the Motorola 68000 (aka 68K) family. Although Linux already provides similar utilities such as **fdisk**, **cfdisk**, and **sfdisk**, a separate utility was developed for Macintosh systems for at least two of the following reasons:

◆ Summary information about the partitions on Macintosh hard disks (known as the *partition map*) is stored differently than it is on any other type of system.

◆ Instructions and data are stored and used in a different order on 68000 and related processors, compared to how they are stored on x86 and Pentium-class processors. (More about this later in this section.)

◆ It was an opportunity to write yet another utility program.

◆ The author of **pdisk** didn't like the way any other Linux disk partitioning tool worked.

On computer systems that use Motorola 68000 chips or their successors, the PowerPC (PPC) chips, instructions, and data are byte-swapped, compared to the order of x86 and Pentium-class instructions and data. If you envision a computer instruction as consisting of two side-by-side bytes, 68000 and PPC read these bytes from right to left, while x86 and similar processors read the bytes left to right. This is known as their *byte-order*—68K and PPC chips are known as *big-endian* (because they read from the "big" or "top" end of a word), while x86 and Pentium-class processors are known as *little-endian*.

Thanks to improvements in higher-end TiVo utilities, such as the MFS Tools and BlessTiVo (itself largely outmoded), it is rarely necessary to use the **pdisk** utility to do most common TiVo tasks. Before BlessTiVo and MFS Tools provided features for automatically creating and adding new partitions, **pdisk** was the only utility in town for doing these sorts of things. However, **pdisk** can still be extremely useful to TiVo hackers because it enables you to manually create partitions of different types, including partitions in the standard Linux **ext2** and swap filesystem types.

 **NOTE**

Like most disk partitioning utilities, **pdisk** focuses on creating and manipulating a disk's partition map (aka *partition table*). Some types of filesystems, such as the TiVo's MFS filesystem, are automatically initialized when an unformatted partition of a specific type is detected. Other types of partitions, such as the Linux **ext2** and swap partitions cannot be used until they have been specially formatted for use as those types of filesystems, using programs such as **ext2fs** and **mkswap**.

The **pdisk** command can be used in two different ways: with command-line options that simply display information and exit, or in interactive mode, where you can enter additional commands to execute specific **pdisk** functionality until you decide to terminate the **pdisk** command. The remainder of this section begins by providing a summary of popular **pdisk** command-line options, and then provides an overview of the internal options provided by the **pdisk** command. For complete information about **pdisk** options, download the source code and associated online reference information for **pdisk** from a URL such as **http://tivohack.sourceforge.net**.

## TiVo Changing Byte-Orders in Mid-Stream

As discussed earlier in this book, Series 1 models use a PPC processor, so it was quite natural for Series 1 machines to adopt the Macintosh partitioning and disk/data format conventions. Series 2 systems use MIPS processors, which can be used as either little-endian or big-endian processors. This was an interesting quandary for TiVo, which obviously had a big investment in the software and tools they had developed for the Series 1, especially system-level software such as the MFS filesystem. All TiVo software obviously had to be recompiled for the Series 2 systems, because MIPS processors use different instructions than PowerPC processors, but recompiling something is different than rewriting it. It's a common misconception that the reason that Series 1 and Series 2 TiVos use different byte-ordering is due to the change in processors, and that Series 2 machines therefore use the MIPS processor in little-endian mode. In reality, examining the TiVo kernel source and the ideturbo (high-speed IDE) module shows that the change in byte-ordering is actually due to extra calls to the `idetivo_bswap_data()` function—in other words, this is totally intentional. Having the kernel source is a great mechanism for a little high-tech detective work. Series 2 TiVos use the MIPS processor in big-endian mode.

The change in byte-ordering between Series 1 and Series 2 TiVos is a small change, but is something that you have to be aware of when you're hacking your TiVo, especially when restoring backups created with different versions of the MFS Tools utilities. For example, Version 1.0 of the MFS Tools utilities is hardwired to use big-endian, PPC byte-ordering because that was the way all TiVo data was organized when Version 1.0 of the MFS Tools utilities was released. Version 2.0 and later of the MFS Tools utilities tries to automatically detect the appropriate type of byte-ordering to use, but can't easily do this since these utilities are designed to run on a PC rather than running natively on the TiVo. For this reason, Versions 2.0 and greater of the MFS Tools utilities add extra command-line options (**-b** and **-B**) that enable you to restore backups created with Version 1.0 of the software, changing the byte-order however you'd like.

 **TIP**

Most versions of the **pdisk** command ignore the first few sectors of the drive where the bootpage is stored. If you format a new disk using the **pdisk** command, you will either need to subsequently use the **bootpage** command to write a valid bootpage or use the **dd** command to bring over the first few sectors from an existing drive.

The following example shows the output of the **pdisk** command, displaying a listing of the partition table on a stock TiVo Series 1 with a 20 MB Quantum disk:

```
# pdisk -l /dev/hdd
Partition map (with 512 byte blocks) on '/dev/hdd'
```

| #: type | name | length | base |
|---|---|---|---|
| ( size ) | | | |
| 1: Apple_partition_map | Apple | 63 | @ 1 |
| 2: Image | Bootstrap 1 | 4096 | @ 64 |
| ( 2.0M) | | | |
| 3: Image | Kernel 1 | 4096 | @ 4160 |
| ( 2.0M) | | | |
| 4: Ext2 | Root 1 | 262144 | @ 8256 |
| (128.0M) | | | |
| 5: Image | Bootstrap 2 | 4096 | @ 270400 |
| ( 2.0M) | | | |
| 6: Image | Kernel 2 | 4096 | @ 274496 |
| ( 2.0M) | | | |
| 7: Ext2 | Root 2 | 262144 | @ 278592 |
| (128.0M) | | | |
| 8: Swap | Linux swap | 260096 | @ 540736 |
| (127.0M) | | | |
| 9: Ext2 | /var | 262144 | @ 800832 |
| (128.0M) | | | |
| 10: MFS | MFS application region | 1048576 | @ 1062976 |
| (512.0M) | | | |
| 11: MFS | MFS media region | 24777728 | @ 2111552 |
| ( 11.8G) | | | |
| 12: MFS | New MFS Application | 1024 | @ 26889280 |
| 13: MFS | New MFS Media | 17104896 | @ 26890304 |
| ( 8.2G) | | | |
| 14: Apple_Free | Extra | 4000 | @ 43995200 |
| ( 2.0M) | | | |

Commonly used **pdisk** command-line options are as follows:

- ◆ *-h*   Displays a usage message for the **pdisk** command and then exits.
- ◆ *-i device*   Starts the **pdisk** command in interactive mode, examining the specified *device*. When running **pdisk** in this mode, you can update any aspect of the specified *device* as long as you have sufficient privileges to do so.
- ◆ *-l device*   Lists the partitions on the specified *device* and then exits.
- ◆ *-r device*   Starts the **pdisk** command in read-only mode, examining the specified *device*. When using **pdisk** in this form, you cannot make any changes to any aspects of the data or partition map for the specified *device*.

◆ *-v*    Displays the version and compilation date of the version of the **pdisk** command that you are using.

You can enter pdisk's interactive mode by using the **-i** command-line option or simply by executing the **pdisk** command followed by the name of the disk you are interested in examining or working with. The most commonly used commands in pdisk's interactive mode are the following:

◆ *C type*    Creates a new partition of the specified *type*.

◆ *c*    Creates a new PPC Linux partition of type **ext2**. The partition is not immediately ready for use—a filesystem must subsequently be created on that partition through the use of the **ext2fs** command.

◆ *d n*    Deletes partition *n*.

◆ *h*    Displays a quick reference list of the **pdisk** commands that are currently available, including a short description of each.

◆ *i*    Initializes the partition map, deleting any existing entries.

◆ *n name*    Assigns the specified *name* to a partition.

◆ *P*    Prints the current partition map, ordered by the base address.

◆ *p*    Prints the current partition table, ordered by the partition number.

◆ *q*    Quits **pdisk** without saving any changes that you have made.

◆ *r n m*    Reorders the entry for partition *n* to entry *m* in the partition map.

◆ *s n*    Changes the size of the partition map to *n* bytes.

◆ *w*    Writes the partition table to disk, saving any changes that you have made.

◆ *x*    Enters expert mode. Once in expert mode, the most useful expert-level commands are as follows:

  ◆ *?*    Displays a quick reference list of the commands available in expert mode, along with short command descriptions.

  ◆ *M n*    Clears the bit identifying partition *n* as an MFS media partition.

  ◆ *m n*    Sets the bit identifying partition *n* as an MFS media partition.

  ◆ *Q*    Exits expert mode and the **pdisk** command without saving any changes that you may have made.

  ◆ *q*    Exits expert mode and returns you to the **pdisk** command's standard interactive mode.

## TiVoMad Utilities

Although largely supplanted by later versions of the MFS Tools utilities, the TiVoMad utilities were an important landmark in TiVo hacking software, and can still be used to upgrade and expand the Series 1 TiVo. For a variety of reasons, explained later in this section, they cannot be used with Series 2 machines. However, since they still work for Series 1 systems and are easily found all over the net (and on the CD that accompanies this book, when mounted in a Series 1 system, byte-swapped mode), they're certainly worth discussing here.

**NOTE**

In general, you should use the latest versions of the MFS Tools rather than the TiVoMad utilities to add a larger or second disk to your TiVo. The MFS Tools and their command-line options are discussed later in this chapter, and their use is explained in Chapter 6, "Expanding Your TiVo's Storage Capacity."

The TiVoMad utilities are a set of scripts, libraries, and executables that enable you to expand the size of the primary drive in your TiVo and to optionally add a second disk at the same time, further expanding your TiVo's storage capacity. TiVoMad (aka Trevor Heartfield) was an early TiVo hacker in the UK who simplified the process of expanding TiVo disk storage by writing a wrapper script that "did the right thing" by using TiVo utilities and libraries that were provided as part of the package.

The basic situation that the TiVoMad utilities are designed for is when you have cloned an existing drive to a larger drive and want to make the additional space on the larger drive available to your TiVo to store additional recording. You can also add a second drive at the same time, and the TiVoMad utilities will make the space that it contains available to your TiVo.

### TiVo With This Software, I Thee Wed

Although discussed in more detail later, it's important to know that when you add a second drive to your TiVo, the two drives are "married" and must be used together. You cannot subsequently remove the second drive and expect your Series 1 system to work correctly with only the A drive. To "un-marry" two drives, you must back them up using the MFS Tools utilities (discussed later in this chapter) and then restore the backup to a single drive, assuming that the single drive has sufficient space to hold the TiVo data that was contained on the previous two drives. This single drive can be used by itself, and then you can recycle the two drives that are its logical parents.

The TiVoMad utilities will only work on Series 1 systems because the utilities and libraries that it installs and attempts to run after rebooting your TiVo are compiled for PPC systems, such as the Series 1 TiVo. They will not run on the MIPS-based Series 2 TiVos, and may actually mess up your machine because some of the libraries that they replace are required for normal functioning of your TiVo.

The TiVoMad utilities are typically found on the Net packaged in two different ways—either bundled in a bootable floppy disk image or in subdirectories of one of the bootable CDs that are available for your TiVo, including the BATBD CD that is provided with this book. Once you have mounted the latter CD (not just booted from it), the TiVoMad utilities are found in the TiVoMad directory as the directories **mad31** and **mad32** (for Versions 3.1 and 3.2 of the software), with a symbolic link to the **mad32** directory (simply referred to as **mad**) to show that this is the latest and greatest version of the utilities. A text file providing additional information about the TiVoMad utilities is also present in this directory.

# TPIP

Todd Miller's **tpip** utility is a handy tool that performs a number of basic tasks such as installing a new kernel, increasing swap space size, displaying partition information, and displaying or updating bootpage information. Thanks, Todd! Originally designed to simplify installing Todd's custom kernels that support disks greater than 137 GB, **tpip** is an excellent example of feature creep in the positive direction. Todd's Web site, providing a good deal of basic TiVo information as well as hosting the latest versions of **tpip** and Todd's enhanced kernels, is located at **http://www.courtesan.com/tivo**. The source code and x86 and TiVo **tpip** binaries are also located in the tpip-1.1 directory on the BATBD CD that accompanies this book.

 **NOTE**

For acronym fans, **tpip** takes its name from the old PIP (Peripheral Interchange Program) utility used to copy and manipulate files on the DEC-10 and CP/M operating systems. Thankfully, Todd didn't preserve PIP's broken syntax—PIP is almost legendary for specifying the name of the file/disk that you are copying to as the first part of its argument list and the name of the file/disk that you are copying from as the second part of the argument list. This is, of course, backward from the popular notion of "copy source-file destination-file." Those wacky DEC guys! Historians, please see **http://www.iso.port.ac.uk/~mike/interests/chistory/documents/cpm-22-manual/ch1.html#Section_1.6.4.**

 **TIP**

If you want to use the **tpip** utility to install one of Todd Miller's LBA-48 kernel on a disk that can hold more than 137GB, you must have restored your backups to the disk *without* using the **mfstool restore** command's **–C** option, and you must have booted from the LBA-enabled kernel (**bigs2**) on the BATBD CD that is provided in this book, even if you are restoring your backups to a Series 1 TiVo.

Like the MFS Tools backup and restore utilities, **tpip** is a smart application that will do byte-swapping as needed when working with TiVo disks, either natively on a TiVo or when installed in a PC booted from a CD, such as the BATBD CD. Todd is a BSD guy, so you can also run **tpip** from an OpenBSD system if you recompile it for that type of system.

The general syntax of the **tpip** command is:

```
tpip [options] device
```

The *device* argument is the basename of your TiVo disk, such as /dev/hda, /dev/hdb, and so on.

The **tpip** command provides the following command-line options:

◆ *-a*   Operate on the alternate kernel partition instead of the primary one. This option can also be specified as **--alternate**. The alternate kernel partition is identified in the bootpage of the TiVo disk, and can be identified by using tpip's **-b** option or the **bootpage -a** *diskname* command, as explained earlier in this chapter.

◆ *-b*   Print the values for the primary and alternate boot partitions and the boot parameters. This option can also be specified as **--bootpage**. The boot and alternate boot partitions can also be identified by using the **bootpage -b -a** *diskname* command, as explained earlier in this chapter.

◆ *-k file*   Write the kernel image in the specified file to the target device. This option can also be specified as **--kernel=***file*.

◆ *-P "bootparams"*   Set the boot parameters in the boot page to the string supplied as *bootparams*. This option can also be specified as **--parameters=***"bootparams"*.

◆ *-p*   Print the partition table on the target device. This option can also be specified as **--partitions**.

◆ *-o file*   Save the current kernel image on the target device to the specified *file*. This option can also be specified as **--old_kernel=***file*.

◆ *-S*   Tells **tpip** that the TiVo disk has been mounted with byte-swapping enabled. You should use this if you have booted using the BATBD disk's **s1swap** boot option or manually specified the **hd***X***=bswap** kernel option when booting a Linux system to which your TiVo drive is attached. This option can also be specified as **--swapped**.

◆ *-s*   Writes a Version 1 (new-style) swap header for any swap partitions found on the target device. Note that you must use a kernel that supports Version 1 swap partitions. The stock TiVo kernel only supports the older, Version 0 swap partitions, which are limited to 128 MB. This option can also be specified as **--mkswap**.

 **TIP**

The **tpip** command's **-s** option is extremely useful to correct the bug in the v2.0 MFS Tools application's swap-size (**-s**) option. If you use MFS Tools to create a larger swap partition when restoring a TiVo backup, you can then run **tpip** to install a custom kernel and use the **-s** option to correctly initialize the swap file header. However, you must only use this option if you are using a nonstandard TiVo kernel—in other words, one that supports Version 1 swap headers. Do not use this option unless you are using a TiVo kernel that was (1) not created by TiVo, Inc., and (2), that you are sure understands Version 1 swap files.

◆ *-V*   Displays the version of **tpip** that you are running and exits without doing anything else. This option can also be specified as **--version**.

◆ *-v*   Causes **tpip** to be more verbose about what it is doing, and displays internal information, such as whether **tpip** believes that the target device is a Series 1 or Series 2 TiVo disk. This option can also be specified as **–verbose**.

As an example, the following **tpip** command line would write the kernel in the file new-s1-kernel to the TiVo disk available as /dev/hdb, save the old kernel to the file old-s1-kernel, and write a version 1 swap header to the swap partition on the same disk:

```
tpip -k new-s1-kernel -o old-s1-kernel -s /dev/hde
```

Additional information about the **tpip** command is available from its page on Todd's Web site: **http://www.courtesan.com/tivo/tpip.html**.

# Useful Linux Tools Outside Most Tools Disks

TiVos are Linux systems, so it isn't surprising that there are a huge number of standard Linux tools that can be useful when hacking your TiVo. This section provides an overview of the most popular of these, all of which are found on the BATBD CD that is included with this book.

The commands described in the previous section are TiVo-specific hacking tools; the ones in this section are just generic Linux tools that will be useful when hacking or simply poking around in your TiVo. The commands in this section are all tools that you will want to run on your x86 system while one or more TiVo disks are attached. These are not commands that you want or need to cross-compile to execute them on your TiVo. Standard Linux commands that are already preinstalled on your TiVo or that you may want to recompile for your TiVo (or install from precompiled versions provided on the BATBD disk) are discussed in Chapter 9 in the section entitled "Popular Linux Software for the TiVo."

## GenROMFS

The **genromfs** command generates a ROM (Read-Only Memory) filesystem image from the contents of a specified directory. ROM filesystems are used on your TiVo to trick it into executing a user-defined set of commands when the system boots. Ordinarily, a TiVo running Versions 2.5 and later of the TiVo software checks the contents of the system's startup files to make sure that the system has not been hacked. (For more information about the details of how the TiVo verifies these files, see the section of Chapter 9 entitled "The TiVo Startup Process.") Creating your own ROM filesystem enables you to cause the TiVo to execute commands stored in this filesystem by using the procedure described in the section of Chapter 7 entitled "Getting a Command Prompt on Your TiVo." This section simply explains the syntax of the **genromfs** command—we'll save the fun stuff for Chapter 7.

The **genromfs** command takes the following command-line options:

- ◆ *-A alignment,pattern*   Aligns all objects matching *pattern* to at least *alignment* bytes, where *alignment* must be at least 16 bytes and must also be a power of 2.
- ◆ *-a alignment*   Aligns regular file data to *alignment* bytes, where *alignment* must be at least 16 bytes and must also be a power of 2.

◆ *-d directory* Uses the specified *directory* as the source of the files that will be written to the ROM filesystem image file. The files and directories in the specified *directory* will appear in the root directory of the ROM filesystem image that you are creating.

◆ *-f file* Writes the ROM filesystem image into the specified *file*.

◆ *-h* Displays a usage message listing the command-line options available for use with the **genromfs** command.

◆ *-V volumename* Assigns the specified *volumename* to the ROM filesystem that you are creating. This is not the name of the file to which the ROM filesystem image will be written, but the internal volume identifier contained in the ROM filesystem.

◆ *-v* Provides verbose output when executing the **genromfs** command.

◆ *-x pattern* Excludes all objects matching *pattern* when creating the ROM filesystem image. Any objects matching *pattern* will not be included in the ROM filesystem image. The specified *pattern* can be any string of characters, and is used as a substring when checking against the names of items that could potentially be written to the ROM filesystem. The specified *pattern* can also use standard Linux/Unix regular expression syntax as long as it is quoted to prevent wildcard characters from being expanded on the **genromfs** command line rather than internally by the **genromfs** command itself. For example, to match any filename containing the words "foo" and "bar," separated by any number of characters, you could use the regular expression **foo*bar**, but you would have to enclose this string within single quotation marks on the **genromfs** command line to prevent the shell from expanding the asterisk wildcard.

# HexEdit

The **hexedit** (hexadecimal editor) command enables you to modify files, disks, and disk partitions directly. On Linux and Unix systems, disk and disk partitions are a series of bytes just like any file in those filesystems, and therefore can be opened, read, and written by any command that can access regular files. As shown in Chapter 2, the **hexedit** command is an interactive, screen-oriented command that makes it easy to search and modify the contents of a disk, disk partition, or file in both ASCII and hexadecimal modes. Figure 5.1 shows a sample hexedit screen.

The **hexedit** command is provided on the BATBD disk that accompanies this book, and is also available as part of the Knoppix Linux distribution. For the truly adventurous, you can read more about the **hexedit** command on its home page at the URL **http://www.chez.com/ prigaux/hexedit.html**. If you find that a newer version is available, and you want to download and compile it yourself, the source is available at the URL **http://merd.net/pixel/hexedit- version.src.tgz,** where *version* is the dot-separated version of the hexedit program. At the time that this book was written, the latest version was Version 1.2.4, which is the version that is provided on the CD that accompanies this book.

**FIGURE 5.1** *Editing a partition using the Linux hexedit utility*

## Script

The **script** command is a standard Linux/Unix utility that captures a transcript of all of the input and output from a single shell until you terminate the script command. It is part of the **linux-utils** package that is part of almost every Linux distribution. The default output file to which everything you type, and every response to each of those commands is captured, is **typescript**. You can write output to a specific file by supplying its name on the **script** command line. If the file does not already exist, it will be created. If the file already exists, its existing contents will be overwritten, so be careful.

Although not a useful diagnostic tool in its own right, the **script** command can be quite useful if you are having problems getting specific commands to work or if you are receiving odd error messages. By keeping a transcript of the shell in which you executed a specific command, you can then exchange this information with other knowledgeable TiVo hackers who may be able to identify the source of the problem once they can see exactly what's happening. For this reason, a copy of the **script** command is included on the BATBD disk for your convenience.

# *Boot Disks*

Previous sections of this chapter discussed various utilities for your TiVo, explaining the function of each and the various options that each provides to customize its behavior. Random collections of software are interesting, but the real key to actually using them successfully is packaging them—making them available for easy use. Packaging system-level software for a system like the TiVo is a more interesting challenge than simply packaging a single application so that you can install it on your current operating system. TiVo systems, and therefore most TiVo-related utilities, run under the Linux operating system and require the power and flexibility of specially-tuned versions of the Linux kernel and core libraries in order to work successfully.

Linux is discussed in greater detail in Chapter 9, but the key fact at this point is that most TiVo utilities require Linux to work correctly. Installing a separate operating system on the personal computer of every potential TiVo hacker is an obvious alternative, but hardly a reasonable solution. Most people use and depend on software that runs under operating systems such as Apple's Mac OS and Microsoft's Windows. While disk space is cheap, installing other operating systems and configuring a home computer to choose between them is impractical.

A practical solution for using tools that run under another operating system is to prepare stand-alone, bootable disks that enable you to run that operating system for as long you need it in order to use those tools. Most modern personal computers can easily be configured to boot from removable media, such as floppy disks and CDs, without requiring any changes to the existing software and operating system that are installed on the system's hard drive. Boot from these, run the tools that they provide, then remove them and reboot the system—no fuss, no muss, no messy dual-booting.

 **NOTE**

This section is in no way a suggestion that people should not run Linux as their primary operating system. It is simply a recognition of the fact that most people could care less what operating system is running on their PCs, and would probably prefer not to know. An operating system exists to enable people to run the software that they need to accomplish whatever they need to accomplish. Since 75 percent of the commercial, home-user software available today is targeted at Windows machines, most people run Windows. Sad but true for a Linux and Mac OS X fan like myself.

Linux is a product of the open source movement, which states that the source code for software should (or must) be freely available. In the case of every aspiring TiVo hacker, Linux and open source means that it's relatively easy for TiVo fanatics to create bootable floppy disks and CDs that contain all of the tools that you may need to hack your TiVo and to freely distribute them. Floppy disks are small and therefore have obvious limitations in terms of how much software they can contain, but their contents are easily downloaded for the same reason. Now that almost every personal computer system has a CD drive, CDs are the way to go whenever possible—they can hold around 600 MB, which is sufficient to hold the operating system and a good-sized collection of relevant software.

Distributing free, bootable floppies and CDs presents an interesting problem. It's easy enough to distribute the software that they contain, but producing a bootable disk is slightly more complex than just installing application software. To be bootable, any media must have boot information in a special location on the disk (the boot block), and must provide special files relevant to the operating system that it provides. These files must also have special names, special attributes, and even must be located in special locations on the disk. Not an easy thing to expect every home computer user to do—most people want to use the hammer rather than making one.

To simplify distributing bootable media, most bootable tools disks are distributed as disk images. Floppy disk images usually have the extension IMG to show that they are a floppy image. CD images usually have the extension ISO to show that these are images of disks in the International Standard Organization 9660 format—a common, portable format for CDs that can be read by multiple types of computer systems. These image files come with special programs that write them directly to the floppy or CD. Rather than writing images to the floppy or CD as standard files and directories, these programs literally start writing at the beginning of the floppy or CD and stop at the end.

Like any software, the programs used to write floppies and CDs are operating system-specific—meaning that you use different programs, depending on the type of computer that you have and the operating system that it runs. Windows users can use programs such as Nero; Mac OS X users can use iTunes or Roxio's (formerly Adaptec's) Toast program; Linux and Unix users can use programs such as **dd** or **cdrecord**. There are many more such utilities for each of these operating systems—these are just my personal favorites. If you want to create (*burn*) your own copies of a TiVo tools disk from an IMG or ISO file, the programs required to do so will be discussed later in this book, along with a general discussion of the TiVo tools that are available for that operating system.

Earlier sections of this book have stressed the differences between Series 1 and Series 2 machines, but nowhere is this difference more important than when deciding which tools disk you want to use when hacking your machine. Selecting the right tools disk is the high-tech equivalent of choosing between buying Torx or slotted screwdrivers—you cannot get the job done if you select the wrong type. In the case of some of the system software provided on TiVo tools disks, you can even permanently screw up your TiVo by selecting the wrong disk. Table 5.1 shows the mapping between tools disks and TiVo models. Make sure that you select the right one!

**Table 5.1    Characteristics of Various TiVo Tools Disks**

| Tools Disk | Type | TiVo Types Disk Series 1 | Is Usable On Series 2 |
|---|---|---|---|
| Dylan's | Floppy | Yes | No |
| TiVoMad | Floppy | Yes | No |
| Kazamyr | CD | Yes | No |
| Johnny Death | CD | With Care | Yes |
| BATBD | CD | Yes | Yes |
| Sleeper | CD | With Care | Yes |
| Knoppix | CD | Somewhat | Somewhat |

The remainder of this section discusses the most common bootable TiVo tools disks available on the Internet, highlighting the type(s) of TiVos that each is designed to work with, the tools that each contains, and any specifics that you need to know when hacking your TiVo using that specific boot disk.

---

 **NOTE**

While you can instantly boot your Pentium-class personal computer using any of the bootable TiVo tools disks discussed in this section, you won't be able to do much unless you have put the disk that you want to work with in your PC. This should either be a new disk that you are preparing for use with your TiVo or an existing TiVo drive. Removing disks from your TiVo and installing new or existing TiVo disks into your PC is explained in the section of Chapter 3 entitled "Working with TiVo Disk Drives."

The discussion of the TiVo tools disks in this section focuses on explaining the contents of the most popular TiVo tools disks. Information on using them is provided in the more task-oriented chapters of this book, such as Chapter 5 ("Backing Up and Restoring Your TiVo data"), Chapter 7 ("Expanding Your TiVo's Storage Capacity"), and Chapter 8 ("Connecting the Universe to Your TiVo").

# BATBD—Bill's Accumulated TiVo Boot Disk

I'm obviously a fan of the bootable TiVo tools disk that comes with this book, BATBD, since I put it together. The name stands for "Bill's Accumulated TiVo Boot Disk," which is intended to highlight the fact that most of the tools on this disk have been rolled up from other TiVo boot disks. Although I built and added a few of my favorite utilities (hexedit, script, etc.), most of the value that this disk provides is that it is designed to work with both Series 1 and Series 2 systems, uses up-to-date kernels, provides preassembled collections of TiVo software that you can easily install on your TiVo, and that it also contains ready-to-install compilers for desktop systems that will enable you to compile your own software. It also makes a dandy coaster.

When you boot your personal computer from the BATBD CD, the boot menu gives you three boot options: working with a Series 2 machine, working with a Series 1 system in byte-swapped mode so that you can mount and access TiVo partitions, and working with a Series 1 model in standard byte-order with Directory Memory Access (DMA) enabled to improve performance when backing up your Series 1. Each of these boot options loads a Linux filesystem that is created in your personal computer's memory. These types of filesystems are generally known as Random-Access Memory (RAM) disks, because they are portions of memory that are configured to look like an actual disk drive to your personal computer. In the case of Linux systems, these are referred to as initial RAM disks, because they are RAM disks that provide the initial filesystem for Linux.

**WARNING**

If you have problems booting from the CD and are running Windows XP, disconnect the primary Windows XP hard drive and reboot.

Each of the initial RAM disks provided by the BATBD disk is tailored to the type of TiVo with which you are going to be working. The BATBD initial RAM disks contain all of the tools (MFS Tools, BlessTiVo, BootPage, PDisk, and so on) discussed in this book for both Series 1 and Series 2 machines—in other words, everything that you will need to back up, restore, and hack your TiVo. The initial RAM disk used by the Series 1 boot options also provides two versions of the TiVoMad utilities for your convenience—using the latest one (3.2) is generally preferable, but you may want to use the older version if your TiVo is running a software release prior to Version 2.0.1.

Another key difference between the BATBD disk and the other TiVo tools disks is the software that the CD provides beyond the scope of the bootable kernel and associated initial RAM disks. Linux systems that boot from a CD load the Linux kernel and associated initial RAM disk into memory, but the CD itself can still contain files and directories that aren't required by the boot process. These aren't available to you until you actually mount the CD, which is Linux-speak for making it available to users so that you can go to that directory and explore its contents.

Installing the software found on the BATBD disk—once you've booted from it—is explained in Chapter 11, "Getting and Installing New Software for Your TiVo." The following items are found in various directories of the mounted BATBD disk:

◆ *bootpage*   A directory containing the source code and Series 1 and Series 2 binaries for tridge's enhanced version of the bootpage utility.

◆ *connectivity*   A directory containing TiVo software for connecting to and communicating with other systems.

◆ *DOS*   A directory containing DOS utilities for unlocking older TiVo hard disks. This directory includes a bootable DOS floppy image that also contains these utilities.

◆ *floppy*   A directory that contains an image of a bootable floppy disk that contains the MFS tools. This directory also contains the RAWRITE.EXE utility used to create a bootable disk from this image file under Microsoft Windows systems.

◆ *hack_dirs*   A directory that contains archive files of complete directories of utilities that have already been compiled for your TiVo, and which are correctly organized so as to make them easy to install on your TiVo. These archive files are stored in the Linux **tar** format. Installing these archives on your TiVo is explained in Chapter 11. All of the software that these archives contain is freely available on the Internet, but as single files and utilities that you would have to download one at a time. Since I've been accumulating these programs for years and have already organized them into the directory structure that they require, sharing them with the readers of this book in an easy-to-install, easy-to-use format seemed like "the right thing to do."

- *HISTORY*   A text file that gives the history of changes made to different versions of the BATBD CD.

- *img*   A directory that contains the files that can be assembled into a hacker's ROM filesystem for 3.x TiVos by using the **genromfs** utility.

- *img_monte*   A directory that contains the files that can be assembled into a hacker's ROM filesystem that uses monte to bootstrap a hacked kernel from a standard one.

- *initrds*   A directory containing replacement initial RAM disks and related utilities, for use when monte'ing a Series 2 system.

- *isolinux*   A directory used by the CD boot process.

- *kernel_modules*   A directory containing loadable kernel modules and related utilities for Series 1 and Series 2 TiVos.

- *killinitrd*   A directory containing versions of a utility used to remove an initial RAM disk (initrd) from various versions of the TiVo kernel.

- *lba48_s1_kernels*   A directory containing Todd Miller's enhanced LBA48 kernels for Series 1 TiVos, which support disk sizes larger than 137 GB on your Series 1 TiVo.

- *macintosh*   TiVo-related utilities for use on a Macintosh personal computer running Mac OS X.

- *man*   Preprocessed versions of the online reference pages for various TiVo and Linux utilities.

- *mfs_ftp*   A directory containing a pointer to the mfs_ftp download site and various utilities related to mfs_ftp.

- *monte-mips*   A directory that contains the Two-Kernel Monte software required to successfully boot hacked versions of later Series 2 machines.

- *mplayer*   A directory containing Linux and Windows versions of the mplayer utility that can play unencrypted TiVo streams. This directory also includes source code for this version of mplayer and related utilities.

- *old_mfstool2.0*   A directory containing the official MFS Tools 2.0 release. This is the version that was widely available before these utilities were released as open source, and is provided in case problems surface with the updated open source version.

- *scrambling*   A directory containing various loadable kernel modules for unscrambling encrypted video on DirecTiVo units.

- *settings-backup*   TCL scripts for backing up personalized information on your TiVo.

- *src*   Source code for many of the TiVo-specific utilities that are provided on the BATBD CD.

- *text*   A directory that contains text files which provide additional information about things like the BlessTiVo program, hacking Series 2 DirecTiVo machines as originally done by TiVo hacker mlar, general information about DMA, the GNU Public License (GPL) under which most of the software on the BATBD disk has been released, using TiVos with network connections and DSL broadband, and the original Series 1 "Hacking the TiVo FAQ," for historical completeness.

- *tivodns-1.0*  A directory containing the source code, library, and a sample binary for doing Domain Name Resolution (DNS) on a TiVo.
- *TiVoMad*  A directory containing the TiVoMad utilities, provided for historical interest.
- *tivopart*  Source code and binaries for a recent repartitioning utility for the TiVos.
- *TiVoWebPlus-1.0-final.tivo.tpm*  A shell script that contains the TiVoWebPlus application, which is a powerful Web server and control application that runs on your TiVo, which you can access from any Web browser, enabling you to program, explore, and generally interact with your TiVo. This is an amazing program! While TiVo, Inc. now offers remote, Web-based scheduling for Series 2, TiVoWebPlus works on both Series 1 and Series 2 TiVos for free. TiVoWebPlus requires some appropriate network configuration to enable you to securely access it from computers outside your home network, but we're all hackers here, right? For detailed information about installing and using the TiVoWebPlus program, see Chapter 8.
- *tpip-1.1*  A directory containing the source code and various executables for Todd Miller's excellent **tpip** utility.
- *TPM*  A directory containing the source code for the Linux-side Tivo Package Manager (TPM), which produced installable packages that can be installed on your TiVo by running them as shell scripts. This directory also contains a tpm_packages subdirectory that provides various TiVo hacks and utilities packaged in this format.
- *TyStudio*  A directory containing source code and binaries for Series 1 and Series 2 versions of the latest version of the TyStudio video extraction and editing tool and related utilities.
- *TyTool*  A directory containing source code and binaries for Series 1 and Series 2 versions of the latest version of the TyTool video extraction and editing tool and related utilities.
- *vplay*  A directory containing source code and binaries for the **vplay** application and its related vserver application. These utilities support video extraction over a network, and also enable direct manipulation of and extraction from a TiVo disk that is mounted in a PC booted from the BATBD CD.
- *windows*  A directory that contains TiVo-related utilities for Microsoft Windows systems.
- *x86bin*  A directory that contains handy TiVo programs precompiled for your Pentium-class desktop system, such as **BlessTiVo**, **bootpage**, **busybox**, various MFS utilities, and the **hexedit** and **script** utilities.
- *xcompilers*  A directory that contains prebuilt compilers that you can install and use on any Linux system to build your own TiVo software. These compilers are known as *cross-compilers* because they run on one type of system but produce executable programs that run on another. In this case, they run on desktop personal computers that use Pentium-class x86 processors, but they produce executables that run on either the PPC or MIPS architectures.

The BATBD is full of fun things that I've accumulated or built over time—I hope you find it useful.

# Dylan's Boot Floppy

Dylan's Boot Floppy is truly the pioneering boot disk for hacking the Series 1 TiVo, but it is somewhat constrained by both its age and the space limitations of a floppy disk. Designed for use on the Series 1, you still can use the software that it contains with extreme care to back up and restore data from the Series 2 TiVo, but I'd advise against it.

Dylan's boot disk contains all of the Series 1-related tools discussed in this book, such as MFS Tools v1.0, BlessTiVo, bootpage, pdisk, and so on, as well as standard Linux utilities (such as **dd**) that you can use to back up TiVo disks in raw format. You can obtain a copy of the IMG image file for Dylan's Boot Disk from **http://www.tivofaq.com/hack**.

# Johnny Death's Boot CD

Johnny Death's CD was created by AVS TiVo community member johnnydeath primarily for use in hacking Series 2 DirecTiVo machines, though it provides options for booting your TiVo in byte-swapped mode to simplify working with TiVo Series 1 disks.

Like the BATBD disk described earlier, Johnny Death's Boot CD contains files and directories not required by the boot process, but which are only available after you mount the CD.

Johnny Death's CD is a great boot CD if you are primarily concerned about hacking the Series 2 TiVo and DirecTiVos. The BATBD CD included in this book owes a tremendous amount to this CD.

# Kazamyr's Boot CD

Kazamyr's Boot CD was created by AVS TiVo community member kazamyr as the ultimate TiVo Series 1 hacking disk, and it still holds that title—if you're only interested in the Series 1. It provides multiple boot options for booting in byte-swapped mode, with and without DMA access for high-speed backups.

Like the BATBD and Johnny Death disks described earlier, Kazamyr's Boot CD contains files and directories not required by the boot process, but which are only available after you mount the CD. The CD primarily contains a number of text files that discuss different aspects of hacking the Series 1 TiVo; the CD also provides an **mfstools.1** directory that contains archives of static and dynamic versions of the MFS Tools utilities, Version 1.

You can obtain a copy of the ISO image of Kazamyr's boot CD from **http://www.9thtee.com/tivobootcd.htm**.

# Knoppix Linux

Knoppix Linux actually has absolutely nothing to do with the TiVo. Rather, Knoppix Linux is a complete Linux distribution that boots and runs from the CD. It is often mentioned on the Net in the context of TiVo hacking because it comes with a copy of the **hexedit** utility that is required to defeat the unknown hash code used by Series 2 machines running Version 4 and later of the TiVo software. (Defeating the hash code is explained in Chapter 2, in the section "Activating Back Door Mode on V3.1 and Later TiVos.") The hexedit utility is included on the BATBD CD provided with this book, so Knoppix Linux may no longer be as exciting as it once was—in terms of TiVo hacking.

Regardless of its value to the TiVo hacking community, Knoppix Linux is still an amazing Linux distribution if you are curious about Linux. It is a complete, up-to-date Linux distribution that includes the latest version (4.3) of the Linux XFree86 X Window System implementation, as well as the complete KDE desktop software suite. And, it's free! I even use Knoppix Linux as a portable diagnostic tools disk when troubleshooting general Windows networking problems, because it contains all of the networking tools I typically need, and it enables me to run Linux on systems that run Windows by default. Impressive, if not amazing!

You can obtain a copy of the ISO image of Knoppix Linux from the Knoppix Linux Web site at **http://www.knopper.net/knoppix/index-en.html**.

 **TIP**

If you're using Knoppix Linux for diagnostics purposes, you won't be able to use the Linux/Unix **su** command to become the root user because this is disabled on most versions of the Knoppix boot CD. However, you can use the **sudo /bin/ bash** command to get a root shell, which is probably a more modern approach to **su**'ing all over the place.

# PTVUpgrade.com

PTVUpgrade.com is one of the premiere vendors of TiVo upgrade kits, networking hardware, and supported software for the TiVos. They used to offer a freely downloadable disk for upgrading your systems, but now they charge for it. Not a big surprise—there is real work involved in collecting software, creating a CD image that boots correctly, and so on. Their boot disk supports disks larger than 137GB and also supports creating backup files that are larger than 2 GB (as does the BATBD CD that accompanies this book). For more information about their upgrade disk, see **http://www.ptvupgrade.com/bootdisk.html/**.

## Sleeper's ISO

You'll see many references to this and the scripts that it contains on the TiVo forums discussed in Chapter 14. Sleeper's ISO provide automated scripts that can monte, back up, and restore your TiVo. Many people swear by these, but I prefer to do things myself (as explained in this book) to make sure that I know exactly what's going on and don't have to worry about how or where I've connected various disk drives. Still, Sleeper's scripts are a great effort and an impressive example of the free software that TiVo-lovers have developed to make all of our lives easier. Current sources for Sleeper's scripts and the ISO that contains them are **http://www.b-lan.com/tivo/sleeper/tivoscripts1_02.zip** and **ftp://tivo: later@ftp.twinbrothers.com/tivoscripts1_02.zip**. A thread discussing Sleeper's ISO and scripts, with additional download locations, is available on the Dealdatabase forum at **http: //www.dealdatabase.com/forum/showthread.php?t=28921**.

## TiVo Hacking for PPC

The TiVo Hacking for PPC project is a SourceForge project (**http://sourceforge.net/ projects/tivo-hack-ppc**) that provides an ISO that is bootable on a PPC Macintosh system, and which provides a port of Sleeper's scripts for automatically monte'ing, backing up, and restoring your TiVo. I have not experimented with this (other than to boot it, which is way cool!), but it's worth looking at if (1) you're a committed Mac user and (2) you've completely backed up your Mac or disconnected your Mac disks. I'm not flaming the author—just being paranoid.

# HACKING THE TiVo

## Chapter 6

SECOND EDITION

## Backing Up and Restoring TiVo Data

**Y**our TiVo is both a computer system and a home entertainment appliance, and should therefore be backed up at various times. Like any other computer system, you should back up your TiVo occasionally simply to guarantee that you don't lose critical data. In the case of the TiVo, settings for features like WishLists and Season Passes are personalized aspects of the TiVo system software that you may want to protect against hardware failures or accidental loss during a TiVo software upgrade—while this has never happened to me, others have reported this problem over the years, and it's always better to be safe than sorry.

The fact that your TiVo is a home entertainment appliance that stores recordings that you may treasure is another motivation for backing up your TiVo. You may want to back up your TiVo to protect recordings that are important to you that you want to continue to view on your TiVo. Saving such "critical" recordings to long-term media like DVD, videotape, or to other computer systems via the network are easy and safe ways of moving or cloning data from your TiVo onto external storage where it is safe from the vagaries of hardware failures and accidental deletion.

## TiVo Physician, Un-Upgrade Thyself

Like all computer systems, your TiVo is ruled by its operating system software, which presents another significant reason for backing up your TiVo, although it might be frowned upon by the head TiVo office—protecting your TiVo against software upgrades, that is. As described earlier, different releases of the TiVo software have different capabilities and different levels of TiVo-induced security measures (for example, hashing). Each software release from TiVo, Inc. provides enhancements such as improved recording quality, increased capabilities in WishLists, the user interface in general, and so on. However, if you've hacked your TiVo and are happy with it as it is, you may not want to get any other TiVo software release. The ability for TiVo, Inc. to remotely upgrade your system can be a good thing if you just want the latest and greatest software, but it's a bad thing if you don't want your system upgraded. You can't apply the mantra, "don't fix it if it isn't broken," if someone else controls the upgrade process. To protect yourself in this case, it's important to have a backup of your TiVo so that you can roll back to the software version that you liked after being upgraded against your will, and it is also useful to discourage your TiVo from upgrading itself by setting special boot parameters. This process is described in later in this chapter in "Changing TiVo Operating System Versions Using Backups."

*Video extraction*, which is the term used to describe the process of transferring saved video from your TiVo to another system, is an especially touchy subject in DVR circles. Video extraction and depriving TiVo, Inc. of revenues from the TiVo service are the two forbidden topics on public TiVo discussion areas, such as the TiVoCommunity and AVS forums, but for two totally different reasons.

Depriving TiVo, Inc. of service revenue (generally known as "stealing service") is wrong for obvious reasons. First, $12.95 a month or $299 for lifetime service simply isn't worth stealing. The folks at TiVo have worked long and hard to make the TiVo the great entertainment appliance it is. Perhaps I'm old-fashioned, but I think that people deserve to be rewarded for good work. If the TiVo service is available in your area and you don't want to pay for it, you are wrong. You should. Things are somewhat different if you live outside the U.S. in an area where the TiVo service is unavailable, but you still want to own and use a TiVo. This book can't help you in that circumstance because some greedy fool would use those techniques in areas where the service is available. However, if you poke around on the Net long enough, you can find posts and pages from people in countries like Canada and Australia who do not have access to the TiVo service but have worked around the problem.

Extracting video from your TiVo so that you can save it to long-term storage that you can watch using devices other than the TiVo is a totally different matter. Recording broadcast television and movies for resale is wrong. Recording them for your own personal use should be totally legal, in my opinion. They broadcast it, we received it, and we probably sat through the commercials at least once—I think we've paid our dues and fulfilled the contract. See Chapter 12, "Extracting, Inserting, and Playing TiVo Recordings" for detailed information on backing up and playing TiVo recordings on other types of computer systems. Information wants to be free—especially if you've already watched the commercials.

# *Overview*

There are two basic ways to back up any computer system:

◆ Unstructured backups, where your backup is essentially an exact copy of a disk or disk partition. This type of backup requires no information about the organization of the data on disk because you are simply making a raw, image copy of a disk or partition.

◆ Structured backups, where your backup is a copy of the data and relevant data structures on the disk. This type of backup must be done by using a program that understands how the data on a disk or disk partition is organized, and then uses that information to traverse the disk or partition in a structured fashion.

Each of these backups techniques has specific advantages. Unstructured backups are easy to do, require no special software, and serve as a complete snapshot of an entire disk or partition at a given moment in time, down to files that the system has marked for deletion but which have not yet been purged from or overwritten on the disk. Unstructured backups of the TiVo use the Linux version of one of the original Unix utilities, an age-old utility called *dd*, which stands for "dump data." The **dd** program does exactly that by leveraging the fact that all native system data on Unix/Linux systems is stored as a stream of bytes and can be accessed in that way. As explained in more detail later in this chapter, the **dd** utility has two mandatory arguments, which are the names of its input and output files or devices.

Structured backups take less space than unstructured backups because they are performed by utilities that understand the organization of the files, directories, and relevant data structures on the filesystems they back up. They access the data on the disk or partition that you are backing up through actual filesystem data structures, and therefore only back up the portions of the filesystem that actually contain data. If you only have 1 GB of data on a 10 GB partition, structured backups will only require 1 GB of storage space (at most, and perhaps less, if you are doing compressed backups).

Several structured backup utilities are available for the TiVo, the best being MFS Tools utilities. The **mfstool backup** utility is specially designed to back up all of the types of filesystems that the TiVo uses, and it features many different options to customize what you are backing up and how you are backing it up. Doing structured backups of your TiVo using the **mfstool backup** command is discussed later in this chapter, in the section "Creating Backups Using MFS Tools." The structured backups of a TiVo drive that do not include your recordings are usually between 100 and 1400 MB in size.

The MFS Tools utilities recognize the format of all of the types of filesystems used by your TiVo, from standard Linux **ext2** filesystems to the MFS filesystems that are specific to the TiVo, and they back up each differently. On a hacked TiVo, you could also choose to back up the data in the TiVo's standard Linux **ext2** filesystems (**hda4**, **hda7**, and **hda9**) by using the standard Linux **tar** (tape archiver) and **cpio** (Copy Input to Output) utilities. Each uses its own archive formats, but they are quite common in Linux/Unix circles. The primary difference between the two utilities is that the **tar** utility cannot back up special Linux/Unix files such as the entries in the /dev and /proc directories, but otherwise is the ubiquitous standard for archiving Linux/Unix directories. The **tar** utility takes the name of one or more directories or files as a command-line argument, and creates an archive file that contains the specified directories and/or files.

The **cpio** utility is much less widely used, but has more sophisticated capabilities. It can back up any type of Linux/Unix file, but requires that a list of files and directories to back up be supplied as its standard input, and it writes an archive of those files and directories to its standard output (which users typically redirect into a file).

---

 **NOTE**

While the Linux/Unix structured backup utilities discussed earlier can be useful for backing up selected portions of the Linux filesystems on your TiVo, using the MFS Tools utilities is the only way to do a structured backup of your TiVo that you can subsequently use to restore your TiVo to a completely usable state.

---

The downside of structured backups is that they are very sensitive to the consistency and condition of the filesystem. If the filesystem is corrupted, the utility that you are using to make structured backups may not be able to follow the organization of files and directories on the disk, and may simply bail out. On TiVo filesystems that store information in a standard Linux filesystem format, such as the root and /var partitions' use of the ext2 filesystem format, you can usually correct this sort of problem by running the **e2fsck** utility to clean up those filesystems before doing the backup. This won't help if there are problems with any of your MFS filesystems. Similarly, if the underlying hardware on which a filesystem is stored begins to go bad, you may not be able to make structured backups due to read errors on the hard drive.

## If TiVos Crash and Structured Backups Fail...

If one of the drives in your TiVo is going bad and occasionally flakes out (i.e., your TiVo crashes or structured backups fail), creating an unstructured backup of that disk may be the solution to your problem. You can use the **dd** program to create an image backup of the entire disk, and then either replace the disk or reformat it. (The former is preferable, but the latter may work.) After you have replaced or reformatted the disk, you can restore the backup to the new disk (as explained later in this chapter), and then retry the structured backup. If you are lucky and the reason that the backup failed and your TiVo crashed was repeated read/write errors to the disk, you just might be able to recover all of your TiVo settings and existing recordings.

# *When to Back Up?*

To some extent, the differences between the two types of backups dictate when it is appropriate to use one or the other. You can make an image backup at any time because it always uses the same amount of space as the total capacity of the media that you are backing up. In other words, making an image copy of a 30 GB disk will always require 30 GB of backup storage, regardless of whether the disk contains 1 byte of data or 29 GB of data. If you can afford the disk space, keeping an image backup around is never a bad idea. However, since unstructured backups save an exact snapshot of the entire disk, people rarely do them except when they first get a TiVo, and perhaps later when the TiVo disk is almost full of recordings that they want to save.

If conserving disk space or minimizing the amount of potentially extraneous information in your backups is a concern, the best time to use the MFS Tools to do a structured backup of your TiVo is the day that you get it, before going through the Guided Setup process. This gives you a completely virginal image of your TiVo's hard drive. You can then restore this to your TiVo at any time to start over from ground zero. A virginal backup image can also come in handy if you or a friend encounters hardware problems and needs to completely restore a TiVo to its original, out-of-the-box state.

For personal reuse, you may find it preferable to use the MFS Tools to do a structured backup of your TiVo immediately after going through the Guided Setup process so that the backup contains the information about your local TiVo dial-up connection. This is especially important for DirecTiVo owners, since the Guided Setup process is the only time that you actually need a phone line for a DirecTiVo. Disk space is cheap nowadays. Similarly, it is also a good idea to do a backup after any new TiVo software release in order to eliminate the need to re-upgrade your system if you have to reinstall from backups for one reason or another.

One thing to remember about backing up your TiVo using the MFS Tools utilities is that, unlike many structured backup utilities, the MFS Tools do not perform incremental backups.

Every backup of a primary TiVo disk done with the MFS Tools is a complete backup of the subset of the partitions on that TiVo disk (and the data that they contain), which is required to successfully boot your TiVo. This means that MFS Tools backups are always relatively large even if little has changed on your TiVo since the last time you did an MFS Tools backup. This also means that restoring one MFS Tools backup to a disk on which a previous MFS Tools backup has been restored will completely overwrite the previous backup data.

# Finding Room for Backups

Whether you're creating structured or unstructured backups, the fact remains that backup files take up a fair amount of space. Unstructured backups of disks and partitions require exactly the same amount of space as each disk or partition that you back up. Structured backups of a TiVo disk, even without saving any of your recordings, generally take between 200 and 800 MB. Full backups of your TiVo that include your recordings can require gigabytes of disk space. Where should you put your backups?

Disk space is cheap nowadays, but getting to it may be an issue. The primary hard drives in most people's computer systems are relatively large, usually ranging from 10 GB to well over 200 GB. TiVo tools CDs, such as BATBD, use RAM disks to hold their filesystems and are primarily designed to give you access to your TiVo disks. Luckily, there's an easy solution to the problem of finding disk space for backups, which capitalizes on the flexibility of Linux and its ability to interoperate with the different types of filesystems used on a variety of personal computers.

 **NOTE**

The versions of Linux provided on the BATBD CD can only access storage located on Windows disks that have been formatted with the FAT32 filesystem. If the filesystems on your personal computer are formatted using the NTFS (NT File System) format, you will not be able to access them after booting from the BATBD CD. See the section later in this chapter entitled "File Size Limitations Under Linux and Windows" for related information.

As discussed earlier, even the kernels on TiVo tools CDs that do byte-swapping only activate byte-swapping for the devices attached as the slave device on your primary IDE interface (/dev/hdb, in Linux terms), the master drive attached to your secondary IDE interface (/dev/hdc, in Linux terms), and the slave drive attached to your secondary IDE interface (/dev/hdd, in Linux terms). The master drive on your primary IDE interface is never byte-swapped and therefore provides access to the native filesystems on your personal computer. All you have to do is make them available to the TiVo tools CD from which you've booted. This can be done with a single Linux command.

**TIP**

When doing backups, you do not need to boot with the byte-swapped kernel even if you are using a Series 1 system. When you restore the backup, the MFS Tools utilities' **mfstool restore** command provides options that make it easy for you to restore both byte-swapped and "normal" backups—as discussed in Chapter 4, the MFS Tools utilities provide internal support for byte-swapping when necessary, regardless of what the kernel provides. However, if you are using a Series 1 system, you always want to boot using a byte-swapped kernel when you are restoring a backup to a TiVo disk. This will enable you to use the **pdisk** command to verify that the TiVo disk has been restored correctly. Mounting and unmounting disks and moving them from one system to another is tedious enough without doing it multiple times because the restore used the wrong byte order.

When you boot from a TiVo tools CD, such as BATBD, you are running Linux. Linux uses its **mount** command to add existing disks and partitions to the filesystem. The syntax of the **mount** command is as follows:

```
mount -t type partition mountpoint
```

In this example, *type* is the type of partition that you are mounting, which would be one of *vfat* (the Linux name for Windows FAT32 partitions), or *ext2* if your desktop system is a Linux system that uses the default *ext2* partition type. The *partition* argument is the Linux name for the disk partition that you want to mount, probably **/dev/hda1** for a Windows C drive and any of /dev/hda1 through /dev/hda8 for a Linux system (depending on how you partitioned your disk when you installed Linux). The *mountpoint* argument is the name of a directory in the Linux filesystem (the RAM disk, if you've booted from BATBD) through which you want to be able to access the partition that you're mounting. Linux traditionally uses the directory /mnt to store directories on which external filesystems are to be mounted (which are therefore known as *mountpoints*).

 **TIP**

You can use the Linux **fdisk** command to quickly list the types of filesystems on a Linux disk. For example, the command fdisk -l /dev/hda would produce a list of all of the partitions on the drive /dev/hda and their types.

If your desktop computer is a Windows system where the C drive is a FAT32 partition and you have booted from the BATBD CD, you could mount your Windows disk on the directory /mnt/windows by using the following command:

```
mount -t vfat /dev/hda1 /mnt/windows
```

After executing this command, you could create TiVo backup files in the directory /mnt/ windows, which you would then find in the C: directory on your Windows system after booting it from its own disk rather than the BATBD CD.

If your desktop computer is a Linux system, use the **df** command to see how its partitions are organized before you reboot your system from the BATBD disk. For example, the output of the **df** on my primary Linux system would look like the following:

```
Filesystem          1K-blocks       Used Available Use% Mounted on
/dev/hda7           10080488     987164   8581256  11% /
/dev/hda1             101089      29810     66060  32% /boot
/dev/hda8           30668576   15242724  13867952  87% /home
none                  515532          0    515532   0% /dev/shm
/dev/hda2            2016044        520   1913112   1% /tmp
/dev/hda5           20161172    4249540  14887492  23% /usr
/dev/hda6           15116836    2799492  11549440  20% /usr/local
/dev/hdb1          196015808   83683884 102374840  45% /opt2
```

In this case, the partition /dev/hda8 is the partition where home directories are located and the partition also has around 13 GB of free disk space, which is enough for most structured TiVo backups. After booting from the BATBD CD, you could mount this filesystem on the directory /mnt/home by using the following command:

```
mount -t ext2 /dev/hda8 /mnt/home
```

In this case, the **-t ext2** argument is actually unnecessary, because **ext2** is the default partition type for the **mount** command on Linux systems—it is shown here for the sake of completeness.

After executing this command, you could create TiVo backup files in the directory /mnt/ home, which you could then find in the /home directory on your Linux system after booting it from its own kernel rather than the BATBD CD.

If you are using a Windows system and your C drive turns out to be formatted using an NTFS filesystem, all is not lost—you can always add another disk to your Windows system, boot into Windows, and format the new drive using the FAT32 filesystem. Then you can shut down the system again, add your TiVo disk to this system, and mount the newly-created FAT32 partition as described earlier, using that disk as storage for your backup files.

If you have absolutely no disk space and want to back up a TiVo disk solely for the purpose of immediately restoring it to another disk, you can take advantage of the capability of Linux to connect the output of one program to the input of another. In Linux terms, this is done using a pipe, which is represented on the command-line as the "|" symbol. In this way, you can use the **mfstool backup** command to back up your existing disk, writing the backup file to what is known as *standard output*, which the corresponding **mfstool restore** command will then use as its *standard input*. This process is described in more detail later in this chapter, in "Connecting Backup and Restore Commands Using a Pipe."

# File Size Limitations Under Linux and Windows

Linux is under continuous development and is therefore constantly improving. Older versions of the Linux kernel, such as all TiVo kernels prior to version 5.x of the TiVo software, cannot create files larger than 2 GB in size. If your personal computer runs Windows and you want to save your backups to a Windows partition, only the Windows NTFS filesystem can store files larger than 4 GB in size, but this filesystem cannot be reliably accessed from Linux. File size isn't a problem in TiVo's MFS filesystem because the MFS filesystem has its own file management scheme, uses multiple chunks for files, and doesn't create files in the standard Linux filesystem.

File size limitations are not a problem if you are doing structured backups that do not include the recordings on your TiVo. However, file size limitations can still be an issue if you want to do a full structured or image backup of your TiVo disk and all of its recordings after booting from the Linux kernels on the BATBD CD that accompanies this book. There are several solutions to this issue:

◆ Use the **bigs2** boot option provided on the BATBD CD that accompanies this book (this is the default boot option if you simply press return at the **Boot:** prompt). This boot option boots a Linux kernel that can create files larger than 4 GB in size. However, you will only be able to access those files when they are booted using this kernel. Also, creating files larger than 4 GB is only useful if the filesystem on your personal computer can store files larger than 4 GB. Windows FAT and FAT32 filesystems can only store files up to 4 GB in size, and you cannot reliably write to NTFS filesystems from Linux at the moment. If the filesystems on your personal computer are formatted using the NTFS (NT File System) format, you will not be able to access them after booting from the BATBD CD. Chalk up another piece of proprietary crap to Microsoft. Newer Linux kernels feature experimental support for writing to NTFS partitions, but related kernel changes make these incompatible with the current TiVo software for now.

◆ Pipe the output of your backup command to the Linux/Unix **split** command, using the **–b 1999mb – tivo_backup** options, which will divide the output of the restore command into files that are 1.9 GB in size, name them using the prefix *tivo_backup*, and give each file a suffix number that shows its order in the sequence of output files. (Note that there is a space between the "-" and *tivo_backup*—the dash tells the split command to read from standard input.) You may want to use a smaller size and compress these files (using gzip, RAR, etc.) if your goal is to store them on removable media, such as a CD-ROM or Zip drive. To restore from these files, you will have to feed these files to your restore utility using a command like "`cat tivo_backup.* | ...`", where the "…" is your restore command, which must use the appropriate option that tells it to read from standard input.

◆ If you simply want to restore the backup to a larger drive, connect the output of the **mfstool backup** command to the **mfstool restore** command using a pipe, as explained later in this chapter. This avoids having to create any files, and thus you avoid any file size limitations.

Unless you absolutely want to back up an entire TiVo drive to files, I suggest that you use the third option when moving to a larger drive or cloning an existing drive for backup purposes. In either case, you will have your old drive as a backup—but treat it kindly, and put it in a safe place!

 **NOTE**

If your primary desktop machine is a Windows system and you don't know what type of filesystem it uses, you can find out from Windows by opening the My Computer folder on your desktop, right-clicking the icon for your system's C drive, and then selecting Properties from the context-sensitive menu that displays. The resulting dialog box displays information about the disk, including the type of filesystem that it contains, as shown in Figure 6.1.

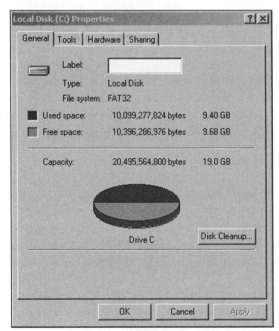

**FIGURE 6.1**  *Determining the type of filesystem on a Windows drive*

# Creating Image Backups Using dd

As mentioned earlier, the **dd** command is one of the oldest and most primal Unix commands around. The **dd** command reads data from one source and writes it to another, with some control over the size of the chunks in which it is read and written at each end, plus the ability to do various forms of data manipulation in between. You'll only need to know about a few of these bells and whistles to use the **dd** command to make image backups of a disk or disk partition from your TiVo. However, it's always nice to know that there are other knobs to turn if future developments in TiVo-land require them.

The first step in creating an image backup of a TiVo disk or disk partition is to take the disk drive out of your TiVo and put it into your desktop PC, as explained in Chapter 4, "Exploring Your TiVo Hardware," in the section "Working with TiVo Disk Drives." As discussed in that section, make sure that you jumper the disk correctly so that it does not conflict with any existing disk in your desktop PC. Also note the IDE interface to which you attached the disk, so that you can be sure that you are backing up the right disk. Few things would be as embarrassing or irritating as trying to use a backup image to restore or expand your TiVo, only to find out that the backup image contained data from the wrong disk or partition.

 **NOTE**

As explained in the section of Chapter 5 that discusses bootable TiVo tools disks, any of the byte-swapped kernels on these disks (necessary for mounting TiVo Series 1 disk partitions) only byte-swap the secondary disk on your primary IDE interface (/dev/hdb) and the primary and secondary disks on your secondary IDE interfaces (/dev/hdc and /dev/hdd, respectively). If you want to access the partitions on a TiVo Series 1 disk, that disk must not be attached to your PC as the master drive on your primary IDE interface.

After the disk is successfully mounted in your PC, you can use the **dd** command to make a backup image of an entire disk at any time, regardless of which of the TiVo kernels on the BATBD disk you have booted from. Reading raw data from an entire disk does not require that you can directly access the specific partitions on the disk, only that you can access the disk itself. (Once you've booted from the BATBD disk, follow the naming conventions given in Chapter 4 for accessing TiVo disks mounted in your PC.) However, if you want to make image backups of specific partitions from a TiVo disk, you will need to boot using a kernel that understands the TiVo's partition table format, and which has the appropriate byte order for the type of TiVo from which the disk you are copying was taken. If you are working with a TiVo Series 1 disk, you will need to use the BATBD boot option that specifies that it is designed to access TiVo partitions. Since the disks from Series 2 machines do not require byte-swapping to access their partition table, you could boot using either of the other boot options from the BATBD CD to access partitions on a TiVo Series 2 disk. These are the Series 2 or nonswapped Series 1 boot options, although the former certainly seems to make more sense.

**TIP**

If you are using a desktop Linux system for your TiVo hacking purposes and want to mount TiVo Series 1 or Series 2 disks without using the BATBD disk, you will need to recompile your kernel. To do so, enable the Macintosh Partition Support in the filesystems section of the kernel Configuration menu, and locate a patch on the TiVo forums that enables support for the partition signature (1492) used on TiVo disks (or add it to the kernel yourself). After you've rebuilt the kernel, you can mount the ext2 partitions from a TiVo Series 2 disk directly. You can also mount the ext2 partitions from a TiVo Series 1 disk by passing the **hdX=swap** boot option on the kernel command line, where **X** is the letter corresponding to the TiVo disk in your system. You can also create an entry for byte-swapped booting in the configuration files used by the Linux boot loaders, GRUB or LILO, to simplify support for Series 1 disks in the future.

Once you've booted your system with the appropriate kernel options, you can use the **dd** command to create an unstructured backup of a TiVo disk by using a command like the following:

```
dd if=disk of=backup-file bs=32k
```

This tells the **dd** command to read from the disk specified as *disk* (probably one of /dev/ hda, /dev/hdb, /dev/hdc, or /dev/hdd) and write to the output file *backup-file*. The **bs** option tells the **dd** command to use 32 K as both the input and output block sizes, which is a convenient value that takes advantage of memory and drive caching.

You can use the **dd** command to create an unstructured backup of a specific partition on your TiVo disk by using a command like the following:

```
dd if=partition of=backup-file bs=32k
```

This tells the **dd** command to read from the disk specified as *disk* (probably one of /dev/hd*XY*, where *X* is the identifier for the disk and *Y* is the partition number) and write to the output file *backup-file*. As in the previous example, the **bs** option tells the **dd** command to use 32 K as both the input and output block sizes, which reflects the block size used on TiVo filesystems.

 **TIP**

If, for some reason, you have problems using the specified **dd** command due to errors, try executing the following **dd** command, which uses some of the **dd** command's "forgiveness" options:

```
dd if=partition of=backup-file bs=32k conv=noerror,sync
```

These options cause the **dd** command to proceed past simple errors that you may encounter if your source drive is having problems. The **sync** option synchronizes, reads, and writes—even after a read error—by padding incomplete reads with the appropriate number of NULL bytes.

## ☖ Exploring Your TiVo through Virtual Filesystems

If you are using a desktop Linux system for your TiVo hacking, making image backups of partitions provides interesting hacking opportunities. Once you use **dd** to clone a disk partition to a file, you can then use Linux's loopback filesystem to mount that file as though it were a physical partition on your Linux system. This only works for partitions that are in a format that your desktop system understands, such as the **ext2** partitions in partitions 4, 7, and 9 of any primary TiVo disk.

If you want to mount partition images from a Series 1 system (which is big-endian) on a standard desktop PC (which is little-endian), you will need to convert the byte order of the filesystem image by using the **dd** command's **conv=swab** conversion option, as in the following example:

```
dd if=series1_hda9.img of=series1_hda9_pc_style.img conv=swab
```

You can then mount the "un-byteswapped" image (**series1_hda9_pc_style.img**, from the preceding example) using the **mount** commands described later in this section. For more information about "endian-ness," see the section of Chapter 5 on the **pdisk** command.

Mounting filesystem images enables you to explore the contents of the parent partition without requiring the disk that contains the filesystem still be physically attached in your desktop system. This can be handy if, for example, you would like to actually use your TiVo at the same time that you are learning more about its internals.

To mount a partition image as a file, use a command like the following:

```
mount -o loop filename mountpoint
```

In this example, *filename* is the name of the file to which you wrote the partition image (using a command like **dd**), and *mountpoint* is the name of the directory on which you want to mount the partition image. For example, the following command would mount the partition image in the file hda_part4.img on the directory /mnt/tivo/part4:

```
mount -o loop hda_part4.img /mnt/tivo/part4
```

After you have mounted a partition image, you can redirect the directory to it, and move around in its files and directories. Also, you can create, edit, and delete files, and generally do anything that you could do if it were an actual disk partition. This also includes running scripts on any Linux system, and even programs—if you happen to be running a compatible version of Linux on a PPC or MIPS box. (Not much chance of that these days, but you never know...)

If you mount an image file, you must unmount it before shutting down your system or, like any other filesystem, you should use the **fsck** command to verify its integrity before reusing it.

The **dd** command takes a while to run, given that it is transferring a fairly large amount of data. Unfortunately, the standard versions of the **dd** command provide no visual feedback while they execute. For people who absolutely must have a progress indicator, a specially hacked version of the **dd** command with a progress indicator is available on the Net at **http://tivohack.sourceforge.net/files/fileutils-4.1.bonehead.tar.gz**. (I have nothing to do with the naming convention for this file, which is intended to reflect the fact that displaying the progress indicator slows down the overall performance of this version of the **dd** command by approximately 10%.) To display the progress indicator, pass the **progress=1** option on the **dd** command line.

Again, whether you are backing up a partition or an entire disk, the **dd** command takes a long time. Creating an image backup of a large TiVo partition is a great opportunity to walk your dog around the block or to have a cigarette. Creating an image backup of an entire TiVo disk is a great opportunity to make dinner or go shopping.

# Creating Backups Using MFS Tools

The unstructured backups discussed in the previous section are typically huge because they are the same size as the disk or partition that you are backing up. The MFS Tools utilities, discussed in detail in Chapter 5, create structured backups of TiVo disks by walking through the disk's partition table and the actual data structures contained in MFS filesystems. The MFS Tools utilities also conserve some space by automatically skipping certain partitions during the backup process, such as the duplicate kernel and root filesystem partitions on a bootable TiVo disk. As explained in Chapter 5, you can further reduce (or increase) the size of the backups produced by the **mfstool backup** utility by passing various command-line options.

This section explains how to perform a variety of different types of backups using the **mfstool backup** command from MFS Tools utilities. As with the previous section, you will need to have mounted the TiVo disk(s) that you want to back up in your PC before preceding; however, you do not have to boot with any special command-line options if you are using Version 2 of the MFS Tools utilities. Knowledge of the partition table and byte-swapping requirements of TiVo disks was built into Versions 2 and later of these utilities—all of which you need to do to execute the appropriate command. (You may need to do a bit more when restoring the data to verify that it was written with the appropriate byte order. (More about that later in this chapter, in the section entitled "Restoring Backups Using MFS Tools.")

---

 **NOTE**

If you are unclear on how to attach a TiVo drive to your personal computer or aren't sure of the naming conventions used to access such drives after doing so, please review the section in Chapter 4, entitled "Working with TiVo Disk Drives."

---

The following information explains how to use the basic capabilities of the MFS Tools utilities, beginning with simple structured backups that use the default settings compiled into the

MFS Tools utilities, then moving on to more advanced types of backups. All of these backup commands use the **mfstool backup** command from MFS Tools utilities, showing how different options to the command can affect the size and contents of the backup files that you create.

# Creating a Simple Backup Using MFS Tools

The simplest type of structured backup that you can do using the **mfstool backup** command requires only one command-line option, which is the name of the backup file that you want the utility to create. After booting from the BATBD disk, to back up a TiVo disk that is attached to your personal computer as the slave drive on your secondary IDE interface, you would execute a command like the following:

```
mfstool backup -o output-file /dev/hdd
```

In this example, *output-file* is the name of the file to which you want to write the backup data. If you followed the conventions discussed earlier in this chapter for mounting a partition from your primary Windows or Linux disk so that you can access it from the BATBD disk, this file should be the full path of a file on the appropriate disk. For example, if your Windows C drive is mounted as /mnt/windows, you could specify a filename such as /mnt/windows/ my_tivo.bak. If the home partition of a desktop Linux system is mounted as /mnt/linux, you could specify a filename such as /mnt/linux/my_tivo.bak. Using the Windows drive as an example, you would execute a command like the following:

```
mfstool backup -o /mnt/windows/my_tivo.bak /dev/hdd
```

The **mfstool backup** command displays output like the following during the backup process:

```
Scanning source drive.  Please wait a moment.
Source drive size is 15 hours
Uncompressed backup size: 1309 megabytes
Backing up NNN of 1309 megabytes (M.MM%)
Backup done!
```

The line beginning with "Source drive" shows the **mfstool backup** command's idea of the capacity of the drive you're backing up, which in this example is a 15 GB Quantum disk from a TiVo Series 1 machine. While the **mfstool backup** command is running, the line reading "Backing up NNN of 1309 megabytes (M.MM%)" is continually updated to show the progress of the backup command. After the command completes its task… Congratulations! You've backed up your TiVo!

 **TIP**

When using the MFS Tools utilities to back up HDTV and DVD-enabled TiVos, you should use a higher FSID value than the default of 2000. A value of 5700 is often suggested—I tend to use 9999, just to be on the safe side, since 5700 doesn't seem to get all of the required settings.

You can determine the actual size of the backup file produced by the **mfstool backup** command by using the Linux **ls** command, as in the following example:

```
ls -l /mnt/windows/my_tivo.bak
-rwxr-xr-x  1 root     root      1374030336 Jun 26 12:19 /mnt/windows/
my_tivo.bak
```

In this case, the file is 1,374,030,336 bytes in size, which is close to what was predicted.

 **NOTE**

The actual size of your backups depends on the size of your original drive, the version of the TiVo software that is installed on the disk, any additional information that you may have put in your drive's /var partition, and the backup options that you specify. The sizes shown in the examples throughout this chapter will almost certainly not match the size of your backups.

Since this backup command used the defaults provided by the **mfstool backup** command, it's useful to know what they are and what the backup file contains. With no options other than the **-o** option to specify the name of the output file, a backup file produced by the **mfstool backup** command contains the following:

◆ A copy of the partition map from the specified disk

◆ A copy of the bootpage from the specified disk

◆ A compressed copy of the active kernel partition from the specified disk

◆ A compressed copy of the active root filesystem partition from the specified disk

◆ A compressed copy of the /var partition from the specified disk

◆ A backup of the entries in the MFS partitions on the specified disk whose filesystem identifier (FSID) is less than 2000. These are all of the files in the MFS Application and Media regions on the disk that are required for normal operation of older TiVos.

 **TIP**

When using the MFS Tools utilities to back up HDTV and DVD-enabled TiVos, you should use a higher FSID value than the default of 2000. A value of 5700 is often suggested—I tend to use 9999, just to be on the safe side, since 5700 doesn't seem to get all of the required settings.

When you restore a backup file created by the **mfstool backup** command, the **mfstool restore** command uses the copy of the original drive's partition map to create the necessary filesystems before restoring their contents. In the case of the Linux swap partition on the TiVo disk, the **mfstool restore** command simply creates an empty partition of the appropriate size (or larger, depending on **mfstool restore** options) and correctly initializes it for use as a swap partition. Backing up a swap partition would be a total waste of time because it is used only by the operating system as a temporary location to provide virtual memory support.

For more details about the restore process and the contents of a backup file created using the **mfstool backup** command, see the section "Restoring Backups Created Using MFS Tools," later in this chapter.

# Creating a Compressed Backup Using MFS Tools

The previous section explained how to create a simple structured TiVo backup using the **mfstool backup** command. While still much smaller than the physical capacity of the TiVo disk that you were backing up, these backups are still fairly large—816 MB or so is nothing to sneeze at. A decade or two ago, this was beyond the maximum storage capacity of a good-sized mainframe. Even though disk space is cheap now (I paid $160 or so for my last 200 GB drive), saving disk space whenever possible is never a bad idea. A classic computer maxim goes like this: "The amount of disk space required by users always expands to fill all available storage." This certainly is even truer when programs create 816 MB files with a single command.

The **mfstool backup** command provides built-in options for compressing backup files as they are created. For the hard-core nerds among us, this is done through the use of the Linux **zlib** library, which implements a standard Lempel-Zev compression scheme to reduce disk consumption in output files. For the rest of us, "the files are smaller."

The **mfstool backup** command provides 10 levels of compression (levels 0 through 9), which reflect the tradeoff between compression and execution time. Obviously, compressing data takes some time, which means that creating a compressed backup takes longer than creating a standard, uncompressed backup file. Higher levels of compression do substantial amounts of extra processing to reduce the size of your backup files, but may not have as radical an impact on the size of your backup files as the middle compression levels do. At some point, the savings provided by higher levels of compression aren't worth the time they take to completely minimize the size of your backup files—saving two or five megabytes of a file that is still a few hundred megabytes in size just may not be worth it.

When using the **mfstool backup** command, compression options are specified using a command-line option that identifies the compression level for which you're looking. These options are therefore -1 through -9, with -9 being the maximum compression level possible. The compression value recommended in the documentation for the **mfstool backup** command itself is -6, which is the one that I typically use. As noted in the MFS Tools documentation, this compression option seems to provide the best tradeoff between savings in backup file size and slower performance of the **mfstool backup command.**

Using a mounted Windows disk as an example of the destination for the backup file that you are creating, the command you would type to perform a compressed backup at compression level 6 is the following:

```
mfstool backup -6 -o /mnt/windows/my_tivo.bak /dev/hdd
```

The **mfstool backup** command displays output like the following during the backup process:

```
Scanning source drive.  Please wait a moment.
Source drive size is 15 hours
Uncompressed backup size: 1309 megabytes
Backing up NNN of 1309 megabytes (M.MM%)
Backup done!
```

This command displays the same output as the **mfstool backup** command without the compressed backup option. The real difference is in the final size of the output file, which you can only determine by actually examining the file by using the Linux **ls** command, as in the following example:

```
ls -l /mnt/windows/my_tivo.bak
-rwxr-xr-x   1 root      root      601924044 Jun 26 12:38 /mnt/windows/
my_tivo.bak
```

In this case, the file is 601,924,044 bytes in size, which essentially is half of the predicted size of the uncompressed backup.

> **TIP**
>
> When using the MFS Tools utilities to back up HDTV and DVD-enabled TiVos, you should use a higher FSID value than the default of 2000. A value of 5700 is often suggested—I tend to use 9999, just to be on the safe side, since 5700 doesn't seem to get all of the required settings.

# Backing Up an Entire TiVo Disk Using MFS Tools

As mentioned earlier, the default action of the **mfstool backup** command is to back up files only within the MFS partitions of a disk whose filesystem identifier is less than 2000. This seemingly arbitrary number is actually a carefully chosen value that guarantees that the backup file will contain all of the portions of the MFS filesystem(s) that are required for normal operation of your TiVo, without backing up the files that truly take up the majority of the space in any MFS filesystem—your recordings. However, there are a few cases in which you would want to back up everything, namely:

◆ When backing up a failing TiVo disk so that you can restore it to an identical disk in order to replace the failing disk.

◆ When backing up a TiVo disk so that you can subsequently restore it to a larger disk and use the additional space provided by the larger disk to increase the storage capacity of your TiVo.

◆ When backing up your existing TiVo disk simply to protect treasured recordings against accidental deletion or loss due to hardware failure (if the disk itself goes bad).

In any of these cases, you can use additional **mfstool backup** options to increase the amount of information that is being backed up, customize the specific types of items being backed up based on the amount of disk space they consume, or simply back up everything.

Backing up the entire contents of a TiVo is easy enough to do, requiring that you add a single command-line option. The **mfstool backup** option for backing up the entire contents of one or more TiVo drives is the **-a** (all) option. The following example shows the sample command and resulting output of backing up the entire contents of a TiVo disk that is connected to your personal computer as /dev/hdd (the slave drive on your secondary IDE interface):

```
mfstool backup -6 -a -o /mnt/windows/my_tivo.bak /dev/hdd
```

The **mfstool backup** command displays output like the following during the backup process:

```
Scanning source drive.  Please wait a moment.
Source drive size is 15 hours
Uncompressed backup size: 1309 megabytes
Backing up NNN of 1309 megabytes (M.MM%)
Backup done!
```

Although in this case, the size of the backup is the same as our previous backup; full-disk backups are typically much larger. This is not surprising because you are backing up everything contained in the entire disk. As long as you can afford the backup space required to save a backup file of this size, it is nice to have the ability to back up all of your favorite recording at one time.

---

 **TIP**

Before doing a complete backup that you plan to keep around for a while, take the time to purge any nonessential recordings from the TiVo. You should also use the **backdoor** commands discussed in Chapter 3, "TiVo Tips and Tricks," in the section "Using Thumb-Thumb-Thumb Codes" to display the listings for any Teleworld or other promotional recordings that may still be stored on your disk and delete. No point in backing up anything that you don't really want to save!

---

# Backing Up Multiple-Disk TiVo Systems

As mentioned when discussing the BlessTiVo command in Chapter 5, "The Hacker's Tool Chest of TiVo Tools," (and discussed in more detail in Chapter 7, "Expanding Your TiVo's Storage Capacity"), adding a second drive to your TiVo effectively marries the two disks so that they must "always" be used together. What this really means is that you cannot remove the second drive and continue to use the TiVo with just its primary disk. Since the TiVo expects to access and use storage on the second drive, it won't take long for the TiVo to attempt to access the second drive and (of course) fail. In the computer biz, this is known as "a bad thing." Fortunately, you can effectively divorce two drives by backing them up together and then restoring the combined backup to a larger, single drive. The **mfstool backup** command stores a copy of the partition map for both the TiVo drives, but it does not require that the restore be performed on two drives—when restoring a dual-drive backup to a single TiVo drive with sufficient space, the **mfstool restore** command simply recreates a sufficient number of partitions to hold the restored data on the new, larger drive.

Backing up a dual-drive TiVo is done exactly like backing up a single-drive TiVo, with two exceptions:

◆ You must supply the **-s** (shrink) command-line option to shrink the set of volumes being backed up as much as possible. This causes the **mfstool backup** command to focus on the data contained in any MFS partitions rather than trying to preserve the actual structure of the volumes and partitions on your disks.

◆ You must supply the names of both TiVo drives on the TiVo command-line—and in the correct order, of course.

A sample command line for backing up a dual-drive TiVo, whose disks are found at /dev/ hdb and /dev/hdd (in other words, as slave drives on both of your IDE interfaces) would look something like the following:

```
mfstool backup -6 -s -o /mnt/windows/my_tivo.bak /dev/hdb /dev/hdd
```

The **mfstool backup** command displays output like the following during the backup process:

```
Scanning source drive.  Please wait a moment.
Source drive size is 15 hours
     - Upgraded to 57 hours
Uncompressed backup size: 1309 megabytes
Backing up NNN of 1309 megabytes (M.MM%)
Backup done!
```

This command displays the same output as any other **mfstool backup** command, with the exception of the information provided about the size of both of the TiVo drives. As with the previous example, the relationship between the estimated, uncompressed size of the backup and the actual size of the backup file is only a guess—you'll need to use the **ls** command to see the actual resulting size of the output file.

After you've created a single backup file that combines information about both drives of a dual-drive TiVo system, you can restore it to a single drive with sufficient available storage, or to a larger set of drives if you want to maximize your storage at the same time. Restoring backups is explained later in this chapter; restoring a single backup file to a pair of disks is explained in Chapter 7, "Expanding Your TiVo's Storage Capacity," as part of the general discussion of how to add a second drive to your system.

# Advanced Backup Options

As discussed in Chapter 4, the **mfstool backup** command provides a few options that enable you to modify the contents of a structured backup file in general and specific ways. This section highlights these options to help you think about ways of customizing your backups. For the most part, I tend to stick with "standard" backups, rarely taking advantage of the more advanced **mfstool backup** options with the exception of the **-v** option (to exclude **/var** from the backups). With other advanced options, it's tricky to know exactly what a specific backup contains (or does not contain) without actually restoring it and seeing what you get. However, your mileage may vary, so here we go.

The discussion of the TiVo's Media File System (MFS) in Chapter 10 presents ways of identifying the MFS entities associated with specific recordings. If you want to create a TiVo backup that is guaranteed to include a specific recording, you can use the **mfstool backup** command's **-f** *fsid* option to ensure that the backup includes the specified recording. This option actually tells the **mfstool backup** command to include all videos with **fsids** less than or equal to the specified *fsid*, which probably means that you'll get other recordings than the one in which you're specifically interested. However, this also means that you won't get other recordings whose fsids are greater than the one in which you are interested.

The **-f** *fsid* option provides a good compromise between minimizing the size of your backup while ensuring that your backup includes a specific recording, without creating a backup of every recording on your TiVo. Continuing with the examples used in the previous sections, the following command would create a compressed backup file containing all video streams with fsids that are less than 2877, which we'll assume is one greater than the *fsid* of the recording we're interested in preserving:

```
mfstool backup -6 -f 2877 -o /mnt/windows/my_tivo.bak /dev/hdb
Scanning source drive.  Please wait a moment.
Source drive size is XX hours
Uncompressed backup size: XXXX megabytes
Backing up NNN of XXXX megabytes (M.MM%)
Backup done!
```

 **TIP**

When using the MFS Tools utilities to back up HDTV and DVD-enabled TiVos, you should use a higher FSID value than the default of 2000. A value of 5700 is often suggested—I tend to use 9999, just to be on the safe side, since 5700 doesn't seem to get all of the required settings. It's a bit slower (since you're backing up more data), but better safe than sorry. When possible, you should test restoring your backups to a scratch disk and try that disk in your TiVo before you can absolutely guarantee that the backups are usable.

An alternative to just backing up streams with fsids that are less than a specified number (or the default value of 2000) is to use the **mfstool backup** command's **-l** *size* option to limit the backup to only streams that are under a certain size. This size is based on the actual amount of data that the files contain, rather than the amount of space allocated to each file (which would differ based on the allocation units used for that TiVo filesystem). The assumption behind this option is that files larger than the specified limit will be recordings (which you would not want to save) because the native animations used by the TiVo are all relatively small. Safe values for this *size* cutoff are 32 or 64 MB. This option cannot be used with the **-f** option, because there may be files with a *fsid* that is less than the specified value, but which is larger than the specified *size* cutoff.

Continuing with the examples used in the previous sections, the following command would create a compressed backup file containing all video streams whose size is less than 32 MB:

```
mfstool backup -6 -l 32 -o /mnt/windows/my_tivo.bak /dev/hdb
```

The **mfstool backup** command displays output like the following during the backup process:

```
Scanning source drive.  Please wait a moment.
Source drive size is XX hours
Uncompressed backup size: XXXX megabytes
Backing up NNN of XXXX megabytes (M.MM%)
Backup done!
```

If you would rather base the size cutoff on the actual amount of space that is actually allocated for a file, rather than the amount of that space that is actually used, you can use the **-t** *size* option instead of the **-l** *size* option. In a final permutation between allocated and actual size, you can use the **-T** *size* option to back up all of the space allocated to files that actually use *size* or less of that space.

# Backing Up Selected Information from Your TiVo

The previous sections discussed how to do backups of your TiVo, which then can be restored to create a new bootable TiVo disk or disk set. While the **mfstool backup** command provides options for reducing (or simply controlling) the items that are included in the backup files that it produces, it does not support incremental backups. *Incremental backups* is the term used for backups that only contain things that have changed since the previous backup was done. The combination of these two facts has the following implications for backups created using the **mfstool backup** command:

- ◆ They are always large.
- ◆ Each backup contains mostly the same files as the previous backup.
- ◆ Each backup contains identical copies of system files that probably have not changed since the previous backup.

If you aren't interested in backing up your recordings and already have a backup of your TiVo system software in a safe location, there are still several things that you have probably spent a fair amount of time crafting, and therefore would be distressed to lose. These are features like Season Passes and WishLists that you've built up over time. Luckily, a thoughtful TiVo hacker named "angra" was kind enough to create backup and restore commands. If you run these commands on your TiVo, it will save and restore these items to and from text files that you can easily preserve for safekeeping by copying them to another machine. These scripts are located in the BATBD CD's settings-backup directory.

 **NOTE**

The settings **backup** and **restore** commands must be executed on your TiVo, unlike the **dd** and MFS Tool utilities. Backing up and restoring your TiVo settings therefore requires that you already have configured your TiVo to display a command-prompt, as explained in Chapter 8, "Connecting the Universe to Your TiVo," in the section "Getting a Command Prompt on Your TiVo."

The easiest way to install the settings-backup software on your TiVo is to recursively copy that directory from the BATBD CD to a partition on your TiVo disk while you have it in your desktop PC. For now, let's assume that we simply want to put the software in its own directory in the TiVo's /var partition. To do so, perform the following steps:

1. Put the TiVo disk in your PC as described in Chapter 4 in the section "Working with TiVo Disks."

2. If your disk is from a Series 1 machine, boot from the BATBD disk using the **bigs1** or **s1swap** options so that you can mount and access your TiVo partitions. If your disk is from a Series 2 machine, boot from the BATBD disk using the default boot option by pressing the Enter or Return key at the boot screen.

3. Mount the partition of your TiVo disk that corresponds to its /var partition. This will be the partition /dev/hdX9, where X is the letter corresponding to where you've attached your TiVo drive to your PC. It could therefore be any of the following /dev/hdb9, /dev/hdc9, or /dev/hdd9—or even /dev/hda9 if you are working with a disk from a Series 2 system. To mount this partition, use a command like the following:

   ```
   mount /dev/hdX9 /mnt/var
   ```

4. Mount the BATBD CD using a command like the following:

   ```
   mount /dev/hdX /mnt/cdrom
   ```

   As in previous examples, replace X with the letter corresponding to your CD-ROM drive. This will be **b** if your CD-ROM drive is attached as the slave on your primary IDE interface; **c** if your CD-ROM drive is attached as the master on your secondary IDE interface; or **d** if your CD-ROM drive is attached as the slave on your secondary IDE interface. If you specified the correct device, you will see a warning message stating that the CD-ROM drive is mounted as read-only, which is true and can be safely ignored.

5. Recursively copy the settings-backup directory from the BATBD CD to the /mnt/var partition using a command like the following:

   ```
   cp -r /mnt/cdrom/settings-backup /mnt/var
   ```

6. Unmount the BATBD CD and TiVo /var partitions by executing the following two commands;

```
umount /mnt/cdrom
umount /mnt/var
```

After you have finished this process, put the TiVo disk back in your TiVo and reboot it. If you are using a serial connection to your TiVo, attach the cable at this point and start the terminal emulation program on your PC; if you have put your TiVo on the network, wait until it has booted successfully and then connect to it using a utility such as Telnet.

When the command prompt displays, change directory to the /var/settings-backup directory by using the **cd /var/settings-backup** command. You can then create a backup file of your Season Passes and WishLists by executing the following command:

```
./backup > settings.out
```

This command writes a copy of your Season Passes and WishLists to the file settings output, which you should then copy back to your personal computer and put in a safe place. To restore the settings from this file in the future, transfer it back to the TiVo, copy it to the /var/settings-backup directory, make sure that it is your working directory by using the **cd** command, and then execute the following command:

```
./restore settings.out
```

 **NOTE**

Restoring Season Pass and WishList settings using the **restore** command provided in the /var/settings-backup directory does not overwrite any existing Season Passes or WishLists, even if they are identical. Before restoring Season Passes or WishLists, you should first clean up your existing Season Passes or WishLists, perhaps deleting or at least renaming any that may have the same names or that might otherwise conflict with the settings that you are restoring. You can then go through the list and delete any duplicates that you do not want to preserve for some reason.

# Finding Backups of the TiVo Software

If you're interested in pursuing many of the hacks discussed in this book, you'll need to have access to backups of specific versions of the TiVo software. This is fine if you've had a TiVo since day one and have religiously made backups of each version and upgrade of the TiVo software immediately after it was installed on your system. If that's the case, pat yourself on the back, and I'm not sure exactly why you bought this book. For the rest of the universe, finding backups of older versions of the TiVo software can be a problem. Several Web sites used to host older backups, but all of the public ones have been pulled down thanks to protests from TiVo, Inc. (Though a stripped-down 3.1u5 RFS and kernel are currently available on one of the DealDatabase forums, which is probably OK because these only contain Linux software.) This is one of the rare cases (aside from video encryption) where TiVo, Inc. has acted in a somewhat hostile fashion towards the TiVo hacking community. Luckily, solutions to this problem are available—read on!

 **NOTE**

I don't understand why TiVo, Inc. cares what version of the TiVo software we run on our TiVos. We've already bought them. We're paying for service, monthly or lifetime—or should be. TiVo, Inc. makes great products with great software. Don't rip them off! On the other hand, I don't see why TiVo cares. Chevrolet doesn't care if I put a different engine in my Chevy. Volkswagen doesn't harass the thousands of people who have built kit cars, dune buggies, and other custom projects after buying an old Volkswagen Beetle or Bug. By opening and hacking your TiVo, you have voided your TiVo warranty. Whatever else you choose to do should be up to you. A little sanity, please.

Peer-to-Peer filesharing, often simply referred to as *P2P*, is the supposed boogeyman of the motion picture and recording industries. Overpriced merchandise, limited availability, and a complete lack of knowledge about implementing modern technology are certainly not the problem. (Sarcasm alert!) Regardless of how you feel about filesharing, P2P has plenty of bona fide uses. One of these, though certainly frowned upon by TiVo, Inc. and therefore perhaps not technically "bona fide," is sharing backups of older versions of the TiVo software.

 **NOTE**

I would like to point out, again, that I am not a lawyer. Though this is not a book about P2P, I'm advocating its use and thus want to point out that I do not believe that it is right to rip off artists by downloading music and films without paying for them. Doing so as a way to preview material seems fine to me—but buy it if you actually like it! At any rate, please exercise the "reasonable person principle," which is the computer equivalent of the golden rule, when downloading things. Pay for what you really use.

Today's Internet is knee-deep in different P2P solutions, but the two that I recommend are eDonkey (**http://www.edonkey2000.com**) and Overnet (**http://www.overnet.com**). You may notice that both of these Web sites seem very similar to each other. The basic idea of these P2P solutions is that you run a core program that knows how to talk to a variety of servers that host shared files. You typically run this core program in the context of a graphical user interface (GUI) that simplifies locating and downloading files. The ed2k-gtk-gui is a great graphical interface for these P2P networks (**http://ed2k-gtk-gui.sourceforge.net/index.shtml**), and is available for Linux, FreeBSD, Mac OS X, and Windows systems.

When you run a P2P client, your system also shares the files that you are downloading, or any other files that you have agreed to share. These P2P networks are loosely connected sets of clients and servers that cooperatively share files back and forth. From the GUI that you're using, you can initiate searches for specific types of files. For example, searching either of these networks for "TiVo" will identify many backup images that you can download and use to customize your TiVo by following the procedures discussed in this book.

**TIP**

Many of the backups that you'll find on P2P networks are archived using the RAR compression utility. Shareware versions of the RAR archiver for Linux, Mac OS X, and Windows systems are available from **http://www.rarsoft.com/**.

By the way, I am not advocating anything that doesn't also impact me personally. For example, a search of these P2P networks for the keyword "TiVo" will turn up a file called "*Premier Press - Hacking the TiVo.pdf*", which is a PDF version of the first edition of this book. I had nothing to do with making it freely available, but am honored to be included in the P2P universe. The people who download this probably aren't going to buy the book anyway—though I'd certainly appreciate it if they would.

**TIP**

Another way to get a disk containing and alternate version of the TiVo software is through PTVupgrade.com. You can send them a disk of any supported size, and they will install a virgin copy of the latest TiVo OS for the system of your choice on that disk. This is known as a drive recertification—more information about this service is available at **http://www.ptvupgrade.com/db/upgrade/category/ products/product_detail_html?product_id=68**. If you want to upgrade your TiVo and don't want to play around with the disks yourself, this is a fast and convenient alternative. Also, if you are interested in hacking a Pioneer 810-H and need a disk with the Pioneer 57-H software, this service is for you.

# General Information About Restoring TiVo Data

The next few sections discuss how to restore different types of TiVo backups, whether as part of a system upgrade or simply as part of the repair process for a formerly ailing TiVo. Before attempting a restore for whatever reason, it's important to understand what TiVo data you can restore and where.

As discussed earlier, image backups of an entire primary TiVo disk always include the entire contents of that disk. Restoring an image backup from one primary TiVo disk to another always produces a bootable disk, complete with all of the files required for daily operation. Similarly, structured backups of primary TiVo disks created using the MFS Tools utilities always contain at least the minimum information required to create a bootable disk. However, all TiVos and bootable TiVo disks are not created equal.

One common mistake made by people who own multiple TiVos or who are restoring backups to a TiVo for some other reason, is to restore a backup of one type of TiVo to another and expect it to work. Series 1 and Series 2 systems use different processors, and they run completely incompatible kernels, libraries, and executables. This is the equivalent of trying to directly execute a Macintosh program on a Windows machine—it simply won't work, ever. There is absolutely no way to restore a Series 2 image to a Series 1 TiVo machine and expect it to work.

Similarly, there are fundamental differences between many of the Series 1 machines, such as the Sony and Phillips/Hughes models. Backups of these systems are also incompatible, even though they may initially appear to work on both types of systems—the TiVo software upgrade process will certainly become confused in the future if, for example, it knows that you have a Phillips TiVo but encounters Sony data when trying to upgrade the system. You can, however, restore backups images to other models of the same series of TiVo from the same manufacturer, as long as sufficient disk space is available to hold the restored data. For example, you can restore a Series 1 Phillips HDR112 image to a Phillips HDR312, and everything will work fine. Similarly, you can restore a backup image from a Series 2 40 GB TiVo to a Series 2 80 GB TiVo with no problems.

 **TIP**

If the first three digits of your TiVo are the same as the first three digits of the TiVo on which a backup was created, the backups are compatible.

 **NOTE**

When restoring backups made on a system with a smaller disk to a system with a larger disk, you will almost certainly want to use the MFS Tools utilities to reclaim the additional space for storing recordings, as discussed later in this chapter in the section entitled "Restoring an MFS Tools Backup to a Larger Drive".

# *Restoring Image Backups Using dd*

Having created an image backup of one of your disks using the **dd** command as explained earlier in this chapter, you can quickly restore this to another disk by essentially reversing the order of the arguments that you supplied to the **dd** command to create the backup. Be extremely careful when supplying arguments to the **dd** command—specifying the wrong disk drive as the target of a restore operation will destroy any data that it previously contained, which would be bad if you accidentally specified the drive containing the Windows or Linux boot information for your personal computer.

**TIP**

It doesn't technically matter which of the kernels on the BATBD CD you boot with to restore an image created with **dd**, but it should be the same one that you booted from when you created the backup using the **dd** command. (This guarantees that no byte-order conflicts arise.) Since it is useful to mount partitions from the restored disk to verify that the restore completed successfully, I suggest that you use the byte-swapped kernel (i.e., the **bigs1** or **s1swap** boot options) when creating or restoring a TiVo Series 1 backup image.

Attach the drive that has the image backup you want to restore to your PC (as explained in Chapter 4 in the section "Working with TiVo Disk Drives") and ensure that you also have access to the partition where the backup is stored (as discussed earlier in this chapter). You can restore the backup image to the new drive using a command like the following:

```
dd if=filename of=/dev/hdX bs=32k
```

The *filename* argument should be the full pathname of the file containing the backup image that you are trying to restore. As always, the *X* in **/dev/hd***X* reflects the drive letter associated with where you have mounted the target hard drive in your PC.

This command will take a long time. After it completes, try mounting partitions from the restored disk. You should be able to mount /dev/hdX4, /dev/hdX7, and /dev/hdX9. You can try mounting these in turn, using a command like the following, where *N* is the partition number (the /mnt/test directory must also exist on your system):

```
mount /dev/hdXN /mnt/test
```

Mounting a Linux filesystem verifies that the core data structures of the filesystem are valid. You can immediately unmount them (before trying to mount another) by using the command **umount /mnt/test**.

After you have restored a backup image and have verified that you can successfully access its partitions, what you do next with the disk depends on why you restored the backup image:

♦ If you were restoring an existing disk image to an identical disk (or even overwriting the original disk) to protect against hardware failures, you can simply put the new disk in your TiVo and begin using it.

♦ If you were restoring an existing disk image to a larger disk to increase the amount of storage available on your TiVo, you can use the MFS Tools utilities to enable the extra space for use by the TiVo (as explained in Chapter 7, in the section "Replacing an Existing TiVo Disk with a Larger One."

**TIP**

If you cannot mount any of the partitions from the restored disk image after the restore finishes, try the following:

◆ Verify that you booted from a kernel that supports access to the TiVo partition tables. On the BATBD disk, these are the **bigs1** or **s1swap** boot options for Series 1 machines and the **bigs2** or default boot options for Series 2 machines (also available at the BATBD CD's boot prompt).

◆ Verify that you are trying to mount the correct partitions. The **ext2** partitions on a TiVo disk are partitions 4, 7, and 9, which you would specify as /dev/hdXN, where **X** is the letter for the drive and **N** is the partition number.

◆ Verify that you did not accidentally create the backup image using a non-byte-swapped kernel if you are restoring it using a byte-swapped kernel. You can reverse byte-swapping when restoring data using the **dd** command by specifying the **conv=swab** option on the **dd** command line, as in the following example:

```
dd if=filename of=disk-or-partition bs=32k conv=swab
```

# Restoring Backups Created Using MFS Tools

As discussed earlier, backups of primary TiVo disks created using the MFS Tools utilities are complete backups of all of the portions of a TiVo disk that are critical for successful operation of your TiVo. They also can be complete backups of your TiVo, if performed as instructed earlier in this chapter in "Backing Up an Entire TiVo Disk Using MFS Tools."

The next few sections discuss different ways of restoring backups created using the MFS Tools utilities. These largely differ in terms of the command-line options used by the **mfstool restore** command, but are organized into separate sections in order to make them easier to find and use.

## Restoring an MFS Tools Backup Without Adding New Space

In most cases, you will be restoring MFS Tools backups to one or more drives that are larger than the drive that you backed up and then automatically devoting any additional space on the drive(s) for use when storing recordings on your TiVo. If that's your goal, skip this section and go to either of the next two sections. However, there are cases where you may want to do a simple restore, either to the same disk that you backed up, to another disk of the same size as the original disk, or to a larger disk on which you do not want to automatically allocate additional space for use with your TiVo. Some cases where these circumstances may be useful are the following:

◆ You suspect that your drive is failing, and you can't afford another one at the moment. In this case, after backing up the original drive, you can use the manufacturer's utilities to low-level format the disk so that it marks any failing sectors as bad and then restores a backup of that drive to the drive to try to continue using it.

◆ You want to preserve your original drive as an on-the-shelf backup and happen to have another drive of the same capacity. In this case, you can put the old disk on the shelf, restore the backup to the duplicate disk, and use the duplicate disk in your TiVo.

◆ You want to restore your original disk to a larger disk on which you plan to use the additional space for some other purposes—in other words, without automatically allocating the additional space for use by the TiVo. In this case, you can restore the backup and then use a command such as **pdisk** (discussed in Chapter 5) to manually create new partitions of types, such as **ext2** or MFS. You may want to do this as your TiVo hacking skills evolve and you need additional **ext2** partitions to store new software that you've put on your TiVo.

Restoring an MFS Tools backup to a disk without doing anything else is the simplest case of restoring data to a TiVo disk. To do this, first put the disk on which you want to restore information into your PC and boot from the BATBD disk. Next, execute a command like the following:

```
mfstool restore -C -i backup-file /dev/hdX
```

The **mfstool restore** command's **-i** option specifies the full pathname of the file that contains your backup (*backup-file*). The **mfstool restore** command's -C option limits the restore process to LBA28 disk addressing, which is necessary if you are using TiVo software Versions 4.x and earlier. The **−C** option is only available in the latest versions of the MFS Tools utilities, such as the one on the BATBD CD that accompanies this book if you boot using the **bigs2**, **bigs1**, or **custs1** boot options.

 **NOTE**

If you are restoring your backups for use with a custom TiVo kernel or version of the TiVo software that supports LBA48 large disk addressing, do *not* use the **−C** option. You must also have booted from the BATBD CD using the **bigs2** option, even if you are restoring to a Series 1 TiVo. Examples of LBA48-aware TiVo kernels are Todd Miller's custom kernels for Series 1 TiVos (found on the BATBD CD that accompanies this book), and systems running Version 5.x or greater of the TiVo software such as the Pioneer 57-H and 810-H, or the HDTV DirecTiVo.

The **mfstool restore** command displays the following output during the restore process:

```
Starting restore
Uncompressed backup size: XXXX megabytes
Restoring NNN of XXXX megabytes (M.MM%)
Cleaning up restore.  Please wait a moment.
Restore done!
```

While the **mfstool restore** command is running, the line reading "Restoring NNN of XXXX megabytes (M.MM%)" is continually updated to show the progress of the restore command. Once the command completes… Congratulations! You've just created a new TiVo drive from an existing backup file! You can shut down the PC, return the drive to your TiVo, and boot from it successfully.

 **NOTE**

After restoring a backup to a TiVo disk and booting from that TiVo, the TiVo may still contain directory entries for recordings that were present on the TiVo disk when it was backed up, even though the recordings themselves were not preserved in the backup. If these are present on your restored TiVo, you should go to the Now Playing screen (TiVo Central, Now Playing) and delete the entries for these shows to minimize confusion as to what recordings are actually residing on your TiVo.

# Restoring an MFS Tools Backup to a Larger Drive

By restoring an existing backup to a drive that is larger than the one from which it was made, you can easily add new storage capacity to your TiVo. The **mfstool restore** command provides the **-x** (expand) option so you can restore a backup to a larger drive and then automatically allocate any additional space on the drive for storage.

To do this, first put the disk on which you want to restore information into your PC and boot from the BATBD disk. Next, execute a command like the following:

```
mfstool restore -i backup-file -x -C /dev/hdX
```

The **mfstool restore** command's **-i** option specifies the full pathname of the file that contains your backup (*backup-file*). The **-x** option tells the **mfstool restore** command to expand the set of volumes on the existing disk to allocate any additional storage available on the drive to MFS partitions that the TiVo can use to store recordings. The **mfstool restore** command's **-C** option limits the restore process to LBA28 disk addressing, which is necessary if you are using TiVo software Versions 4.x and earlier. The **−C** option is only available in the latest versions of the MFS Tools utilities, such as the one on the BATBD CD that accompanies this book if you boot using the **bigs2**, **bigs1**, or **custs1** boot options.

**NOTE**

If you are restoring your backups for use with a custom TiVo kernel or version of the TiVo software that supports LBA48 large disk addressing, do *not* use the **–C** option. You must also have booted from the BATBD CD using the **bigs2** option, even if you are restoring to a Series 1 TiVo. Examples of LBA48-aware TiVo kernels are Todd Miller's custom kernels for Series 1 TiVos (found on the BATBD CD that accompanies this book), and systems running Version 5.x or greater of the TiVo software such as the Pioneer 57-H and 810-H, or the HDTV DirecTiVo.

**TIP**

If you are expanding the storage capacity of your TiVo beyond 100 GB or so, you should consider increasing the amount of swap space on the drive during the restore process. As explained later in this chapter, this will improve the performance and responsiveness of your TiVo. For more information about increasing swap space, see "Increasing Swap Space on a TiVo Disk" later in this chapter.

The **mfstool restore** command displays the following output during the restore process:

```
Starting restore
Uncompressed backup size: 1309 megabytes
Restoring 14 of 1309 megabytes (1.77%)
Cleaning up restore.  Please wait a moment.
Restore done!
Adding pair /dev/hdX12-/dev/hdX13
New estimated standalone size: 79 hours (64 more)
```

While the **mfstool restore** command is running, the line reading "Restoring NNN of 1309 megabytes (M.MM%)" is continually updated to show the progress of the **restore** command. As the example output shows, once the restore itself completes, the **mfstool restore** command creates a new pair of MFS partitions (one application region and one media region) to use the additional space that is available on the drive. It estimates the amount of storage available on the new disk for recordings made at the Basic quality level. The numbers in the example will differ from what you see on your screen because they depend on the size of the drive on which the original backup was made and the size of the drive to which you are restoring the backup.

After the **mfstool restore** command completes… Congratulations! You've just created additional storage for your TiVo recordings and created a new drive for use in your TiVo! You can shut down the PC, put the new drive in your TiVo, and boot from it successfully. Once your TiVo has booted, you can verify the amount of storage available on the expanded TiVo from the System Information screen (TiVo Central, Messages & Setup, System Information).

# Restoring an MFS Tools Backup to a Two-Drive TiVo

The **mfstool restore** command also enables you to restore a single backup to a pair of drives. This actually restores the TiVo system information to the first drive, allocates any free space on the first drive for use by your TiVo, and then allocates the space on the second drive for use by your TiVo. This is accomplished by using the same **-x** (expand) option discussed in the previous section—you simply have to specify both of the drives that you want to restore to on the **mfstool restore** command line.

To do this, first put the disk from which you want to restore your data into your PC and boot from the BATBD disk. Next, execute a command like the following:

```
mfstool restore -i backup-file -x -C /dev/hdX /dev/hdY
```

The **mfstool restore** command's **-i** option specifies the full pathname of the file that contains your backup (*backup-file*). The **-x** option tells the **mfstool restore** command to expand the set of volumes on the target disks to allocate any additional storage available to MFS partitions that the TiVo can use to store recordings. The **mfstool restore** command's **-C** option limits the restore process to LBA28 disk addressing, which is necessary if you are using TiVo software Versions 4.x and earlier. The **−C** option is only available in the latest versions of the MFS Tools utilities, such as the one on the BATBD CD that accompanies this book if you boot using the **bigs2**, **bigs1**, or **custs1** boot options.

 **NOTE**

If you are restoring your backups for use with a custom TiVo kernel or version of the TiVo software that supports LBA48 large disk addressing, do *not* use the **−C** option. You must also have booted from the BATBD CD using the **bigs2** option, even if you are restoring to a Series 1 TiVo. Examples of LBA48-aware TiVo kernels are Todd Miller's custom kernels for Series 1 TiVos (found on the BATBD CD that accompanies this book), and systems running Version 5.x or greater of the TiVo Software such as the Pioneer 57-H and 810-H, or the HDTV DirecTiVo.

The drives specified on the command line must be specified in the order that you will put them in your TiVo: /dev/hdX would be the TiVo boot drive and /dev/hdY would be the TiVo slave drive.

**TIP**

If you are expanding the storage capacity of your TiVo beyond 100 GB or so, you should always increase the amount of swap space on the drive to at least 128 MB during the restore process. You must increase the amount of swap space available, if your new TiVo will contain more than 120 GB of total disk space. As explained later in this chapter, this will improve the performance and responsiveness of your TiVo. You can increase the amount of swap space allocated during a restore by specifying the **-s** *size* option on the **mfstool restore** command line, where *size* is the new amount of swap space that you want to allocate. The default amount of swap space allocated is 64 (MB). A better value for larger drives is 128 (MB). You may even want to increase this to 256 MB if you will be running additional processes, such as an FTP server, Telnet daemon, and TiVoWebPlus on your expanded TiVo. The **-s** *size* option has some issues, though, and is discussed in more detail in the "Advanced Restore Options" section later in this chapter.

The **mfstool restore** command displays the following output during the restore process:

```
Starting restore
Uncompressed backup size: 1309 megabytes
Restoring NNN of 1309 megabytes (M.MM%)
Cleaning up restore.  Please wait a moment.
Restore done!
Adding pair /dev/hdb12-/dev/hdb13
New estimated standalone size: 79 hours (64 more)
Adding pair /dev/hdd2-/dev/hdd3
New estimated standalone size: 103 hours (24 more)
```

While the **mfstool restore** command is running, the line reading "Restoring NNN of 1309 megabytes (M.MM%)" is continually updated to show the progress of the **mfstool restore** command. As the example output shows, once the restore itself completes, the **mfstool restore** command creates a new pair of MFS partitions (one application region and one media region) to use the additional space that is available on the first drive, it creates one or more pairs of MFS partitions on the second drive, and then estimates the amount of storage available on the new disks for recordings made at the Basic quality level. The numbers in the example will differ from what you see on your screen because they depend on the size of the drive on which the original backup was made and the size of the drive to which you are restoring the backup.

After the **mfstool restore** command completes… Congratulations! You've just substantially increased the amount of space available on your TiVo for storing recordings. You can now shut down the PC, put the new drives in your TiVo, and boot from them successfully. When your TiVo has booted, you can verify the amount of storage available on the expanded TiVo from the System Information screen (TiVo Central, Messages & Setup, System Information).

# Advanced MFS Tool Restore Options

The **mfstool restore** command provides a variety of options that you can use to customize different aspects of your disk layout when restoring a backup created using the MFS Tools utilities. Each of these advanced capabilities is activated by specifying an additional option and any associated values on the **mfstool restore** command line. The following sections discuss these advanced options and the situations in which you might want to use them.

## Increasing Swap Space on a TiVo Disk

Like most modern computer systems, your TiVo uses swap space to increase the apparent amount of memory available to the system. Swap space is a specially formatted portion of the disk that the version of Linux running on your TiVo can use as temporary space for processes that are active on your TiVo, but which are waiting for some event to occur in order to continue. Moving paused or lower-priority processes out of main memory and temporarily storing them in the swap space enables the processes that are actively running to use the memory that the paused or lower-priority processes would otherwise have used.

Swap space is also used during certain parts of the boot process. The most important of these is the step where the TiVo verifies that the partitions on your hard drive are usable. Known as a *file system consistency check*, this requires that the process that is doing the check build a table in memory that contains detailed information about your disk drives. The size of this table varies depending upon the size of your disk drives. If your TiVo contains more than 120 GB of total disk space, this process may, at some point, need more than the default 64 MB of swap space provided on TiVo disk drives. If you don't have enough swap space available, you may see the dreaded TiVo "green screen" as your TiVo tries to repair its filesystems.

To increase the amount of swap space that is allocated on your hard drive during a restore, you can use the **-s** *size* command-line option to the **mfstool restore** command. The *size* value is an integer value up to 511 and indicates the number of megabytes of swap space that will be created during the restore process. If you ever plan to have 120 GB or more of disk space in your TiVo, you should allocate a minimum of 128 MB of swap space (by specifying the **-s 127** option to MFS Tools). Larger values would be better, but the current TiVo kernels can only use up to 128 MB of swap space. You cannot easily change the amount of swap space that is allocated on an existing disk, so selecting a larger value during the restore process is a good idea, even if you can't use it now. If you ever get a TiVo update that supports larger amounts of swap space, the larger swap space will already exist on your disk, and you will only need to format it correctly in order to be able to use it.

If you create a swap partition larger than 128 MB, you must use shell access to your TiVo (either through the serial port or over your network) to run the **mkswap** command on the TiVo. This will write the correct information to your TiVo's swap partition, which is usually /dev/hda8 on your TiVo. You should verify the name of your swap partition using **pdisk** before moving the drive from your PC to your TiVo.

After connecting to the TiVo, execute the following commands:

```
# mkswap /dev/hda8
# swapon -a
```

The first command writes the correct header file information to the swap partition. The second command tells your system to use all partitions that are identified as swap partitions.

You can then verify that your swap partition is active and in use by executing the **swapon –s** command, which summarizes swap file use on your system, as in the following example:

```
#   swapon -s
Filename                      Type         Size    Used   Priority
/dev/hda8                     partition    130044  8860   -1
```

## Increasing the Size of the /var Partition on a TiVo Disk

Like all Linux and Unix systems, the TiVo uses a hierarchical set of files and directories to store system information. On Linux and Unix systems, disk partitions used by the system for storing files are mounted on directories in the filesystem, known as *mountpoints*, which are just standard Linux directories that can be recycled as entry points for additional storage. After a partition has mounted on a directory, the storage in that partition is used by any files and directories created in that directory or any of its subdirectories. By default, TiVos only have two Linux partitions: the root partition, which is mounted at the directory named / (the "root" of the Linux filesystem), and the /var partition, which is used to store applications and variable data such as system logs, temporary space for creating noncritical files, upgrades and advertisements that you have received from TiVo headquarters, and so on.

The default size of the /var partition on a TiVo is 128 MB, which is suitable for "normal" use. However, if you decide to install additional applications on your TiVo, you may find that 128 MB is somewhat constraining. The **mfstool restore** command provides the **-v** *size* option to specify the size of the /var partition created when restoring a TiVo from backups. The *size* value that you specify should be an integer value that is interpreted as the number of megabytes that you want to have allocated to the /var partition. If you are planning to do some serious hacking on your TiVo or simply want to prepare for doing so in the future without reformatting your disk, you should specify a higher value when using the **mfstool restore** command. A value of 256 MB should be sufficient for most purposes, though you can certainly use higher values if desired. You can always use the **pdisk** command (discussed in Chapter 5) to manually create additional partitions in the future and mount them wherever you want, as long as your disk contains available space.

**WARNING**

Most TiVo systems running TiVo software releases newer than Version 3.0 use hashing to verify the contents of many of the default files used during system startup. You may not be able to mount additional partitions unless you use some of the techniques explained in Chapter 8 in "Getting a Command Prompt on Your TiVo" to modify the boot sequence and environment on your TiVo. This is probably alright, since you will only be adding and mounting new partitions if you're doing some serious TiVo hacking, but "forewarned is four-armed," as they say ;-).

## Optimizing the Partition Layout on a TiVo Disk

One of the governing factors in the performance of any computer system is the amount of time that it takes your disk drive to read and write information to and from your disk. Regardless of how fast your computer system is electronically, it is still gated by these physical operations, which require moving the heads of the disk to the location where the data is (or is to be) stored. In computer terms, the head movement necessary to locate data is known as *seeking*; the amount of time required to locate a unit of data on the disk is generally referred to as the *seek time*. Minimizing seeking and seek time when using a computer system is an important, but easily overlooked aspect of system performance and optimization.

Newer TiVos, such as the DirecTiVo and newer Series 2 models, use a slightly different partition layout than original Series 1 systems, in an attempt to minimize the movement of your disk's read/write heads and reduce the average seek time. MFS partitions are located on the outside of the disk to minimize the amount of head movement necessary to access them, while the Linux partitions containing application data are put in the center of the disk, since applications are started/stopped less frequently than video data is read and written.

The **mfstool restore** command's **-p** option restores data to the new disk as described in the previous paragraph. Although today's disks are substantially faster than the drives in, for example, original Series 1 machines, using this option can provide a general performance improvement, and may also reduce the amount of noise generated by your disk as a consequence of having to seek less.

## Changing the Block Size When Restoring a TiVo Disk

Different types of computer filesystems use different block sizes when allocating disk space and storing data. The block size of a filesystem is the smallest unit of space that the filesystem can allocate. If a filesystem's block size is 4 MB and you need to store 1 byte of data, the filesystem must still allocate one 4 MB block to store that data. At first, it seems silly to use larger block sizes. Why not simply use a tiny block size and allocate as many blocks as necessary to store a given amount of data?

The reason for larger block sizes is attributed to the system overhead related to allocating and managing blocks in the filesystem. Using a smaller block size means that the system must allocate a greater number of blocks to store files as well as manage a much higher number of blocks within the filesystem, tracking whether each is used or free (i.e., can be allocated). The data structures within a filesystem that track which blocks are associated with that file, and in what order, must also be correspondingly larger. Selecting an appropriate block size is especially important in systems that routinely create and delete large files, as your TiVo does when recording and deleting videos. Larger block sizes tend to "waste" more disk space because the final block of any file is rarely completely filled with data, but significantly less effort is involved in allocating and using the larger blocks of data required for classically large video files.

As a more detailed example, assume that a filesystem's block size was 16 MB and the TiVo was trying to store a recording that required 20 MB of disk space. This would require two blocks and would completely fill the first one but waste 12 MB of disk space in the second. In order to keep track of the recording, the TiVo would keep only information about the two blocks in memory. On the other hand, with a block size of 4 MB, the recording would require 5 blocks but no disk space would be wasted. However, the TiVo would have to keep information about 5 blocks in memory to keep track of that recording.

The **mfstool restore** command's **-r** *value* option enables you to specify the block size used within the MFS partitions, created when restoring a backup file created using the **mfstool backup** command. Acceptable values for this option are 0 (corresponding to a 1 MB allocation unit), 1 (corresponding to a 2 MB allocation unit), 2 (corresponding to a 4 MB allocation unit), 3 (corresponding to an 8 MB allocation unit), and 4 (corresponding to a 16 MB allocation unit). In general, the larger the allocation unit value, the less RAM will be used (making the TiVo more responsive when displaying menus, changing and processing options, and so on), but the greater the amount of storage that may be wasted when storing recordings.

 **TIP**

If you are using a Series 1 TiVo, another way of speeding up your TiVo's responsiveness when displaying menus and so on is to buy and install a CacheCard, made by SiliconDust and sold through WeaKnees.com and other fine TiVo hardware vendors. A CacheCard provides a wired Ethernet connection for your Series 1 TiVo and also provides a DIMM (Dual Inline Memory Module) slot in which you can put additional memory to increase the size of your TiVo's memory cache. The CacheCard was discussed in the section of Chapter 4 entitled "Networking Series 1 TiVos."

The default block size used in partitions created by your TiVo is 1 MB. This was a good value to use with the relatively small drives and small amount of memory used on early TiVos. However, today's larger, faster drives make using a larger block size an attractive option for improving performance.

# Changing Byte Order When Restoring a TiVo Disk

As mentioned over and over throughout this book, the Series 1 models use a big-endian PowerPC processor. The byte order in Series 1 filesystems is therefore different from the byte order used in Series 2 systems (and in desktop Linux systems). The initial version of the MFS Tools utilities didn't concern itself with byte order because there was only one byte ordering at the time. However, with the introduction of Series 2 systems, Version 2 of the MFS Tools utilities introduced two options for manipulating the byte order in a backup file created using the **mfstool backup** command.

You may wonder why this is important. After all, you can still use Version 1 of the MFS Tools utilities to restore backups that it created, and everything will "just work." Unfortunately, this is only true if the kernel that you've booted from uses the same byte order as the one that you were running when you created the backup. A further wrinkle is that Version 2 of the MFS Tools utilities added many other features that increased the power and scope of these utilities. As with so many things, "newer is better."

Tiger, the TiVo hacker who wrote the MFS Tools utilities, took this into account when creating Version 2 of the MFS Tools utilities, adding options that let you permute your backups any way you'd like during the restore process. Ordinarily, the **mfstools restore** command attempts to automatically determine whether byte-swapping should be accomplished by examining the byte order on disks such as **hdb**, **hdc**, and **hdd**. The **-b** option disables this auto-detection and forces a restore to be performed *without* byte-swapping. This option is mandatory when restoring a backup of a Series 2 machine that was created with Version 1 of the **mfstool backup** utility. The parallel **-B** option disables auto-detection and forces a restore to be accomplished *with* byte-swapping. This option is mandatory when restoring a backup of a Series 1 machine, if you are running a nonbyte-swapped kernel, such as the BATBD kernel for Series 2 systems.

 **TIP**

Byte-swapping differences can be a pain in the posterior. When restoring a TiVo backup using **mfstool restore**, you should always boot with a kernel that provides access to the TiVo partition table so that you can query a restored disk's partition table to determine if it was restored correctly. If you are restoring a Series 2 backup, the BATBD disk provides a single boot option because the Series 2 systems don't use byte-swapping. If you are restoring a Series 1 backup, boot with the BATBD's **s1swap** option. If you've gotten the byte order wrong during your first restore, you may need to restore the backup again with the correct byte-swapping options enabled. However, you can be sure that the restored disk will be readable—and hopefully bootable—on your TiVo.

# Verifying TiVo Disks Restored Using MFS Tools

After restoring a backup to a new disk that you want to use in your TiVo, you should always verify that the backup looks reasonably correct by examining the partition table of the new disk by using the **pdisk** command and also by mounting one or two partitions from the restored disk. Moving drives from your PC to your TiVo and back again is something of a pain, and the TiVo is light on feedback if you try to boot from a nonbootable drive. If there's something wrong with your restore, in the best case your TiVo boots to the gray "Just a few more seconds…" screen, and sits there until the end of the universe. In the worst case, you hear lots of disk noise, and the red light displays on the front of the TiVo. What the heck does all that mean? In a nutshell (Sorry, O'Reilly guys!), it means that your restore was unsuccessful for one reason or another.

You can verify that the disk you restored your data to has a valid partition table by executing the command **pdisk -l /dev/hd$X$**, where $X$ is the drive letter corresponding to the restored disk. If this command displays a partition table, the restored disk is at least valid, and there's a good chance that your TiVo will boot from it. If you don't see a valid partition table and instead see a message that the drive does not have one, make sure that you've booted with a kernel that provides access to the TiVo partition table. If you have restored a Series 2 backup, boot from the BATBD disk's Series 2 kernel by pressing the Return or Enter key when you see the BATBD boot screen. If you have restored a Series 1 backup, boot from the BATBD disk's **bigs1** or **s1swap** kernels by entering one of these values at the BATBD boot screen. If you still cannot see the partition table and are backing up or restoring a Series 1 TiVo disk, try experimenting with the byte-swapping options discussed in this chapter in "Changing Byte Order When Restoring a TiVo Disk."

Once you can see the partition table, you should be able to mount one of /dev/hd$X$4 or /dev/hd$X$7, and you also should be able to mount /dev/hd$X$9. As mentioned earlier, the **mfstool backup** command only backs up the currently active root partition from your original TiVo disk to reduce the size of your backup file when doing backups. For this reason, when trying to mount /dev/hd$X$4 and /dev/hd$X$7, one of these will fail because it was the inactive root partition.

 **TIP**

You can use the **bootpage** command to identify the default root partition on a drive. For example, the command **bootpage /dev/hdb** displays the default root partition on the drive /dev/hdb.

You can try mounting each of these in turn by using a command like the following (the /mnt/test directory must exist on your system):

```
mount /dev/hdXN /mnt/test
```

Mounting a Linux filesystem verifies that the core data structures of the filesystem are valid. You can then immediately unmount them (before trying to mount another) by using the command **umount /mnt/test**.

> ## TiVo Cloning the Root Partition on a Restored TiVo Disk
>
> I always prefer to have two root partitions available on any restored TiVo disk. In theory, you will only need the second root partition after a software upgrade has populated it with a new kernel fresh from TiVo HQ. However, in reality, a disk problem could corrupt your existing root partition, leaving you with an unbootable TiVo disk. The truly wizardly among us would just clone the root partition from another TiVo disk using **dd**, but why use your super powers if you don't have to?
>
> After restoring a TiVo disk, try mounting both /dev/hdX4 and /dev/hdX7 to determine which of them actually contains a valid root filesystem (or use the **bootpage** command to query the disk to identify the active root filesystem). Once you know which is valid, you can clone it to the other using the **dd** command. For example, if /dev/hdd4 is the valid root partition on a restored TiVo disk and /dev/hdd7 is just an unmountable hunk of ones and zeroes, you can clone /dev/hdd4 to /dev/hdd7 by using the following command:
>
> ```
> dd if=/dev/hdd4 of=/dev/hdd7 bs=32k
> ```
>
> You then should be able to mount /dev/hdd7. Try it. You'll like it! It's like a free insurance policy. The TiVo won't always be able to switch boot partitions by itself (you may have to do so by using the **bootpage** command), but at least the data will be there.

# Connecting Backup and Restore Commands Using a Pipe

If the disks on your personal computer do not have the space to create a complete or partial backup of an existing TiVo disk, you can clone an existing disk to another disk by using the **mfstool backup** and **mfstool restore** commands together. You can even use this process to add another disk at the same time. As touched upon earlier, you can do this by taking advantage of the capability of Linux to connect the output of one program to the input of another. In Linux terms, this is done using a pipe, which is represented on the command line as the 'I' symbol. In this way, you can use the **mfstool backup** command to back up your existing disk, writing the backup file to standard output, which the corresponding **mfstool restore** command will then use as its standard input.

All of the command-line options for the **mfstool** backup and **mfstool restore** commands work in exactly the same way when writing to a pipe, with the exception of the options that specify input and output files. When writing to a pipe on a Linux or Unix system, the input and output files are specified as a single dash (-). An example of a command that would back up the contents of the drive attached to your PC as /dev/hdb and simultaneously restore that backup to a larger drive attached as /dev/hdc would be the following:

```
mfstool backup -o - /dev/hdb ¦ mfstool restore -i - -x -C /dev/hdc
```

**NOTE**

The **mfstool restore** command's **-C** option limits the restore process to LBA28 disk addressing, which is necessary if you are using TiVo software Versions 4.x and earlier. The **–C** option is only available in the latest versions of the MFS Tools utilities, such as the one on the BATBD CD that accompanies this book if you boot using the **bigs2**, **bigs1**, or **custs1** boot options. If you are restoring your backups for use with a custom TiVo kernel or version of the TiVo software that supports LBA48 large disk addressing, do *not* use the **–C** option. You must also have booted from the BATBD CD using the **bigs2** option, even if you are restoring to a Series 1 TiVo. Examples of LBA48-aware TiVo kernels are Todd Miller's custom kernels for Series 1 TiVos (found on the BATBD CD that accompanies this book) and systems running Version 5.x or greater of the TiVo software such as the Pioneer 57-H and 810-H, or the HDTV DirecTiVo.

You can use this same approach to do more sophisticated backups and restores, such as when you want to clone your existing drive to a larger one but preserve all of your existing recordings, as in the following example:

```
mfstool backup -o - -a /dev/hdb ¦ mfstool restore -i - -x –C /dev/hdc
```

As a final example, here is a sample set of backup and restore commands that back up two TiVo drives and then restore the backup to a set of two (presumably larger) TiVo drives while increasing the amount of swap space to 128 MB and increasing the size of the /var partition to 512 MB. This command is split across two lines for readability in this book (you would ordinarily enter it on a single line, removing the backslash that separates the two commands):

```
mfstool backup -o - -a -s /dev/hda /dev/hdb ¦ \
    mfstool restore -i - -x -s 127 -v 512 –C /dev/hdc /dev/hdd
```

 **NOTE**

This command would not work correctly if you were using the BATBD disk's byte-swapped kernel because the /dev/hda drive is not byte-swapped, while the others are. In this case, a better approach would be to attach the two original TiVo drives so that they show up on your Linux systems as /dev/hdb and /dev/hdc and then attach one of the new drives so that it shows up as /dev/hdd. If the new drive is large enough, you could back up both drives to the new larger drive, shut down the system, remove the old drives, and attach the new drive as /dev/hdb or /dev/hdc. Then use the procedures discussed in Chapter 7 to add the second drive to the new drive that you restored to in the first step. Clear as mud?

# Changing TiVo Operating System Versions Using Backups

The version of the TiVo operating system contained on a bootable TiVo disk is inherently backed up as part of any unstructured backup of an entire TiVo disk, or as part of any structured backup created using the MFS Tools utilities. Therefore, restoring that backup image also restores that version of the operating system to the disk on which you are restoring the data.

 **Software Protection Against TiVo Software Upgrades**

There is no 100% guaranteed way to protect against software upgrades with the exception of disconnecting your TiVo from the phone line or network connection through which it obtains both programming and updated guide data. However, certain versions of the TiVo operating system support boot parameters that prevent software upgrades in most cases. Passed to the TiVo as boot parameters that are stored in the TiVo's bootpage, these options will protect against all but the most aggressive upgrades.

Your TiVo's boot parameters are set by using the **bootpage** command discussed in Chapter 5. Before updating the boot parameters, you'll want to check what they currently are, using a command like the following:

```
bootpage -p /dev/hdX
```

Replace the X with the letter corresponding to where the TiVo disk is located in your PC. This will display something like the following:

```
root=/dev/hda4
```

Once you know your current boot parameters, protecting your TiVo against most software updates is done by using a command like the following:

```
bootpage -P "root=/dev/hdYY upgradesoftware=false" -C /dev/hdX
```

Replace the YY with the appropriate letter and number given in the output of the previous **bootpage** command and replace the X with the letter corresponding to where the TiVo disk is located in your PC. If you want to set other boot parameters, make sure that you add them to this example. After completing this command, only major version TiVo software updates should get through, if anything.

The potential downside of this approach is that the TiVo will continually notice that your TiVo is not upgraded, and it may continue to download the upgrades even if you're not installing them. The folks at TiVo may get cranky about this and could disable your account until you talk to them. The best protection against upgrades is to back up your hacks so that you can easily restore them if your TiVo is forcibly upgraded.

As mentioned at the beginning of this chapter, the TiVo's ability to be remotely upgraded is both an advantage and a potential problem. If you are simply interested in running the latest and greatest version of the TiVo software and aren't necessarily interested in getting a command prompt on your TiVo, logging in over the network, or running TiVoWebPlus, automatic upgrading of the software is a great feature. One morning you wake up, and your TiVo has an enhanced user interface, improved audio or video recording capabilities, or perhaps additional commands and options. It's like Christmas!

On the other hand, if you have carefully hacked your TiVo, you would be dismayed to find that your TiVo has been enhanced behind your back, and typically in a way that stops your careful hacks from working. (In some cases, they will even be deleted!) For this reason, it is important to always have a backup available that contains a snapshot of your TiVo when it was customized just the way you wanted it. If your TiVo has been upgraded and you find that you prefer the hacked version with an older TiVo software release to the new, unhacked TiVo software release, you can always restore your old system from backups, returning your system to the state that you desire.

# HACKING

## THE

# TiVo®

# Chapter 7

**SECOND EDITION**

## Expanding Your TiVo's Storage Capacity

The core aspects of expanding your TiVo's storage capacity have been discussed previously, but only in terms of the commands that enable you to increase the amount of storage available on your TiVo. This chapter provides a central resource for simple processes that you can follow to increase the storage capacity of your TiVo by replacing an existing drive with a larger one, by adding a second disk drive to your TiVo, or a combination of both.

Since detailed information on the various steps involved in the upgrade processes is provided elsewhere in the book, this chapter contains a large number of references to other sections, so it may seem to duplicate information. The goal of this chapter is usability, perhaps occasionally at the cost of redundancy or duplication.

# *Overview*

You can increase the amount of space available for storing your recorded programming on your TiVo by doing one of the following:

◆ Replacing an existing TiVo disk drive with a larger one

◆ Adding a second disk drive to your TiVo

You can perform a number of permutations of these two operations. For example, if you are using a Series 1 TiVo that originally came with two disk drives, both of these drives are relatively small. You can replace both of these drives with a single drive that can store substantially more recordings and is fairly inexpensive. You can add a new (larger) second drive at the same time or add it later. If your TiVo only contains a single drive, you can replace that drive with a larger one. You can add a second drive now or later. If you're happy with the capacity of your current TiVo drive, you can continue using that drive and add a second one.

Table 7.1 gives the approximate ratio between disk storage and TiVo recording capacity at each of the TiVo quality settings. This information will help you calculate how much additional recording time you should get by using a larger drive in your TiVo or adding a second drive. These values are approximations—the actual correlation between different levels of recording quality and the storage that they require are stored in TiVo's MFS filesystem, and may therefore change between different versions of the TiVo software.

**Table 7.1  Comparing Recording Quality and Storage Requirements**

| Recording Quality Level | Hours per Gigabyte |
|---|---|
| Basic (Stand-alone) | 1.2 |
| Medium (Stand-alone) | 0.7 |
| High (Stand-alone) | 0.55 |
| Best (Stand-alone) | 0.35 |
| Best (DirecTiVo) | 1.0 |
| Extreme (Fine - Pioneer) | 0.17 |
| HDTV (Hughes/DirectTV HR10-250) | 0.12 |

The core tasks of the disk upgrade process follows. Since single-drive TiVos are much more common than dual-drive TiVos, these instructions refer to single drives, but the procedure for dual-drive TiVos is the same (except plural):

1. Remove the drive from your TiVo and put it in your PC along with the new drive that you want to use in your TiVo (see Chapter 4).

2. Boot from the BATBD disk and back up the drive from your TiVo (see Chapter 6).

3. Restore the backup to the new drive, using the **mfstool restore** options necessary to allocate any additional space for use by your TiVo (explained in this chapter).

4. Put the new drive in your TiVo and turn it on.

As you can see, the process is actually fairly simple. The details of each of the steps in this process have been outlined earlier in this book; however, at this point, the primary challenge is threading them together correctly, as explained in this chapter.

Determining how you want to upgrade your TiVo is up to you, but here are some suggestions:

◆ If you have an existing dual-drive TiVo, back up both drives to a single backup and restore that to a larger single drive. The drives used in a stock dual-drive TiVo are small by today's standards and are old by anyone's standards. Since the drives in a TiVo run 24 hours a day every day, they will eventually go bad. Also, single drives with more storage capacity than the combination of the drives in a dual-drive TiVo can easily be purchased for less than $100.

◆ If you have an existing single drive TiVo Series 1 system, back up that drive and replace it with a larger drive. Eighty or 100 GB drives can easily be purchased for less than $100, and will at least double the storage capacity of your TiVo. More modern drives are usually quieter and more reliable than older drives. Don't wait for a catastrophe to occur before you expand your storage.

◆ If you have a TiVo Series 2, back up its existing drive and restore it to a larger one. You can then keep the original drive as a spare and add a second drive later.

In general, I prefer to deal with as few variables as possible when upgrading a TiVo. I typically replace the existing drive(s) in an existing TiVo with a single larger drive, making sure that it works (and hack it as needed ;-)), and then add a second drive once I'm sure that the first drive is working and configured correctly. Everyone has his or her own approach—some prefer to do everything at once, but I'd rather take my TiVo apart one more time after verifying that the first part of the upgrade worked correctly.

# TiVo Disk Capacity by Model and Software Version

As discussed in detail in Chapter 10, "Linux and the TiVo," the heart of the Linux operating system is known as a *kernel*. The kernel is the portion of the operating system that loads into memory as the first step of the boot process, and which ultimately manages access to all of the hardware and software on your TiVo. The Linux kernel communicates with specific types of hardware, such as your disk drives, using a combination of built-in information and hardware-specific sets of instructions called *device drivers*. Linux device drivers can be built into the kernel or can load automatically when the hardware that they are associated with is detected during the system's boot process.

The size of the disk drives that you can use with your TiVo and the amount of storage that you can actually use on those disk drives is dictated by the version of Linux used in various TiVo software distributions rather than by physical limitations. All standard TiVo software distributions prior to the 5.x software used on TiVos such as the Pioneer 57H and 810H are limited to being able to address 137 GB of disk space on each disk drive. This puts a rough limit of 274 GB of storage on most TiVos, which is probably enough for day-to-day use, especially given that you can use the techniques described in Chapter 12 to extract video and subsequently reinsert it on your TiVo, eliminating the need to always keep all of your favorite recordings on your TiVo.

The Pioneer 57H and 810H and the Hughes HR10-250 use versions of the Linux kernel and TiVo software (v5+) that provide what is known as *LBA48* (48-bit Logical Block Addressing) support. By using logical disk addresses rather than physical addresses, LBA48 kernels support drives up to 2 TB (Terabytes) in size, which should satisfy even the most compulsive TiVo user.

 **TIP**

TiVo hacker extraordinaire Todd Miller has built a number of LBA48-aware kernels for Series 1 TiVos that you can easily install on your TiVo using his **tpip** utility (discussed in Chapter 5). These kernels are provided for your convenience in the `lba48_s1_kernels` directory on the BATBD CD that accompanies this book. You must mount the CD in order to access this directory, as explained in Chapter 11. Todd has a great online reference to using these on his Web site at **http://www.courtesan.com/tivo/bigdisk.html**.

The potential downside of using these kernels is that they may be incompatible with any future software releases from TiVo. For example, if TiVo ever decides to upgrade the software for Series 1 TiVos and that upgrade does not provide standard LBA48 disk support, you may find that you can no longer address storage beyond the 137 GB limit—and any existing storage that exceeds this limit may be corrupted. If you are going to use these kernels, I strongly suggest that you add **upgradesoftware=false** to your boot parameters, as explained in the section of Chapter 8 entitled "Getting a Command Prompt on a Series 1 TiVo." To be honest, the chances of TiVo ever upgrading the software for Series 1 TiVos is minimal at best, but forewarned is forearmed.

The downside of adding huge disks to your TiVo is, naturally, that you may never have time to watch all of the recordings that can fit on your TiVo. On the other hand, you could go away for a year or so and your TiVo would still capture every *Will & Grace* episode ever released. The potential for overwhelming yourself with TiVo recordings was nicely expressed in a poem by Joel Helgeson (JRHelgeson) that he posted in a TiVo discussion on SlashDot:

```
My TiVo box, a loyal pal,
A friend I truly care for.
Because it guarantees I'll see,
The shows I wasn't there for.
Two-thousand shows I've 'taped' so far,
Each night I 'tape' a new one.
Who knows, perhaps there'll come a day,
I'll find the time to view one...
```

In general, I prefer to err on the side of caution and record anything that I might conceivably want to watch. After all, one can always delete things or move them off to another system for archival purposes.

# What You'll Need for Your TiVo Upgrade

The items that you will need in order to replace the existing drive in your system with a larger one, or to add a second drive to your TiVo, are the following:

- ◆ #10 and #15 Torx screwdrivers for Series 1 and Series 2 TiVos and a Phillips screwdriver for the Pioneer 57H and 810H TiVos
- ◆ One or two IDE disk drives, up to 160 GB in size. (You can use larger disks, but you'll only be able to use up to 137 GB on most of them—see the previous section of this chapter for more information.)
- ◆ This book and the BATBD CD that comes with it
- ◆ An hour or so of free time

If you are adding a second drive to your TiVo rather than replacing an existing TiVo drive with a larger one, you should buy a bracket to mount the new drive in your TiVo. (For sources for these brackets, see the sections of Chapter 4 on 9thTee.com, Weaknees.com, or PVRUpgrade.com, or search the Web yourself for something like "TiVo Drive Bracket.") You can add a second drive to any TiVo Series 1 machine without a bracket, but the drive won't be attached to anything and could easily be damaged when moving your TiVo. All TiVo Series 2 machines with the exception of the TCD130040 and TCD130060 Series 2 stand-alone TiVo machines require a mounting bracket because there is nowhere to put the drive without one.

Once you have these items, you're ready to go!

> **TIP**
>
> A variety of TiVo upgrade kits are available from the vendors of TiVo supplies discussed at the end of Chapter 4 in the section entitled "TiVo Hardware Resources on the Web," or from online sites such as eBay. These kits can be useful if you want to quickly and easily get all of the parts necessary to upgrade a TiVo without getting them all yourself. These kits fall into two classes: upgrade kits that provide a larger drive for use in your TiVo as a replacement for the drive(s) that came with your TiVo, and those that are designed to add a second disk to your TiVo. If you decide to buy an upgrade kit for adding a second drive to your TiVo, make sure that it includes a bracket for mounting the second drive in your machine. Again, some of the replacement brackets that are available are discussed and shown in Chapter 4.

# *Replacing an Existing TiVo Disk with a Larger One*

For most people, the first step in TiVo hacking is to increase the amount of storage available to your TiVo. This is not only practical, but also a good baptismal experience in TiVo hacking. Adding a new drive requires opening your TiVo and your PC, shuffling disk drives between the two, and then using TiVo backup and restore commands. After you've completed this task, you'll be more comfortable with your TiVo and its software—and ready to move on to see what else you can do to take full advantage of your TiVo hardware and the software that is available for it.

After you assemble the items listed in the previous section, "What You'll Need for Your TiVo Upgrade," do the following to increase the storage capacity of your TiVo:

1. Follow the instructions in Chapter 4 to open your TiVo, remove its current disk drive, and put it in your PC along with the new drive that you want to use as a replacement.
2. Insert the BATBD disk in your PC's CD-ROM drive and reboot your PC, selecting the appropriate boot option for the type of TiVo that you are upgrading. For TiVo Series 2 models, you can simply press Return when the BATBD's boot options are displayed. For TiVo Series 1 models, select the **bigs1** (preferred) or **s1swap** boot options.

> **TIP**
>
> If you own a modern PC and it is not configured to boot from the CD before booting from the hard drive, you will need to update your BIOS Setup options. To do this, press the appropriate key (usually Delete or F2) immediately after booting your PC. Search the basic and advanced boot options menus for an entry like Boot Sequence and modify this entry so that your computer tries to boot from the CD-ROM before booting from the hard drive. Exactly where this BIOS option menu is located depends on which BIOS your PC uses, but they're all fairly similar. Exit from the BIOS Setup menus, saving your new settings, and reboot your PC (it will usually reboot automatically at this point).

3.  Create a backup of the drive from your TiVo. Because you are upgrading an existing system and will therefore still have your original TiVo drive, it's easiest to use the MFS Tools **mfstool backup** command for your initial backup. This command would look like the following:

```
mfstool backup -o backup-file /dev/hdX
```

The value of *backup-file* should be the full pathname of a location where you want to store the backup file. You should replace the letter *X* in /dev/hdX with the Linux name of the device corresponding to your TiVo disk drive. The device name would therefore be /dev/hdb if you installed the TiVo drive as the slave drive on your primary IDE interface; it would be /dev/hdc if you installed the TiVo drive as the master drive on your secondary IDE interface; or it would be /dev/hdd if you installed the TiVo drive as the slave drive on your secondary IDE interface.

## TIP

When using the MFS Tools utilities to back up HDTV and DVD-enabled TiVos, you should use a higher FSID value than the default of 2000. A value of 5700 is often suggested—I tend to use 9999, just to be on the safe side, since 5700 doesn't seem to get all of the required settings. You can specify the FSIDs to back up by adding the **–f 9999** option to the previous command.

The previous command only backs up certain sections of your TiVo disk. If you want to back up everything, including any recordings that your TiVo disk currently contains, you must add the **-a** option to the backup command, as in the following example:

```
mfstool backup -o backup-file -a /dev/hdX
```

Using the **-a** option creates substantially larger backup files, and will therefore require substantially more disk space than a minimum backup. However, you don't need to worry about the **–f** option when backing up everything.

## NOTE

If anything about this step is confusing, don't worry. Perhaps you haven't read this book from cover to cover? For more information about installing TiVo and other disk drives in your PC, see the section of Chapter 4, "Working with TiVo Disk Drives." For additional information about this backup command, see the section of Chapter 6, "Creating a Simple Backup Using MFS Tools." For suggestions and additional information about your options for where to store the backup file, see the section of Chapter 6 entitled "Finding Room for Backups." If your PC doesn't have 900 MB of free disk space or if you're simply in a hurry, you can follow the instructions later in this chapter in the section "Replacing a Disk without Using Backup Files," but I'd strongly suggest that you make a backup at this point if at all possible.

4. Restore the backup to the new drive, using the **mfstool restore** options necessary to allocate the additional space for use by your TiVo. This command would look like the following:

```
mfstool restore -i backup-file -x -C /dev/hdX
```

The value of *backup-file* should be the full pathname of the backup file that you created in the previous step. The **-C** option limits the restore process to LBA28 disk addressing, which is necessary if you are using TiVo software Versions 4.x and earlier. The **-C** option is only available in the latest Versions of the MFS Tools utilities, such as the one on the BATBD CD that accompanies this book if you boot using the **bigs2**, **bigs1**, or **custs1** boot options.

---

 **NOTE**

If you are restoring your backups for use with a custom TiVo kernel or version of the TiVo software that supports LBA48 large disk addressing, do *not* use the **-C** option. You must also have booted from the BATBD CD using the **bigs2** option, even if you are restoring to a Series 1 TiVo. Examples of LBA48-aware TiVo kernels are Todd Miller's custom kernels for Series 1 TiVos (found on the BATBD CD that accompanies this book), and systems running Version 5.x or greater of the TiVo Software such as the Pioneer 57-H and 810-H, or the HDTV DirecTiVo.

You should replace the letter *X* in /dev/hdX with the Linux name of the device corresponding to the new drive that you want to use in your TiVo. The device name would therefore be /dev/hdb if you installed the new drive as the slave drive on your primary IDE interface; it would be /dev/hdc if you installed the new drive as the master drive on your secondary IDE interface; or it would be /dev/hdd if you installed the new drive as the slave drive on your secondary IDE interface. (For more detailed information about this restore command, see the section of Chapter 6, "Restoring an MFS Tool Backup to a Larger Drive.")

---

 **WARNING**

Be very careful when entering the name of the new disk drive that you want to use in your TiVo. You can easily overwrite your personal computer's boot drive if you specify the wrong disk drive at this point. The **mfstool restore** command will *not* warn you if you accidentally specify a disk drive that contains Windows or Linux data.

5. Shut down your PC and remove the TiVo drive and the new drive that you want to use in your TiVo. Put the TiVo drive somewhere safe and set the jumpers on the replacement disk correctly to ensure that the drive is identified as a Master disk. For more information about setting drive jumpers, see the section of Chapter 4 entitled "Working with TiVo Disk Drives."

6. After putting the new drive in your TiVo, turn it on. You should see the two gray startup screens as the TiVo boots.

Congratulations! You've upgraded your TiVo. You can go to the System Information screen (TiVo Central, Messages & Setup, System Information) to see the new amount of storage available on your TiVo. The amount of storage that displays depends on the size of the new disk drive, but it will certainly be more. And more is better.

You will want to do some housekeeping on the new TiVo drive before using it. For example, the backup command used in this section does not back up the recordings on your TiVo, so you will need to go to the Now Playing menu (TiVo Central, Now Playing) to delete the empty entries for any recordings that were located on the TiVo disk drive that you backed up. If you want to replace an existing TiVo drive with a new one and preserve your recordings, see the next section. The instructions in that section are largely identical to those in this section, except that they use **mfstool backup** options that preserve the entire contents of your original TiVo disk as part of the backup process.

# Upgrading a Disk Without Using Backup Files

If you do not have sufficient disk space to make a backup of your TiVo, never fear—you can still replace the drive in your TiVo with a larger one by taking advantage of some of the powerful features provided by Linux.

Assemble the items listed in the above section, "What You'll Need for Your TiVo Upgrade," and do the following to increase the storage capacity of your TiVo without creating any intermediate backup files:

1. Follow the instructions in Chapter 4 to open your TiVo, remove its current disk drive, and put it in your PC along with the new drive that you want to use as a replacement.

2. Insert the BATBD disk in your PC's CDROM drive and reboot your PC, selecting the appropriate boot option for the type of TiVo that you are upgrading. For TiVo Series 2 models, you can simply press Return when the BATBD's boot options are displayed. For TiVo Series 1 models, select the **bigs1** or **s1swap**boot options.

 **TIP**

If you own a modern PC and it is not configured to boot from the CD before booting from the hard drive, you will need to update your BIOS Setup options. To do this, press the appropriate key (usually Delete or F2) immediately after booting your PC. Search the basic and advanced boot options menus for an entry like Boot Sequence; then modify this entry so that your computer tries to boot from the CD-ROM before booting from the hard drive. Exactly where this BIOS option menu is located depends on which BIOS your PC uses, but they're all fairly similar. Exit from the BIOS Setup menus, save your new settings, and reboot your PC (it will usually reboot automatically at this point).

## 📺 Resolving Problems Accessing Disk Drives

If you are accessing the TiVo disks in your PC using non-IDE device names, the MFS Tools utilities may occasionally look on the wrong interface for your hard drives. An example of this is the following:

```
# pdisk -l /dev/sda
```

```
Partition map (with 512 byte blocks) on '/dev/sda'
#:                 type name                  length base        ( size )
1:   Apple_partition_map Apple                    63 @ 1
2:                Image Bootstrap 1                1 @ 64
3:                Image Kernel 1               8192 @ 65         ( 4.0M)
4:                 Ext2 Root 1               262144 @ 8257       (128.0M)
5:                Image Bootstrap 2            4096 @ 270401     ( 2.0M)
6:                Image Kernel 2               4096 @ 274497     ( 2.0M)
7:                 Ext2 Root 2               262144 @ 278593     (128.0M)
8:                 Swap Linux swap           260096 @ 540737     (127.0M)
9:                 Ext2 /var                 262144 @ 800833     (128.0M)
10:                 MFS MFS application region    524288 @ 1062977   (256.0M)
11:                 MFS MFS media region      33190912 @ 1587265  ( 15.8G)
12:                 MFS Second MFS application region  524288 @ 34778177  (256.0M)
13:                 MFS Second MFS media region  42990592 @ 35302465  ( 20.5G)
14:          Apple_Free Extra               117078511 @ 78293057 ( 55.8G)
```

```
# mfstool add -x /dev/sda
dev1: /dev/sdb,  size: 2097151
/dev/sdb: Input/output error
/dev/sdb10: Input/output error
mfs_load_volume_header: mfsvol_read_data: Input/output error
Unable to open MFS drives.
```

This problem is caused by a conflict between the non-IDE device names that you are using and the environment variables that the **mfstool** utility can use. The **mfstool** utility can use the environment variables MFS_HDA, MFS_HDB, and MFS_DEVICE to locate your disk drives. You can use the **printenv** command to see which environment variables you are currently using, as in the following example:

```
# printenv ¦ grep MFS
MFS_DEVICE=/dev/sdb10 /dev/sdb11 /dev/sdb12 /dev/sdb13
```

---

## 📺 Resolving Problems Accessing Disk Drives *(continued)*

To resolve this problem, use the **unset** command to unset any of these environment variables and then retry the command, as in the following example:

```
# unset MFS_DEVICE
# mfstool add -x /dev/sda
dev1: /dev/sda,  size: 195371568
Current estimated stand-alone size: 39 hours
Adding pair /dev/sda14-/dev/sda15...
New estimated stand-alone size: 103 hours (64 more)
Done!  Estimated stand-alone gain: 64 hours
```

As you can see, the command now completes successfully, and the storage capacity of your TiVo has been successfully increased.

---

3. Back up your TiVo and pipe the output of the backup command to a restore command. This command would look like the following:

```
mfstool backup -o - /dev/hdX ¦ mfstool restore -i - -x –C /dev/hdY
```

The **mfstool restore** command's -**C** option limits the restore process to LBA28 disk addressing, which is necessary if you are using TiVo software Versions 4.x and earlier. The –**C** option is only available in the latest versions of the MFS Tools utilities, such as the one on the BATBD CD that accompanies this book if you boot using the **bigs2**, **bigs1**, or **custs1** boot options.

---

 **NOTE**

If you are restoring your backups for use with a custom TiVo kernel or version of the TiVo software that supports LBA48 large disk addressing, do *not* use the –**C** option. You must also have booted from the BATBD CD using the **bigs2** option, even if you are restoring to a Series 1 TiVo. Examples of LBA48-aware TiVo kernels are Todd Miller's custom kernels for Series 1 TiVos (found on the BATBD CD that accompanies this book) and systems running Version 5.x or greater of the TiVo Software such as the Pioneer 57-H and 810-H, or the HDTV DirecTiVo.

---

Using dashes as the name of the output file for the backup command and as the name of the input file for the restore command tells these commands not to write to files, but to write to what are known as *standard input* and *standard output*. (This is explained in more detail in Chapter 6, in the section "Connecting Backup and Restore Commands Using a Pipe.") You should replace the letter *X* in /dev/hdX with the Linux name of the device corresponding to your TiVo disk drive and replace the letter *Y* in /dev/hdY with the Linux name of the device corresponding to the new drive. The device name would therefore be /dev/hdb for a drive attached as the slave drive on your primary IDE interface; it would be /dev/hdc for a drive attached as the master drive on your secondary IDE interface; or it would be /dev/hdd for a drive attached as the slave drive on your secondary IDE interface.

 **TIP**

When using the MFS Tools utilities to back up HDTV and DVD-enabled TiVos, you should use a higher FSID value than the default of 2000. A value of 5700 is often suggested—I tend to use 9999, just to be on the safe side, since 5700 doesn't seem to get all of the required settings. You can specify the FSIDs to back up by adding the **–f 9999** option to the **mfstool backup** portion of the previous command.

This command only backs up the mandatory sections of your TiVo disk. If you want to back up everything, including any recordings that your TiVo disk currently contains, you must add the **-a** option to the backup portion of the command line, as in the following example:

```
mfstool backup -o - -a /dev/hdX ¦ mfstool restore -i - -x –C /dev/hdY
```

 **NOTE**

If anything about this step is confusing, don't worry. For more information about installing TiVo and other disk drives in your PC, see the section of Chapter 4 entitled "Working with TiVo Disk Drives." For additional information about the **mfstool backup** and **mfstool restore** commands, see the reference information in Chapter 5 or the appropriate sections of Chapter 6. For information about pipes and connecting commands on a Linux system, see the section of Chapter 6 entitled "Connecting Backup and Restore Commands Using a Pipe."

 **WARNING**

Be very careful when entering the name of the new disk drive that you want to use in your TiVo. You can easily overwrite your personal computer's boot drive if you specify the name of the wrong disk drive at this point. The **mfstool restore** command will not warn you if you accidentally specify a disk drive that contains Windows or Linux data.

4. Shut down your PC and remove the TiVo drive and the new drive that you want to use in your TiVo. Put the TiVo drive somewhere safe and set the jumpers on the replacement disk correctly to ensure that the drive is identified as a Master disk. For more information about setting drive jumpers, see the section "Working with TiVo Disk Drives," in Chapter 4.

5. After putting the new drive in your TiVo, turn it on. You should see the two gray startup screens as the TiVo boots.

Congratulations! You've upgraded your TiVo, and have even taken advantage of a relatively whizzy Linux and Unix feature. You can go to the System Information screen (TiVo Central, Messages & Setup, System Information) to see the new amount of storage available on your TiVo. The amount of storage shown depends on the size of the new disk drive.

# Expanding Drives Using Disk Images

As you probably remember from Chapter 6, there are two ways of backing up your TiVo: unstructured and structured backups. The MFS Tools utilities produce structured backups, which only contain the information required to restore a TiVo disk. Unstructured backups are complete images of TiVo drives, and are therefore the same size as the original drive.

The following sections explain how to back up and restore TiVo disks using unstructured backups. In most cases, the MFS Tools are the preferred mechanism for backing up and restoring TiVo disks because the backups that they produce are smaller. However, you never know—you may need to use disk images to restore a drive if you encounter a bug in the MFS Tools utilities, or if changes in the structure of the MFS filesystem prevent the version of the MFS Tools utilities that you are using from working with a newer TiVo software release. Although disk images are huge, they are nice because they automatically preserve all of your settings, recorded videos, and so on, since they are complete images of your original disk drive.

Another reason for using the **dd** program is when you encounter read errors on the drive and therefore suspect that your disk drive is failing. You can use the **dd** program to create an image backup of the entire disk, and then either replace the disk or reformat it. (The former is preferable, but the latter may work.) After you have replaced or reformatted the disk, you can restore the backup to the new disk (as explained in this section and in more detail in Chapter 6). If you are lucky, you might just be able to recover all of your TiVo settings and existing recordings.

 **TIP**

After using an image backup to attempt to work around a failing hard drive, you should immediately do a structured backup of that disk so that you have a smaller, consistent backup of the drive available.

## Expanding a Drive from a Disk Image

This section explains how to restore an image of an existing TiVo drive to a larger disk, and then how to expand the restored image so that the additional space on the new disk is available for use by your TiVo.

**NOTE**

This section is designed to provide a quick reference for restoring a disk from an image backup and expanding it. For detailed information about various steps of this process, see the appropriate sections of Chapter 6. For detailed information about creating disk images using the Linux **dd** program, see the section of Chapter 6 entitled "Creating Image Backups Using **dd**." For detailed information about restoring disk images using **dd**, see the section of Chapter 6 entitled "Restoring Image Backups Using **dd**."

Assemble the items listed in the section entitled "What You'll Need for Your TiVo Upgrade" and then do the following to increase the storage capacity of your TiVo using an image backup file:

1. Follow the instructions in Chapter 4 to open your TiVo, remove its current disk drive, and put it in your PC along with the new drive.

2. Insert the BATBD disk in your PC's CDROM drive and reboot your PC, selecting the appropriate boot option for the type of TiVo that you are upgrading. For TiVo Series 2 models, you can simply press Return when the BATBD's boot options are displayed. For TiVo Series 1 models, select the **bigs1** (preferred) or **s1swap** boot options.

 **TIP**

If you own a modern PC and it is not configured to boot from the CD before booting from the hard drive, you will need to update your BIOS Setup options. To do this, press the appropriate key (usually Delete or F2) immediately after booting your PC. Search the basic and advanced boot options menus for an entry like Boot Sequence and modify this entry so that your computer tries to boot from the CD-ROM before booting from the hard drive. Exactly where this BIOS option menu is located depends on which BIOS your PC uses, but they're all fairly similar. Exit from the BIOS Setup menus, saving your new settings, and reboot your PC (it will usually reboot automatically at this point).

3. Create a backup of the drive from your TiVo using the Linux **dd** command. This command would look like the following:

```
dd if=/dev/hdX of=backup-file bs=32k conv=noerror,sync
```

You should replace the letter $X$ in /dev/hdX with the Linux name of the device corresponding to your TiVo disk drive. The device name would therefore be /dev/hdb if you installed the TiVo drive as the slave drive on your primary IDE interface; it would be /dev/hdc if you installed the TiVo drive as the master drive on your secondary IDE interface; or it would be /dev/hdd if you installed the TiVo drive as the slave drive on your secondary IDE interface. The value of *backup-file* should be the full pathname of the backup file that you want to create. The **bs** option specifies the block size that the **dd** program should use when reading and writing data. The **conv=noerror,sync** options are usually unnecessary but are handy if you encounter any problems reading from the original TiVo disk. These are conversion options that tell the **dd** program how to react to specific conditions, if encountered. The **noerror** option tells the **dd** program not to abort if an error is encountered. The **sync** option tells the **dd** program to pad incomplete reads with NULL bytes if the program encounters a problem reading from the input drive.

 **NOTE**

For more information about installing TiVo and other disk drives in your PC, see the section in Chapter 4, "Working with TiVo Disk Drives." For suggestions and additional information about your options for where to store backup files, see the section in Chapter 6, "Finding Room for Backups." If your PC doesn't have the gigabytes of free disk space required to create a complete image of your existing TiVo drive, you can follow the instructions in the next section, "Using Disk Images Without Intermediate Backup Files."

4. Restore the backup to the new drive by using the **dd** command. This command should look like the following:

```
dd if=backup-file of=/dev/hdX bs=32k
```

The value of *backup-file* should be the full pathname of the backup file that you created in the previous step. You should replace the letter *X* in /dev/hdX with the Linux name of the device corresponding to the new drive that you want to use in your TiVo. The device name would therefore be /dev/hdb if you installed the new drive as the slave drive on your primary IDE interface; it would be /dev/hdc if you installed the new drive as the master drive on your secondary IDE interface; or it would be /dev/hdd if you installed the new drive as the slave drive on your secondary IDE interface. The conversion options used when creating the disk image are not necessary because you are working from a backup file that was correctly written in the previous step. (For more detailed information about this restore command, see the section of Chapter 6, "Restoring Image Backups Using **dd**.")

 **WARNING**

Be very careful when entering the name of the new disk drive that you want to use in your TiVo. You can easily overwrite your personal computer's boot drive if you specify the name of the wrong disk drive at this point. The **dd** command will not warn you if you accidentally specify a disk drive that contains Windows or Linux data.

5. At this point, you can use either the MFS Tools utilities or the BlessTiVo program to make the extra space on the new drive available to your TiVo. This extra space is the difference between the size of your original TiVo disk and the size of the drive to which you restored the image backup. To use the MFS Tools **mfstool add** command to add this extra space to the drive to which you restored your image backup, use the following command:

```
mfstool add -x /dev/hdX
```

You should replace the letter $X$ in /dev/hdX with the Linux name of the device corresponding to the drive to which you restored your image backup. The device name would therefore be /dev/hdb if you installed the new drive as the slave drive on your primary IDE interface; it would be /dev/hdc if you installed the new drive as the master drive on your secondary IDE interface; or it would be /dev/hdd if you installed the new drive as the slave drive on your secondary IDE interface.

6. Shut down your PC and remove the TiVo drive and the new drive that you want to use in your TiVo. Put the TiVo drive somewhere safe and set the jumpers on the replacement disk correctly to ensure that the drive is identified as a Master disk. For more information about setting drive jumpers, see the section of Chapter 4 entitled "Working with TiVo Disk Drives."

7. After putting the new drive in your TiVo, turn it on. You should see the two gray startup screens as the TiVo boots.

Congratulations! You've upgraded your TiVo. You can go to the System Information screen (TiVo Central, Messages & Setup, System Information) to see the new amount of storage available on your TiVo. The amount of storage shown depends on the size of the new disk drive, but it will certainly be more. As is always true for good things, more is better.

# Using Disk Images Without Intermediate Backup Files

How can you use image backups to back up and restore a drive without creating any intermediate files? As discussed earlier, the backup files created using **dd** are unstructured backup files that are the exact size of the disk drive that you backed up. If you don't happen to have 20 to 60 GB of disk space sitting around but need to do an image backup, such as when you suspect that your existing TiVo disk drive is going bad, no worry. This section explains how to take advantage of some of the powerful features provided by Linux to create and restore an image backup without requiring intermediate disk space. This section concludes by explaining how to expand the cloned disk image on the new drive to use additional space to store TiVo recordings.

After you have the items listed in the section entitled "What You'll Need for Your TiVo Upgrade," take the following steps to increase the storage capacity of your TiVo using an image backup file:

1. Following the instructions in Chapter 4, "Working with TiVo Disk Drives," open your TiVo, remove its current disk drive, and put it in your PC along with the new drive that you want to replace it with.

2. Insert the BATBD disk in your PC's CDROM drive and reboot your PC, selecting the appropriate boot option for the type of TiVo that you are upgrading. For TiVo Series 2 models, you can simply press Return when the BATBD's boot options display. For TiVo Series 1 models, select the **bigs1** (preferred) or **s1swap** boot options.

**NOTE**

This section is designed to provide a quick reference for backing up and restoring a disk using image backup and subsequently expanding the cloned drive. For detailed information about various steps of this process, see the appropriate sections of Chapter 6. For detailed information about creating disk images using the Linux **dd** program, see the section of Chapter 6 entitled "Creating Image Backups Using **dd**." For detailed information about restoring disk images using **dd**, see the section "Restoring Image Backups Using **dd**" in Chapter 6. For detailed information about creating and restoring backups without using intermediate files, see the section of Chapter 6, "Connecting Backup and Restore Commands Using a Pipe." If you are unsure about how to attach or jumper disk drives, see the information about installing TiVo and other disk drives in Chapter 4, the section entitled "Working with TiVo Disk Drives."

 **TIP**

If you have a modern PC that can boot from CD and your PC is not configured to boot from the CD before booting from the hard drive, you will need to update your BIOS Setup options. To do this, press the appropriate key (usually Delete or F2) immediately after booting your PC. Search the basic and advanced boot options menus for an entry like Boot Sequence and modify this entry so that your computer tries to boot from the CD-ROM before booting from the hard drive. Exactly where this BIOS option menu is located depends on which BIOS your PC uses, but they're all fairly similar. Exit from the BIOS Setup menus, saving your new settings, and reboot your PC (it will usually reboot automatically at this point).

3. Create a backup of the drive from your TiVo by using the Linux **dd** command, writing to standard output, and piping the output of this command into another **dd** command that reads from standard input and writes to the new drive. This command should look like the following:

```
dd if=/dev/hdX  bs=32k conv=noerror,sync ¦ dd of=/dev/hdY bs=32k
```

You should replace the letter $X$ in /dev/hdX with the Linux name of the device corresponding to your TiVo disk drive and replace the letter $Y$ in /dev/hdY with the Linux name of the device corresponding to the new drive. The device name would therefore be /dev/hdb for a drive attached as the slave drive on your primary IDE interface; it would be /dev/hdc for a drive attached as the master drive on your secondary IDE interface; or it would be /dev/hdd for a drive attached as the slave drive on your secondary IDE interface. The **bs** options specify the block size that the **dd** program should use when reading and writing data. The **conv=noerror,sync** options are usually unnecessary but are handy if you encounter any problems reading from the original TiVo disk. These are conversion options that tell the **dd** program how to react to specific conditions, if encountered. The **noerror** option tells the

**dd** program not to abort if an error is encountered. The **sync** option tells the **dd** program to pad incomplete reads with NULL bytes if the program encounters a problem reading from the input drive.

 **WARNING**

Be very careful when entering the name of the new disk drive that you want to use in your TiVo. You can easily overwrite your personal computer's boot drive if you specify the name of the wrong disk drive at this point. The **dd** command will not warn you if you accidentally specify a disk drive that contains Windows or Linux data.

4.  Now you can use either the MFS Tools utilities or the BlessTiVo program to make the extra space on the new drive available to your TiVo. This extra space is the difference between the size of your original TiVo disk and the size of the drive to which you restored the image backup. To use the MFS Tools **mfstool add** command to add this extra space to the drive to which you restored your image backup, use the following command:

    ```
    mfstool add -x /dev/hdX
    ```

    You should replace the letter _X_ in /dev/hdX with the Linux name of the device corresponding to the drive to which you restored your image backup. The device name would therefore be /dev/hdb if you installed the new drive as the slave drive on your primary IDE interface; it would be /dev/hdc if you installed the new drive as the master drive on your secondary IDE interface; or it would be /dev/hdd if you installed the new drive as the slave drive on your secondary IDE interface.

5.  Shut down your PC and remove the TiVo drive and the new drive that you want to use in your TiVo. Put the TiVo drive somewhere safe, and set the jumpers on the replacement disk correctly to ensure that the drive is identified as a Master disk. For more information about setting drive jumpers, see the section, "Working with TiVo Disk Drives," in Chapter 4.

6.  After putting the new drive in your TiVo, turn it on. You should see the two gray startup screens as the TiVo boots.

Congratulations! You've upgraded your TiVo. You can go to the System Information screen (TiVo Central, Messages & Setup, System Information) to see the new amount of storage available on your TiVo. The amount of storage shown depends on the size of the new disk drive, but it will certainly be more.

# Adding a Second Drive to Your TiVo

As discussed in the beginning of this chapter, there are two ways to upgrade the storage capacity of your TiVo: by replacing an existing drive with a larger one or by adding a second drive. You can always do both, which is my preferred solution—but I prefer not to do both at the same time. Upgrading an existing disk and verifying that it works correctly is easy enough to do, but it has its own set of potential problems. Rather than combining those problems with any of the potential problems that can arise when adding a second disk, I prefer to upgrade an existing disk first and then verify that everything is working correctly. Then one can easily add a second disk as explained in the following sections.

 **WARNING**

As discussed in more detail in the sections of Chapter 5 that introduced the BlessTiVo and MFS Tool commands, when you add a second drive to your TiVo, the two drives are "married" and must be used together. You cannot subsequently remove the second drive and expect your Series 1 model to work correctly with just the A drive. To "unmarry" two drives, you must back them up using the MFS Tools utilities (also discussed in Chapter 6) and then restore the backup to a single drive, assuming that the single drive has sufficient space to hold the TiVo data that was contained on the previous two drives. This single drive can be used by itself, and then you can recycle the two drives that are its logical parents.

The following sections explain how to use the MFS Tools and BlessTiVo utilities to add a second drive to your TiVo. Each of these utilities has advantages. The MFS Tools utilities enable you to add an entire disk or specific partitions to the storage capacity of your TiVo. The BlessTiVo utility only enables you to add an entire drive to your TiVo and is available for both Linux and the Mac OS X.

# Using the MFS Tools Utilities to Add a Second Drive

The MFS Tools utilities **mfstool** command provides a command-line option that makes it easy to add a second drive to your TiVo, substantially increasing the amount of space available for recordings. The **mfstool add** command enables you to add the entire contents of a second drive quickly, and it also enables you to add specific MFS partitions to the storage capacity of your TiVo. The latter can be quite useful for advanced TiVo hackers who want to create their own standard Linux (**ext2**) partitions on a second drive, but still want to use the majority of that drive to provide increased storage capacity for TiVo recordings.

## Adding an Entire Drive Using MFS Tools

Adding all of the storage space available on a new disk is easy using the MFS Tools utilities. After you have the items listed in the section, "What You'll Need for Your TiVo Upgrade," do the following to prepare a second drive for use in your TiVo by using the **mfstool add** command:

1. Insert the drive that you want to use in your TiVo into your PC as described in Chapter 4.

**WARNING**

Do not use the procedure described in this section to add a second drive to your TiVo unless that drive is blank or is a copy of an existing TiVo drive. Any drive that is not currently used by MFS—that is, does not contain a valid TiVo partition map—is initialized by the **mfstool add** command. To add specific portions of an existing drive to your TiVo, use the procedure described in the section entitled "Adding Specific Partitions of a Second Drive Using MFS Tools" later in this chapter.

2. Insert the BATBD disk in your PC's CD-ROM drive and reboot your PC, selecting the appropriate boot option for the type of TiVo that you are upgrading. For TiVo Series 2 models, you can simply press Return when the BATBD's boot options are displayed. For TiVo Series 1 models, select the **s1swap** boot option.

 **TIP**

If your PC is not configured to boot from the CD before booting from the hard drive, you will need to update your BIOS Setup options. To do this, press the appropriate key (usually Delete or F2) immediately after booting your PC. Search the basic and advanced boot options menus for an entry like Boot Sequence and modify this entry so that your computer tries to boot from the CD-ROM before booting from the hard drive. Exactly where this BIOS option menu is located depends on which BIOS your PC uses, but they're all fairly similar. Exit from the BIOS Setup menus, saving your new settings, and reboot your PC (it will usually reboot automatically at this point).

3. To format and partition the entire contents of the newly attached disk so that it can be used by your TiVo for storing recordings, execute the following command:

```
mfstool add -x /dev/hdX
```

Replace the letter $X$ in /dev/hdX with the Linux name of the device corresponding to the new disk drive. The device name would therefore be /dev/hdb if you installed the new drive as the slave drive on your primary IDE interface; the name would be /dev/hdc if you installed the new drive as the master drive on your secondary IDE interface; or the name would be /dev/hdd if you installed the new drive as the slave drive on your secondary IDE interface.

 **WARNING**

Be very careful when entering the name of the new disk drive that you want to use in your TiVo. You can easily overwrite your personal computer's boot drive if you specify the name of the wrong disk drive at this point. The **mfstool add** command will not warn you if you accidentally specify a disk drive that contains Windows or Linux data, and it will silently initialize that disk for you.

4. Shut down your TiVo and follow the instructions in Chapter 4 to open your TiVo and add the second drive, "jumpering" it correctly so that it does not conflict with the existing drive in your TiVo.

5. Turn on your TiVo. You should see the standard two gray startup screens as the TiVo boots.

That's all there is to it! When you put the new drive in your TiVo and boot the TiVo, the TiVo detects the second drive and adds its disk identifier to the primary drive, thereby making the additional storage that it contains available to your TiVo. After your TiVo displays the startup animation, you can go to the System Information screen (TiVo Central, Messages & Setup, System Information) to see the new amount of storage available on your TiVo. The amount of storage shown depends on the size of the new disk drive, but it will certainly be more. Congratulations!

## Adding Specific Partitions of a Second Drive Using MFS Tools

Adding specific partitions on a second disk to the pool of storage available to your TiVo is easy using the MFS Tools utilities. Once you have the items listed in the section entitled "What You'll Need for Your TiVo Upgrade," do the following to prepare specific partitions of a second drive for use by your TiVo, using the **mfstool add** command:

1. Insert the new drive that you want to use in your TiVo into your PC as described in Chapter 4.

2. Insert the BATBD disk in your PC's CD-ROM drive and reboot your PC, selecting the appropriate boot option for the type of TiVo that you are upgrading. For TiVo Series 2 models, you can simply press Return when the BATBD's boot options are displayed. For TiVo Series 1 models, select the **s1swap** boot option.

 **TIP**

If your PC is not configured to boot from the CD before booting from the hard drive, you will need to update your BIOS Setup options. To do this, press the appropriate key (usually Delete or F2) immediately after booting your PC. Search the basic and advanced boot options menus for an entry like Boot Sequence and modify this entry so that your computer tries to boot from the CD-ROM before booting from the hard drive. Exactly where this BIOS option menu is located depends on which BIOS your PC uses, but they're all fairly similar. Exit from the BIOS Setup menus, saving your new settings, and reboot your PC (it will usually reboot automatically).

3. Use the **pdisk -l** /dev/hdX command to display the partition map on your TiVo to verify the names of the partitions that you want to add. Replace the letter *X* in /dev/hdX with the Linux name of the device corresponding to the new disk drive. The device name would therefore be /dev/hdb if you installed the new drive as the slave drive

on your primary IDE interface; it would be /dev/hdc if you installed the new drive as the master drive on your secondary IDE interface; or it would be /dev/hdd if you installed the new drive as the slave drive on your secondary IDE interface.

> **TIP**
>
> TiVo disks can be initialized and partitions created manually by using the **pdisk** command, as explained in Chapter 5.

4. Once you know the names of the MFS partitions that you want to add, execute the following command:

```
mfstool add /dev/hdXN /dev/hdXM
```

Replace the letter *X* with the identifier for the disk drive, as described previously, and replace the letters *N* and *M* with the numbers corresponding to the partitions containing the MFS application and MFS media regions that you want to add.

5. Shut down your TiVo and follow the instructions in Chapter 4 to open your TiVo and add the second drive, "jumpering" it correctly so that it does not conflict with your existing TiVo drive.

6. Turn on your TiVo. You should see the standard two gray startup screens as the TiVo boots.

That's all there is to it! The TiVo automatically detects the second drive at boot time and adds its disk identifier to the primary drive, making the additional storage that it contains available to your TiVo. After your TiVo displays the startup animation, you can go to the System Information screen (TiVo Central, Messages & Setup, System Information) to see the new amount of storage available on your TiVo. The amount of storage shown depends on the size of the new disk drive.

## Using the BlessTiVo Utility to Add a Second Drive

The BlessTiVo utility is an open source utility that makes it easy to add an entire drive to your TiVo for use in storing recordings. The BlessTiVo utility is available for systems such as Linux (on the BATBD disk) and Mac OS X (on the BATBD CD in the macintosh directory and also downloadable from **http://www.weaknees.com/downloads/OSXv4Blesser.sit.hqx**). For more information about using the BlessTiVo utility on a Mac OS X system, see Chapter 9, "Working with Your TiVo from Windows and Macintosh Systems."

As with the other procedures provided in this chapter, this section provides a procedural guide to using BlessTiVo to add a second drive to your TiVo. For detailed information on the BlessTiVo command, its operation, and any status or error messages that it displays, see the section in Chapter 5, "BlessTiVo." This section is designed to get you up and running with a minimum of fuss and background information. To use the BlessTiVo command to prepare a second drive for use by your TiVo, do the following:

1. Insert the new drive that you want to use in your TiVo into your PC as described in Chapter 4.

2. Insert the BATBD disk in your PC's CD-ROM drive and reboot your PC, selecting the appropriate boot option for the type of TiVo that you are upgrading. For TiVo Series 2 models, you can simply press Return when the BATBD's boot options are displayed. For TiVo Series 1 models, select the **bigs1** (preferred) or **s1swap** boot options.

 **TIP**

If your PC is not configured to boot from the CD before booting from the hard drive, you will need to update your BIOS Setup options. To do this, press the appropriate key (usually Delete or F2) immediately after booting your PC. Search the basic and advanced boot options menus for an entry like Boot Sequence and modify this entry so that your computer tries to boot from the CD-ROM before booting from the hard drive. Exactly where this BIOS option menu is located depends on which BIOS your PC uses, but they're all fairly similar. Exit from the BIOS Setup menus, saving your new settings, and reboot your PC (it will usually reboot automatically at this point).

3. To format and partition the entire contents of the newly attached disk so that your TiVo can use it for storing recordings, execute the following command:

   `BlessTiVo /dev/hdX`

   Replace the letter *X* with the appropriate identifier for the disk that you want to format. The device names used by the BlessTiVo command are `/dev/hdb` for a drive attached as a slave on your primary IDE interface; it would be `/dev/hdc` for a drive attached as a master on your secondary IDE interface; and it would be `/dev/hdd` for a drive attached as a slave on your secondary IDE interface. As a safety feature, the BlessTiVo command does not allow you to specify `/dev/hda` as the drive to be formatted, because this drive is typically the boot disk used by your PC or a Mac OS system.

 **TIP**

When you execute the BlessTiVo command, the program checks first to see if the drive exists and can be opened. If you see error messages such as "No device specified," "Too many command line options," or "Unable to connect to `/dev/hdx`," see the section of Chapter 5 on the BlessTiVo command for suggestions and solutions.

4. If the drive you are blessing already contains DOS or Linux partitioning information, the BlessTiVo command warns you of this fact and asks if you want to proceed. Answer "Y" if you do, or thank your lucky stars and answer "N" if you do not.

5. The BlessTiVo command asks you to verify that you want to proceed even if the specified disk contains no partitioning information. Answer "Y" to continue. The

BlessTiVo command formats and partitions the drive as described in Chapter 5, displaying status messages as it proceeds. When it completes, it displays a final summary message listing the amount of storage available on the newly formatted drive.

 **WARNING**

The summary message displayed at the end of the BlessTiVo process is very important—you should always check this value to make sure that it is within 3 gigabytes of the total size of the disk that you are adding. If the size of the disk that you are blessing is not reported as being within 3 GB of the actual size of the disk, do not add this drive to your TiVo. If you do add it, the two drives will be married, and you will not be able to take advantage of the storage that is actually available on the second disk.

6. Shut down your TiVo and follow the instructions in Chapter 4 to open your TiVo and add the second drive, "jumpering" it correctly so that it does not conflict with your existing TiVo drive.

7. Turn on your TiVo. You should see the standard two gray startup screens as the TiVo boots.

That's all there is to it! The TiVo automatically detects the second drive at boot time and adds its disk identifier to the primary drive, thereby making the additional storage that it contains available to your TiVo. After your TiVo displays the startup animation, you can go to the System Information screen (TiVo Central, Messages & Setup, System Information) to see the new amount of storage available on your TiVo.

# HACKING THE TiVo

## Chapter 8

### Connecting the Universe to Your TiVo

**P**revious chapters of this book have explained how to expand the physical capacity, capabilities, and usability of your TiVo. You've learned how to connect your TiVo to your home network and use an always-on broadband connection as the means for downloading programming and guide updates. This chapter takes your networked TiVo one step further, explaining how to expand the software usability and connectivity of your TiVo by installing software on your TiVo that connects it to the rest of your networked environment.

The key to expanding the software capabilities of your TiVo is getting access to its filesystems. Earlier chapters explained how to attach TiVo disks to other systems and manipulate their contents there, which is all well and good, but that really isn't the sort of interactive computer experience that we've all come to expect. Made a mistake? Shut down the TiVo, remove the disk drive, shut down your PC, install the drive, and reboot from the BATBD CD. That is all fine once or twice, but not suitable for those of us who have come to expect fairly instant gratification. It's as retro as batch mode!

This chapter explains how to start working on your TiVo by starting a command prompt on your TiVo's serial port. When you have your prompt, you can transfer files and software to your TiVo, install and start that software, and generally expand the horizons of your TiVo.

Today's networked universe is all about connectivity—so much of this chapter discusses various system and application software packages that can help make your TiVo a better network and connectivity citizen.

 **NOTE**

At the time this book was updated, the current TiVo software release for Series 2 TiVo systems was 4.0.1b (except for the latest DirecTiVos, which are still running 3.1.x). Newer TiVo systems, such as the Pioneer 57H and 810H systems, run Version 5.2.1a or better of the TiVo software, which includes support for larger disks, the DVD hardware, and so on. The DVD-enabled TiVos are still based on the Series 2 TiVo hardware platform. When referring to Version 4 or better of the TiVo software, I will simply refer to these versions as "Version 4.x+."

The procedures described in this section apply to all Series 2 TiVo hardware systems available at the time that this book was written, including the Pioneer systems. Wherever you need to know something special about a certain type of Series 2 TiVo system, I will insert a note that identifies the type of system and any special concerns.

# Getting a Command Prompt on Your TiVo

Almost all of the truly fun TiVo software hacks require accessing and updating the TiVo's filesystems and boot sequence. While you can do much of this after putting your TiVo disk in your PC and booting from the BATBD CD, hacking different models of TiVos requires different levels of willingness and commitment to hacking your machine. In a Series 1 machine, the key to getting a shell prompt and installing some basic utilities is as simple as making sure that you're running specific versions of the TiVo software. The Series 2 machines have introduced some new wrinkles into getting a shell prompt. If you're willing to run an older version of the TiVo software, you can restore it to your Series 2 TiVo and follow a marginally convoluted procedure to get a shell prompt—with the added bonus of knowing that you are truly the master of your TiVo because there's a fair amount of work involved.

If you (like me) "need" to be running the latest and greatest TiVo software release on your Series 2 machine, things get even more complex, but they still are eminently doable.

Subsequent sections of this book refer to TiVos on which you have a command prompt (and hopefully network access, as well) as "hacked" TiVos. I'm assuming that once you get a shell prompt on your TiVo, you won't be content to stop there, and will explore networking your TiVo so that you can take advantage of the other software packages described in this chapter. And you should. You're not hurting anyone, and you're refining and enhancing the usability of a home entertainment appliance that you've paid for. This seems to me like a good idea.

The next few sections will explain how to get a shell prompt on various models of TiVos, running under various software releases. A shell prompt on your TiVo is essentially a Welcome mat, letting you know that you are indeed the master of your domain and your TiVo—and you can do it easily.

 **TIP**

After following any of the procedures in this chapter to get a command prompt on your TiVo, you may occasionally encounter problems with how the bash shell prompts, displays, or processes input. If this is the case, you can use the Linux command **stty sane** (followed by the Return or Enter key) to make bash work correctly in whatever terminal emulator or other serial connection application you're using. In some truly weird cases, you may need to type **Control-j stty sane Control-j**, where Control-j is typed by holding down the Ctrl key and pressing the letter "j."

 **NOTE**

As always, I want to give credit where credit is due. The folks on the various TiVo forums discussed later in Chapter 14, "Other TiVo Hacking Resources," are the source of much of this information. (I've largely only tweaked processes to make them easier to follow and understand.) The ability to hack your TiVo is a testimonial to the power and flexibility of TiVos in general, but even more so to the commitment and continuing curiosity of the members of the TiVo hacking community. The folks credited in the dedication of this book (and many more) are the real heroes here. Especially in this chapter's Two-Kernel Monte section, TiVo hackers like MuscleNerd, embeem, and d7o did the pioneering work, porting and documenting the **monte** program on the TiVo, based on the original **monte** program for Linux (**http://www.scyld.com/products/beowulf/software/ monte.html**) written by Erik Hendriks. In this section, I am largely playing Boswell to their Samuel Johnsons.

# Getting a Command Prompt on a Series 1 TiVo

As the Homo Erectus of the TiVo hardware family, Series 1 models are great machines that are a pleasure to own and tinker with. As computer systems, they're slower than the Series 2 machines and are essentially end-of-life, in terms of operating system and TiVo software upgrades. For example, TiVo's Home Media Features (formerly known as the "Home Media Option") are not available for the Series 1 and probably never will be. This software depends on kernel and software functionality that TiVo, Inc. has not ported to the Series 1—and (let's face it) why should they? (Actually, the core problem in TiVo's offering things like the Home Media Features on Series 1 machines is that these systems didn't support networking by default—and TiVo certainly can't officially endorse anyone opening up their Series 1 TiVo to add a networking card.)

---

 **NOTE**

If you installed a network card in your Series 1 machine, as described in Chapter 3 in the section "Networking Series 1 TiVos," you do not have to follow the procedure described in this section. The **nic_install** script provided with today's TurboNet and Airnet cards for the Series 1 automatically configures your system to start a command prompt on the serial port, and also starts the FTP and Telnet daemons discussed later in this chapter in "Starting FTP and Telnet on Your TiVo."

---

TiVo's core mission is video recording and playback—in good conscience, they can't guarantee that their older hardware can perform its basic, guaranteed functions and also import and play audio files and display digital photographs. You can only squeeze so much juice out of an orange. TiVo doesn't even sell the Series 1 anymore, so any investment in upgrading its software is just gravy for the TiVo community. That said, the Series 1 TiVo is a hacker's paradise. Since it is essentially end-of-life in terms of software upgrades, why should TiVo care about what version of the OS you run on it, what software you subsequently install, and so on? Some of the more anal aspects of the more recent releases of the TiVo software have reared their ugly heads in the last revs of the TiVo Series 1 software, but these are easiest enough to undo ;-).

To get a command prompt on your Series 1 TiVo, you must be running a version of the TiVo software and operating system that is no newer than version 3.1. This is the latest "non-anal" version of the TiVo OS in which the BASH_ENV environment variable can be added to the boot parameters.

To get a command prompt on a Series 1 TiVo running Version 3.1 or earlier of the TiVo OS, do the following:

1. Shut down your TiVo, remove the drive, and put it in your PC as explained in Chapter 3, "Exploring Your TiVo Hardware."

2. Boot your PC using the BATBD CD and selecting the **bigs1** (preferred) or **s1swap** boot options so that you can mount and access TiVo partitions.

##  Getting a Backup of a Specific Version of the TiVo

I don't see why TiVo cares what version of the TiVo OS you're running, except in the case where you're running a version that's old enough that their servers want to upgrade it. In which case, your TiVo may suck bandwidth each night downloading upgraded versions of the OS. (A bootpage setting for preventing software upgrades was discussed at the end of Chapter 6.)

If TiVo, Inc. would make it easy for users to guarantee that no upgrades would be performed, life for TiVo hackers everywhere would be much better. And hopefully, all TiVo hackers would still be cool enough to pay the monthly or lifetime subscription costs. I know that I do—and I'm happy to do so, because my TiVo is almost as integral to my lifestyle as any other utility.

See the section of Chapter 6 entitled "Finding Backups of the TiVo Software" for general information about finding TiVo backups on the Net. If you are absolutely desperate for a specific version and can't find one on the Net, you can always ask another TiVo fanatic for a copy of one of their backups—but the best solution for having backups available is to make them yourself from your own machine each time that its software version is upgraded.

3. Use the **bootpage** command to determine which of the possible root filesystems is the active one on your TiVo. This will be either /dev/hda4 or /dev/hda7. For example, if the hard drive from your TiVo is available in your PC as /dev/hdd (the slave on your secondary IDE interface), you would execute the following bootpage command:

```
bootpage -p /dev/hdd
```

The **bootpage** command returns a string like root=/dev/hda7, which indicates that your TiVo's active root partition is partition 7 of the drive you're looking at.

### NOTE

The **bootpage** command returns values relative to where the drive would appear in your TiVo, not where it appears in your PC. The **bootpage** command therefore always will return a value on the drive /dev/hda, regardless of where the drive is available in your PC.

4. Mount the specified partition from the drive in your PC so that you can access the files and directories that it contains. For example, if the **bootpage** command returned root=/dev/hda7, and the TiVo drive is available in your PC as /dev/hdd, you would mount the partition using the following command:

```
mount /dev/hdd7 /mnt
```

The files and directories in your TiVo's root partition would then be available under the directory /mnt.

5. Change directory to the /etc/rc.d directory in the partition that you mounted from the TiVo drive. This directory contains default command files that are executed when your TiVo boots. (The directory name rc.d stands for *run command default*.) For example, if you mounted the TiVo partition on the directory /mnt (as shown in the previous example), you would execute the following command to change to the right directory on the TiVo drive:

```
cd /mnt/etc/rc.d
```

6. To verify that you're in the right directory, list its contents by typing the **ls** command and pressing the Return or Enter key on your keyboard. You should see a display like the following:

```
finishInstall.tcl   rc.arch          rc.net              rc.sysinit
```

The files with names that begin with *rc* (run command) are specific command files that your TiVo executes when it boots. The file rc.sysinit contains the basic TiVo system initialization commands. The file rc.arch contains architecture-specific startup commands, and is executed by the rc.sysinit command file. The file rc.net contains network-related configuration commands, and is also executed by the rc.sysinit command file. The rc.sysinit command file is the big kahuna in this directory—it is the file that we will be modifying in the remainder of this procedure.

7. Make a backup copy of the file rc.sysinit by copying it to the file rc.sysinit.save. If you accidentally make any mistakes when editing the "real" rc.sysinit file and your TiVo won't boot for some reason, you can always return to its original state by copying the backup file over the one you've modified. To make a copy of the rc.sysinit file with the name rc.sysinit.save, type the following command and press the Return or Enter key on your keyboard:

```
cp rc.sysinit rc.sysinit.save
```

8. Now comes the moment of truth! Type the following command *exactly as shown* to append the command that starts the bash shell to the end of the rc.sysinit file:

```
echo "/bin/bash </dev/ttyS3 >& /dev/ttyS3 &" >> rc.sysinit
```

Make absolutely sure that this command is exactly as shown before pressing the Return or Enter key on your keyboard. This command uses a feature of the Linux command interpreter to append the series of characters /bin/bash </dev/ttyS3 >& /dev/ttyS3 & to the end of the rc.sysinit file. When you next boot your TiVo with this command at the end of your rc.sysinit, it tells your TiVo to start the command /bin/bash (the Linux command interpreter). The < character tells the TiVo that any input to this command will come from the device /dev/ttyS3, which is your Series 1 TiVo serial port. The >& characters tell the TiVo that any output (>) or error messages (&) should also be sent to the device /dev/ttyS3 (again, your TiVo's serial port). The final ampersand after the second instance of /dev/ttyS3 in this command tells your TiVo to start the command interpreter in the background, which means that your TiVo can execute other commands while the command interpreter runs.

9. Verify that you've typed this command correctly by using the Linux **tail** command to display the last 10 lines of the file rc.sysinit on your screen, as in the following example:

```
tail rc.sysinit
```

You should see the following output on your screen:

```
if [ ! "$vmstat" = "" ]; then
echo "Starting memory statistic gathering"
vmstat 10 &
fi

[ ! -f /etc/rc.d/rc.sysinit.author ] || /etc/rc.d/rc.sysinit.author
echo "rc.sysinit is complete"
/bin/bash </dev/ttyS3 >& /dev/ttyS3 &
```

Before proceeding, compare the last line on your screen with the last line of the output displayed on your screen. If they are not identical, copy the file rc.sysinit.save over the file rc.sysinit using the Linux **copy** command (**cp rc.sysinit.save rc.sysinit**) and begin again at Step 8 of this procedure.

10. If you are absolutely sure that the last line of the rc.sysinit file looks exactly as shown in the previous example, use the Linux **change directory** command to change your working directory to the root of your Linux filesystem and umount the TiVo partition using the following commands:

```
cd /
umount /mnt
```

 **NOTE**

Note that there is no **n** in the command used to unmount drives under Linux. Why type an extra character if you don't have to?

You can now remove the BATBD CD from your PC and turn off the PC, so that you can move the drive back to your TiVo. Make sure that the jumpers on the drive are reset to the way that they were when you first removed the drive from your TiVo. Put the drive back in your TiVo and close it up.

Next, connect a serial cable to the TiVo as explained in Chapter 3, in the section entitled "Attaching a Terminal Emulator or Serial Console," and then reboot your PC. If you're running Windows, start HyperTerminal as explained in Chapter 9 in the "Serial Communications from Windows Systems" and turn on your TiVo. If you're running Linux on your PC (congratulations), start the minicom as explained in Chapter 10 in the section "Using minicom for Serial Communications."

Now, the moment of truth! Plug in your TiVo and wait a few minutes while the normal TiVo boot sequence completes. Watch the terminal emulation program that you're running on your screen. After the TiVo boots successfully, you will see the following message in your terminal emulator:

```
bash: no job control in this shell
bash-2.02#
```

The second line is the prompt from bash, the Linux command interpreter, and you've hacked your TiVo! If you're curious about the "bash: no job control in this shell" message (which is harmless), see "Job Control in Bash" in Chapter 10, "Linux and the TiVo." That section includes a TiVo tip for getting a command prompt with job control on your TiVo, but there are some tradeoffs to consider when doing so.

After you have a command prompt running on your TiVo, you can transfer files to your TiVo over a serial connection. If you're using a Windows system, doing this is explained in Chapter 9, "Working with Your TiVo from Windows and Macintosh Systems," in the section "Transferring Files over a Serial Connection from Windows." If you're using a Linux system, doing this task is explained in Chapter 10, "Linux and TiVo," in the section "Transferring Files Using minicom." Installing software on your TiVo after you've transferred files there is explained in Chapter 11, "Getting and Installing New Software for Your TiVo," in the section "Installing Software on Your TiVo."

# Getting a Command Prompt on a Series 2 TiVo

As mentioned earlier, getting a command prompt on a Series 2 TiVo is much more complex than on a Series 1. This is because later versions of the TiVo software have become progressively more particular about checking various files on the TiVo filesystem that have not been modified. All versions of the TiVo software for Series 2 machines will discard modified files, overwriting them with pristine versions from the TiVo's secret stash of unmodified files. Version 3.2 of the TiVo software even removed the much-beloved BASH_ENV hack described in this chapter.

Luckily, getting a command prompt on a Series 2 TiVo is not impossible, just more complex. You can think of this as being "more of a pain," but I like to think of it as "more of a challenge." This section explains how to get a command prompt on a Series 2 TiVo running Version 3.1 or earlier of the TiVo OS. If you are running a newer version of the TiVo software than this version, see the next section, "Two-Kernel Monte for the Series 2 TiVo," which explains a truly cool way to run any new version of the TiVo software that you want on your TiVo. More pain, but (of course) more gain.

Getting a command prompt on a Series 2 TiVo involves one major step that takes a fair amount of time and requires a bit of forethought. As part of the process of getting a command-prompt on a Series 2 TiVo, you will need to back up and restore your TiVo's current drive. This is necessary because you will need to have at least one new partition available on your Series 2 machine to hack into it. Since you need to do a restore to easily get a new partition, I strongly suggest that you install a larger drive (i.e., do a drive upgrade) while you are following the procedure to get a command prompt on your Series 2 system. You can, of course, immediately restore the backup to the drive that you created it from to create the new partition (unless the drive was completely full of recordings). However, it is much safer to keep your old disk handy as a backup, just in case something goes wrong when you follow the procedure described in this section.

---

### 📺 Getting Older Versions of the TiVo Software

Unless you're interested in features that are specific to a certain version of the TiVo OS (such as the Home Media Features, which weren't available until Version 4 of the TiVo software), you probably don't care which version of the TiVo OS your TiVo is running. If you don't really care what version of the TiVo software your system is running and you just want to hack around with it, you can get a backup of an older version of the OS as described earlier in this chapter in the section entitled "Getting a Command Prompt on a Series 1 TiVo." TiVo software release 3.1 is universally accepted as the best version for easy hacking on a Series 2 TiVo and for bootstrapping things like monte (described in the next section). See the section of Chapter 6 entitled "Finding Backups of the TiVo Software" for general information about finding TiVo backups on the Net.

---

There are three possible hard-drive scenarios for the process of getting a command prompt on your Series 2 machine, as follows:

◆ Upgrade to a larger drive during the procedure. In this case, you can keep your old TiVo disk(s) as backups and do not need to save a physical backup of the original drive(s).

◆ Upgrade to a larger drive during the procedure, keep a backup of your original drive(s) on disk, and keep your old TiVo disk(s) as backups. Backups are always good. You can sleep more soundly knowing that you have one, just in case.

◆ Reuse your existing disk drive(s) during the procedure by first backing up and then restoring the backup to the same drive. This is the least palatable of the hard drive options because you don't get any additional space to store recordings and run the risk of hosing the TiVo if the drive goes bad. Disk drives are relatively cheap so please buy a larger one and use it during the command-prompt procedure if you can.

Both of the last two scenarios require that your PC has sufficient space available to store the backup of your original TiVo disk drive. If your personal computer runs Linux or Windows and has sufficient space available to store a backup, see the section "Finding Room for Backups," in Chapter 6 for tips on mounting existing partitions after booting from the BATDB CD, so you can store your backups there. If your personal computer does not have sufficient space available to store the backup and you are planning to reuse your existing drive, you'll have to add another hard drive to your system to store the backup. If you do this and are running Windows on your personal computer, make sure that you format this disk as a FAT-32 disk so that you can access it from Linux.

To get a command prompt on a Series 2 TiVo running Version 3.1 or earlier of the TiVo OS, make a pot of coffee (this is a long procedure) and do the following:

1. Open your TiVo as described in Chapter 4 in the section "Opening the TiVo," and remove your TiVo's hard drive(s) as described in Chapter 4 in "Removing TiVo Disk Drives."

2. Put your TiVo's disk drive(s) in your PC as described in Chapter 4 in "Attaching TiVo Disk Drives to Your PC." If possible, attach the new drive that you want to use in your TiVo to another IDE interface in your machine at the same time, to minimize the number of times you have to reboot. Boot your personal computer from the BATBD CD by using the boot option for the Series 2 TiVo machines.

3. If you are creating a backup file of your original TiVo drive(s) (and I suggest you do, for the reasons outlined before the beginning of this procedure), mount the partition on the hard disk where you are going to store the backup, as explained in Chapter 5, in the section "Finding Room for Backups." For example, if you are storing your backups on a Windows FAT-32 disk partition that is the first partition on the master drive of your primary IDE interface, you can mount it by using the command:

```
mount -t vfat /dev/hda1 /mnt/backup
```

If you are mounting an **ext2** or **ext3** partition from a Linux machine, you do not have to specify the filesystem type. For example, if you were mounting the Linux partition /dev/hda8, you could simply mount it using the command:

```
mount /dev/hda8 /mnt/backup
```

See the section of Chapter 6 entitled "Finding Room for Backups" if you need more information about identifying the type and location of the partitions on your Windows system or for locating various partitions on a Linux system.

4. Back up your TiVo drive using one of the following commands. The following examples all assume that your TiVo drive is mounted as the slave drive on your secondary IDE interface (/dev/hdd). If your TiVo drive is attached to your PC as a master or on your other IDE interface, substitute the appropriate drive name. For information about mounting and identifying the names of TiVo drives from the BATBD CD, see Chapter 4, the section "Attaching TiVo Disk Drives to Your PC."

 **NOTE**

If your TiVo had two drives, the drives are married and you must back them up together, regardless of whether you are restoring them to one or two new drives. In this case, simply append the name of the second TiVo disk drive—in Linux terms—to the sample command lines shown below.

◆ If you are backing up a single drive and have sufficient space to back up everything (in the worst case, this will require the same amount of space as that available on your original disk), use the following command:

```
mfstool backup -a6so /mnt/backup/tivo-s2.bak /dev/hdd
```

◆ If you are backing up a single drive and don't want to preserve the recordings on your TiVo disk in the backup, use the following command to produce a much smaller backup:

```
mfstool backup -f 4138 -6so /mnt/backup/tivo-s2.bak /dev/hdd
```

◆ If you are backing up a single drive to upgrade to a larger drive, and insist on not creating a backup file, use the following command to create the backup and restore it to another drive (/dev/hdc, in this example) without requiring any intermediate disk space:

```
mfstool backup -aso - /dev/hdd ¦ mfstool restore –C -s 127 -xzpi - /dev/hdc
```

This last command will take a really long time! When it completes, you can skip the next step and move ahead to Step 6. The **mfstool restore** command's **-C** option limits the restore process to LBA28 disk addressing, which is necessary if you are using TiVo software versions 4.x and earlier. The –**C** option is only available in the latest versions of the MFS Tools utilities, such as the one on the BATBD CD that accompanies this book if you boot using the **bigs2**, **bigs1**, or **custs1** boot options.

---

 **NOTE**

If you are restoring your backups for use with a custom TiVo kernel or version of the TiVo software that supports LBA48 large disk addressing, do *not* use the –**C** option. You must also have booted from the BATBD CD using the **bigs2** option, even if you are restoring to a Series 1 TiVo. Examples of LBA48-aware TiVo kernels are Todd Miller's custom kernels for Series 1 TiVos (found on the BATBD CD that accompanies this book), and systems running Version 5.x or greater of the TiVo software such as the Pioneer 57-H and 810-H, or the HDTV DirecTiVo.

---

**5.** When the **backup** command completes, execute the Linux **sync** command to be totally positive that your backup file is consistent and then restore the backup file to the new drive. Skip this step if you used the "all-in-one" backup and restore command in the previous step.

---

 **NOTE**

If you did not have sufficient free IDE interfaces to put the old TiVo drive and the new drive in your personal computer at the same time, you may have to shut down your personal computer, remove the old TiVo drive, put in the new drive, and reboot from the BATBD CD. Before proceeding, make sure that you remount the partition where your backup is stored, as explained in Step 3 of this procedure.

---

The following example uses /dev/hdc as the name of the drive to which you are restoring the backup—make sure that you specify the drive name that is appropriate for your system before restoring your backup to it.

---

 **WARNING**

Be *very* careful when specifying the name of the disk to which you want to restore the backup. The MFS Tools utilities do not warn you if the disk contains data. *Do not* accidentally overwrite a Windows or Linux disk that contains data that you want to see again.

---

Restore your backup to the new disk using a command like the following:

```
mfstool restore -C -s 127 -xzpi /mnt/backup/tivo-s2.bak /dev/hdc
```

The **mfstool restore** command's **-C** option limits the restore process to LBA28 disk addressing, which is necessary if you are using TiVo software versions 4.x and earlier. The **–C** option is only available in the latest versions of the MFS Tools utilities, such as the one on the BATBD CD that accompanies this book if you boot using the **bigs2**, **bigs1**, or **custs1** boot options.

---

 **NOTE**

If you are restoring your backups for use with a custom TiVo kernel or version of the TiVo software that supports LBA48 large disk addressing, do *not* use the **–C** option. You must also have booted from the BATBD CD using the **bigs2** option, even if you are restoring to a Series 1 TiVo. Examples of LBA48-aware TiVo kernels are Todd Miller's custom kernels for Series 1 TiVos (found on the BATBD CD that accompanies this book), and systems running Version 5.x or greater of the TiVo software such as the Pioneer 57-H and 810-H, or the HDTV DirecTiVo.

---

 **TIP**

You may want to reboot your PC at this point (booting from the BATBD CD again) to ensure that the partition changes on your disk are recognized.

---

6. Once the restore process completes successfully, use the **pdisk** command to display the partitions on your newly restored disk, as in the following example:

```
pdisk -p /dev/hdc
```

Write down the name of the last partition on this drive—it will have a blank line after its name and will be identified as being of the type "Apple_Free." You will be using this partition in subsequent steps. This is usually partition 16, but your mileage may vary.

7. Next, identify the name of the default root filesystem on the restored TiVo disk. You will need this information later on, when setting the boot parameters for your system.

Use the **bootpage** command to identify the active root filesystem on your restored drive, as in the following example:

```
bootpage -p /dev/hdc
```

The name of the drive that you provide must be the name of your new TiVo drive, and is not necessarily /dev/hdc. The **bootpage** command should return either the string root=/dev/hda4 or the string root=/dev/hd7. This is the active root partition on your drive.

8. Next, mount the BATBD CD by typing a command like the following:

```
mount /dev/hdb /mnt/cdrom
```

The device associated with your CD-ROM drive may differ from this. If your CD-ROM drive is an IDE drive, its device name will be the same as though it were a disk drive. (Mine is attached as a slave on my primary IDE interface, and is therefore /dev/hdb. For more information about IDE drive names, see Chapter 3, the section entitled "Attaching TiVo Disk Drives to Your PC."

9. Next, we will create a small ROM (Read-Only Memory) filesystem image that the TiVo can mount and use during the boot process. The BATBD CD contains a template for this filesystem. To create the filesystem image in the file /romfs.img, execute the following commands:

```
cd /mnt/cdrom
genromfs -f /tmp/romfs.img -d img
```

---

 **NOTE**

If you're curious about exactly what this ROM filesystem contains, use the **cd** command to change your working directory to the /mnt/cdrom/img directory and examine the file "hacks" in that directory. This file simply waits for the TiVo's /var/hack to be mounted, and then it executes a command file called /var/hack/hackinit on the TiVo. This file is included in the archives of TiVo applications that you will extract in Step 11 of this procedure. The /var/hack/hackinit file simply contains the commands that we want to execute when the TiVo boots.

---

10. Next, write the ROM filesystem image to the empty partition identified in Step 6, using the **dd** command, which copies data from one file or device to another in raw form. To do this, execute the following command, replacing the *Y* in *YXX* with the letter corresponding to the device name of your new TiVo drive, and replacing *XX* with the partition identifier you obtained in Step 6:

```
dd if=/tmp/romfs.img  of=/dev/hdYXX bs=1024 count=1
```

For example, if the new drive for your TiVo was available as /dev/hdc and the partition identified in Step 6 was partition 16, you would execute the following command:

```
dd if=/tmp/romfs.img  of=/dev/hdc16 bs=1024 count=1
```

11. Next, mount partition 9 of the new TiVo disk so that you can create the command file mentioned in Step 9. Partition 9 of any standard TiVo boot disk is the partition that will be mounted as /var when the TiVo boots. To mount this directory, execute a command like the following:

```
mount /dev/hdc9 /mnt/tivo
```

If your TiVo disk has a device name other than /dev/hdc, change the name in this command to match your configuration.

12. Now, create what will be the TiVo's `/var/hack` directory and populate it with some files. Execute the following commands:

```
cd /mnt/tivo

tar xpvf /mnt/cdrom/hack_dirs/hack2.tar
```

The first command makes your working directory the partition that your TiVo will mount as `/var`. The second command extracts the contents of a preprepared archive file on the BATBD CD that contains executable programs that you will want to use on your newly-hacked Series 2 TiVo, as well as the **hackinit** script mentioned in Step 9.

13. The last step is to set the TiVo's boot parameters to mount the ROM filesystem and start the hacks script that it contains, which in turns invokes the `/var/hack/hackinit` script that you installed in the previous step. Type the following command exactly as shown (but on a *single* line—no Return), replacing "XX" with the partition number that you identified in Step 6 and wrote in Step 10. Also, the drive that you specify at the end of the command must be the drive where your new TiVo is located:

```
bootpage -P "root=ROOTDRIVE BASH_ENV=\`mount\$IFS-n\$IFS/dev/hdaXX\
$IFS/mnt;echo\$IFS/mnt/hacks\`" -C /dev/hdc
```

You should replace *ROOTDRIVE* with the value of your default root filesystem, as identified in Step 7 of this procedure. This would be either `/dev/hda4` or `/dev/hda7`.

The value set by the **bootpage** command is relative to the drive names that your TiVo will see when it boots. So `/dev/hda` is correct everywhere but the end of the line, where you specify the drive in your PC where the TiVo drive is currently located. The backslash characters are very important here, because they are used to protect commands that would otherwise be misinterpreted by the TiVo's command interpreter. Make sure that the "backquotes" before the "mount" command and after the directory name `/mnt/hacks` are indeed backward single quotes (found on the same key as the tilde on a U.S. keyboard. They must not be the standard single quotation marks that share a key with the double quotation mark.)

---

 **NOTE**

In case you're wondering, $IFS is an environment variable representing the Linux Internal Field Separator, a value used to separate different elements within a single line. In practice, each instance of the $IFS environment variable is replaced by a space when it is analyzed, enabling us to pass a complex string as a single token using the BASH_ENV environment variable.

After typing this command, execute the following command to make sure that you typed the previous command correctly:

```
bootpage -p /dev/hdc
```

where the drive name you specify is the name of the new TiVo disk. This command should return a string that looks exactly like the one that you entered, except that all of the backslash characters (\) will be gone. If the value displayed does not match the string you entered (minus the backquotes), retype the command shown at the beginning of this step—perhaps a bit more carefully this time.

14. All that's left now is the cleanup. Execute the following commands to **umount** the CD-ROM and your TiVo partition cleanly:

    ```
    cd /
    umount /mnt/cdrom
    umount /mnt/tivo
    ```

    After these commands complete, shut down your PC and put the new TiVo drive back in your TiVo, verifying that the jumpers are set correctly.

You can now remove the BATBD CD from your PC and turn it off. Now you can move the drive back to your TiVo. Make sure that the jumpers on the drive are reset to the way that they were when you first removed the drive from your TiVo. Put the drive back in your TiVo and close it up.

Next, connect a serial cable to the TiVo (as explained in Chapter 4, in the section "Attaching a Terminal Emulator or Serial Console") and reboot your PC. If you're running Windows, start HyperTerminal as explained in Chapter 9, in the section "Serial Communications from Windows Systems," and turn on your TiVo. If you're running Linux on your PC (congratulations), start minicom as explained in Chapter 10, in the section "Using minicom for Serial Communications."

Now, the moment of truth! Plug in your TiVo and wait a few minutes while the normal TiVo boot sequence completes. Watch the terminal emulation program that you're running on your screen. When the TiVo boots successfully, you will see the following message in your terminal emulator:

```
bash: no job control in this shell
bash-2.02#
```

The second line is the prompt from bash, the Linux command interpreter—now you are a TiVo hacker! If you're curious about the "bash: no job control in this shell" message (which is harmless), see Chapter 10, the section "Job Control in Bash." That section also includes a TiVo tip for getting a command prompt with job control on your TiVo, but there are some tradeoffs to consider when doing so.

After you have a command prompt running on your TiVo, you can transfer files over a serial connection to the TiVo. If you're using a Windows system, performing this task is explained in Chapter 9, in the section "Transferring Files over a Serial Connection from Windows." If you're using a Linux system, refer to Chapter 10, the section entitled "Transferring Files Using minicom." Installing software on your TiVo is explained in Chapter 11, in the section "Installing Software on Your TiVo."

# Two-Kernel Monte for the Series 2 TiVo

 **NOTE**

At the time this book was updated, the current TiVo software release for Series 2 TiVo systems was 4.0.1b (except for the latest DirecTiVos, which are still running 3.1.x). Newer TiVo systems, such as the Pioneer 57H and 810H systems, run Version 5.2.1a or better of the TiVo software, which includes support for larger disks, the DVD hardware, and so on. The DVD-enabled TiVos are still based on the TiVo Series 2 hardware platform. When referring to Version 4 or better of the TiVo software, I will simply refer to these versions as "Version 4.x+."

The procedures described in this section can be used on any TiVo Series 2 hardware system available at the time that this book was written, including the Pioneer systems. Wherever you need to know something special about a certain type of TiVo Series 2 system, I will insert a note that identifies the type of system and any special concerns.

 **WARNING**

This section is only for Series 2 TiVo systems, including DVD-enabled systems such as the Pioneer 57-H and 810-H systems. Do not try this on a Series 1 TiVo!

In the procedure described previously, your TiVo booted from a signed kernel, which included an initial RAM disk (**initrd**) that verified the filesystem through hash codes. This procedure effectively makes it impossible to directly modify any of the files that are verified in the TiVo's root filesystem. Some of these files include favorite text-based targets for modification such as /etc/rc.d/rc.sysinit, /etc/rc.d/rc.arch, /etc/inittab, or system binaries such as /bin/bash, /sbin/init, and others that you can replace with personalized versions that do "extra things."

By taking advantage of the BASH_ENV environment variable available in most versions of the Series 2 TiVo software prior to software release 3.2, you can convince your TiVo to run your own processes from another partition (/var, in our case) by creating a ROMFS filesystem image that you can stash in a spare partition on your TiVo. A file in the ROMFS is executed via the BASH_ENV hack, and itself executes a file containing your special hacks (/var/hack/hackinit). This procedure is fine if you're willing to run an older version of the TiVo software forever, but what if you absolutely must have new features like TiVo's Home Media Features? The BASH_ENV hack doesn't work there anymore. Out of luck? Hardly. You just have to be a bit more clever, as explained herein.

## ⎍ 📺 Extracting and Looking at an Initial RAM Disk

If you're curious about the complete list of files on which newer versions of the TiVo software perform signature checks, you'll have to look in the initial RAM (**initrd**) disk used by the TiVo kernel that you're booting. The contents of an **initrd** aren't readily visible ordinarily, but luckily Linux is your friend in this case. Initial RAM disks are just **ext2** filesystem images that have been compressed using the **gzip** program, and you can find where they are located in a compiled kernel image. Since you can find them, you can extract them. The **extract_gzip** program provided on the BATBD CD does just this. You can extract the **initrd** from the partition on which your kernel is located or from an image of that partition created using **dd**. To do this, put your TiVo disk in your PC and boot from the BATBD CD. After you've booted, mount the BATBD CD at /mnt/cdrom and execute the **extract_gzip** program using the following command line:

```
/mnt/cdrom/x86bin/extract_gzip kernel
```

where *kernel* is either the partition where the TiVo kernel is located, or the name of a kernel image file that you extracted from your disk using the **dd** command. The **extract_gzip** command will display a message like the following:

```
gzip magic (0x1f8b0800) detected at 0x0014a160 - saving to file 0x0014a160.gz
```

In this case, the file "0x0014a160.gz" is your **initrd**. You then **un-gzip** this file ("gunzip 0x0014a160.gz") and save the resulting file "0x0014a160" somewhere on your personal computer, and boot to Windows (see Chapter 6 in the section, "Finding Room for Backups"). You can explore like you would any other filesystem image by mounting it under Linux or Mac OS X, or by using a Windows tool (e.g., **explore2fs** on Windows). The file containing the signatures and filenames used by the newer TiVo software releases is located at the root of the **initrd**, and is called *signatures*.

The next sections explain how to use a program called **monte** to boot one kernel as part of the boot process of another kernel. If the second kernel doesn't happen to do signature checks (for example, if its **initrd** has been neutered), it can use a filesystem that contains any modified or new files that you want. The **monte** program, named after the old "three-card Monte" card game, is included in the monte-mips directory on the BATBD CD. Using **monte** is only necessary when hacking into Series 2 systems, so only the MIPS version of this utility and associated files are provided on the CD. Series 1 machines can't run the latest versions of the TiVo OS, and I don't see much difference between 3.0, 3.1, 3.2, and so forth on the Series 1 TiVo systems.

# Monte Overview

Before configuring your TiVo to do the two-kernel monte, it's useful to visualize the new boot process that your TiVo will use once monte'd. The following is the boot process for a monte'd TiVo:

1. At power-up, your TiVo reads its boot parameters, which tell it to boot from an older 3.x kernel and matching root filesystem, which passes the signature checks but also supports the BASH_ENV hack.

2. The TiVo boots from the old kernel and does the signature check on the matching root filesystem.

3. Once the signature check passes, the BASH_ENV hack directs the TiVo to mount another filesystem that is contained in a spare partition somewhere on your TiVo drive. This is usually the highest partition on your drive, though you can put it anywhere if you want to manually tweak your partition map. This partition is usually in ROMFS (ROM filesystem) format so that it is read-only and thus never has fsck problems.

4. After the new partition is mounted, the BASH_ENV hack also directs the TiVo to run a script (command file) from that partition.

5. The script inserts the monte.o module into the running kernel, and it directs the TiVo to load a more modern kernel from which the initial RAM disk signature checks have been removed by replacing the initial RAM disk in the kernel image.

6. Because the updated initial RAM disk does not do signature checks, the initial RAM disk does not scan the root filesystem that matches the new kernel. This root filesystem can therefore contain modified files, such as an updated /etc/rc.d/rc.sysinit, /etc/rc.d/rc.arch, or any other files that you want to use to start up your favorite hacks on the TiVo.

The **monte** hack is one of those things that is elegant in its simplicity once you understand how it actually works, but which can be daunting if you're not sure why you're doing all of the steps in the procedure described in the next section. Be fruitful and monte!

## Special Considerations for Large Disks, DVD TiVos, and Monte

Because the **monte** hack depends on being able to boot an older TiVo kernel, you are subject to the limitations of that kernel when you boot your TiVo. This means that if the old TiVo kernel doesn't understand how to address disks that are larger than 137 MB (i.e., LBA 24 rather than LBA 48), you won't be able to monte off one of those at this time. In other words, if the old TiVo kernel can't access the storage that the BASH_ENV hack points to, you can't access it in order to insert the monte module and switch kernels.

There are two solutions to this problem:

◆ Use disks that are less than 137 MB

◆ Manually rearrange the partitions on your TiVo disk so that the partition where monte lives is located within the first 137 GB of your TiVo disk. Doing this is described on the TiVo forums, but is very complex. Rearranging partitions is outside the scope of this book but is described on the TiVo forums.

The Pioneer 810 is a popular TiVo because it includes a DVD burner that makes it easy to save recordings to permanent storage (even though they still contain commercials). They also use a newer version of the TiVo kernel that can address huge (LBA 48) disks. However, many people, including myself, have experienced problems upgrading the amount of storage on these systems using backups of the TiVo 810 software. Luckily, the 810s can run the Pioneer 57 software, which is easily used on larger disks. To avoid problems, you should obtain a backup of the Pioneer 57 software and install it on your 810. At some point, TiVo may prevent this from working on an 810, but it currently does. I cannot control TiVo, Inc., but if you prevent software upgrades using the procedures described at the end of Chapter 6, you should be fine.

## Doing the Monte

The following procedure explains how to use **monte** to boot a hacked version of the 4+ version of the TiVo software from a system that starts by booting a hacked version of release 3.x of the TiVo software. You can use this same trick to boot unhackable 3.x versions of TiVo software, but I don't see much point in that. Why not go for the Version 4.x+ brass ring? If you thought that hacking a Series 2 running 3.x TiVo software was fun, wait until you finish reading this one!

To follow the instructions in this section, you will need the following:

◆ The BATBD CD that came with this book.

◆ A Series 2 machine running Version 4.+ of the TiVo software.

◆ If you are working with a Pioneer 810, you will need a backup image of the Pioneer 57H software. Some people have been able to upgrade an 810 with the actual 810 software, but this is problematic. See the section of Chapter 6 entitled "Finding Backups of the TiVo software" for more information about finding specific TiVo backups.

◆ A backup of a hackable version of the 3.x TiVo software—that is, a version that supports the BASH_ENV hack, release 3.1 or earlier. If you're lucky, you can also simply obtain image files of a hackable 3.1 kernel and root filesystem, as described later in this section.

◆ Approximately 150 MB of free disk space to store images of the 3.x system's kernel and root filesystem (only necessary if you do not have image backups of a hackable 3.1 kernel and root filesystem).

◆ You also will need one of the following:

 ◆ A larger disk, which is optional. It is strongly recommended that you do this as part of a disk upgrade so that you have your original TiVo disk to fall back on if something goes wrong.

 ◆ Sufficient disk space to store a backup of your Series 2 TiVo running Version 4.+.

 The procedure in this section requires that you restore 3.x to a TiVo disk drive as an intermediate step. You *must* either have a backup of Version 4.+ to subsequently restore it, or you must be upgrading to a larger drive as part of the process. Also, something could go wrong, and backups are a good thing.

◆ An hour or so of your time.

**WARNING**

These instructions assume that you're starting with a system that runs Version 4.0 of the TiVo software. If you're using a stand-alone Series 2 TiVo, your TiVo should have been automatically upgraded to this software release in April, 2003. If you're still running an older version of the TiVo OS on your Series 2, you can always upgrade your system manually by backing it up and then restoring a 4+ backup to it—but make sure that you've saved your recordings first, as described in Chapter 12. Frankly, in that case, it's probably easier to let your Series 2 upgrade itself and then follow the instructions in this chapter so that you don't lose anything. If you are running a Series 2 TiVo that hasn't been upgraded, you know what you did to prevent upgrades, and should undo that. ;-)

The following procedure begins with creating a backup of your Series 2 TiVo and then installing a backup of the 3.x so that you can extract image files containing the 3.x kernel and root filesystem. You always need to do the backup (just in case!), but you do not have to restore the 3.x backup if you already have image files of a 3.x kernel and root filesystem. These are currently available on some of the forums, but may not always be because TiVo is needlessly paranoid about older versions of their filesystems floating around. Check the following forum posts to see if the 3.x kernel and root filesystem are still available:

◆ Kernel: **http://www.dealdatabase.com/forum/showthread.php?t=25743**

◆ Minimal Root Filesystem: **http://www.dealdatabase.com/forum/showthread.php?s=&threadid=25219**

If these are still available, download them and reassemble the root filesystem by concatenating the two parts and extracting the root filesystem from the concatenated file using the **gunzip** command. You can then skip Steps 5 through 8 in the following procedure.

To use **monte** to get a command prompt on a hacked version of release 4.x+ of the TiVo software, do the following:

1. Open your TiVo (described in Chapter 4 in "Opening the TiVo") and remove your TiVo's hard drive(s) (described in Chapter 4 in "Removing TiVo Disk Drives").

2. Put your TiVo's disk drive(s) in your PC (described in Chapter 4 in "Attaching TiVo Disk Drives to Your PC"). If possible, attach the new drive that you want to use in your TiVo to another IDE interface in your machine at the same time—this minimizes the number of times you have to reboot. Boot your personal computer from the BATBD CD by using the Series 2 boot option.

3. If you are creating a backup file of your original TiVo drive(s) (and I suggest you do, for the reasons outlined in the previous section), mount the partition on the hard disk where you are going to store the backup, as explained in Chapter 6 in "Finding Room for Backups." For example, if you are storing your backups on a Windows FAT-32 disk partition that is the first partition on the master drive of your primary IDE interface, you can mount it using the command:

```
mount -t vfat /dev/hda1 /mnt/backup
```

If you are mounting an **ext2** or **ext3** partition from a Linux machine, you do not have to specify the filesystem type. For example, if you were mounting the Linux partition /dev/hda8, you could simply mount it by using the command:

```
mount /dev/hda8 /mnt/backup
```

(See Chapter 6, the section "Finding Room for Backups," if you need more information about identifying the type and location of the partitions on your Windows system, or for locating various partitions on a Linux system.)

---

 **NOTE**

If you are following this procedure as part of a disk upgrade and insist on not creating a backup file of your 4.x+ system, skip Step 4, but don't send me cranky mail or make me say "I told you so," if something goes wrong.

---

4. Back up your TiVo drive using one of the following commands. If possible, put the backup on the same partition on your PC where the 3.1 or earlier image required by this process is located. You will need access to both the backup image of your TiVo and the 3.x image during this process, and putting them in the same place makes sense.

   The following examples all assume that your TiVo drive is mounted as the slave drive on your secondary IDE interface (/dev/hdd). If your TiVo drive is attached to your PC as a master or on your other IDE interface, substitute the appropriate drive name. For information about mounting and identifying the names of TiVo drives from the BATBD CD, see Chapter 4, the section entitled "Attaching TiVo Disk Drives to Your PC."

---

 **NOTE**

If your Series 2 machines had two drives, the drives are married, and you must back them up together, regardless of whether you are restoring them to one or two new drives. In this case, simply append the name of the second TiVo disk drive—in Linux terms—to the sample command lines shown below.

---

   ◆ If you are backing up a single drive and have sufficient space to back up everything (in the worst case, this will require the same amount of space as that available on your original disk), use the following command:

   ```
   mfstool backup -a6so /mnt/backup/tivo-s2.bak /dev/hdd
   ```

   ◆ If you are backing up a single drive and don't want to preserve the recordings on your TiVo disk in the backup, use the following command to produce a much smaller backup:

   ```
   mfstool backup -f 4138 -6so /mnt/backup/tivo-s2.bak /dev/hdd
   ```

**NOTE**

If you are backing up a Pioneer TiVo like the 57H or 810H, use 9999 instead of 4138. The Pioneer TiVos store much more system information in MFS, and you'll need this to be able to use the restored system correctly.

Once the backup command completes, execute the Linux **sync** command to be totally positive that your backup file is consistent.

5. Next, you will restore the 3.x backup image to your new drive (or to your existing TiVo drive if you don't have another and you made a backup of 4.x+). You need to restore a version of 3.x that supports the BASH_ENV hack to extract its kernel and root filesystem. However, you do not need to perform this step if you already have image backups of a 3.x kernel and root filesystem.

 **WARNING**

Do *not* perform this step if you didn't create a backup of your Version 4.x+ system or you are upgrading to a new drive—reread the list of requirements earlier in this section instead.

 **NOTE**

If you did not have sufficient free IDE interfaces to put in the old TiVo drive and the new drive that you will be using in your personal computer at the same time, you may need to shut down your personal computer, remove the old TiVo drive, put in the new drive, and reboot from the BATBD CD. Before proceeding, make sure that you remount the partition where the backup of your TiVo and the 3.x backup that this process requires are stored, as explained in Step 3 of this procedure.

The following example uses /dev/hdc as the name of the drive to which you are restoring the backup. Make sure that you specify the drive name that is appropriate for your system before restoring your backup to it.

 **WARNING**

Be *very* careful when specifying the name of the disk that you want to restore the backup to. The MFS Tools utilities will *not* warn you if the disk contains data. *Do not* accidentally overwrite a Windows or Linux disk that contains data—if you ever want to see it again.

Restore your 3.x backup to the new disk using a command like the following:

```
mfstool restore -C -s 127 -xzpi /mnt/backup/tivo-s2.bak /dev/hdc
```

The **mfstool restore** command's **-C** option limits the restore process to LBA28 disk addressing, which is necessary if you are using TiVo software versions 4.x and earlier. The **–C** option is only available in the latest versions of the MFS Tools utilities, such as the one on the BATBD CD that accompanies this book if you boot using the **bigs2**, **bigs1**, or **custs1** boot options.

---

 **NOTE**

If you are restoring your backups for use with a custom TiVo kernel or version of the TiVo software that supports LBA48 large disk addressing, do *not* use the **–C** option. You must also have booted from the BATBD CD using the **bigs2** option, even if you are restoring to a Series 1 TiVo. Examples of LBA48-aware TiVo kernels are Todd Miller's custom kernels for Series 1 TiVos (found on the BATBD CD that accompanies this book), and systems running Version 5.x or greater of the TiVo software such as the Pioneer 57-H and 810-H, or the HDTV DirecTiVo.

---

 **TIP**

You may want to reboot your PC at this point (booting from the BATBD CD again) to ensure that the partition changes on your disk are recognized.

---

6. Once the restore process completes successfully, use the **pdisk** command to display the partitions on your newly restored disk, as in the following example:

```
pdisk -p /dev/hdc
```

If these partitions are not visible, the restore failed. Do not proceed.

7. If the partitions on the restored 3.x disk are visible, use the **bootpage** command to determine the active root partition on the restored drive, as in the following example:

```
bootpage -p /dev/hdc
```

This should return either the string **root=/dev/hda4** or **root=/dev/hd7**. This is the root partition on the restored 3.x drive. The kernel image for this drive will be located in the partition numbered one less than the root filesystem. For example, the default kernel for a drive whose root partition is /dev/hda4 will be located in partition 3 of the same drive.

8. Use the Linux **dd** command to extract the kernel and root filesystem from the 3.x disk and save them to files. The name of the drive in these examples will be the name of the drive where your 3.x TiVo disk is found in your PC, not the drive name returned by the **bootpage** command.

To extract a copy of the active root filesystem from the 3.x TiVo disk, execute a command like the following:

```
dd if=/dev/hdcX of=30_rootfs.img bs=32k
```

Replace the letter *X* in this command with the number at the end of the drive name returned by the **bootpage** command.

To extract a copy of the active kernel from the 3.x disk, execute a command like the following:

```
dd if=/dev/hdcX of=30_kernel.img
```

Replace the letter *X* in this command with the value that is one less than the number at the end of the drive name returned by the **bootpage** command.

That's all you need to use the 3.x disk for—now you can restore the 4.x+ image to the new drive (or to your only drive if you created a backup of your 4.x+ disk and don't have a new disk).

9. Restore your 4.x+ backup image to the drive that you will be using in your TiVo—either a new, larger drive if you are upgrading during this process, or your original drive.

 **NOTE**

If you are monte'ing a Pioneer 810, you will want to restore the 57H backup that was discussed at the beginning of this chapter. If you are working with a larger drive that already contains a 57H image and it contains a free partition (labeled Apple_Free) at the end of the disk, you do not have to do the restore, but can work directly with that disk.

The following example uses /dev/hdc as the name of the drive to which you are restoring the backup. Make sure that you specify the drive name that is appropriate for your system before restoring your backup to it.

Restore your backup to the new disk using a command like the following:

```
mfstool restore -C -s 127 -xzpi /mnt/backup/tivo-s2.bak /dev/hdc
```

The **mfstool restore** command's **-C** option limits the restore process to LBA28 disk addressing, which is necessary if you are using TiVo software versions 4.x and earlier. The **-C** option is only available in the latest versions of the MFS Tools utilities, such as the one on the BATBD CD that accompanies this book if you boot using the **bigs2**, **bigs1**, or **custs1** boot options.

 **NOTE**

If you are restoring your backups for use with a custom TiVo kernel or version of the TiVo software that supports LBA48 large disk addressing, do *not* use the **-C** option. You must also have booted from the BATBD CD using the **bigs2** option, even if you are restoring to a Series 1 TiVo. Examples of LBA48-aware TiVo kernels are Todd Miller's custom kernels for Series 1 TiVos (found on the BATBD CD that accompanies this book), and systems running Version 5.x or greater of the TiVo software such as the Pioneer 57-H and 810-H, or the HDTV DirecTiVo.

**TIP**

You may want to reboot your PC at this point (booting from the BATBD CD again) to ensure that the partition changes on your disk are recognized.

**10.** Once the restore process completes successfully, use the **pdisk** command to display the partitions on your newly restored disk, as in the following example:

```
pdisk -p /dev/hdc
```

Write down the name of the last partition on this drive—it will have a blank line after its name and will be identified as being of type "Apple_Free." You will be using this partition in subsequent steps. This is usually partition 16, but yours may vary.

**11.** Use the **bootpage** command to identify the active root filesystem on your restored 4.x+ drive, as in the following example:

```
bootpage -p /dev/hdc
```

This should return either the string **root=/dev/hda4** or the string **root=/dev/hd7**. This is the active root partition on the 4.x+ drive. The kernel image for this drive will be located in the partition numbered one less than the root filesystem. For example, the default kernel for a drive whose root partition is /dev/hda4 will be located in partition 3 of the same drive.

**12.** Use the **dd** command to clone the root filesystem and bootable kernel on your 4.x+ disk to the backed up versions of those same partitions:

◆ If the **bootpage** command in the previous step returned **root=/dev/hda4**, you will be cloning partition 4 of your 4.x+ drive to partition 7 of your 4.x+ drive, and you will be cloning partition 3 of your 4.x+ drive to partition 6 of your 4.x+ drive.

◆ If the **bootpage** command in the previous step returned **root=/dev/hda7**, you will be cloning partition 7 of your 4.x+ drive to partition 4 of your 4.x+ drive, and you will be cloning partition 6 of your 4.x+ drive to partition 3 of your 4.x+ drive.

To clone the root filesystem partition, execute a command like the following:

```
dd if=/dev/hdcX of=/dev/hdcY bs=32k
```

where the name of the drive is the name of your new TiVo drive in your personal computer, $X$ is the number at the end of the string returned by the **bootpage** command in the previous step, and $Y$ is the other partition identified in the previous list.

To clone the kernel partition, execute a command like the following;

```
dd if=/dev/hdcX of=/dev/hdY
```

where the name of the drive is the name of your new TiVo drive in your personal computer, $X$ is the number one less than the number at the end of the string returned by the **bootpage** command in the previous step, and $Y$ is the other partition identified in the previous list.

**NOTE**

You may get an error message when cloning the kernel. This is because some TiVo disks have different-sized partitions for the primary and alternate kernels. TiVo kernels, at the time of this book's writing, are always less than 2 MB, which is the size of the smaller of these two partitions. Again, at the time of this book's writing, you could safely ignore this message. You *do* have a backup image or your original 4.x+ disk, right?

13. Next, mount the BATBD CD by typing a command like the following:

```
mount /dev/hdb /mnt/cdrom
```

The device associated with your CD-ROM drive may differ from this. If your CD-ROM drive is an IDE drive, its device name will be the same as though it were a disk drive. (Mine is attached as a slave on my primary IDE interface and is therefore /dev/hdb. For more information about IDE drive names, see Chapter 4, the section entitled "Attaching TiVo Disk Drives to Your PC."

14. Next, you will create a small ROM (Read-Only Memory) filesystem image that the TiVo can mount and use during the boot process. The BATBD CD contains a template for this ROM filesystem. To create the filesystem image in the file /romfs.img, execute the following commands:

```
cd /mnt/cdrom
genromfs -f /romfs.img -d img_monte
```

 **NOTE**

If you're curious about exactly what this ROM filesystem contains, **cd** (change directory) to the /mnt/cdrom/img_monte directory and examine the file **runmonte** in that directory. This file loads a kernel module used by **monte** and then executes the **monte** command, passing the kernel partition that contains the root filesystem that holds the hacked 4.x+ image and several other command-line arguments to the kernel that **monte** will run for you.

15. Next, write the ROM filesystem image to the empty partition identified in Step 10, using the **dd** command discussed in Chapter 6, which copies data from one file or device to another in raw form. To do this, execute the following command, replacing the *Y* in *YXX* with the letter corresponding to the device name of your new TiVo drive, and replacing *XX* with the partition identifier you obtained in Step 10:

```
dd if=/romfs.img  of=/dev/hdYXX
```

For example, if the new drive for your TiVo was available as /dev/hdc and the partition identified in Step 10 was partition 16, you would execute the following command:

```
dd if=/romfs.img  of=/dev/hdc16
```

**16.** Next, write the backups of your 3.x kernel and root filesystem to partitions 3 and 4 of your new TiVo disk, respectively.

To write the backup of your 3.x kernel to partition 3 from the backup image you created in Step 8, execute the following command:

```
dd if=30_kernel.img of=/dev/hdc3
```

where the name of the drive is the name of your new TiVo drive in your personal computer.

To write the backup of your 3.x root filesystem to partition 4 from the backup image you created in Step 8, execute the following command:

```
dd if=30_rootfs.img of=/dev/hdc4 bs=32k
```

where the name of the drive is the name of your new TiVo drive in your personal computer.

**17.** Next, mount partition 9 of the new TiVo disk so that you can install your favorite TiVo hacks. Partition 9 of any standard TiVo boot disk is the partition that will mount as **/var** when the TiVo boots. To mount this directory, execute a command like the following:

```
mount /dev/hdc9 /mnt/tivo
```

If your new TiVo disk has a device name other than /dev/hdc, change the name in this command to match your configuration.

**18.** Next, create what will be the TiVo's /var/hack directory and populate it with some files. Execute the following commands:

```
cd /mnt/tivo
tar xpvf /mnt/cdrom/hack_dirs/hack2.tar
```

The first command makes your working directory the partition that your TiVo will mount as /var. The second command extracts the contents of a preprepared archive file on the BATBD CD, which also contains executable programs that you will want to use on your newly hacked Series 2 TiVo.

**19.** Now, remove the initial RAM disk in the v4.x+ kernel on your system. To do this, execute the following commands:

```
cd /mnt/cdrom/initrds
replace_initrd /dev/hdX6 null-linuxrc.img.gz /path/to/backup-file
```

where *X* is the drive letter of the drive you've been working with—your new TiVo drive. The third argument to the **replace_initrd** command (/path/to/backup-file) should be the full path to a directory on your PC that has at least 2 MB of free space, and where the **replace_initrd** command can store a backup copy of your standard 4.x+ kernel in case something goes wrong.

**20.** Add the commands to get a shell prompt for the startup file on the 4.x+ root filesystem. You can do this by executing the following commands:

```
cd /
sync
```

```
umount /mnt/tivo
mount /dev/hdX7 /mnt/tivo
cp /mnt/tivo/etc/rc.d/rc.sysinit /mnt/tivo/etc/rc.d/rc.sysinit.old
cat /mnt/cdrom/initrds/rc.sysinit.upd >> /mnt/tivo/etc/rc.d/rc.sysinit
```

Be very careful that you specify two right angle brackets (>), not just one. If you accidentally specify only 1, you have just truncated the contents of your new TiVo disk's startup file. Oops! Copy the file /mnt/tivo/etc/rc.d/rc.sysinit.old back to the file /mnt/tivo/etc/rc.d/rc.sysinit and type more carefully this time.

21. The last step is to set the TiVo's boot parameters to mount the ROM filesystem and run **monte**, handling all of the kernel switching, and so on. Type the following command exactly as shown (except on a single line—no Return), replacing *XX* with the partition number that was identified in Step 10, and written in Step 15. Also, the drive that you specify at the end of the command must be the drive where your new TiVo is currently located:

```
bootpage -P "root=/dev/hda4 dsscon=true BASH_ENV=\`mount\$IFS-n\
$IFS/dev/hdaXX\$IFS/mnt;echo\$IFS/mnt/runmonte\`" -C /dev/hdc
```

This command is relative to the drive names that your TiVo will see when it boots, so /dev/hda is correct everywhere but at the end of the line, where you specify the drive in your PC where the TiVo drive is currently located. The backslash characters are very important here, because they are used to protect commands that would otherwise be misinterpreted by the TiVo's command interpreter. Make sure that the back quotes before the "mount" command and after the filename /mnt/hacks are indeed backwards single quotes (found on the same key as the tilde on a U.S. keyboard. They must not be the standard single quotation marks that share a key with the double quotation mark.)

After typing this command, execute the following command to make sure that you typed the previous command correctly:

```
bootpage -p /dev/hdc
```

where the drive name you specify is the name of the new TiVo disk. This command should return a string that looks exactly like the one that you entered, except that all of the backslash characters (\) will be gone. If the value displayed does not match the string you entered (less the back quotes), retype the command shown at the beginning of this step—perhaps a bit more carefully this time.

---

 **NOTE**

In case you're wondering, $IFS is an environment variable representing the Linux Internal Field Separator, a value used to separate different elements within a single line. In practice, each instance of the $IFS environment variable is replaced by a space when it is analyzed, enabling us to pass a complex string as a single token by using the BASH_ENV environment variable.

**TIP**

When you monte a Series 2 TiVo, you may also want to add the **upgradesoftware=false** boot parameter to your TiVo's bootparams. This will prevent your system from being updated and overwritten but may cause folks at TiVo central to notice that there's something odd about your TiVo. For more information about this boot parameter and its implications, see the TiVoGuide section near the end of Chapter 6 entitled "Software Protection Against Upgrades."

**22.** All that's left now is the cleanup. To ensure that your newly monte'd TiVo will boot without requiring any filesystem cleanup, use the **fsck** (filesystem consistency check) program to check the ext2 partitions on your new TiVo drive, as in the following examples:

```
fsck /dev/hdc4
fsck /dev/hdc7
fsck /dev/hdc9
```

where the drive name you specify is the name of the new TiVo disk. You may see errors about being unable to check if the drive is mounted. These can safely be ignored. The **fsck** command should report that the filesystems are "clean" when it completes.

**23.** Execute the following commands to umount the CD-ROM and your TiVo partition cleanly:

```
cd /
umount /mnt/cdrom
umount /mnt/tivo
```

After these commands complete, you can now remove the BATBD CD from your PC and turn off the PC, and you can move the drive back to your TiVo. Make sure that the jumpers on the drive are reset to the way that they were when you first removed the drive from your TiVo. Put the drive back in your TiVo and close it up.

Next, connect a serial cable to the TiVo, as explained in Chapter 4 in the section "Attaching a Terminal Emulator or Serial Console," and reboot your PC. If you're running Windows, start HyperTerminal, as explained in Chapter 9 in the section "Serial Communications from Windows Systems," and turn on your TiVo. If you're running Linux on your PC (congratulations), start minicom as explained in Chapter 10 in "Using minicom for Serial Communications." Set your communication speed to 115,200—the speed of the Series 2 TiVo serial port.

Now, the moment of truth! Plug in your TiVo and wait a few minutes while the normal TiVo boot sequence completes. Unlike when booting previous kernels, you will see all of the boot messages for both the 3.x and 4.x+ kernels displayed on the serial port, and you will see the complete TiVo startup process. The instructions in this section set the system console to the serial port using the command **dsscon=true** so that you can easily see if something goes wrong during the boot process. Watch the terminal emulation program that you're running on your screen. When the TiVo boots successfully, you will see the following message in your terminal emulator:

```
bash: no job control in this shell
bash-2.02#
```

The second line is the prompt from bash, the Linux command interpreter, which means you are a certified TiVo hacker! The procedure described in this section is not for the weak, and you should be proud if everything works correctly the first time.

If you're curious about the "bash: no job control in this shell" message (which is harmless), see the section "Job Control in Bash" in Chapter 10. That section also includes a TiVo tip for getting a command prompt with job control on your TiVo, but there are some tradeoffs to consider when doing so.

After you have a command prompt running on your TiVo, you can transfer files to it over a serial connection. If you're using a Windows system, doing so is explained in Chapter 9 in "Transferring Files over a Serial Connection from Windows." If you're using a Linux system, this part of the process is explained in Chapter 10 in "Transferring Files Using minicom." Installing software on your TiVo after you've transferred files there is explained in the Chapter 11 in "Installing Software on Your TiVo."

# Starting FTP and Telnet on Your TiVo

Admittedly fairly simple, this section explains how to start the Telnet and FTP daemons on your TiVo. Telnet is a network-based terminal emulation program that enables you to log in on remote systems over a network. In order to connect to a remote system, a Telnet daemon must be running, waiting for incoming connections. (A *daemon* is the Unix/Linux term for a program that is always running when a system is active, and constantly waits to service appropriate requests.) FTP is a *file transfer protocol* client that you can use to send files to your TiVo and retrieve them from the TiVo, as long as an FTP daemon is running on the TiVo.

If you are hacking your Series 1 TiVo and have installed a network card in it as described earlier in this chapter in the section "Networking Series 1 TiVos," you do not have to follow the procedure described in this section. The **nic_install** script provided with today's TurboNet and Airnet cards for the Series 1 TiVo automatically adds entries that start the FTP and Telnet daemons to the /etc/rc.d/rc.sysinit script, along with other modifications. If you are hacking your TiVo Series 1 and installed a network card without also using the **nic_install** program, you can install Series 1 versions of the Telnet (**tnlited**) and FTP (**tivoftpd.ppc**) daemons by installing the directories of TiVo software included in the hack_dir directory on the BATBD CD, explained in Chapter 11, in the section "Installing Software on Your TiVo." You can add them to your TiVo's startup procedure by adding the following lines to the /etc/rc.d/rc.sysinit file on your TiVo:

```
/var/hack/bin/tivoftpd.ppc &
/var/hack/bin/tnlited 23 /bin/bash -login &
```

If you are hacking your Series 2 machine running a version of the TiVo OS earlier than 3.2, you should have installed the Series 2 software from the BATBD CD as explained in "Getting a Command Prompt on a Series 2 TiVo," earlier in this chapter. In that case, the following startup commands are already present in the /var/hack/hackinit file that was installed for you:

```
/sbin/tnlited 23 /bin/bash -login &
/var/hack/bin/tivoftpd &
```

If you are hacking your Series 2 using the two-kernel monte method and are running a TiVo software version later than 3.1 that **monte** boots for you, you also should install the Series 2 software from the BATBD CD, as explained in "Two-Kernel Monte for the Series 2 TiVo," earlier in this chapter. If you followed the procedures for the two-kernel monte described earlier in this chapter, the FTP and Telnet startup commands were automatically added to your TiVo's system startup file, but this section may still be useful to you in order to see what is actually going on when your system starts these commands.

If for some reason you need to manually update the rc.sysint file on a Series 2 TiVo, you must remount the TiVo's root filesystem so that it is writable before you can append to this file. To remount the root filesystem from a running TiVo in read-write mode, execute the following command:

```
mount -o rw,remount /
```

You can then add the following two commands to the end of the /etc/rc.d/rc.sysinit file in the root partition that is actively being used by the TiVo to which **monte** has been applied:

```
/sbin/tnlited 23 /bin/bash -login &
/var/hack/bin/tivoftpd &
```

You should remount the root filesystem in read-only mode, as it should be, using the following command:

```
mount -o ro,remount /
```

The next time you start your TiVo, these daemons will automatically start.

# Integrating Your TiVo with AOL Instant Messenger

If you're a fan of AOL's Instant Messenger and are using a hacked Series 1 TiVo on your home network, you may want to be notified when a buddy arrives or when someone sends you an instant message ("*IMs you*," to use the vernacular). In this case, you'll be happy to know that software is available for your TiVo that enables any networked TiVo to display onscreen messages—and, of course, it's free software.

### TIVO Opening Your 4.x+ TiVo for Networking

Aside from the inherent pain in hacking a Series 2 machine running Version 4.x+ of the TiVo OS (and the related satisfaction when you succeed), Version 4.x+ of the TiVo OS is more modern in other aspects; for example, its paranoia about network connections.

Version 4.x+ of the TiVo OS uses a Linux application called **iptables** to set up a firewall on your TiVo that it uses to block most types of network connections. In order to Telnet or FTP to your 4.x+ TiVo, even after you have used monte, you will need to enable the ports used by those services. The easiest way to do this is to turn off the firewall, but my membership in the International Brotherhood of Unix SysAdmins and Circus Geeks would be revoked if I did not point out that this is a BIG security hole. (No more so than running an earlier version of the TiVo OS, but I'm not sure that's a good argument.)

To disable the firewall on your hacked 4.x+ TiVo system so that you can Telnet in and FTP files to and from the TiVo, execute the following command on your TiVo:

```
/sbin/iptables -F
```

This flushes (i.e., removes from memory) all of the rules used by the firewall, making it completely open to all network communications. If your TiVo has an IP address that makes it visible on the Internet, this means that school kids in China can now log in to your TiVo, create and destroy files, and configure it so that they can suck your recorded pornography down to their home systems. Don't do this unless your machine is isolated on your home network, or you don't care if someone hacks into it and turns it into an electronic paperweight or hacking zombie. If you're comfortable with not running a firewall, you may want to add this command to your 4.x+ root filesystem `/etc/rc.d/rc.sysinit` file when you append the commands that start the Telnet and FTP servers.

More subtle approaches to the firewall problem are preferable but would take too long to explain here in all their glory. For more details about using **iptables**, especially in a more graceful mode than the sledgehammer proposed in this tip, see the project's home page at **http://www.netfilter.org**.

Displaying instant messages and buddy notifications on your TiVo requires that you use an instant messaging client known as *GAIM* (GTK AOL Instant Messenger). GAIM is an open source project with a home page located at **http://gaim.sourceforge.net**. GAIM is completely compatible with the most popular instant messaging protocols, including AOL, MSN, Yahoo, Jabber, IRC, Gadu-Gadu(GG), Napster, and Zephyr, and it provides a central instant messaging console for anyone using any of those services.

Both the Windows and Linux versions of GAIM are freely available from the GAIM project's download page at **http://gaim.sourceforge.net/downloads.php**. The latest version for Linux at the time of this book's writing is provided in the connectivity directory on the BATBD CD that accompanies this book. The latest version for Windows at the time of this book's writing is provided in the Windows directory on the BATBD CD that accompanies this book. See Chapter 10 for information about accessing the software on the BATBD CD. Figure 8.1 presents the initial login or sign-on screen in the Linux version of GAIM. Figure 8.2 shows GAIM after signing on, which should be remarkably familiar to AOL Instant Messenger users.

**FIGURE 8.1**   *GAIM's login screen on a Linux system*

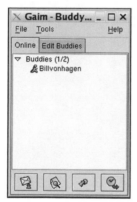

**FIGURE 8.2**   *GAIM's main screen on a Linux system*

After you install GAIM on your Linux or Windows system, you will have to install two additional components: an application that you must run on your TiVo to enable displaying instant message notifications and a plug-in to GAIM itself that can talk to the TiVo software. Both of these pieces of software were written by the TiVo hacker "hermanator" (who also ported GAIM to Windows). A zip file named gaim2tivo-0.2.zip contains this software and is available in the connectivity directory on the BATBD CD included with this book. This zip file also can be downloaded directly from the DealDatabase Forum thread on this subject, located at **http://www.dealdatabase.com/forum/showthread.php?s=&threadid=14453**. At the time this book was written, the latest version was Version 0.2.

To integrate GAIM with your TiVo, unpack the zip file and transfer the file `tivo_messenger` to your TiVo. Make sure that it's executable on your TiVo (**chmod 755 tivo_messenger**) and execute it in the background (**./tivo_messenger &**). You may eventually want to integrate it with the `/etc/rc.d/rc.sysinit` startup file that you use to start your favorite TiVo hacks. The `gaim2tivo-0.2.zip` archive file on the BATBD CD includes the source code for the TiVo messenger application, so you should recompile it yourself for the Series 2 TiVo, though there seem to be some problems with the onscreen display module.

After you have the **tivo_messenger** application running on your TiVo, you must install the appropriate plug-in on your Windows or Linux system.

To install the gaim2tivo plug-in on a Linux system, do the following:

1.  Copy the file `gaim2tivo.so` from the directory where you extracted the gaim2tivo archive to the directory used for GAIM plug-ins. This is usually the `lib` directory corresponding to the binary directory where the "gaim" program is installed on your Linux system. For example, if the gaim binary is located in `/usr/bin` on your Linux system, GAIM plug-ins probably are stored in the directory `/usr/lib/gaim`.

2.  After starting GAIM, select the Tools menu's Plugins command. Click the Load button in the dialog box that displays, browse to the directory where you copied the GAIM plug-in in the previous step, select the plug-in, and click OK (see Figure 8.3).

**FIGURE 8.3**    *GAIM's plug-in screen on a Linux system*

3.  Click Configure (see Figure 8.4 ). Enter the IP address or hostname for your TiVo. Don't change the specified port number. Click Close to close the configuration dialog box.

To install the gaim2tivo plug-in on a Windows system, do the following:

1.  Copy the file `gaim2tivo.dll` from the directory where you extracted the gaim2tivo archive to the directory used for GAIM plugins. This is usually the directory `C:\Program Files\Gaim\Plugins`.

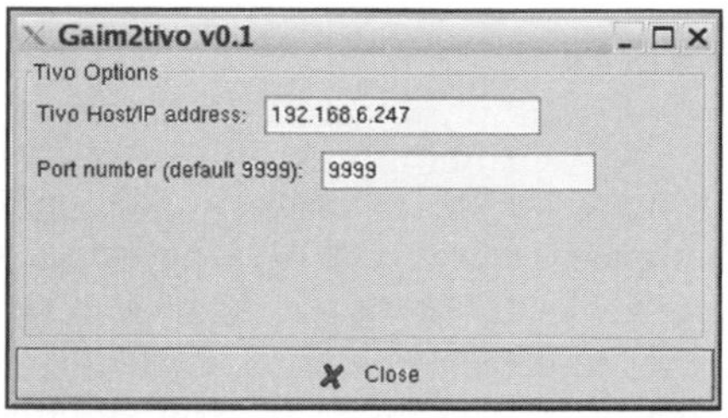

**FIGURE 8.4**   *GAIM's plug-in configuration screen on a Linux system*

2. After starting GAIM, select the Tools menu's Plugins command. Click the Load button in the dialog box that displays, browse to the directory where you copied the GAIM plug-in in the previous step, select the plug-in, and click OK.

3. Click Configure and enter the IP address or hostname for your TiVo. Don't change the specified port number. Click Close to close the Configuration dialog box.

At this point, you can test GAIM by sending yourself an Instant Message. Your screen will display a message like the one shown in Figure 8.5. If you are connected to your TiVo through a serial connection, you will also see text like the following:

```
192.168.6.32:32879 connected
RECEIVED: Billvonhagen: You there?
```

The next time you or any of your GAIM buddies sign on, a sign-on message will display on your TiVo screen, as shown in Figure 8.5. This is a great way to watch TV while not missing any of those "important" messages from any of your friends or coworkers.

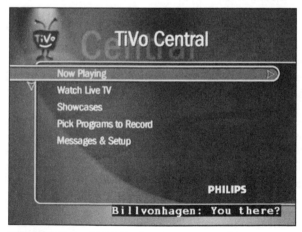

**FIGURE 8.5**   *GAIM's plug-in screen on a Linux system*

# Caller ID and Your TiVo

Today, Caller ID is almost a fact of life—regardless of how many don't-call lists that state and local governments set up. Even if you are actually interested in talking to someone, Caller ID gives you some advance warning as to who is calling, long before you pick up the phone. This is all well and good if your Caller ID box is glued to a wall where you can always see it, or if you're willing to run over to it each time the phone rings. But what if you're doing something else, like watching your TiVo, and don't feel like moving unless absolutely necessary?

If you have a spare modem card lying around and your personal computer runs Windows, YAC, which stands for "Yet Another Caller ID Program," just may be the answer.

 **NOTE**

Unix and Linux have a long tradition of "Yet Another..." programs, the best known of which is **yacc**, which stands for "Yet Another Compiler Compiler." Since the fundamental design philosophy of Unix (and thus Linux) is to have many small, specialized utilities that work together to do more complex tasks, it's only natural that different people have different ideas about how those small utilities should work. Consequently, there was often one application to do a task, followed by another application that did the same task slightly differently, followed by yet another application that did the same task differently.... I think you get the idea.

Jensen Harris's YAC program is a client/server Caller ID program that is available from **http://www.sunflowerhead.com/software/yac**. The server component runs on a Windows 2000 or later system and requires that an internal modem be present in order to monitor incoming calls and retrieve Caller ID information. Once an incoming call is received, the YAC server broadcasts the Caller ID information to any YAC client (known as a *listener*) running on the local network. Each listener receiving the broadcast formats the information and displays it on the device where it is running—in our case, a Series 1 TiVo. The current version of the TiVo's YAC client is only supported on the Series 1 TiVo. Maybe if we ask really nicely....

The YAC server software for Windows is provided in the file yac-0.16-win32.zip in the Windows directory on the BATBD CD. The TiVo listener software is provided in the file yac-0.15-tivo.tar.gz in the connectivity directory on the BATBD CD. If newer versions of this software are available, you should be able to download them from the Web site listed in the previous paragraph.

After you install and configure the YAC software on your TiVo, your TiVo will display messages like the one shown in Figure 8.6 when an incoming call is received.

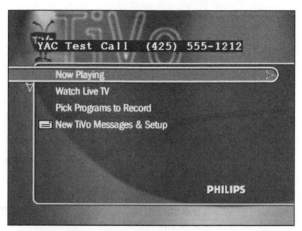

**FIGURE 8.6**    *A Caller–ID notification from YAC on a TiVo screen*

# News, Sports, Weather, and Your TiVo

After you've networked your TiVo, extracting information from a variety of online services is just an *LMOP* (Large Matter of Programming). TiVo hacker Zirak has a TiVo Control Station application, available at **http://www.zirakzigil.net/tivo/TCS.html**, which enables you to connect to, extract data from, and display summary information from a variety of online sources. Written in TCL, it displays up-to-date sports, stock quotes, and eBay and weather information on your TiVo. The application is easy to install and easily expandable by writing additional TCL modules. TCS currently works only on Series 1 machines. Figure 8.7 shows a sample screen from TCS, displaying recent stock quotes.

**FIGURE 8.7**    *A weather map displayed by the TiVo Control Station*

A copy of an archive file of the TiVo Control Station software is located in the file `TCS_1.0.0.tar.gz` in the connectivity directory on the BATBD CD. You can also download this file from its Web site (listed in the previous paragraph). To execute this program on your TiVo, transfer the file and unpack it in a directory such as `/var/hack`. This will create the directory `/var/hack/tcs`. To start TCS, simply **cd** to this directory and execute the file "starttcs," which starts TCS in the background.

>  **NOTE**
>
> TCS depends on other applications that may not be located on your TiVo. These programs are **jpegwriter** (for displaying weather maps), **newtext2osd** (for most onscreen displays), and a nonbusy-box version of the **ps** command. Archive files containing all of these are located in the connectivity directory on the BATBD CD.

The TiVo Control Station enables you to execute the following special TCS commands from your remote:

- ◆ *(clear)(0)(clear)*     Lists running hacks on the screen
- ◆ *(clear)(7)(clear)*     Displays stock quotes (requires an Internet connection)
- ◆ *(clear)(8)(clear)*     Displays local weather (requires an Internet connection)
- ◆ *(6)(0)(clear)*     Displays the available sports commands
- ◆ *(6)(1)(clear)*     Major League Baseball scores, schedule, and standings
- ◆ *(6)(2)(clear)*     National Football League scores, schedule, and standings
- ◆ *(6)(3)(clear)*     NCAA college football, scores, schedule, and AP/ESPN, *USAToday* polls
- ◆ *(6)(4)(clear)*     National Hockey League scores, schedule, and standings
- ◆ *(7)(1)(clear)*     Various interest rates
- ◆ *(8)(1)(clear)*     Changes the weather zip code from using the remote (valid until you restart your TiVo)
- ◆ *(8)(2)(clear)*     Displays local (600 mile) weather radar
- ◆ *(8)(3)(clear)*     Displays national weather radar
- ◆ *(9)(0)(clear)*     Shows all TCS remote and network commands
- ◆ *(9)(6)(clear)*     Displays any updates available from the TCS Web site
- ◆ *(9)(7)(clear)*     Displays all background processes/timers
- ◆ *(9)(8)(clear)*     Resets all background timers—updates everything NOW
- ◆ *(9)(9)(clear)*     Quits TCS
- ◆ *(mute)(mute)(clear)*     Toggles the execution of greedy processes (NICE/MEAN)

As you can see from this list, TCS enhances your TiVo experience in a big way, providing access to a tremendous amount of extra information, all from your TiVo. As another example, Figure 8.8 shows stock quotes as displayed by TCS on a TiVo screen—uh-oh, time to sell!

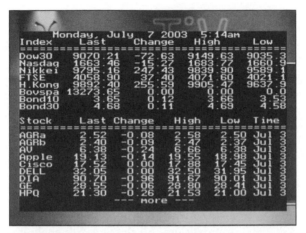

**FIGURE 8.8**    *Stock quotes displayed by the TiVo Control Station*

TCS also provides commands that enable you to control other hacks that may be running on your TiVo. Since controlling these commands is somewhat specific to how they're installed and started on your TiVo, these command aren't discussed here. See Zirak's Web site (address below) for details.

 **NOTE**

A new version of the TiVo Control Station is available from the URL **http:// www.zirakzigil.net/tivo/TCSdownload.html**. More info about TCS can also be found on the TiVoCommunity forum thread at **http://www.tivocommunity.com/tivo-vb/ showthread.php?s=&threadid=166708**. The latest versions of TCS are shareware, so please pay for it if you use it. Frankly, you should pay for previous versions, too, even though they were not officially shareware. Supporting the TiVo hackers who bring you great software like TCS is important if you expect to see more of it!

 **TIP**

A version of TiVo Control Station for Series 2 TiVos is under development but requires a fair amount of work to get the underlying utilities that it uses to work correctly on Series 2 systems. Watch the forums for updates!

# Programming Your TiVo over a Network Using TiVoWebPlus

Long before TiVo introduced its own Internet connectivity software, the Home Media Features (discussed later in this chapter), a free package of software known as the *TiVo Web project* (or, more familiarly, TiVoWeb) enabled you to access, manage, and explore your TiVo over a network, from any Web browser. This was an amazing piece of work by well-known TiVo hackers lightn, embeem, and many others, and has recently received a major upgrade known as *TiVoWebPlus*, thanks to the TiVo hackers falcontx, mrblack51, and others. The latest TiVoWebPlus software is available at the TiVoWebPlus home page, **http://tivo.fp2000.org/twp/**or at **http://www.dealdatabase.com/forum/showthread.php?t=30564** on the Deal-Database forum. (A copy of the latest revision of the TiVoWebPlus software at the time this book was updated is also included on the CD that accompanies this book.)

The ability of TiVoWeb and TiVoWebPlus to schedule recordings from any Web browser is only a tiny subset of the bells and whistles that they provide. TiVoWeb and TiVoWeb-Plus enable you to access your TiVo remotely, get information about its status, view its log files, view program listings, and much more. Most impressively, they provide access to the internals of TiVo's MFS filesystem and include an easily expanded resource editor that you can even use to peek and poke at resource values. All this in a free application that "just works." It's absolutely incredible!

TiVoWeb was primarily targeted for older Series 1 TiVos, though some later versions also worked on Series 2 TiVos, as described in the first edition of this book. TiVoWebPlus brings the functionality of TiVoWeb to dual-tuner DirecTiVos, Series 2 TiVos, and even the latest DVD-equipped TiVos from Toshiba and Pioneer. This section focuses on TiVoWebPlus, since it is the version of TiVoWeb that I now use everywhere and is the version under active development (and support) at the moment.

## Installing TiVoWebPlus

To install TiVoWebPlus on your TiVo, you already must have a shell prompt or network service enabled—TiVoWebPlus isn't all that useful without the latter anyway. This section assumes that you have put your TiVo on a home network, as discussed earlier in this chapter. Once your TiVo is on your home network, do the following:

1. Mount the BATBD CD on your PC and change the directory to the top level of the CD.

2. Open an FTP connection to the TiVo and send the file `TivoWebPlus-1.0-final.tivo.tpm` to your TiVo using the following commands:

   ◆ *bin*    Puts the transfer in binary mode.

   ◆ *hash*    Turns on hashing to see packet transfers.

   ◆ *cd /var*    Changes directory to a writable directory on your TiVo.

   ◆ *put TivoWebPlus-1.0-final.tivo.tpm*    Transfers the file.

3. After the file has transferred, quit the FTP connection and open a Telnet connection to your TiVo.

4. When you're connected, change directory to the directory where you put the FTP file, `TivoWebPlus-1.0-final.tivo.tpm` (`/var` if you followed the previous examples) and make sure that the archive that you downloaded is executable by using the following command:

```
chmod 755 TivoWebPlus-1.0-final.tivo.tpm
```

5. Extract the contents of the tar file by using the following command:

```
./TivoWebPlus-1.0-final.tivo.tpm
```

You will see some introductory messages, such as the following:

```
Packaged with Tivo Package Manager (TPM) Version: 1.0 Release: 5
TivoWebPlus is a comprehensive TiVoWeb package meant to support all existing
TiVos. This initiative was started by falcontx with his addition of dual
tuner DirecTiVo support and has been further updated and enhanced by
mrblack51 and several other members of the TiVo hacking community.
This project is based upon TivoWeb 1.9.4 final. TiVoWeb credits can be
found in the README file in the tivoweb-tcl directory.
Would you like to install "TivoWebPlus-1.0-final.tivo.tpm" now? [yes]:
```

6. Enter "yes" or press the Return or Enter key. The installation procedure will prompt you for the directory in which you want to install TiVoWebPlus:

```
Where would you like to install "TivoWebPlus-1.0-final.tivo.tpm" ?
[/var/local/tivoweb-tcl]:
```

7. Press the Return or Enter key to accept the default install location, or enter the full pathname of another directory if you want to install TiVoWebPlus somewhere else. (I recommend that you simply accept the default value.) The installation procedure will display some additional information as it installs TiVoWebPlus and then displays a message asking if you want to add TiVoWebPlus to your system's startup files:

```
Extracting archive...
Decompressing archive...
Unpacking archive...
"TivoWebPlus" can optionally start everytime your tivo boots, this way
you do not have to start it manually each time your system boots.
Do you want to configure automatic startup? [yes]:
```

8. Unless you have a specific reason not to, enter yes or press the Return or Enter key. The installation procedure will display a number of periods as it scans your system startup files. It will then display messages offering to delete the archive file `TivoWebPlus-1.0-final.tivo.tpm`, and offering to start TiVoWebPlus. I suggest that you keep the archive file around until you're sure that TiVoWebPlus has installed correctly (answer "no"), and that you let the install automatically start TiVoWebPlus for you (answer "yes").

9. Though it's optional, I suggest that you password-protect your copy of TivoWebPlus. This will prevent randoms from accessing your TiVoWebPlus server, which is especially important if you are planning to make your TiVo available on the Internet.

To password-protect your TiVoWebPlus installation, change directory to the new `tivoweb-tcl` directory and edit the file `tivoweb.cfg`. Put a username after the equal sign at the end of the line beginning with UserName and put a password after the equal sign on the line beginning with Password. This isn't the most elegant security, since anyone on your home network can telnet to the machine and examine this configuration file, but I hope that you can trust the people on your home network. Your `tivoweb.cfg` file should now look something like the following:

```
UserName = wvh
Password = mypassword
Port = 80
Prefix =
Theme =
DescriptionHover = 1
MultiDelete = 1
TyShowLinks = 0
```

10. During installation, the TiVoWebPlus installation procedure offered the option of adding TiVoWebPlus to your system's startup procedure, so that TiVoWebPlus will automatically start whenever you restart your TiVo. If you answered "yes" to that option, skip to Step 15 in this list. If you answered "no," you will have to manually add the TiVoWebPlus startup command to your system. Proceed to the next step.

11. Execute the following command so that you can modify your TiVo's `/etc/rc.d/rc.sysinit` file:

```
mount -o rw,remount /
```

12. If you are running a hacked Series 1 TiVo or a monte'd Series 2 TiVo, use a text editor to add the following line to the end of the `/etc/rc.d/rc.sysinit` file so that TiVoWebPlus will automatically start each time you reboot your TiVo:

```
/var/local/tivoweb-tcl/tivoweb &
```

13. If you are running a hacked Series 2 TiVo and are not using the two-kernel monte approach (and are therefore probably running a 3.x version of the TiVo operating system), use a text editor to modify the file `/var/hack/hackinit`, adding the following command to the end of the file so that TiVoWebPlus will start each time you reboot your TiVo:

```
/var/local/tivoweb-tcl/tivoweb &
```

14. Now, execute the following command to make sure that your root partition is read-only again:

```
mount -o ro,remount /
```

15. If you did not tell the TiVoWebPlus installer to automatically start TiVoWebPlus for you, you can now start the TiVoWebPlus application manually by executing the following command at the Telnet prompt:

```
/var/local/tivoweb-tcl/tivoweb &
```

After you have TiVoWebPlus running on your TiVo, you can connect to it by using any Web browser using a URL like *http://your-tivos-IP-address* (which you can find on the TiVo Messages and Setup screen's System Information screen). Because you set a username and password when installing TiVoWebPlus, your browser will prompt you for the username and password before you can log in. After you enter the correct username and password, your browser displays TiVoWebPlus's main menu as shown in Figure 8.9.

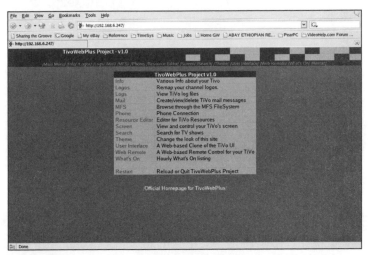

**FIGURE 8.9**    *The TiVoWebPlus main screen on a Series 1 TiVo*

The menu bar across the top of the screen provides access to all the TiVoWebPlus screens, as does the list of links on its main menu page.

 **NOTE**

The TiVoWebPlus screen that you see in your Web browser may differ slightly, depending on the version of TiVoWebPlus that you have installed and whether you are using a Series 1 or Series 2 TiVo. TiVoWeb was originally developed for Series 1 TiVos (since the Series 2 didn't exist at the time)—only the most popular features have been brought forward to the version of TiVoWebPlus that runs on the Series 2 TiVo. Features that are only available in TiVoWebPlus for the Series 1 TiVo will be identified throughout the remainder of this section. Don't worry—all of the most exciting features are still there!

Figure 8.10 shows the main screen of TiVoWebPlus when running on a stand-alone Series 2 TiVo.

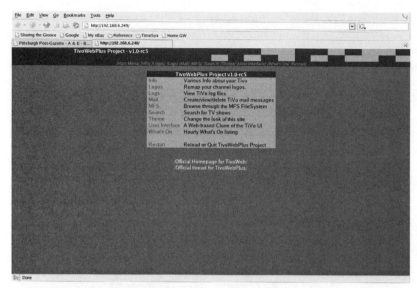

**FIGURE 8.10** *The TiVoWebPlus main screen on a Series 2 TiVo*

# Exploring the TiVoWebPlus Menus

Once you have installed TiVoWebPlus, you're ready for a guided tour. As mentioned earlier, TiVoWebPlus makes it easy for you to schedule programs over the Internet without using TiVo's Home Media Features—which is certainly useful on Series 1 and other TiVos that can't run the Home Media Features! However, that's not all that TiVoWebPlus enables you to do.

The version of TiVoWebPlus (1.0-final) included on the CD with this book provides the following items in the menu bar across the top of the TiVoWebPlus screen in your Web browser:

◆ *Main Menu* Displays the main menu screen, as shown in Figure 8.9.

◆ *Info* Provides a variety of information about your TiVo, including the channel and program that it is currently displaying, the version of the TiVo software and Linux kernel that it is running, memory use, and filesystem status and usage information. The latter is especially useful because it tells you how much free space is available on your TiVo for recording new programs. This screen takes a while to display in its entirety, because it does such a detailed analysis of your system!

◆ *Logos* Shows the graphical logos associated with various channels, which are used throughout TiVoWebPlus. You can click the "Automatically Associate Logos" link at the top to have TiVoWebPlus do its best to match its collection of channel and network logos to the channels that you receive.

◆ *Logs* Displays a list of the log files stored on your TiVo. These log files are used by the TiVo software and the Linux operating system to record internal messages and other status information. You can view the actual contents of any log file in the list by clicking on its name. This part of TiVoWeb (known as a *module*) was written by

Jeff Keegan, a well-known TiVo hacker and the author of an excellent TiVo hacking book that largely focuses on the Series 1 TiVos.

◆ *Mail*   Views TiVo service messages over the Web and allows you to post your own. This is a great way to leave messages on your TiVo for your wife and kids!

◆ *MFS*   Displays a number of entries in the Media File System (MFS) used by the TiVo, and enables you to explore their values by clicking on them. TiVo's MFS is discussed in the section of Chapter 10 entitled "MFS—TiVo's Media File System"

◆ *Phone (Series 1 only)*   Displays information about the last time your TiVo received information from TiVo headquarters, the last time it tried to call home, the next scheduled call, the amount of programming data currently available on the system, and the version of the TiVo software that your system is running. Links are available to have the TiVo make a test to call or to make its daily call now.

◆ *Resource Editor (Series 1 only)*   Modifies specific values related to recording quality that are stored in MFS. You should not modify these unless you know what you are doing!

◆ *Screen (Series 1 only)*   Shows the name of the program that is currently being displayed on the TiVo's screen.

◆ *Search*   Displays a search dialog that enables you to search for upcoming recordings in various TiVo categories. This screen is a fancier version of the "Pick Programs to Record" screen's "Search by Title" screen, because it also enables you to search by title, title keyword, description keyword, actor, director, or various combinations of these.

◆ *Theme*   Changes the appearance of TiVoWebPlus in your Web browser, as described in the next section.

◆ *User Interface*   Displays a concise screen that gives you easy access to your Season Passes, the Now Showing screen, your ToDo list, suggested shows that the TiVo plans to record, the ability to undelete shows that you have already deleted (within reason), your preferences and WishLists, a list of the channels that your TiVo currently received, and information about your TiVo's recording history. As discussed later in this chapter, the ability to undelete shows on your TiVo is an incredibly good reason for installing TiVoWebPlus on your system!

◆ *Web Remote (Series 1 only)*   Displays a graphical image of a TiVo remote control and enables you to operate it over the Web, just as if you were standing in front of it clicking your physical remote.

◆ *What's On*   Browses the shows that your TiVo is receiving. You can select between those shown on all channels and those shown on just your favorite channels, and you can also specify the date and hour for which you want TiVoWebPlus to display a listing.

◆ *Restart*   Restarts or shuts down TiVoWebPlus remotely.

The next few sections highlight some of the more useful tasks you can do with these menu items. As with any hacking project, the best thing to do is to simply explore all of the menus—the next few sections are simply my favorites.

# Changing the Appearance of TiVoWebPlus

Figure 8.9 showed the initial TiVoWebPlus screen that you'll see when you connect to it from your favorite Web browser. This screen is a bit dark for my tastes, but luckily, TiVoWebPlus is fully configurable in terms of its appearance. How TiVoWebPlus looks in your browser is controlled by different themes that you can change from within TiVoWebPlus. (Web aficionados may recognize these as *Cascading Style Sheets*.) The graphically inclined can even create their own cascading style sheets and use them as themes for TiVoWebPlus.

To change the appearance of TiVoWebPlus, select the Themes item from the TiVoWebPlus menu bar (see Figure 8.11).

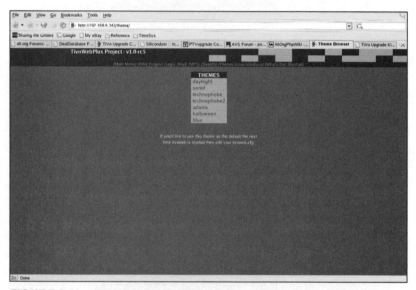

**FIGURE 8.11**   *TiVoWebPlus Themes screen*

Selecting any of the items on this screen loads a different theme, which changes the appearance of TiVoWebPlus in your browser. Figure 8.12 shows TiVoWebPlus after the daynight theme has been selected, which I'll use throughout the rest of this chapter for readability purposes.

---

 **TIP**

You can permanently change the theme used by TiVoWebPlus by modifying the configuration file that it uses. We modified this after installing TiVoWebPlus so that a username and password was required. To change the theme loaded by TiVoWebPlus, modify the Theme entry in the configuration file (usually `/var/local/tivoweb-tcl/ tivoweb.cfg`). For example, to always use the daynight theme when starting TiVoWeb-Plus, you would modify the Theme entry to look like the following:

```
Theme = daynight
```

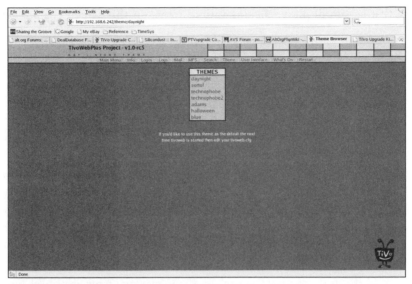

**FIGURE 8.12** *TiVoWebPlus after selecting the daynight theme*

# Browsing and Recording Upcoming Shows Using TiVoWebPlus

TiVoWebPlus makes it easy for you to access your TiVo's programming guide information over your local network. Clicking on the What's On menu item displays the screen shown in Figure 8.13.

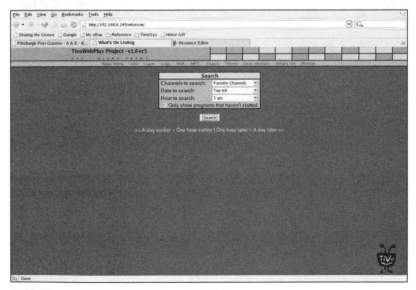

**FIGURE 8.13** *The TiVoWebPlus What's On screen*

Once that screen displays, clicking various items on this screen enables you to refine your search:

◆ *Channels to Search* This drop-down box searches all of the channels that you received (Channels Watched) or only those channels that you have identified as your favorites (Favorite Channels). On a stand-alone TiVo, favorite channels are set by selecting Messages & Setup from the TiVo Central menu, selecting the Preferences screen, and then selecting the Customize Channels screen.

◆ *Date to Search* This drop-down box selects the day whose programming you want to display.

◆ *Hour to Search* This drop-down box selects the hour whose programming you want to display.

◆ *Only show programs that haven't started* As the name suggests, clicking this check box enables you to limit your search to programs that have not yet started, which is useful if you are hoping to schedule recordings, but do not want to schedule any partial recordings.

Figure 8.14 shows the results of a search for shows playing on my favorite channels between 6 and 7 A.M. on April 6, 2004.

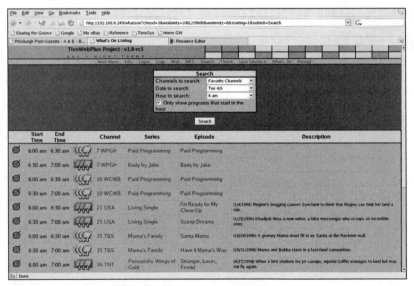

**FIGURE 8.14** *The TiVoWebPlus Now Showing screen*

The first field in each entry on this screen displays a green circle overlaid by a red check mark if no entry is currently scheduled for recording in the specified hour. If you were searching the current hour, this column would display a button labeled Watch that you could click to cause the TiVo to change to the selected channel and display the selected show.

Once this screen displays, you can do any of the following:

◆ Click the hyperlink to any channel in the Channel column to display a screen that lists any Season Passes that are currently associated with the selected channel, as shown in Figure 8.15. This figure shows the results of my clicking the Channel WPGH from the screen shown in Figure 8.14, and shows that I have a Season Pass for syndicated episodes of the series "Friends" shown on that channel.

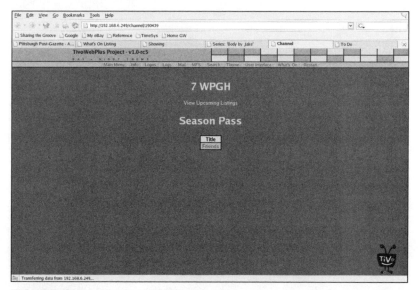

**FIGURE 8.15** *The TiVoWebPlus Channel screen*

◆ Click the hyperlink to the name of any series in the Series column to display a screen that lists all upcoming episodes of the selected series (see Figure 8.16). Note that the upcoming episodes of the selected series are not limited to the instances of this show on the selected channel—this screen shows all upcoming episodes of the series on any channel that you receive. This screen enables you to schedule recordings of selected upcoming episodes, in exactly the same way as clicking on the name of any individual episode does, as described in the next bullet. Figure 8.16 shows the results of my clicking the "Body by Jake" entry in the Series column from the screen shown in Figure 8.14.

◆ Click the hyperlink to any upcoming episode in the Episode column to display a screen that provides information about the episode that is currently showing (hence the name of the screen), as shown in Figure 8.17. This enables you to schedule re-cording the selected episode. Figure 8.17 shows the results of my clicking the "Body by Jake" entry in the Episode column from the screen shown in Figure 8.14.

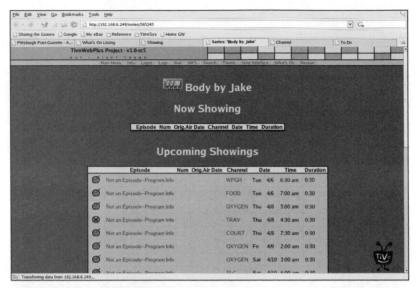

**FIGURE 8.16** *The TiVoWebPlus Series screen*

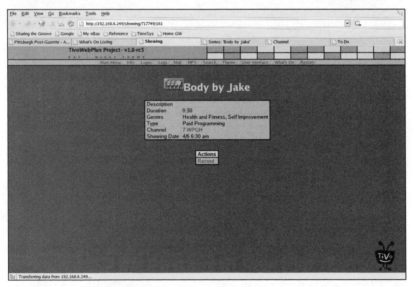

**FIGURE 8.17** *The TiVoWebPlus Showing screen*

After you have displayed information about any episode that you want to record, clicking on the Record hyperlink displays a screen that enables you to specify the recording options that you want to use for that episode (see Figure 8.18).

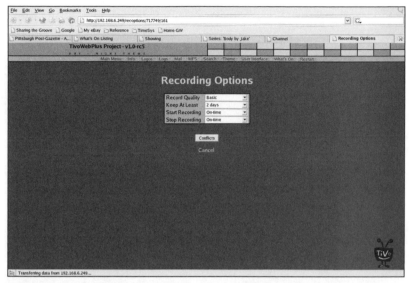

**FIGURE 8.18** *The TiVoWebPlus Recording Options screen*

Once you've set the recording options that you want to use in the recording you're scheduling, you can click the Conflicts button to identify any currently-scheduled recordings that the recording you are scheduling might conflict with. In this example, there are no conflicts, so clicking this button displays that information, as shown in Figure 8.19.

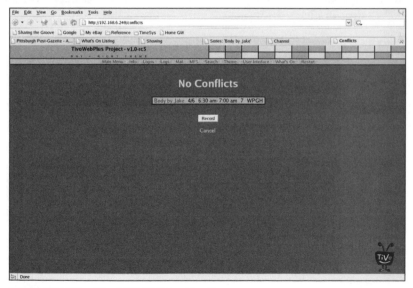

**FIGURE 8.19** *The TiVoWebPlus Conflicts screen*

To record the selected episode, click the Record button. Clicking this button displays a screen that confirms the scheduled recording (see Figure 8.20).

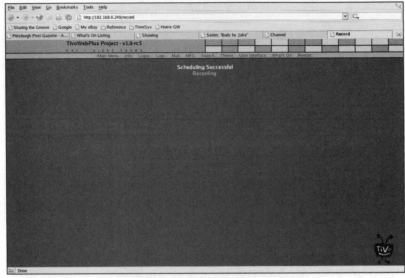

**FIGURE 8.20** *The TiVoWebPlus Recording Scheduled screen*

The screen in Figure 8.20 provides the "Recording" hyperlink that enables you to review summary information about the scheduled recording. In this example, clicking this link shows the screen in Figure 8.21.

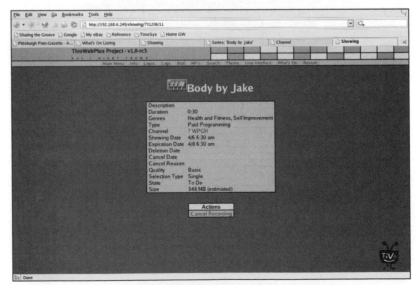

**FIGURE 8.21** *The TiVoWebPlus Recording Summary screen*

The screen shown in Figure 8.21 also enables you to cancel the scheduled recording (if you've changed your mind) by clicking the "Cancel Recording" link. Clicking this link displays a screen that requests confirmation of the cancellation. Confirming the cancellation by clicking on this link cancels the scheduled recording.

It's quite impressive that a free tool provides you with this much power and flexibility—in many ways, TiVoWebPlus is superior to the online scheduling capabilities of TiVo's own Home Media Features (described later in this chapter). Of course, TiVo's Home Media features have some advantages—you don't have to hack your TiVo in order to use it and they are officially supported by TiVo, Inc., which means that you have someone to complain to if it doesn't work correctly. On the other hand, you're reading this book, so…

 **TIP**

If you want to review all of the channels that you currently receive on your TiVo, TiVoWebPlus provides a convenient summary through the Logos command in the TiVoWebPlus menu or on its main screen. A screen displays like the one shown in Figure 8.22, but is customized for the list of channels that you receive. This screen enables you to associate graphical logos with various channels, and automatically displays logos for any stations associated with known networks or broadcasting systems. You can display this same list by clicking the User Interface menu item and selecting the Channel Guide link, but the Logos screen is an easy one-click reference.

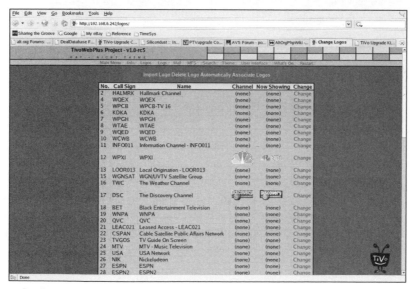

**FIGURE 8.22**  *TiVoWeb Project's Change Logos screen*

# Undeleting Recordings Using TiVoWebPlus

One of the cooler things that you can do with TivoWebPlus is to undelete shows that you have deleted on your TiVo. Much like undeleting files on old DOS or Windows systems, undeleting recordings depends on the fact that the MFS files associated with TiVo recordings are not actually wiped out when you delete a show using your TiVo remote control—the directory entry is marked as deleted and the MFS files for a deleted recording are simply marked as being reclaimable by the MFS filesystem. Therefore, if the MFS files associated with your recording have not been reused by the TiVo filesystem, the recording can be undeleted. For more information about the TiVo's MFS filesystem, see Chapter 10—we don't really have to know anything about its internals in order to take advantage of them using TiVoWebPlus!

To undelete recordings that are still available but marked as deleted on your TiVo, do the following:

1. Click the User Interface command in the TiVoWebPlus menu bar (see Figure 8.23).

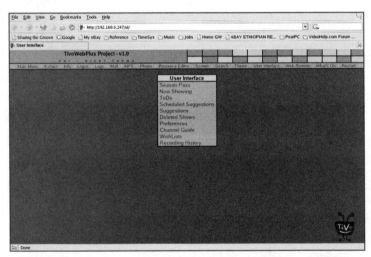

**FIGURE 8.23** *The TiVoWebPlus User Interface screen*

2. Click the Deleted Shows menu entry (see Figure 8.24).
3. Locate the show that you want to undelete and click the icon that looks like the universal recycling icon in the left column beside that entry. Figure 8.25 shows the results of clicking the icon beside the entry for the episode of "Sue Thomas, F.B.Eye" entitled "Elvis Is In The Building," shown in Figure 8.24.

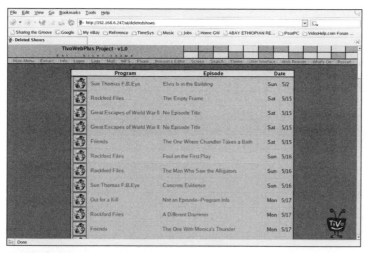

**FIGURE 8.24**    *The TiVoWebPlus Deleted Shows screen*

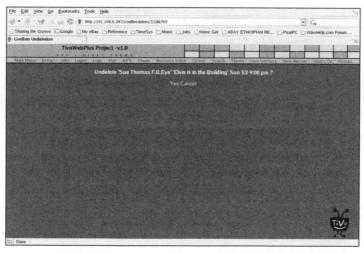

**FIGURE 8.25**    *Selecting an Episode to Undelete in TiVoWebPlus*

4. To undelete the selected show, click Yes (see Figure 8.26). To skip undeleting this recording, click Cancel, which returns you to the Deleted Shows screen. If you selected Yes, you can continue undeleting shows by clicking the Deleted Shows menu entry that is displayed after a show has been successfully undeleted.

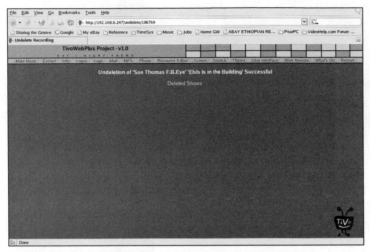

**FIGURE 8.26** *Successfully undeleting a show in TiVoWebPlus*

# Getting Status Information about Your TiVo in TiVoWebPlus

You can also use TiVoWebPlus to get a variety of general information about your TiVo through its Info menu entry. Clicking the Info entry in the TiVoWebPlus title bar shows a screen like the one in Figure 8.27, which provides information about the show that is currently being displayed on your TiVo, and information about your TiVo such as your TiVo service number and the version of the TiVo software that is running. This screen also displays detailed information about the version of the kernel that your TiVo is running, how it is using memory, the state of the filesystems on your TiVo, and the amount of free space that is available on your TiVo.

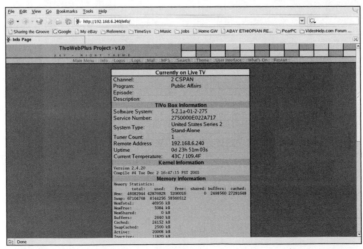

**FIGURE 8.27** *Displaying status information about your TiVo in TiVoWebPlus*

# Enabling Internet Access to Your TiVo

Using TiVoWebPlus on your home network is easy, since all of the machines on your home network can presumably access your networked TiVo. Accessing TiVoWebPlus from the Internet requires that you make your TiVo accessible from outside your home network. There are two ways to do this: through a proxy if you are running your own Apache Web server or a similar application, or through port forwarding on a home gateway, if that's what you're running to connect your home network to the Internet.

If your home network is connected to the Internet through a home gateway, the easiest way to make your TiVo available from the outside world is to set up port forwarding on the gateway. This means that when requests are received on a specific port of the IP address that corresponds to your home gateway, the gateway automatically forwards those requests to your TiVo. Needless to say, the gateway also handles outgoing communication from your TiVo for any connections that have been established using port forwarding. Figure 8.28 shows the port-forwarding panel of the LinkSys gateway that I use at home. The TiVoWeb Project entry shows that any requests received on port 99 of my home gateway's external IP address will automatically forward to port 80 on my TiVo, which has the internal IP address 192.168.6.247.

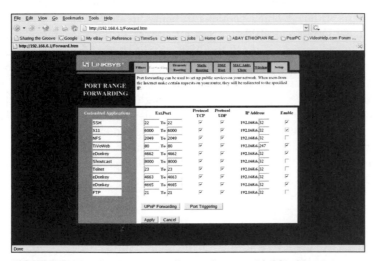

**FIGURE 8.28**   *Setting up port forwarding on a LinkSys home gateway*

---

 **WARNING**

Using port forwarding on your TiVo is a serious security hole on your home network if your gateway does not require authentication before forwarding a connection or if the applications that you are forwarding requests to do not require authentication.

# Using TiVo's Home Media Features

TiVo's Home Media Option (HMO), introduced in early April, 2003, extended the basic capabilities and network awareness of Series 2 machines. As of June, 2004, the capabilities formerly known as the Home Media Option were integrated into the standard TiVo service offering, and are now known as "Home Media Features." TiVo's Home Media Features require that your Series 2 is running Version 4.0 or better of the TiVo OS. The basic capabilities of the Home Media Features are discussed in the section of Chapter 1 entitled "What Was TiVo's Home Media Option?"

TiVo's Home Media Features require that you have a USB (Universal Serial Bus) network adaptor for your Series 2 machine. A list of suggested USB adaptors for the Series 2 was discussed in earlier in this chapter, in the section "Networking Series 2 and DVD TiVos." If you want to take advantage of remote scheduling over the Web or want to play online audio or browse digital photographs stored on other people's TiVos, you must have an always-on, broadband connection to the Internet.

If it isn't clear already, TiVo's Home Media Features are only available for stand-alone Series 2 machines, and then only for Series 2 systems running Version 4.0 or better of the TiVo operating system. Although online petitions are being circulated to request that TiVo make the Home Media Features available for Series 1 systems, I don't see much chance of this happening. The last revision of the TiVo OS for Series 1 machines was 3.2; DirecTiVos are still running a version of 3.1 (officially), and porting 4.0 to a Series 1 TiVo is a large effort. More importantly, the Series 1 systems are also somewhat underpowered by today's standards, and only have networking support through third-party products that are not officially endorsed by TiVo. (See the section earlier in this chapter entitled "Networking Series 1 TiVos" for more information about Series 1 networking products.) While the performance issue could be addressed by clever programming, the core networking requirements of the Home Media Features make it unlikely that we'll ever be seeing the Home Media Features on a Series 1. I'd be ecstatic to be proved wrong, however!

 **TIP**

Version 4.x+ of the TiVo software will run on the Series 2 DirecTiVos. If you get it running on one of these through some mfstool backup/restore mechanism, the patch is available at **http://www.dealdatabase.com/forum/showthread.php?t=35209** to enable access to Home Media Features from these systems. This is somewhat controversial, but shouldn't be, since the patch could just go away if DirectTV would just upgrade their Series 2 systems to Version 4.x+. I once heard the saying *"Give the people what they want,"* which would seem to apply here since *"The customer is always right."*

# Playing Music or Displaying Photos Using Your TiVo

Playing MP3 files stored on an online service or on a networked personal computer in your home is easy. TiVo provides software for Macintosh and Windows systems that makes it easy for you to export your online audio files so that they can be browsed and played from Series 2 TiVos. Known as the TiVo Desktop, this software is free and can be downloaded from the TiVo Web site. Downloading and using the TiVo Desktop software for Windows systems was explained in Chapter 9 in "Installing and Using the Windows TiVo Desktop." Downloading and using the TiVo Desktop software for Macintosh systems was explained in Chapter 9 in "Integrating Macintosh Systems with TiVo's Home Media Features."

If your online audio files are stored on a Linux system or on a Windows system in a format other than MP3, don't despair. While not officially supported by TiVo, Inc., it is possible to integrate Linux systems with TiVos running the Home Media Features, and thus play other audio formats from a Windows system. Integrating Linux systems with the Home Media Features is accomplished through freely-available, open-source applications such as the *Java Home Media Option* or the *Portable Open TiVo Home Media Option*, which are explained in Chapter 10 in the section "Working with TiVo's Home Media Features from Linux." The folks at TiVo are certainly open source advocates and one of the best success stories ever for the power of Linux and the open source movement in general, so they released documentation and a sample plug-in for the Apache Web server written in the Perl language that showed how the Home Media Option/Home Media Features software worked. (This is available from the page at **http://www.tivo.com/developer**.) This source code is the conceptual parent of the Portable Open TiVo Home Media Option project.

If your online audio files are stored in a format other than MP3 and are stored on a Windows system (or a system that you can mount from your Windows system over your home network), you can use J. River's Media Center software to export these audio collections so they can be accessed from your TiVo. For more information about this, see Chapter 9, the section entitled "Playing Windows Audio Formats Other than MP3."

After you've exported your audio collection from your personal computer using one of these techniques, you can browse the list from the "Music & Photos" menu on your TiVo (TiVo Central, Music & Photos). Selecting this menu displays the screen shown in Figure 8.29.

This screen displays the name of each system exporting music and photos in a format compatible with the Home Media Features. The audio and photo collections on each system are listed separately, organized by the name of the system.

To play audio files or display photographs from any of these systems, select the name of the audio or photo collection that you want to browse. The TiVo displays a list of all files in the specified format available on that system, as shown in Figure 8.30.

When a collection displays, select the folder containing the music that you want to play or which contains the photos that you want to display. Photo collections in a selected folder display immediately, while audio files are listed and can be played by selecting specific files or playlists.

**FIGURE 8.29** *Browsing for available music and photograph collections*

**FIGURE 8.30** *Browsing an online music collection.*

That's all there is to it. The Home Media Features' ability to access online music collections from any TiVo/TV combination in one's home is incredibly handy at parties or when you simply want to listen to online music without sitting at your personal computer.

# Scheduling Recordings on Your TiVo over the Internet Using Home Media Features

Hearing about an interesting upcoming show that you'd love to record is traditionally frustrating if you're not near your VCR. I've certainly seen things mentioned in the morning paper that I wanted to record. And what if you're held up at work, out of town, or simply forget to schedule a recording. You could always call your significant other or a friend, but that's somewhat embarrassing. The best solution for solving the problem of remote scheduling is scheduling its recording over the Internet. Network-capable DVRs, such as the TiVo, make this easy to do through an official, TiVo-supported solution for the Series 2 TiVo owners, or through an excellent TiVo application written by TiVo hackers.

For Series 1 and hacked Series 2 machines that cannot or simply do not run TiVo's Home Media Features software, you already have an excellent tool for scheduling recordings over a network in the TiVo Web Project software, known more familiarly as TiVoWeb and now TiVoWebPlus. These were discussed in detail earlier in this chapter. As explained there, using TiVoWeb or TiVoWebPlus from machines on the Internet requires some special configuration of your TiVo or home gateway so that your TiVo is accessible from the outside world.

If you are using a Series 2 machine running a current version of the TiVo software, life is much easier. Stock Series 2 users can connect to TiVo, Inc.'s primary Web site, browse the shows that the TiVo will receive, and schedule recordings from anywhere on the Web. This capability, officially known as the *Remote Scheduling option*, was formerly a part of TiVo's Home Media Option, but is now available to all Series 2 users as part of the enhanced network-awareness of Version 4.x+ of the TiVo software.

Once you've remotely scheduled a recording, the request to create that recording is pushed to your TiVo during a specially scheduled call. This makes remotely scheduling recordings quite convenient because you can access the TiVo Web site from any machine that is connected to the Internet, and TiVo handles getting the data down to your machine.

To schedule a recording over the Web:

1.  Connect to the TiVo Web site and select the "I Have TiVo!" entry in the left-hand menu. Click the "TiVo Central Online" entry that displays in the left-hand menu (see Figure 8.31). A shortcut to this screen is **http://www.tivo.com/tco**, but there is no guarantee that this URL will stick around forever.

2.  Enter the email address and password that you used when you created your tivo.com account and click "Sign In" (see Figure 8.32 ).

 **TIP**

If you do not already have an account at tivo.com, you can click Register and create one by starting from this screen.

3.  Click the Schedule Recordings for TiVo DVR drop-down box and select the TiVo on which you want to schedule this recording. All DVRs that you have registered with your TiVo account will be listed in this drop-down box, but you only have the ability to schedule recordings for other DVRs that support the Home Media Features. All others will be shown with two leading asterisks in the list, indicating that they cannot be remotely programmed.

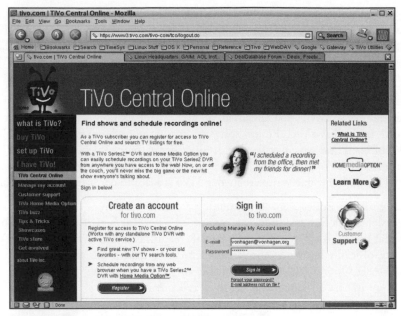

**FIGURE 8.31**  *The TiVo Central Online sign-on screen*

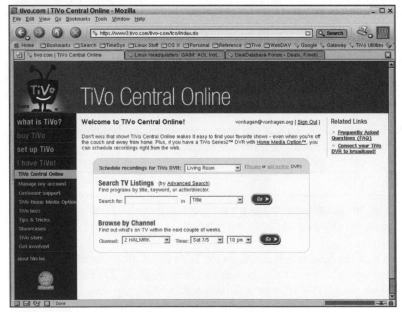

**FIGURE 8.32**  *The TiVo Central Online scheduling screen*

4. To search TV Listings in your area, enter a string that you want to search for, select where you want to search for that field (Title, Title or Description, or Actor/Director, for example), and click Go. After a few moments, a screen like the one shown in Figure 8.33 displays, which shows the results for my search for "Rockford Files" in the title.

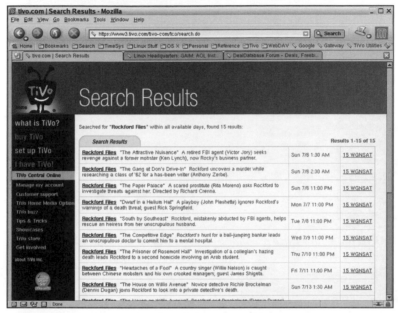

**FIGURE 8.33**   *The results of a TiVo Central Online search*

5. Browse the list of results and click on the title of anything that you want to record. A screen like the one in Figure 8.34 displays, providing more detailed information about the show, its cast and crew (when available), and a list of the times that this show will be broadcast in the near future.

6. To record this show, click Record this episode (see Figure 8.35). This screen shows your recording options for the selected episode, and enables you to change the TiVo on which you want to record this show, set recording options such as quality and priority, and lets you select a check box that results in tivo.com sending you email about the status of scheduling this recording (not the status of the recording itself).

7. After selecting appropriate options, click Schedule It! to schedule the recording. A screen like the one shown in Figure 8.36 displays, confirming that the recording will be scheduled the next time the specified DVR connects to the TiVo service.

That's all there is to it! Barring communication failure or other acts of God, the selected recording will be scheduled on your DVR and should be waiting for you one of these evenings.

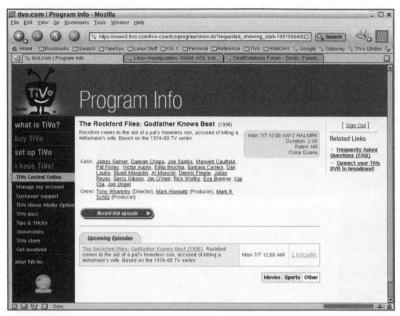

**FIGURE 8.34** *A selected recording from a TiVo Central Online search*

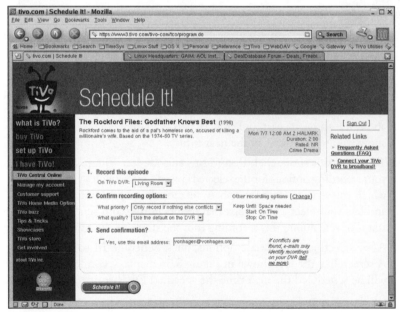

**FIGURE 8.35** *Scheduling a selected recording at TiVo Central Online*

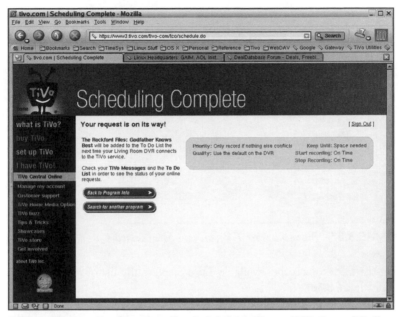

**FIGURE 8.36**   *Confirmation of a scheduled recording at TiVo Central Online*

# Multiroom Viewing on Your TiVo

TiVo's Home Media Features provide built-in support for multiroom viewing, which is the ability to browse and view stored recordings on other networked TiVos in your home that are running the Home Media Features. When you have multiple Series 2 stand-alone TiVos in your home, each machine shows up on the Now Playing lists of the other TiVos by name. You can set the name of your TiVo from TiVo's Web site using the "Manage My Account" portion of the site. These TiVo names are really only a convenience, and have nothing to do with the networked host name of your TiVo. I tend to give my machines descriptive names such as "Bedroom," "Living Room," and "Bathroom," which reflect where each TiVo is located.

Viewing a recording stored on a remote TiVo actually transfers that recording to your TiVo over your home network. You can watch the show as it is being transferred or simply transfer it and watch it later at your convenience. Depending on the speed of your home network (and especially on slower wireless networks), watching a show while it is being transferred can result in delays while you "catch up" with the portion of the show that has been transferred, and then have to wait while enough of the show transfers so that you can continue viewing. Even on wired networks, I prefer to transfer the shows and watch something else until the transfer has been completed.

To view a recording stored on one networked Series 2 stand-alone TiVo from another, simply browse to the Now Playing list (TiVo Central, Now Playing on TiVo) and browse to the bottom of the list. Each other available TiVo on your home network displays, (see Figure 8.37).

**FIGURE 8.37** *Browsing other TiVos on your home network*

Selecting the name of another available TiVo displays the list of recordings stored on that DVR (see Figure 8.38).

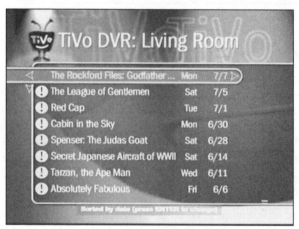

**FIGURE 8.38** *Browsing the Now Playing list on a remote TiVo*

After you have identified a recording that you want to view on the TiVo you're currently using, selecting its name displays the screen shown in Figure 8.39.

At this point, you can select Watch On This TV to transfer the recording to the TiVo that you are currently using, or select Don't Do Anything, which returns you to the list of shows available on the remote TiVo that you are currently browsing. If you select Watch On This TV, a "Please wait..." message displays as the transfer begins. Once the recording begins transferring, the screen shown in Figure 8.40 displays.

**FIGURE 8.39**   *Selecting a recording stored on a remote TiVo*

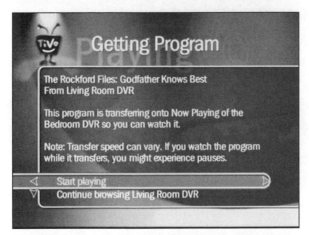

**FIGURE 8.40**   *Options when transferring a show from a remote DVR*

At this point, you can either select Start playing to begin watching the recording on the TiVo that you are using as it is being transferred, or you can select Continue browsing *tivo-name* to continue browsing the list of recordings stored on the remote TiVo.

As shows are transferred from one TiVo to another, they show up in the Now Playing list of the TiVo to which they are being transferred with a red dot next to the filenames, just as if that TiVo was actively recording them. Recordings are transferred from one TiVo to another sequentially. If you select multiple shows from a remote TiVo, they are transferred in the order that they were selected. You can only view subsequently selected shows once the first has finished transferring.

# HACKING THE TiVo

## Chapter 9

SECOND EDITION

### Working with Your TiVo from Windows and Macintosh Systems

Although the TiVo is a Linux system, most of today's home computers are not. The ABATBD TiVo tool disk included with this book provides all of the tools you need for TiVo hacking on a standard desktop personal computer, but it works by booting Linux on that PC. All of the TiVo tools discussed in the other chapters of this book require the Linux operating system. So what can you do for a TiVo from a personal computer while actually running an operating system like Microsoft Windows? Luckily, you can do quite a bit.

If you are interested in investigating any of the other TiVo tools disks that are available on the Internet, you'll need to use your personal computer to burn copies of the CDs from the ISO images that you download. If you have hacked your TiVo to enable a bash prompt over a serial connection, you'll need to connect to the serial port to do anything interesting. If you've put your TiVo on your home network, you'll need to run an application on your personal computer to connect it to the network. If you want to export music or digital photographs stored on your personal computer so that your TiVo can play or display them using TiVo's Home Media Features (formerly known as the Home Media Option), you'll need to install the TiVo desktop software on your personal computer to export that music. All of these TiVo-related tasks require software that runs on your personal computer under its existing operating system. Whether you're using Mac OS X, older versions of the Mac OS, or some version of Microsoft Windows, you can do a lot for your TiVo from your existing desktop.

In addition to the native software discussed in the previous section, there are also a fair number of "hacker-oriented" tools available for Microsoft Windows and Mac OS X. The open source foundation of Linux makes it quite easy to port Linux (and therefore TiVo) software to other platforms, but differences in the graphical user interfaces for Linux and the PC/Mac software often makes it tough to port graphical tools. However, one area of Linux where this doesn't apply is supporting low-level components such as the **ext2** filesystem. Although there are some restrictions on what (and how) you can work with the TiVo's **ext2** filesystems, support for these filesystems is available for both Windows and Mac OS X, and you can easily use this to preview and explore TiVo filesystems, even when you're not directly connected to your TiVo.

 **NOTE**

This chapter uses the colloquial term "Windows" to refer to any version of Microsoft Windows. I realize that Microsoft believes that it owns the copyright to the term *Windows*, but I wanted this chapter to be readable and also didn't want it to look like I'd blasted the book with a shotgun loaded with copyright and trademark symbols. If you're a Microsoft Windows user, you know what I'm talking about when I say Windows. If you're not, you probably don't care. Similarly, this chapter uses the term "Mac OS" to refer to versions of the Macintosh operating system prior to any version of Mac OS X. Because Mac OS X is very different than previous versions of the Mac OS, it is explicitly identified where necessary.

# Communicating with Your TiVo from Windows

After you have a command prompt running on your TiVo (described in Chapter 8, "Connecting the Universe to Your TiVo") or have your TiVo on your home network (described in Chapter 4, "Exploring Your TiVo Hardware"), you're ready to start talking to your TiVo from your personal computer. This section explains how to use and configure Windows software to communicate with your TiVo, discussing software packages that come with Windows or are freely available on the Internet.

---

### 📺 Differences Between Serial and Network Logins

Serial and network connections to your TiVo are different in one important respect—whether or not you should log out when you're finished using them. The command-line prompt on your TiVo is a bash shell that is started by an entry in the `/etc/rc.d/rc.sysinit` startup file on your TiVo. It is a single process that is started once. Therefore, you do not want to terminate it before closing down your serial connection to the TiVo. If you do terminate it (by using the **exit** command or pressing Control-D, depending on how you've configured bash on your TiVo), it will not restart. You will have to reboot your TiVo in order to get another command-line prompt (unless you manually start another one using a network connection, which would be somewhat backward but functional).

Network connections to your TiVo work differently because each network connection is an individual connection that is started by the Telnet and FTP servers that you are running on your TiVo. Terminating a network connection doesn't terminate the server. It only terminates one particular connection. The next time you connect to your TiVo over the network, the appropriate server (Telnet or FTP) creates a new connection for you and starts the appropriate processes to communicate with it.

---

# Serial Communications from Windows Systems

After you've attached a serial cable to your TiVo (as described in Chapter 4, in the section entitled "Attaching a Terminal Emulator or Serial Console") and have configured a command prompt on your TiVo (described in Chapter 8), you can connect the serial cable from the TiVo to your Windows system's serial port and begin exploring your TiVo from your Windows system. While there are a number of different serial communication software packages available for Windows, this section focuses on the default terminal emulator provided with Windows systems.

All versions of Microsoft Windows come with a simple but functional terminal emulator called *HyperTerminal*, which is available from the Programs, Accessories, Communications menu. (If you can't find HyperTerminal on your Windows system for some reason, you can download it from **http://www.hilgraeve.com/htpe/download.html**.) After starting HyperTerminal by selecting it from the menu, the HyperTerminal application displays the screen shown in Figure 9.1, which prompts you to give the new serial connection that you are defining a name. Each HyperTerminal connection contains its own configuration settings, so you'll want to enter a name that will help you remember what this connection is for—perhaps "TiVo Serial Connection," as shown in Figure 9.1. Click OK to continue.

**NOTE**

HyperTerminal is primarily designed for communicating with remote computer systems over a modem. If this is the first time that you are running the HyperTerminal program, it will display an initial dialog box that prompts you for some basic modem configuration information, such as your area code and any numbers that you have to dial to get an outside line. Although irrelevant in this case, you still have to supply your area code. Enter it and click OK to continue.

**FIGURE 9.1**   _Creating an initial HyperTerminal connection_

Next, HyperTerminal displays a Connect To dialog box where you supply information about the connection that you are establishing, as shown in Figure 9.2. If you have connected the TiVo's serial cable to your Windows system's first serial port, select COM1 in the Connect To drop-down list and click OK to continue.

**FIGURE 9.2**   _Specifying your communications port_

Next, HyperTerminal displays a screen in which you can specify the communications settings used for this connection (see Figure 9.3). Specify 9600 baud as the Bits per second rate and select None as the type of flow control to use. The other settings (8 data bits and no parity) are already correct. Click OK to continue.

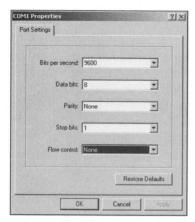

**FIGURE 9.3** *Specifying your communication settings*

At this point, HyperTerminal closes its Configuration dialog boxes and displays its standard communication window. Press Control-l followed by the Return (Enter) key on your keyboard once or twice, and you should see a prompt from the TiVo's command-line interpreter, as shown in Figure 9.4.

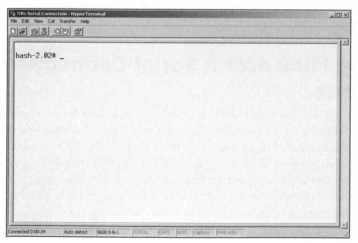

**FIGURE 9.4** *A command-line prompt from your TiVo in HyperTerminal*

Congratulations. You're connected! To ensure that HyperTerminal saves your configuration information, select the File menu's Save command. Your HyperTerminal configurations are saved on a special HyperTerminal menu that is added to the Programs, Accessories, Communications menu. In the future, you can start HyperTerminal using the settings you just created by selecting these settings by name from this menu.

**TIP**

If you're not excited by the performance or appearance of HyperTerminal, an excellent alternative is Tera Term, which can be found at **http://hp.vector.co.jp/ authors/VA002416/teraterm.html**. You can download a version of Tera Term for Windows 95/NT from **http://hp.vector.co.jp/authors/VA002416/ttermp23.zip**. This version worked fine on my Windows 2000 system, and IMHO (In My Honest Opinion) is visually and functionally superior to HyperTerminal for standard serial communications. Figure 9.5 shows a sample Tera Term screen after establishing a connection to your TiVo.

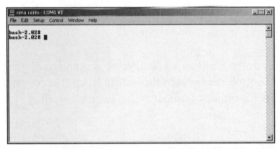

**FIGURE 9.5** *A command-line prompt from your TiVo in Tera Term*

# Transferring Files over a Serial Connection from Windows

If you're using a serial connection to your TiVo because you don't have a network card for your Series 1 machine or a USB network adapter for your Series 2 system, you may wonder how you can ever get some of those cool hacks from the BATBD CD (or ones that you've downloaded yourself) to your TiVo. Don't despair. You can still transfer files to your TiVo using tried and true serial protocols for file transfer. Unless you've been using computers for quite a while, you may never have transferred files in this way, but this was the default file transfer mechanism used by millions of home computer users long before graphical interfaces and networks were just gleams in Xerox PARC's eye. No worries, it's really quite easy. Most serial communication programs, including HyperTerminal and Tera Term, provide built-in support for serial file transfers. Your TiVo also comes with built-in applications for sending and receiving files over serial connections.

Serial file transfer protocols include xmodem, ymodem, and zmodem. The first of these was xmodem, which was invented in the late 1970s by Ward Christensen. All of these protocols automatically perform error-checking as they transfer data back and forth. The latest generation of serial communications protocols (from the early 1980s) is Chuck Forsenberg's zmodem, which includes support for restarting serial file transfers if a connection is interrupted for one reason or another, and also supports more sophisticated recovery from transfer errors (a problem on phone lines in the 1980s). TiVos provide the **rz** (Receive Zmodem) and **sz** (Send Zmodem) commands in all versions of the TiVo software.

To transfer a file to your TiVo using HyperTerminal (perhaps one of the archives of pre-compiled TiVo applications provided in the **hacks_dir** directory on the BATBD CD?), do the following:

1. After connecting to your TiVo as described in the previous section, start the **rz** program on your TiVo by typing **rz** at the bash prompt and pressing Return. HyperTerminal will display something like the screen shown in Figure 9.6.

**FIGURE 9.6**    *Starting a serial file transfer on your TiVo*

2. In HyperTerminal, pull down the Transfer menu and select the Send File command. The dialog box displayed in Figure 9.7 displays.

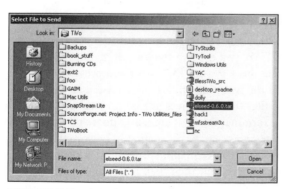

**FIGURE 9.7**    *Selecting the file to transfer in HyperTerminal*

3. Click Browse, navigate to the directory containing the file that you want to transfer, select that file, and click OK to close the Browse dialog box.

4. In the Protocol field at the bottom of HyperTerminal's Send File dialog box, select either the "Zmodem with Crash Recovery" or "Zmodem" entries. Different versions of HyperTerminal (and Windows) provide different serial transfer protocols. "Zmodem with Crash Recovery" is preferred, but "Zmodem" will do just fine.

5. Click Send to begin the file transfer. The dialog box shown in Figure 9.8 displays. The different fields in this dialog box provide status information about the file transfer as it proceeds, including a histogram that graphically displays the percentage of the file that has been transferred.

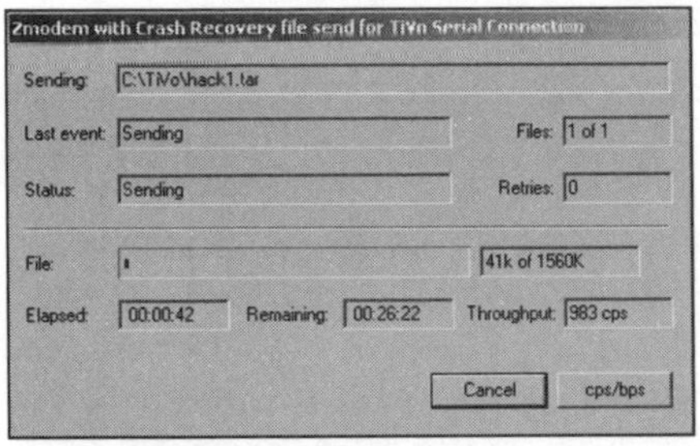

**FIGURE 9.8**    *Transferring a file in HyperTerminal*

6. Remember that this is a serial file transfer, and will therefore take a while, depending on the size of the file that you are transferring. The dialog box shown in Figure 9.8 closes automatically when the file transfer completes, and automatically terminates the **rz** command running on your TiVo. (You may need to press Return once or twice to see the bash prompt again.)

Once the serial transfer completes, you can install the software you just uploaded to your TiVo by using one of the mechanisms described in Chapter 11, "Getting and Installing New Software for Your TiVo."

Sending files from your TiVo to your PC works in much the same way as transferring them the other way. On the TiVo, you execute the **sz** command, followed by the name of the file that you want to send back to your PC. After you press Return, HyperTerminal should automatically start the receiving end of the transfer, as shown in Figure 9.9. HyperTerminal will store the files that it receives at the top level of your Windows boot drive. If the version of HyperTerminal that you are using doesn't automatically start the receiving end of the file transfer, you can start it manually by selecting the Receive File command from HyperTerminal's Transfer menu, specifying "Zmodem with Crash Recovery" or "Zmodem" as the protocol, and then manually selecting the directory where you want to store the files you receive.

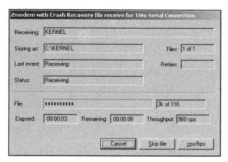

**FIGURE 9.9** *Receiving a file in HyperTerminal*

# Networked Communications from Windows

If you have added a network card to your Series 1 machine or a USB network adapter to your Series 2 TiVo, you will certainly want to connect to it over the network. The command-line prompt access discussed in the previous section is always useful, but serial file transfers are slow and clunky, although elegant in their simplicity. This section describes how to use standard Windows software to log in and transfer files to and from your TiVo over a network. The instructions in this and the next few sections assume that you installed (and started) the versions of the FTP and Telnet daemons that are provided in the archives of TiVo hacks provided on the BATBD CD, or that were installed and started for you as part of installing the TurboNet or AirNet card in your TiVo. For information on installing the software from the BATBD CD on your TiVo, see Chapter 11, "Getting and Installing New Software for Your TiVo." For information on installing a TurboNet or AirNet card on your PC, see Chapter 4, in the section entitled "Networking Your TiVo."

 **TIP**

If you're new to networking, see the general information about networking provided in Chapter 4, in the section entitled "Networking 101." Everybody must start somewhere—and what better motivation than your TiVo!

## Using HyperTerminal for Network Communications

As discussed earlier in the section on serial communications using Windows systems, all versions of Microsoft Windows come with a simple but functional terminal emulator called *HyperTerminal*, which is available from the Programs, Accessories, Communications menu. The instructions for configuring a network connection in HyperTerminal are much the same as the instructions for configuring a serial connection.

**TIP**

If you already have configured a serial connection to your TiVo, don't select that connection from the HyperTerminal menu when configuring a network connection. Instead, select the standard HyperTerminal command from the Programs, Accessories, Communications menu. This enables you to define a new connection without accidentally overwriting your serial communication settings.

After starting HyperTerminal by selecting it from the menu, the HyperTerminal application displays the screen shown in Figure 9.10, which prompts you to name the new serial connection that you are defining. Each HyperTerminal connection contains its own configuration settings, so you'll want to enter a name that will help you remember what this connection is for (try "TiVo Network Connection," which I've used in this case, as shown in Figure 9.10. Click OK to continue.

 **NOTE**

HyperTerminal is primarily designed for communicating with remote computer systems over a modem. If this is the first time that you are running the HyperTerminal program, it will display an initial dialog box that prompts you for some basic modem configuration information, such as your area code and any numbers that you have dial to get an outside line. Though irrelevant in this case, you still have to supply your area code. Enter it and click OK to continue.

**FIGURE 9.10** *Creating an initial HyperTerminal connection*

Next, HyperTerminal displays a Connect To dialog box that enables you to supply information about the connection that you are establishing, as shown in Figure 9.10 above. Select TCP/IP (Winsock) from the Connect To drop-down list, which displays the dialog box shown in Figure 9.11.

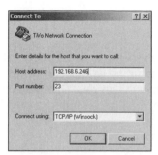

**FIGURE 9.11** *Specifying a network connection in HyperTerminal*

Enter your TiVo's IP address in the dialog box shown in Figure 9.11 and click OK to continue. At this point, HyperTerminal closes its configuration dialog boxes and displays its standard communication window. Press the Return (Enter) key on your keyboard once or twice, where you should see a prompt from the TiVo's command-line interpreter, as shown in Figure 9.12.

**FIGURE 9.12** *A network connection to your TiVo in HyperTerminal*

Congratulations—you're connected! To be sure that HyperTerminal saves your configuration information, select the Save command in the File menu. Your HyperTerminal configurations are saved on a special HyperTerminal menu that is added to the Programs, Accessories, Communications menu. In the future, you can start HyperTerminal using the settings you just created by selecting these settings by name from this menu.

**TIP**

If you don't know your TiVo's IP address (which may be the case if it is allo-cated dynamically, using DHCP), you can determine what it is by executing the **/sbin/ifconfig -a** command from a serial connection to your TiVo. This command displays information about all of the Ethernet interfaces that are active on your TiVo in the following format:

```
lo      Link encap:Local Loopback
        inet addr:127.0.0.1  Bcast:127.255.255.255  Mask:255.0.0.0
        UP BROADCAST LOOPBACK RUNNING  MTU:3584  Metric:1
        RX packets:0 errors:0 dropped:0 overruns:0 frame:0
        TX packets:0 errors:0 dropped:0 overruns:0 carrier:0 coll:0
eth0    Link encap:Ethernet  HWaddr 00:40:36:01:B0:11
        inet addr:192.168.6.246  Bcast:192.168.6.255  Mask:255.255.255.0
        UP BROADCAST RUNNING MULTICAST  MTU:1500  Metric:1
        RX packets:0 errors:0 dropped:0 overruns:0 frame:0
        TX packets:0 errors:0 dropped:0 overruns:0 carrier:0 coll:0  Interrupt:29
```

You will want to enter the IP address shown in the `eth0` (for "Ethernet Connection Zero") section. Your TiVo's IP address may change if you reboot your TiVo after using other network devices that dynamically allocate IP addresses, but you can always use a serial connection to your TiVo and the **/sbin/ifconfig -a** command to find out your TiVo's current IP address.

**TIP**

There are several shareware and freeware clients that enable Microsoft Windows systems to access other systems using network protocols such as Telnet and Secure Shell (SSH). If you plan on using your Windows system to connect to Linux (or Unix) systems other than the TiVo, you will want to use a network com-munications client that supports SSH, which is a new, more secure replacement for Telnet. The Tera Term program, mentioned earlier, is one of the most popular free applications for standard telnet connections, but requires an add-on module to support SSH (available at **http://www.zip.com.au/~roca/ttssh.html**). This may not work correctly with newer versions of SSH. One of the most commonly used and freely available clients with up-to-date SSH support is PuTTY, which you can download from **http://www.chiark.greenend.org.uk/~sgtatham/putty/**. The easiest way to download PuTTY and related utilities for Windows systems from this site is as a single Zip file. After you have downloaded the Zip file, you can install PuTTY and its companion applications by creating a directory and extracting the contents of the Zip file into it. You can then start PuTTY like any other Windows application, by clicking on its icon.

## Using FTP from Windows

FTP (File Transfer Protocol) is both the protocol for simple networked file transfers and the application that you execute to perform those sorts of transfers on most systems (including Windows). In terms of Microsoft's graphical standards, Windows provides a truly tragic version of FTP as part of all network-capable versions of Windows. However, it works, so it's hard to argue with that. And, it should be immediately familiar to anyone who is familiar with using command-line FTP clients on other types of computer systems. Figure 9.13 shows the FTP client provided with Windows, in all its glory.

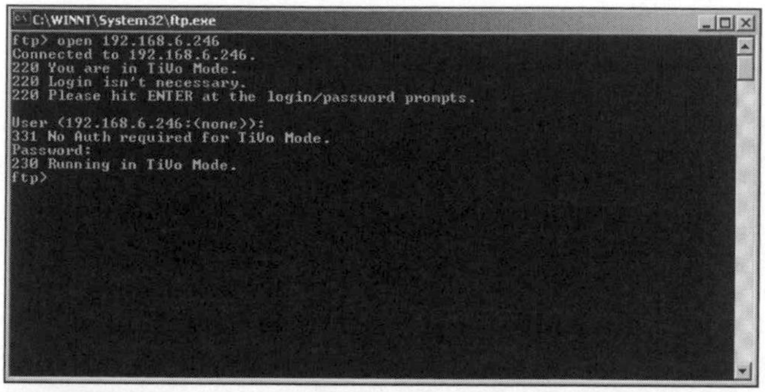

**FIGURE 9.13**    *The default Windows FTP client*

To transfer a file to or from your Windows system using the standard Windows FTP client, do the following:

1. Select the Start menu's Run command and enter FTP in the Open text entry box. The Windows FTP client displays (see Figure 9.13).

2. Type the command **open IP-Address** in the FTP client window, where IP-Address is your TiVo's IP address. The FTP client displays a connection message, and eventually prompts you for the name of the user you want to connect to the TiVo. Since TiVos don't have user logins, press Return to continue.

3. The FTP client prompts you for the password of the user you are connecting as. Since TiVos don't have user logins, press Return.

4. The FTP client displays the standard "ftp>" prompt. At this point, you can use the commands shown in Table 9.1 to navigate to and transfer any file to or from your TiVo.

That's all there is to it. As an example, a transcript of the commands that you would type in the FTP client to transfer the file C:\sample.tar to your TiVo's /var directory and exit the FTP client would be the following:

```
ftp> lcd c:\
Local directory now C:\.
ftp> cd /var
250 Directory change successful.
```

```
ftp> hash
Hash mark printing On  ftp: (2048 bytes/hash mark) .
ftp> bin
200 Type set to I.
ftp> put sample.tar
200 PORT command successful.
150 Opening BINARY mode data connection for KERNEL.
#####
226 File transfer complete.
ftp: 11047 bytes sent in 0.00Seconds 11047000.00Kbytes/sec.
ftp> quit
```

 **TIP**

If you're not excited by the performance or appearance of Windows' command-line FTP client, an excellent alternative is SmartFTP, which you can find at **http://www.smartftp.com**. You can download a version of SmartFTP for any flavor of Windows from **http://www.smartftp.com/get/SFTPFull.exe**. SmartFTP is free for personal, noncommercial use, although it turns into nag-ware after 30 days. If you're going to be using FTP in the future and need to talk to FTP servers directly, buying a copy of SmartFTP is a good investment. Figure 9.14 shows a sample SmartFTP screen after establishing an FTP connection to your TiVo. It's hard to argue that this isn't superior to the standard Windows FTP client shown in Figure 9.13.

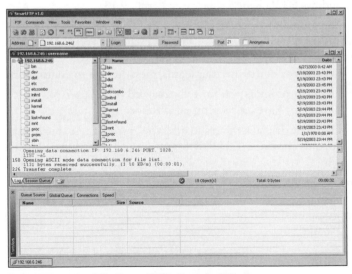

**FIGURE 9.14** *The SmartFTP client for Windows*

**Table 9.1   Common FTP Commands**

| FTP Command | Meaning | Action |
| --- | --- | --- |
| bin | binary mode | Puts the FTP client into the mode necessary to transfer binary files. |
| cd *directory* | change directory | Changes to the specified *directory* on the TiVo. |
| get *file* | get file | Retrieves the specified *file* from the TiVo to your Windows system. |
| hash | display hashes | Causes the FTP client to display a hash mark ('#') for each 1K sent to or retrieved from the TiVo. |
| lcd *directory* | local change directory | Changes to the specified *directory* on your Windows system. |
| put *file* | put file | Sends the specified *file* to the TiVo from your Windows system. |
| quit | quit FTP client | Terminates the FTP session and the Windows FTP client. |

# Creating TiVo Tools Disks under Windows

This book comes with the BATBD CD, a bootable TiVo tools disk that enables you to run Linux on your PC in order to perform the TiVo tasks and hacks discussed in this book. Though I believe that this contains a good selection of software for all Series 1 or Series 2 machines, any CD is just a software moment frozen in time. As new software or new versions of existing software become available, you're probably going to want to download and run it on your PC or TiVo. That isn't a problem for software designed to run on the TiVo, since you can download archive files to your PC, transfer them to your TiVo, and run the applications after unpacking the archives. If the software you're interested in runs under Windows, you have no problem at all and can install and execute it like any other Windows software.

However, if the TiVo software that you're interested in, for example, a new version of the BATBD CD, is only available as a CD-ROM image file, you may have a problem. CD-ROM images are usually referred to as ISO images because they contain images of a CD-ROM filesystem that is compliant with the International Standards Organization 9660 filesystem standard. Even if you have a CD/RW drive, Windows does not come with software that enables you to burn CDs from ISO images. Newer versions of Windows Media Player (8.x and greater) provide the ability to create CD playlists and burn audio CDs, but do not support burning CDs from ISO images.

Your CD/RW drive should have come with software to burn CDs from ISOs; if not, there are several excellent software packages on the Internet for doing this under Windows. There are commercial software packages that provide a demonstration mode that you can use to burn CDs in emergencies or until you decide to purchase the software. Since the companies that wrote and continue to support these packages were cool enough to provide usable demonstration versions, you should be cool enough to actually pay for them after using them—but that's an ethical issue. The two packages that I recommend for burning CDs under Windows are the following:

◆ Ahead Software's **Nero — Burning ROM** package. Ahead Software's Web site is **http://www.nero.com/en**, and you can download a demonstration copy of Nero from **http://www.nero.com/en/content/download.html**. The latest version at the time this book was written was Version 5.5. Aside from having one of the funniest and coolest names of any burning software that I've ever used, Nero is a great, usable package with a nice GUI that makes it easy to burn a CD from an ISO or create lists of files that you want to burn to audio or data CDs. Figure 9.15 shows the "Nero—Burning ROM" software in action. You can purchase a license for this software for $49 if you download the software over the Net rather than a physical CD. (You can always burn one using the software ;-).

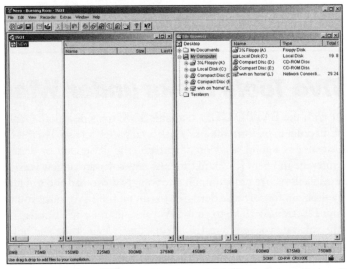

**FIGURE 9.15**   *The Nero—Burning ROM CD-burning software for Windows*

◆ VSO Software's **Blindwrite Suite**. VSO Software's Web site is **http://www.vso-software.fr**, and you can download a demonstration copy of Blindwrite Suite from the URL, **http://www.vso-software.fr/download.htm**. Blindwrite Suite is a simple, easy-to-use package that makes it almost trivial to burn a CD from an ISO, although it also supports creating audio and data CDs from lists of files that you assemble. Figure 9.16 shows the Blindwrite Suite software in action. You can purchase a license for this software for $29 if you download the software over the Net.

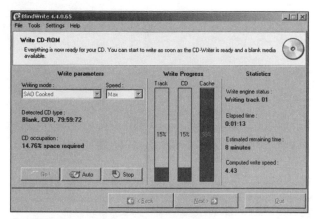

**FIGURE 9.16** *The Blindwrite Suite CD-burning software for Windows*

There are plenty of other packages available to do this sort of thing—these are just my favorites. Of the two, I find Blindwrite Suite simpler for burning CDs from ISOs. Your mileage may vary.

After downloading and installing Blindwrite Suite, the procedure for using it to burn a CD from an ISO is as follows:

1. Double-click the desktop shortcut created when installing the software or execute Blindwrite Suite by clicking its entry in the Programs, Blindwrite Suite menu. The dialog box shown in Figure 9.17 displays. Click the icon on the right to start the CD burning portion of Blindwrite Suite.

**FIGURE 9.17** *Starting the Blindwrite Suite application*

2. If you're using the demonstration version of the software, the dialog box shown in Figure 9.18 displays. Click Test to continue (or enter the license that you received when your purchased the software, and then click Unlock). Accept the license that displays in the next dialog box (not shown—we've all seen licenses before).

3. The primary Blindwrite Suite dialog box displays (see Figure 9.19). Make sure that the Start CD writing wizard entry is selected and click Next.

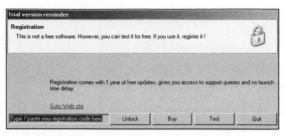

**FIGURE 9.18** *Blindwrite Suite's register or demonstration dialog box*

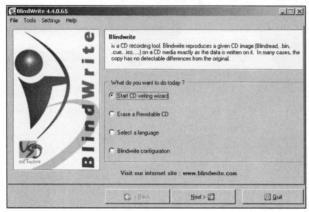

**FIGURE 9.19** *Blindwrite Suite's Primary Tasks dialog box*

4. The Select a CD-Writer dialog box displays (see Figure 9.20). If your CD writer is not already selected, click the drop-down arrow at the right of the dialog box and select the CD writer that you want to use from the drop-down list. After you've selected your CD writer, click Next.

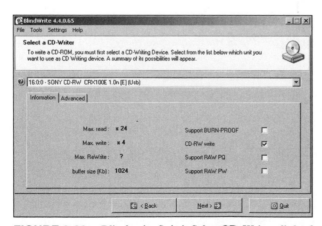

**FIGURE 9.20** *Blindwrite Suite's Select CD Writer dialog box*

5.  The Select a CD-ROM Image dialog box displays, as shown in Figure 9.21. Click the leftmost of the three icons near the top of this dialog box to browse for the location of the ISO file that you want to write to CD.

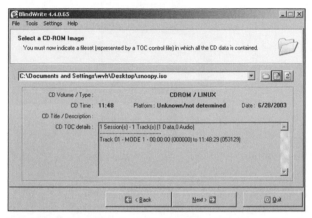

**FIGURE 9.21**   *Blindwrite Suite's Select CD Image dialog box*

6.  The CD Image verification dialog box shown in Figure 9.22 displays. Click Start to verify the consistency of the ISO image that you want to write to CD. This is handy to verify that no errors were introduced when downloading and to avoid wasting a CD by burning crap to it. After the image has been verified, click Next.

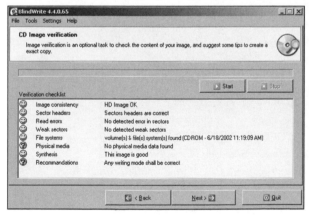

**FIGURE 9.22**   *Blindwrite Suite's CD Image Verification dialog box*

7.  The Write CD-ROM dialog box shown in Figure 9.23 displays. Click Go! to begin burning the CD. The dialog box displays the progress of the write process.

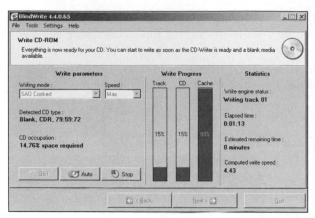

**FIGURE 9.23** *Blindwrite Suite's Write CD-ROM dialog box*

8. After the CD has been written successfully, the summary CD writing complete dialog box displays (see Figure 9.24). Click Quit to exit Blindwrite Suite. You can now eject the CD you just burned by pressing the Eject button on the drive or by right-clicking on its entry in the My Computer dialog box and selecting the Eject command from the context-sensitive menu.

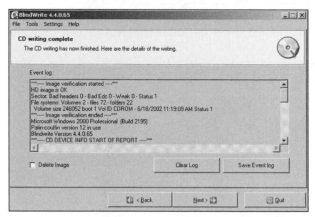

**FIGURE 9.24** *Blindwrite Suite's CD Writing Complete dialog box*

After ejecting the CD, you can reinsert it in your CD drive to verify its readability or simply shut down Windows and boot from the CD to try the one true test. As you can see from this process, burning a CD from an ISO under Windows is quite easy, and probably takes less time than downloading the ISO itself.

# TiVo Disks and Windows Systems

As discussed earlier in this book, putting your TiVo drives in a personal computer that you can boot using the BATBD CD is a critical step in doing most TiVo hacking. The reason that you boot from the BATBD CD is that Windows systems can't read or work with TiVo disks. There are two primary reasons that you might want to access your TiVo disks directly from Windows:

◆ To use Windows while browsing the contents of your TiVo filesystems

◆ To simplify copying large files or a number of files from your Windows disk to your TiVo disk

Even if you can't access TiVo disks from Windows directly, there are easy solutions to both of these problems. There may be a few warts in the solutions, but this book is all about hacking, right? Perhaps you'll come up with a better solution—if so, please let me know!

## Exploring ext2 Disk Images under Windows

As discussed in Chapter 6 in the section entitled "Creating Image Backups Using **dd**," after booting your personal computer using the BATBD CD and selecting a boot option that provides access to TiVo partitions, you can use the **dd** command to create an image backup of a specific partition from your TiVo disk. You can create this image backup by using a command like the following:

```
dd if=partition of=backup-file bs=32k
```

This command tells the **dd** command to read from the disk specified as *disk* (probably one of /dev/hd*XY*, where *X* is the identifier for the disk and *Y* is the partition number), and write to the output file *backup-file*. The **bs** option tells the **dd** command to use 32 K as both the input and output block sizes, which reflects the block size used on TiVo filesystems.

Some interesting hacking opportunities present themselves to Windows users once you have an image backup of a TiVo partition that contains an **ext2** filesystem. Specifically, you can use a freely available Windows application called **explore2fs** to browse the contents of the partition image as though it were an actual disk partition. Figure 9.25 shows the explore2fs application examining an image backup of one of my TiVo's **ext2** partitions. Pretty amazing! The explore2fs utility can't be used to update the disk images, but it does make it easy to use your Windows system to browse a TiVo's **ext2** filesystem to your heart's content, learning the location of files, viewing the contents of bash, TCL, and iTCL command scripts, and so on. Remember that this only works for image backups of TiVo partitions that are in **ext2** format, such as partitions 4 (your root or backup root filesystem), 7 (your root or backup root filesystem), and 9 (the /var partition) of any primary TiVo disk.

Versions of the explore2fs application for Windows 95 and NT are available from its Web site at **http://uranus.it.swin.edu.au/~jn/linux/explore2fs.htm**. This application worked fine on my Windows 2000 system, so I would assume that it will work on versions of Windows such as 98,

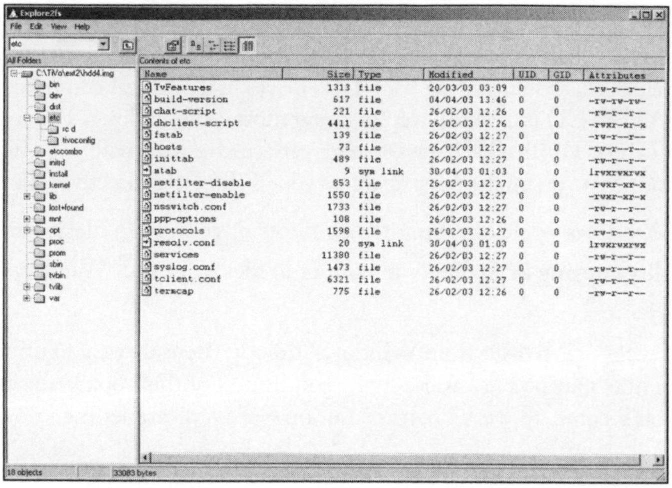

**FIGURE 9.25**   *Exploring an ext2 filesystem image under Windows*

ME, and XP. You can download the application itself from **http://uranus.it.swin.edu.au/~jn/
explore2fs/explore2fs-1.00pre6.zip**. This is a prerelease, but it's free and worked great for me.

After you've downloaded the explore2fs archive, extract its contents into a directory in your
system and copy an image backup of one of your TiVo's **ext2** partitions to that same directory.
Open explore2fs, select the File menu's Open File command, navigate to the disk image, and
click Open. The explore2fs application displays a collapsed version of the **ext2** filesystem in
the All Folders pane at the left. Click the plus sign to expand the image, and voila! All of the
directories in the filesystem image display in the All Folders pane, while any files or symbolic
links in a selected directory are listed in the pane at the right of the explore2fs application.
You can then use standard Windows techniques to navigate through the filesystem. If you
find a file that you actually want to examine, right-click on the filename in the right pane
and select View from the context-sensitive menu. The explore2fs application invokes your
default viewer, and you can explore the file to your heart's content. Figure 9.26 shows the
file /etc/rc.d/rc.sysinit displayed in WordPad.

Admittedly, exploring an **ext2** filesystem image is only an interesting hack. Not having the
ability to change the files is something of a drag, and it would (of course) be nicer if Windows
could simply understand TiVo partition maps as well as **ext2** filesystems. There are some
useful applications for Windows that understand **ext2** filesystems, the most promising of
which is the Paragon Software Group's MountEverything software (**http://www.mount-
everything.com**). Available for $39.95 from their Web site, this software enables you to
mount **ext2** and **ext3** partitions from Windows 95, 98, ME, XP, NT, and 2000 systems, as
well as access NTFS partitions from Windows 95, 98, and ME. Maybe if we all ask them
really nicely... I know I have!

```
#!/bin/bash
# Copyright (c) 2001, 2002 TiVo Inc.
#
# /etc/rc.d/rc.sysinit - run once at boot time
#
#
# Useful functions
#

function nthword () {
   n=0
   for foo in $* ; do
      if [ $n -eq $1 ]
      then
         echo $foo
      fi
      n=$(($n+1))
   done
}

function runme () {
   echo "Scanning for $1 repair scripts"
   for foo in /var/persist/*.$1 ; do
      if [ -f $foo ]
      then
         echo "Running repair program $foo"
         rm -f $foo.old
         mv $foo $foo.old
         chmod 555 $foo.old
         if /tvbin/crypto -vfs $foo.sig $foo.old /tvlib/misc/service-v3-s.pub ; then
            $foo.old || echo "$foo failed."
         else
            echo "$foo failed signature check."
         fi
         rm -f $foo.old $foo.sig
      fi
   done
}
```

**FIGURE 9.26**  *Viewing a file from an ext2 filesystem image under Windows*

# Accessing Windows Disks from Your TiVo

The corollary of accessing TiVo disks from Windows systems is accessing Windows disks from TiVo systems. If you've put your TiVo on your network, you can take advantage of the power of Linux to mount any shared Windows disk on your TiVo. File copying doesn't get much easier than that.

The keys to mounting shared Windows disks on your TiVo are a loadable kernel module (**smbfs.o**) that knows how to access Windows shares via the SMB (Server Message Block) protocol, and a companion application (**smbmount**) that knows how to mount SMB filesystems on a Linux directory. These are both located in the BATCD's **kernel_modules** directory, in subdirectories called **Series1** and **Series2** that contain the version specific to Series 1 and Series 2 TiVos—make sure that you copy the right kernel module and binaries to your system.

 **TIP**

If you are using the Series 2 **smbmount** application, you must also copy the files *.dat from the BATBD CD's **kernel_modules/Series2** directory to the directory /var/hack/lib on your TiVo and use the **touch** command to create an empty file called /var/hack/lib/smb.conf .

To use the **smbmount** command to mount a Windows share on your TiVo, do the following:

1. After transferring **smbfs.o** and **smbmount** to your TiVo, load the **smbfs.o** module into the kernel using the following command:

```
insmod -f -s smbfs.o
```

This command inserts the module into the running TiVo kernel, forcing the kernel to ignore version differences and redirecting any error messages from the module to the system log (/var/log/messages).

2. Remount the TiVo's root filesystem so that the system can update the file containing the list of mounted filesystems (**/etc/mtab**). To remount the root filesystem in read/write mode, execute the following command:

```
mount -o rw,remount /
```

3. Use the **smbmount** command to mount a share from your Windows system. If you are using the Series 1 version of **smbmount**, use a command like the following:

```
./smbmount //system/share mountpoint -U user -P password -I IP-address
```

When executing this command, *system* is the Windows name of your Windows system; *share* is the name of the Windows share that you are mounting; *mountpoint* is the name of the directory on your TiVo where you want to mount the Window share; *user* is your username on the Windows system; *password* is your password; and *IP-address* is the IP address of the Windows system. Specifying an IP address rather than a host name is necessary because your TiVo does not run DNS or the Windows equivalent (WINS), and it can't map the host name of your Windows system to its IP address without your help. If you are using the Series 2 version of the **smbmount** command, use a command like the following:

```
smbmount//system/share mountpoint -o username=user,password=
password, ip=IP-Address
```

A sample command to mount a share named TiVo from the Windows host named win2k on the directory /var/mnt/win (which must already exist) using the username wvh, password guessme, and where the IP address of the host win2k is 192.168.6.244 would be the following:

```
./smbmount //win2k/TiVo /var/mnt/win -U wvh -P guessme -I 192.168.6.244
```

If you are using the version of **smbmount** provided for Series 2 TiVos on the BATBD CD, the equivalent example command would be the following:

```
./smbmount//win2k/TiVo /var/mnt/win -o username=wvh,password=guessme,
ip=192.168.6.244
```

After executing this command, your Windows disk would be available through the TiVo's /var/mnt/win directory, and you would have the same privileges there as the user whose name and password you specified.

> ⊻
> **TiVO** **NFS, Anyone?**
>
> As discussed in Chapter 10, "Linux and the TiVo," in the section entitled "NFS," the TiVo supports the NFS (Network File System) distributed filesystem protocol, just like any other Linux system. There are a number of NFS utilities available for Windows systems, the least expensive of which ($40) is LabTam's ProNFS (**http://pronfs.com**). While a demonstration version of this software is available, it times out too quickly to be useful to your TiVo in demonstration mode. Another alternative is installing Cygwin (**http://www.cygwin.com**), which is a complete GNU/Linux environment for Windows systems. As a complete GNU/Linux system, Cygwin provides built-in support for NFS and works just like NFS under standard, desktop Linux. Unfortunately, Cygwin is far outside the scope of this book—it deserves its own.

# Integrating Windows Systems with TiVo's Home Media Features

Shortly after the release of Version 4.0 of the TiVo software, TiVo unveiled its long-awaited Home Media Option (HMO). Available only for Series 2 models and priced at $99 for your first TiVo (and $49 for each additional TiVo), the Home Media Option provided some exciting extensions to the functionality of your TiVo, as described in the section of Chapter 1 entitled "What Was TiVo's Home Media Option?"

As of June, 2004, HMO capabilities (now known as Home Media Features) are now built into the standard TiVo service for stand-alone Series 2 machines at no extra cost. The next section focuses on exploring some of the in and outs of exporting MP3 files from Windows systems using the TiVo Desktop, providing a few tips and tricks along the way.

## Installing and Using the Windows TiVo Desktop

You can download the Windows version of the TiVo Desktop from the TiVo Web page at **http://www.tivo.com/4.9.4.1.asp**. After you download and install it, exporting your MP3 collections (known as *publishing* in TiVo Desktop terms) so that you can access them from any networked, stand-alone Series 2 TiVo that is running 4.x TiVo software is easy. To do so, perform the following steps:

1. Select the TiVo Publisher command from the Start, Programs, TiVo Desktop menu on your PC. The TiVo Desktop displays(see Figure 9.27).

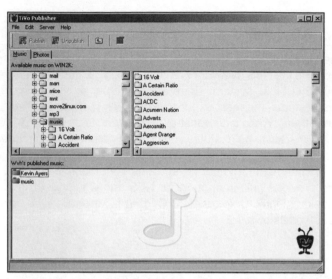

**FIGURE 9.27**  *TiVo Publisher for Windows via the TiVo Desktop menu*

2. To export a directory containing MP3 files, use the directory tree in the upper left corner of the TiVo Publisher to navigate to the directory that you want to export. After you've found a directory that you want to publish, click the Publish button on the TiVo Publisher toolbar. Figure 9.28 shows the TiVo Publisher after navigating to and exporting a directory of music by *The Cynics*.

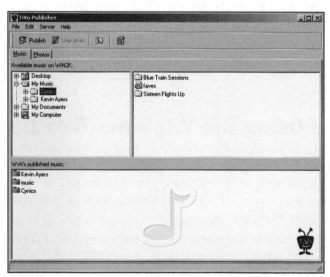

**FIGURE 9.28**  *Publishing a directory of MP3 files in the TiVo Publisher*

That's all there is to it—the TiVo Desktop is as easy to use as you would hope that a Windows program should be. Any directories of MP3 files and playlists that you publish from the TiVo Publisher will be visible on your TiVo under the TiVo Central, Music & Photos menu. The name of a TiVo Server on a Windows system is created by combining your login name on your PC and the Windows name of that PC. For example, my Windows box is named "win2k" and my login there is "wvh," so my published collections show up on my TiVo as "Wvh's Music from WIN2K."

## TiVo Sharing MP3 Files from Linux Systems Using Samba

Samba is an application that you can run on a Linux system to export selected Linux directories so that they can be accessed from Windows systems, exactly as if they were standard Windows shares. Samba also includes applications that enable you to access standard Windows shares from your Linux systems. Explaining how to install and configure Samba on your Linux system is outside the scope of this book—there are already books dedicated to that topic.

If you are storing your MP3 audio files on a Linux system, you can make these files available to any stand-alone Series 2 TiVo that is running 4.x TiVo software by running the Personal TiVo Home Media Option software on your Linux system, as explained in Chapter 10, "Linux and the TiVo," in the section entitled "Working with TiVo's Home Media Option from Linux." If you don't want to use that option, another option is to share the directory containing your Linux music archive using Samba, permanently mount it on your PC like any other network drive, and then publish that directory using the TiVo Publisher. The TiVo server running on your Windows server will then deliver those files to any suitable TiVo DVR, just as if they were directly stored on your Windows system.

To configure some aspects of how the TiVo Publisher delivers music to your TiVo, take the following steps:

1. In the TiVo Publisher, select the Server menu's TiVo Server Properties command. The TiVo Server is a component that is installed as part of the TiVo Desktop for Windows, and is the component that actually services incoming network requests for access to Publisher music, and then delivers them from your PC to your TiVo (see Figure 9.29).

2. To automatically start the TiVo Server each time you log in to your Windows system, make sure that the Start the TiVo Server when I log on to Windows check box is selected.

3. To pause or terminate the TiVo Server, click the appropriate button.

4. To configure some aspects of the performance of the TiVo Server component, click the Performance tab at the top of the TiVo Server Properties dialog box (see Figure 9.30).

**FIGURE 9.29**    *The TiVo Publisher's TiVo Server Properties dialog box*

**FIGURE 9.30**    *The TiVo Server Properties Performance tab*

5. To change the size of the cache used when delivering audio files to a TiVo, drag the Cache Options slider to the right (to increase the size of the cache) or to the left (to decrease the cache size). When the TiVo requests a file, it is copied to the cache directory. Playing that song again will be faster if the song is already located in the cache. Changing the cache size determines the number of songs that can be cached. If the cache fills up, the oldest entries in the cache will be deleted to make room. Files are deleted from the cache, not from your music collection, of course!

6. To modify the amount of CPU time that your system dedicates to the TiVo Server process, drag the Server Activity slider up and down. The top setting, High (best performance), dedicates the majority of your PCs resources to the TiVo Server process, and should therefore be used only while your PC is essentially dedicated to exporting audio files and digital photographs. The lowest setting, Low (moderate

performance), should be used if you are actively executing processor-intensive tasks like audio/video editing, creating or editing large graphics files, or playing games. The two intermediate settings, Medium (good performance) and Medium High (better performance), can be selected to provide better trade-offs between local computing power and serving MP3 files and digital photographs.

7. To manage the Tivo DVRs that can access the collections of online audio and digital photographs that you publish using the TiVo Server, select the Access Control tab at the top of the TiVo Server Properties dialog box (see Figure 9.31).

**FIGURE 9.31**    *The TiVo Server Properties Access Control tab.*

8. To make your audio and digital photograph collections available to any TiVo that can access your home network, make sure that the Allow all TiVo DVRs to access published media files radio button is selected.

9. To limit the TiVo DVRs that can access your audio and digital photograph collections, select the Only allow the selected TiVo DVRs to access media files radio button and then click the check boxes next to the TiVo DVRs that you want to access your published files.

Once you execute the TiVo Publisher, an icon for the TiVo Server displays in the system tray at the right or bottom of the Windows task bar. This icon indicates that the TiVo Server is running, and can be used to access the TiVo Server properties dialog boxes discussed previously or to shut down the TiVo Server. If you selected the Start the TiVo Server when I log on to Windows check box in the TiVo Server Properties dialog box, this icon also displays any time you reboot and log in.

The TiVo Desktop is a great application if all of your online audio files are stored in MP3 format. What if they aren't? Luckily, third-party software exists that enables you to export collections of audio files in other formats to your TiVos that support the Home Media Features.

# Playing Windows Audio Formats other than MP3

TiVo's Home Media features use open APIs that make it easy for software vendors to integrate it into their software. This is no surprise coming from a Linux and Open Source advocate like TiVo. TiVo sells TiVos, its service, and the Home Media Option that enables TiVos to play published collections of online audio files and digital photographs. Software vendors of digital audio and image software can integrate support for Home Media Features into their software, enabling it to publish audio and image files in other formats. The end result of these sorts of partnerships is that life is better for everyone because users have more options, especially where non-MP3 audio files are concerned.

An excellent example of this is J. River's Media Center. The Media Center software is easily integrated with a TiVo that supports the Home Media Features and supports audio and video files in a zillion different formats, including a ton that I've never heard of. Most critical to Linux and open source fans is the Media Center's support for audio files encoded in the popular, open source OGG audio format. Windows fans should be delighted in the Media Center's support for audio formats such as ASX, ASF, WM, WAV, WAX, WMA, and RealMedia formats. Fans of classic audio file formats such as AIF, AIFC, AIFF, AU, and SND files will also be happy to know that J. River's Media Center enables them to publish audio in these formats so that they can be played through your TiVo. When used with the TiVo Home Media Features, my guess is that the Media Center converts files in all of these formats into MP3 on-the-fly and delivers the MP3 streams to your TiVo, but who cares—it works, and all my OGG files play fine through my TiVos!

 **TIP**

If your music is stored in OGG format, you're probably encoding and storing it on a Linux system (unless you're a very up-to-date Windows or Mac user who is clued in to the powerful, excellent, and open source OGG format). If you're storing your music on a Linux system and want to publish it to your TiVo directly, check out the Personal TiVo Home Media Option and JavaHMO software discussed in Chapters 10 and 11 . These open source software packages enable you to publish music from your Linux box directly without using Samba or any Windows-based software.

J. River's home page is **http://www.musicex.com/mediacenter/index.html**. You can download a 30-day demonstration version of the Media Center from **http://www.musicex.com/mediacenter/download.html**. After that, it's $39.95, which is a cheap price to pay for the power and flexibility it gives you.

> **NOTE**
>
> Even if you plan to use J. River's Media Center to publish your audio and digital image files to TiVos running the Home Media Features, you still will want to download and install the TiVo Desktop software as described earlier. The Media Center makes use of one of the components of the TiVo Desktop, the TivoBeacon, which advertises the presence of systems that are publishing music and digital images for use by your TiVos. The TiVo Server and J. River's Media Center can even run simultaneously on a single PC, though the rationale for doing so is unclear, and is only sanctioned by the Department of Redundancy Department.

After downloading and installing the Media Center software, the first time you execute the Media Center, it offers to search your disk for audio and digital image files in compatible formats, as shown in Figure 9.32.

**FIGURE 9.32**   *The Media Center's Import Media Files dialog box*

You can restrict this search to specific types of files by clicking Advanced and checking or unchecking various file formats. For more information about doing this, see the Media Center documentation. Now let's worry about interacting with your TiVo.

Once the Media Center has located files to publish, you can take the following steps to configure J. River's Media Center to serve files to any TiVo DVR that is running the Home Media Features:

1. Within the Media Center application, enable its Media Server by selecting the Media Server command from the Tools menu's More Tools submenu (see Figure 9.33).

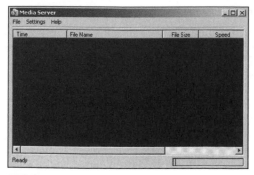

**FIGURE 9.33**   *The Media Center's Media Server dialog box*

2. Select the Settings menu's Options command (see Figure 9.34).

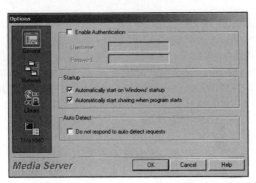

**FIGURE 9.34** *The Media Server's Options dialog box*

3. Click the Network icon at the left and make sure that Automatic port selection (recommended) is selected (see Figure 9.35).

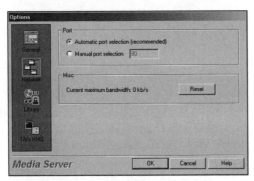

**FIGURE 9.35** *The Network Panel in the Options dialog box*

4. Click the TiVo HMO icon at the left (see Figure 9.36). Click the Support TiVo HMO on Port 8079 (with beacon on port 2190) radio button, and make sure that the Support all audio formats check box is selected. Click OK.

5. If the Media Server is already running, a dialog box appears, displaying the message "Media Server is connected. Do you want to reconnect?" Click Yes. If this dialog box does not appear, select the File menu's Share command to start the J. River Media Center's Media Server.

That's all there is to it. You can now go to any networked TiVo DVR that is running the Home Media Features and browse and play music or display digital images exported by the Media Center. Any directories of audio files and playlists that are published by the Media Center will be visible on your TiVo under the TiVo Central, Music & Photos menu. Much

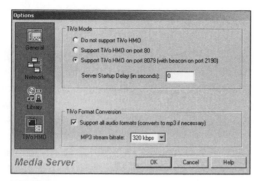

**FIGURE 9.36**   *The TiVo HMO Panel in the Options dialog box*

like the TiVo Server, the name of the Media Center on a given Windows system is created by combining your login name on your PC and the Windows name of that PC. For example, my Windows box is named "win2k" and my login there is "wvh," so my published collections show up on my TiVo as "wvh's Media Center Music on win2k."

As you might suspect, J River's Media Center is much more than an alternative to the TiVo Publisher, but discussing its other bells and whistles is outside the scope of this book. For more information about J. River's Media Center and other configuration options, see its documentation. And buy a copy of the software.

# TiVos and Mac OS X

Today's Macintosh computer and its operating system is truly a work of art. Macs have always been the sexiest computers around, both in terms of appearance and usability. The Macintosh pioneered the graphical user interfaces in the home computer market, even though they got the idea for the GUI from Xerox PARC like everybody else. The Macintosh operating system, now simply known as Mac OS, has always been incredibly usable and eminently user-friendly.

The latest version of the Mac OS, known as Mac OS X, is better than ever before, largely because Apple used the NeXT Computer's NeXTStep and its underlying Mach operating system as the underpinnings of Mac OS X. As a Unix sysadmin for over 20 years, I never thought that I would see any version of Unix on the shelf at my local CompUSA, even in my wildest, nerdiest dreams. First, there was Linux, and now there's the Mac OS X—Unix-like systems with actual usable GUIs. Was that a pig that just flew overhead? What is next? Are the Cubs going to win the World Series?

As a popular personal computer operating system and as a system with its conceptual roots in Unix, Mac OS X is a natural for developing applications for and interacting with your TiVo. The fact that Mac OS X runs a Unix-like operating system makes it "easy" to port various TiVo software to Mac OS X, such as the BlessTiVo software discussed later in this chapter.

> **TiVo | The TiVo Hacking for PPC Project**
>
> If you are interested in hacking your TiVo from a Mac using a tools CD just like the x86 guys do, you should definitely check out the TiVo Hacking for PPC project at **http://sourceforge.net/projects/tivo-hack-ppc/**. This is a fantastic project dedicated to developing bootable disks that enable TiVo hacking on Mac OS X systems. They are currently working on porting Sleeper's scripts and ISO to work on PPC systems, and have a bootable ISO that you can use on your Mac OS X system in much the same way that you can use the BATBD CD that accompanies this book on x86 systems. This ISO is still Beta (so be very, very careful and back up first) but has fantastic promise for brings many of the standard Linux TiVo hacking software to Macs with a minimum amount of fuss.

# TiVo Disks and Mac OS X Systems

Putting your TiVo drives into a personal computer that you can boot using the BATBD CD is a critical step in doing most TiVo hacking. Unfortunately, booting from this CD requires a Pentium personal computer. Fortunately, there are a few things that you can do from your Mac OS X system without running Linux or having an x86-style PC—thanks largely to the fact that Mac OS X is based on Unix, which makes it much easier for Linux software to be recompiled for use under Mac OS X:

◆ Put Series 1 or Series 2 TiVo disks in your Mac OS X system and mount and access their ext2 and MFS partitions.

◆ Mount **ext2** partition images so that you can browse their contents from your Mac OS X system. This can be useful if you're familiar with using the Mac OS X Finder and want to use it to explore a TiVo filesystem while learning the bash, TCL, or iTCL command languages.

◆ Bless new TiVo disks from Mac OS X. You can easily use the Mac OS X version of the BlessTiVo program (called *OSXv4Blesser*) to prepare a second disk that you can then add to your TiVo, expanding the space that it has available for storing recordings.

## ext2 Filesystem Support for Mac OS X

Though you can't read TiVo hard drives directly under Mac OS X, you can install ext2 filesystem support on your Mac OS X system, thanks to the efforts of the open source community. After this support is installed, you can install a TiVo disk in your Mac OS X system or transfer a filesystem image to your Mac. You can then mount and access ext2 partitions directly from the Mac OS X Finder, or use the standard OS X disk image manipulation commands to mount and access and explore an ext2 filesystem image.

The ExtFS Manager, a System Preferences pane that enables you to mount and access ext2 filesystems from Mac OS X, is available from SourceForge's Mac OS X Ext2 Filesystem project, located at **http://sourceforge.net/projects/ext2fsx**. The current version at the time that this book was written is 1.w, which you can download as a mountable Mac OS X disk image from **http://prdownloads.sourceforge.net/ext2fsx/Ext2FS_1.2.dmg?download**. A copy of this disk image is also provided in the Macintosh directory at the top level of the BATBD CD that is included with this book.

> **NOTE**
>
> The disks used by Series 1 TiVos are byte-swapped, which means that these drives (or partition images taken from them) will not look like standard ext2 filesystems to Mac OS X. In order to support accessing Series 1 TiVo disks or partition images from Mac OS X, you will need to install Josh Graessley's **TiVo-PartitionScheme**, a kernel extension for Mac OS X that enables byte-swapping as needed on disks that match the byte-swapped TiVo disk signature. Installing this kernel extension is explained in the next section.

After you've downloaded or copied the ExtFS Manager disk image to your Mac OS X system, double-click the disk image file to mount it on your Mac OS X desktop, open it, and click the file Ext2FS_1.1.1.pkg to begin the installation process. Ext2 support is provided through a Mac OS X kernel extension, so you'll be prompted for the administrative password for your system during the installation process; otherwise, installing ext2 support is exactly like installing application software on your OS X system.

After the ext2 kernel extension is installed, you will need to restart your system so that the kernel extension is correctly registered.

## Putting Series 1 and Series 2 Disks in Your Mac OS X System

If you're lucky enough to have a Mac OS X system that has a free IDE disk connection, you can put a TiVo disk in your system and browse the contents of both its ext2 and MFS partitions. Using the ExtFS Manager kernel extension enables you to mount and browse the ext2 partitions of a TiVo disk, while the MFS Browser tool enables you to explore your TiVo's Media Filesystem (MFS) and even extract recordings by MFS filesystem identifier (FSID).

The disks from Series 2 TiVo systems read and write data to disk using the same byte order as the disks used by Mac OS X. However, the disks from Series 1 TiVo systems swap each pair of bytes on the disk for some sort of "*security through obscurity*" reason. In order for any of the partitions on a Series 1 TiVo disk to work, you will need to install Josh Graessley's TiVoPartitionScheme kernel extension, which is available on the Web as a Macintosh disk image (DMG) at **http://josh.graessley.net/tivo/TiVoPartitionScheme.dmg**. A copy of this disk image is also provided in the macintosh directory on the BATBD CD that accompanies this book.

To install the TiVoPartitionScheme on your Mac OS X system, do the following:

1. Download the TiVoPartitionScheme.dmg disk image to your Mac or copy it from the macintosh subdirectory of the BATBD CD that accompanies this book.

2. Mount the disk image file by double-clicking on it.

3. Start the Mac OS X Terminal application and **cd** to the directory /Volumes/ TiVoPartitionScheme.

4. Execute the following commands from the terminal window:

   ```
   sudo cp -r TiVoPartitionScheme.kext /System/Library/Extensions
   sudo touch /System/Library/Extensions
   ```

5. Shut down your Mac OS X system by selecting the Shutdown command from the Apple menu.

After your Mac OS X system shuts down, you can attach a TiVo Series 1 or Series 2 disk to your spare IDE connector. Make sure that you set the jumpers on the TiVo disk as needed to configure it as a slave drive. (The required jumper settings should be printed on the top of the disk drive. You can buy jumpers at your local Radio Shack or other electronics store if you don't have any.)

When you reboot your Mac OS X system with a TiVo drive attached, you should see icons for the TiVo drives displayed on your desktop, often with a "?" or "UNTITLED" disk label. This is because ext2 partitions do not provide standard Macintosh partition labels. As mentioned earlier, the ext2 partitions on a standard TiVo drive are the following:

◆ *hda4*  A root partition (mounted as /, depending on your TiVo boot parameters). If your TiVo disk is installed in your Mac OS X system as a slave on the primary IDE bus, this partition will be available as /dev/disk1s4—IDE disk 1, slice 4.

◆ *hda7*  Another root partition (mounted as /, depending on your TiVo boot parameters). If your TiVo disk is installed in your Mac OS X system as a slave on the primary IDE bus, this partition will be available as /dev/disk1s7—IDE disk 1, slice 7.

◆ *hda9*  A user partition mounted as /var on your TiVo. If your TiVo disk is installed in your Mac OS X system as a slave on the primary IDE bus, this partition will be available as /dev/disk1s9—IDE disk 1, slice 9.

You can open and examine these disks like any other Macintosh volume by double-clicking on the desktop icon.

## [TiVo] Checking TiVo Partition Consistency

When you first boot your Mac with a TiVo drive inside, it will usually only mount the two root partitions from the TiVo drive. The partition that would normally be mounted as /var on your TiVo will not be mounted automatically, because it is not "clean" in ext2 terms. Like most types of Unix and Linux disk partitions, ext2 partitions cannot be mounted if there is any question whether the filesystem is consistent. Most Unix and Linux systems unmount disk partitions as part of their shutdown procedure, and mark them as clean at that time, which means that the filesystem is in a totally consistent state—no writes to the filesystem were pending when the disk was unmounted. TiVos do not have an official shutdown process—the shutdown process consists of pulling the plug. Therefore, any ext2 partitions that were writable when the system was turned off must be checked for consistency using an application called **fsck** (filesystem consistency check), and repaired, as necessary.

The version of the fsck utility provided by the Mac OS X Ext2FS Manager is called *fsck_ext2*, and must be run from a Mac OS X Terminal window (or an xterm if you have installed a version of the X11 Window System on your Mac). The output from running this command on a Mac OS X system looks like the following:

```
macosx:~ williamvonhagen$ sudo fsck_ext2 -f /dev/disk1s9
e2fsck 1.34 (25-Jul-2003)
Pass 1: Checking inodes, blocks, and sizes
Pass 2: Checking directory structure
Pass 3: Checking directory connectivity
Pass 4: Checking reference counts
Pass 5: Checking group summary information
/dev/disk1s9: 128/32768 files (12.5% non-contiguous), 8940/131072 blocks
```

If you are prompted to fix any problems, answer *yes*, because that is what your TiVo would do automatically the next time it booted using that drive. After your Terminal or xterm prompt redisplays, you can then use the Ext2FS Manager to manually mount the specified partition, as explained in the next section.

# Mounting and Exploring ext2 Partitions under Mac OS X

You can use the ExtFS Manager System Preferences pane to get additional information about the mounted ext2 partitions from your TiVo disk. To do so after installing the ExtFS Manager as explained in "ext2 Filesystem Support for Mac OS X" (earlier in this chapter), start the System Preferences application and click the Show All button in the upper left-hand corner. In the Other section at the bottom of the System Preferences list, click on the ExtFSManager preference to display the ExtFSManager Preferences pane, as shown in Figure 9.37.

**FIGURE 9.37**   *The ExtFSManager System Preferences pane*

To view information about any partition on your TiVo disk (which will be the disk that contains partitions identified as MFS Application and Media Regions), click on the name of that partition at left, and the ExtFSManager will display information about that partition at right. Figure 9.37 shows information about the partition that would be mounted as /var on your TiVo.

The ExtFSManager provides buttons that make it easy for you to mount and unmount ext2 partitions without needing to learn the command-line commands that do the same thing. If the partition you select is already mounted, an Unmount button will be displayed above the partition list in the ExtFSManager—simply click this button to unmount that partition. If the partition that you select is not mounted, a Mount button will be displayed above the partition list in the ExtFSManager—simply click this button to mount that partition, and an icon for that drive will display on your Desktop. You can double-click this icon like any Mac OS X volume to display its contents in the Finder (see Figure 9.38). You can then explore the contents of this partition like any other volume on your Mac OS X system.

**FIGURE 9.38**   *A TiVo ext2 partition in a Mac OS X Finder window*

The ExtFSManager also enables you to set mount options for each ext2 partition by clicking the Options button above the partition list. This displays the pane shown in Figure 9.39.

**FIGURE 9.39** *Options for ext2 Filesystems in the ExtFSManager*

The ExtFSManager Options pane enables you to set the following options:

◆ *Don't Automount*   Do not automatically mount this partition the next time you boot your Mac OS X system. By default, all consistent ext2 partitions detected at boot time are automatically mounted.

◆ *Mount Read Only*   Mount the partition so that you can view its contents but cannot write to it. This setting is useful for maintaining ext2 filesystem consistency, because an ext2 partition that is successfully mounted as read-only is always marked as being consistent.

◆ *Enable indexed directories*   Newer ext2 and ext3 (the journaling version of an ext2 filesystem) filesystems support indexing, which provides faster file and directory access for directories containing large numbers of files (typically 5000 or more). Selecting this option enables this feature, but this feature is not used on the ext2 filesystems used by the TiVo.

To maintain the consistency of your ext2 filesystems, you should always unmount them by dragging them to the trash before shutting down your Mac OS X system.

# Exploring ext2 Filesystem Images under Mac OS X

As discussed in Chapter 6 in the section entitled "Creating Image Backups Using **dd**," you can use the **dd** command on a Pentium-class system to create an image backup of a specific partition from your TiVo disk. If you don't have a free IDE slot in your Mac OS X tower system or are using a laptop to which you can't add a drive, don't despair. Thanks to the power of Unix and Mac OS X, you can still mount and access ext2 partitions on your system, by using the Unix/Linux **dd** command to make a copy of a TiVo ext2 filesystem (see Chapter 6), transferring the image to your Mac OS X system, and then mounting and accessing it just like an ext2 partition of a physical disk.

After installing the ExtFSManager discussed in the section of this chapter entitled "ext2 Filesystem Support for Mac OS X" and extracting an ext2 filesystem image from a TiVo disk as explained in the section of Chapter 6 entitled "Creating Image Backups Using dd," transfer the ext2 filesystem image from the other system on which it is located, start the Mac OS X Terminal application, and perform the following steps to mount the ext2 image on your Mac OS X system:

1. At the shell prompt, use the **sudo** command to execute the Mac OS X **hdid** command to map the filesystem image to a device on your Mac OS X system, using the following command:

```
sudo hdid image-file
```

Replace *image-file* with the name of your ext2 filesystem image (including the extension, such as img, dmg, etc.). The **sudo** command will prompt you for your system's administrative password. Enter that password and press the Return key.

The **hdid** command will automatically load the ext2 filesystem driver and will mount the image file as UNTITLED. An icon for the filesystem image will appear on your Desktop, as shown in Figure 9.40.

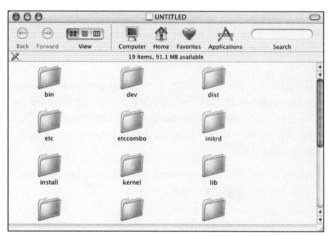

**FIGURE 9.40**    *Viewing a mounted TiVo filesystem image in the Finder*

Alternatively, you can mount the filesystem manually by performing the following steps:

1. At the shell prompt, use the **sudo** command to execute the Mac OS X **hdid** command to map the filesystem image to a device on your Mac OS X system, using the following command:

```
sudo hdid -nomount image-file
```

The **-nomount** option tells the **hdid** command not to mount the image, but just to map it to a device node. Replace *image-file* with the name of your ext2 filesystem image (including the extension, such as img, dmg, etc.). The **sudo** command will prompt you for your system's administrative password. Enter that password and press the Return key.

The **hdid** command will return something like /dev/disk1, which is your new handle for the image file that you want to mount.

2. Use the **sudo** command and the standard Mac OS X Mount command to mount the image on a directory on your Mac OS X system, using a command like the following:

```
sudo mount -t ext2 handle mountpoint
```

In this command, replace *handle* with the value returned from the **hdid** command (something like /dev/disk1), and replace *mountpoint* with the name of the directory on which you want to mount the TiVo ext2 filesystem image (something like /mnt, or the name of any other directory on your system).

That's all there is to it. At this point, you can use the Terminal window or the Mac OS X Finder to navigate through the virtual TiVo filesystem that you've mounted.

 **NOTE**

You will only be able to use the Finder to navigate through a mountpoint if it was automatically created by the **hdid** command. If you manually mounted the directory, the Finder will not understand how to traverse the mountpoint and will refuse to display its contents.

The following example shows the contents of this directory from a Mac OS X Terminal window:

```
# ls /Volumes/UNTITLED
bin        etc        install    lost+found proc       tmp        var
dev        etccombo   kernel     mnt        prom       tvbin
dist       initrd     lib        opt        sbin       tvlib
```

 **TIP**

As a good sysadmin, you should unmount the filesystem image before shutting down your Mac. You can do this by using a command like the following:

```
sudo umount mountpoint
```

Where *mountpoint* is the directory on which you mounted the ext2 filesystem image.

# Mounting and Exploring MFS Partitions under Mac OS X

Mac OS X users can also browse filesystems that use the TiVo Media Filesystem (MFS) thanks to Josh Graessley's MFSBrowser, which brings the power and ease-of-use of the Mac GUI to TiVo filesystem exploration. The TiVo Media Filesystem, its contents, and organization are explained in Chapter 10—this section focuses on explaining how to install and use the Mac OS X MFSBrowser utility.

The MFSBrowser utility is available as a Macintosh Disk Image (DMG) file on the Net at the **http://josh.graessley.net/tivo/**, and is also available as the file **mfs_browser_3.dmg** on the BATBD CD that accompanies this book in the macintosh directory. The disk image file contains the MFSBrowser utility, its source code, and a short README file explaining how to use the application.

To install the MFSBrowser on your Mac OS X system, download this file there or copy it from the CD; then double-click to mount the disk image file as a volume on your Mac OS X desktop. You can then drag the MFSBrowser utility to your /Applications folder to install it on your system.

Double-click the MFSBrowser icon to run the MFSBrowser, which will scan the disks in your OS X system for MFS partitions. To display the contents of any MFS partition, click the Disk menu and select the name of any of the MFS partitions on the drop-down list. A dialog like the one shown in Figure 9.40 displays, showing the contents of that MFS partition.

| Name | Type | Size | ID |
|------|------|------|-----|
| MessageItem | Dir | 48 | 1893 |
| Package | Dir | 3632 | 34522 |
| Person | Dir | 32 | 2472 |
| PostalCode | Dir | 16 | 3019 |
| Preference | Dir | 12 | 60370 |
| Recording | Dir | 356 | 2709 |
| RecordingQueueItem | Dir | 4 | 107095 |
| Resource | Dir | 92 | 1377 |
| Rubbish | Dir | 20 | 2470 |
| Schedule | Dir | 1092 | 2698 |
| SeasonPass | Dir | 96 | 29482 |
| Server | Dir | 1708 | 4 |
| Service | Dir | 24 | 29584 |
| Setup | Obj | 3356 | 2697 |
| Showcase | Dir | 436 | 34571 |
| ShowcaseIndex | Dir | 216 | 29449 |
| ShowcaseIndex.temp | Dir | 4 | 29523 |
| Star | Dir | 36 | 2474 |
| State | Dir | 264 | 2701 |
| StationTms | Dir | 5532 | 44426 |
| SwModule | Dir | 124 | 5 |
| SwSystem | Dir | 40 | 2469 |
| Table | Dir | 52 | 21 |

**FIGURE 9.41** *An MFS Filesystem in the MFSBrowser*

To view the contents of any MFS directory object or object, double-click its name. If the selected object is a directory, MFSBrowser displays another window showing the items in that directory. If the selected item is an MFS object, MFSBrowser displays another window showing the contents of that object. You can drill down into the MFS filesystem as deeply as you want. Figure 9.42 shows an MFSBrowser window showing the MFS objects in the /Recording/NowShowingByBucketTitle directory of the MFS partition on one of my stand-alone TiVo disks.

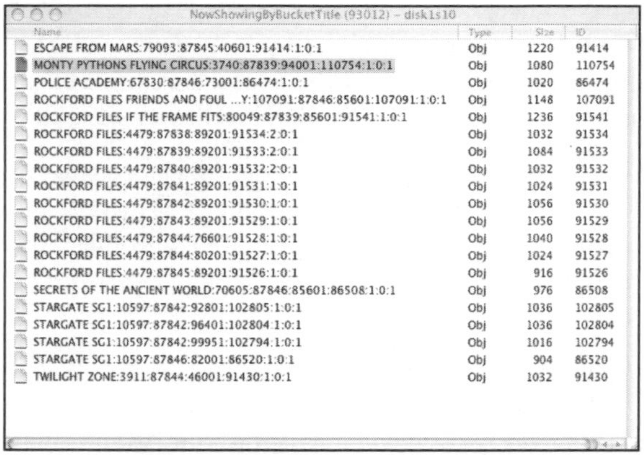

**FIGURE 9.42** *The /Recording/NowShowingByBucketTitle directory in an MFS Filesystem*

You can drill down into the MFS filesystem until you encounter MFS database objects (see Figure 9.43). This figure shows an MFSBrowser window displaying the contents of the Monty Python item shown in Figure 9.42. This item holds the metadata about one of the recordings that is currently stored on this TiVo disk.

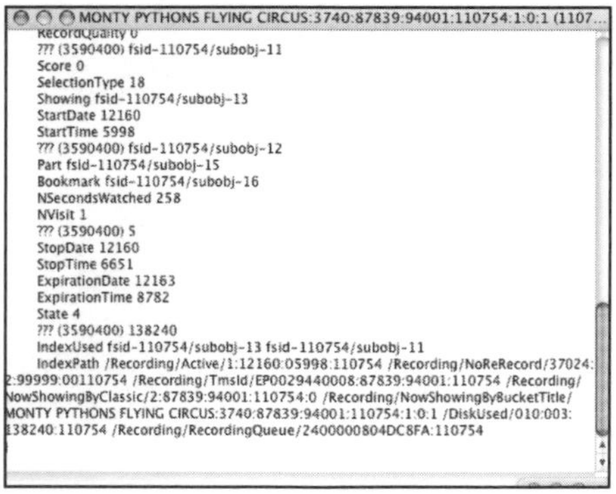

**FIGURE 9.43** *The Monty Python item in my /Recording/NowShowingByBucketTitle directory*

The MFSBrowser is a truly incredible tool for viewing and exploring TiVo filesystems on a Mac OS X system. It has no equivalents on Windows and Linux systems.

# Blessing a Disk under Mac OS X

A TiVo devotee named Eric Wagner was kind enough to port the BlessTiVo utility to Mac OS X. While his old home page at mac.com is long gone, the Mac OS X version of BlessTiVo lives on thanks to the folks at Weaknees.com. You can download the Mac OS X version of BlessTiVo from **http://www.weaknees.com/mactivo.php**. The downloadable version of a StuffIt archive file containing a binhexed version of the Mac OS X BlessTiVo application is located at **http://www.weaknees.com/downloads/OSXv4Blesser.sit.hqx**.

Most modern Macintosh towers contain one IDE drive and have a spare connection to which you can attach another. Open up your tower, jumper the IDE drive to be a slave, and connect it to the spare IDE connector on your system's primary IDE cable. You can usually place the second drive in the tray on top of the existing one (in the bottom of your Mac) while you're working with it.

Next, use StuffIt Expander to unpack the archive that you downloaded. This will produce a version of the BlessTiVo application that you can execute from the Mac OS X command line inside a terminal window. The syntax of the command is as follows:

```
./OSXv4Blesser device devicesize extratype extrasize
```

The last two arguments are optional, and enable you to create additional partitions of types such as "swap" or "ext2." In this example, let's assume that you simply want to devote the entire drive to storage that your TiVo can use for recordings.

Figure 9.44 shows the OSXv4Blesser command's Help message when the command is executed with no arguments inside the Mac OS X Terminal application.

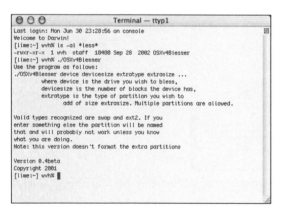

**FIGURE 9.44**   *The OSXv4Blesser's Help message in a terminal window*

The tricky parts of the OSXv4Blesser command are identifying the disk drive you've added to your Mac, and then determining how many blocks it has. To paraphrase Eric's original instructions:

> *"Now for the hard part. You need to determine how many blocks the drive has and under what /dev file its located. The best way I've found for this is the IORegistryExplorer*

*program provided by Apple as part of their development package/CD. The program presents a hierarchy that you traverse in the following layers:*

*Root, Computer, PCI, Bus, Harddrive"*

After you traverse this tree to the level where you can actually see your drive (for example, something like "MAXTOR 4k080H4 Media"), you will see two properties: the BSD Name String, and the Size field. They will look something like the following:

```
BSD Name String disk0
Size Number 80026361344
```

When you have this information, you can determine the actual block count by dividing the specified number by 512. You then can run the **OSXv4Blesser** command, as in the following example:

```
sudo ./OSXv4Blesser /dev/BSDname blockcount
```

Where *BSDname* is the value of the BSD Name String property, and *blockcount* is the Size Number property divided by 512. The **sudo** command will prompt you for you system's administrative password and then format the disk for use by the TiVo. The disk should then be ready to be added to your TiVo!

To verify that the blessing process worked correctly, re-execute the OSXv4Blesser command, as in the following example:

```
sudo ./OSXv4Blesser /dev/BSDname partitions
```

where *BSDname* is the value of the BSD Name String property, and *partitions* is the word "partitions." This displays a list of the TiVo partitions that were created on the disk.

 **WARNING**

Be very careful when blessing a disk from the Mac OS X command line. You can easily destroy your current Mac OS X boot disk if you accidentally enter the wrong name. Enter a value and check it twice.

# Creating TiVo Tools Disks under Mac OS X

Unlike Windows, Mac OS X comes with an application that is capable of burning CDs from CD images that you have downloaded from the Internet. CD-ROM images are usually referred to as ISO images because they contain images of a CD-ROM filesystem that is compliant with the International Standards Organization 9660 filesystem standard. Even though you will not be able to run the majority of these on your Mac OS X system (or boot the system from any CDs that you create), you still may want to burn them on your Mac OS X system if your Mac is the only machine in your home with a CD burner.

The Disk Copy (Mac OS X 10.2, Jaguar, and earlier) or Disk Utility (Mac OS X 10.3, Panther) applications provided with Mac OS X do an excellent job of burning CDs. This application is located in your Application folder's Utilities submenu. To create a CD from an ISO image using the Disk Utility application, take the following steps:

1. Start the Disk Utility application and select the Images menu's Burn command. The Open dialog box displays (see Figure 9.45).

**FIGURE 9.45** *Selecting an ISO Image in the Disk Utility application*

2. Select the image that you want to burn to a CD and click the Burn button. After a bit of processing, the dialog box shown in Figure 9.46 displays. Click Burn to continue.

**FIGURE 9.46** *Preparing to burn a CD using the Disk Copy utility*

3. The Disk Copy utility displays a progress bar as it burns the CD. When the CD is complete, the primary Disk Copy dialog box displays a success message, as shown in Figure 9.47.

   After the status message displays, you can remove the CD from your CD burner and exit the Disk Copy utility.

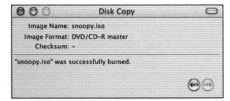

**FIGURE 9.47**    *A status message indicating successful CD creation*

# Integrating Macintosh Systems with TiVo's Home Media Features

The general characteristics of the Home Media Features, formerly known as TiVo's Home Media Option, were explained earlier. TiVo provides a free version of the TiVo Desktop software for Mac OS X that enables you to publish all music or selected playlists from your iTunes Library so that you can play it from any networked stand-alone Series 2 TiVo that is running 4.x TiVo software . Unfortunately, the OS X version of the TiVo Desktop is tightly integrated with iTunes—so the only way to export MP3 files from your Mac is if they have been integrated into iTunes. You cannot simply export a selected directory of music, as you can with the Windows version discussed earlier in this chapter.

You can download the Mac OS X version of the TiVo Desktop from TiVo's Web page at **http://www.tivo.com/4.9.4.1.asp**. Once you download and install it, exporting your iTunes Library is almost trivial. To do so, take the following steps:

1. Start your OS X system's System Preferences application. This application is located in your Applications folder's Utilities folder.

2. Select the TiVo Desktop icon from the Other section at the bottom of the System Preferences dialog box. The Mac OS X TiVo Desktop displays (see Figure 9.48).

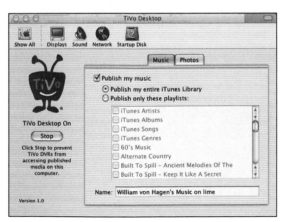

**FIGURE 9.48**    *The TiVo Desktop application on Mac OS X.*

3. To publish your entire iTunes Library, make sure that the Publish my entire iTunes Library radio button is selected. To publish only selected playlists, select the Publish only these playlists radio button and check the playlists that you want to publish.

4. If the TiVo Server is not already running on your Mac OS X system, click the Start button at the left of the TiVo Desktop dialog box. If a button labeled Stop displays at the left side of this dialog box, then your TiVo server is already running.

That's all there is to it! The name at the bottom of the TiVo Desktop dialog box shows the name under which you can find the music from your Mac in your TiVo's Music & Photos screen (TiVo Central, Music & Photos).

# HACKING THE TiVo

## Chapter 10

SECOND EDITION

## Linux and the TiVo

Linux is a freely available operating system that is gaining in popularity in the desktop, server, and embedded computing markets. The conceptual parent of Linux is the Unix operating system, written at Bell Labs in the 1970s. Many different versions of Unix have appeared since then, and Unix-like operating systems are the most popular operating systems used in server environments today.

One of the most attractive aspects of Linux as a Unix-like operating system is its source code that is downloaded easily from hundreds of sites on the Internet, and runs on a variety of hardware platforms and architectures including x86, MIPS, PPC, Super-Hitachi, SPARC, ARM, and XScale.

This chapter provides a basic introduction to Linux, its organization and operating model, the enhancements that TiVo, Inc. has made to Linux, and how to perform basic TiVo-related tasks under Linux.

# Introduction to Linux and Open Source Software

Development of Linux began in 1991 when a Finnish college student named Linus Torvalds announced that he had begun work on a new operating system that was similar to MINIX. MINIX was a popular Unix-like operating system written by Professor Andrew Tanenbaum. It was widely used in academic circles because its complete source code was available in Tanenbaum's *Operating Systems* book. Written in the C programming language with some assembly language, MINIX was designed for 8086 systems but provided a basic Unix-like environment and command set. Unfortunately, there were licensing requirements associated with doing extensive work or commercial deployments of MINIX, which made it unsuitable for wide deployment. In addition, MINIX was written as an academic tool rather than as an industrial-strength operating system.

Development of the Linux MINIX-like operating system was facilitated by the Open Software Foundation's GNU project (**http://www.gnu.org**). Its goal was to develop a complete, free, Unix-like operating system and all the associated utilities. Founded by a legendary MIT hacker named Richard Stallman, the GNU Project popularized the concept of free software, which means that the source code for all GNU software is freely available and the source code for subsequent enhancements made to GNU software will also be available. As the GNU Web site states, "Free software is a matter of liberty, not price." This principle of freely available program source code is known as *open source*, a term coined by Eric Raymond and popularized by the high quality and ideals of the GNU Project.

An operating system is just that—it operates your hardware, communicating with devices, scheduling and executing tasks, managing system-level resources such as memory, and so forth. However, without programs for users to execute, it isn't very exciting. The software developed by the GNU Project was a perfect fit for a newly developed operating system. One of the earliest software packages developed by the GNU Project was GCC, the GNU C Compiler, an open source compiler for programs written in the C programming language. GCC was designed to be easily portable to multiple operating systems, and comprised a complete development environment, which is tightly integrated with the GNU C Library that provides the function libraries that C programs require to run. The fact that most of the software from the GNU Project forms the core set of utilities that all Linux users depend on is the reason why Linux is often referred to as GNU/Linux.

Given a free C compiler and other applications, such as a command-line interpreter (bash) for actually running commands, Linux was born. In 1991, Linux sent a second, now famous email message to subscribers of the comp.os.minix newsgroup, an Internet newsgroup dedicated to MINIX support and development. This message announced the wider availability of the Linux source code. GNU utilities such as bash, gcc, the GNU-make program, and others were successfully running on Linux. This was Linux 0.02. Since then, Linux has been ported to various platforms, extended by thousands of free utilities including a graphical user environment (GUI) based on MIT's X Window System, text editors, word processors, games, and just about everything else. And all of it is still free. While it is possible to buy CDs containing GNU Project and Linux software from a variety of companies, the charge for these CDs is for their packaging, production, and support—not for the GNU and core Linux software itself, which is and will always be free.

---

 **NOTE**

The vendors of other operating systems, which are therefore competitors to Linux, like to confuse people by claiming that open source software is viral in nature, infecting any commercial products that it touches and spelling the end of commercial software products. This could not be further from the truth. GNU software conforms to licenses (GNU General Public License [GPL], and Lesser GNU Public License [LGPL]). The licenses guarantee that it will remain free, and they also explicitly state that no software that interacts with GNU software is affected by its open source nature unless it specifically incorporates code from Linux. These licenses also explicitly state that software compiled with open source libraries is not affected by its open source nature. So much for Fear, Uncertainty, and Doubt from companies such as Microsoft! The open source licenses used by Linux and the GNU Project are available at **http://www.gnu.org/licenses/licenses.html**. TCL and iTCL use the slightly different BSD license (for more information, see the section of this chapter that discusses TCL and iTCL).

---

# Overview of the Linux Boot Process

The process of starting an operating system on a computer is known as *booting* the system, which refers to the old expression "pulling up one's self by your bootstraps." The heart of the Linux operating system is known as the *kernel*, which is compiled specifically for the different hardware architectures. When you boot a Linux system, the hardware loads a relatively small program known as a *boot-loader* from a special location on the disk, and then executes this boot-loader. Next, the boot-loader loads the kernel into memory and transfers control of the system to the kernel. The kernel probes the hardware and gathers information about its characteristics and the devices that are attached to the system, and then it loads any device drivers that are required to communicate with that hardware.

Device drivers are small programs that are loaded by an operating system and contain the specific sets of instructions necessary for the operating system to communicate with those devices (drives). In Linux, device drivers can be either compiled into the kernel or loaded separately. Each method has its advantages. Some device drivers are required for the kernel to communicate with a computer system's screen, disk drives, and other critical pieces of hardware, and are therefore compiled into the kernel. It would be impossible for the kernel to load a device driver from disk if it didn't understand how to obtain information from the drive at the hardware level. Similarly, the kernel must understand how information on that disk is organized so that it can find the specific data that it requires.

---

 **NOTE**

Device drivers that load separately are examples of what are known as *loadable kernel modules*. Device drivers that can load as modules are those for devices that aren't directly required by the boot process. As the name suggests, loadable kernel modules are complete sections of code that the kernel can load, and they follow well-known conventions for integrating with it. Common examples of device drivers that are loaded as modules are drivers for network devices, sound cards, mice, special-purpose hardware such as USB or PCMCIA hardware, and so forth. All loadable kernel modules are not necessarily associated with specific physical devices. They also can be associated with logical devices and higher-level protocols, such as those used by network-based filesystems, kernel processes such as firewalling, and so forth.

After the kernel loads into memory and completes its probe of the hardware, it sets a logical or physical device as its primary storage device (known as *mounting a filesystem*) and begins to execute programs from there.

## Linux Filesystems and Initial RAM Disks

To access information on a storage device such as a hard disk, floppy disk drive, or CD-ROM, the information on that device must be organized in a way that the computer can uniquely locate specific pieces of information. A *filesystem* is the term used for the organization of files and directories on a physical storage device, such as a disk drive. Files are discrete sets of related information that the computer can locate and use. Directories provide a hierarchical way of organizing files, much like the drawers in a filing cabinet provide for the files that it contains.

As an example, a standard directory found in the initial filesystems used by most Linux systems is a directory containing administrative and configuration information, **/etc**. The slash (/) at the beginning of the name of this directory indicates that it is available under the very top level of the Linux filesystem, which is known as the *root* of the filesystem. The directory /etc contains files such as those that provide information about users on the Linux system, which are stored in a file named /etc/passwd, and commands that the system should execute when it starts (stored in the directory /etc/rc.d, which stands for "Run Command Default"), and so on. Using a filesystem comprised of files and directories, known as a *hierarchical filesystem*, makes it easy for programs and users to locate files by name, as well as to explore the contents of the filesystem by simply traversing the directory structure of the disk.

Linux supports many different types of filesystems, each with its own advantages and disadvantages. The types of standard Linux filesystems relevant to the TiVo are filesystems located on a Linux disk in a format known as *EXT2* (Extended Filesystem 2), and in-memory filesystems known as *initial RAM disks* (also commonly referred to as an *initrd*). As we'll see later in this chapter in the section "TiVo Disk Information," TiVo also provides its own type of filesystem, known as *MFS*, which is a cross between a database and a filesystem that is specially designed to fulfill the performance and allocation requirements of recording and storing digital video in real-time.

Linux kernels can be set to use an in-memory filesystem known as an *initial RAM disk* as their initial root filesystem. These initial RAM disks are separate filesystems that are bundled into a Linux kernel when it is compiled, and provide certain advantages to a Linux system. In embedded systems that may not have disk drives attached, an initial RAM disk enables the system to boot without a disk, CD-ROM, or floppy drive. Similarly, if the kernel requires that special device drivers load into the kernel, but you don't want to compile them into the kernel, they can be stored in an initial RAM disk and loaded from there.

 **TIP**

RAM disks can be created in a number of formats, although those that are typically bundled into a kernel are either EXT2 or ROMFS filesystems stored in a compressed format known as *gzip* (GNU zip). By examining a kernel for the special sequence of bytes that identifies the beginning of a gzip file, you can extract an initial RAM disk from a compiled kernel. The extract_gzip.c file provided in the **src** directory of the CD that accompanies this book enables you to do just that. After uncompressing the extracted file (using the Linux command **gunzip** *filename*), you can then mount this filesystem using a Linux command such as **mount -o loop** *filename* **/mnt**. When mounted, it can be explored just like any other Linux filesystem.

When a Linux kernel that has been configured to use an initial RAM disk boots, it does the following:

◆ Formats a special portion of system memory to look like a disk drive

◆ Loads the initial RAM disk into that portion of memory

◆ Sets that RAM disk as its root filesystem

◆ Executes any prespecified commands from that root filesystem, including loading any specified loadable kernel modules (explained in the next section)

As the last stages of executing the startup commands specified in the initial RAM disk, the system typically mounts a standard Linux device as its "real" root filesystem, changes the / directory of its filesystem to that new device (known as "pivoting" to the new root filesystem), and begins executing commands from that filesystem.

# The Linux Boot Sequence for Initial RAM Disks

If your system uses an initial RAM disk, the boot sequence uncompresses and mounts the initial RAM disk and then executes the file /linuxrc. This file must therefore be executable, but can be a stand-alone binary, a command file that lists other commands to execute, a multicall binary such as BusyBox, or a symbolic link to another binary.

Executing the file /linuxrc is done as a step in the initial ram disk's mount process, as specified in the kernel source file init/do_mounts_initrd.c. A sample /linuxrc file, where the /linuxrc file in your initial RAM disk is actually a command script (taken from a Red Hat 9 system) is the following:

```
#!/bin/nash
echo Mounting /proc filesystem
mount -t proc /proc /proc
echo Creating block devices
mkdevices /dev
echo Creating root device
mkrootdev /dev/root
echo 0x0100 > /proc/sys/kernel/real-root-dev
echo Mounting root filesystem
mount -o defaults --ro -t ext3 /dev/root /sysroot
pivot_root /sysroot /sysroot/initrd
umount /initrd/proc
```

As you can see from this example, the /linuxrc file executes a number of commands that help initialize the system. The last commands in this example command file mount the root filesystem on your storage device and use the **pivot_root** command to change the system's idea of the / directory. The **pivot_root** or **chroot** commands are Linux commands that are commonly used to change the system's root directory from an initial boot device to the device that actually provides your long-term storage. The system then executes the /sbin/init process. The Linux kernel performs a sequential search for the init process (as specified in the kernel source file init/main.c).

On TiVos running software versions greater than 3.1, the /linuxrc file in the system's initial RAM disk performs a series of checks on the contents of critical files in the TiVo's root filesystem. This is discussed in detail later in this chapter in the section entitled "The TiVo Startup Process."

# Obtaining the Source Code for TiVo's Linux

As mentioned previously, Linux is and must remain open source, as are many of the utilities used by the version of Linux running on your TiVo. This means that TiVo must provide the source code for its version of Linux and any other open source utilities included in the software that ships with the TiVo. You can download these from the TiVo Web site at **http://www.tivo.com/linux/index.html**.

The downloadable files from TiVo for the current version of the TiVo OS are organized into several component files, organized into modules (loadable kernel modules), commands (GNU and other open source commands), libraries (GNU and other open source libraries for things such as MPEG encoding, display, and so on), Linux (the source for TiVo's kernel), and development (tools and libraries required for successful compilation and linking). Version 4.0 of the TiVo software is for Series 2 machines only, which use MIPS processors. The source code for earlier versions of TiVo's Linux kernel provides both PPC and MIPS versions.

 **NOTE**

It is important to differentiate between TiVo's use of Linux and TiVo's development and use of proprietary software. Your TiVo runs Linux as its operating system, but the user interface and many associated programs are all proprietary products of TiVo, Inc. TiVo provides the code for the open source modules that help make your TiVo the great machine that it is. You will find the source code for the open source Linux utilities and libraries used by your TiVo on the TiVo Web site. You won't find the source for their proprietary tivoapp or any similar programs there. We all want TiVo to survive, right? It's hard to do that if you give away your intellectual property.

Linux is completely supported on the MIPS platform, and many TiVo users actually use the **monte** approach discussed in Chapter 8, "Connecting the Universe to Your TiVo," to boot versions of Linux such as Debian-MIPS on their TiVos. Explaining how to integrate a standard version of Linux with the TiVo kernel, libraries, and command modifications is somewhat outside the scope of this book, but you can find lots of useful information on this topic on the TiVo forums discussed in Chapter 14, "Other TiVo Hacking Resources."

# *Overview of the TiVo Application Environment*

Your TiVo is different from almost any other Linux system. For one thing, it's running in your living room. More seriously, your TiVo differs from a generic Linux system in a variety of user-level and system-level ways. This was necessary both to protect TiVo, Inc.'s intellectual property and to provide the performance and application environment required for a heavy-duty digital video recording appliance. Of course, this book is about hacking the TiVo, so I've already explained many of the ways that you can customize its startup sequence, configuration, and so on.

If you're already familiar with Linux, this section will help you identify aspects of the TiVo that are unique to its software and Linux configuration. If your TiVo is your first introduction to Linux, the topics in this section provide a convenient reference for things that you wouldn't expect to read about in generic Linux text.

# The TiVo Startup Process

Like many computers, your TiVo boots from a Programmable Read-Only Memory chip (PROM). This PROM uses configuration information stored in permanent but rewritable memory (known as *flash memory*) to determine where to boot from, how to boot, and so on.

When you boot your TiVo, first it reads information about the location of your TiVo's root filesystem from the bootpage of your primary hard drive (which is stored in the first sector of the hard drive), and then it checks the kernel partition associated with that root filesystem to verify that the kernel is correctly signed—in other words, that a value in the kernel header matches a calculated checksum for the kernel that it plans to boot. The convention used by TiVo is that the kernel partition associated with a root filesystem is always one less than the partition identifier of the root filesystem. For example, if your root filesystem is set to /dev/hda4, the TiVo will first try to boot the kernel stored in the partition /dev/hda3. If this signature check fails, the TiVo attempts to boot from the other kernel/root filesystem pair on your disk. This initial check by the PROM against the contents of the kernel that you are trying to boot is the reason that you must boot a valid TiVo kernel/initrd combination as the first step in hacking a Series 2 machine, as explained in Chapter 8, "Connecting the Universe to Your TiVo."

Assuming that the TiVo has found a valid, bootable kernel and an initial RAM disk, it boots that kernel using the initial RAM disk as its primary root filesystem. As explained earlier, the initial command executed in an initial RAM disk is the file /linuxrc (Linux Run Commands). On a TiVo, after temporarily mounting the system's actual root filesystem, this program performs a variety of system consistency checks, including checking the boot parameters with which you booted against hashed values stored in **/linuxrc** itself to verify that you haven't modified them. (Hence, no more BASH_ENV hacks when your TiVo uses recent operating system versions and PROMs.) The most clever (or irritating) of these is calculating SHA1 hash signatures of the majority of the files on the TiVo's actual root filesystem, and then comparing them against values listed in a file called /signatures that is stored on the initial RAM disk. Files that do not match the precalculated signatures in the signatures file are simply deleted, with the exception of three files that are replaced with standard, unmodified TiVo versions if they don't pass the signature check. These files are as follows:

◆ /etc/rc.d/rc.arch   Command script containing architecture-specific startup commands

◆ `/etc/rc.d/rc.sysinit` Command script containing diagnostic and startup commands

◆ `/etc/inittab` Table of commands to run at various points during system initialization

The virgin copies of these three files are located in the **/fixes** directory in the initial RAM disk.

 **TIP**

If you are hacking your TiVo, as described in Chapter 8, and receive the message "Can't find init" in your boot messages, you probably used a kernel/initrd combination with a signature file that didn't match the contents of your root partition. Your TiVo probably purged the root filesystem of files that didn't match. First, try to boot using your other root partition. If that fails, you will have to restore your root filesystem from an unstructured backup (best case), or completely restore your TiVo from a structured backup. It can happen to you—I have to confess that it has certainly happened to me.

If all of the previous tests have succeeded, your TiVo will execute the **/sbin/init** process, which will then execute the command script `/etc/rc.d/rc.sysinit`. This unmounts the initial RAM disk, performs various system consistency checks and diagnostics, checks for updates from TiVo, and then starts all of your favorite TiVo applications, such as the primary TiVo application (tivoapp, aka myworld).

# TCL and iTCL

Though most GNU projects and Linux itself are primarily written in the C programming language, a wide variety of free programming languages are available for Linux systems. A very popular language, and the primary language used for most application development on TiVo systems, is the Tool Command Language (TCL). TCL is an interpreted language and associated interpreter for that language, which was written in 1988 by John Ousterhout.

iTCL, more formally known as "[incr TCL]," is a set of object-oriented extensions to TCL, designed to simplify the structure of complex TCL applications. iTCL adds support for objects to TCL, which can be used as building blocks in iTCL/TCL applications. Objects consists of data structures and associated procedures (known as *methods*) that create, delete, and manipulate those objects. To further simplify things, objects are organized into classes that can inherit methods from others or can override existing methods with methods more appropriate to a given class.

Both TCL and iTCL are open source projects hosted at **http://www.sourceforge.net**. The home page for TCL is located at **http://sourceforge.net/projects/tcl**. The home page for [incr TCL] is located at **http://incrtcl.sourceforge.net/itcl**.

Providing an in-depth guide to writing and debugging TCL and iTCL applications is outside the scope of this book; however, a variety of books on TCL are already available. Good online sources of information are the *TCL Reference Manual* at **http://tmml.sourceforge.net/doc/tcl** and the [incr TCL] online reference information, which is located at **http://www.tcl.tk/man/ itcl3.1**. A Web search for TCL, iTCL, or projects using them could keep you busy for days.

Many people initially find it odd that TiVo would select an interpreted language for initial GUI and user application development. Actually, given that TiVo began to develop and debug its software while the hardware that supported it was under development, using an interpreted language makes a lot of sense. Interpreted languages are often easier to debug than applications written in compiled languages, and they are inherently portable across different operating systems, Linux versions, and even different Linux platforms. I would assume that much of the early TiVo development was initially done on more common Linux platforms, such as x86 systems. At this point, little of the TiVo interface is written in TCL for performance reasons.

 **NOTE**

If you've downloaded the updated open source code from TiVo's Web site, you will notice that it does not contain the source code for any modifications to TCL made by TiVo. TCL and, therefore, iTCL are released under a slightly different license than the GPL or LGPL license, known as the *BSD license*, which does not require this level of redistribution. For more information, see the general information about the BSD license at **http://www.opensource.org/licenses/bsd-license.html** .

## TiVo's TiVoSH Application

Command scripts written for interpreted languages other than standard Linux shell commands typically identify the command interpreter that they are supposed to run under as the first line in the script. For example, Perl scripts typically begin with a line to tell the Linux command interpreter to execute these commands using the Perl interpreter, such as the following:

```
#!/usr/bin/perl -w
```

TCL and iTCl scripts on the TiVo begin with the similar line:

```
#!/tvbin/tivosh
```

The previous section prepared you for finding lots of command scripts on your TiVo with extensions such as .tcl and .itcl, the extensions used by TCL and iTCL applications, respectively. It may, therefore, be somewhat confusing that the most common command scripts found for the TiVo, even those posted on the forums or Web sites discussed in Chapter 14, all invoke another application as their command interpreter—namely **/tvbin/tivosh**. The tivosh application is TiVo's enhanced version of TCL, and contains a large number of commands designed to make it easier to manipulate values and resources stored in the TiVo's MFS filesystem or to send specific events to the primary TiVo application. Tivosh is designed to use as a command-line application, so it has no direct control over the TiVo interface other than by manipulating the data that is used by the myworld application, the primary TiVo application.

 **NOTE**

Like TiVo applications such as myworld, the switcher, and many more, the actual **tivosh** command is actually a symbolic link to TiVo's monolithic "one app does all" application called *tivoapp*. These all were originally stand-alone applications (myworld was actually the name of an earlier version of tivoapp), but began to be merged together in TiVo software release 2.0. Like the Linux **busybox** command (discussed later in this chapter), nowadays tivoapp does different things depending on how it is called. For this reason, tivoapp weighs in at an impressive 16 MB in size.

Tivosh is based on TCL Version 8.0p2, using the TCLsh interpreter that it includes. Tivosh incorporates iTCL Version 3.0a1 and also adds a number of TiVo-specific commands to transactionally manipulate the MFS filesystem or to manage events on the TiVo. Given that most of the truly fun tivosh applications explore and manipulate the TiVo's MFS filesystem, see the sections later in this chapter entitled "MFS—TiVo's Media File System" and "Exploring MFS" for more detailed information (and examples) on using **tivosh**.

 **WARNING**

Never type Control-c to exit from the tivosh application once you have executed any command there that accesses the TiVo's MFS filesystem—this will cause your TiVo to reboot instantly. Instead, use the **exit** command.

# TiVo Disk Information

Because the TiVo Series 1 used a Power-PC processor, these TiVos inherited much of their disk formatting and layout information from applications originally developed for various versions of PowerPC Linux for Macintosh computer systems. Because PowerPC Linux had to understand the disk formats and disk partition layout used by Macintosh systems, the Series 1 machines based their disk layout and organization on the Macintosh partition format. The final partition table used in the TiVos is very close to the Macintosh partition format, but is slightly different at the kernel-level. By the time the MIPS-based Series 2 models were released, information about this partition format was too deeply ingrained into the TiVo software to remove it. Consequently, today's MIPS-based TiVo still uses the Apple partition format, even though the data itself is now byte-swapped compared to the TiVo Series 1.

The following sections discuss the organization of Apple Macintosh disks, explain the different types of partitions used on each, and then provide a detailed discussion of TiVo's own MFS filesystem, specially designed to support the requirements of real-time video recording and playback.

## TiVo Disk and Partition Map

If you've ever installed a computer system or disk drive from scratch, you'll remember that one of the first steps in the process is partitioning and formatting the drive. Partitioning a drive divides it into discrete sections that are formatted separately and therefore can be separately addressed by your operating system.

 **NOTE**

A slight extension of the partitioning concept is extended partitions, which is a special type of partition that contains other logical partitions. These extended partitions are largely an artifact of the disk drive sizes that grew faster than the ability of some operating systems to make use of the huge amounts of the additional space.

If you have hacked into your TiVo and want to look at the organization of your disk, you may be tempted to use the **df** command, which shows the disk usage for all mounted filesystems. This command returns something like the following, which isn't exactly what we wanted:

```
# df
Filesystem         1K-blocks      Used Available Use% Mounted on
/dev/hda7          10080488    988948   8579472  11% /
/dev/hda1            101089     29810     66060  32% /boot
/dev/hda8          30668576  23059468   6051208  80% /home
none                 515532         0    515532   0% /dev/shm
/dev/hda2           2016044      2276   1911356   1% /tmp
/dev/hda5          20161172   4249740  14887292  23% /usr
/dev/hda6          15116836   2918980  11429952  21% /usr/local
/dev/hdd1         196015808  76972756 109085968  42% /opt2
```

The numbers in the device names at left show the organization of each mounted partition on each disk. On a standard Linux system, what we actually need is the output of the **fdisk** command, which presents something like the following:

```
# fdisk -l /dev/hda
 Disk /dev/hda: 255 heads, 63 sectors, 10011 cylinders
Units = cylinders of 16065 * 512 bytes
    Device Boot    Start      End   Blocks   Id  System
/dev/hda1    *         1       13   104391   83  Linux
/dev/hda2             14      268  2048287+  83  Linux
```

```
/dev/hda3        269       395   1020127+  82  Linux swap
/dev/hda4        396     10011  77240520    f  Win95 Ext'd (LBA)
/dev/hda5        396      2945  20482843+  83  Linux
/dev/hda6       2946      4857  15358108+  83  Linux
/dev/hda7       4858      6132  10241406   83  Linux
/dev/hda8       6133     10011  31158036   83  Linux
```

The **fdisk** command is used on standard Linux systems. To examine the partition map on a Macintosh-format drive, you must use the **pdisk** command, which was discussed in detail in Chapter 5, "The Hacker's Tool Chest of TiVo Tools."

 **TIP**

To view disks formatted on Macintosh systems from a standard Linux system, your kernel must support the Macintosh partition map format, which is located on the Partition Types menu in the File Systems section of your Linux kernel configuration menus. You also must have a version of the **pdisk** program on your system to interpret the filesystem map.

Sample output from the **pdisk** command is as follows:

```
# pdisk -l /dev/hdd
 Partition map (with 512 byte blocks) on '/dev/hdd'
 #:                  type name                       length    base     ( size )
 1: Apple_partition_map Apple                            63 @ 1
 2:                Image Bootstrap 1                    4096 @ 64       (  2.0M)
 3:                Image Kernel 1                       4096 @ 4160     (  2.0M)
 4:                 Ext2 Root 1                       262144 @ 8256     (128.0M)
 5:                Image Bootstrap 2                    4096 @ 270400   (  2.0M)
 6:                Image Kernel 2                       4096 @ 274496   (  2.0M)
 7:                 Ext2 Root 2                       262144 @ 278592   (128.0M)
 8:                 Swap Linux swap                   260096 @ 540736   (127.0M)
 9:                 Ext2 /var                         262144 @ 800832   (128.0M)
10:                  MFS MFS application region      1048576 @ 1062976  (512.0M)
11:                  MFS MFS media region           24777728 @ 2111552  ( 11.8G)
12:                  MFS New MFS Application            1024 @ 26889280
13:                  MFS New MFS Media              17104896 @ 26890304 (  8.2G)
14:          Apple_Free Extra                          4000 @ 43995200  (  2.0M)
```

The first partition of an Apple format disk drive contains the disk's partition map and boot information. As shown in the above list, partitions 2, 3, 5, and 6 contain raw data that is not in any recognizable filesystem format. Partitions 2 and 5 contain the bootstrap code for use by TiVo (but not actually used, as far as I can tell), loaded by the TiVo's PROM. Partitions 3 and 6 contain the TiVo's Linux kernel—one is a primary, and the second is used as a failsafe. (If you've hacked a Series 2 machine running TiVo's Version 4.0 software as explained in Chapter 8, one contains your original TiVo kernel, and the other one contains your hacked kernel image.)

Partition 8 is used as swap space by Linux, which is a specially formatted partition that Linux can use to store sections of programs from memory when they are not actually running, such as when they are waiting for user input or other events. This enables a Linux system to appear to have more memory than it physically contains. Inactive applications or code pages can be written to disk, the physical memory associated with them can be reused, and the programs can be loaded again from swap space when they are ready to run. This is known as _virtual memory_.

Partitions 4, 7, and 9 are standard Linux partitions in the standard Linux ext2 partition format. Partitions 4 and 7 are the root filesystems associated with the kernels in partitions 3 and 6, respectively. (Only one of partitions 4 and 7 is used at any given time—you can have only one root partition at a time.) Partition 9 is the ext2 partition that is mounted as /var on a running TiVo, and is used to hold variable data.

The most interesting and unique aspects of a TiVo disk are partitions 10, 11, 12, and 13, which are TiVo Media File System (MFS) partitions. Discussed in more detail in the next section, MFS partitions are not mounted as are ext2 partitions, but are addressed directly through a library of MFS access functions provided on your TiVo.

The last partition of the sample TiVo disk drive is Partition 14, which is free space that has not been allocated to any partition. If you've hacked your Series 2 system as explained in Chapter 8, you'll remember that all of the Series 2 hacks take advantage of this free space—if not, you have something to look forward to.

 **TIP**

Disks using an Apple-style partition map can have a maximum of 16 partitions.

# MFS—TiVo's Media File System

MFS stands for the _Media File System_, and is a hybrid of a filesystem and database that was created by TiVo. Unlike most classic filesystems, MFS partitions are not mounted to use, but accessed through a user-space library. For this reason, you will not find TiVo's MFS filesystem listed in the kernel configuration options in the TiVo kernel source.

Each MFS filesystem actually consists of a pair of allocated partitions. Each has an MFS Application Region that holds administrative and internal information, and an MFS Media Region where data is actually stored. There currently can be no more than six MFS partition pairs present on all of the disk drives in a TiVo system.

For the most part, MFS is a simple database populated by four types of elements:

- ◆ Directories (tyDir)
- ◆ Files (tyFile)
- ◆ Objects (tyDb)
- ◆ Streams (tyStream)

In MFS, each directory, file, and stream is indexed by a unique number called a *filesystem ID (fsid)*. Many different objects can be associated with a single filesystem ID, leading to the sub-objects mentioned earlier. Filesystem IDs are allocated incrementally for each new element that is created in an MFS filesystem, and provide a mechanism for objects to reference other elements within MFS, much as inodes do in traditional Unix and Linux filesystems. Unlike standard Linux filesystems, where inode numbers are specific to a given filesystem, filesystem IDs are allocated sequentially across all MFS filesystems in a TiVo.

# Exploring MFS

As explained in the previous section, MFS stores four basic types of information in different types of elements. The following sections provide more details about certain aspects of MFS and explain how to access them. These sections provide some examples that will help you get started exploring MFS on your own. Maybe TiVo will even document it at some point....

 **NOTE**

As with most hacking in general, much of the information about the contents and organization of MFS filesystems has been found by exploring and reverse-engineering the filesystem. The tivosh application is your friend!

## Exploring Directories in TiVo's Media File System

One of the tivosh application's most useful commands is **mls**, which enables you to list an MFS directory. The **mls** command is equivalent to the **ls** command in Linux or the DIR command in DOS and Windows, and it provides a directory listing relative to some point in the MFS filesystem. The tivosh environment does not have the notion of a current directory, and so it always requires an argument that begins at the root of the MFS filesystem. The **mls** command also only lists the first 50 commands in the specified directory—you must specify a prefix to use when listing subsequent entries.

A sample listing of the root of your MFS directories produced by **mls** looks like the following:

```
bash-2.02# tivosh
% mls /
```

```
Directory of / starting at ''

    Name                    Type      FsId      Date   Time    Size
    ----                    ----      ----      ----   ----    ----
    Anchor                  tyDir    79392   07/10/03  08:30   2496
    AreaCode                tyDir     3078   04/19/03  14:59     16
    Avalanche               tyDir    79395   06/03/02  08:23     20
    AvalanchePP             tyDir   219041   04/29/03  16:59      4
    CaptureRequest          tyDir    75720   07/06/03  15:42     92
    Clips                   tyDir    79387   06/03/02  08:32     44
    Component               tyDir      190   01/07/02  23:25     40
    CorrelationIndexPart    tyDir    75717   06/02/02  11:43     16
    DataSet                 tyDir       24   07/11/03  09:45    692
    DataSetVersion          tyDir   220684   07/12/03  12:29    804
    Database                tyDir     1891   07/13/03  05:01    444
    DiskUsed                tyDir   220662   07/13/03  19:59   3016
    Genre                   tyDir       40   04/19/03  15:48   2856
    GuideIndex              tyDir     3126   06/02/02  12:19      4
    GuideIndex.temp         tyDir     2741   06/01/02  20:18      4
    GuideIndexV2            tyDir    75493   07/13/03  05:07    372
```

This isn't a complete list, which would waste paper and would discourage you from looking yourself.

 **TIP**

The **mls** command will only list a maximum of 50 entries at a time. If you are exploring directories with more than this number of entries, you can see the next set by supplying the name of the last result in the previous listing as an argument to the **mls** command.

Like most filesystems, different directories in MFS store different types of information. Table 10.1 shows some of the more interesting directories on your TiVo and summarizes the types of information they can contain.

**Table 10.1    Interesting MFS Directories and Their Contents**

| | |
|---|---|
| Avalanche | Stores the downloaded data from "Advanced Paid Programming" showings that TiVo broadcasts |
| Clips | Video clips broadcast during the "Teleworld Paid Programming" programming |
| Component | The definitions of the IR codes for the IR blaster and the programmable remote |
| Famous | A list of famous actors and directors |
| Genre | The genre definitions for a stand-alone TiVo |
| GuideIndexV2 | The indexes used to sort shows by title, keyword, actor, directory, and so forth. These indexes are used for finding the listings for when a program or series airs, as well as for a few internal purposes. |
| Headend | A listings of headends, which is the TiVo term for the groups of channels on cable, satellite, and over-the-air transmissions that you might receive |
| MenuItem | The definition of the extra menu item in TiVo Central |
| MessageItem | Any mail items or messages that you receive from TiVo |
| Package | Information used to build the TiVo Central Showcases menus |
| Person | The definitions of actors, directors, and writers used in the preferences engine when building lists of your personal preferences |
| Preference | All of the primary ThumbsUp or ThumbsDown data that any user of your TiVo has entered |
| Recording | Organized listings of all of the recordings requested by any user of your TiVo, including recordings that were automatically recorded by the TiVo |
| Resource | All of the fonts, images, sounds, and backgrounds used in the main TiVo interface |
| Schedule | The listings for all of the guide data by station and day |
| SeasonPass | All of the user's Season Passes plus some behind-the-scenes capture requests from TiVo |
| Server | A link to every object in the database with a ServerId attribute set. (Objects and attributes are explained in the next section.) ServerIds are allocated by TiVo and used when making series, program, station, day, and broadcast selections. |
| Setup | TiVo's original configuration data, now deprecated and only used for a few things. (See the State directory.) |
| State | The new configuration data, split into a number of subdirectories |
| SwModule | The software upgrade packages for your current TiVo software release |
| SwSystem | The resource group data for your current TiVo software release. The first database object in this directory contains the version number information for your current TiVo software release. |
| Theme | Information about your WishLists |

Each directory can, of course, contain other directories. All file and directory names in the MFS filesystem are case sensitive. As a continuing example for use in the next section, the following example shows the contents of the TiVo's /Setup directory as listed from the **mls** command in tivosh:

```
bash-2.02# tivosh
% mls /Setup
Directory of / starting at 'Setup'
```

| Name | Type | FsId | Date | Time | Size |
|------|------|------|------|------|------|
| ---- | ---- | ---- | ---- | ---- | ---- |
| Setup | tyDb | 2697 | 07/06/03 | 16:35 | 3392 |
| Showcase | tyDir | 32165 | 07/12/03 | 12:29 | 508 |
| ShowcaseIndex | tyDir | 78865 | 07/13/03 | 04:59 | 216 |
| ShowcaseIndex.temp | tyDir | 78844 | 07/13/03 | 04:59 | 4 |
| Star | tyDir | 2474 | 01/07/02 | 23:36 | 36 |
| State | tyDir | 2701 | 05/01/03 | 03:42 | 248 |
| StationTms | tyDir | 92842 | 07/07/03 | 10:01 | 5468 |
| SwModule | tyDir | 5 | 05/02/03 | 21:09 | 164 |
| SwSystem | tyDir | 2469 | 05/01/03 | 21:59 | 40 |
| Table | tyDir | 21 | 01/07/02 | 23:23 | 52 |
| Theme | tyDir | 62475 | 07/07/03 | 23:32 | 56 |
| TuikRes | tyDir | 219587 | 04/29/03 | 17:03 | 44 |
| Uri | tyDir | 92843 | 06/10/02 | 13:19 | 20 |
| User | tyDir | 2703 | 04/30/03 | 06:07 | 4 |
| Uuid | tyDir | 32110 | 07/07/03 | 10:00 | 4284 |
| tmp | tyDir | 75524 | 07/13/03 | 21:59 | 4 |

## Exploring Objects in TiVo's Media File System

An object holds a number of values in predefined fields called *attributes*. Continuing with the previous example, let's look at the /Setup object using the **dumpobj** command in tivosh:

```
bash-2.02# tivosh
% dumpobj /Setup
  Setup 75622/10 {
    IndexPath    = /Setup
    Source       = 75622/2108 75622/2459
    Version      = 2637
  }
```

The first line of the **dumpobj** command contains the string "Setup 75622/10." In the output from the **dumpobj** command, "Setup" refers to the type of the object and "75622/10" is the filesystem ID (fsid) and subobject ID (subobjid) of the object. When multiple objects are stored under a single fsid, a subobjid is used to identify those subobjects. All objects can be referenced by their fsid/subobjid; objects that can only be referenced by their fsid are known as *primary objects*. Primary objects are the only objects that can be referenced by the file system. Generally, any object that is only referenced from another object and not the filesystem will be the subobject of that primary object. All primary objects should have an IndexPath or IndexUsedBy attribute set, which identifies their location in the filesystem.

"IndexPath," "Source," and "Version" are all attributes of this particular object. The types of objects that can be created in MFS and the attributes they can hold are dictated by a hardcoded list of valid MFS combinations known as a *schema*. At last, it's time to write our first tivosh script to extract the schemas from the MFS filesystem. Let's create the following script to dump all attribute/schema information from MFS:

```
#!/tvbin/tivosh
# 2002, embeem
#
set db [dbopen]
transaction {
  set types [db $db schema types]
  set i 1
  foreach type $types {
    set attrs [db $db schema attrs $type]
    set j 1
    foreach attr $attrs {
      set ai [db $db schema attrinfo $type $attr]
      puts "$i $type $j $attr $ai"
      set j [expr $j+1]
      #13-15 never seem to be used -- embeem
      if { $j == 13 } { set j 16 }
    }
    set i [expr $i+1]
  }
}
```

After creating a file named queryschema.tcl with the previous code example as its contents on the TiVo and making it executable, you could simply run it by typing **./queryschema.tcl**. However, since it dumps the schema for every object in the TiVo's MFS filesystem, you can pipe its output to the Linux **grep** command (installed in /var/hack/bin when you hacked your TiVo), using the following command:

```
./queryschema.tcl ¦ grep Setup
```

The first few lines of schema information for the Setup object look something like the following:

```
43 Setup 1 Version int optional {} base
43 Setup 2 Expiration int optional {} base
43 Setup 3 Path string optional {} base
43 Setup 4 IndexPath string multi {} derived
43 Setup 5 IndexUsed object multi {} derived
43 Setup 6 IndexUsedBy object multi {} derived
43 Setup 7 IndexAttr object multi {} derived
43 Setup 8 ServerId string optional {} base
43 Setup 9 ServerVersion int optional {} base
43 Setup 10 Uuid string optional {} base
43 Setup 11 Unsatisfied string multi {} base
43 Setup 12 Bits int multi {} base
  ...
43 Setup 70 FrontIRBlasterOBSOLETE int optional {} base
43 Setup 71 AlternateBitratesOBSOLETE int optional {} base
43 Setup 72 TunerCountOBSOLETE int optional {} base
```

 **NOTE**

I've eliminated 60 or so lines, so this book doesn't turn into a telephone book. There's a lot of data in there. Also note that the format of this output is the result of the formatting commands in the **queryschema.tcl** script, not of any inherent format in the data itself.

The first 12 attributes in this listing are common to all objects, while the others are unique to a specified type of object—the /Setup object, in this case.

The first and third fields of each line, both numbers, aren't important when you are manipulating objects in tivosh. The second field is the name of the object type, and the fourth field shows you an attribute of that type of object. The fifth field is the type of value that particular attribute can contain, and the sixth field specifies how many entries can or must be present for that attribute. The last item is either "base" or "derived," indicating if this is a value that is set externally or is derived from other data in the object.

The main commands for manipulating database objects in MFS are the **db** and **dbobj** commands. All **db** and **dbobj** commands need a database handle and also must be open inside a transaction. To get a database handle, you simply execute the command **set db [dbopen]** and wrap the transaction within a transaction statement. The outline of a simple tivosh query script would look something like the following:

```
#!/tvbin/tivosh
#
set db [dbopen]
transaction {
 CODE GOES HERE
}
```

If you are executing a transaction inside a tivosh script that requires a resource that may be busy, the basic skeleton of your script would look like the following:

```
#!/tvbin/tivosh
#
EnableTransactionHoldoff true
 set db [dbopen]
RetryTransaction {
  CODE GOES HERE
}
```

In a tivosh script that may need to retry a transaction, the EnableTransactionHoldoff variable takes a Boolean value that tells tivosh that it can wait until the specified transaction completes—in other words, until the database is available.

A bit of activity goes on behind the scenes when you manipulate an object. If you are dealing with a primary object, the database automatically increments the Version attribute, rebuilds the IndexPath and other derived types, and then relinks the object into the directory where it was located.

# Exploring Resources and Resource Groups in TiVo's Media File System

Resource groups are an interesting part of MFS and provide a variety of information that you can examine and hopefully determine how to change in a useful way. A *resource* is an external definition of a string that the main program loads at runtime. This allows TiVo developers to customize applications in various ways without touching the executable, by essentially passing parameters. (Needless to say, it enables us to do the same thing!)

The current resource groups available on your TiVo are stored in the MFS database object /SwSystem/ACTIVE. Once you open this object, the ResourceGroup attribute for each entry in the list of the resource groups contains a list of items. These entries contain all of the text in the user interface, constants that control the bit rate of your mpeg encoder, the backdoor password, all kinds of default values, and a variety of other things that have not yet been identified.

The following script can be used to dump all the strings from the MFS resource groups:

```
#!/tvbin/tivosh
#
# 2002, embeem
 EnableTransactionHoldoff true
 set db [dbopen]
transaction {
  set swsysa [db $db open "/SwSystem/ACTIVE"]
  set resgrp [dbobj $swsysa get ResourceGroup]
  set groupn 0
  foreach group $resgrp {
    set items [dbobj $group get Item]
    set itemn 0
    foreach item $items {
      puts "$groupn $itemn [dbobj $item get "String"]"
      incr itemn
    }
    incr groupn   }
}
```

These sections are obviously an introduction to tivosh and the MFS filesystem—the complete story isn't currently known and may never be known unless TiVo decides to share additional information with the TiVo hacking community. As mentioned earlier, none of this is documented, so exploring is the only way to figure it out, determine what different MFS objects do, and see what you can do with the information you've obtained. If you're serious about TiVo hacking, share your scripts and the information that you obtain on the various TiVo forums for the benefit of the entire TiVo community!

# Using Serial Communications Under Linux

Like most other tasks under Linux, there are a variety of ways to do serial communications. This section explains how to use minicom, a popular serial communication utility for Linux that works fine from a terminal or a GUI command window such as an xterm. The minicom application is typically installed by default as part of most Linux distributions.

**NOTE**

If the minicom application is not installed on your system and you are running a Linux distribution that uses RPM packages, you can obtain a binary version for most Linux distributions from the central Linux resource at **http://www.rpmfind.net**. You can also download the source for minicom from a minicom site such as the one at **http://alioth.debian.org/projects/minicom/** and then build and install it yourself.

# Using minicom for Serial Communications

The first time you run minicom on your system, you must execute the command as the root user on your Linux system, as well as specify the **-s** command-line option to cause minicom to create its initial configuration file, /etc/minirc.dfl.

 **TIP**

In general, when you first configure minicom, you should run through the instructions in this section as the root user on your Linux system to correctly configure minicom for communication with your TiVo. You can then use the Save setup as **dfl** command on the main minicom menu to save these settings as your system's default settings. This will enable you to subsequently run minicom using a standard Linux account.

The basic serial communications settings necessary for communicating with your TiVo are the following:

- ◆ The name of the serial port on your Linux system that you've attached the serial cable to that connects to your TiVo. On your Linux host, this is /dev/ttyS0 for the first serial port and /dev/ttyS1 for the second.
- ◆ Set the appropriate communication speed. The serial ports on a Series 1 machine run at 9600 baud. The serial ports on a Series 2 model run at 115,200 baud.
- ◆ 8N1 communications settings (8-bit communications, no parity, 1 stop bit)
- ◆ No software or hardware flow control

To configure minicom with these settings, do the following:

1. Start minicom from the command line. Most Linux distributions install minicom as /usr/bin/minicom.
2. Type the key sequence **Control-a z** to display the minicom command summary. (To type this key sequence, hold down the Control key while pressing the letter **a**, then release the Control key and press the letter **z**.)

3. Type the letter **w** to enable line wrapping in minicom. You should see the message "Linewrap ON" display on your screen. If the message "Linewrap OFF" displays on your screen, press the letter **w** again to enable line wrapping. Some of the output that you may want to see in your serial console can be rather long. By enabling line wrapping, you can read everything that you are typing.

4. Type the key sequence **Control-a z** to redisplay the minicom command summary.

5. Type the letter **o** to display the Configure Minicom dialog box.

6. A menu of generic configuration options displays. Use the down-arrow key to scroll down and select the Serial Port Setup option; then press the Return key to display a Configuration dialog box.

7. The current configuration settings for the serial port display—first, verifying that the serial port that you have connected to your TiVo's serial cable is the same one listed in the minicom Serial Port Setup dialog box. Type the letter **a** to enter the name of the correct device, if necessary. The name of the default serial port on most Linux systems is /dev/ttyS0.

8. Next, make sure that both Hardware flow control and Software flow control are set to No. If Hardware flow control is currently set to Yes, press the **F** key to change the setting to No. If Software flow control is currently set to Yes, press the **G** key to change the setting to No.

9. The current communications settings are displayed next to the Bps/Par/Bits entry dialog box. If these are not 9600 8N1 or 115200 8N1 (depending on the model of TiVo that you want to communicate with), type the letter **e** to display the Communication Options dialog box. After this dialog box displays, type the letter **q** followed by the letter **e** (for 9600 baud) or **i** (for 115200 baud) to configure minicom with these settings. Next, press the Return key to close the Communications Parameters dialog box and return to the Configure minicom dialog box.

10. Use the down-arrow key to scroll down to the **Exit** command and press the Return key to close the dialog box.

At this point, press Control-1 followed by the Return key to see if you are successfully connected to the TiVo board. If you see a "bash-2.02#" prompt each time you press the Return key, you are successfully connected to your TiVo. If you don't get a response, check your cables, settings, and (of course) make sure that you have enabled a command-line prompt on your TiVo using one of the mechanisms described in Chapter 8.

 **TIP**

If you are using your TiVo's serial port to control your cable box or dish, you shouldn't be running a bash shell on your serial port.

## TIP

If you are experiencing intermittent problems or lost characters when communicating with the TiVo over a serial connection, you should check your Linux system to ensure that no other process is running on the serial port to which you have connected your TiVo. The most common processes you may see already running on this port are the Linux **agetty**, **mingetty**, or **mgetty** commands, which support various types of logins on serial ports. For more information on these commands, see the Linux online manual.

# Transferring Files Using minicom

After you have established a connection to your TiVo from the minicom application, the next thing that you will want to do (unless your TiVo is on a network) is to transfer some files there. The minicom application provides built-in support for popular serial file transfer protocols including xmodem, ymodem, and zmodem, kermit, and even pure ASCII file transfers. TiVos provide the **rz** (Receive Zmodem) and **sz** (Send Zmodem) commands in all versions of the TiVo software, so let's use that protocol.

To transfer a file to your TiVo using minicom (perhaps one of the archives of precompiled TiVo applications provided in the hacks_dir directory on the BATBD CD), do the following:

1. After connecting to your TiVo as described in the previous section, start the rz program on your TiVo by typing **rz** at the bash prompt and pressing the Return key. (Make sure that you're in a directory where you can create files, such as /var.)

2. In minicom, press **Control-a** followed by the **s** key. A menu of file transfer protocols displays, with the zmodem entry highlighted. Press the Return key (see Figure 10.1).

**FIGURE 10.1** *Selecting the file to transfer in minicom*

3. Click Browse, navigate to the directory containing the file that you want to transfer, press the spacebar to highlight the file, and press the Return key.

4. A screen, like the one shown in Figure 10.2, displays. The different fields of this dialog box provide status information about the file transfer as it proceeds, including a histogram that provides a graphical display of the file transfer percentage.

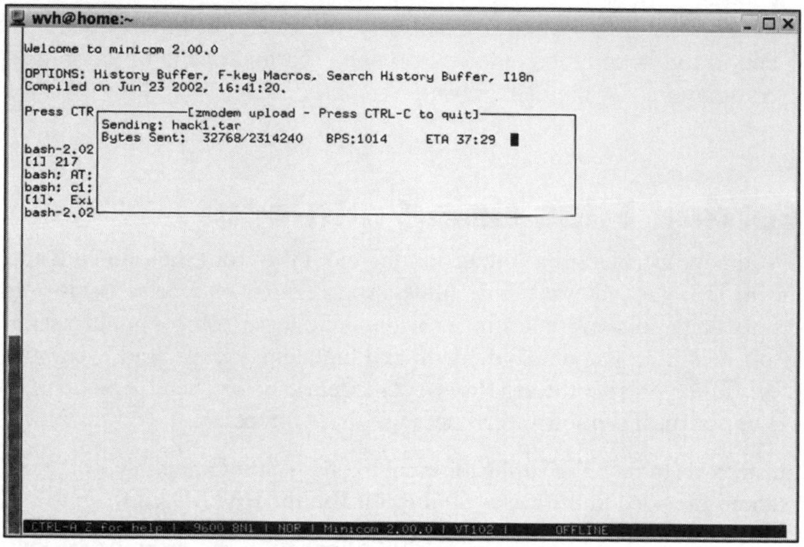

**FIGURE 10.2** *Transferring a file in minicom*

5. Remember that this is a serial file transfer and will take a while, depending on the size of the file that is transferring. The dialog box shown in Figure 10.2 closes automatically when the file transfer completes, and it automatically terminates the **rz** command running on your TiVo. (You may have to press the Return key once or twice to see the bash prompt again.)

When the serial transfer completes, you can install the software you just uploaded to your TiVo using one of the mechanisms described in Chapter 11.

Sending files from your TiVo to your Linux system works in much the same way as reverse transferring them. On the TiVo, you execute the **sz** command, followed by the name of the file that you want to send back to your PC. After you press Return, minicom should automatically start the receiving end of the transfer, and it will store the files that it receives in the directory where you started minicom.

# Using a Linux Shell

A *Linux shell* is the name given to a Linux command interpreter. When you log in to a Linux system, the login process typically starts a command interpreter in each terminal or console that you are running. As with most Linux applications, a variety of shells are available. The most common and popular of these is *bash*, which stands for "Bourne-Again Shell," and is a pun on the name of the author of the original Unix shell, Stephen Bourne. The remainder of this section applies specifically to the bash shell, although the basic concepts are the same in Unix and Linux shells, such as the C-Shell (/bin/csh), the Korn Shell (/usr/bin/ksh), and the others that you commonly find on modern Linux systems.

A shell displays a series of characters known as a *prompt* to let you know that it is ready to receive input. The standard bash prompt is the word "bash," followed by the version number of bash that you are running, followed by a hash mark if you are logged in as the root user. This bash prompt for Version 2.02 of bash (the version commonly found on a TiVo) would look like the following:

```
bash-2.02#
```

A shell reads the characters you type at a console or terminal window. Once you press Return, the shell first checks if the command that you typed is built into the shell. If it is, the shell executes the command immediately and redisplays its prompt to inform you that it is ready for another command. If the command is not built into the shell, the shell searches an internal variable known as an *environment variable* to find the command that you requested. The environment variable used by bash to locate commands is the PATH environment variable. The PATH environment variable is set to a colon-separated list of directories in which you want the shell to search for commands, in order. You can examine the current value of your PATH environment variable in bash in the following way:

```
bash-2.02# echo $PATH
/var/hack/bin:/bin:/sbin:/tvbin:/devbin
```

In this case, you tell the shell to echo the current value of the PATH environment variable, identifying it as an environment variable by preceding its name with a dollar sign ($). If you install new commands or simply want to search an additional directory for commands, you can use the bash **export** command to add a directory to the PATH environment variable, as in the following example:

```
bash-2.02# export PATH=/var/wvh/bin:$PATH
bash-2.02# echo $PATH
/var/wvh/bin:/var/hack/bin:/bin:/sbin:/tvbin:/devbin
```

In this example, the first mention of the PATH environment variable uses only its name (no dollar sign) because you are setting the value of the environment variable. The second mention of PATH, preceded by a dollar sign, ensures that the current contents of your PATH are included in the new value that you are setting.

A number of other environment variables are used in bash, but the PATH variable is the most critical one for finding and executing programs on your TiVo (or any Linux system, for that matter). A number of excellent books and online tutorials are available on bash. One of my personal favorites is the "Beginner's Bash" at **http://linux.org.mt/article/terminal**.

## Job Control in the Bash Shell

Job Control is a feature of many Unix and Linux shells that enables a user to manage multiple processes within a particular shell. Job control enables you to suspend commands that are currently running, to interrupt running commands, restart suspended commands, and much more.

>  **NOTE**
>
> The information in this section is generic to all Linux command interpreters and, therefore, also applies to the Unix command interpreters that they were modeled after. Since the TiVo runs Linux, I'm just going to say "Linux" from now on, but you may want to remember that this information also applies to all Unix or Unix-like systems, just in case you see one that isn't running Linux at some point.

Each time you type a command at a prompt on a Linux system and press Return or Enter, the shell runs that command for you, accepting any further input required by the command, and then sending the output of the command to the shell from where you started it. Normally, you can't execute another command until the first one has finished. This is usually a good thing, because you generally want the commands that you run to complete. However, Linux also enables you to run commands in ways that don't tie up your current shell. You can do this by running a command in the background or by suspending a command that is currently running. You can always run a command in the background from a Linux shell because this is a standard bash process control feature, but you can't suspend, interrupt, or restart them unless Job Control is available.

The next sections explain how to run commands in the background, how to redirect the output of your commands to files, and how to suspend, restart, interrupt, and manage commands from a bash shell.

## Running Commands in the Background

Running a command in the background means that the shell executes the command for you, but doesn't tie up the shell—it runs the command in parallel with the shell, while enabling you to type and run other commands from the shell prompt. All the examples of getting a command prompt on your TiVo are done by running a copy of the bash shell in the background, usually started from the /etc/rc.d/rc.sysinit file on your TiVo's root partition.

To start a command in the background on a Linux system, you simply put an ampersand (&) at the end of the command. When running commands that display output in the background, you typically use Linux redirection commands to send the output of the command to a file so that it doesn't display on the same screen where you're currently using the command interpreter. Redirecting the output of a command to a file is accomplished by using the > symbol on the command-line. For example, to run the **ls** command in the background and redirect its output to the file "ls.out," you would type the following command at a shell prompt:

```
ls > ls.out &
```

The shell would display a message like the following after you pressed Return or Enter:

```
[1] 20903
```

This means that, in this case, the shell is running the **ls** command as its first job (often referred to as a *subprocess*), and that the process ID of this process is 20903. The process ID you see will always be different, because the ID number assigned to a given process depends on the number of other processes that are running or have been run on your system.

While a command runs in the background, you can check on its status by using the bash shell's built-in **jobs** command, which lists all background tasks running under the current shell and displays their status. Executing the **jobs** command while our sample **ls** command runs in the background would produce output something like the following:

```
[1]+  Running                 ls >ls.out
```

This shows the same job number shown before, displays a plus sign (+) to show that the command actually is running, and displays the name of the command and the first 20 or so characters of any arguments supplied to the command on the command-line. When the command finishes, you will see a message like the following displayed by the bash shell:

```
[1]+  Done                    ls >ls.out
```

This means that the command completed successfully.

# Managing Commands in the Bash Shell

As mentioned earlier, you can always run a command in the background from a Linux shell, but you can't suspend, interrupt, or restart them unless job control is available. Job control is only available if the shell that you are running is associated with a specific device on your Linux system. Starting a command in the background and redirecting its input and output to a device is not the same thing as you did to start the bash prompt on your TiVo, as explained in Chapter 8. This is because the TiVo startup process that executed the command-prompt started the process in the background and then exited. Once the parent of any process exists, that process is no longer associated with a specific device, even though it can still send and receive input from any devices specified on the command line. A process that is not associated with a specific device is known as a *detached process* in Linux-speak.

When a command is running in the background and it isn't attached to a specific physical or network device, it can't receive the special commands that enable it to manage background or suspended processes. These special commands are Control-z (hold down the Ctrl key and press the letter "z"), which suspends a command, and Control-c (hold down the Ctrl key and press the letter "c"), which interrupts and terminates a command.

When job control is available, an alternative to running a command in the background is to run a command, suspend its execution for some period of time, and then restart it. This is a more advanced feature of job control, but it can be quite useful if you're executing some command that takes a long time to run and you suddenly remember that you want to execute some other, relatively quick command without restarting the first one. To suspend a command, you can type Control-z while the command is running, and you will see a message like the following displayed in your shell:

```
[1]+  Stopped                 /bin/ls>ls.out
```

If job control is available and you can suspend a running command, you can restart this command in the background by typing the bash shell's **bg** (background) command, which would display output like the following:

```
[1]+ /bin/ls>ls.out &
```

You can also use job control to bring a background task into the foreground by specifying its job number and using bash's **fg** command. For example, to bring whatever job is running as job number 1 into the foreground, you could type the command **fg %1**. The percent sign identifies the number as a job identifier. Similarly, to terminate a job that is running in the background, you could use the shell's built-in **kill** command. For example, to terminate whatever job is running as job number 1 into the foreground, you could type the command **kill %1**.

If you are running a command in the foreground that you want to terminate, you can simply terminate the task if job control is active by typing Control-c. This tells the shell to terminate the command, regardless of whether it's finished.

**TiVo** **Getting a Command Prompt with Job Control on Your TiVo**

As mentioned earlier, you can only get complete job control in processes that are actually associated with a specific device. If your only goal is getting job control in your TiVo command prompt, you can do this by not running the bash command in the background. The downside of this is that this must be the last command in your /etc/rc.d/rc.sysinit command file; because it never exits, no commands after that line will be executed from the /etc/rc.d/rc.sysinit command file. To get a serial prompt with job control enabled on a TiVo Series 1, remove any other command that starts a bash shell in your /etc/rc.d/rc.sysinit command file, and put the following command as the last line of the file:

```
exec </dev/ttyS3 &> /dev/ttyS3; /bin/bash
```

To do the same thing on a hacked TiVo Series 2, modify the file /var/hack/hackinit, remove the existing bash startup command, and add the following command as the last line of the file:

```
exec </dev/ttyS2 &> /dev/ttyS2; /bin/bash
```

You now can start, stop, suspend, and manage other processes from within the bash shell running on your TiVo's serial port.

Like most aspects of Linux, there are a zillion more nuances to the concept of job control and the larger aspect of process management in Linux. Explaining all of these would be fun, but it is somewhat outside the scope of this book. Many Web sites provide a good discussion of job control and process management on Linux systems, such as the about.com information on process management at **http://unix.about.com/library/weekly/aa062501a.htm**, and the information about job control available at **http://unix.about.com/library/weekly/aa072301a.htm**. Most Linux books with reasonably large coverage of bash also will explain job control and process management in great, gory detail.

# Popular Linux Software for the TiVo

Since the TiVo runs Linux, a large amount of freely available software is available for your TiVo. In many cases, this software is provided in archive files located in the hack_dirs directory on the CD that accompanies this book. This directory contains a complete set of my favorite Linux utilities for both Series 1 and Series 2 machines. Instructions for installing these on your TiVo are presented in Chapter 11, and also in the sections of Chapter 8 on getting a command-line prompt on your model of TiVo under most common versions of the TiVo operating system.

In other cases, you'll have to compile certain software packages for your TiVo yourself—perhaps using one of the cross-compilers provided in the xcompilers directory on the same CD. Cross-compilers are compilers that run on one type of computer system, but which provide output for another. The popular GNU compiler, GCC, is a great example of a freely-available, open source compiler that is easy to configure and use as a cross-compiler. Versions that produce executables for both the TiVo Series 1 and Series 2 machines are provided on the BATBD CD.

The next few sections discuss applications that you will probably want to use on your TiVo after you get a command-line prompt there.

## BusyBox

BusyBox is a truly impressive software package primarily designed for use in embedded Linux systems. Billing itself as "The Swiss Army Knife of Embedded Linux," BusyBox is a single executable that behaves differently based on how it was invoked. For example, if you create a symbolic link named *ls* to the busybox executable and then type **ls**, BusyBox produces the same output as the standard Linux **ls** command. You can get the same result by executing busybox directly and specifying the name of the command that you want it to work like as the first argument on the command line. For example, executing the command **busybox ls** would have the same effect as executing the symbolic link to BusyBox described in this paragraph.

The version of BusyBox included in the hack_dir archives on the BATBD CD is a slightly older version, but it does everything I've asked of it. The version on the BATBD CD (for both Series 1 and Series 2 systems) displays the following message when executed with no arguments:

```
BusyBox v0.48 (2000.12.22-03:36+0000) multi-call binary -- GPL2
 Usage: busybox [function] [arguments]...
   or: [function] [arguments]...
```

```
     BusyBox is a multi-call binary that combines many common Unix
utilities into a single executable.  Most people will create a
link to busybox for each function they wish to use, and BusyBox
will act like whatever it was invoked as.
Currently defined functions:
     [, ar, basename, busybox, cat, chgrp, chmod, chown, chroot, clear,
     cmp, cp, cut, date, dc, dd, df, dirname, dmesg, dos2unix, du,
     dutmp, echo, expr, false, find, free, freeramdisk, fsck.minix,
     getopt, grep, gunzip, gzip, halt, head, id, init, kill, killall,
     length, linuxrc, ln, logger, logname, ls, lsmod, makedevs, md5sum,
     mkdir, mkfifo, mkfs.minix, mknod, mkswap, mktemp, more, mount,
     mv, poweroff, printf, ps, pwd, readlink, reboot, renice, reset,
     rm, rmdir, rmmod, rpmunpack, sed, sh, sleep, sort, swapoff, swapon,
     sync, tail, tar, tee, test, touch, tr, true, tty, umount, uname,
     uniq, unix2dos, update, uptime, usleep, uudecode, uuencode, wc,
     which, whoami, xargs, yes, zcat
```

That's one impressive list! Needless to say, BusyBox doesn't support all of the 10 zillion options available to some of the commands that it emulates, such as **ls** and **ps**, but it supports enough commands to help get the basic information you expect from certain commands.

The primary reason that you might want to have a single binary that does the same thing as so many others is to save space on systems with small amounts of available storage. BusyBox was originally written for the Debian Linux boot floppies by Bruce Perens, but was substantially rewritten and enhanced for general use in any small footprint system by Erik Anderson. The size of each statically linked, stand-alone executable on a TiVo system generally ranges from 40K to 400K. BusyBox itself is only 248K in size, and each symbolic link to the busybox binary requires 7 characters (the number of characters in the word "busybox," which is what each symbolic link actually contains).

Not only does having a multicall binary (the name for an application that can be called in many different ways) save space, it also saves time. Building (and supporting) one binary and invoking it in 50 different ways is much faster than building 50 applications.

BusyBox has several homes, the most open of these is **http://www.busybox.net**. The source code for the current version of BusyBox is available from **http://www.busybox.net/downloads**.

# Emacs

The choice of a text editor is a religious issue. However, I have been using versions of Emacs since 1983, and my fingers think in terms of Emacs' keystrokes. Hence, I highly recommend a version of Emacs for use on your TiVo, and have included one in the archives of popular TiVo applications provided on the CD that accompanies this book.

Emacs stands for "Editor Macros," and was originally compiled as a set of macros for a long-gone, but little-lamented, text editor that was known as *TECO* (Text Editor and Corrector). Ironically, the Emacs' macros were originally compiled and maintained by none other than Richard Stallman, founder and guru of the GNU Project. Because these ran on top of (and therefore required) TECO, a version of Emacs was written for Unix systems in the early 1980s by James Gosling, who later went on to create Java. This version of Emacs, colloquially known as *gosmacs*, was eventually superceded by a free version of Emacs from the GNU project (big surprise) known as *GNU Emacs*.

Over the years, there have been many suggestions for alternate expansions of the Emacs acronym. One of my favorites has always been "Eight Megabytes and Constantly Swapping," which was a problem in the 1980s, but is somewhat outdated since my home Linux box has a gigabyte of memory. Regardless, Emacs is big, requires a relatively large amount of memory by any standards, and also requires a fair amount of auxiliary disk space for hundreds of configuration files.

For this reason, many smaller reimplementations or versions of Emacs are freely available. The one included on the BATBD CD is *NanoEmacs*, which (as its name suggests) is designed to be small with relatively low memory requirements. It does not support configuration files, but does require that your terminal type (TERM environment variable) be set to something like "linux" or "xterm" because it uses a minimal version of the TERMINFO, terminal information database.

 **TIP**

I'm sure that lovers of quaint modal text editors have already started composing nastygrams about my love for Emacs on a TiVo. For you guys, an open source version of vi, known as "vim" (Vi iMproved) is also provided for the Series 1 and Series 2 machines on the BATBD CD.

# FTP

FTP is the classic, networked file transfer application. Its name stands for *File Transfer Protocol*, which is the protocol that the FTP command implements. Both an FTP client and server are commonly found on Linux systems, but only the FTP daemon is included in the application archives on the BATBD CD. This enables you to use standard Linux to initiate a file transfer to or from a TiVo that is running the FTP daemon.

To start the FTP daemon on a hacked, networked Series 1 or Series 2 system, execute the following command:

```
/var/hack/bin/tivoftpd &
```

This starts the TiVo FTP daemon in the background, where it accepts standard FTP commands, such as those shown in Table 10.2.

**NOTE**

Originally, TiVos were not intended to be logged in to, so they do not support authentication. When you connect to a TiVo running the FTP daemon, it will respond with a series of messages like the following:

```
Connected to 192.168.6.247.
220 You are in TiVo Mode.
220 Login isn't necessary.
220 Please hit ENTER at the login/password prompts.
Name (192.168.6.247:wvh):
331 No Auth required for TiVo Mode.
Password:
230 Running in TiVo Mode.
Remote system type is UNIX.
ftp>
```

You must press Return or Enter at both of the authentication prompts. At that point, you will be connected to the TiVo and can move around the filesystem to send or receive files, using standard FTP commands such as those shown in Table 10.2.

**Table 10.2 Popular FTP Commands**

| FTP Command | Meaning | Action |
| --- | --- | --- |
| bin | binary mode | Puts the FTP client into the mode necessary to transfer binary files. |
| cd *directory* | change directory | Changes to the specified <directory> on the TiVo. |
| get *file* | get file | Retrieves the specified <file> from the TiVo to the system from where you connected. |
| hash | display hashes | Causes the FTP client to display a hash mark (#) for each 1K sent to or retrieved from the TiVo. |
| lcd *directory* | local change directory | Changes to the specified <directory> on the system from where you are connected. |
| put *file* | put file | Sends the specified <file> to the TiVo from the system from where you connected. |
| quit | quit FTP client | Terminates the FTP connection to the TiVo and closes your local FTP client. |

# GCC

As discussed earlier in this chapter, one of the earliest software packages developed by the GNU Project was GCC, the GNU C Compiler. GCC is an open source compiler for programs written in the C programming language. GCC was designed to be easily portable to multiple operating systems, and forms the core of a complete development environment for Linux systems. GCC is an excellent cross-compiler, which means that it is capable of producing binaries on one system that are formatted and designed to run on another type of system.

Cross-compilers that run on x86 desktop Linux systems and produce output for both the Series 1 (PPC) and Series 2 (MIPS) TiVos are found in the appropriate subdirectories of the xcompilers directory on the BATBD CD included with this book. For information on installing and executing them on your desktop Linux system, see the section of Chapter 11 entitled "Installing Cross-Compilers for TiVo Development."

# NFS

The Network File System, *NFS*, is a relatively easy way to move or share large numbers of files among networked computer systems. NFS, originally developed by Sun Microsystems, was one of the earliest network-oriented filesystems. Sun released the protocol specification for NFS early in its history, and versions of NFS quickly became available for every Unix machine on the planet. NFS is supported on all Linux distributions, and is generally installed on any Linux machine as part of a full or server installation (depending on the Linux distribution that you are installing).

NFS support for both Series 1 and Series 2 systems is provided as a loadable kernel module in the hack_dirs/kernel_modules directory on the BATBD CD. Different versions are available for different kernel versions for both types of systems. You can insert a loadable kernel module into the TiVo kernel by using a command like the following:

```
insmod -f -s nfs.o
```

The **insmod** command's **-f** switch forces the **insmod** command to suppress errors about different kernel versions, while the **-s** option causes any error or logging messages to be directed to the system-error log.

After the NFS kernel module is loaded into the TiVo kernel, you must make sure that your Linux system is running an NFS server that is exporting the filesystem that you want to mount on your TiVo. The filesystems exported from a NFS server are defined in the file /etc/exports. A sample entry to export the /home/wvh directory to any IP address on the 192.168.6 network, enabling read-write access and ignoring authentication issues when a remote NFS client tries to connect as root is the following:

```
/home/wvh   192.168.6.*(no_root_squash,rw)
```

**WARNING**

Be very careful when exporting NFS filesystems to systems that do not support authentication. Typically, NFS systems use an authentication package to validate that users have sufficient privileges to access, read, and write remote directories using NFS. Since the TiVo does not support authentication, your NFS server must enable connections from the TiVo that are interpreted as being equivalent to requests from the root user on your system. This gives anyone logged in on your TiVo complete access to any exported directory. You should restrict NFS connections so that they come from only trusted hosts (such as hosts on a private network), or only provide access to directories that you can afford to restore from backups should someone accidentally delete them. Exporting the root directory of a Linux system via NFS to an unauthenticated host is almost never a good idea.

Once you have created the /etc/exports entry for the directory that you want to export via NFS, you can start the NFS server on your Linux system by issuing the following commands as the root user:

```
/etc/rc.d/init.d/nfslock start
/etc/rc.d/init.d/nfs start
```

 **NOTE**

Different Linux distributions use different types of NFS servers (kernel or user space) and start them differently. These examples are from a Red Hat Linux system. You can often simply start the appropriate NFS components on your system by simply executing the command **exportfs –a** as the root user.

You should then be able to use the **exportfs** command on your Linux system to verify that the directory that you want to export via NFS is successfully exported. Using the /etc/exports entry cited previously, this command and its output would look like the following:

```
# exportfs
/home/wvh            192.168.6.*
```

After a filesystem exports from your Linux host, return to the TiVo and create the directory on which you want to mount the remote filesystem in a local directory that you have write access to (I typically use /var, and create the directory /var/nfs). You can then mount the remote directory on your TiVo using a command like the following:

```
mount -t nfs 192.168.6.32:/home/wvh /var/nfs
```

After mounting this directory, the output from the **df** command on your TiVo should show something like the following:

```
Filesystem          1k-blocks        Used Available Use% Mounted on
/dev/root              126911        15695    104663  13% /
```

```
/dev/hda9                126911      36307      84051   30% /var
192.168.6.32:/home/wvh 30668576   23093232   6017444   79% /var/nfs
```

You now can read and write files from your TiVo in the /var/nfs directory, and quickly and easily copy files to and from your TiVo using this directory.

For more information about using NFS on Linux systems, see the NFS FAQ at **http:// nfs.sourceforge.net**. Keep in mind that not all of the discussion about authentication will be relevant, so you must be even more careful to export only a limited number of directories, and then only to trusted hosts. However, NFS can save an incredible amount of time in large file transfers, in either direction.

# Rsync

Rsync (*remote sync*) is a file and directory synchronization program that makes it easy to copy files and directories from one host to another. When both a local and remote copy of a file or directory hierarchy exist, rsync is able to leverage built-in features that help reduce the amount of data that needs to be transmitted in order to ensure that the local and remote copies of those files and directories are identical. The remote-update protocol used by the rsync utility enables rsync to transfer only the differences between two sets of files and directories. A copy of the rsync utility is installed for you on your TiVo when you install the sets of binaries that are found in the archive files in the hack_dir directory on the BATBD CD (as explained in Chapter 11).

You must make changes to certain security-oriented system configuration files on a Linux system in order to be able to use the rsync utility. These changes are the following:

- ◆ Make sure that inbound rsync connection are enabled. This is controlled by settings in the file /etc/xinetd.d/rsh. The entry on the **disable** line must be set to **no**—in other words, enabling incoming rsync connections. If you have to change this file, you must then restart the xinet (Extended Internet Daemon) daemon by executing the command /etc/rc.d/init.d/xinetd **restart** as the root user on your system.
- ◆ Create (or edit) the rsync configuration file /etc/rsyncd.conf.

The /etc/rsyncd.conf file on my system looks like the following:

```
[tivo]
    path = /home/wvh/tivo_rsync
    uid = wvh
    read only = no
```

This file identifies a synchronizable entity known as *tivo* that maps to the directory /home/ wvh/tivo_rsync on my Linux system. Synchronization to this directory is done as the user wvh on my Linux system, and the directory is both readable and writable.

Once you have made these changes and restarted your xinet daemon, if necessary, you should be able to use the rsync command to push or pull files or directories from your TiVo to your

Linux system. The basic syntax of the **rsync** command when pulling files or directories from your Linux system to your TiVo is the following:

```
rsync -Haz Linux-system-addr::sync-dir target-tivo-dir
```

The arguments to the **rsync** command have the following meaning:

- ◆ *-H* Preserve hard links if these exist in any directories that are being copied
- ◆ *-a* Use archive mode, which preserves ownership, symbolic links, device files, and so on, and is essentially a shortcut that saves you specifying a large number of other options
- ◆ *-z* Use compression when transferring files, which improves throughput

For example, when logged in on a TiVo, I can make a backup copy of the contents of /var/hack on my TiVo to the synchronization directory *tivo* (which maps to the physical directory /home/wvh/tivo_rsync through my /etc/rsyncd.conf file) on a Linux system whose IP address is 192.168.6.32 by using the following command:

```
rsync -Haz  /var/hack 192.168.6.32::tivo
```

This creates the directory /home/wvh/tivo_rsync/hack on my Linux system, which contains an exact copy of /var/hack from the TiVo. On the Linux system, I can then add files to that directory and pull the changes back to the TiVo using the command:

```
rsync -Haz  192.168.6.32::tivo /var
```

Note that in this example, I do not need to specify the name of the hack directory because I am synchronizing the entire contents of the tivo synchronization directory on my Linux system to the /var directory on my TiVo. If I explicitly only wanted to synchronize the hack directory from my Linux system, I could have used the following command:

```
rsync -Haz  192.168.6.32::tivo/hack /var
```

You can also use the rsync command to push or pull individual files to your Linux system, as in the following example, which pushes the file /etc/rc.d/rc.sysinit from my TiVo to the synchronization directory *tivo* on my Linux system:

```
rsync -Haz /etc/rc.d/rc.sysinit 192.168.6.32::tivo
```

If you have problems using **rsync**, you can use its verbose argument (-v) to display additional information about the files that are being transferred and the checking that is taking place. On your Linux system, you can get information about what the **rsync** command is doing by examining the file /var/log/messages, which logs information about every **rsync** connection attempt, file transfer, and so on.

# Telnet

Telnet is the original application for network-oriented access to remote systems via virtual terminals. Like the FTP command, the Telnet application features both clients (running on your local system) and servers (that wait for incoming connections on a remote system).

Like the FTP daemon, only the Telnet daemon is provided on a TiVo system—however, this daemon (/sbin/tnlited, a "lite" version of the standard Linux Telnet daemon) is already provided as a part of all standard TiVo software distributions, and does not have to be separately installed.

To start the Telnet daemon on your TiVo, execute a command like the following:

```
/sbin/tnlited 23 /bin/bash -login &
```

This tells the Telnet daemon to run on port number 23 (the standard Telnet port on Unix and Linux systems) and to execute **/bin/bash** in login mode in response to any incoming connections. Because the TiVo does not support authentication, any incoming connection will be logged in instantly as the root user on your TiVo. This is unquestionably a security hole, so do not put your TiVo on a public network where randoms may be able to initiate Telnet connections—unless you don't care if the entire machine is deleted.

You may want to add this command to the end of your hacked TiVo's /etc/rc.d/rc.sysinit file so that the Telnet demon is automatically started each time your TiVo boots.

 **TIP**

If you don't know your TiVo's IP address (which may be the case if it is allocated dynamically, using DHCP), you can execute the **/sbin/ifconfig -a** command from a serial connection to your TiVo. This command displays information about all of the Ethernet interfaces that are active on your TiVo in the following format:

```
lo        Link encap:Local Loopback
          inet addr:127.0.0.1  Bcast:127.255.255.255  Mask:255.0.0.0
          UP BROADCAST LOOPBACK RUNNING  MTU:3584  Metric:1
          RX packets:0 errors:0 dropped:0 overruns:0 frame:0
          TX packets:0 errors:0 dropped:0 overruns:0 carrier:0 coll:0

eth0      Link encap:Ethernet  HWaddr 00:40:36:01:B0:11
          inet addr:192.168.6.246  Bcast:192.168.6.255  Mask:255.255.255.0
          UP BROADCAST RUNNING MULTICAST  MTU:1500  Metric:1
          RX packets:0 errors:0 dropped:0 overruns:0 frame:0
          TX packets:0 errors:0 dropped:0 overruns:0 carrier:0 coll:0
          Interrupt:29
```

You will want to enter the IP address (192.168.6.246) shown in the eth0 (for "Ethernet Connection Zero") section for the name of the host that you want to Telnet to from your Linux system. Your TiVo's IP address may change if you reboot your TiVo after using other network devices that dynamically allocate IP addresses, but you can always use a serial connection to your TiVo and the **/sbin/ifconfig -a** command to find out your TiVo's current IP address.

# Wget

Wget (*Web get*) is a file transfer utility that makes it easy to retrieve files from a Web server. A copy of the **wget** utility is installed for you on your TiVo when you install the sets of binaries that are found in the archive files in the hack_dir directory on the BATBD CD (as explained in Chapter 11).

In its simplest form, you need only specify the file that you want to retrieve from a remote Web server, as in the following example, which retrieves the file tivo_test.tgz from the files directory of a Web server running on the host 192.168.6.32:

```
wget http://192.168.6.32/files/tivo_test.tgz
```

The **wget** command displays a progress bar as it transfers the file to your TiVo. A complete man page for the **wget** command is provided in the man directory on the BATBD CD that accompanies this book.

---

 **NOTE**

The **wget** command is very similar to the **http_get** command that is provided in the /tvbin directory on the TiVo, and which the TiVo uses to retrieve files when updating your system. The syntax of the **http_get** command to do the same thing as the **wget** example would be the following:

```
http_get -T 0 -C 0 -D /var/hack -U http://192.168.6.32/files/tivo_test.tgz
```

In this example, the **–T** and **–C** options are mandatory options that identify the transaction and caller ID, and which can safely always be set to 0. The **–D** option identifies the directory to which the file should be retrieved, and the **–U** option identifies the URL of the file that you are retrieving.

---

# Burning CDs on Linux Systems

This section explains how to burn CD images from existing ISO images using a Linux system. Creating ISO images on Linux systems is accomplished using the robust and complex Linux **mkisofs** command. For more information about mkisofs, see the online manual page or download the latest version of the Linux package that contains it, CDRTools, from **http://www.fokus.gmd.de/research/cc/glone/employees/joerg.schilling/private/mkisofs.html**.

You can create CDs from ISO images using a number of Linux applications. The CD creation application most commonly found on Linux systems is **cdrecord**, and it is most commonly found in the directory /usr/bin.

**TIP**

Many versions of the cdrecord application require a SCSI CD drive, or require that your CD drive has been designated as using the IDE-SCSI emulation mode provided by the Linux kernel. If you are using an IDE CD drive and a 2.4.x Linux kernel, you can usually enable this mode by updating the configuration file used by the Linux boot loader that your system uses. The LILO boot loader uses the configuration file /etc/lilo.conf, while the GRUB boot loader uses the configuration file /etc/grub.conf. Regardless of which boot loader you are using, you can enable IDE-SCSI mode by appending an appropriate boot parameter to the kernel command line. For example, to enable IDE-SCSI mode on /dev/hdc, which is the CD drive in my primary 2.4.x Linux system, I would append the following:

```
hdc=ide-scsi
```

Newer versions of the **cdrecord** application do not require SCSI emulation. If you have a CD burner that is supported by Linux and you can't locate it, try loading the ide-scsi module or upgrading to a later version of the **cdrecord** application. The IDE-SCSI module and its use by the **cdrecord** application has been the subject of many long-running, embarrassing arguments that you can find on the Web if you like that sort of thing.

Your CD drive should be listed in the output from the **cdrecord** command's **-scanbus** command-line option. Executing the **cdrecord -scanbus** command causes the cdrecord application to probe all actual or emulated SCSI interfaces in your system and to list any CD drives that it finds, as shown in the following sample output:

```
# cdrecord -scanbus
Cdrecord 1.10 (i686-pc-linux-gnu) Copyright (C) 1995-2001 Jorg Schilling
Linux sg driver version: 3.1.24
Using libscg version 'schily-0.5'
scsibus1:
        1,0,0   100) 'TOSHIBA ' 'DVD-ROM SD-R1202' '1026' Removable CD-ROM
        1,1,0   101) *
        1,2,0   102) *
        1,3,0   103) *
        1,4,0   104) *
        1,5,0   105) *
        1,6,0   106) *
        1,7,0   107) *
scsibus2:
        2,0,0   200) 'SanDisk ' 'ImageMate II    ' '1.30' Removable Disk
        2,1,0   201) *
```

```
2,2,0   202) *
2,3,0   203) *
2,4,0   204) *
2,5,0   205) *
2,6,0   206) *
2,7,0   207) *
```

In my case, my system's CD drive was found as device 1,0,0 on the system's first SCSI bus (hence the leading "1").

To write an existing ISO image to CD, you simply specify the device that the **cdrecord** command should write to, the speed at which it should write, and the name of the ISO file to write to the specified CD drive. The following command would write the file "sample.iso" to the device reported as device 1,0,0, at speed 16x:

```
cdrecord dev=1,0,0 speed=16 sample.iso
```

If you're interested in seeing the intermediate progress of this command, you can specify the **-v** command-line option, which puts the **cdrecord** command in verbose mode and displays numeric messages about the percentage of the disk that it has burned.

# Working with TiVo's Home Media Features from Linux

In April 2003, TiVo released its Home Media Option, now known simply as TiVo's Home Media features, which was discussed in terms of Windows and Macintosh connectivity in Chapter 9, "Working with Your TiVo from Windows and Macintosh Systems." (For more information about the name change and the capabilities of the Home Media Features, see the section of Chapter 1 entitled "What Was TiVo's Home Media Option?") The Home Media Features' ability to play MP3 files is facilitated by software for Windows and Macintosh systems that enables those systems to export MP3 collections and iTunes libraries, respectively. Finally, the documentation from the TiVo Web site, where the TiVo Desktop software is available, (**http://www.tivo.com/4.9.4.1.asp**) states that no desktop software for Linux is available at the present time.

A fair amount of information on the internals of the Home Media Features is available from TiVo's Developer Web site at **http://www.tivo.com/developer**. After you accept their license agreement, you can download documentation and a sample Apache plug-in written in Perl that enables an Apache Web server to export collections of MP3 files and digital photographs to a TiVo running the Home Media Features.

 **TIP**

Make sure that you read the license before you actually accept it.

Unfortunately, TiVo does not provide an official Linux-based server for those of us who store our music files on a Linux system. However, thanks to the power of open source software and the ingenuity of various members of the TiVo hacking community, several excellent solutions are available—and for free, of course! The next few sections discuss each of these, explaining the installation and configuration process for each, and discussing the pluses and minuses of each solution.

# The Personal TiVo Home Media Option

When the Home Media Option was first announced, I was, of course, irritated that TiVo didn't provide a Linux client. I was initially able to play my music files by exporting my music directory from my Linux system to a Mac OS X or Windows system using Samba (the excellent SMB suite from TiVo hero Andrew Tridgell *et al.*, available at **http://www.samba.org**), and then making it available through the official Home Media Desktop client for those systems, but that's certainly the long way around. It also required that I keep two machines running at all times to perform the tasks that one machine would normally do.

In frustration, I asked about this issue on the TiVoCommunity forum, and received replies from several members of SourceForge's Personal TiVo Home Media Option project (**http://sourceforge.net/projects/ptivohmo**). From their SourceForge site, you can freely download various files which, when installed, built, and configured on a desktop Linux system, enable you to export both MP3 and OGG-format audio files from your desktop Linux system to any TiVo running the Home Media Option. A tar file of this project is also located in the connectivity subdirectory of the CD that accompanies this book.

To install, configure, and start this software on your desktop Linux system, follow the steps below.

1. Extract the contents of the archive file from the CD that accompanies this book to a writable directory on your Linux system. Assuming that the BATBD CD was mounted at /mnt/cdrom, you could do this with the following command:

   ```
   tar zxvf /mnt/cdrom/connectivity/TiVoServer-0.16.tar.gz
   ```

   This creates the directory TiVoServer-0.16 in your working directory.

2. Change the directory to the TiVoServer-0.16 directory and execute the following commands as the root user on your system:

   ```
   perl Makefile.PL
   make
   make install
   ```

3. Make sure that the file tivoserver.pl has been copied to your /usr/bin directory (copy it there if not), making sure that it is executable by using the command:

   ```
   chmod 755 /usr/bin/tivoserver.pl
   ```

**NOTE**

The TiVoServer software requires that Perl and various Perl libraries be installed on your system. If any required libraries are missing, the **perl** command listed previously will list them and explain how to retrieve and install them. You should do this as the root user on your Linux system.

4. Copy the sample configuration file, `tivoserver.conf`, to the `/etc` directory in your Linux system and edit its contents. Specifically, you must correctly set the following entries, and all of the directories that they specify must exist:

◆ Create the directories specified by the **tivo_cache_dir** and **tivo_image_cache_ dir** entries.

◆ Set the **tivo_mp3_path** variable to the name of the directory that contains the MP3 and/or OGG files that you want to export from your Linux system to your TiVo.

◆ Set the **tivo_photo_path** variable to the name of a directory containing any digital photographs that you want to export from your Linux system to your TiVo.

You can change other options, but these must be in the correct order for the server to start.

5. Start the TiVoServer using the following command:

```
/usr/bin/tivoserver.pl --conf_file=/etc/tivoserver.conf
```

That's all there is to it! You can check the log file (`/tmp/tivo.log` unless you changed it in the configuration file) for the status of your Linux TiVoServer; or, you can simply go to a TiVo Series 2 that is running the Home Media Features, select Music & Photos from the TiVo Central menu, and start enjoying the music that you have stored on your Linux system from the comfort of your home theater. (See also the following tip for creating a Linux tivoserver startup command.)

# The Java Home Media Option

As discussed in the previous section, TiVo's Home Media Option for the TiVo Series 2 machine running Version 4.0 or better of the TiVo software is an impressive extension to the power and usability of your TiVo. However, the lack of similar software from TiVo for those of us who store our audio files on Linux systems (and in Linux-based formats such as OGG) is irritating to many people.

SourceForge's Personal TiVo Home Media Option Project is an excellent solution to this problem. An alternative to this project is the Java Home Media Option project, which is also hosted on SourceForge and is available at the URL **http://javahmo.sourceforge.net**. JavaHMO started as a simple server to bring Internet content to TiVo with HMO, but grew into a replacement of the Publisher server software provided by TiVo. An advantage to using this software is that it runs on Mac OS X, Linux, and Windows systems (the latter under Cygwin). Because TiVo provides its TiVo Desktop software for Mac OS X and Windows systems, I've primarily

**TIP**

You may eventually want to create a Linux startup file for this command. I created the file `/etc/rc.d/init.d/tivoserver` with the following contents:

```
#! /bin/bash
#
# tivoserver            Start/Stop the tivoserver application
#
# Source function library.
. /etc/init.d/functions
RETVAL=0
# See how we were called.     prog="tivoserver"
 start() {
     echo -n $"Starting $prog: "
     /usr/bin/tivoserver.pl --conf_file=/etc/tivoserver.conf
     RETVAL=$?
     echo
     return $RETVAL
}
 stop() {
     echo -n $"Stopping $prog: "
# this kills all running copies of perl - heavy-handed but ???
     killall /usr/bin/perl
     RETVAL=$?
     echo
     return $RETVAL
}

 restart() {
     stop
     start
}
 case "$1" in
   start)
     start
     ;;
   stop)
     stop
     ;;
   restart)
     restart
     ;;
  *)
     echo $"Usage: $0 {start|stop|status|reload|restart}"
     exit 1
esac
exit $?
```

Depending on the run level at which you start your Linux system, you can then link this file into the standard directories of startup scripts in `/etc/rc3.d` or `/etc/rc5.d`.

used JavaHMO under Linux (since that's where I store my music archives). All of the files that you need to install in order to run this package on your Linux system are provided in the connectivity/JavaHMO subdirectory of the CD that accompanies this book. The rest of this section explains how to install and configure this software package.

As far as I'm concerned, the only downside of JavaHMO is that it only (currently) supports MP3 files, while most of my music archives are in the superior and open source OGG format. I'm not much of a Java programmer, but the JavaHMO project is always looking for volunteers—maybe this is your chance to give something to the TiVo community by adding OGG support!

You shouldn't run the JavaHMO server and any other TiVo publishing software at the same time, because they use the same ports.

◆ On Linux systems, you can't run both the Personal TiVo Home Media Option and the Java Home Media Option at the same time. You must modify your system's startup scripts to start only one or the other. Experiment with both and see which one works better for you. If all of your music is stored in MP3 files, the Java Home Media Option is probably a better choice.

◆ On Mac OS X systems, you should stop the TiVo Desktop Publisher by selecting it in the Other section of the System Preference pane, de-selecting "Publish my music" and "Publish my photos", and clicking the Stop button.

◆ On Windows systems, the standard TiVo Desktop software must not be running when you install the Java Home Media Option. To disable the TiVo Desktop software on your Windows system, either uninstall it using the Control Panel's Add-Remove Programs application, or at least disable the TiVo Beacon service that it requires. To do this, close the TiVo Publisher program (if it is displayed in your toolbar) by right-clicking on its icon and selecting Exit from the pop-up menu. You must then shut down the TiVo Beacon service by selecting the Start menu, opening the Control Panel, selecting the Administrative Tools icon, and double-clicking on Services. Right-click on the "TiVo Connect Beacon" entry, and select Stop from the pop-up menu. You should then modify its startup settings to prevent the TiVo Connect Beacon service from starting up each time that you boot your Windows system. You can do this by double-clicking the TiVo Connect Beacon entry and selecting the appropriate entry from the General tab on the Properties panel. I generally use the "Manual" setting.

 **TIP**

If you are running J. River's Media Center on your Windows system, the Media Center requires that the TiVo Beacon service (part of the TiVo Desktop for Windows) be running. If you need to be able to export non-MP3 audio files from your Windows system, the Media Center application is your only option, and you should probably not install the JavaHMO server.

To install, configure, and start the JavaHMO software on your desktop system, you must first make sure that Java and other required packages are installed on your system.

◆ Linux users must have installed Java and the Java Advanced Imaging (JAI) packages on your system. The main page for Sun's Java 2, Standard Edition (J2SE) is **http://java.sun.com/j2se**. At the time this book was written, the version that JavaHMO has been tested with is version 1.4.2, which can be downloaded from **http://java.sun.com/j2se/1.4.2/download.html**. I tend to download the J2SE Software Development Kit (J2SDK), but the standard J2SE works fine. Installable versions of the J2SDK (`j2sdk-1_4_2_03-linux-i586.bin`) and JAI (`jai-1_1_2-lib-linux-i586-jdk.bin`) packages are provided in the BATBD CD's `connectivity/JavaHMO/Linux` directory. To install these packages, execute these files using the command "**sh** *name-of-package-file.*"

◆ Mac OS X users must install the Java Advanced Imaging (JAI) package on their systems—Java is installed by default on all Mac OS X systems. An installable version of the JAI package is provided as a Macintosh Disk Image (DMG file) in the BATBD CD's `connectivity/JavaHMO/Mac_OS_X` directory. After double-clicking on this disk image to mount it on your Mac OS X desktop as a disk named ***Java3D and Java Advanced Imaging***, open that drive and double-click the `Java3D_and_JAI.mpkg` file to install the JAI package on your system. Once the installation completes, you can drag the virtual drive to the Trash icon to dismount it.

◆ Windows users don't have to do anything special, for once. Java and the Java Advanced Imaging (JAI) package are installed as part of the JavaHMO installation. The Windows installer for the JavaHMO package is provided in the BATBD CD's `connectivity/JavaHMO/Windows` directory. Double-click the `JavaHMO-1.2.exe` file to install Java, JAI, and the JavaHMO package on your system. You will have to accept Sun's licensing agreements for Java and JAI during the installation process.

---

 **TIP**

Like any open source software package, JavaHMO is always being updated and enhanced. You can check for the latest versions of JavaHMO or any related packages at the URL **http://javahmo.sourceforge.net/download.html**.

Once Java and JAI are installed, you can install JavaHMO as follows:

◆ *Linux* Install the JavaHMO-1.2.rpm package if you are running Red Hat Linux or any other version of Linux that supports archive files in Red Hat Package Manager (RPM) format. If your Linux distribution doesn't support RPMs or you haven't installed support for them, you can use the **cd /** command to change your working directory to / and extract the contents of the `JavaHMO-1.2.tgz` file as root to install the JavaHMO package. Both of these files are provided in the BATBD CD's `connectivity/JavaHMO/Linux` directory.

◆ *Mac OS X* Double-click the JavaHMO.dmg disk image file (provided in the BATBD CD's connectivity/JavaHMO/Mac_OS_X directory) to mount it on your desktop as a disk named JavaHMO, open that drive, and then double-click the JavaHMO.mpkg package file to install JavaHMO on your system. Once the installation completes, you can drag the virtual drive to the Trash icon to dismount it. Once installed, you must restart your computer in order to correctly start the JavaHMO server.

◆ *Windows* Everything was installed when you double-clicked on the JavaHMO-1.2.exe file in the previous list.

Once installed, JavaHMO is configured through a Web interface that you can access at **http://127.0.0.1:8081/configure**, as shown in Figure 10.3. You must start the JavaHMO server before you can configure it. When you install JavaHMO on a Windows system, a shortcut for JavaHMO Configuration (labeled *JavaHMO*) is created on your desktop.

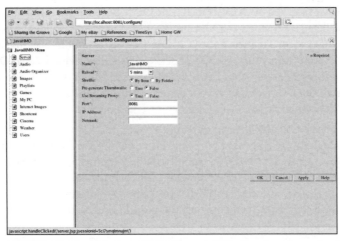

**FIGURE 10.3** *The JavaHMO Server's Web-based configuration interface*

To start the JavaHMO server, do the following:

◆ *Linux* Restart your system or, as root, manually execute its startup script by typing the command **/etc/rc.d/init.d/JavaHMO start**.

◆ *Mac OS X* Double-click the JavaHMO Control application in the system's Applications folder.

◆ *Windows* The server is automatically started by the installation process and will be automatically started after each reboot.

After you have started the JavaHMO server, you can configure it by using your favorite Web browser. Figure 10.4 shows the JavaHMO server's configuration interface on a Mac OS X system in Apple's Safari browser. Figure 10.5 shows the JavaHMO server's configuration interface on a Windows XP system in Microsoft's Internet Exploder browser.

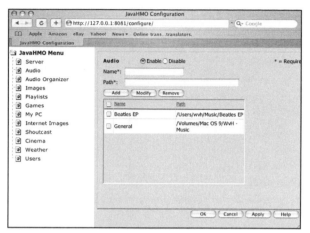

**FIGURE 10.4**   *The JavaHMO Server's audio configuration pane on Mac OS X*

 **TIP**

If you are using a Mac OS X system and have not integrated your online audio collection with iTunes, JavaHMO is much easier to use than the official TiVo Desktop application that TiVo provides. The TiVo Desktop application is completely integrated with iTunes, and it does not enable you to export audio files that have not been imported into (or indexed by) iTunes. The JavaHMO server is directory-oriented, enabling you to quickly export directories containing MP3 audio files, regardless of whether iTunes knows about them or not.

The JavaHMO project has a great deal of excellent documentation that is available on their SourceForge site, which I therefore won't duplicate here. However, to get started, the most critical aspect of setting up JavaHMO to serve MP3s to your TiVo is to tell it where to find the audio files that you want to export from your system. To do this, click the Audio item in the left pane of the configuration interface in your browser. A dialog like the one shown in Figures 10.4 and 10.5 displays. To enable audio export in general, click the Enable radio button at the top of the right pane. To add a specific directory to the list of those exported by the JavaHMO server, enter the name that you want to associate with this directory in the Name field, enter the full path to the directory containing the files that you want to export in the Path field, and click Apply.

On the television attached to any TiVo running the Home Media Features, any of the items that you have enabled in the JavaHMO Menu pane of the JavaHMO server's configuration interface will be visible in the TiVo's Music & Pictures menu. My personal focus in using the JavaHMO server is in exporting audio files, but the JavaHMO server also enables you to export images, access ShoutCast audio streams, display local movie listings, and even display weather information about a selected zip code. The JavaHMO project is another excellent example of the power and usability of open source software!

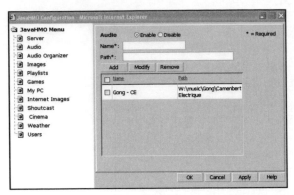

**FIGURE 10.5** *The JavaHMO Server's audio configuration pane on Windows XP*

# HACKING *THE* TiVo

## Chapter 11

SECOND EDITION

### *Getting and Installing New Software for Your TiVo*

One of the best aspects of hacking your TiVo is that with a hacked TiVo it is possible to install a variety of interesting software on the machine beyond the great software that your TiVo already runs out of the box. As explained in Chapter 8, "Connecting the Universe to Your TiVo," a lot of free software for your TiVo is already available on the Internet (or on the CD that accompanies this book). This software is all ready-to-run once you install and execute it on a hacked TiVo. In addition to the software on the CD, Chapter 14, "Other TiVo Hacking Resources," provides a variety of sources of free software that wouldn't fit on the CD, or that I didn't have much experience with personally.

Unfortunately, just because software is available doesn't always make it easy to understand or install and use. Throughout this book, I've explained how to install and use a good number of interesting software packages, but you're bound to find something that sounds intriguing that isn't covered here. New packages are coming out every day, especially now that hackers and books such as this one have explained how to get into the TiVo Series 2 machines. Many of the most popular TiVo hacks were written in the early days of the TiVo revolution, when folks like Tridge, embeem, and others hacked into their Series 1 machines. Opening up the Series 2 machines, which are obviously faster and more powerful, extends that same hackability to the Series 2. Who knows what cool new software for your TiVo may appear tomorrow?

This chapter explains how to unpack and install software in the most common archiving and compression formats used in TiVo and Linux development, how to install the compilers provided on the BATBD CD so that you can compile your own software for your TiVo, and discusses some of the more interesting TiVo development projects going on at various spots on the Internet.

# Mounting the BATBD CD on Your System

In order to access some of the TiVo software discussed in this book, you'll need to mount the CD that accompanies this book so that you can access its contents. If you're using a Mac OS X or Windows system, this is usually a NO-OP (a null operation, in computer terms), because most Windows and Mac systems are configured to automatically mount data CDs when they are inserted into your personal computer's CD-ROM drive. This is generally known as *auto-mounting*. The BATBD CD that accompanies this book is readable on Linux, Mac OS X, and Windows systems, so you should be able to access its contents regardless of the type of computer system that you happen to be using.

Things can be slightly more complex for Linux users. Linux desktop environments, such as GNOME and KDE, are usually configured to auto-mount data CDs; however, if you're using an X Window system window manager rather than a full-fledged desktop (as I do), or if you want to access the contents of the BATBD CD after you've booted from it, you may have to *mount* the CD manually so that you can browse its contents. The Linux **mount** command makes the contents of a CD available through a standard directory on your Linux system. Although I discuss mounting the BATBD CD as part of various sets of instructions given elsewhere in this book, this section provides a convenient central location for that information.

Windows systems transparently make the contents of your CD-ROM drive available in the My Computer folder. Mac OS X systems, although they run Unix under their covers, usually make the contents of a mounted CD visible as an icon on your desktop, though this can be configured in the Finder's Preference menu. Linux (and Un*x) systems require that you make the CD available through a directory that must already exist on your system. Mac OS X systems automatically create an appropriate directory for you in the /Volumes folder on your Mac before mounting the CD. On many Linux systems, you'll need to create an appropriate directory (known as a *mount-point* in Un*x terms) before trying to mount the CD. Most Linux users mount CDs on the directory /mnt/cdrom. This directory already exists if you've booted from the BATBD CD, but if you want to access the BATBD from a system that is already running Linux, you may have to create it manually, as in the following example:

su

*Password:*

 mkdir /mnt/cdrom

The Linux **su** (substitute user-id) command with no arguments enables you to become the superuser (aka the *root* user) on your system. The **mkdir** (make directory) command will then create the directory /mnt/cdrom.

---

 **NOTE**

The alternative Linux **sudo** command is a popular way to execute privileged commands on a Linux system without simply using the **su** command with no arguments. The **sudo** command enables you to execute a command as another user on your Linux system (sudo stands for *substitute-userid do,* i.e., perform some action using a substitute user-id), and is configured by modifying a file called /etc/sudoers. This is the easiest way to execute privileged commands on a Linux system without simply using the **su** command with no arguments to become the superuser, which is often frowned upon nowadays. I'm not using the **sudo** command here because the chances that you're hacking your TiVo on a Linux system where you don't have the root password are probably pretty small.

---

After you've created this directory, you can mount the BATBD CD using a command like the following:

 mount -r /dev/hdX /mnt/cdrom

When issuing this command, you should replace the letter *X* with the letter corresponding to your CD-ROM drive. This will be **b** if your CD-ROM drive is attached as the slave on your primary IDE interface, **c** if your CD-ROM drive is attached as the master on your secondary IDE interface, or **d** if your CD-ROM drive is attached as the slave on your secondary IDE interface. If you specified the correct device, the drive will mount correctly and silently. If you accidentally leave out the **–r** option, you will see the following warning message stating that the CD-ROM drive is mounted as read-only, which is true and can be safely ignored:

mount: block device /dev/hdc is write-protected, mounting read-only

You can now access the contents of the BATBD CD by using the Linux **cd** command to change directory to /mnt/cdrom, and explore the contents of the CD just like any other directory on your Linux system.

**NOTE**

Before shutting down your Linux system, you should unmount the CD using the Linux **umount** command. (Note the missing 'n'—who wants to type that extra character, anyway?) Unmounting and removing the CD ensures that your system doesn't try to remount it the next time you boot your Linux box. To unmount a CD, you cannot be accessing it through Linux—in other words, you can't unmount a CD when you're exploring it from a Linux shell, or when any process is running that was started in any directory on the CD. To unmount a Linux CD, you must usually still be the superuser, as explained earlier. (It never hurts to be the superuser ;-) Terminate any processes that you may have started when working in any directory on the CD, use the Linux **cd** command to change directory to some other directory on your Linux system, and then issue the **umount** command as in the following example:

```
cd ~
umount /mnt/cdrom
```

You can then eject the CD by issuing the Linux **eject** command:

```
eject
```

If you see a message like the following, you still have some process running in or on the CD:

```
umount: /mnt/cdrom: device is busy
```

If you can't figure out what process it is, you can simply shut down your system and manually eject the CD the next time you restart it—not the best Linux etiquette, but a solution is a solution.

# Installing Software on Your TiVo

Once you've found an interesting package that is supposedly already compiled for your TiVo, figuring out how to extract software from the various archive file formats can be quite challenging.

## Identifying Binary File Formats

After you've located some interesting TiVo software, you need to figure out whether it's for the TiVo model that you actually have. This is hard to do when just looking at a file. Ones and zeroes that are designed to run on a PPC-based TiVo Series 1 look much like the ones and zeroes that are designed to run on a MIPS-based Series 2 machine.

If you're using a Linux system as your personal computer, you can easily get information about the platform any binary application was compiled for by using the **file** command. The **file** command has a number of options, but is usually used with a single argument, which is the name of the file in which you're interested. For example, using the **file** command to examine a file called tnlited from a TiVo Series 1 would look like the following:

```
# file tnlited
tnlited: ELF 32-bit MSB executable, PowerPC or cisco 4500,
        version 1 (SYSV), dynamically linked (uses shared libs),
            stripped
```

### NOTE

The output of the **file** command typically displays on a single line—these examples are broken across multiple lines for readability.

While this is all very interesting, the most important part of the **file** command's output is the fact that this executable is compiled for use on a PowerPC system (such as the TiVo Series 1).

Similarly, using the **file** command to examine a version of the tnlited file from a TiVo Series 2 would look like the following:

```
# file tnlited
tnlited: ELF 32-bit MSB MIPS-I executable, MIPS, version 1 (SYSV),
        for GNU/Linux 2.2.15, dynamically linked (uses shared libs),
            stripped
```

In this case, the file is an executable compiled for a MIPS system, such as a TiVo Series 2.

# Uncompressing ZIP and GZ Files

Most applications for systems like those for the TiVos are distributed in single files that have been compressed in special formats. This reduces the amount of space they consume, as well as reducing the time that it takes to transfer the file from one system to another. Two of the most common formats for compressing files for Linux systems (such as the TiVo) are the zip format and gzip formats. (Windows and DOS users should be quite familiar with zip files.)

### TIP

Binaries of the unzip utility for both Series 1 and Series 2 machines are found in the hack archives provided in the BATBD CD's hack_dirs directory. The gzip utility (which can both compress and decompress archives) is provided as part of the Series 2 software from TiVo. A version of the gunzip utility (which decompresses) is provided courtesy of BusyBox in the archives on the BATBD CD.

Files compressed using the zip utility generally have the file extension ".zip" at the end of their names. Zip archives can contain one or more files, but generally contain a number of files. These files may be included as standard files, or they may be contained within a directory that is also archived in the zip file.

The **unzip** command decompresses archive files with a .zip extension, as in the following example:

```
$ unzip tivovbi-1.03.zip
Archive:  tivovbi-1.03.zip
   creating: tivovbi/
  inflating: tivovbi/tivovbi
  inflating: tivovbi/README
  inflating: tivovbi/LICENSE
  inflating: tivovbi/CHANGES
   creating: tivovbi/src/
  inflating: tivovbi/src/osd.c
  inflating: tivovbi/src/makefile
  inflating: tivovbi/src/osd.h
  inflating: tivovbi/src/font.h
  inflating: tivovbi/src/tivocc.c
```

In this case, the zip archive contains a directory—when the contents of the archive file are extracted, the directory is created first, and then all of the extracted files are created inside the directory.

The gunzip utility extracts the contents of archived files compressed using **gzip**. The gzip utility itself provides a **-d** option to enable it to perform decompression. (The gzip and gunzip binaries are often the same file on standard Linux systems.) Compressed files with the .gz extension are usually either single files or archives of some other type, which then must be extracted. On Linux systems, these archived files are usually tar format files, as discussed in the next section.

Both gzip and gunzip work silently, unless told to be verbose using other command-line options. To use gunzip to extract the contents of an archived file, simply issue the **gunzip** command followed by the name of the archived file that you want to decompress, as in the following example:

```
$ gunzip newtext2osd-1.4.tar.gz
```

This command would create the file `newtext2osd-1.4.tar` in the current directory, which then could be extracted using the **tar** command, as explained in the next section.

To use the **gzip** command to extract the contents of an archived file, simply issue the **gzip** command with its **-d** (decompress) option, followed by the name of the archived file that you want to decompress, as in the following example:

```
$ gzip -d newtext2osd-1.4.tar.gz
```

As in the previous example, this command would create the file `newtext2osd-1.4.tar` in the current directory, which could then be extracted using the **tar** command, as explained in the next section.

---

 **TIP**

If you aren't sure if an archive file contains a directory or whether it simply will dump files in your working directory, you can use the **unzip** command's **-t** (test) option to see what the archive contains without actually extracting files, as in the following example:

```
$ unzip -t tivovbi-1.03.zip
Archive:  tivovbi-1.03.zip
    testing: tivovbi/              OK
    testing: tivovbi/tivovbi       OK
    testing: tivovbi/README        OK
    testing: tivovbi/LICENSE       OK
    testing: tivovbi/CHANGES       OK
    testing: tivovbi/src/          OK
    testing: tivovbi/src/osd.c     OK
    testing: tivovbi/src/makefile  OK
    testing: tivovbi/src/osd.h     OK
    testing: tivovbi/src/font.h    OK
    testing: tivovbi/src/tivocc.c  OK
No errors detected in compressed data of tivovbi-1.03.zip.
```

# Extracting Files from TAR and TGZ Archives

The **tar** command, which stands for "tape archiver," is one of the oldest Unix commands, and it's not surprising that the format of the outputted files it produces (known as *tar files*) is probably the most common way in which directories are archived on Unix and Linux systems.

---

 **TIP**

Binaries of the tar utility for both Series 1 and Series 2 machines are provided in the hack archives found in the BATBD CD's hack_dirs directory. The **tar** command for a Series 1 system is provided courtesy of BusyBox. The **tar** command for a Series 2 machine is a stand-alone command.

### TiVo Extracting the Contents of Tar Files without the tar Command

Extracting the contents of the first tar file you have on a TiVo can be challenging. The **tar** command is provided in the tar files provided on the BATBD CD. If you extract the contents of the tar file while your TiVo drive is in your PC and you've booted from the BATBD CD, it's no problem—the BATBD CD comes with a built-in version of the **tar** command. However, what if you forget, or need to transfer the file to a networked TiVo manually?

All TiVo software distributions include another early Unix archiving utility, **cpio** (which stands for *Copy Input To Output*). The version of this command provided on the TiVos can extract the contents of a tar file (specified as TARFILE in this example) by using the following syntax:

```
cpio -iduvH tar <  TARFILE
```

The **cpio** command options have the following meanings:

- *I*  Extract files from its input
- *d*  Create directories as needed
- *u*  Unconditionally creates files, even if they already exist
- *v*  Be verbose about what's going on
- *H*  Use the specified archive format (tar, in this case)

An example of using this command on a TiVo is as follows:

```
# cpio -iduv -H tar < newtext2osd-1.4.tar
newtext2osd-1.4
newtext2osd-1.4/README
newtext2osd-1.4/LICENSE
newtext2osd-1.4/CHANGES
newtext2osd-1.4/src
newtext2osd-1.4/src/osd.c
newtext2osd-1.4/src/makefile
newtext2osd-1.4/src/osd.h
newtext2osd-1.4/src/font.h
newtext2osd-1.4/src/osd.o
newtext2osd-1.4/src/newtext2osd.o
newtext2osd-1.4/src/testgrid
newtext2osd-1.4/src/newtext2osd.c
newtext2osd-1.4/newtext2osd
388 blocks
```

To extract the contents of a tar file, you use the **tar** command's **x** (extract) and **f** (file) options. The **f** option must be followed by the name of the tar file that contains the contents you want to extract, as in the following example:

```
$ tar xf newtext2osd-1.4.tar
```

This command would extract whatever was in the specified tar file to the current directory. Since most people usually like to see what they're getting from an archive, it is common to include the **v** (verbose) option, as in the following example:

```
$ tar xvf newtext2osd-1.4.tar
newtext2osd-1.4/
newtext2osd-1.4/README
newtext2osd-1.4/LICENSE
newtext2osd-1.4/CHANGES
newtext2osd-1.4/src/
newtext2osd-1.4/src/osd.c
newtext2osd-1.4/src/makefile
newtext2osd-1.4/src/osd.h
newtext2osd-1.4/src/font.h
newtext2osd-1.4/src/osd.o
newtext2osd-1.4/src/newtext2osd.o
newtext2osd-1.4/src/testgrid
newtext2osd-1.4/src/newtext2osd.c
newtext2osd-1.4/newtext2osd
```

You may also encounter archived files with the extension .tgz. These are tar files that also have been compressed using gzip, typically in a single operation. To extract the tar file contents on a TiVo, you can use a Linux pipe to tell the **gzip** command to decompress a file, write the uncompressed output, and then pipe that to a **tar** command that actually extracts the contents of the stream of data that it is receiving from the **gzip** command, as in the following example:

```
$ gzip -cd newtext2osd-1.4.tar.gz ¦ tar xvf -
newtext2osd-1.4/
newtext2osd-1.4/README
newtext2osd-1.4/LICENSE
newtext2osd-1.4/CHANGES
newtext2osd-1.4/src/
newtext2osd-1.4/src/osd.c
newtext2osd-1.4/src/makefile
newtext2osd-1.4/src/osd.h
newtext2osd-1.4/src/font.h
```

```
newtext2osd-1.4/src/osd.o
newtext2osd-1.4/src/newtext2osd.o
newtext2osd-1.4/src/testgrid
newtext2osd-1.4/src/newtext2osd.c
newtext2osd-1.4/newtext2osd
```

This is just another example of the power and flexibility of Linux. The version of tar provided on many desktop Linux systems has built-in support for gzip compression and decompression. You usually can do all of this with a single **tar** command, such as the following:

```
$ tar zxvf newtext2osd-1.4.tar.gz
newtext2osd-1.4/
newtext2osd-1.4/README
newtext2osd-1.4/LICENSE
newtext2osd-1.4/CHANGES
newtext2osd-1.4/src/
newtext2osd-1.4/src/osd.c
newtext2osd-1.4/src/makefile
newtext2osd-1.4/src/osd.h
newtext2osd-1.4/src/font.h
newtext2osd-1.4/src/osd.o
newtext2osd-1.4/src/newtext2osd.o
newtext2osd-1.4/src/testgrid
newtext2osd-1.4/src/newtext2osd.c
newtext2osd-1.4/newtext2osd
```

# Installing Software Packaged with TPM

TPM, the TiVo Package Manager, is an application developed by the wizardly TiVo hacker "Sleeper," and provides a convenient way of packaging many of the latest TiVo hacks. Although TPM packages are usually zipped to save space, unzipping them generally produces two files, a file with the .meta extension, which provides meta information (information about information) about the packaged hack, and a file with the .tpm extension, which is the actual file that you will want to install. TPM files are actually Linux shell scripts, which are Linux command files that you can either execute directly or execute by executing the Linux command interpreter, **/bin/bash**, with the name of the TPM file as an argument, as in one of the following two examples:

```
chmod 755 30SecondSkip-1.0-2.tivo.tpm ; ./ 30SecondSkip-1.0-2.tivo.tpm
/bin/bash 30SecondSkip-1.0-2.tivo.tpm
```

This will prompt you for a number of things during the installation process, but will "do the right thing."

**TIP**

At one point in the installation process, you will be prompted for the name of the directory in which you want to install the software contained in the TPM archive that you are installing. Unless you want to change the directory in which the software is installed, always press the Return key at this point. If you accidentally answer "yes" (as I have done once or twice), the TPM program will become confused because it thinks that you want to install software into a local directory named "yes."

TPM provides a nice way of installing software on your TiVo because it keeps track of what is installed on your system and does a lot of work for you automatically as part of the installation process. Thanks, Sleeper! Information about the packages that have been installed on your TiVo from archives produced using TPM is stored in the file /etc/tpm/ installed.packages on your TiVo.

 **TIP**

Not all TPM archives are completely alike—different versions of TPM had slightly different capabilities. If you have problems installing a TPM archive using the **/bin/bash** command as explained previously, try making the archive executable on your TiVo by executing the following command:

chmod 755 *tpm-archive-file*

Replace *tpm-archive-file* with the name of the TPM file that you are trying to install. You should then be able to install whatever is in the TPM archive by executing the command *./tpm-archive-file*.

The TPM program is available on the BATBD CD in the directory TPM. Some hacks packaged with TPM are provided on the BATBD CD in the directory TPM/tpm_packages.

# Installing Hacks from the BATBD CD

The BATBD CD that accompanies this book contains archive files in tar format that contain collections of my favorite hacks for Series 1 and Series 2 TiVos. Information about installing these on their respective types of TiVos is integrated into the sections of Chapter 8 that describe how to get a command prompt on Series 1 and Series 2 TiVos. This section explains how to install or reinstall the hacks in those archive files in case you want to do it manually. Some TiVo upgrades or problems (such as running out of disk space on your /var partition) may cause your TiVo to delete all non-essential directories in /var, which usually includes the /var/hack directory where your TiVo hacks are usually stored.

If you've already hacked your TiVo and want or need to re-install the hacks from the BATBD CD manually, do the following:

1. Remove the drive from your TiVo and put it in your PC as described in the section of Chapter 4 entitled "Working with TiVo Disk Drives."

2. Boot your PC from the BATBD CD and mount the BATBD CD as described earlier in this chapter.

3. Mount the /var partition from your TiVo drive on the directory /mnt/tivo, as in the following example:

   ```
   mount /dev/hdX9 /mnt/tivo
   ```

   Replace the letter *X* with the drive letter that corresponds to the letter associated with the TiVo drive in your PC. This will be **b** if your TiVo drive is attached as the slave on your primary IDE interface, **c** if your TiVo drive is attached as the master on your secondary IDE interface, or **d** if your TiVo drive is attached as the slave on your secondary IDE interface.

4. Change directory (**cd**) to the directory /mnt/tivo.

5. Extract the contents of the archive file that is appropriate for your TiVo. If yours is a Series 1 TiVo, execute the following command:

   ```
   tar xvf /mnt/cdrom/hack_dirs/ hack1.tar
   ```

   If yours is a Series 2 TiVo, execute the following command:

   ```
   tar xvf /mnt/cdrom/hack_dirs/ hack2.tar
   ```

6. Change directory to the root directory (**cd** /) and unmount the CD-ROM and TiVo partition:

   ```
   umount /mnt/tivo
   umount /mnt/cdrom
   ```

7. You can now shutdown your PC by using the **halt** command, remove the TiVo drive from your PC and replace it in your TiVo, restart the TiVo, and you should have access to your favorite hacks again.

The instructions in this section only explain how to install the basic archives of hacks provided with the BATBD CD. If you have installed other hacks using TPM, you will have to copy the TPM archive files over to your TiVo and reinstall those hacks manually.

# Safe Locations for Storing Your TiVo Hacks

As mentioned earlier in this book, most TiVos perform a number of file and general sanity checks on the contents of their root partitions. TiVo's software update process can overwrite any of the default partitions on your TiVo, which may cause you to lose your hard-won TiVo hacks if they're stored in the filesystems mounted at / or /var. Also, newer versions of the TiVo software are more and more paranoid about verifying the integrity and source of every piece of software in standard TiVo partitions. Versions of the TiVo software newer than Version 2.5 will delete modified versions of standard TiVo command files, programs, and libraries, replacing them with "stock" versions of the same files from the original TiVo software distributions. In some cases, directory hierarchies that are not present in the partitions provided with original TiVo software distributions will be automatically deleted.

As you amass a collection of your favorite TiVo hacks, you may want to consider creating a special partition on your TiVo disk in which to store these and mounting this partition elsewhere on your TiVo to access your favorite tweaks. As a special partition, it will not be affected by TiVo software updates—its mount point may be deleted, but nothing else.

Manually creating a partition on your disk and formatting it with the right type of filesystem is complex, but it can be done as part of a disk upgrade if you create a new swap partition, leaving the old one (usually 64 MB in size) available for reuse, For some suggestions and troubleshooting pointers, see the TiVo forums discussed in Chapter 14.

# Installing Cross-Compilers for TiVo Development

With a Linux system, an exponentially larger amount of free software is available in source form that you may want to run on your TiVo. However, figuring out how to build software on a desktop system that is compiled to run on your TiVo can be perplexing, unless you're already familiar with software such as GCC and the concept of cross-compiling applications on one machine so that they will run on another.

The BATBD CD included with this book includes cross-compilers for both Series 1 and Series 2 machines. As discussed in Chapter 10, cross-compilers run on one type of system, but produce binary output targeted for another type of system. In the case of the cross-compilers included with this book, they run on an x86 Linux system and produce output targeted for the TiVo Series 1 or the TiVo Series 2.

The BATBD CD includes the following cross-compilers for your TiVo:

- ♦ *macintosh/usr.local.powerpc–TiVo.dmg*   A cross-compilation environment for the TiVo Series 1 that runs on the Macintosh (only under Mac OS X). This is a Macintosh Disk Image (DMG) file that you can open as a virtual disk on any Mac OS X system. You can then execute the usr.local.tivo.pkg installer that it contains, which will install /usr/local/powerpc-TiVo on your Mac OS X system.

- ♦ *macintosh/osx-mips-xcomp.tgz*   A cross-compilation environment for the TiVo Series 2 that runs on the Macintosh (only under Mac OS X).

- ♦ *xcompilers/Series1/usr.local.powerpc–tivo.tgz*   An early cross-compiler for the TiVo Series 1 that requires relatively little disk space.

- ♦ *xcompilers/Series1/tivodev-2.5_linux-x86_dtype1.tgz*   Version 1 of an extensive cross-compilation environment for the TiVo Series 1

◆ *xcompilers/Series1/tivodev-2.5_linux-x86_dtype2.tgz*  Version 2 of the same extensive cross-compilation environment for the TiVo Series 1. It is somewhat larger, but much improved and enriched.

◆ *xcompilers/Series2/usr.local.tivo-mips_bu211.tgz*  A cross-compiler for the TiVo Series 2 that uses Version 2.11 of the binutils package. (The binutils package contains compilation-related software like the GNU assembler, archiver, linker, loader, and so forth.)

◆ *xcompilers/Series2/usr.local.tivo-mips_bu213.tgz*  A cross-compiler for the TiVo Series 2 that uses Version 2.13 of the binutils package.

◆ *xcompilers/usr.local.tivo-s2.tgz*  A cross-compiler for the TiVo Series 2 that includes Version 3.4.0 of GCC.

# Selecting and Installing a Cross-Compiler for the TiVo Series 1

If you are using a Series 1 machine, the usr.local.powerpc-tivo.tgz cross-compiler on the BATBD CD is a good starting point for your Linux-based, cross-compilation experiments. It is easier and smaller to install, though much less powerful. To install it, **cd** to the root of your computer and extract its contents, as in the following example:

```
# cd /
# tar zxvf PATH-TO-CD/xcompilers/Series1/usr.local.powerpc-tivo.tgz
```

After a hundred yards or so of output, the installation will complete. Your Series 1 cross-compiler then is installed in the appropriate subdirectories of /usr/local/tivo. To begin cross-compiling, all you have to do is add the directory /usr/local/tivo/bin to your PATH, as in the following example:

```
$ export PATH=/usr/local/tivo/bin:${PATH}
```

You should be ready to compile applications for your Series 1 machine using the standard **gcc** command.

 **WARNING**

When using cross-compilers that have the same names as your desktop Linux system's compiler, make sure that you add this directory only to your PATH environment variable when you want to build applications for your Series 1 machine. If you arbitrarily add the directory /usr/local/tivo/bin to the front of your PATH, the cross-compiling GCC will be the first C compiler in your PATH at all times, and everything you compile will execute only on your TiVo—probably not what you had in mind.

For a much more complete TiVo development environment, install the xcompilers/Series1/tivodev-2.5_linux-x86_dtype2.tgz cross-compiler and general all-around development environment from the BATBD CD. This is Version 2 of a complete Series 1 development environment used by well-known TiVo hackers to build their favorite TiVo software. To do so, make sure your working directory is /home and extract the contents of xcompilers/Series1/tivodev-2.5_linux-x86_dtype2.tgz, as in the following example:

```
# cd /home
# tar zxvf /PATH-TO-CD/xcompilers/Series1/tivodev-2.5_linux-x86_dtype2.tgz
```

After extracting the contents of the archive, **cd** to the directory /home/tivodev and read the README file for complete instructions about taking advantage of this impressively complete and robust development environment. It contains much more than the us.local.powerpc cross-compiler, but it also requires substantially more disk space.

**NOTE**

Version 1 of the same development environment is provided in the file xcompilers/Series1/tivodev-2.5_linux-x86_dtype1.tgz on the BATBD CD, primarily for comparative purposes, but also in case you encounter problems with Version 2.

**TIP**

As mentioned earlier, the file macintosh/usr.local.powerpc-TiVo.dmg on the BATBD CD contains a cross-compilation environment for the TiVo Series 1 that runs under Mac OS X on the Macintosh. This is a Macintosh Disk Image (DMG) file that you can open as a virtual disk on any Mac OS X system. After it is mounted, you can double-click the usr.local.tivo.pkg installer that it contains in order to install /usr/local/powerpc-TiVo on the system. You can then invoke the compiler from any command-line window under Mac OS X, such as a Terminal window or an **xterm** (if you are running X11 on your Mac OS X system).

# Selecting and Installing a Cross-Compiler for the TiVo Series 2

The decision as to which Linux-based, cross-compiler to install on your Series 2 machine is much simpler. Two are provided on the BATBD CD—the only difference is based on the version of the GNU binutils package that they include. The binutils package contains compilation-related software like the GNU assembler, archiver, linker, loader, and so on. I would definitely suggest that you try first the version based on binutils 2.1.3 (usr.local.tivo-mips_bu213.tgz), by changing the directory to the root directory of your Linux system and extracting its contents, as in the following example:

```
# cd /
# tar zxvf /PATH_TO_CD/xcompilers/Series2/usr.local.tivo-mips_bu213.tgz
```

After a huge amount of output listing the files that are installing, the installation will complete. Your Series 2 cross-compiler will be installed in the appropriate subdirectories of /usr/local/tivo-mips. To begin cross-compiling, all you have to do is add the directory /usr/local/tivo-mips/bin to your PATH, as in the following example:

```
$ export PATH=/usr/local/tivo-mips/bin:${PATH}
```

You now should be ready to compile applications for your Series 2 system by using the standard **gcc** command.

 **WARNING**

When using cross-compilers that have the same names as your desktop Linux system's compiler, make sure that you add this directory only to your PATH environment variable when you want to build applications for your Series 2 machine. If you arbitrarily add the /usr/local/tivo-mips/bin directory to the front of your PATH, the cross-compiling GCC will be the first C compiler in your PATH at all times and everything you compiled will only execute on your TiVo—probably not what you had in mind.

If you subsequently have problems using this cross-compiler, you can try falling back to the other version by deleting your current version and installing the older one in its place, as in the following example:

```
# cd /
# rm -rf /usr/local/tivo-mips
# tar zxvf /PATH_TO_CD/xcompilers/Series2/usr.local.tivo-mips_bu211.tgz
```

If you continue to have problems with the cross-compiler, the TiVo forums are your friends. Many people are actively using forums, so the problems that you are experiencing are likely configuration issues or slight cases of "pilot error."

 **TIP**

As mentioned earlier, the file macintosh/osx-mips-xcomp.tgz on the BATBD CD contains a cross-compilation environment for the TiVo Series 2 that runs under Mac OS X on the Macintosh. To install this cross-compiler on a Mac OS X system, create the directory /usr/local/tivo-mips, **cd** there, and extract the contents of the archive using the **tar zxvf osx-mips-xcomp.tgz** command. You can then invoke the compiler from any command-line window under Mac OS X, such as a Terminal window or an xterm (if you are running X11 on your Mac OS X system) by typing **/usr/local/tivo-mips/bin/gcc** or (just to be on the safe side) by typing **/usr/local/tivo-mips/bin/mips-TiVo-linux-gcc**.

# Cross-Compiling Software on a Linux System

The syntax required to cross-compile applications can be somewhat arcane. If you are lucky and the application that you are cross-compiling uses a simple Makefile, you may simply be able to cross-compile an application for your TiVo by using a command line such as the following:

```
CC=/path/to/tivo/gcc make
```

where */path/to/tivo/gcc* is the full path of the gcc executable for the TiVo cross-compiler that you have installed (something like **/usr/local/tivo-s2/bin/gcc**).

If the application that you are cross-compiling requires access to system header files, you may need to modify its Makefile to tell the cross-compiler where to look for those header files. This can usually be added to the CFLAGS setting in your Makefile, as in the following example:

```
CFLAGS= -O2 -I/path/to/tivo/compiler/include
```

where */path/to/tivo/compiler/include* is the full path of the include directory that is part of your cross-compiler installation (something like /usr/local/tivo-s2/include). If you are modifying the Makefile, you may also want to set the CC variable to the */path/to/tivo/compiler* mentioned earlier.

More modern and complex open source applications use an automated configuration process (known as a **configure** script) that generates the Makefiles required in order to build your application. These automatically generated Makefiles are hard to read and should rarely be edited manually. Instead, you should set appropriate environment variables and pass arguments to the configure script that tell it what you're trying to do, as in the following example:

```
CFLAGS="-static -I/usr/local/tivo-s2/include -D_FILE_OFFSET_BITS=64" \
    ./configure  --build=i686-pc-linux-gnu --host=i686-pc-linux-gnu \
                --target=mips-TiVo-linux --prefix=/usr/local/tivo-s2
```

This example uses the tivo-s2 MIPS cross-compiler provided on the BATBD CD that accompanies this book, and configures the compilation of your application to generate a static binary, look in the /usr/local/tivo-s2/include directory for header files, create binaries that support large files, and shows that I am cross-compiling on an i686 Linux system. Commands like this one should be typed on a single line, though you can use the backslash character ('\') as shown in the example to escape any carriage returns that you press when typing it in.

If you have configured your application using as shown in this example, you could then cross-compile your application using a command line like the following:

```
PATH=/usr/local/tivo-s2/bin:${PATH} make
```

More detailed information about using **configure** scripts, using GCC in general, and cross-compiling is available in the GCC documentation or in one of the books about GCC. My personal favorite is "The Definitive Guide to GCC" by Kurt Wall and yours truly. I never have trouble finding information in there, for some reason.

# Stand-Alone TiVo Tools and Development Projects

This section highlights some of the more active TiVo development projects and tools that are available on the Web today.

## An Alternate UI in the TiVo Web Project

The TiVo Web Project, aka *TiVoWeb*, is one of the more impressive bits of TiVo software I've ever seen. The TiVoWeb Project was created by a TiVo hacker, lightn (along with other contributors such as embeem), who deserves all of the kudos he's ever received for this truly amazing piece of software. The home page of the TiVo Web Project is at `http://tivo.lightn.org`. The ability of the TiVoWeb Project to schedule recordings from any Web browser is only a tiny subset of the bells and whistles that it provides.

As cool as the TiVo Web Project was, it didn't work all that well on Series2 machines due to changes in the TiVo filesystem and associated utilities. Therefore, it has recently received a major upgrade known as *TiVoWebPlus*, thanks to the TiVo hackers falcontx, mrblack51, and others. The official TiVoWebPlus Web site is **http://tivo.fp2000.org/twp** and provides a link to the latest TiVoWebPlus software, which is also always available at the URL **http://www.dealdatabase.com/forum/showthread.php?t=30564** on the DealDatabase forum. (A copy of the latest revision of the TiVoWebPlus software at the time this book was updated [1.0-final] is also included on the CD that accompanies this book, as the file `TiVoWebPlus-1.0-final.tivo.tpm`.) As discussed in more detail in Chapter 8, the TiVoWebPlus Project enables you to control your TiVo remotely, get information about its status, view its log files, request updates from TiVo, and so forth. Most impressively, TiVoWebPlus provides access to the internals of TiVo's MFS filesystem, and includes an easily expanded resource editor that lets you use TiVoWebPlus to peek and poke resource values. All this in a free application that "just works." It's absolutely incredible!

Older versions of TiVoWeb (anything numbered 1.9.x) were primarily targeted for older Series 1 TiVos, but TiVoWebPlus brings the functionality of TiVoWeb to dual-tuner DirecTiVos, Series 2 TiVos, and even the latest DVD-equipped TiVos from Toshiba and Pioneer.

## The TiVo Enhancement Development Team

The TiVo Enhancement Development Team is the current home of many of the original TiVo hacks, instructions, and development efforts. Hosted at SourceForge at http://tivohack.sourceforge.net, it is a useful repository. If you're looking for older TiVo Series 1 tips, tricks, or Linux add-ons, this Web site is a great place to look.

# The Personal TiVo Home Media Option

As discussed in Chapters 9 and 10, TiVo's Home Media Features for the TiVo Series 2 machine running Version 4.0 or better of the TiVo software are an impressive extension to the power and usability of your TiVo. Playing online audio files and displaying digital photographs stored on Windows and Macintosh systems makes your TiVo an even more powerful part of your home theater system. However, the lack of similar software from TiVo for those of us who store our audio files on Linux systems (and in Linux-based formats such as OGG) is irritating to many people.

In frustration, I asked about this issue on the TiVoCommunity Forum, and received replies from members of SourceForge's Personal TiVo Home Media Option Project (**http://sourceforge.net/projects/ptivohmo**). This project provides a free, Linux-based server for digital audio and photographs to which your TiVo can instantly connect. Installing and configuring this software was explained in Chapter 10 in "Working with TiVo's Home Media Option from Linux." This project seems to be defunct (sadly enough), so a tar file of the last version of this project that I could find is also located in the connectivity subdirectory of the CD that accompanies this book.

This is simply a great project. If you store your music on a Linux system, this software is great. It works reasonably well for me, but has some bugs. If you fix the version of the source that is included with this book, please try to re-contribute your fixes (and let me know!).

# The Java Home Media Option

As mentioned in the previous section, TiVo's Home Media Features for the TiVo Series 2 machine running Version 4.0 or better of the TiVo software are an impressive extension to the power and usability of your TiVo. However, again, the lack of similar software from TiVo for those of us who store our audio files on Linux systems is irritating to many people.

SourceForge's Personal TiVo Home Media Option Project, discussed in the previous section, is an excellent solution to this problem. An alternative to this project is the Java Home Media Option project, which is also hosted on SourceForge and is available at the URL **http://javahmo.sourceforge.net**. JavaHMO started as a simple server to bring Internet content to TiVos with Home Media Features, but grew into a replacement of the Publisher server software provided by TiVo. An advantage to using this software is that it runs on Mac OS X, Linux, and Windows systems (the latter under Cygwin). Because TiVo provides its TiVo Desktop software for Mac Os X and Windows systems, I've primarily used JavaHMO under Linux (since that's where I store my music archives). Installing and configuring this software was explained in Chapter 10 in "Working with TiVo's Home Media Option from Linux." All of the files that you need to install in order to run this package on your Linux system are provided in the `connectivity/JavaHMO` subdirectory of the CD that accompanies this book.

The only downside of JavaHMO is that it only (currently) supports MP3 files (as TiVo's official HMO Publisher software for Windows and Macs does), while most of my music archives are in the open source (and superior) OGG format. I'm not much of a Java guy, but the JavaHMO project is always looking for volunteers—maybe this is your chance to give something to the TiVo community by adding OGG support!

**TIP**

You can't run both the Personal TiVo Home Media Option and the Java Home Media Option at the same time because they both use the same network ports. Experiment with both and see which one works better for you. If all of your music is stored in MP3 files, the Java Home Media Option is probably a better choice.

# Closed Captioning Support Using TiVoVBI

TiVoVBI was an early TiVo hack that led to many of the onscreen display routines used by almost every project that displays text on a TiVo screen, and it is still a great piece of software. TiVoVBI enables the TiVo to decode and display closed caption and XDS data to the television screen, file, or console.

**TIP**

TiVoVBI is especially useful because even the TiVo's rewind command doesn't always enable you to catch what's being said, regardless of how many times you listen to it. To solve this problem, install TiVoVBI on your TiVo, activate closed captioning, rewind, and there you go! The missing phrases are displayed on your TiVo screen.

You can download a copy of the current version (1.03) from **http://tivo.samba.org/download/mbm/tivovbi-1.03.zip**. The software is also available in the connectivity directory on the BATBD CD. Work on porting TiVoVBI to Series 2 TiVos is in progress—check threads on the DealDatabase forums such as **http://www.dealdatabase.com/forum/showthread.php?t=34159** for up-to-date information on TiVoVBI and related software for onscreen display (OSD).

**NOTE**

Installing this software on a Series 1 TiVo running Version 3.0 or greater of the TiVo software also requires that you download the tvbi-test.o module from **http://tivo.samba.org/download/mbm/bin** (or get it from the connectivity directory on the BATBD CD), transfer it to your TiVo, and use the **insmod** command to insert it into your running kernel by using the following command:

```
insmod -f tvbi-test.o
```

This module is only for Series 1 TiVos – I haven't seen an equivalent for the Series 2 TiVos. If you will be running TiVoVBI in the future, you may want to permanently add this statement to your rc.sysinit or other system startup files.

# TiVo Utilities Home Page

The TiVo Utilities Home is yet another fine repository of good TiVo software. The TiVo Utilities Home Page is hosted by SourceForge at **http://tivoutils.sourceforge.net**. This is a great place to look for Series 1 and Series 2 system software. Unlike many other TiVo sites, they've made a noble attempt at posting as much of whatever documentation is available for various TiVo hardware, and there is also a link to TiVo's own developer documentation and resources.

# HACKING THE TiVo

# Chapter 12

SECOND EDITION

## Extracting, Inserting, and Playing TiVo Recordings

**V**ideo extraction has been a contentious topic in TiVo (and other DVR) circles for quite a while. On the one hand, you have the networks that don't want people to see any type of entertainment without getting it directly from them or at least having commercials embedded in it. On the other hand, you have people like TiVo, Inc., who want to make their customers happy but need to maintain a good working relationship with the networks. Let's face it, the broadcast media folks are unhappy about anything that they don't control and sell to you. They were extremely cranky about cassette, BetaMax, and VCR tapes. Who can forget various proposals to tax these over the years? Broadcast media executives and their pet lawyers were probably similarly unhappy about dictaphones, wire recorders, and reel-to-reel tapes in their day. Come to think of it, we're probably lucky that we don't have to pay entertainment tax on pencils, since we can conceivably write down things that people say on the radio and TV without also copying down all of the commercials.

**NOTE**

As an aside, I'd like to discuss how much I hate buying a videotape or DVD and having previews and commercials embedded in SOMETHING THAT I PAID FOR. However, that might be inappropriate, so I won't go into it.

The ethics of extracting recorded video from a TiVo is such a contentious topic that video extraction was actually the original motivating factor for the great TiVo forums that are now available on DealDatabase.com. Discussing video extraction is verboten on the TiVoCommunity.com forums—threads that raise the topic are purged, people who initiate them repeatedly can be banned, and even the name DealDatabase.com is a forbidden term in any post there. (You have to refer to it through some obtuse language that can't be a direct link, such as "the forbidden forum site.") All of the energy spent suppressing this information and issuing warnings could probably power a thousand TiVos for a hundred years. That said, the first version of this book didn't discuss it either, for the simple reason that this was the first "Hacking the TiVo" book available, and I didn't want to alienate TiVo or sour their relationship with the networks.

Regardless of any historical concerns that one might have about extracting video from a TiVo, I'd say the fact that the latest TiVos from Pioneer come with internal DVD burners seems to be the nail in the coffin of video extraction as a taboo topic. TiVos have always been able to dump recordings to videotape, and now they can burn DVDs directly. What's the difference between extracting a recorded program from the hard drive on your TiVo and burning it onto a DVD? My vote is "nothing." Similarly, Chapter 1 discusses TiVo's TiVo To Go service, an official mechanism for watching recordings originally captured on a TiVo from personal computer and other systems.

This chapter discusses mechanisms for extracting recordings from your TiVo that you can use today, for free, on all types of personal computers—not just those supported by TiVo To Go and TiVo's software partners. If you don't want to invest the time in extracting recordings yourself and are using a supported type of personal computer system, use TiVo To Go— it has tech support and is official. If you want to get started now or are using a type of personal computer not supported by TiVo To Go, let's extract away!

# Overview: Extraction, Insertion, and Conversion

Extraction, insertion, and conversion are the three core things that most people do with recordings on a TiVo (aside from simply watching them, which is my true favorite). This section explains what I mean by each of these and why it's important to consider your goal when thinking about the software setup that you need in order to accomplish what you're trying to do.

In a nutshell, *extraction* is the ability to transfer a recording from a TiVo to some other system or medium. There are several different flavors of extraction. The most obvious of these is that you want to transfer the recording to some other system so that you can watch it there, but don't want to have to step back in time by copying it to videotape. As we'll see later in this chapter, there are a variety of different ways to do this. You can simply stream the video from your TiVo over your home network to an application that understands TiVo's video format, such as mplayer, or you can extract the recording as a file in TiVo format and play it back in applications such as mplayer, TyTool, or TyStudio.

Another common extraction scenario is that you may transfer a recording to another system or medium simply to save the recording without wasting TiVo disk space on it until the next time that you want to see it. A good example of this sort of extraction is seasonal programming. Most fans of a traditional western Christmas have at least one Christmas special that has special meaning to them—but do you really want to have to keep "Mr. Magoo's Christmas Carol," "Christmas Vacation," or "Suzy Snowflake" on your TiVo all year round? I don't, which is why I roll these off onto my home file server after each Christmas and copy them back to the TiVo after Thanksgiving each year.

 **WARNING**

I am not a lawyer (IANAL) and have never even played one on TV. Decrypting video is your choice, and some people feel that TiVo hates the whole idea. I disagree —the folks at TiVo are smart people who have created a great system and service. While they'd probably prefer to sell you a solution, I can't see why they would take the pipe over the fact that people can extract videos from their TiVos, even if the data on the TiVo is encrypted. As far as extraction is concerned, you could just as easily have dumped shows from your TiVo to videotape or DVD, recorded broadcast television on a videotape and dumped it to your computer's disk, or simply recorded a show using a video capture card from a direct television feed. Getting a television broadcast to a computer system is not rocket science nowadays. Given this, I don't see any reason why you shouldn't be able to pull things off your TiVo disk and, if necessary, decrypt them so that you can watch them. And finally, as mentioned previously, the latest Pioneer TiVos have integrated DVD burners. Given that some means for creating portable recordings directly from a TiVo is now commercially available, what's the problem with extracting a recording and processing it yourself? Unfortunately, my opinions are not the law.

However, let's be reasonable—to paraphrase the documentation from Extract-Stream, one of the earliest TiVo video extraction tools, "I urge you to understand the difference between 'fair use' and copyright violation when using copyrighted video. The people who wrote and distribute video extraction tools for the TiVo feel strongly that the code should be used only in a legal manner. It is legal for you to view the video captured on your TiVo (or any video capture device) at any time and using any playback device. However, it is not legal to distribute or publicly play back copyrighted material."

Finally, it is completely reasonable to want to extract recordings from your TiVo because you want to back them up like you would any other data that is important to you. However, storing all of your favorite recordings on your TiVo is a "single point of failure solution" that puts you at the mercy of a hard disk crash. One crash, and you've lost everything. If you've been smart and extracted your favorite recordings, you can always put them back on your TiVo after you install and configure a new hard drive.

Which is a nice segue into *insertion*, which is the ability to take an existing recording from some other medium and put it onto a TiVo. It is certainly easiest to insert recordings that you've previously extracted from a TiVo, but you can also use the TiVo's inputs to attach things like VCRs, video cameras, and so on, record from them, and thereby "insert" recordings from other sources. (This is explained later in this chapter.)

Finally, there's *conversion*, which is the term for taking a recording that was made on a TiVo and converting it into some other video format so that you can play it on other devices or in other applications. There are a variety of different ways to do this—some complex, some time-consuming, but all rewarding if you want to share your favorite shows with your friends, or simply want to be able to watch them without having to carry a TiVo everywhere that you go.

# Video File Formats

Computer technology is always acronym city, where articles, online discussions, and even books are peppered with three-letter acronyms (known as *TLAs* in computer circles) that are convenient if you're already an expert, but which are mystifying to someone who's actually trying to learn what's going on. This is especially the case when discussing online audio and video because of the potentially bewildering number of formats in which these types of data can be stored.

If you're new to computer video or are curious about the various types of video files that you'll see referenced throughout this chapter, the next two sections explain the most popular TLAs used when referring to the format in which video is stored on your TiVo, the formats in which you can extract video from your TiVo, and the target formats to which you may want to convert your extracted TiVo recordings.

## TiVo Video File Formats

All TiVos store video in the same format on disk. The data itself may differ depending on whether the video is encrypted, but the objects in which that data is stored and its format on your TiVo disks are the same. As discussed in Chapter 10, "MFS—the Media File System," TiVo's MFS is essentially a database to which access is controlled through user-space libraries. This enabled TiVo to keep the structure of MFS and its data formats as proprietary technology, since it is not integrated into the Linux kernel as other filesystems are. Recordings are stored in the MFS Media regions of your TiVo disk(s), in objects known as tyStream objects.

The TiVo hacking community has created various formats that are used when extracting and working with recordings from a TiVo. The file extensions used on an extracted video file identify the format of those files, and are the following:

- ◆ *ty* The .ty extension stands for tyStream, the name of the objects in MFS filesystems that are used to hold recordings or portions of recordings. The data in tyStream objects contains both audio and video information. TY files are typically used for conversion or straight playback on other systems.

- ◆ *ty+* The .ty+ extension indicates that the file is a standard tyStream file, but it also contains information at the end of the file that can be used to insert the recording back onto a TiVo. The end of a TY+ file contains 512 '#' symbols, followed by the contents of the showing.xml file that described the recording, followed by another 512 '#' characters. Because these markers and the data between them are simply appended to a standard tyStream file, you can process .ty+ files using the same tools used to process standard .ty files—there will always simply be some unusable excess characters at the end. (For example, the TY files produced by applications such as **mfs_ftp** are actually TY+ files.) TY+ files are typically used for conversion or playback on other systems, and were the first TiVo file format that enabled reinserting recordings back into a TiVo, because they preserve the metadata about a recording that is stored in the showing.xml file.

- ◆ *tmf* The .tmf extension stands for TiVo Media Format, and it indicates that the file is a Unix tape archive (tar) file whose first entry is showing.xml file that provides insertion information, and which is followed by however many separate .ty files are required to hold the entire recording. TMF files are similar to .tyx files, which were a short-lived predecessor that were also tar files, but which contained clear text header information before the tar archive. (These .tyx files were rarely used, are largely extinct, and are only mentioned here for completeness.) TMF files are used for archiving, insertion, and can also be used for conversion if you extract their contents. The following series of Linux commands extract the contents of a TMF file and produce a TY file from them:

```
# tar xvf showing.tmf
# cat part*.ty > ty-file-name.ty
```

# Identifying TiVo Video Files on Linux and Mac OS X Systems

The Un*x **file** command enables users to identify the type of data that a file contains by examining the first few bytes of that file and matching it against a set of canned file signatures. On most Linux systems, these are stored in the file /usr/share/magic. On Mac OS X systems, the file command uses canned file signatures stored in the file /usr/share/file/magic. Unfortunately, TiVo video formats aren't widespread, and therefore, by default, the **file** command returns the following when you ask it to identify a TiVo video file:

```
$ file Friends-Viewers-Choice-WPXI-687802.ty
Friends-Viewers-Choice-WPXI-687802.ty: data
```

The description "data" simply means that the **file** command recognized the file as a binary file, but that it was in an unknown format. Luckily, the **file** command's signature file is a text file that is designed to be easily extended by appending appropriate entries to the file. Most Unix-like systems provide the **file** command, but the location of the magic file containing file signatures differs—if you're using a Un*x system other than Linux or Mac OS X, you can usually execute the command "man magic" to determine where the file is located on your system.

If you're going to be extracting recordings from your TiVos, TiVo video files have well-known signatures that you can add to the magic file so that you can easily identify them. This is especially important if you are extracting files for different purposes and from different TiVos. For example, I extract TY files from my Series 1 TiVos for conversion purposes, TMF and (historically) TY+ files from my Series 1 and Series 2 TiVos for archival and insertion purposes, and so on. Since I have both Series 1 and Series 2 TiVos, some of which store encrypted video, I've added some entries to the magic file on my primary Linux box to make sure that I can tell one file from another.

To enable the **file** command to identify different types of TiVo video files, append the following entries to your system's magic file (which, again, is probably /usr/share/magic on a modern Linux box, and is /usr/share/file/magic on a Mac OS X system):

```
# TiVo video files or chunks
0 belong 0xadbd6726 TiVo TY file, scrambled
0 belong 0xf5467abd TiVo TY file, unscrambled
0 belong 0xfb3da7ef TiVo TY+ file, scrambled
```

After saving the file, you'll need to force the **file** command to update its cached signature information, which you can do by executing the **file -C** command as the superuser. Once you do this, you should be able to execute commands like the following:

```
$ file Friends-Viewers-Choice-WPXI-687802.ty
Friends-Viewers-Choice-WPXI-687802.ty: TiVo TY file, unscrambled
$ file 708965-Friends-The-One-With-the-Unagi.ty+
708965-Friends-The-One-With-the-Unagi.ty+: TiVo TY+ file, scrambled
```

Unfortunately, since TMF files are Unix tape archive (**tar**) format files, there's no easy way to uniquely identify them. If you use the file command to look at a TMF file, you will still see the following:

```
$ file When-Your-Body-Gets-the-Blues-WQED-308571.tmf
When-Your-Body-Gets-the-Blues-WQED-308571.tmf: GNU tar archive
```

# Target Video File Formats

If you're extracting files from your TiVo for the simple purpose of archiving them, the format of those files depends on the software that you use to extract them, and you probably don't care about the formats to which others may want to convert them. However, if you're extracting files in order to convert them to files that you can watch on something other than a TiVo, it's useful to understand the most popular file formats to which TiVo recordings are converted and their associate file extensions.

## MPEG Files

MPEG (pronounced *M-peg*) stands for the Moving Picture Experts Group, and is used as the name of a family of standards used for coding audio-visual information such as motion pictures and audio in a compressed, digital format. The Motion Picture Experts Group works under the joint direction of the International Standards Organization (ISO) and the International Electro-Technical Commission (IEC). The MPEG family of standards includes MPEG-1 (ISO/IEC-11172), MPEG-2 (ISO/IEC-13818), and MPEG-4 (ISO/IEC-14496). The MP3 audio file format, commonly used to record and exchange music, is actually an MPEG format, and stands for MPEG-1 Audio Layer 3.

One interesting fact is that MPEG formats with higher suffixes are not replacements for other MPEG formats, but are related formats with different goals. For example, MPEG-2 is not a successor for MPEG-1. MPEG-1 is targeted for medium-bandwidth usage, while MPEG-2 is meant for high-bandwidth/broadband usage. MPEG-2 is therefore the MPEG format that is used in digital TVs, DVD-videos, and in SVCDs.

Though there are many other audio and video formats, MPEG formats are quite popular because they are usually smaller than the same quality audio or video encoded in other formats. All MPEG standards use sophisticated compression techniques to minimize file size, although MPEG compression is generally known as "lossy" compression. In a nutshell, MPEG compression works by sampling the incoming audio or video at various rates, reducing its resolution, analyzing the change between previous and subsequent samples, and then building compressed audio or video that contains an optimized combination of actual data and data about subsequent changes.

If you're deeply interested in MPEG file formats, compression, techniques, and other gory details, see the official MPEG site at **http://www.mpeg.org**. This site provides a tremendous amount of local information, and also provides links to hundreds of other MPEG-related sites (some of which are always down, but you still can't beat the price).

## VCD, DVD, and VOB Files

Video CDs (VCDs) are an older video disc format that uses MPEG-1 rather than MPEG-2 encoding. VCDs are recorded on standard CD-ROMs and can therefore be played in all CD players as well as many DVD players. VCDs suffer from the capacity and performance limitations of CD-ROMs but are good for shorter video recordings that you may want to play on computer systems that may not have a DVD drive.

Digital Video Disks (DVDs, also sometimes known as *Digital Versatile Disks*) are a storage technology much like the traditional CD-ROM disk, but provide much higher storage capacity and data delivery rates. Standard DVDs hold around 4.7 GB of data, as opposed to the 600 MB or so that you can store on a data CD-ROM.

Another term that you may encounter when researching DVDs is VOB. VOB stands for DVD Video Object and is one of the core types of files found on any DVD if you look at one on a system that can read DVDs as data disks. VOB files are the files that contain the actual movie data. VOB files are basically a standard MPEG-2 system stream, consisting of a multiplexed MPEG-2 video stream, one or more audio streams (normally AC3 format), and subtitle streams.

# Saving Recordings to Media— Built-In Methods

For computer systems, backups typically refer to external media that contain copies of critical system programs, system configuration data, and user data. In this last sense, your TiVo provides a built-in mechanism for backing up its equivalent of user data, which consists of the programs that you've recorded. Because most of us still have an old dusty VCR sitting around somewhere from our pre-TiVo days or for the occasional retro video rental, it's also useful to back up some of your more precious recordings onto videotape. This is also useful for sharing them with Luddite friends who may have missed a specific episode of your favorite show. Although videotapes are somewhat retro in the age of the DVR, they're still a useful exchange medium—similar to what floppy disks are to today's personal computers.

Regardless of how you feel about extracting video from your TiVo system, various models of TiVos provide built-in capabilities for saving recordings to external devices (such as VCRs) and internal devices (if you have a DVR that has a built-in DVD burner, like the Pioneer TiVos). If you want to spend a few extra bucks and buy a video capture card for your PC, a tremendous amount of software is available that enables you to capture recordings that are coming into the video capture card—which could, of course, be connected to your TiVo. In this case, you're not doing anything that isn't officially supported by hundreds of software and hardware vendors.

The next few sections provide quick discussions of recording from your TiVo to a VCR, burning a DVD on a TiVo with a DVD burner, and showcasing an overview of some of the most popular software that you can use with video capture cards on Linux, Mac OS X, and various flavors of Windows. Some of these software packages were also discussed in the section of Chapter 1 entitled "Software Competitors."

EXTRACTING, INSERTING, AND PLAYING TIVO RECORDINGS

# Saving Recordings to Videotape

Your TiVo provides built-in support for backing up recordings onto videotape through the Save to VCR command, which is available on the Now Playing screen for any recording. On TiVos with DVD burners, this menu item is labeled Copy to DVD or VCR, and requires an additional step to select which of the two backup mediums you want to save to. Saving recordings to DVD is discussed in the next section—this section focuses on saving recordings to a VCR.

After selecting the "Save to VCR" menu item and connecting your VCR to your TiVo (explained in great detail in the TiVo Installation Guide that came with your TiVo), make sure that your VCR is set to record from the input source to which you attached your TiVo. Now put a videotape in the VCR.

 **NOTE**

If you don't have your TiVo Installation Guide handy and never bothered to connect your VCR after getting your TiVo, you can download PDF versions of the TiVo documentation for your TiVo from **http://www.tivo.com/4.2.2.asp**. (If this URL changes, you can always find it through a link to this page on the Customer Support portion of the TiVo Web site at **http://customersupport.tivo.co**m.) You'll probably be most interested in downloading the "TiVo Viewer's Guide," but if you have to reinstall your TiVo and are having problems, you may find the "TiVo Installation Guide" to be extremely useful.

Viewing PDF files requires that you have installed a PDF viewer such as Adobe Acrobat Reader on your system, which you can freely download from **http://www.adobe.com/products/acrobat/readermain.html**. Linux systems generally come with the **xpdf** application, which works just as well. Mac OS X systems provide the **Preview** application, which is automatically executed if you double-click on a PDF file.

After selecting the recording that you want to save to videotape from the Now Playing screen, highlight the Save To VCR screen option and press Select. This displays an auxiliary screen from which you should then select "Start saving from the beginning." This means your TiVo will begin to play the recording from the beginning—regardless of whether you've been watching it and are therefore positioned in the middle of it somewhere. At this point, your TiVo gives you about 10 seconds to press the Record button on your VCR before actually starting to play the recording on your TiVo.

Saving a recording to videotape takes as much time as the recording would take to play. This is because dumping a recording to videotape occurs in real-time, not in any whizzy streaming mode. If you've begun saving a recording to your VCR and you decide that it's taking too long (or you simply want to do it later), you can stop the process by pressing the Live TV or TiVo buttons on your TiVo remote control. A videotape icon will display as a warning—to proceed, press the same button again, and a confirmation screen displays.

This screen gives you the option of resuming this operation later or you can cancel saving altogether. When selecting either of these options, make sure that you also press stop on your VCR, or you'll record a lot of garbage.

**TIP**

Although the TiVo displays the recording in real-time so that any VCR can record it successfully, any of the TiVo backdoor commands that you already may have activated are available while the recording is playing. If you have activated the 30-second-skip backdoor (described in the section of Chapter 3 entitled "Using Select-Play-Select Codes"), you can use this command (or even the standard fast-forward commands) to skip or fast-forward through any sections of the recording that you may not want to preserve on videotape.

## Saving Recordings to DVD on DVD TiVos

TiVos with built-in DVD drives provide built-in support for backing up recordings to DVD-R or DVD-RW drives through the Copy to DVD or VCR command, which is available on the Now Playing screen for any recording.

After selecting the Copy to DVD or VCR menu item and the subsequent Save to DVD menu item, your TiVo displays a series of menus that prompt you to insert a DVD in your TiVo's DVD drive, prompts you for whether you want to copy just the selected recording or multiple recordings, and initiates the DVD burning process on your TiVo. All of this is explained in excellent detail in the TiVo Viewers Guide—my goal in mentioning this here is not to repeat their documentation but to discuss copying TiVo recordings to DVD as a valid and legal way of extracting video from your TiVo in the generic sense.

## Using a TV Tuner Card and Video Capture Software

As discussed in the introduction to this chapter, video extraction is one of the touchier subjects in TiVo-land. This is not surprising, because the entertainment industry has one of the highest profit margins in the known universe. One has only to look at the industry's reaction to MP3s and other forms of online audio to see a comic-tragedy of greed unfold. (I'm lumping audio and video entertainment together because they are essentially the same thing, digitally.)

One sure-fire mechanism for backing up videos from your TiVo is to purchase a TV tuner card or external device that will work with your personal computer system. These work with Linux, PCI-based Macintosh, and Windows systems. TV tuner cards and external TV tuners are available online from many sites (including eBay, of course) at prices ranging from $20 to hundreds of dollars, depending upon quality, sophistication, and any software packages that are included with them.

Many of the TV tuner cards provide built-in video capture capabilities, and some provide full DVR functionality. Why discuss potentially competing products in a book about hacking the TiVo? Because TiVos offer features such as TiVo Suggestions, Season Passes, and WishLists that are superior to any similar features found on any of the "competing" products that I've seen. If you don't want to network your TiVo or don't want to bother with the TiVo-oriented extraction and conversion software that is the focus of this chapter, that's fine with me. You can piggyback the advantages of the TiVo on the functionality provided by TV tuner cards and associated capture software to get the best of both worlds.

The next few sections provide details about using TV tuner cards, external tuners, and associated software on various operating systems.

## Using TV Tuner Cards Under Linux

If you're using Linux, you should verify that the TV tuner card that you're interested in is supported under Linux before randomly purchasing one. The good news is that most are. For example, many of the more common TV tuner cards use BrookTree chips, which are well supported in the BTTV drivers, which are included with most Linux distributions. The latest versions of these drivers are always available from **http://bytesex.org/v4l2/bttv.html**. For details about people's experiences with various TV tuner and capture cards under Linux, see **http://pvrhw.goldfish.org/bttv/bttv-gallery.html**. This page provides an incredible amount of information about any BrookTree-based card that I've ever encountered.

The open source movement has produced a number of excellent video displays, and in some cases, capture packages such as the following:

◆ *DVR*   DVR is an open source project that records Windows Audio Video Interleave (AVI) files from a video input source such as a TV tuner card. The AVI file format is a special case of the Resource Interchange File Format (RIFF), was defined by Microsoft, and is a perfect example of a de facto standard defined because no one knows any better. If you're willing to deal with converting AVI files to a format that is an actual standard (or if your goal is to capture videos that people can watch on their Windows boxes), DVR is an excellent package. For more information about DVR, see **http://dvr.sourceforge.net**.

◆ *ebox*   This is a combination hardware and software project that uses xawtv as its core display engine. I've never experimented with this package and am listing it here to be complete. For more information, see the ebox home page at **http://www.bluelightning.org/ebox**, or see the sourceforge page for the GUI that the ebox uses at software at **http://eboxy.sourceforge.net**.

◆ *FreeVo*   FreeVo is an open source project that displays TV programming and also provides the capability of scheduling and recording shows. It uses the open source mplayer application to display video (**http://www.mplayerhq.hu**), and uses a variety of open source plug-ins such as **mencoder** (part of mplayer), **ivtv_record** (**http://ivtv.sourceforge.net**), and so on. For more information about FreeVo, or to download it, see **http://freevo.sourceforge.net**.

- *mythTV* MythTV is probably the best known TV display and recording package for Linux. MythTV is a flexible, powerful DVR software package that is easily extended through modules and tightly-coupled applications such as MythDVD (a separate application that rips DVDs and displays them within MythTV), MythGallery (a separate application that displays photos and slideshows within MythTV), MythMusic (a module for playing and visualizing music in MythTV), MythVideo (a separate application that enables you to play videos that are stored in formats that are not directly supported by MythTV), MythWeather (a module that displays information about your local weather within MythTV), and MythWeb (a separate application that provides a Web interface to MythTV). For TiVo fans, one of the most interesting MythTV modules is MythTiVo, which is a module for locating TiVos on your network and listing their recordings. The MythTiVo module is available at **http://tivo-mplayer.sourceforge.net/mythtivo.html**. For more information about MythTV, see **http://www.mythtv.org**.

- *tvtime* The tvtime package for displaying video input from a tuner card on Linux and other Unix-like systems is available from **http://tvtime.sourceforge.net**. This package does not provide capture capabilities but is handy if you want to watch your TiVo on the screen of your Linux box. The tvtime package requires the X Window system, expects drivers for bt848 and bt878-based TV tuner cards, but should be portable to other Unix-like systems with a fairly small amount of effort. The tvtime package is easily integrated with the xmltv project discussed later in this section.

- *xawtv* The xawtv software for displaying video input from a tuner card under Linux is available from **http://bytesex.org/xawtv/index.html**. The xawtv package is easy to set up and use, and works with a large number of available TV tuner and related video input cards. A list of supported cards is included in the source code, although many more have probably been used successfully. If you are using xawtv with a BrookTree-based TV tuner card, you will probably want to get the specific set of fonts that it uses, which is available on the page at **http://linux.bytesex.org/xawtv/tvfonts.html**.

 **TIP**

Most TV-oriented software for Linux, such as FreeVo, MythTV, and tvtime, can be integrated with the xmltv package, which is a software package that retrieves programming information over the Net. This data can then be used by the applications to display TV listings, show information, and so on, and can be stored in flat files or in a database such as MySQL for fast and easy access. The home page for xmltv is at **http://membled.com/work/apps/xmltv**. It also has a SourceForge project page at **http://sourceforge.net/projects/xmltv**. One especially impressive aspect of xmltv is that it is incredibly internationalized—it includes listing grabbers for the U.S., Canada, Germany, Denmark, Spain, Finland, France, Hungary, Italy, Japan, the Netherlands, New Zealand, and the UK.

## Using TV Tuner Cards and Devices Under Mac OS X

If you're using a Mac OS X system, several internal and external TV tuners are available that enable you to display incoming video signals in a window on your Mac's screen. Unlike the Linux and Windows solutions described in the previous and following sections, most of the TV tuners that I'm familiar with for the Mac are external devices that attach to the USB, audio, or Firewire ports on your Mac.

**TIP**

Apple's iMovie and QuickTime software for Mac OS X are tremendous assets when capturing and fine-tuning from a TV tuner on Mac OS X. The professional version of QuickTime, an inexpensive upgrade from the standard version, can read the video formats captured by most Mac TV tuners, such as MotionJPEG, MPEG-1, or MPEG-4. You can export these in the format used by the iMovie video editor, which is an uncompressed digital video (DV) format. Then you can use iMovie to trim the beginning and end of shows, and even accidentally remove commercials if you want.

Some of the most popular TV tuners for Mac OS X are the following:

- ◆ *Alchemy TV*   Alchemy TV is a cooperative product of Miglia Technology Ltd and Meilenstein's Televio internal TV tuner for Power Macs. This is a sweet package that consists of an internal PCI card and software for Power Macs running OS X 10.2.4 or better, and includes an infrared remote control for controlling the card—and which you can even use to control other applications. Alchemy TV can capture video and audio to various formats supported by QuickTime. For additional information about the Televio video card itself, see **http://www.televio.com/**. For detailed information about the Alchemy TV package, see **http://www.miglia.com/products/video/alchemytv/index.html**.

- ◆ *Canopus ADVC1394 Video Capture card*   I've never used one of these but would be happy to do so if someone would send me one. The retail package includes drivers for newer Macs so that you can use packages like iMovie and Final Cut Pro to edit captured DV video. The card supports analog and DV capture, and it includes a 1394 Firewire interface for high-speed data capture.

- ◆ *EyeTV*   A product of Elgato systems, EyeTV is an inexpensive TV tuner with DVR capabilities that attaches to your Mac's USB port. The EyeTV digitizes both video and audio over the USB port, and it does not require a separate audio connector. EyeTV also shares many built-in features with the TiVo, such as the ability to pause video and skip commercials in existing recordings.

  The EyeTV only displays video on your Mac's screen—it does not have separate video outputs for connecting directly to a television or VCR (retro alert!). The EyeTV only captures video in MPEG-1 format, which means that you'll have to use QuickTime to generate DV data, which often results in the loss of your audio data. Elgate provides a free utility called *bbDEMUX* that splits out the MPEG-1 audio data, which you can convert into an AIFF file, and then import everything into QuickTime. I'd expect Elgato to change or fix this at some point in the future. However, if you just want to watch recordings on your Mac and are OK with MPEG-1 quality, everything works out of the box.

◆ *Formac Studio TVR* The most expensive but most powerful Mac solution, the Formac Studio TVR, is an external device that connects to your Mac OS X system via Firewire. It is a full-blown DVR package that is inherently designed for capturing recordings—hence the new acronym, TVR, for TV Recorder. Like the EyeTV, the Formac Studio TVR shares many built-in features with the TiVo, such as the ability to pause video and skip commercials in existing recordings. The TVR captures video in DV format, which eliminates the QuickTime conversion necessary with most of the other Mac-based TV tuners. This also explains why the Studio TVR is a Firewire device because DV data is fast and big. For more information about the Formac Studio TVR, see **http://www.formac.com**. The Format Studio TVR is a replacement for Formac's older Studio DV/TV, provides a number of new features that weren't present on the DV/TV, and includes a substantially enhanced software package for controlling the TVR.

◆ *MyTV and MyTV2GO* Products of Eskape Labs, both of these devices are inexpensive external devices that connect to your Mac's USB port. In order to capture audio with these, you'll need to connect your Mac's audio input port to the MyTV and MyTV2GO devices. If you're using a Mac without audio input or output ports (like my iBooks), you'll also want to get Griffin Technology's iMic, which is available through Eskape Labs or directly from Griffin Technology. For more information about MyTV, see **http://www.eskapelabs.com/mytv.html**. Additional information about MyTV2GO is available at **http://www.eskapelabs.com/mytv2go.html**. More information about Griffin Technology's iMic is available at **http://www.griffintec hnology.com/products/imic**. The iMic's audio output are incredibly useful even if you're not doing video capture—my iBook's internal speaker is pitiful, and I highly recommend the iMic!

◆ *Televio* See the discussion of Alchemy TV earlier in this list.

## Using TV Tuner Cards Under Windows

If you're using a Windows system, most TV tuner cards come with software tailored to the card that enables you to display incoming video signals in a window on your PC screen. You can put the card in your PC, use the PC as a display device for the TiVo by connecting the TiVo's Cable Out or S-Video (and audio) connectors to it, and then use the software provided with the card to capture the video and audio that is being displayed on your PC.

You can hardly buy a TV tuner card without Windows-based software falling out of the box and cluttering up the place. For this reason, it's hardly worth noting that there is plenty of Windows-based TV display and capture software. Some of the best-known software for this purpose is available both stand-alone and bundled with PCI video cards or USB capture devices. The best-known packages that I have seen or am aware of are:

◆ *Hauppage WinTV*   A product of Hauppage, one of the first computer TV Tuner vendors, WinTV is available as a stand-alone from Hauppauge or bundled with most of the video cards in the known universe. It is also available with USB capture devices, and a new HDTV version is also available. For more information, see **http://www.hauppauge.com**. Don't worry if you misspell it—Hauppage has bought up most of the orbital URLs that reflect popular typos for their name.

◆ *Pinnacle Studio*   A product of Pinnacle Systems, this is an impressive software package that is often bundled with video cards from popular vendors, such as ATI. Pinnacle Studio simplifies capturing, editing, and converting video, and also makes it easy to generate output that you can save to videotape, DVD, or even for display on the Web. For more information about this package, see h**ttp://www.pinnaclesys.com/ProductPage_n.asp?Product_ID=1501&Langue_ID=7**. A copy of this came with a friend's ATI All-In_Wonder card, and it's pretty impressive.

◆ *SnapStream BeyondTV*   SnapStream's BeyondTV is a great video capture and recording package for Windows. It requires DirectX 9.0 or better, the Microsoft .NET framework v1.1 or better, Windows Media 9 components, and probably most other infrastructure from Microsoft. The software is incredibly powerful and makes it easy to locate and schedule recordings. BeyondTV is available as a stand-alone and supports most popular PCI TV tuners, but can also be bought bundled with various tuner cards for convenience. Unlike other TV display and capture software for Windows, BeyondTV uses guide data that can be retrieved over the Internet directly from SnapStream, which is a true convenience. For more information about BeyondTV or a 21-day demo version, see **http://www.snapstream.com**.

# Extracting Recordings from Your TiVo (Overview)

Now we get to the fun part—actually explaining how to extract video from your TiVo so that you can store and use it on your home computer system, regardless of whether you're using Linux, Mac OS X, or even Windows. As discussed in the introduction to this chapter, video extraction has been a hot and contentious topic in TiVo circles since the first TiVo guy swung and slid his way onto a TV screen. Being able to extract recordings from a TiVo is the key to doing anything else with it, whether you're simply planning to archive recordings or want to convert them to a more standard, portable format so that you can watch them in another application or on another computer system.

The next sections provide general information and tips that you should consider before using any of the software discussed later in this chapter. Subsequent sections discuss general issues about extracting video from your TiVo over a home network, but a network isn't manda-tory—another section explains how to extract TiVo recordings directly from a TiVo hard drive in your personal computer system. Most of the extraction and conversion utilities discussed later in this chapter are also oriented toward stand-alone Series 1 TiVos. The fact that DirecTiVo systems have always encrypted video can be a problem. Similarly, the heightened paranoia, er, security, that is built into the Series 2 TiVos, whether stand-alone or DirecTiVo systems, makes it more challenging to back up videos from these systems in the first place. However, don't worry—solutions to all of these problems are discussed throughout the rest of this chapter.

# Overview of Extraction and Processing Software

There are a huge number of TiVo extraction utilities and conversion processes. Some of these are historical and no longer work correctly due to changes in TiVo's TyStream recording format. Some are outdated, having been replaced by more elegant and usable packages, and some are for video wizards only. Throughout this chapter, I'll focus on the packages that I've used successfully and which are at least reasonably usable.

The DealDatabase.com forum on Extraction, Insertion, & Streaming Support (**http: //www.dealdatabase.com/forum/forumdisplay.php?f=48**) is a truly tremendous source of information about extracting TiVo recordings and converting them to more portable formats. However, it is a public forum, so it's not always easy to mine zillions of messages for the nuggets of information that you actually want or need. To simplify things, Table 12.1 provides a summary of the most commonly used packages that are freely available for various models of TiVo, what models of TiVo they work with, what they do, the output formats that each of them supports, and the TiVo and PC-side software that is required to use each of them.

**TABLE 12.1 Extraction, Processing, and Viewing Software Summary**

| SOFTWARE | SUPPORTED ON | | CAPABILITIES | | FORMATS | SOFTWARE | |
|---|---|---|---|---|---|---|---|
| | SERIES 1 | SERIES 2 | EXTRACTION | PROCESSING | | TIVO-SIDE | CLIENTS |
| mfs_ftp | Y | Y | Y | N | TY, TY+, TMF, ASX | mfs_ftp | any ftp |
| mplayer | Y | Y | Y | N | TY | vserver | W,L,M |
| TiVoWebPlus | Y | Y | Y | N | TY, TMF | TiVoWebPlus | any browser |
| TyTool | Y | Y | Y | Y | TY | tserver | W |
| TyStudio | Y | Y | Y | Y | TY, TY+ | tyserver, tyindex | W,L,M |

KEY: W—Windows, L—Linux, M—Mac OS X

The packages listed in Table 12.1 are the most popular packages used to extract and, in some cases, process recordings that you've made on your TiVo. TyTool and TyStudio are the most dedicated TiVo tools for extracting and processing TiVo recordings. This doesn't mean that they're sanctioned or supported in any way by TiVo—like 90% of the software discussed in this book, they're the work of wizardly and dedicated TiVo hackers. By TiVo tools, I mean that they were designed expressly for the purpose of extracting TiVo recordings and converting them into more standard, portable formats. The mfs_ftp program is an impressive TiVo-side FTP server that provides a set of virtual directories that makes it easy to extract and insert recordings in a variety of formats. TiVoWebPlus is listed in this table because thoughtful TiVo hackers have developed TCL scripts that make it easy to integrate **mfs_ftp** with TiVoWebPlus (and which also work with later versions of TiVoWeb), simplifying extraction in various formats for those who would prefer to never have to fire up a generic FTP client.

# Tips for Extracting Recordings over a Network

As discussed throughout this book, putting your TiVo on your home network has a number of advantages. The TiVo Connectivity software discussed in Chapter 8 is high on this list—if you are using a hacked Series 1 or Series 2 TiVo that can't run the Home Media Features for one reason or another, you'll be ecstatic to program your TiVo over your home network or the Internet by using TiVoWebPlus. Similarly, if you're interested in extracting recordings from your TiVo, pulling them down over your home network is the way to go—it's extremely easy, doesn't require a screwdriver, and doesn't require that you move your TiVo's hard drive anywhere.

One thing to remember when buying a network adaptor for any model of TiVo is that wireless networking is convenient, but wired networking is much faster. This is especially significant when you transfer huge files over the network. For example, even at the lowest TiVo recording resolution (Basic), a half hour television show takes up at least half of a gigabyte of disk space. That's a lot of data to be moving back and forth over a wireless network!

Remember that extracting recordings from a DirecTiVo or stand-alone Series 2 TiVo for the purpose of converting them to a more portable format such as MPEG-2 is useless unless you disabled encryption before the recording was made. Disabling video encryption is discussed in the section of this chapter which, oddly enough, is entitled "Disabling Video Encryption." Extracting recordings for archival and subsequent reinsertion purposes is a good idea at any time. If you follow the instructions in this section for disabling encryption, you will always be able to play archived recordings after reinserting them. This assumes, of course, that TiVo, Inc. doesn't change anything fundamental, but was accurate at the time this book was updated.

# Extracting Recordings Directly from a TiVo Disk

If you're willing to take your TiVo down for a while by removing its hard drive, you can use the vplay tools to extract TiVo recordings directly from a TiVo hard drive that you've put in your PC. This is faster than transferring them over a network but does cause an interruption in your TiVo viewing pleasure. However, this approach is basically your only option if your TiVo hard drive has crashed, and you want to see if you can recover some of your precious recordings before throwing your new paperweight (the hard drive) out the window.

> **TIP**
>
> If your TiVo is hacked and on your network, and can therefore run the servers associated with the extraction utilities described throughout this chapter, I suggest that you extract your recordings using the network rather than directly from your TiVo's hard disk. Though reading from a local disk is usually faster than reading the same data over the network, the network-oriented extraction utilities do a lot of the grunt work of mapping recordings to all of the FSIDs that contain them, extracting and correctly concatenating these, and so on. Extracting recordings directly from your TiVo disk is best left as a last resort to save precious recordings from a crashed or otherwise dysfunctional TiVo drive.

Extracting recordings directly from a TiVo disk is done using utilities that are part of the *vplay* package, originally written by Andrew Tridgell (Mr. Samba), and subsequently enhanced by TiVo hackers such as Alphawolf and many others. This package is often referred to as the *vserver* package, since that's one of the primary binaries that it produces, but I'll use the original name in this book. A statically-linked set of the **vplay** binaries is provided in the x86bin directory on the BATBD CD that accompanies this book. See Chapter 11, "Mounting the BATBD CD", for instructions for mounting the BATBD CD. After you've mounted the BATBD CD, you can add the directory containing those binaries to this list of directories where Linux looks for programs through the following command:

```
# export PATH=/path-to-batbd-cd-mountpoint/x86bin:${PATH}
```

In order to extract recordings from a TiVo hard drive using the tools provided as part of the vplay package, you will need to know the FSIDs of the recordings that you want to extract. Don't worry—if your TiVo disk is readable at all, you will probably also be able to get this information directly from the TiVo disk by following the instructions in this section.

After putting the TiVo's hard drive in your PC and either booting from the BATBD CD or running Linux in the first place, you must set an initial environment variable called *MFS_DEVLIST* to the base name of the disk device corresponding to that disk. For example, if your TiVo hard drive is mounted as a slave drive on your first IDE interface, you would set MFS_DEVLIST to /dev/hdb, as in the following example:

```
# export MFS_DEVLIST="/dev/hdb"
```

Other common possibilities are /dev/hda (the primary drive on your first IDE interface), /dev/hdc (the primary drive on your second IDE interface), and /dev/hdd (the secondary drive on your second IDE interface). I often attach TiVo disks to my Linux box using an external USB case. In this case, the appropriate settings are usually /dev/sda (the first SCSI storage device on your system, since USB storage devices typically appear to be SCSI devices to many Linux systems) or /dev/sdb (the second SCSI storage device on your system)—it depends what other USB storage devices you may have on your system. I typically use a SanDisk compact flash reader as /dev/sda on my Linux system, so /dev/sdb is where my external USB drive shows up. I'll use /dev/sdb in the following examples, because they came directly from my desktop Linux system.

After setting this environment variable, you can use the **mfs_info** command to get information about the MFS partitions on your TiVo drive, as in the following example:

```
# mfs_info
Found 4 MFS partitions
Super:
    state=0 magic=abbafeed
    devlist=/dev/hda10 /dev/hda11 /dev/hda12 /dev/hda13
    zonemap_ptr=1121 total_secs=39081984 next_fsid=18
    backup_zonemap_ptr=ffffe zonemap_size=1
/dev/sdb has 40019968 sectors
zone(0):
    sector=1121 type=0 start=1122 next_zonemap=263266
    size=262144 per_chunk=262144 limit=263266 zone_size=262144
    backup_sector=ffffe zonemap_size=1
    backup_next_zonemap=ffff5 next_zonemap_size=9
    buddy_size=1
zone(1):
    sector=263266 type=2 start=1048576 next_zonemap=263275
    size=24776704 per_chunk=2048 limit=25825280 zone_size=24776704
    backup_sector=ffff5 zonemap_size=9
    backup_next_zonemap=fffb3 next_zonemap_size=66
    buddy_size=15
zone(2):
    sector=263275 type=1 start=263341 next_zonemap=25826305
    size=785152 per_chunk=8 limit=1048493 zone_size=785152
    backup_sector=fffb3 zonemap_size=66
    backup_next_zonemap=18a17fd next_zonemap_size=2
    buddy_size=18
zone(3):
    sector=25826305 type=2 start=25827328 next_zonemap=0
    size=13254656 per_chunk=8192 limit=39081984 zone_size=13254656
    backup_sector=18a17fd zonemap_size=2
    backup_next_zonemap=deadbeef next_zonemap_size=0
    buddy_size=12
```

The information in the first section, superblock information, lists the MFS partitions on your TiVo disk relative to the name of the device as it would appear to your TiVo. In this example, it listed the following MFS partitions:

```
devlist=/dev/hda10 /dev/hda11 /dev/hda12 /dev/hda13
```

You can then use these values to set the MFS_DEVICE environment variable, which contains a list of the MFS partitions on your TiVo drive, but relative to the location of the hard drive in your PC. The appropriate MFS_DEVICE setting for a TiVo drive whose MFS_DEVLIST is set to /dev/sdb would be the following:

```
export MFS_DEVICE="/dev/sdb10 /dev/sdb11 /dev/sdb12 /dev/sdb13"
```

After setting these environment variables appropriately, you can begin browsing MFS directories to start searching for FSIDs, as in the following example:

```
# mfs_ls "/Recording"
Found 4 MFS partitions
dir: fsid=1883 count=14
     fsid    type      name
     ---------------------------------
    49695   tyDir    Active
    42050   tyDir    Cancelled
     1884   tyDir    Complete
    50619   tyDir    DiskUsed
    50624   tyDir    History
    49709   tyDir    InProgress
    49710   tyDir    LiveCache
    49697   tyDir    NoReRecord
    49696   tyDir    NowShowing
    50621   tyDir    NowShowingByClassic
    50622   tyDir    NowShowingByExpiration
    50623   tyDir    NowShowingByTitle
    41965   tyDir    Pending
     1885   tyDir    ProgramId
```

This shows the contents of the recording directory on your TiVo drive. It is useful to list the directories in /Recording before proceeding, because the directories on your TiVo where you must look for FSID information differ between Series 1 and Series 2 TiVos (as do the contents of the /Recording directory). On Series 1 TiVo disks, I find it most useful to look in the directory /Recording/NowShowingByTitle. On stand-alone Series 2 TiVo disks, the equivalent place to look is /Recording/NowShowingByBucketTitle. (The names of the relevant directories differ based on the version of the TiVo software used on the disk.) The examples in this chapter are taken from a Series 1 disk, but I'll highlight the differences whenever appropriate.

**NOTE**

This is a good time to remind you that extracting scrambled TY files from a Series 2 TiVo isn't all that useful unless your sole purpose in doing so is being able to reinsert them sometime later. If you want to extract TY files for conversion purposes, you must have already configured your Series 2 TiVo not to scramble recordings. There is currently no way of unscrambling Series 2 recordings after the fact. See the section of this chapter entitled "Disabling Video Encryption" for more information.

Next, use the **mfs_ls** command to list the titles that are available on your TiVo, as in the following example (I'm only showing the first recording as an example):

```
# mfs_ls "/Recording/NowShowingByTitle"
Found 4 MFS partitions
dir: fsid=50623 count=13
     fsid    type     name
     --------------------------------
     1882    tyDb     1:WELCOME TO THE TIVOLUTION:89194:96399:1882
     [...]
```

Doing an equivalent list of the /Recording/NowShowingByBucketTitle directory on a Series 2 TiVo would produce entries for each recording that looked like the following:

```
     679011   tyDb     7 DAYS:190929:87517:35201:679011:1:0:1
```

In these examples, the value in the FSID field is the important one. However, this is the FSID for the MFS object that contains the metadata about that recording stored on the TiVo, not the data for the recording itself. We'll need one more step to actually find out the FSID(s) for the recording associated with that directory entry. To get this information, use the **mfs_dumpobj** command with the FSID of the metadata object to dump the contents of the metadata node, as in the following example:

```
# ./mfs_dumpobj 1882
Found 4 MFS partitions
Showing 1882/11 {
    Program[16]=1881/-1
    Station[17]=1880/-1
    Date[18]=10805
    Time[19]=3600
    Duration[20]=225
    IndexUsedBy[6]=1882/10
}
```

```
RecordingPart 1882/12 {
    Begin[16]=0
    End[17]=225000
    File[18]=1879
}
(null) 1882/15 {
    UNKNOWN(126,16)[16]=1
    UNKNOWN(126,17)[17]=2
    UNKNOWN(126,18)[18]=1
    UNKNOWN(126,19)[19]=1
    IndexUsedBy[6]=1882/10
}
Recording 1882/10 PRIMARY {
    Version[1]=11
    State[16]=4
    Showing[17]=1882/11
    SelectionType[18]=3
    RecordQuality[40]=100
    BitRate[21]=0
    Score[22]=0
    StartDate[24]=10805
    StartTime[25]=3600
    StopTime[27]=3825
    Part[34]=1882/12
    ExpirationDate[19]=24855
    ExpirationTime[20]=0
    DeletionTime[39]=0
    DeletionDate[38]=0
    StopDate[26]=10805
    StreamFileSize[54]=188416
    UNKNOWN(14,59)[59]=10
    UNKNOWN(14,57)[57]=1882/15
    NSecondsWatched[47]=737
    NVisit[48]=4
    IndexUsed[5]=1882/11 1882/15
    IndexPath[4]=/Recording/Active/1:10805:03600:1882 \
            Recording/NowShowingByClassic/2:89194:96399:1882 \
          /Recording/NowShowingByExpiration/2:24855:00000:1882 \
```

```
        /Recording/NowShowingByTitle/1:WELCOME TO THE TIVOLUTION:89194:
96399:1882 \
        /Recording/DiskUsed/10/1882:188416
}
```

The RecordingPart section(s) of the **mfs_dumpobj** output contain the significant information. In this case, there's only one RecordingPart entry, but most recordings will consist of multiple parts, depending on the length of the recording and the quality level at which you're recording. The File entry in each RecordingPart gives the FSID of the TY file associated with that part of the recording—in this case, a single segment with the FSID 1879.

Once you know the FSID(s) associated with the recording that you want to extract from your TiVo's hard disk, you can extract it from the disk using the **mfs_export** command, as in the following example:

```
# ./mfs_export 1879 welcome.ty
Found 4 MFS partitions
exporting fsid 1879 of size 192937984 to welcome.ty
starting at 0 for 192937984 bytes
100%
```

That's all there is to it! If your recording has multiple parts, you should extract and save each of them to your system. You're now ready to begin converting them to some other format, or to reinsert them on any TiVo. If you're going to insert them onto a TiVo, it's easiest to insert each part as a separate TY file—you can try manually creating a nowshowing.xml file and manually packaging the parts as a TMF file, but that's extremely complex and error-prone—the smallest typo can screw up your TiVo. Also, remember that scrambled recordings can only be viewed on the exact system that they came from, and then only if the master encryption key there has not changed.

 **TIP**

If the recording that you're extracting from the disk has multiple parts and you want to convert it to another format, you can concatenate all of its parts into a single TY file using the Linux **cat** command. Assuming that you had three TY files that you'd saved as *part1.ty*, *part2.ty*, and *part3.ty*, you could produce a single TY file for your entire recording using the following command:

```
cat part1.ty part2.ty part3.ty > entire_show.ty
```

# Disabling Video Encryption

Like most technologies, TiVos have been increasing in performance and reliability since they were first introduced. Unfortunately, they have also been increasing in paranoia about hacking. As explained in the section of Chapter 9 on "Using Two-Kernel Monte," Series 2 TiVos perform an extremely anal set of hash-bashed security checks to verify the integrity of the system when it boots. Along the same lines, Series 1 DirecTiVos and Series 2 TiVos encrypt the video that they record. This is totally transparent when you watch a recording on your TiVo because the recordings are decrypted on-the-fly, but it does make video extraction "challenging."

If you have a Series 1 stand-alone TiVo, you don't need to read this section. Series 1 stand-alones don't encrypt their recordings. However, if you have a Series 1 or Series 2 DirecTiVo or a Series 2 stand-alone TiVo (running Version 4+ of the TiVo software), this section is for you! DirecTiVos have always encrypted the recordings that they make, presumably because the data downloaded from satellite is pure digital information and is higher quality on disk than the recordings made by stand-alone TiVos. Series 2 TiVos introduced anti-hacking measures such as PROM and initial RAM disk hashing checks, and also began encrypting recordings with Version 4.0 of the TiVo software. I've heard the theory that hashing and encrypting recordings were initiated because of the network-readiness of Series 2 TiVo models, so that randoms couldn't simply connect to a TiVo and pull off recordings that they weren't entitled to. This is almost plausible, and certainly sounds good.

Luckily, the TiVo hacking community is knee-deep in smart people, and there are hacks to enable you to get access to your TiVo and your recordings, regardless of hashing and video encryption. If you're uncomfortable using these but still want to back up your precious recordings, try one of the TV tuner/video capture solutions discussed earlier in this chapter. If you, like me, believe that you paid for your TiVo and its service, and you should be able to do anything that you want with it as long as you don't actively rip off anyone, read on—this section is full of cool information and neat hacks!

 **NOTE**

This section owes a tremendous debt to TiVo hackers such as AlphaWolf, rc3105, ScrambleThis, and many others who developed, consolidated, and originally posted much of this information.

Early fixes to the encryption problem on DirecTiVos and some Series 2 stand-alones involved patching kernel memory (known as *kmem patches*) and loadable kernel modules (commonly referred to as *noscramble* or *unscramble modules*, since those are the base names of the modules themselves). The standard method for undoing encryption to give you clear access to your recordings involves patching the tivoapp application. This application is the core application that creates and plays recordings on your TiVo. The unscramble module is still useful for decrypting encrypted streams on Series 1 DirecTiVo systems after you've corrected the encryption problem in the tivoapp application.

The instructions in this section explain how to eliminate encryption for new recordings made using TiVo software Versions 3.1.X and greater—at this point, most Series 2 and DirecTiVo users have probably upgraded to newer software releases (or should), so older versions of the TiVo software are not supported. If you insist on running an older version of the TiVo software, you can either use the older kmem or noscramble module approaches, or you can try posting on the DealDatabase thread on this topic (**http://www.dealdatabase.com/forum/showthread.php?t=31213**) to see if someone can supply you with the information that you need.

## WARNING

The instructions in this section are designed for use with hacked TiVos—in other words, they should be executed from a serial or Telnet connection to your TiVo. If you are using a Series 1 DirecTiVo, you can actually follow these instructions after putting your TiVo drive in a PC and booting from a boot CD, such as the BATBD CD that accompanies this book. However, if you are using an unhacked Series 2 TiVo and try following these instructions from a PC, the **tivoapp** binary will fail to pass the hash checks, and your TiVo will be dead in the water. Don't try this!

## TIP

If you are using any previous kmem patches or noscamble/unscramble modules, disable them and reboot before fixing the **tivoapp** application. These patches and modules can interfere with the **tivoapp** repair process, and can also interfere with your ability to play back recordings made prior to the patch procedure described in this section.

To eliminate encryption on DirecTiVo and stand-alone Series 2 models, do the following:

1. Connect to your TiVo over a serial or Ethernet connection and make sure that your root partition is writable, by executing the following command:

   ```
   mount -o remount,rw /
   ```

2. Make a backup copy of the tivoapp binary, located in /tvbin/tivoapp, and make sure that you are working on a version of the tivoapp that isn't running. Trying to edit the copy of the tivoapp that is actually running will fail, displaying the message "tivoapp: text file busy." To do this, execute the following commands:

   ```
   cd /tvbin
   cp tivoapp tivoapp.orig
   mv tivoapp tivoapp.save
   cp tivoapp.orig tivoapp
   chmod 755 tivoapp
   ```

3. Consult Table 12.2 to see which command to execute to correct the **tivoapp** binary on your system and execute that command on your TiVo.

**TABLE 12.2  Commands for Disabling TiVoApp Encryption**

| TiVo | Software # | Command |
|------|-----------|---------|
| S1 | 3.1.0b | ```echo -ne "\x48\x00\x00\x38" ¦ dd conv=notrunc of=tivoapp bs=1 seek=4678456``` |
| S2 | 3.1.1b | ```echo -ne "\x3C\x02\x00\x00" ¦ dd conv=notrunc of=tivoapp bs=1 seek=6493084``` |
| S2 | 3.1.1c | ```echo -ne "\x3C\x02\x00\x00" ¦ dd conv=notrunc of=tivoapp bs=1 seek=6495772``` |
| S2 | 4.0 ONLY | ```echo -ne "\x3c\x02\x00\x00" ¦ dd conv=notrunc of=tivoapp bs=1 seek=8593192``` |
| S2 | 4.0.1 or 4.0.1b | ```echo -ne "\x3c\x02\x00\x00" ¦ dd conv=notrunc of=tivoapp bs=1 seek=8618248``` |

4. If you are using **mfs_ftp**, remove its cache of XML files that describe various recordings on your TiVo. These are located in the cache subdirectory of the directory in which you installed **mfs_ftp**. As an example, if **mfs_ftp** was installed in /var on your TiVo, you would execute the following command on the TiVo to flush the XML cache:

```
rm /var/mfs_ftp/cache/*.xml
```

5. Next, remount your root filesystem in read-only mode to avoid any possible filesystem corruption, as in the following example:

```
mount -o remount,ro /
```

6. Reboot your TiVo so that the newly patched version of the **tivoapp** binary is the version that is running on your system. Any recordings that you subsequently make should be unencrypted.

```
Reboot
```

If you're a Series 2 stand-alone TiVo user, you're done. New recordings have to be unencrypted (in technical terms, their CSO attribute will be set to zero). You will be able to play both newly created unencrypted recordings and any existing scrambled recordings—make sure that you remember which is which if you are planning to extract and convert them because the **tivoapp** patch cannot retroactively decrypt recordings that were made while encryption was enabled. There is currently no way to decrypt existing Series 2 recordings, but who knows—the TiVo hacker community is full of incredibly clever people. As a suggestion, at this point you may simply want to archive all of your existing encrypted recordings to your PC. That will make it easier for you to remember what's encrypted and what's not, because everything on your Series 2 will be unencrypted (at least until your next TiVo software upgrade).

**TIP**

You can check the encryption status of your TiVo and any saved recordings by running the **ciphercheck4.tcl** script that is provided in the BATBD's scrambling directory. Thanks, AlphaWolf! Transfer it to your TiVo, make it executable, and execute it to see the encryption status of your TiVo and any recordings that it contains, as in the following output:

```
bash-2.02# chmod 755 ciphercheck4.tcl bash-2.02
# ./ciphercheck4.tcl
TyStream encryption is currently disabled.
Here is the status of your current recordings:
Encrypted CSO Set Stream Name
----------------------------------------------------------------
No         No       welcome.ty
No         No       Rockford Files
No         No       Touching Evil
No         No       Friends
[...]
```

If you are a Series 1 DirecTiVo user, various kernel modules and scripts are available to unscramble existing recordings, enable extraction, and so on. I used the tivoapp patch described earlier in this section to ensure that new recordings weren't scrambled, and used the unscramble.o module to unscramble my existing recordings. This seems to be the most popular and reliable approach. Your mileage may vary.

You can decrypt existing scrambled recordings by installing the unscramble.o loadable kernel module that is found in the scrambling/s1_unscramble on the BATBD CD that is included with this book. To install this module, transfer it to your TiVo (in binary mode) and add the command to load it at the end of your /etc/rc.d/rc.sysinit file. Note that the path to the module in the following example assumes that you transferred the module to your /var/hack directory. If you put it somewhere else, change the path to reflect the directory in which you actually installed the module:

```
insmod /var/hack/unscramble.o
```

After rebooting, you can use this module to decrypt any recordings made before you patched the **tivoapp** binary by simply playing the first few seconds of those recordings. You should wait at least 10 seconds between decrypting recordings. Then you can use the extraction tool of your choice to extract the recording. This module actually exploits a bug in the **mfs_stream** utility (used by most tools to extract recordings over the Net). It will not decrypt recordings that you extract from your TiVo disk while that disk is in a PC (discussed in the previous section).

**TIP**

If you had previously been using one of the older methods for disabling encryption, such as an older loadable kernel module or a kernel memory (kmem) patch, recordings that you made when using these mechanisms will no longer play back. In order to get them to play, you will have to remove their CSO keys so that the patched version of **tivoapp** doesn't try to use them unnecessarily. You can use AlphaWolf's **csoscout.tcl** script, also provided in the scrambling directory on the BATBD CD, to punt any CSO keys for existing unscrambled recordings without disturbing them for scrambled recordings. This script assumes that you have a copy of **mfs_export** on your TiVo, which is also provided in the `scrambling/s1_unscramble` directory on the BATBD, just in case you can't find or build it easily.

# Using TyTool

TyTool is a totally amazing software package for extracting and converting unscrambled TiVo recordings. Written by TiVo hacker and forum moderator extraordinaire jdiner, it's the best argument for having a Windows box in your home that a Linux/Mac OS X geek like myself can think of. TyTool is also under very active development—which means that it just keeps getting better and better. The BATBD CD that accompanies this book contains the latest version that was available when this book was updated (TyTool9r14), but you owe it to yourself to check the appropriate DealDatabase.com forum to see if a newer version is available when you want to begin experimenting with it. TyTool has its own sticky thread on the "Extraction, Insertion, & Streaming Support" forum there, at **http://www.dealdatabase.com/forum/showthread.php?t=34402**. I really can't say enough good things about this package—except my heartfelt thanks to jdiner!

**TIP**

If you don't have a Windows box but want to use TyTool, VirtualPC and VMWare are excellent commercial products that enable you to run Windows on Mac OS X and Linux systems, respectively. Microsoft bought Connectix, the company that originally developed VirtualPC, but has not yet killed off the product and has even updated it since the acquisition. Still, you might want to get it soon... For more information about the Mac version of VirtualPC, see **http://www.microsoft.com/mac/products/virtualpc/virtualpc.aspx**. For more information about VMWare, see **http://www.vmware.com/products/desktop/ws_features.html**. I've used VMWare for years at home and at work, and think it's an awesome product.

An earlier version of TyTool currently forms the core of PTVupgrade.com's DVRchive product, which is great in terms of getting some official support for the package through PTVupgrade.com. A description of this product and related support information are available at **http://www.ptvupgrade.com/db/cs/DVRchive** and **http://www.ptvupgrade.com/ support/DVRchive**. If you're a convert from the ReplayTV universe, PTVupgrade.com's DVRchive product is totally different than the DVArchive software that is available for extracting recordings from ReplayTV systems. If you're still using a ReplayTV system, isn't it time to bite the bullet, give up on your BetaMax DVR, and get a TiVo?

This section explains how to use TyTool to extract and convert an unscrambled recording from your TiVo, removing commercials and any other interruptions from the recording as part of the process. (After all, you already watched them when you first watched the show, right?) TyTool has many options and bells and whistles, and probably deserves its own book—discussing all of them would certainly bloat this one. The DealDatabase.com forum on TyTool is very active, and is a great place to ask about specific options, their implications, and general usage techniques.

Using TyTool to extract recordings directly from your TiVo requires that your TiVo be networked, and that you install its tserver application and a companion TCL script on your TiVo. This is not necessary if you simply want to use it to process recordings in TY format that you've already extracted using **mfs_ftp** or some other application, but the server is pretty lightweight and you might as well run it unless you're having memory problems from running too many other hacks on your TiVos. The TyTool9r14.zip archive provided in the TyTool directory on the BATBD CD includes the server software for both Series 1 and Series 2 TiVos. Unzipping this archive on your Windows system to install TyTool will create the TyTool9r14 directory (where the TyTool application lives) and the TyTool9r14/ TSERVER_Series1 and TyTool9r14/TSERVER_Series2_MIPS directories on your system. Use whatever mechanism you want to transfer the contents of the appropriate TSERVER directory to your TiVo and then telnet to the TiVo to start them manually or add them to your TiVo's /etc/rc.d/rc.sysinit script and restart your TiVo.

Once the server is running on your TiVo, return to your Windows system and double-click on the TyTool9r14 icon (or whatever icon corresponds to any newer version that you're using) to start the main TyTool application. A screen like the one shown in Figure 12.1 displays

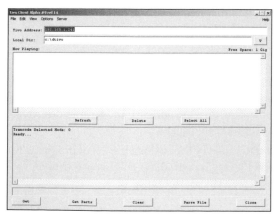

**FIGURE 12.1** *TyTool's startup screen*

**TIP**

If you get confused about what to do next when using TyTool and don't have this book handy, TyTool's File menu displays a quick "cheat sheet" that highlights the significant steps in the extraction and conversion process (see Figure 12.2). Nice one, jdiner!

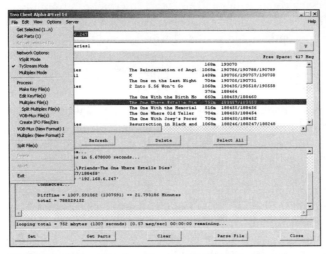

**FIGURE 12.2** *The cheat sheet on TyTool's File menu*

At this point, to extract and convert a TiVo recording to standard MPEG-2 format, do the following:

1. Pull down the File menu and verify that TyStream Mode is selected; select it if it is not.

2. Enter your TiVo's IP address in the TiVo Address text box.

3. Click the down-arrow icon to the right of the Local Dir text field. The Pick Directory dialog shown in Figure 12.3 displays.

4. Double-click the ".." entry to move to the root of your Windows system's hard drive and navigate to find the directory where you want to store TY files, parts of TY files, intermediate files produced when using TyTool, and the MPEG-2 file that you will eventually produce using TyTool. When you've navigated to that directory, click the OK button to set that directory as your current working directory. The dialog closes, and the main TyTool screen displays.

5. Click the Refresh button to cause TyTool to load the list of programs that are available on your TiVo's Now Playing screen. After this list is retrieved, TyTool should look something like the screen shown in Figure 12.4.

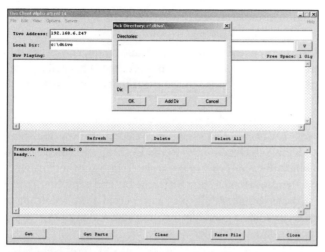

**FIGURE 12.3** *Selecting a directory for local storage in TyTool*

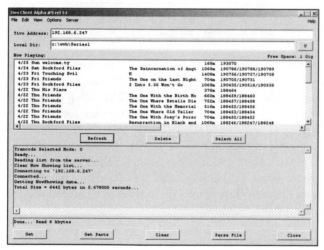

**FIGURE 12.4** *Retrieving your TiVo's Now Playing List in TyTool*

6. Select the show that you want to extract from your TiVo and click Get at the bottom of the TyTool screen to retrieve that recording. The general status box in the middle of the TyTool screen displays some summary information about the selected file, and the active status box at the bottom of the TyTool screen will display information about the transfer, including a time estimate for completing the retrieval. Depending on the speed of your network and your TiVo, this might be a good time to get a cup of coffee. If you're extracting a recording from a Series 1 TiVo, this is not a good time to decide to watch something on it, as the screen may break up due to the processing power needed to extract and send the recording over your network.

7. Once the extraction completes, you'll want to verify a few of the TyTool option settings before proceeding with the conversion process:

   ◆ Pull down the Options menu, select the Audio menu, and either select or make sure that the Patch Audio Holes option is selected. This will ensure synchronization between audio and video in the event that drop-outs are encountered in the audio stream.

   ◆ For MPEG-2 conversion that you may want to subsequently burn to a DVD, select the #5 - DVD - 48 @ 192 option. Selecting this option transcodes your audio to 48 KHz, which conforms to the DVD specification. Transcoding is a process in which the audio stream is translated into another format (in this case, PCM), and then re-encoded at a different bit and sampling rate. This is not necessary in order to successfully play a converted TiVo recording on all DVD players, but is generally a good idea because stand-alone TiVos typically record audio at approximately 33 KHz.

**TIP**

You only have to perform Steps 8 through 11 if you want to edit the extracted recording. If you want to convert it to MPEG as it is, you can skip straight to Step 12.

8. Pull down the File menu and select Make Key File(s). Key files are files that contain information about the video in the selected TY file, and are used to identify the segments of the file that you want to convert. The dialog shown in Figure 12.5 displays, showing any TY files and MPEG files that are located in the directory you selected when you first started the TyTool process. In the window at the upper right, select the name of the file associated with the recording you just extracted and click the Add button to add it to the listing in the File(s) to process window. Click the Process button. TyTool will index the file, displaying status messages in the general status dialog. When processing completes, a Done message is displayed in TyTool's general status window.

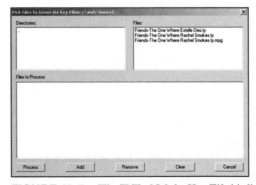

**FIGURE 12.5** *The TyTool Make Key File(s) dialog*

9. Pull down the File menu and select the Edit Keyfile(s) command. The dialog shown in Figure 12.6 displays, showing any key files that are located in the directory you selected earlier in TyTool. In the window at the upper right, select the name of the key file associated with the recording you just indexed and click the Add button to add it to the listing in the File(s) to process window. Click the Process button.

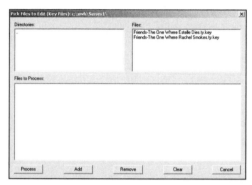

**FIGURE 12.6** *The TyTool Edit Keyfile(s) dialog*

10. TyTool displays its GOP (Group of Pictures) Editor dialog (see Figure 12.7). Using this dialog, you can select the beginning and end of any portions of the TY video that you want to eliminate when converting the TiVo video to MPEG-2. To move backward and forward in the video, click the buttons that display the right and left arrow keys. To move through the video more quickly, press and hold the right and left arrow keys on your keyboard.

 **NOTE**

To save processing time and screen space, the GOP Editor's video display window does not attempt to display the TY file using the correct aspect ratio. The aspect ratio of your recording is still preserved.

To define the starting point of a range that you want to delete, click the left bracket ([) button. To define the end of a range that you want to delete, click the right bracket (]) button. As you define ranges of video to delete, the start and end points of those ranges are listed in the Start and Stop fields below the Cut List window at the upper right of the GOP Editor dialog. After you define the start and stop points for a range that you want to delete, click the Add button to add it to the Cut List window at the upper right.

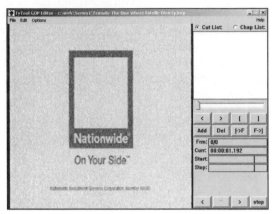

**FIGURE 12.7** *The TyTool GOP Editor dialog*

 **NOTE**

The starting and ending points of these ranges are not 100% exact. Because of the way in which MPEG videos predict motion from one frame to another, TyTool is able to do an extremely impressive job in seamlessly eliminating these ranges from its eventual output.

11. When you're done selecting all of the portions of the recording that you want to eliminate, pull down the GOP Editor's File menu and select the Save Cut List menu item. A somewhat cryptic dialog displays, showing the name of the cut list that you just created. Click the OK button to close this dialog. Next, pull down the File menu again and select the Exit command to close the GOP Editor and return to the main TyTool window.

12. Pull down the File menu and select the Multiplex File(s) command. The dialog shown in Figure 12.8 displays, showing any TY files and MPEG files that are located in the directory you selected when you first started the TyTool process. In the window at the upper right, select the name of the TY file that you are converting and click the Add button to add it to the listing in the File(s) to Process window. Click the Process button. TyTool processes the video, removing any sections identified in your Cut List, generating an MPEG-2 file, and displaying status messages in the general status dialog. When processing completes, a Done message is displayed in TyTool's general status window. Your MPEG-2 file will be stored in the directory you selected previously, and will have the same name as that of your TY file, except that it will also have an .mpg extension appended to the name of the file.

That's all there is to it! You can now play the MPEG-2 file that you generated in Windows Media Player, any other MPEG-2 compliant Windows application, or move it to another system for display in a Linux or Mac OS X application that understands the MPEG-2 video format.

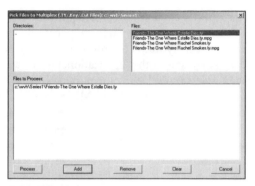

**FIGURE 12.8**  *Selecting the File to multiplex in TyTool*

# Using TyStudio

As discussed in the previous section, TyTool is Windows-only, which can be a problem for people who use other types of personal computers. Luckily, an excellent alternative is available for Linux, Mac OS X, and Windows users in TyStudio. TyStudio does a great job of extracting and converting TY files. It's the only open source GUI conversion solution for Linux and Mac OS X users, and works equally well on Windows systems. I tend to stick with TyTool on Windows systems, but TyStudio has many fans there. Unfortunately, TyStudio development isn't as active as TyTool development—actually, at the time this book was written, the last update to TyStudio was in 2003. The versions included in the TyStudio directory on this book's BATBD CD are actually beta versions from that time. That said, they work fine.

The home page for the TyStudio project in on SourceForge at **http://dvd-create.sourceforge.net/tystudio/index.shtml**. The TyStudio directory at the top level of the BATBD CD that accompanies this book includes archive files of the latest Linux, Mac OS X, and Windows applications at the time this book was written.

This section explains how to use TyStudio to extract and convert an unscrambled recording from your TiVo, removing commercials and any other interruptions from the recording as part of the process. (After all, you already watched them when you first watched the show, right?)

 **TIP**

Most of this section assumes that you are using Windows or Linux. If you are using Mac OS X, you can find one person's discussion of extracting and processing video on a Mac OS X system using TyStudio at **http://minnie.tuhs.org/twiki/bin/view/Howtovideoextract/ExtractVideoonOSX**. The process described there uses Fink, which is a Linux execution layer that runs on Mac OS X and is roughly analogous to the way that Cygwin enables you to execute Linux applications on a Windows system. It also suggests additional software packages that you can use if you have problems with the beta version of TyStudio on Max OS X.

Using TyStudio to extract recordings directly from your TiVo requires that your TiVo be networked and that you install TyStudio's **tyserver** and **tyindex** applications on your TiVo. This is not necessary if you simply want to use TyStudio to process recordings in TY format that you've already extracted using **mfs_ftp** or some other application, but the server is pretty light-weight, and you may as well run it unless you're having memory problems from running too many other hacks on your TiVos. The PPC (Series 1) and MIPS (Series 2) versions of these applications are located in the TyStudio directory at the top level of the BATBD CD. To install these applications on a Series 1 TiVo, copy the file **tyserver.ppc.sh** to your TiVo and execute it to install these applications in the directory /var/index. To install these applications on a Series 2 TiVo, copy the file **tyserver.mips.sh** to your TiVo and execute it to install these applications in /var/index. The shell scripts will automatically create this directory if it does not already exist. You can then start these applications manually (in the background) or by adding them to your TiVo's /etc/rc.d/rc.sysinit script and restarting your TiVo.

Once these applications are running on your TiVo, you'll need to install the TyStudio software on your personal computer. All of the installers referenced in this list are located in the TyStudio directory at the root of the BATBD CD that accompanies this book:

◆ To install TyStudio on a Linux system, execute the tystudio.i386.sh shell script as root. This will install the TyStudio software in /usr/local/bin. You can then execute the **/usr/local/bin/tystudio** command to start TyStudio. Most of the examples in this section show TyStudio running on a Linux system.

◆ To install TyStudio on a Mac OS X system, transfer the tystudio-0.5b3a1.dmg disk image file to your Mac and double-click it to mount it on your OS X desktop. You can then drag the tystudio folder from the mounted disk image to your Applications folder in order to install TyStudio. Note that TyStudio is an X Windows system application on Mac OS X, and you will therefore have to install Apple's X Windows system distribution or a commercial X Windows system application for OS X before you can actually run the graphical portion of TyStudio (**tyeditor**). After the X Window system is running on your Mac, start an X terminal application (xterm) if one isn't already running, and start the **tyeditor** process by executing the **/Application/tystudio/tyeditor** command. Figure 12.9 shows TyStudio running on a Mac OS X system.

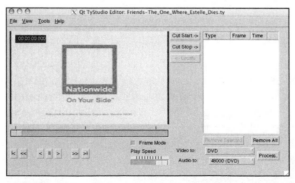

**FIGURE 12.9** *TyStudio running on a Mac OS X system*

◆ To install TyStudio on a Windows system, transfer the file setup.exe to your Windows system and double-click it to start the installation process. The TyStudio applications will install into \Program Files\tystudio. You can then select the tystudio Editor menu item or icon to start TyStudio (see Figure 12.10).

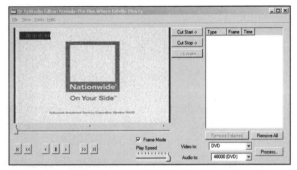

**FIGURE 12.10**  *TyStudio running on a Windows System*

After you've installed the TiVo and personal computer portions of TyStudio, to extract and convert a TiVo recording to standard MPEG-2 format, do the following:

1. Start the TyStudio application as described earlier (see Figure 12.11).

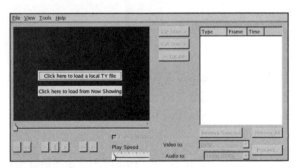

**FIGURE 12.11**  *TyStudio's Startup screen on a Linux system*

2. To extract a TY file from your TiVo, click the Click Here To Load From Now Showing button. The Now Showing dialog displays. Enter your TiVo's host name or IP address in the text entry field at the top of the dialog and click the Refresh button to retrieve a list of all of the programs in the Now Showing list on your TiVo (see Figure 12.12).

3. Select the name of the recording that you want to extract and convert. To retrieve the file to your computer before doing any processing (recommended), select the Copy to PC First check box. Click OK to retrieve the file from your TiVo. TyStudio displays a dialog in which you can navigate to the directory in which you want to store the extracted recording. After you select this location and change or accept the

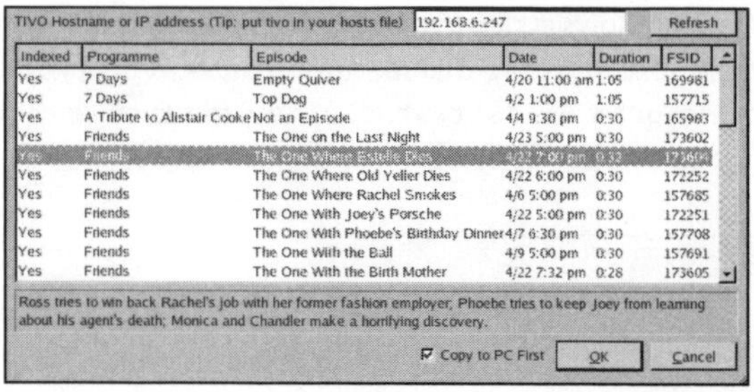

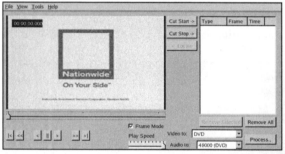

**FIGURE 12.12** *Selecting a show from the Now Showing list in TyStudio*

file name, go have a cup of coffee. After the file is retrieved, TyStudio will index the file, which makes it easy for TyStudio to identify the ranges of the recording that you may want to eliminate before generating an MPEG-2 file.

4. Once indexing is complete, TyStudio should look something like Figure 12.13. Note that, unlike TyTool, TyStudio displays the extracted recording using the correct aspect ratio.

**FIGURE 12.13** *TyStudio displaying an extracted TY file*

5. Next, click the down arrow beside the Video to field and select Generic MPEG2. Click the down arrow beside the Audio to field and select 48000 (DVD). This audio setting conforms to the DVD specification in case you ever want to burn your MPEG-2 file to a DVD. This setting is used during transcoding, which is a process in which the audio stream is translated into another format (in this case, PCM), and then re-encoded at a different bit and sampling rate. As mentioned before, this is not necessary in order to successfully play a converted TiVO recording on all DVD players, but is generally a good idea because stand-alone TiVos typically record audio at approximately 33 KHz.

6. You can now begin to define the beginning and end of any portions of the TY video that you want to eliminate when converting the TiVo video to MPEG-2, as shown in Figure 12.14. To move backward and forward in the video, click the buttons that display the right arrow and left arrow keys. To move backward and forward through the video more quickly, click the double-left and double-right arrow buttons.

To define the starting point of a range that you want to delete, click the Cut Start button. To define the end of a range that you want to delete, click the Cut Stop button. As you define ranges of video to delete, the start and end points of those ranges are listed in the window at the upper right of the TyStudio dialog.

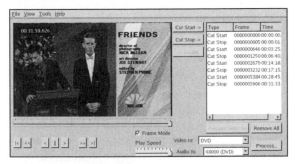

**FIGURE 12.14** *TyStudio showing Cut Start and Cut Stop entries*

7. Once you've defined all of the portions of the extracted recording that you want to eliminate when converting it to MPEG-2, click the Process button in the lower left corner of the TyStudio dialog. A progress dialog displays (see Figure 12.15).

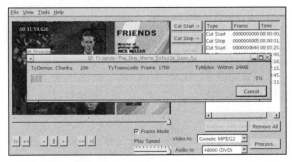

**FIGURE 12.15** *TyStudio processing an extracted video*

That's all there is to it! You can now play the MPEG-2 file that you generated in your favorite MPEG-2-compliant application on Linux, Mac OS X, or Windows.

# Using mfs_ftp

The **mfs_ftp** application is by far the coolest and easiest way of extracting recordings from a TiVo and subsequently reinserting them. It has various features that make it incredibly powerful and easy to use:

◆ Any PC-side FTP client is suitable for use with **mfs_ftp**. No special PC-side tools are required in order to extract TiVo recordings in TY, TY+, or TMF formats, exec files for Windows Media Player (ASX files), or batch files for **mplayer** running under Cygwin on Windows systems, or meta-information about your recordings in text or XML formats.

◆ The **mfs_ftp** server on the TiVo can run side-by-side with your existing FTP server, since it uses its own port (3105), rather than the generic FTP port (21).

◆ It presents a virtual set of directories that provide entry points to the recordings on your TiVo in different formats. To extract a recording in TY format, you simply **cd** to the ty directory once you've established an FTP connection to your TiVo and extract any of the TY files that it contains.

Truly impressive! The **mfs_ftp** program is free for personal use but cannot be redistributed, so it is not included on the CD that accompanies this book. You should retrieve your own copy from DealDatabase.com at **http://www.dealdatabase.com/forum/showthread.php?t=21915**. If you are planning on running mfs_ftp on a Series 2 TiVo, you must also retrieve the Series 2 binaries from the thread at **http://www.dealdatabase.com/forum/showthread.php?s=&threadid=29459**.

 **NOTE**

The author's PayPal address is rc3105@hotmail.com—donations are always cheerfully accepted (and justified), and you can also purchase a license to redistribute a single copy of **mfs_ftp** if you'd like to bundle it with a single hacked TiVo that you are reselling.

In order to use **mfs_ftp** on a Series 1 system, simply retrieve the mfs_ftp.tar.zip archive from the URL in the previous paragraph, unzip it, and transfer the resulting mfs_ftp.tar file to your TiVo. Change directory (**cd**) to /var, and untar the archive using the **tar** command or the native cpio equivalent (**cpio -i -H tar -d -F mfs_ftp.tar**). This will create the directory /var/mfs_ftp and any mandatory subdirectories and symbolic links. You can then start the **/var/mfs_ftp/mfs_ftp.tcl** script in the background (and probably add this to your TiVo's /etc/rc.d/rc.sysinit startup file).

In order to use **mfs_ftp** on a Series 2 system, retrieve both the Series 1 mfs_ftp.tar.zip archive and the s2bins.tar.zip archive from the Dealdatabase.com threads given earlier, unzip them, and transfer the resulting tar files to your Series 2 TiVo. Install the Series 1 version of **mfs_ftp** as described in the previous paragraph; then extract the contents of the s2bins.tar file using the **tar** command or the local cpio equivalent. This will overwrite the Series 1 binaries in the /var/mfs_ftp directory with the Series 2 equivalents. You can then start the **/var/mfs_ftp/mfs_ftp.tcl** script in the background (and probably add this to your TiVo's /etc/rc.d/rc.sysinit startup file).

An example of using a command-line FTP client to connect to an **mfs_ftp** server that is running on a TiVo is the following (I've added some blank lines to make it easier to see specific FTP commands and their results):

```
$ ftp 192.168.6.247 3105
Connected to 192.168.6.247.
220 Mfs_Ftp ver 1.2.9k - {sock22} from "192.168.6.32:33413"
 Name (192.168.6.247:wvh):
331 User name okay, need password.
Password:
230 Running in TiVo Mode.
Remote system type is UNIX.

 ftp> hash
Hash mark printing on (1024 bytes/hash mark).

 ftp> bin
200 Type set to I

 ftp> passive
Passive mode off.

 ftp> ls
200 PORT command successful.
150 Opening ASCII mode data connection for file list.
dr--r--r--   1 0          0               1024 Jan 01  1972 tmf
dr--r--r--   1 0          0               1024 Jan 01  1972 ty
dr--r--r--   1 0          0               1024 Jan 01  1972 ty+
dr--r--r--   1 0          0               1024 Jan 01  1972 xml
dr--r--r--   1 0          0               1024 Jan 01  1972 txt
dr--r--r--   1 0          0               1024 Jan 01  1972 bat
dr--r--r--   1 0          0               1024 Jan 01  1972 asx
-r--r--r--   1 0          0                  0 May 31 19:00 phoenix.txt
-r--r--r--   1 0          0                  0 May 31 19:00 shutdown.txt
#
226 Transfer complete.

 ftp> cd ty
```

```
250 Directory change successful.

 ftp> ls
200 PORT command successful.
150 Opening ASCII mode data connection for file list.
-rwxr-xr-x   1 0         0       0192937984 Aug 01  1999 1882 - Welcome to
the TiVolution - .ty
-rwxr-xr-x   1 0         0       1602224128 Apr 02 01:00 157715 - 7 Days -
Top Dog.ty
-rwxr-xr-x   1 0         0       0738197504 Apr 03 07:00 157682 - Friends -
The One With the Holiday Armadillo.ty
-rwxr-xr-x   1 0         0       1677721600 Apr 04 08:00 165980 - Master-
piece Theatre - Daniel Deronda.ty
-rwxr-xr-x   1 0         0       0559939584 Apr 04 09:30 165983 - A Tribute
to Alistair Cooke - .ty
[...]
```

 **NOTE**

You must specify that you want to connect to port 3105 in order to use **mfs_ftp**. If you do not specify a port number, you will be connected to the standard FTP server (installed from the hack archives contained on the BATBD CD that accompanies this book), which is useful but irrelevant in the extraction context.

Like all TiVo FTP clients, no authentication is necessary, so you can just press the Enter key when prompted for a Name and Password. After initiating a connection to the mfs_ftp server, you must issue some standard FTP configuration commands:

◆ *bin*   The bin command sets all future file transfers to be in binary mode, which is necessary in order to preserve the integrity of any TiVo recordings that you extract.

◆ *passive*   The passive command turns FTP's passive mode off. Whether an FTP connection is active or passive (the default) determines whether the client initiates the connection to the server's data port and the server sends an acknowledgement (active), or if the server initiates the connection to the client's data port and the client sends an acknowledgement (passive). Many FTP clients have problems with passive mode FTP, so active FTP is generally preferred for use with **mfs_ftp**. (You may see problems if you are going through a firewall or using a Web browser as an FTP client. My suggestion is simple—don't do that.)

◆ *hash*   (optional) The hash command causes a hash-mark (#) to be displayed for each 1K of data transferred between the server and the client in either direction. I generally find this useful in large files transfers (such as TiVo recordings) to make sure that I can see that something is happening. TiVo recordings are huge and take a long time to transfer—without the hash marks, it's hard to tell what is going on.

The files and directories shown when you first connect to mfs_ftp are the following:

- ◆ *asx* A virtual directory that lists your recordings as ASX files that can be used to stream TiVo recordings directly into Windows Media Player, assuming that you have installed d7o's **TyShow** application (provided in the mfs_ftp directory of the BATBD CD that accompanies this book). Retrieving any of these files causes the mfs_ftp server to create and send an ASX file for the specified recording.

- ◆ *bat* A virtual directory that lists your recordings as BAT (batch) files that can be used to stream TiVo recordings directly into mplayer running under Cygwin on Windows systems. Retrieving any of these files causes the mfs_ftp server to create and send a BAT file for the specified recording.

- ◆ *phoenix.txt* Retrieving this file from your FTP client causes the TiVo-side mfs_ftp server to restart.

- ◆ *shutdown.txt* Retrieving this file from your FTP client causes the TiVo-side mfs_ftp server to shut down and exit without restarting.

- ◆ *tmf* A virtual directory that lists your TiVo recordings as TMF files. Retrieving any of these files will cause the mfs_ftp server to create and send a version of the specified recording in TMF format (see the section entitled "TiVo Video File Formats").

- ◆ *txt* A virtual directory that lists text files that provide meta-information for your TiVo recordings. Retrieving any of these files will cause the mfs_ftp server to extract and send meta-information about the specified recording in text format.

- ◆ *ty* A virtual directory that lists your TiVo recordings as TY files. Retrieving any of these files will cause the mfs_ftp server to create and send a version of the specified recording in TY format (see the earlier section entitled "TiVo Video File Formats"). (These are actually TY+ files, but what are a few extra bytes between friends?)

- ◆ *ty+* A virtual directory that lists your TiVo recordings as TY+ files. Retrieving any of these files will cause the mfs_ftp server to create and send a version of the specified recording in TY+ format.

- ◆ *xml* A virtual directory that lists XML files that provide meta-information for your TiVo recordings. Retrieving any of these files will cause the mfs_ftp server to extract and send meta-information about the specified recording in XML format.

To retrieve a recording or information about one of your recordings in a particular format, use the **cd** command to change directory to the directory associated with that format, and use the **get** command to retrieve a specific recording. Since the names of your recordings contain spaces, it's generally a good idea to enclose the name of the file that you want to retrieve within double quotation marks inside your FTP client.

That's all there is to extracting a recording from your TiVo using **mfs_ftp** and your favorite FTP client! Amazing and easy. Insertion is similarly easy. Connect to the **mfs_ftp** server, **cd** to the appropriate directory for the format in which your TiVo recording was created, change to binary mode by executing the **bin** command, and use the **put** command to insert the recording into your TiVo.

---

**TiVo** **Integrating mfs_ftp with TiVoWebPlus**

You can integrate **mfs_ftp** and TiVoWebPlus through a great TiVoWeb module known as `extract.itcl`. This module is available in the `mfs_ftp` directory on the BATBD CD that accompanies this book, but actually lives at **http://www.dealdatabase.com/forum/showthread.php?t=32049**.

To integrate **mfs_ftp** and TiVoWebPlus, ftp the `extract.itcl` file to your TiVo and put it in the modules subdirectory of your TiVoWebPlus home directory (typically `/var/local/tivoweb-tcl/modules`). Next, create symbolic links to the **mfs_ftp** binaries from within the appropriate binaries' directory for TiVoWebPlus. These are the `bin_ppc` and `bin_mips` directories found in your TiVoWebPlus home directory. You will need to create symbolic links in this directory to the **mfs_stream** and **mfs_tarstream** binaries, as in the following example for a Series 2 TiVo:

```
ln -s /var/mfs_ftp/mfs_stream /var/local/tivoweb-tcl/bin_mips/mfs_stream

ln -s /var/mfs_ftp/mfs_tarstream /var/local/tivoweb-tcl/bin_mips/mfs_tarstream
```

You should then restart TiVoWebPlus. An Extract command will show up in its heading when you connect to TiVoWebPlus using your Web browser. Clicking on this displays the Web page shown in Figure 12.16. Note that this figure shows a different theme than the default TiVoWebPlus theme. Using different themes was explained in the section of Chapter 8 on TiVoWebPlus.

To retrieve a TMF file through this interface, simply click on its name. To retrieve a TY file for one of your recordings, click on the ty entry at the end of the listing for that recording.

Note that TiVoWebPlus is *not* multithreaded, and will therefore be totally unresponsive until extraction of the recording that you have selected completes.

---

# Playing TY Files with mplayer

The **mplayer** (movie player) application for Linux is an incredibly powerful and popular player for different video file formats under Linux and other Unix-like systems. The mplayer application requires the X11 Window system. Its home page is located at **http://www.mplayerhq.hu**. You can find a more readable version at **http://www.mplayerhq.hu/homepage/design5/news.html**.

Enterprising TiVo hacker cwingert has taken **mplayer** to the next level for TiVo hackers by integrating TiVo TY file support into **mplayer**. These enhancements are slated for submission and integration into the mplayer mainline, but are currently available on SourceForge at **http://tivo-mplayer.sourceforge.net**, and are also located in the mplayer directory on the BATBD

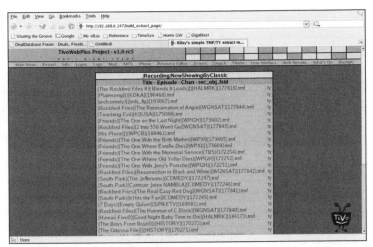

**FIGURE 12.16** *The mfs_ftp extraction interface in TiVoWebPlus*

CD that accompanies this book. If you're lucky enough to have all of the right libraries on your Linux system, you may be able to simply run the mplayer-x86-binary that is located in this directory. Otherwise, you will have to unpack the archive file `mplayer-1.0pre1-tivo-0.19.tar.gz` (the latest version of the TiVo mplayer available when this book was updated) and build mplayer yourself. The file `mplayer.HOWTO` on the BATBD CD is an excerpt from one of the text files provided with the TiVo version of mplayer, and it provides an overview of building and using mplayer.

In order to play recordings directly from your TiVo, you must also run mplayer's server application, **vserver**, on your TiVo. Series 1 and Series 2 versions of this server are provided in the `mplayer` directory on the BATBD CD, and have the names **vserver-ppc-s1-exec** and **vserver-mips-s2-exec**, respectively.

In a nutshell, you can do the following using the TiVo-enhanced version of mplayer:

◆ Play a locally stored TY file:

```
# mplayer stream.ty
```

◆ Retrieve the Now Showing list from a TiVo using the hostname or IP address of your TiVo (requires that **vserver** be running on the TiVo):

```
# mplayer tivo://hostname-or-ip-address/list
```

◆ Play a recording that is still stored on your TiVo over your network. This requires that **vserver** be running on your TiVo, and it requires that you know the FSID of the recording:

```
# mplayer tivo://hostname-or-ip-address/12345
```

◆ Play a single part of a recording that is still stored on your TiVo over your network. This requires that **vserver** be running on your TiVo, and it also requires that you know the FSID of the recording. The following example only plays the first segment of the recording identified in FSID 12345:

```
# mplayer tivo://hostname-or-ip-address/12345/1
```

◆ Extract a part of a recording that is still stored on your TiVo. This requires that **vserver** be running on your TiVo, and that you know the FSID of the recording that you want to extract. The following example extracts part 1 of the recording identified in FSID 12345:

```
# mplayer -dumpfile stream.ty -dumpstream tivo://hostname-or-ip-
address/12345/1
```

The **mplayer** application is quite powerful and is great for watching unscrambled TY recordings directly from your TiVo, watching extracted, unscrambled recordings made on your TiVo, or even for extracting portions of the recordings stored on your TiVo. For complete documentation on building and using **mplayer**, see the README files that are contained in the archive files on its Web site or on the BATBD CD.

# HACKING THE TiVo

## Chapter 13

SECOND EDITION

## TiVo Repairs and Troubleshooting

Like any hardware device, TiVos occasionally break. TiVo will be happy to repair most TiVo-branded systems, but service on the older TiVos such as most Series 1 TiVos is trickier—you often have to contact the vendor for repair information. Similarly, if you have a DirecTiVo, you will have to get hardware support through DirecTV. The customer support pages at **http://customersupport.tivo.com** provide information about hardware support for various models of TiVos based on a number of drop-down lists.

TiVo hardware and upgrade vendors such as 9thTee.com, Hinsdale, PTVupgrade.com, and Weaknees.com (discussed in the section of Chapter 4 entitled "TiVo Hardware Supplies on the Net") will all also repair broken TiVos. However, like any problem, the first thing to determine is whether your TiVo is actually broken or whether you've simply messed up something during one of your hacking sessions.

This chapter discusses the most common problems that you may encounter with your TiVo hardware and software, whether you've hacked it or not. Each problem description is followed by a list of possible causes for the problem you're seeing, as well as a list of potential solutions.

# Dealing with a Blown Modem

The TiVo's modem and phone line are potentially weak links in your TiVo enjoyment. If the modem or phone line goes bad, your TiVo will run out of guide information in a week or so, at which point your TiVo may become less fun than usual. For example, on stand-alone TiVo with full service, where the modem is used to retrieve the programming information, services such as WishLists and Season Passes will no longer work. On DirecTiVo boxes, where programming information comes in over the satellite stream, you won't be able to order pay-per-view movies and other pay-as-you-go services. Either way, not the whole ball of wax that you're used to! Fixing a bad phone line is fairly easy to do, but fixing a blown modem can be a problem if you are not a hardcore electronics geek. You can send the TiVo off to be serviced, but—gasp—you will be without a TiVo for some period of time. If the modem is the problem, you may be tempted to buy a new TiVo. This is good news for TiVo, but expensive for you. It is especially bad news for you if you've purchased lifetime service for your TiVo, since lifetime service is tied to your TiVo's serial number, which is stored in an EPROM (Erasable Programmable Read-Only Memory) on your TiVo's motherboard and cannot be moved easily (or legally, probably) from one TiVo to another.

The modems in TiVo Series 1 machines often go bad, which is not all that surprising since they're a few years old now and are custom-built machines. Modem problems manifest themselves in different ways:

◆ Your TiVo has problems dialing and holding the phone line, but downloads work correctly if you dial the number manually and connect the phone line when you hear the remote modem answer.

◆ You repeatedly get a no dial tone message when trying to connect over a phone line that you know to be good — that is, the phone line works fine with a telephone connected to it.

If you're handy with a soldering iron, you can generally fix these problems by replacing and resoldering a few parts on your TiVo. You can diagnose the scope of the parts that you need by consulting the TiVo Repair Kit guide at http://www.9thtee.com/images/E-Legstivomodem.jpg. ElectricLegs, a well-known TiVo hacker, developed these tests and the parts kits associated with them. The parts kits are sold through 9thTee.com, an excellent vendor of a variety of

TiVo-related parts and services, as I discussed in the section of Chapter 4 entitled "TiVo Hardware Supplies on the Net."

Actually repairing the modem in your TiVo when possible requires some ability to use and control a soldering iron. If you aren't a wizard with a soldering iron or simply aren't willing to take the chance that your repair efforts might increase the amount of damage to your TiVo, you can pay to have the repairs done or find an alternative solution.

Getting someone to attempt to repair your modem is usually successful, but there are no guarantees that the problem is actually fixable. Sometimes, things just break and stay that way. You'll also be without your TiVo for some period of time, which can be hard to deal with. Luckily, there are quick and easy alternatives to repairing your modem—use an external modem (described in the next section) or use a an Internet connection to download programming and guide information (described in Chapter 8).

# Using External Modems with the TiVo

Before PCs became the center of most people's computing universe and the price of internal modems dropped to under $10, people commonly bought external modems. Because modems were external to a computer system, they didn't depend on the bus architecture or characteristics of a given computer and could, therefore, be used with any computer system. External modems are largely a thing of the past, but they have special value for TiVo owners whose internal modems have gone bad. Picking up an inexpensive external modem will enable you to get your TiVo up and running within minutes, and usually for less than $15 (search eBay for external modem). If you already have an old modem in a drawer in your basement, you can fix your TiVo for free. The default speed of the TiVo's built-in modem is 33,600 baud (usually referred to as a "33.6" modem), but you can use any external modem as long as it is 9600 baud or better.

To use an external modem rather than your TiVo's internal modem, your TiVo needs to be running system software Version 3.0 or greater. You'll also need the following:

◆ External modem, preferably 33.6 or better
◆ Power supply for the external modem
◆ 25-pin-male to 9-pin-female serial adapter
◆ $^1/_8$-inch DSS to 9-pin male serial cable

Most external modems have old-style, 25-pin-female serial connectors. You will need the 25-pin-male to 9-pin-female adapter to attach the external modem to the $^1/_8$-inch serial cable that you should have received with your TiVo. If you don't have this cable, you can buy one from one of the sources listed in the section of Chapter 4 entitled "TiVo Hardware Supplies on the Net", or you can make one as described in the section "Attaching a Terminal Emulator or Serial Console" earlier in Chapter 4. I've used older US Robotics Sportster modems to repair various friends' TiVos with absolutely no problems.

Many external modems provide some external configuration settings through DIP switches, which are a row of numbered up and down switches that should be visible on the back of the modem. Different modems support different settings, but the settings for a 33.6 US Robotics Sportster in Table 13.1 provide a good idea of the configuration settings that your modem may require.

**Table 13.1  DIP Switch Settings on an External Modem**

| DIP Switch | Position | Meaning |
| --- | --- | --- |
| 1 | DOWN | DTR Ready Override |
| 2 | UP | Verbal Result Codes |
| 3 | DOWN | Display Result Codes |
| 4 | UP | Echo Offline Commands |
| 5 | DOWN | Auto Answer Off |
| 6 | UP | Carrier Detect Normal |
| 7 | UP | Load NVRAM Defaults |
| 8 | DOWN | Smart Mode |

You will also need to configure your modem to disable DTR, RTS, and flow control. On most Hayes-compatible modems, you can do so by sending the following two sequences of characters (strings, in programmer-speak) to the modem from your computer by using a terminal emulator (and null-modem cable) before you attach it to your TiVo:

```
AT&D0&H0&I0&R1&W0
AT&D0&H0&I0&R1&W1
```

These strings disable DTR, RTS, and flow control and write this configuration to two different saved configuration profiles in the nonvolatile random access memory (NVRAM) where your modem stores its default configuration information. The entries in these strings have the following meanings:

- ◆ *AT*  Get the attention of the modem, telling it that you are going to be sending it commands.
- ◆ *&D0 (D zero)*  Ignore DTR.
- ◆ *&H0 (H zero)*  Disable CTS and Xon/Xoff flow control.
- ◆ *&I0 (I zero)*  Disable RX flow control.
- ◆ *&R1 (R one)*  Ignore RTS.
- ◆ *&Wn*  Writes the configuration information to profile *n*. Profile 0 is usually used when your modem initially powers on, but saving it to both profiles can't hurt.

Some modems do not implement the **&H** and **&I** commands correctly. If you receive errors when you enter the previous strings in your terminal emulator, try removing the **&H0** and **&I0** commands from the previous strings and entering the **AT&K0** (K zero) command on a separate line, which disables all flow control on many modems. You can then execute the **AT&W0** and **AT&W1** commands to save the updated profile information.

Finally, if your modem's speaker is active, you'll hear the classic modem song as your modem negotiates communication speeds and until it establishes a connection. To keep things quiet on most modems, add the **&M0** (M zero) command to the previous strings to turn off the speaker.

---

### ◆ TIP

For a complete list of the Hayes modem commands used by most modems, see Web sites such as **http://readthetruth.com/modems.htm** or **http://www.lisa.univ-paris12.fr/Electronik/Hayes.htm**. The Hayes command set is named after an early pioneer in reliable, affordable modems that were subsequently cloned by hundreds of other vendors (who also adopted the command set, which, therefore, became a standard).

---

###  Guaranteeing Correct Settings in an External Modem

If your modem is old or you experience frequent power failures, you may find that your modem may forget its settings. If you have a network connection to your TiVo and aren't using the serial line as a console, you can leave the external modem connected to your TiVo and add a command like the following to the end of the `/etc/rc.d/rc.sysinit` file, which is executed each time your TiVo reboots. In order to add these commands, you will have to first make your root partition writable, using the command "**mount –o rw,remount /**." On a Series 1 machine, add this command:

```
echo "AT&D0&H0&I0&R1&W0" > /dev/ttyS3
```

On a Series 2 machine, add this command:

```
echo "AT&D0&H0&I0&R1&W0" > /dev/ttyS2
```

Both these commands will write the correct profile settings for your modem and cause it to resave them. Your modem should be reset correctly each time your TiVo reboots for one reason or another.

Of course, if you had to modify the strings you used to get your modem to work, make sure you enter the values your modem requires—don't just retype these strings and expect it to work!

After you make the specified settings, detach the modem from your PC and null-modem cable. You can then attach the 25-to-9 adapter to the modem's serial connector, attach the TiVo's serial cable to the 9-pin connector, and plug the 1/8-inch jack into the Serial Cntrl Out connector on the back of your TiVo.

The final step for using an external modem with your TiVo is to set your Dial Prefix so that the TiVo knows to communicate via the serial port and uses the correct speed for the modem you're using. The Dial Prefix command is found in different places in the TiVo menus, depending on the version of the TiVo software you are running. For TiVo 3.x and earlier systems, the Dial Prefix is located in the Change Dial Options menu (select TiVo Central, Messages and Setup, Recorder & Phone Setup, Phone Connection, Change Dial Options). For TiVo 4.x systems, an equivalent Set Dial Prefix command is located in the Phone Dialing Options screen (TiVo Central, Messages and Setup, Settings, Phone & Network Settings, Edit Phone or Network Settings, Phone Dialing Options).

After you've located the Dial Prefix or Set Dial Prefix command, use one of the settings in Table 13.2 to tell the TiVo to use PPP over the serial port at the specified speed to make your daily calls. Make sure you do not try to use a speed setting that is faster than the maximum speed of your modem—that simply won't work.

**Table 13.2    Dialing Prefixes for Different Modem Speeds**

| Modem Speed | Dial Prefix |
| --- | --- |
| 9600 | ,#396 |
| 19,200 | ,#319 |
| 38,400 | ,#338 |
| 57,600 | ,#357 |

 **TIP**

To get the comma, press Pause on your TiVo remote. To get the hash mark, press Enter on your TiVo remote.

At this point, you should be able to execute the Make a Test Call command from the same menu, and the call should succeed! If it does, congratulations! You now have another notch in your TiVo hacking belt! If not, check the call log in /var/log/0tclient on the TiVo to see if an error was reported. If the end of the log file does not show an error message, try setting the Dial Prefix to use a slower call speed. On my favorite U.S. Robotics Sportster modems, I typically use the 19,200 communication speed simply because the phone lines in my area have a fair amount of noise.

# TiVo Troubleshooting

If you're reading this section, chances are that something went wrong in one of the upgrade or hacking procedures discussed elsewhere in this book. No need to panic—everyone hoses his or her TiVo once or twice in the course of hacking it. It's a baptismal experience. It's also one of the world's best arguments for doing backups of your TiVo disks before making any modifications to them, and immediately after you receive any software upgrade.

Aside from drastic hardware failures, there are relatively few potential problems when upgrading or hacking your TiVo. The next few sections discuss each of these problems and their most common causes.

## No Picture or Welcome Screen

When you first turn on your TiVo, it displays a welcome graphic as it initializes and validates the TiVo software. On a TiVo Series 1, this is a screen that features the TiVo character that displays the message "Your recorder is starting up. Please wait a moment..." at the bottom of the screen. On a TiVo Series 2, this is a gray screen that displays the message "Welcome, powering up" in the center of the screen. Seeing either of these screens is relatively good news because it means that the TiVo was able to find its disk and begin loading software. If you do not see a picture or either of these screens on your TiVo, you will want to do the following:

◆ If you have a Series 1 stand-alone TiVo, check the fuse in the power supply, located near the external power connector. It is rare for this to fail, unless there are actual problems with the power supply, but it can happen.

◆ If you have a TiVo Series 2, verify that the stiff white cable that connects the power supply to the motherboard is seated correctly at both ends.

If you still cannot get the TiVo to power on, you may simply have a bad power supply. Companies such as 9thTee.com, PTVUpgrade.com, and Weaknees.com will all assess and repair TiVo problems. Trying to get a TiVo Series 1 through TiVo Inc. is especially frustrating because Phillips and Hughes handles hardware support, and they can be hard to track down.

## Your TiVo Is Stuck at the Welcome Screen

If your TiVo displays either of these graphical screens: "Your recorder is starting up. Please wait a moment..." or "Welcome, powering up." your power supply is obviously fine, so at least you can cross one thing off your list.

If your system seems stuck at the Welcome screen or constantly reboots to this screen, your TiVo is not booting successfully. Some common reasons for this are as follows:

◆ You are trying to boot your system with a kernel or root filesystem intended for another model of TiVo.

◆ Your /etc/rc.d/rc.sysinit file doesn't execute correctly. The most common problem with this file is that it has been edited elsewhere and then moved back to the TiVo. This file must *not* be edited on a Windows system without using a Linux-safe editor. Windows systems end each line in a file with a carriage return and linefeed characters (aka *CRLF*). Linux systems only end each line with a linefeed character. In general, the best idea is never to edit Linux files on a Windows system.

 **TIP**

If you must edit TiVo or Linux text files on a Windows system, you must use an editor like UltraEdit (**http://www.ultraedit.com**) or GNU Emacs (the world's greatest text editor: **http://www.gnu.org/software/emacs/**), which is smart enough to end lines "the right way." You can download a demonstration copy of UltraEdit from **http://www.ultraedit.com/downloads/index.html**. You can get a copy of Emacs for Windows from **http://ftp.gnu.org/gnu/windows/emacs/latest**. Emacs will sense the end of line characters in any file that it edits and will preserve them in that same fashion.

◆ You are trying to boot a signed kernel on a Series 1 or 2 system and have modified the kernel so that it no longer passes the boot PROM's signature check (perhaps by deactivating the initial RAM disk). Unfortunately, you can do that only on TiVo software releases prior to Version 3.1 of the TiVo software. You will have to fall back to an older version of the TiVo software if you want to keep your modifications, or follow a procedure like the Two-Kernel Monte to chain-boot a hacked kernel, described in Chapter 8.

◆ You have modified entries in the root filesystem and want to boot a 3.2 or later version of the TiVo software that is still comparing the entries in the root filesystem against the hash signatures. Ordinarily, the TiVo will simply replace modified files such as /etc/rc.d/rc.sysinit with virgin copies, but if you've been clever and tried to make this process immutable using the **chattr** command, your TiVo will try to delete them, fail, reboot, try to delete them again, fail.... I think that you get the idea. As in the previous point, you'll either have to fall back to an older version of the TiVo software if you want to keep your modifications, or follow a procedure like the Two-Kernel Monte procedure to chain-boot a hacked kernel.

◆ On Series 2 machines, you may have accidentally detached or loosened the ribbon cable that connects the motherboard to the front keypad. Make sure that this is seated correctly!

◆ You have hacked a Series 2 machine, but there is a syntax error in the boot parameters that you set using the **bootpage** command. This is especially common when entering the boot parameters on a system that you are hacking using the Two-Kernel Monte Method described in Chapter 8. It is extremely important that you escape both of the back quotes (`) in this entry by preceding them with a backslash (\). Make sure that they are indeed back quotes and not standard single-quotes, and that you have also escaped all of the dollar signs ($) in this entry by preceding them with a backslash (\). The back quote character is located in the upper-left corner of most standard, non-Dvorak U.S. keyboards. You can use the **bootpage -p** *drive* command to examine your current settings after the TiVo drive is back in your PC.

◆ You have hacked a Series 2 machine, as described in previous sections, but there is a syntax error in the startup script that is being executed through the BASH_ENV entry in the boot parameters that you set using the **bootpage** command. Check this carefully. This script and any applications that it runs must be marked as executable (**chmod 755** *filename*) in the directory from which you built your ROMFS image.

◆ Last and least, your disk drive may be corrupted to the point where it is temporarily unbootable or a permanent paperweight. This is truly rare because you can rarely restore a backup or mount partitions (as you probably did when you were hacking it) from a bad drive. However, it is possible. Try restoring a backup to another drive and booting from that one. If the replacement drive boots successfully, try restoring a backup to the drive that you suspect is bad and see what happens. Sorry to say it, but disk problems are usually pilot error—unless the disk is actually on fire, no longer spins, or is making clicking sounds (indicating a problem with the disk surface or heads).

Those are all the ways in which I've shot myself in the foot—er, I mean, that I've ever heard about going wrong. If your TiVo is continually rebooting and you're sick of messing with it for the time being, restore the disk from a backup, use it for a while, and try hacking it again. Better yet, buy another one just for hacking so that you're never inconvenienced by a typo or a versioning problem.

# Your TiVo Is Stuck at the Second Welcome Screen

When your TiVo successfully loads a kernel and begins the boot process, it displays a second screen with a message like "Almost there, a few more seconds." Seeing this screen is even more exciting than the previous one because it means that your disk is good, your kernel passed any signature check, and your boot parameters haven't invalidated the boot process. However, if the system hangs at this point or reboots shortly after displaying this screen, the most common sources of problems are as follows:

◆ You are trying to boot a signed kernel on a Series 1 or 2 system and have modified the kernel so that it no longer passes the boot PROM's signature check (perhaps by deactivating the initial RAM disk). Unfortunately, you can do that only on TiVo software releases prior to Version 3.2 of the TiVo software. You will have to fall back to an older version of the TiVo software if you want to keep your modifications, or follow a procedure like the "Two-Kernel Monte for the TiVo Series 2" described in Chapter 8 to use **monte** to chain-boot a hacked kernel.

◆ You have passed the **noinitrd** command as one of your boot parameters. This trick only worked on the 2.03 kernel distributed with original Series 2 machines. If you are using **monte**, you must disable the **initrd** in the kernel that you are attempting to monte using the **replace_initrd** or **killinitrd** commands.

◆ You are trying to use **monte** to boot a kernel in which the **initrd** has been disabled, and the program **/sbin/init** isn't found in your root filesystem. See the section in Chapter 8 on "Two-Kernel Monte for the TiVo Series 2" for information about getting around this.

◆ You are trying to use **monte** to boot a kernel and root filesystem whose MFS software versions do not match. This could be the case if you are trying to monte a 4.0 OS from a 3.0 kernel, and have simply overlaid the 4.0 filesystems on top of a restored 3.0 disk. You should do this in reverse, overlaying a 3.0 kernel and root filesystem over a restored 4.0 disk, as explained in the "Two-Kernel Monte for the TiVo Series 2" section of Chapter 8.

◆ If you have two drives in your TiVo, verify that you correctly set the jumpers on the disk drives when you put them back in the TiVo. The TiVo is unable to mount and access the second drive if its jumpers are not set correctly.

If you are hacking a Series 2 machine, one good way to see what's actually going wrong is to connect a serial cable to the TiVo's serial port, and then watch the diagnostic and kernel messages that display. Add the entry **dsscon=true** to the boot parameters that you set using the **bootpage** command and connect a terminal emulator to your serial cable, running at a connection speed of 115,200. You then will see all of the boot messages from the kernel's signature check to the actual kernel boot messages—hopefully, one of these messages will help you identify the problem you're experiencing.

# Your TiVo Displays a Green Screen

After your TiVo begins executing the /etc/rc.d/rc.sysinit startup file, MFS problems or inconsistencies can cause your TiVo to display a green screen, almost as though it was a Microsoft Windows system. If you find your TiVo displaying a green screen, *do not unplug it!* The green screen indicates that an error has been detected in the TiVo's MFS filesystem, and that the TiVo is running diagnostic and repair routines to try to correct the problem. Be patient, and the problem will usually resolve itself. The amount of time required to repair MFS filesystem inconsistencies depends on the amount of storage in your TiVo. Larger-capacity systems take longer.

Unplugging your TiVo at this point would cause the filesystem repair routines to fail, potentially corrupting the MFS filesystem even further. Get a cup of coffee. Have a cigarette. Walk the dog. Do not unplug the TiVo!

# HACKING THE TiVo

# Chapter 14

**SECOND EDITION**

## Other TiVo Hacking Resources

**A**s Carl Sagan or Johnny Carson might have said, "There are billions and billions of Web sites on the Internet devoted to the TiVo." That might be a slight exaggeration, but the fact remains that there are a huge number of sites that mention the TiVo, provide reviews of TiVo hardware and TiVo software, compare and contrast TiVos with other DVR hardware and software, and (best of all) provide tips and tricks for getting the most out of your TiVo.

**NOTE**

None of the sites discussed in this chapter is unilaterally endorsed by TiVo, Inc., including the TiVo Community Forum, which is partly sponsored by TiVo. That doesn't mean that they like everything they see there. Some employees of TiVo, Inc. may occasionally post messages or tips on various forums, but this does not mean that TiVo, Inc. endorses or even sanctions those posts.

To the best of my knowledge, none of the sites discussed in this chapter provides illegal software or instructions that describe illegal techniques. If it turns out that they do, I'm sorry. I do not maintain any of these sites, although I've certainly benefited from them. If you have a general problem, seek medical attention. If you have a problem with any of the sites or Web pages discussed in this chapter, take it up with their owners or maintainers.

Don't play with matches. Don't run with scissors. Don't look at things that offend you. Don't ruin things for other people.

Articles about the TiVo frequently note that the TiVo is unique among DVRs and in terms of the fanatical devotion of its owners. The TiVo has been discussed on the Oprah Winfrey and David Letterman shows, has been mentioned in a variety of situation comedies, and has been a central "character" in an episode of *Sex and the City*. It has become a verb (as in "I tivo'd that last night"), and it was even the favorite Christmas gift of FCC Chairman Michael Powell, who referred to the TiVo as "God's Machine" in an interview at a consumer electronics show. I can't think of anything since the original Volkswagen Bug that has the same sort of fanatical army of devotees as TiVo—and it took the Bug a decade or so to achieve cult status. Apple's iPod is coming up fast, though….

One aspect of the TiVo's overwhelming online presence and vocal advocate groups is the fact that TiVos run Linux, which provides a lot of cross-over between TiVo groupies and Linux fanatics, the latter of whom are well-known for their missionary zeal. Given that the TiVo is one of the stellar successes of Linux in a commercial setting and that it displays none of the command–line awkwardness that people often associate with Linux—you've got a winning combination for every Linux advocate in the known world to say, "See, I told you so!" (The author included.) Add in the fact that the TiVo is eminently hackable, and you've got a winning combination that just begs for Web sites, newsgroups, blogs, and discussions on SlashDot.

Another fun aspect of the TiVo's popularity on the Internet is the frequency with which industry observers and related pundits delight in predicting its imminent demise. This seems to come largely from a bunch of "late to the .com crash" critics with a last-shark-at-the-shipwreck mentality, wanting to make sure that they get a piece, too. "Let's see, who's still around that might go down and make me look like Nostradamus?" To be fair, many aspects of the TiVo reek of the dot.com days, but even the most jaded among us has to admit that the cute TiVo guy is a lot more pleasant than a sock puppet. Among TiVo detractors are a huge number of bitter ReplayTV and UltimateTV fans out there, endlessly griping about how much better their now-deceased platforms were. You can't blame people for being sad when their pets have been put to sleep. I was a Berkeley Unix/SunOS fanatic for years—but sorry, it's over. (Though there's always the Mac OS X—but I digress!)

This book wouldn't have been possible without the hundreds of Web sites, posts, questions, and discussions of TiVo tips, ticks, gotchas, and everything else. I want to give credit where credit is due by highlighting some of the most extensive and useful TiVo sites that are available on the Internet. In the discussion of each site, you will find the type of TiVo the site is relevant to and, where necessary, any information that may be invalid or superceded.

# A Byte of Fun—TiVo Advocacy Articles

TiVo advocacy is somewhat in decline, largely because the TiVo is a fact of life nowadays. Like Linux itself, the time and the need to proselytize is largely past—it's time to put the technology to work. However, if you just happened to stumble upon the TiVo or heard about it from someone who wasn't a rabid TiVo fanatic, you might enjoy reading a few articles and bits of commentary about TiVo and the TiVo phenomenon. If you're having a hard time convincing your siblings, parents, coworkers, or even a complete stranger that the TiVo is a great thing, perhaps a photocopy of this page could save you a lot of talking.

Here are some of my favorites from the past two years (organized alphabetically by author):

Christine Chen's "My Life with TiVo" in *Fortune Magazine* online (**http://www.fortune.com/fortune/technology/articles/0,15114,366870,00.html**) is a fun article from May of 2001.

Marjorie Dorfman's "What Is This Thing Called TiVo?" available at **http://www.bytebackonline.com/Articles_p/tivo_p.html** is a humorous look from 2003 at the TiVo phenomenon and some of the advantages of the TiVo.

Brendan Koerner's doom and gloom article at **http://slate.msn.com/id/2072037**, entitled "TiVo, We Hardly Knew Ye," is my favorite entry in the "Funny, but Wrong" sweepstakes. Published in October, 2002, it would seem that rumors of the demise of the TiVo have been much exaggerated. It is somewhat surprising that a humor publication from MSN (the Microsoft Network) would criticize the TiVo when its own Ultimate TV was the Ultimate Tur-Key.

Heather Newman's posts for the *Detroit Free Press* are a great source of information for TiVo fans and advocates. A representative article from April, 2003 entitled, "This Is a Recording: TiVo Is a Must for the Viewer," is available at **http://www.freep.com/money/tech/newman24_20030424.htm**.

David Pogue, writer of the "Circuits" column for *The New York Times*, the "Missing Manual" series of computer books, and a zillion other computer books over the years, is a well-known and vocal TiVo fan. Links to abstracts of his "Circuits" columns are available from **http://www.davidpogue.com/TimesArchives.html,** but you have to pay money to see them (unless you subscribe and wait for the next one). One of them (from January, 2003) has been preserved on the TiVo site itself, and is available in

PDF at **http://www.tivo.com/pdfs/productreviews/ny_times_0103_pogue.pdf**.

Ernest Svenson (aka Ernie the Attorney) has a fun "TiVo Changed My Life" blog at **http://radio.weblogs.com/0104634/stories/2002/12/14/tivoChangedMyLife.html** (2003). This is an entertaining site that also features links to other TiVo advocacy sites and information.

# Online Forums for TiVo Information and Discussion

The best sites on the Web for discussing and sharing TiVo information are known as *discussion forums* or simply *forums*. These sites enable people to read and participate in online discussions of TiVo-related topics. These online discussion topics are organized into different categories that reflect specific subjects or levels of expertise with the subject matter. Within each category and forum, each set of posts and replies on a single topic is organized into a sequence of messages known as a *thread*, which makes it easy to follow a specific online discussion. Organizing topics and discussions hierarchically makes it easier to find information on a specific subject or know where to post a specific question.

Forums work much like Web logs (*blogs*) or bulletin board systems (depending on what is familiar to you). After you've selected the forum that you want to view, your browser displays the first page of the threads that are available in that forum. Once you click on a thread, the first page of messages in that thread displays. You can scroll through various posts in that thread, reply to the thread, or reply to the specific individual who posted a given message.

Many of the forums discussed in this section use a software package called vBulletin (**http://www.vbulletin.com**) from Jelsoft Enterprises Limited to manage the forum and its threads (the TiVo Community Forum, **http://www.tivocommunity.com**, is a notable exception—it started out using UltimateBB). The vBulletin software is powered by great open source software such as PHP (the Personal Hypertext Preprocessor: **http://www.php.net**) and MySQL (My Structured Query Language: **http://www.mysql.com**), but is a commercial product with reasonable licensing charges.

The vBulletin software is a great framework for a wide variety of online communities, providing not only the software to power the site, but the associated administrative utilities and infrastructure required to manage it. Most online forums enable anyone to view forums and threads, but require that you actually log into the forum site to post messages. In order to log in, you must register with the forum and create a user account there. Requiring user accounts to post messages helps eliminate the possibility that people would post SPAM or offensive messages there, since each thread and reply to a thread is tagged with the online identity of the person who posted it.

Unfortunately, simply tagging each message with the community identity of the person who posted it doesn't always stop people from posting offensive, off-topic, or inappropriate messages. Everyone's standard of offensive language or subject matter is different. Off-topic or inappropriate messages (such as advertisements for commercial services) are different—while not offensive, they waste people's time. In order to eliminate these types of offenses, online forums are moderated. This means that someone is responsible for managing and maintaining the threads within each forum, deleting offensive or inappropriate messages whenever necessary, and offering suggestions to people who have asked questions or posted information that isn't relevant to the topic being discussed in a particular thread. Most moderators have a good knowledge of the forum topic themselves, and are willing to invest some of their time in order to ensure that the forums are as useful and understandable as possible. When reading the messages in a thread on a forum that uses the vBulletin software, you'll see several icons displayed at the end of each message. These provide convenient shortcuts for replying to the message or editing it (if you posted it originally). Each message also provides a convenient link for reporting a specific message to the moderator if you find it offensive, feel that it is inappropriate, or feel that it is unrelated to the topic.

Because the same software powers all of the forums discussed in this section, they have a similar look and feel. However, different forum sites host different categories and forums, they have different notions of the topics that are valid to discuss in each forum, and they provide different levels of online support and service to the TiVo community as a whole. The forums discussed in this chapter are organized alphabetically—not in terms of usability, relevance, or general good times.

 **TIP**

If you are new to the TiVo or new to the notion of online communities, the various TiVo forums discussed in this chapter can be somewhat overwhelming. I've found lots of great information on all of these sites, but it helps to know where to start and what different forums specialize in.

To dip your toe in the water, I'd suggest trying the TiVo Community forum and beginning your online community experience by reading one of the Newbie or general discussion groups there. If you are interested in topics that cannot be discussed there, you should try the DealDatabase or PTVUpgrade forums. Both of these places discuss topics such as Video Extraction that are forbidden on the TiVo Community forum because it is partially sponsored by TiVo, Inc.

If you are specifically looking for information related to networking a Series 1 TiVo or DirecTiVo, the SiliconDust forums are dedicated to helping with TurboNet, AirNet, and CacheCard issues. If you are generally interested in audio-visual issues and systems similar to the TiVo, you may want to check out the AVS Forum. If you are a Macintosh lover (as I am), check out (and contribute to) the MacTiVo forum.

Finally, if you are already a hard-core Linux or TiVo developer, you should visit the alt.org forums for the latest in detailed, hard-core software and internals information.

# The alt.org Forums

Located at **http://www.alt.org/forum**, the alt.org forums are an excellent resource for hard-core TiVo hackers or those interested in learning about the internals of the TiVo, its filesystems, and advanced TiVo hacking. These forums are not for newbies or the naïve, and off-topic or introductory questions will be quickly filed in the conceptual bit-bucket. The alt.org site offers a smaller number of high-level forums than any other forum site discussed in this chapter—two—but this is because the audience and its members are focused on TiVo software development and nothing else. Figure 14.1 shows the main page of the alt.org forum site.

**FIGURE 14.1** *The home page of the alt.org forums in a Web browser*

The two forums provided on the alt.org forum site are the following:

◆ *TiVo Software Development* As the name suggests, this forum is dedicated to the development of software for the TiVo.

◆ *Off Topic* This forum is used as a repository for topics that were posted on the alt.org TiVo Software Development forum, but which are viewed as off-topic for one reason or another—usually because they are newbie questions that would be best asked on one of the other TiVo forums.

The alt.org site's focus on topics related to serious TiVo software development or internals does not mean that the people who run this site are unfriendly—quite the contrary! The page at **http://alt.org/tivo** is a Wiki (a type of editable Web site) that contains many links to some of the best TiVo-related sites on the Internet. This is an excellent starting point if you're looking for information on a specific TiVo topic, a specific piece of TiVo-related software, or are just curious regarding what's available.

# AVS Forum

The AVS (AV Science or Audio-Visual Science) forum (**http://www.avsforum.com**) is often confused with the TiVo Community forum. The TiVo Community forum is dedicated to TiVo-related topics and discussions, while the AVS forum views the TiVo as a single instance of an audio-visual device. You will certainly find TiVo-specific information on the AVS forum, but the site in general has a much wider focus. The AVS forum is operated and managed by the AV Science Corporation of Rochester, NY, USA.

The AVS forum is a great site for anyone interested in any type of audio-visual equipment, associated rumors, or AV industry trends. I'm historically more of a computer guy than an AV fan, but my first visit to the AVS forum changed all that. After reading a few posts about high-definition televisions, plasma screens, and whizzy devices that I hadn't even heard of before, I found myself picturing a much more hi-tech living room and lifestyle than I'd ever dreamed. Use caution when visiting this site ;-).

Figure 14.2 shows the home page of the AVS forum in a Web browser. The page where you can see all of the forums available on the AVS forum is located at **http://www.avsforum.com/avs-vb**.

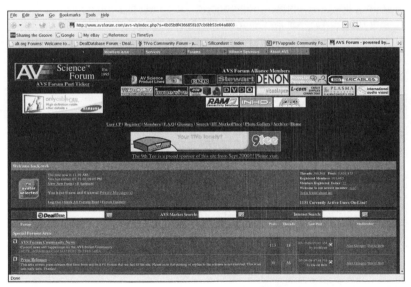

**FIGURE 14.2** *The home page of the AVS forum in a Web browser*

The AVS forum is the largest and most extensive of any of the forums discussed in this chapter, largely because it is not just limited to DVRs, but discusses the entire spectrum of high-tech home entertainment gear. The AVS forum was the original TiVo hacking forum, so it contains a seemingly endless archive of posts relating to hacking TiVo; some of the hacks date back to the earliest days of TiVo hacking. Eventually, the TiVo portion of AVS forum branched off to its own site, TiVo Community forum, where it remains today.

**TIP**

If you're a regular visitor to the AVS forum, an easy way to view a listing of the most recent posts on any of its forums is to click on the AVS forum Post Ticker link, which is available at the top of each Web page on the AVS forum (currently in the upper left corner). Clicking this link pops up a small dialog box that displays a scrolling list of the most recent posts made to any of the AVS forums. To view a specific post from this list, just click on its listing in the scrolling dialog box, and a new browser window opens on your screen, containing the selected post.

 **TIP**

The AVS forum can be somewhat unreadable as originally displayed. If you register as a user, you can modify your user profile to use a different style sheet that makes it more readable. To do this, click on the link for your user control panel, select Edit Options, and then change the Style Set entry from AVS Black to AVS White. Click the Submit Modifications button to save the new setting. Subsequent visits to the AVS forum will look like the screen shown in Figure 14.3, which is much more readable than the default.

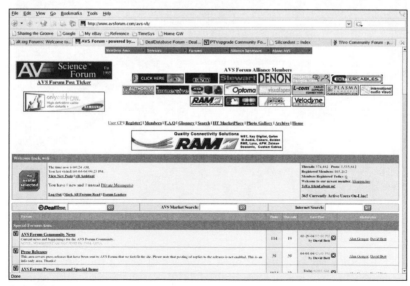

**FIGURE 14.3** *The home page of the AVS forum using the AVS White Style Set*

Remember that each of the categories and forums on the AVS forum site contains its own threads, fanatics, and range of useful information. If you are interested in high-tech audio/visual gear, you owe it to yourself to visit the site and search through all of its forums. The ones in the following list are simply my favorite AVS forum areas, although your mileage may vary:

♦ *Digital Recorders (PVRs) General*   A forum for discussing any type of digital or personal video recorder. This forum is the place for general questions about cable boxes with built-in DVRs, as well as do-it-yourself hardware and software for putting one together on your own. The TiVo, ReplayTV, and Microsoft UltimateTV DVRs have their own forums, so discussion of these on this general forum will quickly be moved elsewhere. This forum prohibits any discussions of theft of service from any of the providers of DVRs. Posts on such topics will be squashed like a bug.

♦ *Dish Network PVRs*   A forum for questions, answers, and general discussion of the DishNetwork and the DishPVR Digital Receiver/Recorder. Competing devices and systems such as the DirecTiVo should not be discussed here, only slandered. No discussion of hacking these systems is permitted.

♦ *HDTV Hardware*   A forum for questions, answers, and general discussion of HDTV tuners and associated hardware. This is a great place to do research or to have your HDTV questions answered before buying a system. Different types of HDTV displays have their own forums (*Screens, Plasma and LCD flat panel displays*, and so on) in the *Display Devices* section of the AVS forum.

♦ *Microsoft UltimateTV PVR*   A forum for questions, answers, and general discussion of the evolutionary dead-end, also known as the UltimateTV.

♦ *ReplayTV & Showstopper PVRs*   A forum for questions, answers, and general discussion regarding the dearly departed ReplayTV and ShowStopper Digital Recorders.

♦ *TiVo Community Forums*   A hyperlink to the TiVo Community forums, discussed later in this chapter.

♦ *Tweaks and Do-It-Yourself*   Discussions of off-the-shelf and do-it-yourself items that can help improve the image, sound, or overall performance of your audio and home theater. This forum even discusses details like interconnects, speaker cables, power cords, and how to isolate one system from another. It's amazing how much of a difference a type of wire or connector can make in certain circumstances.

# The DealDatabase Forums

DealDatabase.com is a Web site that specializes in helping you find the best prices for a variety of online purchases. They do this by providing a number of categories in which one can post "deals" that are relevant to those categories. Standard categories include Auto(mobiles), Baby Stuff, Books & Magazines, Business & Office, Casinos, Clothing & Footwear, Computers, DVDs & VHS, Electronics, Rewards, Food, Freebies, Health & Beauty, Home & Garden, Jewelry, Music, Pets, Sporting Goods, Toys & Games, and a Miscellaneous category for anything that doesn't fit into any of the above categories. At any given time, you're likely to find special deals from online sites such as Amazon.com, Barnes&Noble.com, BestBuy.com, Buy.com, Dell.com, DVDPlanet.com, JCrew.com, Staples.com, and many more.

The aspects of DealDatabase.com are quite interesting if you're going online shopping, but not so much if your primary interest is TiVo hacking. To TiVo hackers, the most interesting aspect of the DealDatabase site is its Message Board section (**http://www.dealdatabase.com/forum**), which provides a forum for online discussions on a number of different topics—including TiVo hacking, of course!

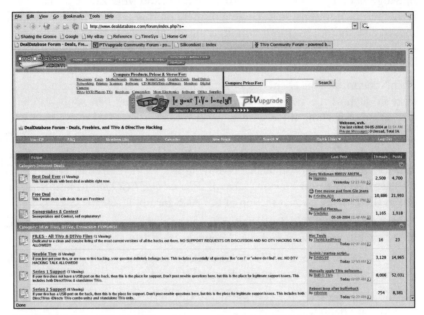

**FIGURE 14.4** *The DealDatabase.com forums in a Web browser*

Unlike the AVS and TiVo Community forums, the DealDatabase forum does not provide menus across the top, but rather provides a table of quick links to commonly-used features of the site; for example, getting to the home page, submitting a deal, a list of the top deals that are currently available, a free email service, getting to its forums, and a page containing general and contact information for DealDatabase.com.

> ### NOTE
>
> The DealDatabase forum recently underwent a major reorganization to make it more useful and to clarify the forums in which to discuss specific topics. If you haven't been there for a while, you should check it out—focus on the forums in the category labeled *NEW TiVo, DtiVo, Extraction FORUMS*.

The DealDatabase forum provides a tremendous amount of useful information about TiVos and other types of DVRs. Since TiVo, Inc. is not one of its sponsors, topics such as video extraction and related software are fair game here, making this site a great repository for this sort of information.

### TIP

To download attachments to any post (such as the ZIP, GZ, TGZ, or other files that you're probably interested in, you'll need to become a registered member of the DealDatabase forum.

The following list describes the DealDatabase forums that I have found most useful in my DVR and TiVo education, along with a short description of each. These are listed alphabetically, rather than in the order that they appear on the DealDatabase forum Web pages:

◆ *Broken TiVos (Hardware problems & Troubleshooting)*   If the Troubleshooting chapter of this book hasn't identified and helped you resolve any problems you're having with your TiVo, this forum is a great place to check for up-to-date tips on identifying and resolving hardware and software problems with your TiVo.

◆ *Extraction, Insertion, & Streaming Support*   At last! A forum dedicated to information and software for extracting and processing video from Series 1 and Series 2 stand-alone and DirecTiVo systems. This forum is not the place for philosophy, flames, trolling, or any other irrelevant activity. All Linux systems come with a special forum for discussing the latter topics, known as **/dev/null**.

◆ *FILES – All TiVo and DTiVo Files*   A single source for posts to which the latest and greatest versions of TiVo and DirecTiVo hacks are attached. This forum is one-stop-shopping for most of the TiVo hacks you've been looking for, and is certainly a great place to look for updates to any of the software included on the BATBD CD that is provided with this book. Development never stops!

◆ *General TiVo Development*   A general forum intended to host general questions, answers, and discussions about developing software for your TiVo. This forum is a great source for scripts and TCL hacks that will work on both Series 1 and Series 2 TiVos.

◆ *Newbie TiVo*   This forum is targeted toward TiVo users who are new to the TiVo or to TiVo hacking. This forum is a great place to research your new-user questions—chances are that someone has asked the same questions before and that they have already been answered here.

◆ *Series 1 Development*   A forum for technical and development-oriented questions, answers, and discussions that are specific to the PPC-based Series 1 TiVo. If you own a stand-alone Series 1 TiVo or a Series 1 DirecTiVo, this forum is a great source of technical information, tips, and up-to-date development information.

◆ *Series 1 Support*   A forum for general questions and answers that are specific to any PPC-based Series 1 TiVo or DirecTiVo. If you own any TiVo Series 1 model, this forum is a great place to ask (and answer) questions related to using or hacking it.

◆ *Series 2 Development*   A forum for technical and development-oriented questions, answers, and development discussions that are specific to the MIPS-based Series 2 TiVo. The latest versions of these machines are harder to hack than any other TiVo. If you own a TiVo Series 2, this forum is a great source of technical information, tips, and up-to-date development information.

◆ *Series 2 Support*   A forum for general questions and answers that are specific to the MIPS-based Series 2 TiVos and DirecTiVos. These systems are harder to hack and debug problems on than the Series 1 systems, and this forum is a great source of information, assistance, and up-to-date hacking information.

◆ *XBOX Hacking*   A forum dedicated to questions, answers, and discussion of hacking Microsoft's X-Box home gaming systems. Now that they run Linux (although not without software and optional hardware hacking), these appliances are probably worth a look. They're quite sexy as video game systems, but I'm prejudiced against supporting the evil empire unless necessary. The discussion of hacking them is quite cool, and it would be nice to have a box stamped "Microsoft" running Linux at home. See back issues of 2600 for details on running Linux on an X-Box.

## MacTiVo Forums

Apple's adoption of Mach and FreeBSD as the underpinnings of Mac OS X in its Darwin kernel provided a huge boost in capabilities and potential for its Macintosh line of personal computers. It also opened the door to making the Macintosh a more hacker-friendly environment due to the inherent power and flexibility of Un*x. To paraphrase Walt Kelly, "We have met those hackers, and some of them is us." The MacTiVo forums at **http://www.mactivo.com/forums/index.php**, shown in Figure 14.5, promise to help keep you

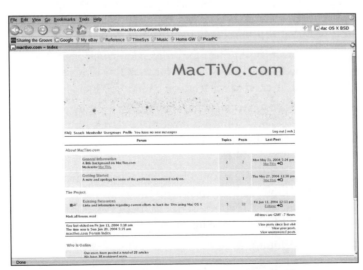

**FIGURE 14.5**   *The MacTivo.com forums in a Web browser*

up to date with the latest information about hacking TiVos from Macs. This site only has a few forums at present, but already contains a lot of good information and can grow to be a significant resource if interested parties join and contribute.

## PTVupgrade Forums

As discussed in Chapter 4, PTVupgrade.com is a firm that specializes in upgrading TiVos, and providing auxiliary hardware, software, and services for use with your TiVo. They also host forums related to the software and hardware that they sell. PTVupgrade.com supports Series 1 networking products such as the TurboNet and CacheCard, and also provides a variety of software and software-related services. The PTVupgrade forums are available at **http://forum.ptvupgrade.com** (see Figure 14.6).

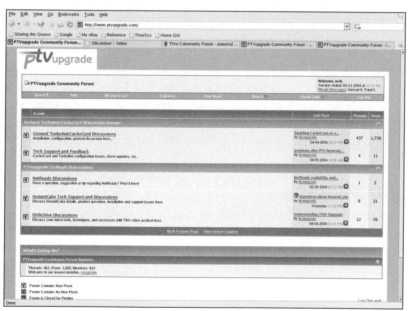

**FIGURE 14.6**   *The PTVupgrade Community forums in a Web browser*

Unlike the more general TiVo-related forums, such as the DealDatabase and TiVo Community forums, the PTVupgrade forums focus on the products available from PTVupgrade.com—no surprise, really, and it's quite useful to have a place to report or discuss any problems that you might encounter in using these. One thing that makes these forums especially interesting is that PTVupgrade.com has a very close relationship with TiVo, Inc., and offers upgrade kits that eliminate the need to scrounge around on the Net or beg for backups of various versions of the TiVo software.

The PTVupgrade forums that were available when this book was last updated are the following:

- ◆ *DVRchive Discussions*   DVRchive is a prepackaged toolkit from PTVupgrade.com that makes it easy to extract and archive video from any Series 1 TiVo. See **http://www.ptvupgrade.com/products/DVRchive/** for detailed information about this product.

- ◆ *General TurboNet/CacheCard Discussions*   General discussions of installing and using the TurboNet or CacheCard network devices for Series 1 TiVos.

- ◆ *InstantCake Tech Support and Discussions*   InstantCake is a prepackaged CD and TiVo system image that makes it easy for you to upgrade any Series 1 or Series 2 TiVo. See **http://www.ptvupgrade.com/products/instantcake/** for detailed information about this product.

- ◆ *NetReady Discussions*   NetReady is the term used by PTVupgrade.com to emphasize the fact that any TiVo system upgrade that you purchase from them already incorporates all of the modules, startup scripts, and related applications necessary to put your TiVo on your home network as soon as you install network hardware, such as a TurboNet card, CacheCard, or a USB Ethernet device on a Series 2 TiVo or DirecTiVo. This forum provides a place for reporting or discussing problems that you might have when using any Series 1 or Series 2 TiVo or DirecTiVo whose storage was upgraded by purchasing an upgrade kit from PTVupgrade.com.

- ◆ *Tech Support and Feedback*   A central location for obtaining the latest drivers for the TurboNet or CacheCard network devices for Series 1 TiVos and DirecTiVos.

## pvrhax0r Forums

The pvrhax0r forums, shown in Figure 14.7, are a relatively new set of forums dedicated to hacking various types of PVRs, including TiVos. You can find these forums at **http://www.pvrhax0r.com/forum/**, and will understand their name if you are 31337. At the time this book was updated, the site was fairly young and thus there wasn't much content there, but the site has promise and is worth a look. You can't beat the price! The pvrhax0r site provides forums dedicated to TiVo hacks, TiVo technical information, and general reference information about hacking PVRs.

## SiliconDust Forums

SiliconDust is the corporate identity of the people who commercialized the original network device for Series 1 TiVos, the TiVoNet card, which used a "standard" ISA Ethernet card in a Series 1 TiVo. Since then, they developed and support the TurboNet, AirNet, and CacheCard network devices for Series 1 TiVos—some seriously impressive hardware! These are all stand-alone Ethernet devices that make it almost trivial to put a Series 1 TiVo on your home network (see Chapter 4 section entitled "Networking Your TiVo"). Without the efforts of Nick at SiliconDust, far too many people would still be using PPP over a serial

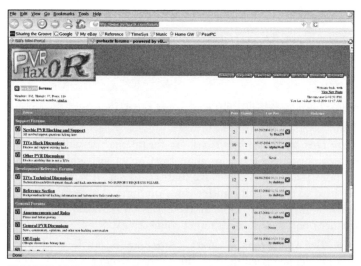

**FIGURE 14.7** *The pvrhax0r Community forums in a Web browser*

connection to connect to their TiVos over a "network"—which is painfully slow if you're trying to do anything such as extracting or inserting video to your TiVo.

Located at **http://www.silicondust.com/forum/**, the SiliconDust forums are dedicated to providing information and support for the AirNet, CacheCard, and TurboNet cards and the software that they use to support network connectivity (see Figure 14.8).

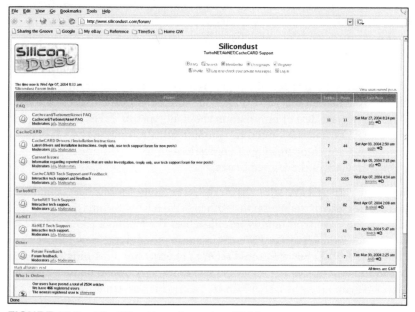

**FIGURE 14.8** *The SiliconDust forums in a Web browser*

The SiliconDust forums that were available when this book was last updated are the following:

◆ *AirNet Tech Support*   A general forum for asking questions and reporting problems related to using an AirNet card in a Series 1 TiVo or DirecTiVo. An AirNet card enables you to use a variety of wireless, PCMCIA Ethernet cards in a Series 1 TiVo or DirecTiVo.

◆ *CacheCard/TurboNet/AirNet FAQ*   A great central location for obtaining general information about any of these products.

◆ *CacheCard Drivers/Installation Issues*   A forum that provides the latest software and related information about installing the CacheCard, which is an Ethernet card for the Series 1 TiVo and DirecTivo that includes a DIMM slot that expands the memory used to cache and transfer video on Series 1 systems. The CacheCard is the latest Ethernet card available for the Series 1 TiVos, and provides an impressive performance boost as well as Ethernet connectivity.

◆ *CacheCard Tech Support and Feedback*   A general forum for asking questions and reporting problems related to using the CacheCard in a Series 1 TiVo.

◆ *TurboNet Tech Support*   A general forum for asking questions and reporting problems related to using a TurboNet card in a Series 1 TiVo or DirecTiVo. A TurboNet card is a dedicated Ethernet card that directly connects any Series 1 TiVo or DirecTiVo to a home network, just like any other Ethernet device.

# TiVo Community Forums

Located at **http://www.tivocommunity.com**, the TiVo Community forums (see Figure 14.9) are probably the best-known sites for TiVo information, discussion, sharing TiVo hacks and software, and for any other TiVo-related topics. This site and its forums were one of the earliest TiVo community sites (if not the earliest) and were founded to provide TiVo users and fans with a place to discuss and exchange ideas, software, and TiVo tips. The TiVo Community forums actually began as a part of the AVS forums discussed earlier in this chapter, but split off because of the huge volume of traffic that these forums attracted. They provide a great deal of information about all types of TiVos, including sections dedicated to using TiVos in the United Kingdom (UK), a community of TiVo fans and hackers whose postings are unfortunately often overlooked or buried under the flood of postings from TiVo-maniacs in the United States.

As one of the earliest TiVo sites, the TiVo Community forums have a much stricter set of rules on posting and participation than other TiVo-related forums discussed in this chapter. Specifically, the TiVo Community forums reflect the paranoia about video extraction that is still rampant in much of the TiVo community—though the new Pioneer Series 2 TiVos with integrated DVD burners would seem to obviate any remaining concerns about these issues. On the other hand, the recording and motion picture industries have a long history of isolationism and secretism to maximize profit margins rather than trying to innovate in order to simply give people what they want at an affordable price. At any rate, any talk of video extraction on the TiVo Community forums is verboten. If you post questions about video extraction or—gasp!—software to help people do it, your posts will be deleted, your medals and insignia will be torn from your uniform, your sword will be broken in half, and 80 pizzas will be delivered to your house, collect. Don't try it!

**FIGURE 14.9**  *The TiVo Community forums in a Web browser*

 **TIP**

If you're a regular visitor to the TiVo Community forum, an easy way to view a listing of the most recent posts on any of its forums is to click the TiVo Forum Post Ticker link, which is available near the top of each page within the TiVo Community site (currently in the upper left corner). Clicking this link pops up a small dialog box that displays a scrolling list of the most recent posts made to any of the TiVo Community forums. To view a specific post from this list, just click its listing in the scrolling dialog box, and a new browser window opens on your screen that contains the selected post.

The TiVo Community forum is all about TiVos, and it provides more dedicated information about TiVos and TiVo hacking than any other site. (Sites such as the alt.org and DealDatabase forums provide more technical information, in most cases, but the alt.org forums are small and the DealDatabase forums also discuss types of systems other than TiVos.) Folks from TiVo even participate in the forums and threads on this site, making it more authoritative than others. It's also a great place to pick up hot TiVo rumors. However, because TiVo, Inc.

is one of its sponsors, topics such as video extraction and related software are forbidden, and evil topics are eliminated without mercy whenever they appear (and they do. Who reads the FAQ anyway?). The following list therefore contains almost all of the forums on the TiVo Community site, since most of them are relevant, along with a short description of each. They are listed alphabetically, rather than in the order that they appear on the TiVo Community forum Web pages:

- ◆ *DIRECTV Receiver with TiVo*   A forum dedicated to discussing DirecTiVo systems. This forum prohibits any discussions of hacking the Digital Subscriber Service required to use the DirecTiVo (and other TiVo models, although the DirecTiVos have many special requirements and associated hacks).

- ◆ *HDTV TiVo Powered PVRs*   A forum dedicated to discussing TiVo PVRs that support HDTV (High-Definition Television). In late April, 2004, DirecTV introduced a DirecTivo with HDTV support, a truly amazing unit. Though still emerging technology, these systems are quite impressive—this forum is specific to any TiVo that has integrated support for HDTV. Rumors abound that TiVo, Inc. intends to produce an OpenCable-compatible HD TiVo, which would be an integrated HD TiVo/Cable box following industry standards, but this is certainly waiting for the adoption of the OpenCable standard, expected to take effect in July, 2004 For more information about the OpenCable standard, see **http://www.opencable.com/primer/**.

- ◆ *Now Playing—TV Show Talk*   A general forum for discussing your favorite TV shows, with occasional tips and tricks for locating and recording upcoming episodes.

- ◆ *Season Pass Alerts*   Like it or not, TiVo guide data is not always up-to-date, largely due to broadcast networks changing their schedules, misidentifying something, and so on. This forum provides a place for TiVo fanatics to post "alerts" about Season Pass problems or other scheduling weirdness that might cause you to miss a show that you expected to see on TiVo. These alerts also include messages suggesting when you should pad various shows (i.e., increase the amount of time after the normal conclusion of the show to continue to record) due to interruptions, over-runs, and other random events. This is an incredibly useful forum if you keep up with it.

- ◆ *TiVo Coffee House—TiVo Discussion*   A chatty, general-purpose forum for discussing TiVo news, TiVos, TiVo culture, and upcoming devices that will feature the TiVo software. If we're lucky, upcoming devices from Toshiba and Pioneer that feature integrated DVD recording support should finally squash the prohibition against discussing video extraction on any of the TiVo Community forums.

- ◆ *TiVo Help Center*   A general-purpose forum for asking questions about using the out-of-the-box TiVo software. You should not ask questions about hacked, upgraded, or otherwise-modified TiVos here—they have their own forums. This forum provides lots of useful tips and tricks for getting the most out of your TiVo without taking a Torx screwdriver to it.

- ◆ *TiVo Home Media Option*   A forum dedicated to questions, answers, and discussion of the Home Media Option (HMO) introduced by TiVo for the Series 2 systems in mid-2003. This forum prohibits discussions of Home Media Option hacking or related topics. See the HMO-related sections of this book for more information, especially if your MP3 or digital photograph server is a Linux box, you store your Music in OGG/Vorbis format, or anything else along those lines. The Linux-specific section of Chapter 10 entitled "Working with TiVo's Home Media Option," or various sections of Chapter 9, "Working with Your TiVo from Windows and Macintosh Systems," might be useful to you.

◆   *TiVo Suggestion Avenue*   This forum provides a place for posting suggestions that you'd like TiVo, Inc. to consider in upcoming software releases. The folks from TiVo read this forum, and some of the suggestions posted here have made it to subsequent releases of the TiVo software. Maybe you'll get lucky, too....

◆   *TiVo UK*   A forum dedicated to questions, answers, and general discussion of using TiVos in the UK. Discussion of Skybox, the connectivity service in the UK, is also a valid topic here.

◆   *TiVo Underground*   A forum dedicated to discussions of TiVo hacking. It's sometimes hard to differentiate general topics from topics specific to certain models of TiVos, but this is still a great forum. It is populated by smart, friendly wizards and is knee-deep in software, good instructions, and so on. Information specific to hacking the TiVo Series 2 is easily found on the DealDatabase forum. As always, any discussion of theft of service or video extraction is forbidden here, and will be terminated quickly. Long-time TiVo hackers remarked to me with some sadness that TiVo Underground has become little more than a glorified support section for topics forbidden in the TiVo help forum, such as hacked TiVos.

◆   *TiVo Upgrade Center*   This forum is dedicated to discussions, questions, and answers about upgrading your TiVos. This forum provides reviews of various upgrade kits, dealers, and discusses potential problems and their solutions. Discussions of TiVo hacking, even if related to an upgrade, should be posted in the "TiVo Underground" forum in the same category of the TiVo Community site. As always, any discussion of theft of service or video extraction is forbidden here.

# TiVo.net Forums

The TiVo.net forums, shown in Figure 14.10, are a relatively new set of forums dedicated to TiVo hacking. You can find these forums at **http://www.tivo.net**. At the time this book was updated, the site was fairly young but the amount of content there was growing fairly quickly thanks to active participation. As with any other online resource, you can't beat the price! Besides some general-purpose forums, the TiVo.net site provides forums dedicated to General TiVo Discussions, TiVo Help, TiVo HDTV DVR, and TiVo Hacks and Easter Eggs. Unfortunately, they currently follow TiVoCommunity.com's stance of not allowing discussion of video extraction, but that will hopefully have been fixed by the time you read this. Check them out—the more TiVo forum sites, the merrier!

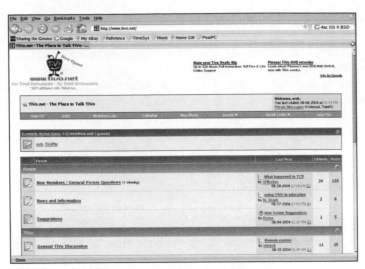

**FIGURE 14.10** *The TiVo.net forums in a Web browser*

# TiVo Hardware Web Sites

Relatively few sites on the Web actually discuss the TiVo hardware beyond discussing the types of hard drives and networking devices that you can use with your TiVo. Specific sites for obtaining TiVo upgrades, network hardware, or related tools and parts are discussed in Chapter 4 in the section, "TiVo Hardware Supplies on the Net." The following sites provide useful information about stock TiVos and related hardware:

- ◆ *Inside DirecTiVo*   Part of the 9thTee.com Web site discussed elsewhere in this book (and this chapter), the page can be found at **http://www.9thtee.com/ insidedirectv-tivo.htm**, which provides lots of great photos of the internals of a Series 1 DirecTiVo, even providing information about the chips that it contains, the purpose of each, and (in many cases) links to reference information about those chips. Truly a labor of love.

- ◆ *Inside Series 1 TiVo*   Part of the 9thTee.com Web site discussed elsewhere in this book (and this chapter), the page can be found at **http://www.9thtee.com/insidetivo.htm**, which provides lots of great photos of the internals of a Series 1 TiVo, even providing information about the chips that it contains, the purpose of each, and (in many cases) links to reference information about those chips. This was the first site to provide this sort of detailed information about TiVo internals, and has been a great asset to the TiVo community for years (as has 9thTee.com itself).

- ◆ *Inside Series 2 TiVo*   Part of the 9thTee.com Web site discussed elsewhere in this book, the page can be found at **http://www.9thtee.com/insideseries2tivo.htm**, which provides some photographs of the internals of a Series 2 TiVo.

- *JTAG Support for Series 1 TiVos* This site, available at **http://penguinppc.org/embedded/tivo/hardware/jtag.shtml**, discusses how to attach JTAG devices to the edge connectors found on Series 1 systems. JTAG (Joint Test Action Group) is a low-level hardware/software debugging interface used for hardware and operating system development. Since the edge connector discussed on this site is only available on the Series 1 stand-alone and Series 1 DirecTiVo motherboards, this site is of limited utility for anyone but the true hobbyist.

- *Linux/PPC for PowerPC 4xx* This site, available at **http://www.borg.umn.edu/~grant/Linux**, provides hardware and software information about the IBM reference hardware on which the Series 1 systems were originally based. It is largely only useful for historical purposes. (Any discussion of software here is not only outdated, but doesn't include any discussion of the TiVo-specific software that makes the TiVo what it is.)

- *PVR Comparisons* This site, available at **http://www.pvrcompare.com**, provides comparisons of various TiVo, ReplayTV, and UltimateTV models. Although parts of it are outdated, this is a good site for getting some comparative information about the hardware and hardware capabilities of various types of PVRs.

- *Series 1 Edge Connector Information* This site, available at **http://penguinppc.org/embedded/tivo/hardware/edgecon.shtml**, provides detailed information about the edge connector on the TiVo Series 1 motherboards.

- *SiliconDust.com* This site, available at **http://silicondust.com**, is the home page of the makers of the TiVoNet, TurboNet, and AirNet network adaptors for Series 1 TiVos. As such, it deserves a special mention here. Networking your Series 1 systems would be impossible without the pioneering work done by Andrew Tridgell and the subsequent amazing developments done by Nick Kelsey (aka jafa) at SiliconDust.

- *TiVo Hardware Questions* Part of the TiVo Forum FAQ discussed later in this section, available at **http://www.tivofaq.com/index.html?http://www.tivofaq.com/Hardware.html**, this site is a good source of useful information about working with and using the TiVo hardware without taking a Torx screwdriver to it. It explains what the lights mean on the front of the TiVo, how different remotes and services work, and how to hook up your TiVo to almost everything but your toaster or Jini network.

- *TiVo Rev 0 PPC 403 Oak Evaluation Kit* This site, available at **http://penguinppc.org/embedded/tivo/hardware/oak.shtml**, discusses the IBM reference board that was the parent of the Series 1. Historically interesting, but it is largely irrelevant these days.

# Various TiVo FAQs and Help Sites

FAQs, which stands for "Frequently Asked Questions," are a common way of disseminating commonly asked information on specific topics, making it available to a much wider audience than paper documentation could ever hope to read (with the exception of this book, I hope). FAQs are generally simple text or HTML files that provide a centralized source of information about a given topic. Like its companion acronym, RTFM (Read The F***ing Manual), FAQs hope to reduce the number of times any given question is asked by writing it down once, so that people who are inclined to read documentation can do so—as well as to provide an online source for information that is searchable on the Internet.

Much of the online documentation for Internet-related topics can be downloaded from **ftp://rtfm.mit.edu/pub**, including many general FAQs (available in **ftp://rtfm.mit.edu/pub/faqs**). Unfortunately, this does not include various FAQs about the TiVo and TiVo-related topics. The next few sections discuss the primary TiVo FAQs that I've found over the years, providing URLs where they can be found and an overview of contents and relevance today.

## Hacking the TiVo FAQ

No relation to this book (except in spirit), the Hacking the TiVo FAQ was the original TiVo FAQ, providing general and increasingly detailed information about hacking your TiVo. The latest version of this FAQ is available at **http://www.tivofaq.com/hack/faq.html** in its entirety.

Unfortunately, to quote this FAQ itself, "This FAQ is obsolete." It deals entirely with Series 1 topics, and even in that context discusses hacks and hacking techniques that were first-generation solutions. For example, it focuses on doing backups using Dylan's Boot Disk, which was the first TiVo tools floppy available. This aside, it focuses on doing backups using **dd** (explained in this book) but does not discuss using the newer, faster, and less disk-intensive MFS Tools utilities (also discussed in this book).

If you are a hard-core Microsoft Windows user, this FAQ does contain some information available nowhere else, such as how to back up the TiVo using some dedicated Windows utilities. However, these are superceded by improvements in tools disks, such as the one included on the CD with this book.

This is an interesting FAQ, but is basically no longer relevant except for historical purposes.

## Hinsdale FAQs

Bill "Hinsdale" Regnery's TiVo upgrade FAQs, available at **http://www.newreleasesvideo.com/hinsdale-how-to**, are the standard by which most TiVo upgrade information is judged. These FAQs are eminently usable discussions of the complete procedures necessary to add disk space and generally upgrade your TiVo. These FAQs are constantly kept up-to-date, and contain a tremendous amount of information oriented towards Microsoft Windows users that explains caveats and additional information to think about when upgrading a TiVo using your Windows PC.

The URL referenced in the paragraph above actually contains pointers to two additional Hinsdale FAQs, as well as to the Hinsdale site where you can buy prepackaged upgrade kits or even send your TiVo for repair or upgrading. (The URL for this section is **http://www.newreleasesvideo.com/hinsdale-how-to/upgradeservice.html**). The latest Hinsdale upgrade FAQ is at **http://www.newreleasesvideo.com/hinsdale-how-to/index9.html**, and uses Version 2.0 of the MFS Tools utilities as the core of the backup and upgrade procedure. An older version of the FAQ is also available at **http://www.newreleasesvideo.com/hinsdale-how-to/index2.html**. The older version uses TiVoMad, BlessTiVo, and Version 1.1 of the MFS Tools utilities in its upgrade procedure. If you are upgrading a Series 1 system, the information in this older FAQ (all of which is also discussed in this book) may still be useful to you.

The TiVo community would be a much poorer place without the Hinsdale FAQs and the work that has gone into them.

## OzTiVo Site

If you're lucky enough to live in Australia, you have great beer but face a unique set of problems in getting your TiVo to work, since TiVo, Inc. doesn't provide TiVos or programming information down under. Shame on them! The OzTiVo site at **http://minnie.tuhs.org/twiki/bin/view/Main/WebHome** focuses on the information that you need in order to help get your TiVo up and running there, including information about obtaining programming guide data. This site is truly a labour (Aussie spelling) of love, with tons of information contributed by true TiVo wizards. It's worth looking at from anywhere in the world if only to see the fanatic devotion of some TiVo owners and the extent to which people will go to use a TiVo anywhere.

## Seth's TiVo FAQ

Seth's TiVo FAQ, available at **http://www.sethb.com/TiVo**, is a site that contains lots of good information, maintained by Seth Bokelman, a long-time TiVo evangelist. It provides a good deal of general TiVo information, as well as a good listing of USB network adaptors that work with various models of TiVos. It's generally a good read, and it is a good source of introductory TiVo information for people new to the TiVo. It also features a picture of the front cover of this book, so it must be good ;-).

## TiVo Network Hack How-To Guide

Steve Jenkins is a long-time TiVo hacker and knows his stuff. His Network Hack FAQ, available at **http://tivo.stevejenkins.com/**, is a great source of information about hacking and networking your TiVo. This FAQ focuses on networking TiVo rather than on upgrading their disks, which makes it a great central source of information not easily found elsewhere online. The FAQ is frequently updated and almost always reflects the latest and greatest in TiVo networking techniques. Links that enable you to download any of the files referenced in the FAQ are provided at **http://tivo.stevejenkins.com/downloads**.

Steve's site at **http://tivo.stevejenkins.com** is also fun, in general, with a good sense of humor. One especially cool thing that it provides is a downloadable graphic that represents a hacked TiVo. This is available at **http://www.stevejenkins.com/tivo/downloads/sticker.zip**. The idea is that you download it, print it off on transparent, adhesive paper, and then affix it to your TiVo. Voila! TiVo Hacks inside.

## TiVoHelp.com

Though not a FAQ per se, this site contains a good deal of information about getting started with your TiVo, fixing various problems, as well as links to many other TiVo sites. This site is available at **http://www.tivohelp.com**, and is designed to perform some blog-like functions, enabling you to add to or update it. If you have problems with any aspect of the site, you can check out a static version of the site at **http://www.tivohelp.com/archive/tivohelp.swiki.net/6.html**.

One especially useful section of this site is its "Home/LAN Configuration" section, which goes into great detail about setting up a home network. Another useful section discussed Microsoft Windows utilities for connecting to and interacting with your TiVo, including text editors that you can use on Windows systems without changing the end-of-line characters that Linux systems, such as the TiVo, require.

## Weaknees Interactive TiVo Upgrade Instructions

Weaknees.com, discussed earlier in this book and a great source for upgraded TiVos, TiVo upgrade kits, and other TiVo-related niceties, sponsors a useful interactive Web interface for TiVo upgrade instructions and information at **http://tivo.upgrade-instructions.com/**. You select the type of TiVo system that you are upgrading, and subsequent pages walk you through the upgrade process. The site is quite usable and provides links to tools disks (and, of course, hardware) that you may need while upgrading.

## DirecTiVo Sites and Information

As mentioned in the Introduction to this book, I don't own a DirecTiVo and therefore don't know as much as I'd like to about the internals of these systems. Large parts of community forums such as the AVS, DealDatabase, and TiVo Community forums (discussed earlier in this chapter) are devoted to DirecTiVo (aka DTiVo) hacking. One of these days I'll move beyond the five stand-alone TiVos that I currently own, and will branch out into DirecTiVo-land. Feel free to send me one! Until then, I can only dream....

## TiVo Software Download Sites

The CD that accompanies this book provides a good collection of software that you will need to hack your TiVo, compile programs for it, or work with it from other systems. Unfortunately, a single CD can't hold everything—even a DVD would be hard-pressed to keep up with the flood of TiVo software, kernels, source code, and associated documentation that is available for TiVos on the Internet. This section attempts to fill in any gaps left unfilled by the CD that accompanies this book, providing links to my favorite online sources of TiVo-related software and general information.

The entire TiVo community benefits from the work and dedication of TiVo hackers everywhere. This includes those who collect available software and provide Web sites that make it easy for all of us to obtain the latest and greatest software, tips, and tricks. To the best of my knowledge, none of the sites listed in this section provides illegal software or instructions, or explains illegal techniques. In general, don't look at things that offend you, and don't use things that are illegal. That's just the "right thing" to do.

The following are my favorite sites for browsing and downloading some of the vast armada of TiVo-related software available on the Internet:

- ◆ *Craig Leres' TiVo Downloads* Available at **http://www.xse.com/leres/tivo/ downloads**, this site provides older downloads for the Series 1 TiVo but still can be useful if you're running an older TiVo.

- ◆ *DarkWing's (aka Wanker) DTiVo Links* Available at **http://www.angelfire.com/ darkside/wanker**, this is a great software download site for all things DirecTiVo.

- ◆ *TiVo Hacking for PPC* Available at **http://sourceforge.net/projects/tivo-hack-ppc/**, this is a great project dedicated to developing bootable disks that enable TiVo hacking on Mac OS X systems. This is absolutely fantastic! They are currently working on porting Sleeper's scripts and ISO to work on PPC systems, and have a bootable ISO that you can use on your Mac OS X system in much the same way that you can use the BATBD CD that accompanies this book on x86 systems. This ISO is still beta (so be very, very careful and back up first) but has fantastic promise for brings many of the standard Linux TiVo hacking software to Macs with a minimum amount of fuss.

- ◆ *TiVoWeb Project* The other sites in this section provide links to a variety of software. This one provides just one. While the site only contains the TiVoWeb software, "only" is a misnomer here. Long before TiVo introduced the Home Media Option, TiVoWeb enabled you to access and manage your TiVo over a network from any Web browser. This is an amazing piece of work, and has recently received a major upgrade known as TiVoWebPlus (available at **http://tivo.fp2000.org/twp**, and discussed on the DealDatabase forum at **http://www.dealdatabase.com/forum/ showthread.php?t=30564**). A copy of the latest revision of the software at the time this book was updated is also included on the BATBD CD that accompanies this book. The original TiVoWeb software is available at **http://tivo.lightn.org**. TiVoWeb and TiVoWebPlus are discussed in more detail in Chapter 8 in the section entitled "Programming Your TiVo Over a Network Using TiVoWebPlus."

- ◆ *TiVo Hacking Links* Primarily a hard-core developer/download site (and part of the alt.org forums, discussed earlier in this chapter), this site provides links to a variety of TiVo-related hacking and download sites and also maintains a TiVo hacking wiki and some traditional forums at **http://alt.org/wiki/index.php/TivoHackingLinks**.

# Sites Specific to Video Extraction, Archiving, Processing, and Insertion

This section lists sites that provide software or information specific to extracting and archiving video from various TiVo and DirecTiVo systems. If you are having problems with any of the software on the CD that accompanies this book, check these sites and the DealDatabase.com forums to see if updates are available.

The following are my favorite sites for information about extracting, archiving, and manipulating:

◆ *Extracting Video from a TiVo Series 1 Using Mac OS X*   For Mac OS X fans (such as myself), this site provides some useful information about the process of extracting and processing video from a Series 1 TiVo using Mac OS X. See **http://www.fajkowski.com/tivo/** for more information.

◆ *Extracting TiVo Video to a VCD or DVD on Mac OS X*   You can find one person's discussion of extracting and processing video on a Mac OS X system using TyStudio at **http://minnie.tuhs.org/twiki/bin/view/Howtovideoextract/ExtractVideoonOSX.** The process described there uses Fink, which is a Linux execution layer that runs on Mac OS X and is roughly analogous to the way that Cygwin enables you to execute Linux applications on a Windows system. It also suggests additional software packages that you can use if you have problems with the beta version of TyStudio on Max OS X.

◆ *TiVo Mplayer*   TiVo Mplayer is an enhanced version of the standard Linux mplayer application that enables you to play TiVo recordings in TiVo's tystream format on your Linux or Windows system. (Using mplayer on Windows requires the Cygwin Linux-on-Windows environment, which is available at **http://www.cygwin.com**.) TiVo Mplayer itself is available at **http://tivo-mplayer.sourceforge.net/**.

◆ *TiVo Video to DVD for Windows*   This site provides a step-by-step description of extracting and processing TiVo video using TyTool and creating DVDs from the processed video. See **http://themurrays.homeip.net/downloads/tivo/extraction_articles/tivo_dvd.html** for details.

◆ *TyStudio*   TyStudio is a Linux and Windows framework for receiving and processing TiVo video recordings in the *tystream* format, consisting of a suite of tools for receiving, processing, and converting this type of video, and a server that runs on the TiVo to deliver the video stream. The Linux and Windows TyStudio tools enable you to transform TiVo TY (tyStream) recordings to more standard formats, such as MPEG, that can be played on most computer systems or burned to standard DVDs. TyStudio also enables you to edit recordings prior to converting them, which makes it extremely handy for removing commercials and other irritations. The latest version of TyStudio is available at **http://dvd-create.sourceforge.net/tystudio/**. See Chapter 12, "Extracting, Inserting, and Playing TiVo Recordings," for more information about using TyStudio.

◆ *TyTool* TyTool is a Windows-only tool for receiving and processing TiVo video recording in the *tystream* format, consisting of a Windows application for receiving, processing, and converting this type of video, and a server that runs on the TiVo to deliver the video stream over the network. (Not the same server as used by TyStudio.) Like TyStudio, TyTool enables you to convert TiVo TY (tyStream) video to MPEG and also provides editing capabilities for eliminating irritations such as commercials. The latest version of TyTool is always available on a dedicated thread on the DealDatabase forum, at **http://www.dealdatabase.com/forum/showthread.php?t=32985**.

# Index

\* wildcard character, 83
0-ThumbsUp keys, 56
3 0 BC code, 77
8 command, 81
9-inch gender changer, 88
9thTee.com Web site, 48, 111,
   115, 135, 173, 225, 480
10-Base2, 108
10-BaseT, 108
30-second skip button, 50
30-Second Skip mode, 67, 75–76
100-BaseT, 108
160 GB hard disks, 93
#401 dialing prefix, 125
1000-BaseT, 108
8160/8170/8170S emitters, 47

## A

About Unix Web site, 391
Acrobat Reader, 441
active root filesystem, 269
active root partition, 267
Adobe Photoshop Album 2.0, 15
Adobe Web site, 15, 441
Advanced Paid Programming
   entries, 70
Advanced Wishlist, 83–85
advertising, 9, 14
agetty command, 385
AirNet cards, 135, 248
   changing options, 117–118
   Daily call option, 119
   dynamic IP address
      information, 118
   easy-to-use installer for
      software, 115
   firmly seating, 125
   installing software for, 113–120

   PCMCIA adapter, 113
   SSID value, 117
AirNet Tech Support forum, 504
Alchemy TV, 445
All Programs option, 53
alternate boot partitions
   number of, 146
   printing values, 163
alternate kernel partition, 163
alt.org forums, 494
Amiga computer, 10
Angry IP Scanner utility, 133
AOL, 12, 276
AOL Instant Messenger,
   275–279
application software, 140
architecture-specific startup
   commands, 250
archive files, 170
Arpanet, 107
ASCII file transfers, 385
asx directory, 475
ASX format, 7
AT&T Series 2 TiVos
   adding disk drives, 102
   air circulation, 104
   auxiliary fans, 104–105
   removing disk drives, 95–97
attributes, 378–380
audio files, 15, 429
   alternate Windows formats,
      342–345
   exporting, 303–304
   MP3 format, 303
   OGG audio format, 342
authentication, 394
   information, 16
   NFS (Network File System),
      396

automatic key-press generation,
   72
automatically recording shows,
   81
auto-mounting, 412
AutoTest mode, 50, 72
Avalanche directory, 377
AVI (Audio Video Interleave)
   file format, 443
Avid One Media Composer, 10
Avid Technology, 10
AVS forum, 495–497
AVS Forum Web site, 23

## B

Backdoor codes
   known, 54
   verifying, 51
Backdoor mode, 50
   activating, 51–60
   automating, 74–78
   CCEE (Clear-Clear-Enter-
      Enter) codes, 61
   key sequence to activate, 51
   V 3.0 and earlier TiVos, 53–55
   V 3.1 and later TiVo models,
      55–60
backdoors
   accessing TiVo Advanced
      WishLists, 84
   brute force attempts to identify,
      53
   Disk Space Usage screen,
      55–56
   DVD-equipped TiVos, 55
   enabling, 51, 76–78
   Home Media features, 56
   patching tivoapp binary to
      enable, 74–76

**"Backdoors enabled!" message, 53**

**backup files, 265**

checking consistency, 266

disk images without, 236–238

mfstool backup command, 192

**backup images, restoring, 266–268**

**backups, 92, 253–255**

advanced options, 196–198

advanced restore options, 211–215

-C option, 207

changing operating system versions using, 219

compatible, 203

compressed, 152, 193–194

creation of, 190–198

dd command, 186–188, 190

entire TiVo disks, 194–195

excluding /var directory from, 154

expanding, 141

filesystems, 180

finding room for, 182–184

hard disks, 99, 152–154, 265–266

-i option, 207

image backups, 181

including video streams with fsid, 153

incremental, 181, 198

limiting stream size, 197–198

locating, 200–202

MFS Tools, 190–198

multiple-disk TiVo systems, 195–196

name of output file, 153

of operating system, 249

personalized information, 171

protecting against software upgrades, 177

RAR compression utility, 202

rc.sysinit file, 250

reasons for, 177–178

reducing backup image size, 153

before replacing hard disks, 227

restoring, 141, 256

byte-swapped and normal, 183

files, 154–156

to larger hard disk, 185, 207–208

MFS Tools backups, 205–216

to two-drive TiVos, 209–210

without adding space, 205–207

Season Passes, 200

selected information backups, 198–200

Series 2 TiVo, 264

simple, 191–193

special format, 149

streams with fsids, 197

structured, 179

unstructured, 179

video stream size calculation, 153

virginal image, 181

when to make, 181–182

WishLists, 200

*Bamboozled at the Revolution* **(Motavelli), 11**

**Barton, Jim, 11**

**bash (Bourne-Again Shell), 259, 315, 387–391**

myworld (tivoapp) command, 65

problems with, 247

setting ROM monitor password, 80

**BASH_ENV environment variable, 248, 252, 258, 260, 272, 487**

**BASH_ENV hack, 262–263, 266**

**"bash:no job control in this shell" message, 259**

**bat directory, 475**

**BATBD boot option, 187**

**BATBD boot screen, 38, 41**

**BATBD (Bill's Accumulated TiVo Boot Disk) CD, 36, 38, 40–41, 57, 140, 169–173**

bigs1 boot option, 199, 205, 226, 234, 236, 243, 248

bigs2 boot option, 185, 205, 228–229, 231, 255–256, 268

boot options, 169

bootpage directory, 170

connectivity directory, 170

cross-compilers, 423–424

DOS directory, 100–101, 170

extract_gzip program, 261

floppy directory, 170

GAIM (GTK AOL Instant Messenger), 277

hack_dirs directory, 170, 415

HISTORY file, 171

img directory, 171

img_monte directory, 171

initrds directory, 171

installing hacks from, 421–422

isolinux directory, 171

kernel_modules directory, 171

killinitrd directory, 171

lba48_s1_kernels directory, 171

macintosh directory, 171, 348, 354

man directory, 171

mfs_ftp directory, 171

monte-mips directory, 171

mounting, 256, 270, 412–413

mplayer directory, 171

old_mfstool2.0 directory, 171

RAM (Random-Access Memory) disks, 169–170

s1swap boot option, 199, 205, 217, 226, 229, 234, 236, 240, 243, 248

scrambling directory, 171

scripts directory, 132

settings-backup directory, 171, 199–200

src directory, 148, 171

text directory, 171

tivodns-1.0 directory, 172

TiVoMad directory, 172

TiVoMad utilities, 170

tivopart directory, 172

TiVoWebPlus-1.0-final.tivo.tpm shell script, 172

tpip-1.1 directory, 172
TPM directory, 172
TyStudio directory, 172
TyTool directory, 172
unmounting, 259, 414
vplay directory, 172
windows directory, 172
x86bin directory, 172
xcompilers directory, 172
bbDEMUX, 445–446
"Beginner's Bash" Web site, 387
BeyondTV, 447
bg (background) command, 390
big-endian processors, 157–158
bin command, 284, 474–475
binary file formats, 414–415
/bin/bash command, 250, 260, 420–421
BIOS (Basic Input Output System), 98
Setup options, 226, 229, 234, 237, 240–241, 243
blessing hard disks, 141
BlessTiVo, 41, 141–144, 172–173, 235, 238
adding second drive, 242–244
bpage option, 144
command-line arguments, 142
erase option, 144
id option, 144
Mac OS X, 356–357
part option, 144
reporting drive size incorrectly, 143
status message, 143
summary message, 143, 244
versions, 141
Blindwrite Suite, 328–331
blown modem, 480–481
BMP file format, 7
BNC (Bayonet Neill-Concelman, or Baby N Connector), 108
Boat Anchor Mode, 63

boot disks, 57, 166–167
BATBD (Bill's Accumulated TiVo Boot Disk), 169–173
distributing, 168
Dylan's Boot Floppy, 173
Johnny Death's Boot CD, 173
Kazamyr's Boot CD, 173
Knoppix Linux, 174
partition 9, 271
boot drive, 98
boot page, setting boot parameters from, 163
boot parameters, 219
listing, 147
setting, 147, 272
upgradesoftware-false, 224
boot partition, 81, 144–146
boot sequence for initial RAM disks, 366
bootable CD, 99
bootable disks, 167, 170
bootable DOS floppy image, 170
bootable floppy, 99
bootable FreeDOS floppy, 101
bootable kernel, cloning, 269
booting, 363
boot-loader, 363
BootPage, 144–147, 173
bootpage, 158, 172
bootpage -a *diskname* command, 163
bootpage -b -a *diskname* command, 163
bootpage command, 145–147, 158, 170, 216–217, 219, 249, 256, 258, 267–269, 486–488
bootpage directory, 145, 170
bootparam command, 81
bootrom password, 78–79
Bourne, Stephen, 387
broadcast networks and TiVo, 13
broadcasts, information about upcoming, 13–14

Broken TiVos (Hardware problems & Trouble-shooting) forum, 499
Browse By Name screen, 53
browsing shows, 289
BSD license, 370
buddy notifications and instant messages, 276
"Bullwinkle" mode, 50
burning CDs
Linux, 400–402
Windows, 327–332
business partners and integrators, 12–13
BusyBox, 172, 391–392
busybox command, 371
BusyBox Web site, 392
byte-order, 157–158
Bytesex Web site, 443
byte-swapped boot configuration, 57
byte-swapping, 182–183, 215

# C

cable service
DirecTiVo units, 20
DVRs, 24
stand-alone TiVo, 16
cables, 88–89, 94
CacheCard cards, 214
changing options, 117–118
Daily call option, 119
downloading latest drivers, 120
firmly seating, 125
incremental CacheCard installer, 115
installing software for, 113–120
revision 2.2, 112
RJ-45 Ethernet adapter, 112
CacheCard Drivers/Installation Issues forum, 504
CacheCard Tech Support and Feedback forum, 504
CacheCard/TurboNet/AirNet FAQ forum, 504

Caller ID, 280

Canopus ADVC1394 Video Capture card, 445

"Can't find init" message, 369

Cascading Style Sheets, 290

cat command, 455

Cat5 (Category 5) cabling, 108

CCEE (Clear-Clear-Enter-Enter) codes, 50, 61

cd command, 200, 257, 413, 475

cdrecord application, 168, 400–402

cdrecord -scanbus command, 401

CD-ROM drives and jumpers, 37–38

CD/RW drives, 327

cd/var command, 284

cd/var/settings-backup command, 200

CEC (Clear-Enter-Clear) codes, 50, 62–65

cell phones, programming TiVo over, 15

cfdisk, 156

Change Dial Options menu, 125

change directory command, 251

Channel Down key, 52

channels
  clearing current list, 61
  favorite, 292
  reviewing received, 297
  searching for future shows, 291–297

Channels You Watch screen, 61

Charter Communications, 24

chattr command, 486

checksums, 52

Chen, Christine, 491

Christensen, Ward, 318

chroot command, 366

CHS (Cylinder:Head:Sector) geometry, 92

Cinemax, 13

CinePlayer, 15–16

ciphercheck4.tcl script, 459

Cisco 802.11b cards, 113

classes, 369

Clips directory, 377

Clips On Disk screen, 70

clock, 67

cloning
  bootable kernel, 269
  hard disks, 36, 39–40, 57
  root filesystem, 269
  root partition, 217
  TiVo disks, 39–40

closed caption support, 430

Cntrl Out port, 88

codes, automating, 74–78

COM1 port, 89

Comcast, 24

command files, 250

command interpreter, 386–391

command prompt, 246–247
  job control, 390
  Series 1 TiVos, 248–252
  Series 2 TiVos, 252–259

command scripts, 370

command-line prompt, 315

commands
  bash shell management, 389–391
  checking status, 389
  emulating, 391–392
  running in background, 388–389
  secret, 49–51
  suspending, 389–390
  terminating, 389–390

commercials
  automatically skipping, 13
  skipping, 67
  skipping over, 22

Component directory, 377

comp.os.minix newsgroup, 363

compressed backups, 152, 193–194

configuration
  saving changes, 81
  updating information, 105

configure script, 427

connecting backup and restore commands, 217–218

connectivity directory, 170

connectors, 17

Control-a z key sequence, 383–384

convergence, 2–3

conversion, 434–436

copy command, 251

Copy to DVD or VCR command, 442

copying
  data from one file or device to another, 257
  files, 251

Courtesan Web site, 224

cpio (Copy Input to Output) utility, 180, 418

Craig Leres' TiVo Downloads Web site, 513

crashing hard disks, 181

Create WishList screen, 84

creeping featurism, 3

cross-compilers, 172
  installing, 423–424
  Series 1 TiVos, 424–425
  Series 2 TiVos, 425–426

C-Shell, 387

CSLIP (Compressed SLIP), 107

csoscout.tcl script, 460

custom remote controls, 44

CVS (Concurrent Versioning System), 148

Cygwin, 337

**D**

d70, 247

daemon, 274

daily calls, 124–134

DarkWing's (aka Wanker) DTiVo Links Web site, 513

data verification and hashing, 52

databases
  handles, 380
  hashing algorithm, 52

date, displaying, 70
db command, 380–381
dbobj command, 380–381
dd command, 57, 158, 168, 179, 181, 217, 233–234, 237, 257, 261, 267, 269–270
  backups, 186–188, 190
  bs option, 188, 234, 237
  byte-order conflicts, 204
  conv=noerror,sync options, 234–235, 237–238
  conv=swab option, 205
  "forgiveness" options, 188
  image backups, 333–334
  Mac OS X, 352
  progress indicator, 190
  progress=1 option, 190
  restoring image backups, 203–205
  sync option, 188
DealDatabase forum, 48, 148, 175, 201, 264, 284, 302, 497–500
DealDatabase Web site, 277, 428, 460, 472
debug messages, writing to log file, 71
debugging, 61
decrypting video, 435
default command files, 250
default hostname, 146
default IP address, 146
default MAC address, 146–147
Delay: prompt, 66
Deleted Shows screen, 298–299
Denebian Web site, 383
Denon and Marantz, 22
detached processes, 389
/dev/hdb device drive, 142
/dev/hdc device drive, 142
/dev/hdd device drive, 142
device drivers, 224, 364
devices
  listing partitions, 159
  summary boot sector information, 147

writing bootpage information, 146–147
/dev/ttyS0 serial port, 89, 91
/dev/ttyS1 serial port, 91
/dev/ttyS2 serial port, 91
/dev/ttyS3 serial port, 91
df command, 184, 372, 396
DGM (Disk Image) file, 354
DHCP (Dynamic Host Control Protocol), 110, 127–128, 131
DHCP client ID, 128
DHCP (Dynamic Host Control Protocol) servers, 118, 125, 129, 131
diagnostic features, 50, 61
diagnostic tools, 49
Dial Prefix screen, 125
Dial-in Configuration code, 61
DIB file format, 7
Digeo, 24
digital photographs, 15, 428
Digital Recorders (PVRs) General forum, 497
DIMM (Dual Inline Memory Module), 112, 214
Direct TV systems, 3
DirecTiVos, 8, 16, 20, 75
  AirNet cards, 113
  basic level of programming, 4
  cable service, 20
  connectors, 16–17
  disconnecting fan, 94
  disconnecting phone line, 106
  Guided Setup, 181
  HDTV-enabled, 20
  loadable kernel modules, 171
  maximum hard disk capacity, 93
  networking cards, 111
  phone line, 105
  power supplies, 104
  tivoflash utility, 120
  TOTAL CHOICE package, 4
  tuners, 17
  two-pin connector, 30
  Web sites and information, 512

directories, 375–377
  case sensitivity, 378
  changing, 251, 257
  listing, 250, 375–376
  ROM (Read-Only Memory) filesystem image, 164–165
  synchronizing, 397–398
DIRECTTV Receiver with TiVo forum, 506
DirecTV, 12, 21
  dish receivers and DirecTiVo, 16
  UltimateTV, 23
disabling video encryption, 455–460
Discovery Channel, 13
Dish Network PVRs forum, 497
Dish Networks, 24
Disk Copy, 358
disk images, 168
  expanding drives with, 233–238
  without intermediate backup files, 236–238
Disk Space Usage screen, 55–56
Disk utility, 358
DISKUTIL.EXE utility, 101
DISKUTIL.TXT file, 101
D&M Holdings, 22
DMA (Directory Memory Access), 169
DNS (Domain Name Resolution), 172
DNS (Domain Name Server) Address, 128
DNS servers, 110, 128
dongles, 16
Dorfman, Marjorie, 491
DOS
  partitioning information, 41
  utilities, 170
DOS directory, 170
double quotation marks ("), 83
drive brackets, 40
drive racks, 100
drive recertification, 136, 202
dsscon=true command, 274

dumpobj command, 378–379

DVD-enabled TiVos
    backdoors, 55
    hash strings, 55
    monte, 262–263
    multiroom viewing, 7
    networking, 120–124
    removing screws, 27

DVDs (Digital Video Disks), 440, 442

DVR capture package, 443

DVRchive, 136

DVRchive Discussions forum, 502

DVRs (Digital Video Recorders), 2, 24

Dylan's Boot Floppy, 173

dynamic IP addresses, 110, 127, 129

## E

e2fsck utility, 180

Easter eggs, 49, 67

eBay, 100

ebox capture package, 443

echo "rc.sysinit is complete" command, 119

EchoStar Communications Corporation, 24

ed2k-gtk-gui, 201

eDonkey Web site, 201

EE (Enter-Enter) codes, 50, 65–67

elapsed time display, 67

Emacs, 130, 392–393

embeem hacker, 247, 284

EnableTransactionHoldoff variable, 381

Encore, 13

encryption and hashing, 52

environment variables, 387

"Error - Unable to find complete string" message, 119

error messages, 270

Eskape Labs Web site, 446

/etc directory, 364

/etc/grub.conf file, 401

/etc/inittab file, 260, 369

/etc/lilo.conf file, 401

/etc/minirc.com file, 383

/etc/mtab file, 336

/etc/passwd file, 364

/etc/rc.d directory, 250, 365

/etc/rc.d/init.d/tivoserver file, 405

/etc/rc.d/init.d/xinetd file, 397

/etc/rc.d/rc.arch file, 260, 262, 368

/etc/rc.d/rc.net file, 133–134

/etc/rc.d/rc.sysinit file, 75, 77, 111, 119, 133–134, 260, 262, 274, 286, 315, 334, 369, 390, 398, 486

/etc/rsyncd.conf file, 397–398

/etc/tmp/installed.packages file, 421

/etc/xinetd.d/rsh file, 397

ethereal, 126, 130

Ethernet, 107

Ethernet cables, 108

exit command, 315, 371

exit (Ctrl-D) keyboard shortcut, 315

expanding drives with disk images, 233–238

expired recordings, 50

expired showcases, 50

explore2fs, 333–334

export command, 387

exportfs command, 396

exporting
    audio files, 303–304
    collections of MP3 files and playlists from, 7

ext2 (Extended Filesystem 2), 97, 180, 314, 365
    disk images and Windows, 333–334
    images, 261
    Mac OS X, 346–347, 351–353

ext2 partitions, 157, 184, 205–206, 265
    checking, 273
    mounting, 254

ext2fs, 157

Ext2FS_1.1.1.pkg file, 347

EXT3, 97

ext3 partition, 254, 265

extended partitions, 372

external modems, 481–484

ExtFS Manager, 347, 349–351

extract_gzip program, 261

extract_gzip.c file, 365

extracting files from TAR and TGZ archives, 417–420

Extracting TiVo Video to a VCD or DVD on Mac OS X Web site, 514

Extracting Video from a TiVo Series 1 Using Mac OS X Web site, 514

extraction, 434–436

Extraction, Insertion, & Streaming Support forum, 499

EyeTV, 445–446

## F

factory password, 78, 80

fakecall31-1.0-5.tivo.tpm package, 106

fakecall31.tcl script, 106

fakecall40-1.0.5.tivo.tpm package, 106

fakecall40.tcl script, 106

falcontx hacker, 284

Famous directory, 377

FAQs (Frequently Asked Questions), 140, 509–512

fast-forward speeds, 65–66

FAT filesystem, 185

FAT Telnet, 89

FAT-32 (32-bit File Allocation Table), 97

FAT32 filesystem, 184–185

FAT-32 partition, 254
favorite channels, 292
fdisk command, 156, 183, 372–373
fg%1 command, 390
file command, 415, 437–438
File-> Save command, 317
file system consistency check, 211
files, 375
 copying, 251
 extracting from TAR and TGZ archives, 417–420
 larger than 4GB, 185
 minicom transfer, 385–386
 modifying, 165
 MP3 format, 7
 restoring from backup, 149
 saving current kernel image to, 163
 sending from TiVo to PCs, 320
 serial connection transfer, 318–320
 size limitations, 185–186
 synchronizing, 397–398
 transferring, 400
FILES—All TiVo and DTiVo Files forum, 499
filesystem images, 257
filesystems
 adding disks and partitions, 183–184
 backups, 180
 determining active, 249
 hard disk usage for mounted, 372
 hierarchical, 365
 Linux, 364–366
 listing, 183
 mounting, 204, 364
 mounting images, 189
 NTFS (NT File System) format, 185
 root, 364
 unmounting, 204
 verifying with hash codes, 260
 virtual, 189

Final Cut Pro, 445
finding backups, 200–202
firewall, 276
flash memory, 368
flat IR emitter, 47
Flix, 13
floppy directory, 170
floppy disk images, 168
Formac Studio TVR, 446
formatting disk drives, 35
Forsenberg, Chuck, 318
fort, 47
FreeBSD, 201
FreeDOS, 101
FreeDos Web site, 101
FreeVo capture package, 443
fsck (filesystem consistency check) command, 189, 273, 349
fsck_ext2, 349
fsid (filesystem ID), 375, 379
FSN (Full Service Network), 10–11
FTP (File Transfer Protocol), 127, 393–394
 commands, 327
 starting, 274–275
 Windows, 325–327
FTP daemon, 120
ftp> prompt, 325
full backups, 182
full structured backups, 185
full TiVo service, 105–106
future trends, 24

**G**

GAIM (GTK AOL Instant Messenger), 276–277, 279
gaim2tivo plug-in, 278–279
gaim2tivo-0.2.zip archive file, 277–278
Gateway (Router) Address, 128
gateways, 109–110, 128

GCC (GNU C Compiler), 362, 395
Gemstar-TV Guide, 24
GenAddDiskTiVoID program, 144
gender bender, 88–89
gender changer, 78
general features, 21
General TiVo Development forum, 499
General TurboNet/CacheCard Discussions forum, 502
Genre directory, 377
genromfs command, 164–165, 171
get command, 475
GG (Gadu-Gadu), 276
GIF file format, 7
gigabit Ethernet, 108
GNOME, 412
GNU Emacs, 393
GNU project, 362
GNU Web site, 363
Goldfish Web site, 443
gold-star TiVo advertising, 14
Gosling, James, 393
GPL (GNU General Public License), 363
Graessley, Josh, 347, 354
grep command, 379
Griffin Technology Web site, 446
GRUB bootloader, 188, 401
guide data, updating, 124–134
Guided Setup, 105, 181
GuideIndexV2 directory, 377
gunzip utility, 415–416
gz files, uncompressing, 415–417
gzip (GNU zip) command, 261, 365, 415–416, 419

**H**

hack_dir directory, 274, 397
hack_dirs directory, 170, 417

**hack_dirs/kernel_modules directory, 395**
**"Hacking the TiVo FAQ," 140**
**Hacking the TiVo FAQ Web site, 510**
**hackinit script, 258**
**halt command, 422**
**hard disks, 92**
  160 GB, 93
  accessing
    with non-IDE device names, 230–231
    Windows, 335–336
  adding, 101–103, 150–152
    to filesystem, 183–184
    larger, 38–40
    partitions, 241–242
    second, 40–41, 238–244
    space to, 235–236
  allocation units, 151
  attaching to PC, 97–99
  automatically detecting, 98
  backing up, 57, 99, 149, 152–154, 227, 265–266
  blessing, 141
  cables, 94
  capacity by model and software version, 223–225
  changing block size, 213–214
  changing byte order, 215
  CHS (Cylinder:Head:Sector) geometry, 92
  cloning, 36, 39–40, 57, 217
  conflicts, 37, 98
  copying operating system and data from, 35
  crashing, 181
  data storage on, 97
  delays between spinning up, 104
  from different manufacturers, 104
  easily preparing second hard disk, 141–144
  editing partitions, 59–60
  efficiency of storage, 151
  erasing partition information, 144

expanding
    with disk images, 233–238
    MFS volumes, 150–152
  EXT2, 97
  EXT3, 97
  formatting, 35
  hda4 partition, 348
  hda7 partition, 348
  hda9 partition, 348
  IDE (Integrated Drive Electronics), 30, 94, 97
  identifier, 142
  identifying default root partition, 216
  image backups, 181, 186–188, 190
  increasing
    size of /var partition, 212
    swap space, 211–212
  information about, 371–372
  initializing, 240, 242
  jumper settings, 38, 99
  jumpers, 37, 57, 97–98, 102
  LBA (Logical Block Addressing), 92, 143
  LBA 48 (48-bit logical block addressing), 92
  Mac OS X, 346–377
  Macintosh partition format, 371–372
  Macintosh-formatted, 373–374
  manually creating, 242
  manually detecting, 98
  married, 40, 143, 254, 265
  master drive, 31, 37, 97, 142
  maximum partitions, 374
  MFS (Media File System) partitions, 374
  modifying, 165
  mounted with byte-swapping enabled, 163
  mounting bracket, 31–33, 225
  NTFS (NT File System), 97
  optimizing partition layout, 213
  overwriting, 255

partition creation, 144
  partition map, 57–58, 372–374
  partition table, 216
  partitioning, 156–164, 372
  power connector, 94
  prices, 92
  putting in PCs, 35–38
  RAM required to track usage, 151
  reading and writing boot information, 144–147
  removing, 29–35, 93–96
  replacing with larger, 226–229
  reporting size of, 143
  restoring backup to larger, 185
  restoring or expanding backup to, 141
  room for backups, 182–184
  seek time, 213
  seeking, 213
  sizes, 92–93
  slave drive, 31, 37, 97, 102, 142
  specifying names of, 149–150
  swap space, 208, 210
  testing, 40
  tools for adding, 101–102
  unlocking, 40, 100–101
  unstructured backup, 188
  upgrading, 222–223, 225
    without backup files, 229–233
  usage, 55–56, 372
  valid partitions, 142
  verifying restored, 216
  verifying usage, 143
  video extraction directly from, 449–455
  virginal image, 181
  Windows, 333–336
  writing valid bootpage to, 144
**hardware, 3**
  diagnostic log file, 9
  manufacturers, 13
  models and features, 16–19
  Web sites, 508–509
**hardware supplies, 134–138**

Harmony H688 Universal Remote, 45
Harris, Jensen, 280
hash codes, 174, 260
hash command, 284, 474
hash keys, 51
hash values, 51
hashing, 52–53, 213
Hauppage Web site, 447
Hauppage WinTV, 447
Hayes Modem Web sites, 483
HBO, 13
hda4 partition, 348
hda7 partition, 348
hda9 partition, 348
hdid command, 352–353
HDRs (Hard Disk Recorders), 2
HDTV Hardware forum, 497
HDTV TiVo Powered PVRs forum, 506
HDTV-enabled DirecTiVos, 20
HDTV-enabled disks, 191
Headend directory, 377
heat considerations, 104–105
Helgeson, Joel, 225
Helvetica Italic font, 71
Helvetica screen font, 71
Hendriks, Erik, 247
hermanator, 277
hexadecimal editor, 57
hexedit (hexadecimal editor) command, 57, 59–60, 165, 172, 174
hexedit home page, 165
hidden recordings, 69–70
hidden screens, 50
hierarchical filesystems, 365
HiFi Remote Web site, 45
high-performance video workstations, 10
Hilgraeve Web site, 315
Hill, Mike, 141
Hinsdale FAQs Web site, 510–511
Hinsdale Web site, 135–136

HISTORY file, 171
HMO (Home Media Option), 5, 6–7
Home Media, 248, 342
displaying photographs, 303–304
features, 15, 302–311
information about features, 56
integrating Windows with, 337–345
Linux, 402–409
Mac OS X, 359–360
multiroom TiVo viewing, 309–311
playing music, 303–304
scheduling recordings over Internet, 304–307
stand-alone Series 2 TiVos, 302–311
USB (Universal Serial Bus) network adapter, 302
/home/tivodev directory, 425
/home/wvh/tivo_rsync directory, 398
host IP addresses, 109
http_get command, 75–76, 400
hubs, 108–109
Hughes, 13
Hughes HDVR2 systems, 19
Humax T800 and T2500 models, 19
Humax USA Web site, 19
HyperTerminal, 78, 88–89, 251, 259, 273, 315–317, 319–323

**I**

IBM PowerPC 403GCX processor, 16
IDE cables, 37, 97, 103
IDE drives, 97
identifying manufacturer, 17
idetivo_bwap_data() function, 158
ideturbo (high-speed IDE) module, 158

IEDs (Intelligent Entertainment Devices), 2
ifconfig command, 125–126, 130
$IFS environment variable, 258, 272
image backups, 181
creation of, 186–188, 190
dd command, 333–334
file size limitations, 185
restoring, 203–205
of specific partitions, 187
image files, 189
image of bootable FreeDOS floppy, 101
images, mounting partition, 189
img directory, 171
IMG extension, 168
img_monte directory, 171
iMic, 446
iMovie, 445
incremental backups, 181, 198
information about upcoming broadcasts, 13–14
init/do_mounts_initrd.c file, 366
initial RAM disks, 169, 364–366
initialization commands, 250
initrd (initial RAM disk), 116, 260–261, 365, 487
initrds directory, 171
insertion, 434–436
Inside DirecTiVo Web site, 508
Inside Series 1 TiVo Web site, 508
Inside Series 2 TiVo Web site, 508
insmod command, 395
installing
cross-compilers, 423–424
hacks from BATBD CD, 421–422
software, 414–423
software packaged with TPM (TiVo Package Manager), 420–412
instant messages, 275–279
InstantCake Tech Support and Discussions forum, 502

int.disabled prompt, 66
int.enabled prompt, 66
Inter: prompt, 66
Intercil Prism2 or Prism2.5
chipset, 113
internal values, setting, 65–67
International Standards
Organization 9660
filesystem standard, 327
Internet, 11, 107
broadband connection, 302
early connectivity, 107–108
enabling access, 301
hardware supplies, 134–138
RFCs (Request for
Comments), 109
scheduling recordings, 6,
304–307
TiVo-related information on,
140
interstitials, 66
IP addresses, 109, 399
assigning, 110, 128
DNS (Distributed Name
Service) servers, 110
gateways, 128
information about, 324
managing for networked TiVos,
133–134
manually assigning, 118–119,
133–134
TiVos, 131–133
iptables, 276
IR (infrared) amplifier, 48
IR Blaster, 46–47
IR receiver, 47
IRC, 276
ISA bus slot, 111
ISO extension, 168
ISO images, 327, 400–402
isolinux directory, 171
iTCL (incrTCL), 369–370
.itcl file extension, 370
iTunes, 168, 409
ivtv_record plug-in, 443

**J**

J2SDK (Java 2 Software
Development Kit), 407
J2SE (Java 2, Standard
Edition), 407
Jabber, 276
JAI (Java Advanced Imaging)
package, 407
Java Home Media Option, 303,
342, 404–409, 429–430
Java package, 407
job control, 388, 390
jobs command, 389
Johnny Death's Boot CD, 173
jpegwriter, 282
JPG file format, 7
JTAG Support for Series 1
TiVos Web site, 509
jumpers, 37

**K**

Kazamyr's Boot CD, 173
KDE, 412
KDE desktop software suite, 174
Kelly, Walt, 500
kermit, 385
kernel_modules directory, 171
kernels, 223–224, 363–364
byte-swapping, 182–183
Configuration menu, 188
configured for initial RAM
disk, 365
extracting, 267–268
LBA48-aware, 224
monte.o module, 262
source, 158
writing to partition, 271
kill%1 command, 390
killinitrd command, 487
killinitrd directory, 171
kmem patches, 456–458
Knoppix Linux, 165, 174
Knoppix Linux Web site, 174

Koerner, Brendan, 491
Korn Shell, 387

**L**

Lang, Steven, 147
LBA (Logical Block
Addressing), 143
LBA28 disk addressing, 218,
228, 231, 255–256, 267–268
LBA48 disk addressing, 92, 224
LBA48 kernels, 171
LBA48-aware kernels, 224, 255
lba48_s1_kernels directory, 171
Lempel-Zev compression
scheme, 193
Levin, Gerald, 10
LGPL (Lesser GNU Public
License), 363
lifetime service, 138
lifetime subscription, 5
lightn hacker, 284
LILO bootloader, 188, 401
Linux, 3, 21, 167, 189, 361–362
actively modifying data in
partitions, 57
agetty command, 385
BlessTiVo, 242
boot process, 363–364
boot sequence for initial RAM
disks, 366
booting PC into miniature
version of, 98
boot-loader, 363
burning CDs, 400–402
busybox command, 371
cd command, 413
change directory command, 251
copy command, 251
cross-compilers, 172
cross-compiling software, 427
dd command, 234
detached processes, 389
device drivers, 224, 364
directories, 364

DVR capture package, 443
ebox capture package, 443
ed2k-gtk-gui, 201
/etc directory, 364
/etc/rc.d directory, 365
ethereal, 126
EXT2, 97
EXT3, 97
extra space for emergencies, 56
fdisk command, 183, 372–373
file command, 415
file size limitations, 185–186
files, 364
filesystems, 364–366
FreeVo capture package, 443
GAIM (GTK AOL Instant
    Messenger), 276–277
GNOME, 412
grep command, 379
history of, 362–363
Home Media, 402–409
identifying video files, 437–438
initial RAM disks, 364–366
installing gaim2tivo plug-in, 278
iptables, 276
JAI (Java Advanced Imaging)
    package, 407
Java Home Media Option,
    404–409
Java package, 407
KDE, 412
kernel, 92, 143, 185, 223–224,
    363–364
LBA48 (48-bit Logical Block
    Addressing) support, 224
linux-utils package, 166
listing log files, 288–289
ls command, 192, 388–389
mgetty command, 385
mingetty command, 385
minicom, 251, 273, 382–386
MIPS platform, 367
mkdir (make directory)
    command, 413

mkisofs command, 400–402
monte program, 247
mount command, 183–184, 412
mounting
    filesystem, 216
    SMB filesystems, 335
    TiVo Series 1 or Series 2 disks
        without BATBD disk, 188
mountpoints, 212, 413
MythTV capture package, 444
network packet-sniffing utility,
    126, 130–131
obtaining source code, 367
older kernel versions, 185
open source movement, 167
open source software, 7
partitioning information, 41
pdisk (Partition Disk) utility,
    156–164
Personal TiVo Home Media
    Option, 339, 403–404
pipe (|), 184, 217–218
programming languages, 369
RAR archiver, 202
redirection commands, 388
running commands in
    background, 388–389
serial communications,
    382–386
sharing MP3 files with Samba,
    339
startup file, 405
stty sane command, 247
su (subsitute user-id)
    command, 413
sudo command, 413
swap space, 211
sync command, 255, 266
tail command, 251
tar format, 170
tcpdump, 126
TV tuner cards, 443–444
tvtime capture package, 444
TyStudio, 468

xawtv capture package, 444
"Yet Another..." programs, 280
zlib library, 193
**Linux command interpreter, 89**
**Linux shells, 386–391**
**Linux software**
    BusyBox, 391–392
    Emacs, 392–393
    FTP (File Transfer Protocol),
        393–394
    GCC (GNU C Compiler), 395
    NFS (Network File System),
        395–397
    rsync (remote sync), 397–398
    telnet, 398–399
    Wget (Web get), 400
**Linux tools, 164**
    genromfs command, 164–165
    hexedit (hexadecimal editor)
        command, 165
    script command, 166
**Linux XFree86 X Window
    System implementation, 174**
**Linux/PPC for PowerPC 4xx
    Web site, 509**
**/linuxrc file, 366, 368**
**linux-utils package, 166**
**listener, 280**
**little-endian processors,
    157–158**
**LMOP (Large Matter of
    Programming), 281**
**loadable kernel modules, 171, 364**
**log files, displaying, 64**
**log files, listing, 288–289**
**logical partitions, 372**
**logs, 61**
**loopback address, 75**
**ls command, 192, 250, 388–389**

**M**

**M3U format, 7**
**Mac OS 9 and BlessTiVo,
    141–142**

**Mac OS X, 345**

Alchemy TV, 445

/Applications folder, 354

BlessTiVo, 141–142, 242, 356–357

Canopus ADVC1394 Video Capture card, 445

checking partition consistency, 349

dd command, 352

Disk Copy, 358

Disk Utility, 358

ed2k-gtk-gui, 201

ext2 filesystem, 346–347, 351–353

ExtFS Manager, 347

EyeTV, 445–446

Formac Studio TVR, 446

fsck_ext2, 349

hard disks, 346–357

hdid command, 352–353

Home Media, 359–360

identifying video files, 437–438

iMovie, 445

iTunes, 409

JAI (Java Advanced Imaging) package, 407

Java Home Media Option, 406

mounting and exploring ext2 partitions, 349–351

mounting and exploring MFS partitions, 354–355

mounting and unmounting ext2 partitions, 350

MyTV and MyTV2GO, 446

QuickTime, 445

RAR archiver, 202

Series 1 and Series 2 hard disks, 347–348

terminal application, 352

TiVo Desktop, 359–360

TiVo Hacking for PPC project, 346

TiVo tools disks, 357–358

TiVoPartitionScheme, 347–348

TV tuner cards, 445–446

TyStudio, 467–468

viewing partition information, 350

**Macintosh**

bootable ISO, 175

communicating with TiVo, 89

exporting audio files, 303–304

exporting collections, 7

instructions and data stored and used, 157

partition map, 157

pdisk (Partition Disk) utility, 156–164

shutting down system, 143

TiVo-related utilities, 171

**Macintosh DGM (Disk Image) file, 354**

**macintosh directory, 171**

**Macintosh formatted disks, 373–374**

**Macintosh Partition Support, 188**

**macintosh/osx-mips-xcomp.tgz cross-compiler, 423, 426**

**macintosh/usr.local.powerpc-TiVo.dmg cross-compiler, 423**

**MacTiVo forums, 500–501**

**Main Street, 11**

**Make Test Call command, 67**

**Makefile, 427**

**man directory, 171**

**manually assigning IP address to network card, 118–119**

**manufacturers, 17–18**

**married disk drives, 40**

**married hard disks, 143**

**master disks, 31, 37, 97, 142, 182**

boot and alternate boot partition information, 144–145

reading and writing TiVo boot information, 144–147

**Media Center, 303, 342–345, 406**

**Media Composer, 10**

**Media Jukebox, 15**

**mencoder plug-in, 443**

**Menu Item backdoor screen, 70**

**MenuItem directory, 377**

**MessageItem directory, 377**

**Messages & Setup, Recorder & Phone Setup, Cable/ Satellite Box, Cable Box Setup menu, 48**

**Messages & Setup, Settings, Phone & Network Setup path, 127**

**Messages & Setup screen, 20**

**.meta file extension, 420**

**Metcalf, Bob, 107**

**methods, 369**

**MFS (Multimedia File System), 147, 180, 185, 190, 197, 365, 374–382**

automatically allocating free space, 154

displaying number of values in, 289

recording quality values, 289

unformatted partition, 157

video file formats, 436–437

**MFS Application Region, 374**

**MFS Browser, 347, 354–355**

**MFS disks, information about, 149**

**MFS files, 298–299**

**MFS Media Region, 374**

**MFS partitions, 206, 242, 374**

allocation unit size, 155

layout, 213

MFS Application Region, 374

MFS Media Region, 374

mounting and exploring, 354–355

pairs of, 374

specifying device names of, 152

**MFS Tools, 141–142, 147–156, 171, 173, 179–180, 233, 235, 238**

adding entire drive, 239–241

adding second drive, 239–242

adding specific partitions, 241–242

advanced restore options, 211–215

backups, 190–198
  entire disk, 194–195
  HDTV and DVD-enabled TiVos, 153, 227
  binary version, 149
  complete backups, 182
  compressed backups, 193–194
  conserving space, 190
  DVD-enabled TiVos, 191
  filesystems formats, 180
  fixing and enhancing, 148
  HDTV-enabled TiVos, 191
  higher FSID value, 232
  incremental backups, 181
  mfstool utility, 148
  overwriting hard disks, 255
  restoring backups, 205–216
  -s (swap-size) option, 163
  simple backup, 191–193
  static and dynamic versions, 173
  structured backups, 190
  verifying disks restored, 216
  Version 2, 156, 190
  versions, 150, 158

**MFS utilities, 172**

**MFS volumes**
  dumping raw data from, 149
  expanding, 150–152
  information about, 154
  using all available space, 151–152

**mfs_browser_3.dmg file, 354**

**MFS_DEVICE environment variable, 149, 230–231**

**MFS_DEVLIST environment variable, 149, 450, 452**

**mfs_dumpobj command, 453–455**

**mfs_export command, 455, 460**

**mfs_ftp, 448, 458**
  TiVoWebPlus, 476
  video extraction, 471–475

**mfs_ftp directory, 171**

**mfs_ftp download site, 171**

**mfs_ftp.tar.zip archive, 472**

**MFS_HDA environment variable, 150, 230–231**

**MFS_HDB environment variable, 150, 230–231**

**mfs_info command, 451**

**mfs_ls command, 453**

**mfs_stream utility, 459, 476**

**mfs_tarstream binary, 476**

**mfstool add command, 144, 150–152, 235, 238–241**

**mfstool backup command, 39–40, 152–154, 179–180, 184–185, 190, 216, 229, 254–255, 265**
  -a option, 227, 232
  -a (all) option, 195
  actual size of backup file, 192
  advanced backup options, 196–198
  backing up entire TiVo disk, 194–195
  backup file, 192
  command-line options, 152–154
  compressed backups, 193–194
  connecting with mfstool restore command, 217–218
  copy of partition map for both TiVo drives, 196
  -f 9999 option, 232
  -f fsid option, 197
  -f option, 198, 227
  -l size option, 197–198
  multiple-disk TiVo systems, 195–196
  -o option, 192
  output displayed by, 191
  progress of, 191
  restoring backup file created by, 192–193
  -s (shrink) command-line option, 196
  selected information backups, 198–200

simple backup, 191–193
  -T size option, 198
  -t size option, 198
  -v option, 197

**mfstool command, 57, 148–150**

**mfstool info command, 154**

**mfstool restore command, 153–156, 183–185, 192, 196, 228, 232, 266**
  - option, 206
  - x (expand) option, 207
  -B option, 215
  -b option, 215
  -C option, 206, 209, 218, 228, 231, 255–256, 267–268
  command-line options, 154–156
  connecting with mfstool backup command, 217–218
  -i option, 209
  -p option, 213
  progress of, 207–208, 210
  -r value option, 214
  -s size option, 209, 211–212
  -v size option, 212
  -x (expand) option, 209

**mfstools directory, 148**

**mfstools.1 directory, 173**

**mfstools_15jun04.tgz archive, 148**

**mfstools_orig.tgz archive, 149**

**mfstools_rt.tgz archive, 149**

**mgetty command, 385**

**Microsoft Ultimate TV PVR forum, 497**

**Microsoft Web site, 460**

**Miglia Web site, 445**

**Miller, Todd, 171, 172, 224, 255**

**mingetty command, 385**

**minicom, 78, 88–89, 251, 273, 382–386**

**MINIX, 362**

**MIPS platform, 367**

**MIPS processors, 158**

**mkdir (make directory) command, 413**

**mkisofs command, 400–402**

**mkswap command, 157, 211**
**mls command, 375–376**
**/mnt directory, 249–250**
**/mnt/cdrom/img directory, 257**
**/mnt/tivo directory, 422**
**/mnt/tivo/etc/rc.d/rc.sysinit file, 272**
**/mnt/tivo/etc/rc.d/ rc.sysinit.old file, 272**
**mobile racks, 100**
**models**
  features, 16–19
  selecting, 20
**modems, 105–106**
  external, 481–484
  slow speed of, 107
  troubleshooting, 480–481
**modes, secret, 49–51**
**monte, 93, 171, 247, 487–488**
  boot process, 262
  DVD TiVos, 262–263
  large disks, 262–263
  overview, 261–262
  running, 272
  usage, 263–274
**monte command, 270**
**monte-mips directory, 171**
**monte.o module, 262**
**MoodLogic Web site, 15**
**Motorola 68000 chips, 157**
**mount command, 183–184, 265, 412**
**MountEverything, 334**
**mounting**
  BATBD CD, 256, 270, 412–413
  ext2 partition, 254
  ext3 partition, 254
  FAT-32 partition, 254
  filesystem images, 189
  filesystems, 364
  Linux filesystem, 216
  partition image as file, 189
  partition images, 189
  partitions, 249, 251, 254

**ROM filesystem, 272**
**root filesystem, 366**
**/var directory, 271**
**mounting bracket, 94, 225**
**mountpoints, 183, 212, 413**
**MP3 files, 7, 15**
  Java Home Media Option, 406, 429–430
  playing, 303–304
  sharing from Linux with Samba, 339
**MPEG (Motion Picture Experts Group) files, 439**
**MPEG Web site, 439**
**MPEG-2 format**
  TyStudio, 469–471
  TyTool, 462–466
**mplayer application, 171, 443, 448**
  playing TY files, 476–478
**mplayer directory, 171**
**mrblack51 hacker, 284**
**MSN, 276**
**multiple-disk TiVo systems, 195–196**
**multiroom viewing, 6–7, 309–311**
**MuscleNerd, 247**
**Music & Photos menu, 303**
**music, playing, 303–304**
**Musicex Web site, 342**
**MusicExchange.com Web site, 15**
**mwstate Insert file, 63–64**
**MyDVD, 15–16**
**MySQL, 492**
**MythTV capture package, 24, 444**
**MyTV and MyTV2GO, 446**
**myworld application, 63–65, 371**

**N**

**NanoEmacs, 393**
**Napster, 276**
**NAT (Native Address Translation), 110, 128**
**NBC, 13**

**NDS Web site, 21**
**NEC MIPS processor, 16**
**Nero - Burning ROM package, 328**
**NetReady Discussions forum, 502**
**network adapter, 125**
**network cards**
  DirecTiVos, 111
  Series 1 TiVos, 248
  stand-alone Series 1, 111
**network communications**
  HyperTerminal, 321–323
  Windows, 321–327
**network connections, 108, 315**
**network packet-sniffing utility, 126, 130–131**
**network-enabled Series 2 TiVo, 15**
**networking**
  basics, 107–111
  DVD TiVos, 120–124
  Ethernet, 107
  Series 1 TiVos, 111–120
  Series 2 TiVos, 120–124
  TCP/IP (Transmission Control Protocol/Internet Protocol), 107
  UDP (Universal Data Packet), 107
**networking TiVo, 106–107**
**network-related configuration commands, 250**
**networks, 108**
  connectivity between, 109
  correct configuration, 130
  DHCP servers, 125
  enabling Internet access, 301
  making daily calls from, 124–134
  programming TiVo over, 283–301
  Series 1 TiVos daily calls, 125–126
  Series 2 TiVos daily calls, 127–131
  speed of, 108
  Subnet Mask, 128

verifying connectivity, 125
video extraction, 449
**Newbie TiVo forum, 499**
**Newman, Heather, 491**
**news, 281–283**
**NewTek, 10**
**newtext2osd, 282**
**NFS (Network File System), 337, 395–397**
**NFS FAQ Web site, 397**
**nic_install script, 111, 133, 248, 274**
**nic_install scruot, 113–120**
**Nickolas, Steve, 101**
**"No device specified" error message, 41, 142, 243**
**Node Navigator, 62**
**non-DirecTiVo systems, 120**
**non-DVD Series 2 TiVos, 93**
**non-IDE device names, 230–231**
**nonroutable IP addresses, 109**
**noscramble modules, 456–457**
**Now Playing - TV Talk Show forum, 506**
**Now Playing list, 309, 311**
displaying hidden recordings, 69
sorting, 72–73
**Now Playing menu, 229**
**Now Playing Options screen, 72**
**Now Playing screen, 70, 72, 74, 207, 441**
**Now Showing screen, 289, 292**
**NTFS (NT File System), 97, 185**
**null modems, 90**
**null-modem adapter, 78**
**null-modem connectors, 88–89**

**O**

**objects, 369, 375**
**ODIN Web site, 101**
**Offset: prompt, 67**
**OffTopic forum, 494**

**OGG audio format, 342**
**old_mfstool2.0 directory, 171**
**OmniRemotePro, 48–49**
**online forums, 492–507**
**online reference pages, 171**
**Open: prompt, 66**
**open IP-Address command, 325**
**Open Software Foundation GNU project, 362**
**open source movement, 167**
**open source software, 7, 362–363**
**open source TiVo, 5**
**open source Web site, 370**
**opening TiVos, 26–29, 91–92**
**operating systems, 167**
backups of specific, 249
changing with backups, 219
release 3.1, 253
Series 2 DirectTiVos, 302
Version 4.0, 264
Version 4.x+, 276
**OSX4Blesser, 356–357**
**Ouija screen, 50, 53, 65, 129**
**Overnet Web site, 201**
**overshoot correction, 62, 66–67**
**OzTiVo Web site, 511**

**P**

**p command, 81**
**P2P (Peer-to-Peer filesharing), 201–202**
**PACELink Web site, 137**
**Pacific Neotek Web site, 48**
**Package directory, 377**
**packaging system-level software, 166–167**
**packets, 109**
**PalmOS 3.0, 48**
**partition 9, 271**
**partition map, 57–58, 157, 372–374**
displaying, 241–242
**partition table, 163**

**partitioning hard disks, 156–164**
**partitions, 142**
adding, 149, 183–184, 241–242
allocation unit size, 151
creation of, 144
displaying, 256, 267, 269
editing, 57, 59–60
ext2, 157
image backups, 186–188, 190
maximum number, 374
modifying, 165
mounting, 189, 249, 251, 254
optimizing layout, 213
organization of, 184
rearranging, 262
scrolling lists, 58
TiVo ID string, 144
unable to mount, 205
unstructured backup, 188
**passive command, 474**
**patching kernel memory, 456–457**
**PATH environment variable, 387, 424**
**PCMCIA 802.11b cards, 113**
**PCMCIA adapter, 113**
**PCMCIA cards, 113**
**PCs**
attaching disk drives to, 97–99
BIOS (Basic Input Output System), 36, 98
BIOS Setup options, 226, 229, 234, 237, 240–241, 243
boot drive, 98
drive racks, 100
IDE cables, 97
non-IDE device names, 230–231
primary (IDE-1) interface, 97
putting disk drive in, 35–38
restoring and expanding backups, 141
secondary (IDE-2) interface, 97
serial ports, 88
shutting down system, 143
terminal emulators, 78

PC-style ISA networking cards, 111

PDA as remote control, 48–49

pdisk command, 144, 154, 157–159, 173, 183, 189, 206, 211–212, 216, 242, 256, 267, 269, 373–374

pdisk (Partition Disk) utility, 57–58, 156–164

pdisk-l/dev/hdX command, 216, 241

PDRs (Personal Digital Recorders), 2

Pentium-class desktop system, 172

Perens, Bruce, 392

perl command, 404

Person directory, 377

personal desktop viewing systems, 10

Personal Television Service, 12

Personal TiVo Home Media Option, 339, 342, 403–404, 429

Philips Consumer Electronics, 12, 13

Philips DSR6000 DirecTiVo model, 19

Philips HDR312 TiVo model, 19

Philips HDR612 TiVo model, 19

Phillips screwdriver, 91

phoenix.txt file, 475

Phone & Network Settings, Wireless Settings, Connect path, 129

Phone & Network Setup menu, 128

Phone & Network Setup screen, 127–129

phone jacks, 106

photographs, displaying, 303–304

PHP (Personal Hypertext Preprocessor), 492

Picasa Digital Picture Organizer, 15

Picasa Web site, 15

Pick Programs To Record menu, 53, 82

Pick Programs To Record screens, 50, 55–56

Pinnacle Studio, 447

Pioneer 57-H Series 2 TiVos, 14, 45, 88, 93, 246

Pioneer 57H software, 39

Pioneer 810, 268
    backup image of Pioneer 57H software, 39
    DVD burner, 263

Pioneer 810-H Series 2 TiVos, 14, 93
    current software release, 246
    release 5.2, 88
    remote controls, 45

Pioneer Series 2 TiVos, 33
    DVD burners, 96
    DVD players, 96
    removing disk drives, 96–97

Pioneer TiVos, 5–6, 91, 266

pipe (|), 217–218

PIP/Window button, 45

pivot_root command, 366

Play bar, 68

playing music, 303–304

playlists, 7

PLS format, 7

PNG file format, 7

Pogue, David, 491–492

port forwarding, 301

Portable Open TiVo Home Media Option, 303

Powell, Michael, 488

power supplies, 26, 93, 103–104

PowerTrip device, 104, 137

PPC (PowerPC) chips, 157

PPC processors, 158

PPP (Point-To-Point Protocol), 107

PPV (Pay-Per-View) movies, 105

Preference directory, 377

Price Watch Web site, 100

Primary Master hard drives, 98

primary objects, 379

primary partition, 163

Primary Slave hard drives, 98

Prism2 chipset, 113

Prism2 PCMCIA cards, 114

privacy concerns, 9–10

programming
    over cell phones, 15
    TiVo over network, 283–301
    updating, 124–134

programming guide, 291–297

programs
    information about episodes, 293
    operating-system specific, 168
    scheduling, 81–82
    viewing name of, 289

Programs, Accessories, Communications menu, 315, 321

PROM (Programmable Read-Only Memory), 81, 368

ProNFS, 337

ps command, 282

PTCMs (Pre-TiVo-Central Messages), 9, 51

PTVs (Personal Television Receivers), 2

PTVupgrade forums, 501–502

PTVupgrade.com Web site, 48, 104, 136, 174, 202, 460–461

publishing, 337

put command, 284, 475

PuTTY Web site, 324

PVR Compare Web site, 21

PVR Comparisons Web site, 509

pvrhax0r forums, 502

PVRs (Personal Video Recorders), 2, 24

PVRUpgrade.com Web site, 225

## Q

quality assurance and system test personnel, 50

queryschema.tcl file, 379–380

QuickTime, 445
QUNCLOCK.EXE utility, 101

# R

RAM (Random-Access Memory) disks, 116, 169–170, 271, 365
Ramsay, Mike, 11
randomly generating key presses, 50
RAR compression utility, 202
RARsoft Web site, 202
Rate1: prompt, 66
Rate2: prompt, 66
RAWRITE.EXE utility, 170
Raymond, Eric, 362
rc.arch file, 250
rc.net file, 250
rc.sysinit file, 75–76, 250–251, 275
rc.sysinit.save file, 250–251
rebooting TiVo, 63
receiving programming and guide data updates, 124–134
Record by Time or Channel menu, 82
Recording directory, 377
recording programs
  Advanced WishLists, 83–85
  based on a keyword, or specific actor or director names, 83
  canceling, 297
  confirming, 296
  conflicts, 295
  conversion, 434–436
  expired, 50
  extraction, 434–436
  insertion, 434–436
  MFS files, 298–299
  saving to DVD, 442
  saving to media, 440–447
  saving to videotape, 441–442
  scheduling over Internet, 304–307
  searching for future, 289

on specific channel for specific period of time, 82
summary information about, 296
undeleting, 298–299
WishLists, 83
redirection commands, 388
remote controls, 44–46, 48
  graphical image of, 289
  modes and codes, 50
  PDAs as, 48–49
  Pioneer 57-H, 45
  Pioneer 810-H, 45
  PIP/Window button, 45
  resolving problems, 46–48
  Series 1 TiVo, 44–45
  Series 2 TiVo, 44–45
  Sony, 44
  universal, 45
remote scheduling, 304–307
remote systems, accessing, 398–399
removing disk drives, 29–35, 93–96
repartitioning utility, 172
replace_initrd command, 271, 487
Replay TV & Showstopper PVRs forum, 497
ReplayTV, 12–13, 22–23
ReplayTV Advanced FAQ Web site, 22
ReplayTV and TiVo FAQ Web site, 23
ReplayTV FAQ Web site, 22
ReplayTV Revealed Web site, 22
ReplayTV vs. TiVo Comparison Web site, 22
Resource directory, 377
resource groups, 381–382
ResourceGroup attribute, 381
resources, 381–382
Restart or Reset System menu, 105
restore command, 200
restoring
  advanced options, 211–215
  backup files, 154–156

backup image, 266–268
backups, 185, 205–210, 228, 231, 255–256, 267–268
basic information about, 202–203
byte-swapped and normal backups, 183
changing block size, 213–214
changing byte order, 215
created by mfstool backup command, 192–193
files from backup, 149
full pathname of file containing, 206
image backups, 203–205
increasing swap space, 211–212
LBA28 disk addressing, 207
MFS Tools backups, 205–216
RFCs (Request for Comments), 109
RIFF (Resource Interchange File Format), 443
RJ-45 connectors, 108
RJ-45 Ethernet adapter, 112
ROM (Read-Only Memory) filesystem, 164–165, 257, 270, 272
ROM monitor, 78–80
ROMFS filesystem image, 260
ROMFS (ROM filesystem) format, 262
/romfs.img file, 257, 270
ronnythunder hacker, 148
root filesystem, 256, 271, 275, 366
  extracting, 267–269
root partition, 217, 267
routers, 108–109
Roxio, 168
RPMFind Web site, 383
rsync (remote sync), 397–398
runmounte file, 270
running commands in background, 388–389
rz (Receive Zmodem) command, 319, 385

# S

safe locations for storing TiVo hacks, 422–423

Samba, sharing MP3 files from Linux, 339

Samba Web site, 403

Sanyo TiVo systems, 96–97

satellite television service, 24

Save to DVD command, 442

Save to VCR command, 441

saving

recordings to DVD, 442

recordings to media, 440–447

recordings to videotape, 441–442

/sbin/bootpage file, 145

/sbin/ifconfig -a command, 324, 399

/sbin/init file, 260, 366, 369, 488

/sbin/tnlited daemon, 399

Schedule directory, 377

scheduled downloads, 8

scheduled shows, 44

Scheduled Suggestions, 69

turning on and off, 62

scheduling programs, 81–82

schema, 379–380

Scientific Atlanta, 24

scrambling directory, 171

scraping Web sites, 5

screens

changing display fonts, 71

hidden, 50

script command, 166

scripts, 172

scripts directory, 132

SDRAM, 112

Search By Title screen, 53, 65

search prompt, 60

searching

for future recordings, 289

for future shows, 291–297

Season Pass Alerts forum, 506

Season Passes, 4, 21, 82

backups, 200

easy access to, 289

listing, 293

restoring settings, 200

SeasonPass directory, 377

Secondary Master hard drives, 98

Secondary Slave hard drives, 98

secret commands and modes, 49–51

security key, 15–16

seek time, 213

seeking, 213

sendkey command, 75–76

serial cables, 90

serial communications

Linux, 382–386

minicom, 383–384

necessary to communicate with TiVos, 383

Windows, 315–317

serial connections, 315

intermittent problems or lost characters, 385

transferring files, 318–320

serial consoles, attaching, 88–91

serial file transfer protocols, 318–319

serial number, 17–18

serial ports, 91

correct network configuration, 125–126

displaying serial prompt, 88

number of, 90

series, listing upcoming episodes, 293

Series 1 Development forum, 499

Series 1 Edge Connector Information Web site, 509

Series 1 Support forum, 499

Series 1 TiVos, 5, 20

adding disk drives, 102

adding second drive to, 19

Audio Right/Left and Video inputs and outputs, 16

big-endian PowerPC processor, 215

byte-swapped disks, 347

byte-swapped kernel, 183

CacheCard, 112, 214

command prompt, 248–252

connectors, 16

cross-compilers, 424–425

daily calls on network, 125–126

differences between, 203

drive bracket, 93

hacking, 20, 140, 173

IBM PowerPC 403GCX processor, 16

IDE and power connections, 30

LBA 48 kernels, 171

Macintosh partitioning and disk/data format conventions, 158

maximum hard disk capacity, 93

modules for using networking, 115

mounting bracket, 94

multistrand IDE cable, 94

network adapter, 125

network card, 248

networking, 111–120

power connector for second drive, 103

PPC processors, 158

processors, 203

rear of, 27

remote controls, 44–45

removing cover, 91

removing disk drive, 93–94

removing screws, 27

separating top of case, 28–29

slotted tabs on top, 28

special brackets, 102

static IP addresses, 110

S-Video inputs and outputs, 16

telephone connectors, 16

TiVoWeb, 287

TurboNet network card, 111–112

Verify password: prompt, 78
"Warranty void if this seal is broken" sticker, 92
**Series 2 60-MB AT&T TiVos, 103**
**Series 2 Development forum, 500**
**Series 2 DirecTiVos, 13**
  hacking, 173
  operating system version, 302
**Series 2 expansion brackets, 137**
**Series 2 Support forum, 500**
**Series 2 TiVos, 5, 13, 20**
  accessing online music and digital photograps, 6
  adding disk drives, 102
  adding second drive to, 19
  Audio Right/Left and Video inputs and outputs, 16
  backing up and restoring hard disks, 252
  backups, 264
  command prompt, 252–259
  connectors, 16
  cross-compilers, 425–426
  current software release, 246
  disconnecting fan, 94
  drive bracket, 95
  hacking, 20
  heat considerations, 104–105
  Home Media Option, 5, 6–7, 110–111
  IDE cables, 103
  maximum hard disk capacity, 93
  MIPS processors, 158
  multiroom viewing, 7
  NEC MIPS processor, 16
  network for daily calls, 127–131
  network-enabled, 15
  networking, 120–124
  Now Playing lists of other networked, 6
  power considerations, 103–104
  power supplies, 103–104
  processors, 203
  rc.sysint file, 275

  recognizing USB adapter, 124
  remote controls, 44–45
  remote scheduling, 305
  removing cover, 91
  removing disk drives, 95–97
  removing screws, 27
  ribbon cable, 94
  separating top of case, 28–29
  sharing recordings between, 6
  smbmount command, 336
  special brackets, 102–103, 105
  static IP addresses, 110
  S-Video inputs and outputs, 16
  telephone connectors, 16
  TiVo Control Station, 283
  two kernel monte, 260–274
  two-pin connector, 30
  upgradesoftware=false boot parameter, 273
  USB connectors, 17
  USB (Universal Serial Bus) network adapter, 302
  USB ports, 120, 127
  V4.0 or better version, 127
  "what is password? prompt, 78
  Y-power cable, 103
**Series 3.2 software, 52**
**Server directory, 377**
**service fees, 4–5**
**service levels, 5–6**
**service messages, viewing, 289**
**set db [dbopen] command, 380**
**Seth's TiVo FAQ Web site, 511**
**settime command, 67**
**settings-backup directory, 171**
**Setup directory, 377**
**/Setup object, 378–379**
**sfdisk, 156**
**SHA1 (Secure Hash Algorithm, Version 1.0), 52–53**
**shell prompt, 271–272**
**shells, 166**
**showcases, 13–14**
  displaying and hiding, 70–71
  expired, 50

**Showcases screen, 70**
**showing.xml file, 437**
**shows**
  automatically recording, 81
  browsing, 82, 289, 291–297
  detailed information about, 4
  identifying by name and scheduling, 82
  locating and selecting to record, 82
  recording upcoming, 291–297
  refining search for, 292
  undeleting, 289
**Showtime, 13**
**shutdown.txt file, 475**
**signatures, 261**
**/signatures file, 368**
**Silicon Graphics, 11**
**Silicon Graphics machines, 10**
**SiliconDust, 48**
**SiliconDust forums, 120, 502–504**
**SiliconDust.com Web site, 111, 115, 135**
**skinnable, 49**
**skipping commercials, 22, 67**
**Sky+ systems, 21**
**slave drives, 31, 37, 97, 102, 142, 144, 182**
**Sleeper hacker, 420**
**Sleeper's ISO, 175**
**slideshows, 15**
**SLIP (Serial Line Internet Protocol), 107**
**Slow 0 Record ThumbsUp key sequence, 72**
**SmartFTP, 326**
**SmartHome Web site, 47**
**SmartStart Power Supply Protector, 104**
**SMB filesystems, 335**
**smbfs.o loadable kernel module, 335–336**
**smbmount command, 335–336**
**Snapstream Web site, 447**

**software**
application software, 140
BlessTiVo, 141–144
Bootpage, 144–147
brute force attempts to identify backdoor, 53
competitors, 23
diagnostic log file, 9
download sites, 512–515
extracting files from TAR and TGZ archives, 417–420
finding backups of older versions, 200–202
hash codes for releases, 51
identifying binary file formats, 414–415
installing, 414–423
installing packaged with TPM (TiVo Package Manager), 420–412
MFS Tools, 147–156
pdisk (Partition Disk) utility, 156–164
releases and hashes, 59
responsibility for updates, 12
secret control codes, 51
software protection against upgrades, 219
system software, 140
tools overview, 141
uncompressing zip and gz files, 415–417
Version 4.0, 264
versions, 19–20
**software partners, 15–16**
**SONICblue Web site, 22**
**Sony, 12–13**
**Sony remote controls, 44**
**Sony SAT-T60 DirecTiVo unit, 19**
**Sony SVR-3000, 19**
**sorting Now Playing list, 72–73**
**SourceForge Web site, 148, 157, 175, 190, 276, 347, 369–370, 403–404, 428–429, 443–444, 467**

**special call to TiVo headquarters, 61**
**special characters, 83**
**Speed1: prompt, 65**
**Speed2: prompt, 66**
**Speed3: prompt, 66**
**spinning up the drive, 104**
**split command, 185**
**splitter, 103**
**sports, 281–283**
**SPS (Select-Play-Select) codes, 50, 67–68**
**src directory, 148, 171**
**SSH (secure shell), 324**
**SSID (Secure Set Identifier), 129**
**Stallman, Richard, 362, 393**
**stand-alone bootable disks, 167**
**stand-alone Series 1 TiVos, 75**
AirNet cards, 113
drive bracket, 31, 33
networking cards, 111
**stand-alone Series 2 TiVos, 75**
drive bracket, 31, 33
Home Media, 302–311
multiroom viewing, 309–311
**stand-alone TiVos, 4, 16, 20**
Channel 3/Channel 4 selector switch, 16
home cable boxes, 46
retrieving programming over phone line or Internet, 8
**standard input, 231**
**standard output, 231**
**star menu item, 70–71**
**startup file, 271–272**
**startup process, 368–369**
**Starz, 13**
**State directory, 377**
**static IP addresses, 127–128**
**status information about TiVos, 300**
**status message, displaying, 68**
**stored program, 68**
**storing recorded programming, 222–223**

**storing TiVo hacks, 422–423**
**streams, 375**
**structured backups, 179**
advanced options, 196–198
after Guided Setup, 181
compressed, 193–194
disk space, 182
entire TiVo disks, 194–195
file size limitations, 185
MFS Tools, 190
sensitivity to consistency and condition of filesystem, 180
simple backups, 191–193
space necessary for, 179
utilities, 179–180
**stty sane command, 247**
**su (substitute user-id) command, 174, 413**
**Subnet Mask, 128**
**subobjid (Subobject ID), 379**
**subprocess, 389**
**sudo /bin/bash command, 174**
**sudo command, 352–353, 413**
**Suggestions screen, 69**
**Sun Web site, 407**
**Sundance Channel, 13**
**SunflowerHead Web site, 280**
**superuser, 140**
**Sutter operating system, 22**
**Svenson, Ernest, 492**
**swap partitions, 157, 163**
**swap space, 208, 210–212**
**switches, 108–109**
**SwModule directory, 377**
**SwSystem directory, 377**
**/Swsystem/ACTIVE object, 381**
**sync command, 255, 266**
**System Information screen, 51, 55, 61, 144, 208, 210, 229, 236, 238, 241–242, 287**
**system software, 140**
**system-level software, packaging, 166–167**
**systems, listing available, 56**

sz (Send Zmodem) command, 319–320, 385

# T

tail command, 251

Tanenbaum, Andrew, 362

TAR archives, 417–420

tar command, 416–420, 472

tar files, 417

  extracting contents, 285

  without tar command, 418

tar format, 170

tar (tap archiver) utility, 180

target device, 163

TCD130040 AT&T Series 2 model, 19

TCD140060 Series 2 model, 19

TCD230040 TiVo Series 2 systems, 19

TCD240080 TiVo Series 2 systems, 19

TCL (Tool Command Language), 369–370

.tcl file extension, 370

*TCL Reference Manual*, 370

tcpdump, 126, 130

TCP/IP (Transmission Control Protocol/Internet Protocol), 107

TCP/IP Settings menu, 124

TCS_1.0.0.tar.gz file, 282

Tech Support and Feedback forum, 502

TECO, 393

Televio Web site, 445

television buffer, 81

TeleWorld, 12

Teleworld, 70

telnet, 89, 127, 398–399

  starting, 274–275

  Windows, 324

Telnet daemon, 120

tent, 47

Tera Term, 318, 324

TERM environment variable, 393

terminal emulation program, 89

terminal emulators, 78, 88–91, 251–252

TERMINFO, 393

text directory, 171

text editors, 392–393

TGZ archives, 417–420

.tgz file extension, 419

Theme directory, 377

themes, 290

Thomson, 12, 13

ThumbsDown key, 64

ThumbsDown ThumbsDown ThumbsDown Enter code, 71

ThumbsDown ThumbsDown ThumbsUp InstantReplay code, 69

ThumbsDown ThumbsUp ThumbsDown Clear code, 71

ThumbsDown ThumbsUp ThumbsDown Instant Replay code, 70

ThumbsDown ThumbsUp ThumbsDown Record code, 70–71

ThumbsUp key, 56, 64

time-shifting, 2

timestamp messages, 61

TimeWarner, 24

TiVo, Inc., 178–179

TiVo, ReplayTV, and UltimateTV Feature Comparison Web site, 23

TiVo advocacy articles, 491–492

TiVo Basic, 5–6, 8

TiVo Central, 20

TiVo Central, Messages & Setup, Recorder & Phone Setup, Phone Connection, Change Dial Options, 125

TiVo Central, Messages & Setup, Recorder & Phone Setup, Phone Connection, Make Test Call, 67

TiVo Central, Messages & Setup, Restart or Reset System, Guided Setup, 105

TiVo Central, Messages & Setup, Settings, Phone & Network Settings, Edit Phone or Network Settings, 124

TiVo Central, Messages & Setup, System Information, 61–62, 144, 208, 210, 229, 236, 238, 241–242

TiVo Central, Music & Photos menu, 303, 339, 344

TiVo Central, Now Playing, 70, 72, 207, 229

TiVo Central, Now Playing on TiVo path, 309

TiVo Central, Pick programs to Record, Record by Time or Channel, 82

TiVo Central, Pick Programs To Record, Schedule Suggestions, 62

TiVo Central, Pick Programs To Record, Search By Title, Category, 65

TiVo Central, Pick Programs To Record, TiVo's Suggestions, 69

TiVo Central, Pick Programs To Record, To Do List, 69

TiVo Central, Programs to Record, Search Using Wishlists page, 84

TiVo Central, Showcases, 70

TiVo Central button, 46

TiVo Central menu, 9, 53

TiVo Central screen, 70–71

TiVo Coffee House - TiVo Discussion forum, 506

TiVo Community Forum, 492

TiVo Community forum, 497

TiVo Community Forums, 504–507

TiVo Control Station application, 281–283

**TiVo Customer Care telephone number,** 9

**TiVo Customer Support Web site,** 6, 137, 479

**TiVo Desktop,** 7, 303, 343
installing and using Windows version of, 337–341
Mac OS X, 359–360

**TiVo Developer Web site,** 303, 402

**TiVo Enhancement Development Team,** 428

**TiVo FAQ Web site,** 173

**TiVo Hacking for PPC project,** 175, 346

**TiVo Hacking for PPC Web site,** 513

**TiVo Hacking Links Web site,** 513

**TiVo Hardware Questions Web site,** 509

**TiVo headquarters**
retrieving updates from, 75
special call to, 61

**TiVo Help Center forum,** 506

**TiVo Home Media Option forum,** 506–507

**TiVo HQ Web site,** 111

**TiVo ID string,** 144

**TiVo Installation Guide,** 441

**TiVo Messages,** 9

**TiVo Messages & Setup, Setup, Phone & Network Setup screen,** 133

**TiVo Messages & Setup menu,** 9

**TiVo Mplayer Web site,** 514

**TiVo Network Hack How-To Guide Web site,** 511–512

**TiVo Plus,** 5–6, 8

**TiVo Publisher,** 338–341

**TiVo Repair Kit guide,** 480

**TiVo Rev 0 PPC 403 Oak Evaluation Kit Web site,** 509

**TiVo ROM monitor,** 78–80

**TiVo Server,** 339–341

**TiVo Server Properties dialog box,** 339–341

**TiVo service,** 4, 7–8
full, 105–106
identifying manufacturer, 17
licensing, 14
subscriptions to, 13

**TiVo sleeper scripts Web site,** 175

**TiVo Software Development forum,** 494

**TiVo Store Web site,** 136

**TiVo Suggestion Avenue forum,** 507

**TiVo Suggestions screen,** 62

**TiVo System Information screen,** 61–62

**TiVo ToGo software,** 15

**TiVo tools disks**
characteristics, 168
Mac OS X, 357–358
Windows, 327–332

**TiVo UK forum,** 507

**TiVo Underground forum,** 507

**TiVo Upgrade Center forum,** 507

**TiVo Utilities Home Page,** 431

**TiVo Video to DVD for Windows Web site,** 514

**TiVo *vs.* UltimateTV Comparison Web site,** 23

**TiVo Web Project.** *See* **TiVoWeb**

**TiVo Web site,** 6, 15, 337, 441
documentation, 402
I Have TiVo! entry, 305
Linux source code, 367
Manage My Account portion, 309
TiVo Central Online entry, 305

**tivoapp application,** 74–76, 371, 457–458

**TiVoBasic service level,** 105

**tivo.com accounts,** 305

**TiVoCommunity,** 48

**tivodns-1.0 directory,** 172

**tivoflash utility,** 120

**TiVoHelp.com Web site,** 512

**TiVo-like devices,** 2, 5

**TiVolution showcase,** 14

**TiVoMad directory,** 172

**TiVoMad utilities,** 170, 172

**tivo_messenger file,** 278

**tivo_mp3_path variable,** 404

**TiVoNet boards,** 111

**TiVoNet cards,** 113–120, 125, 135

**TiVo.net forums,** 507

**TiVoNet/TurboNet/ CacheCard/AirNet software,** 118

**tivopart directory,** 172

**TiVoPartitionScheme,** 347–348

**tivo_photo_path variable,** 404

**TiVo-related information on Internet,** 140

**TiVos,** 2
accessing Windows hard disks, 335–336
adding hard disks, 38–41, 101–103
affecting behavior, 50
application environment, 367–368
authentication, 394
backing up, 92, 171
broadcast networks and, 13
business partners and integrators, 12–13
changing behavior, 44
checking packet and sending and receiving, 126
codes available on different versions, 50
command prompt, 246–259
configuring to send three digits, 48
connectors, 17
convergence, 3
correctly connected to hub or switch, 125
cryptographic chip, 8
Direct TV systems, 3
displaying additional information about, 50
duplicate kernel and root filesystem partitions, 147

dynamic IP addresses, 127
expanding software capabilities, 246
future trends, 24
hardware, 3, 19
hardwiring specific remote to, 45
history of, 10–12
Home Media Option, 6–7
identifying, 7, 17
information about, 288
IP addresses, 131–133
ISA bus slot, 111
last received information from headquarters, 289
lifetime service, 138
Linux, 21
Linux software for, 391–400
listing log files, 288–289
modifying behavior, 62–65
multiroom viewing, 309–311
network connections, 315
networking, 106–107
obtaining IP addresses via DHCP, 110
opening, 26–29, 91–92
phone line, 105
port forwarding, 301
power supplies, 26
programming over cell phones, 15
programming over network, 283–301
protecting against backups, 177
rebooting, 63
receiving signals from any other IR sources, 48
reliability, 3
requiring pressing Enter, 48
restarting, 65
sending files to PCs, 320
serial connections, 315
Series 1, 5
Series 2, 5
service fees, 4–5
service levels, 5–6
setting default hostname, 146

simulating usage, 72
stand-alone, 4
standard kernels, 26
startup process, 368–369
static IP addresses, 127
status information about, 300
superuser, 140
TiVo service number, 7–8
unplugging, 26, 93
user interface, 21
user-level security, 140
viewing service messages, 289
voiding warranty, 26
Windows communicating with, 314–327
Windows-centric focus, 16
**tivoserver, 405**
**TiVoServer-0.16 directory, 403**
**tivoserver.conf file, 404**
**tivoserver.pl file, 403**
**tivosh application, 370–371**
  mls command, 375–376, 378
  scripts, 381
**TiVo-specific utilities, 171**
**TiVoVBI, 430**
**TiVoWeb, 107, 287, 428**
**TiVoWeb Project Web site, 513**
**tivoweb.cfg file, 286**
**TiVoWebPlus, 77, 107, 127, 172, 283–301, 428, 448**
  adding startup procedure, 286
  automatically starting, 285
  built-in Web server, 75
  Cancel Recording hyperlink, 297
  changing appearance of, 290
  Conflicts button, 295
  connecting to, 287
  default install location, 285
  Deleted Shows menu entry, 298
  enabling Internet access, 301
  graphical logos associated with channels, 288
  Info menu, 288
  installing, 284–287
  introductory messages, 285

Logos menu, 288
Logs menu, 288–289
Mail menu, 289
Main Menu, 288
manually starting, 286
menus, 288–289
mfs_ftp, 476
password-protecting, 285–287
Phone (Series 1 only) menu, 289
Record button, 296
Record hyperlink, 294
Recording hyperlink, 296
remotely shutting down or starting, 289
Resource Editor (Series 1 only) menu, 289
Restart menu, 289
reviewing channels received, 297
scheduling recordings over Internet, 305
screen, 287
Screen (Series 1 only) menu, 289
Search menu, 289
status information about TiVo, 300
Theme menu, 289
undeleting recordings, 298–299
User Interface command, 298
User Interface menu, 289
username, 287
Web Remote (Series 1 only) menu, 289
Web-based remote control, 75
What's On menu, 289
**TiVoWebPlus Web site, 284, 428**
**TiVoWebPlus-1.0-final.tivo.tpm file, 172**
**TiVoWebPlus-1.0-final.tivo.tpm file, 285**
**tivoweb-tcl directory, 286**
**TLC (The Learning Channel), 13**
**TMC (The Movie Channel), 13**
**TMF (TiVo Media Format), 437**
**tmf directory, 475**
**.tmf file extension, 437**

**/tmp/mwstate file, 63–64**

**TMP/tmp_packages directory, 106**

**Toast program, 168**

**Todd's Web site, 164**

**ToDo list**

activating display of scheduled suggestions, 69

easy access to, 289

**ToDo List screen, 62**

**"Too many command line options" error message, 41, 142, 243**

**tools overview, 141**

**Torvalds, Linus, 362**

**Torx screwdriver, 91**

**Toshiba SDH400, 14**

**Toshiba TiVos, 6**

**TOTAL CHOICE package, 4**

**touch command, 335**

**ToVp Suggestions, 4**

**tpip command, 163–164**

**tpip utility, 172**

**tpip-1.1 directory, 172**

**TPM (TiVo Package Manager), 172, 420–412**

**TPM directory, 172**

**tpm_packages subdirectory, 172**

**transferring files, 318–320, 385–386, 400**

**Tridgell, Andrew, 111, 145, 403, 450**

**troubleshooting**

blown modem, 480–481

external modems, 481–484

green screen, 488

no picture or welcome screen, 485

stuck at welcome screen, 485–488

**TTSSH Web site, 324**

**TTT (Thumb-Thumb-Thumb) codes, 50, 69–71**

**TurboNet cards, 111–112, 124, 135, 248**

changing options, 117–118

Daily call option, 119

dynamic IP address information, 118

easy-to-use installer for software, 115

firmly seating, 125

installing software for, 113–120

**TurboNet Tech Support forum, 504**

**TV tuner cards, 442–447**

**tvtime capture package, 444**

**Tweaks and Do-It-Yourself forum, 497**

**Twin Brothers Web site, 175**

**two-kernel monte, 171, 260–274**

**txt directory, 475**

**ty directory, 475**

**ty+ directory, 475**

**.ty file extension, 437**

**.ty+ file extension, 437**

**TY files and mplayer, 476–478**

**tyindex application, 468**

**typescript file, 166**

**tyserver application, 468**

**tyserver.mips.sh file, 468**

**tyserver.ppc.sh file, 468**

**tyStream objects, 436–437**

**TyStudio, 172, 448, 467–471**

**TyStudio directory, 172**

**TyStudio Web site, 514**

**TyTool, 136, 172, 448, 460–466**

**TyTool directory, 172**

**TyTool Web site, 515**

**TyTool9r14.zip archive, 461**

**U**

**UDP (Universal Data Packet), 107**

**UltimateTV, 23**

**UltimateTV Hacking Forum Web site, 23**

**UltraEdit, 486**

**umount command, 251, 259, 414**

**umount/mnt/test command, 204, 216**

**"Unable to connect to /dev/hdx" error message, 41, 142, 243**

**uncompressing zip and gz files, 415–417**

**undeleting recordings, 298–299**

**universal remote controls, 45**

**Unix**

mountpoints, 212

"Yet Another..." programs, 280

**unlocking hard drives, 40, 100–101**

**unplugging TiVo before modifying, 26**

**unscramble modules, 456–457**

**unscramble.o loadable kernel module, 459**

**unset command, 231**

**unstructured backups, 179, 236**

advantages, 179

crashed hard disks, 181

disk space, 182

hard disks, 188

image backups, 181

partitions, 188

**unzip command, 416–417**

**updating configuration information, 105**

**upgrade kits, 226**

**upgradesoftware=false boot parameter, 273**

**upgrading**

hard disk without backup files, 229–233

hard disks, 222–223, 225

**uplink port, 109**

**Uranus Web site, 333–334**

**USB adapters, 120–123, 129–131, 302**

**USB ports, 120, 127**

**User Interface, 21**

**user-level security, 140**

**/usr/bin directory, 400**

**/usr/bin/minicom file, 383**

**usr.local.powerpc-tivo.tgz cross-compiler, 424–425**

usr/share/file/magic file, 437–438

usr/share/magic file, 437–438

## V

V 3.0 and earlier TiVos, 53–55

V 3.1 and later TiVo models, 55–60

v command, 81

V.3.x TiVos, 72–73

/var directory, 154, 271

/var partition, 271, 422
  increasing size of, 212
  size of, 156

/var/hack directory, 258, 421

/var/hack/hackinit file, 257, 258, 275, 286, 390

/var/hack/lib/smb.conf file, 335

variables, setting, 50

/var/log/kernel file, 126, 130

/var/log/tverr log file, 61

/var/log/tvlog log file, 71

/var/lon/tvdebug log file, 61

/var/packages directory, 76

vBulletin, 492

VBWare Web site, 460

VCDs (Video CDs), 439–440

Vector Web site, 318

verifying integrity, 189

Version 4.0 of TiVo software, 72

vi, 393

video
  decrypting, 435
  disabling encryption, 455–460

video capture software, 442–447

video extraction, 177, 179, 433–434
  directly from hard disks, 449–455
  disabling video encryption, 455–460
  extraction and processing software, 448–449
  mfs_ftp, 471–475

networks, 449
  overview, 447–449
  TV tuner card, 442–447
  TyStudio, 467–471
  TyTool, 460–466
  video capture software, 442–447

video file formats, 436
  DVDs (Digital Video Disks), 440
  MFS (Media File System), 436–437
  MPEG (Motion Picture Experts Group) files, 439
  VCDs (Video CDs), 439–440
  VOB (Video Object), 440

video on demand, 11

Video Toaster, 10

video-editing capabilities, 10

videotapes, saving recordings to, 441–442

viewing habits, 8–9

vim (Vi iMproved), 130, 393

virtual filesystems, 189

virtual memory, 374

VirtualPC, 460

VOB (Video Object), 440

voiding warranty, 26, 27, 91

vplay application, 172

vplay directory, 172

vplay package, 450

vserver application, 172, 477

vserver package, 450

VSO Software Web site, 328

## W

Wagner, Eric, 356

Wall, Kurt, 427

warranty, voiding, 91

"Warranty void if this seal is broken" sticker, 92

Weaknees.com Web site, 45, 48, 102, 104, 137, 141, 214, 225, 242, 356, 512

weather, 281–283

Web browsers, scheduling recordings from, 284

Web sites, 5

WebPlus-1.0-final.tivo.tpm TiVo, 284

WebTiVoPlus
  browsing upcoming shows, 291–297
  changing appearance, 289
  modifying configuration file, 290
  Now Showing screen, 292
  recording upcoming shows, 291–297
  themes, 290
  What's On menu item, 291

Westerns, 13

Wget (Web get), 400

Windows
  accessing hard disks from TiVos, 335–336
  alternate audio formats, 342–345
  Angry IP Scanner utility, 133
  BeyondTV, 447
  bootable disks, 170
  browsing partition image, 333–334
  burning CDs, 327–332
  checking filesystem type, 186
  communicating with TiVos, 314–327
  ed2k-gtk-gui, 201
  explore2fs, 333–334
  exporting audio files, 303–304
  exporting collections, 7
  exporting MP3 files directory, 338
  ext2 disk images, 333–334
  FAT-32 (32-bit File Allocation Table), 97
  FAT32 filesystem, 184
  file size limitations, 185–186
  FTP (File Transfer Protocol), 325–327
  GAIM (GTK AOL Instant Messenger), 276–277

**Windows** *(continued)*

hard disks, 333–336

Hauppage WinTV, 447

HyperTerminal, 251, 259, 273, 315–317

installing and using TiVo Desktop, 337–341

installing gaim2tivo plug-in, 278–279

integrating with Home Media, 337–345

Java Home Media Option, 406

Media Center, 406

network communications, 321–327

NFS utilities, 337

NTFS (NT File System), 97, 185

Pinnacle Studio, 447

RAR archiver, 202

reformatting or damaging TiVo drive, 99

serial communications, 315–317

SSH (secure shell), 324

Start, Programs, TiVo Desktop menu, 337

telnet, 324

TiVo Publisher command, 337

TiVo tools disks, 327–332

TiVo-related utilities, 172

transferring files over serial connection, 318–320

TV tuner cards, 446–447

TyStudio, 469

**Windows CE**, 23

**windows directory**, 172

**Windows FTP client**, 325

**Windows-centric focus**, 16

**wired Ethernet adapter**, 125

**wired USB Ethernet device**, 128

**wireless network**, 129

**wireless phone jack**, 106

**Wireless Settings menu**, 124, 129

**wireless USB adapters**, 120–123

**wireless USB Ethernet device**, 129

**WishLists**, 4, 21, 44, 82–84

backups, 200

restoring settings, 200

**World Wide Web**, 107

**X**

**X (extended) command**, 80

**x86bin directory**, 172

**xawtv capture package**, 443–444

**XBOX Hacking forum**, 500

**xcompilers directory**, 172, 395

**xcompilers/Series1/tivodev-2.5_linux-x86_dtype1.tgz cross-compiler**, 423

**xcompilers/Series1/tivodev-2.5_linux-x86_dtype2.tgz cross-compiler**, 424–425

**xcompilers/Series1/usr.local.powerpc-tivo.tgz cross-compiler**, 423

**xcompilers/Series2/usr-local.tivo-mips_bu211.tgz cross-compiler**, 424

**xcompilers/Series2/usr-local.tivo-mips_bu213.tgz cross-compiler**, 424

**xcompilers/usr-local.tivo-s2.tgz cross compiler**, 424

**xml directory**, 475

**xmltv capture package**, 444

**xmodem**, 318, 385

**XTV**, 21

**Y**

**YAC (Yet Another Caller ID Program)**, 280

**YAC client**, 280

**yac-0.16-win32.zip file**, 280

**yacc (Yet Another Compiler Compiler)**, 280

**Yahoo**, 276

**ymodem**, 318, 385

**Y-power cable**, 103

**Z**

**Zephyr**, 276

**Zero key**, 56

**ZeroWing game**, 52

**.zip file extension**, 416

**zip files, uncompressing**, 415–417

**Zirak**, 281

**Zirak Zigil Web site**, 281, 283

**zmodem**, 318–319, 385

# *About The CD*

The CD included with this book is both bootable and mountable. You can boot Linux from the CD on any Pentium-class personal computer in order to work with TiVo disks and partitions. If you boot from the CD, you can subsequently mount the CD using the Linux **mount** command in order to access other software stored on the disc. You can also mount the CD on a Windows or Macintosh personal computer by inserting it into your CD drive in order to access the software that is stored on the CD. The contents of the CD are explained in the section of Chapter 5 entitled "BATBD—Bill's Accumulated TiVo Boot Disk."

The CD includes TiVo-related software for Windows, Mac OS X, and Linux systems, plus the most popular TiVo-side tools for your Series 1 or Series 2 TiVo. Highlights of the software on the CD include all of the software needed for adding larger disks to your TiVo, software for extracting and processing recordings stored on your TiVo from your Windows, Mac OS X, or Linux system, the TiVoWebPlus Web server for scheduling recordings over the network and undeleting recordings, an FTP server for the TiVo, cross-compilers for compiling your own software for the TiVo, dozens of popular Linux applications ready to run on any TiVo, and much more.

# License Agreement/Notice of Limited Warranty

By opening the sealed disc container in this book, you agree to the following terms and conditions. If, upon reading the following license agreement and notice of limited warranty, you cannot agree to the terms and conditions set forth, return the unused book with unopened disc to the place where you purchased it for a refund.

### License:

The enclosed software is copyrighted by the copyright holder(s) indicated on the software disc. You are licensed to copy the software onto a single computer for use by a single user and to a backup disc.

You may not reproduce, make copies, or distribute copies or rent or lease the software in whole or in part, except with written permission of the copyright holder(s). You may transfer the enclosed disc only together with this license, and only if you destroy all other copies of the software and the transferee agrees to the terms of the license. You may not decompile, reverse assemble, or reverse engineer the software.

### Notice of Limited Warranty:

The enclosed disc is warranted by Thomson Course Technology PTR to be free of physical defects in materials and workmanship for a period of sixty (60) days from end user's purchase of the book/disc combination. During the sixty-day term of the limited warranty, Thomson Course Technology PTR will provide a replacement disc upon the return of a defective disc.

### Limited Liability:

THE SOLE REMEDY FOR BREACH OF THIS LIMITED WARRANTY SHALL CONSIST ENTIRELY OF REPLACEMENT OF THE DEFECTIVE DISC. IN NO EVENT SHALL THOMSON COURSE TECHNOLOGY PTR OR THE AUTHOR BE LIABLE FOR ANY OTHER DAMAGES, INCLUDING LOSS OR CORRUPTION OF DATA, CHANGES IN THE FUNCTIONAL CHARACTERISTICS OF THE HARDWARE OR OPERATING SYSTEM, DELETERIOUS INTERACTION WITH OTHER SOFTWARE, OR ANY OTHER SPECIAL, INCIDENTAL, OR CONSEQUENTIAL DAMAGES THAT MAY ARISE, EVEN IF THOMSON COURSE TECHNOLOGY PTR AND/OR THE AUTHOR HAS PREVIOUSLY BEEN NOTIFIED THAT THE POSSIBILITY OF SUCH DAMAGES EXISTS.

### Disclaimer of Warranties:

THOMSON COURSE TECHNOLOGY PTR AND THE AUTHOR SPECIFICALLY DISCLAIM ANY AND ALL OTHER WARRANTIES, EITHER EXPRESS OR IMPLIED, INCLUDING WARRANTIES OF MERCHANTABILITY, SUITABILITY TO A PARTICULAR TASK OR PURPOSE, OR FREEDOM FROM ERRORS. SOME STATES DO NOT ALLOW FOR EXCLUSION OF IMPLIED WARRANTIES OR LIMITATION OF INCIDENTAL OR CONSEQUENTIAL DAMAGES, SO THESE LIMITATIONS MIGHT NOT APPLY TO YOU.

### Other:

This Agreement is governed by the laws of the State of Massachusetts without regard to choice of law principles. The United Convention of Contracts for the International Sale of Goods is specifically disclaimed. This Agreement constitutes the entire agreement between you and Thomson Course Technology PTR regarding use of the software.